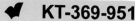

KT-369-951

hugo

POCKET DICTIONARY

SPANISH

SPANISH-ENGLISH
ENGLISH-SPANISH

HUGO'S LANGUAGE BOOKS LTD.
LONDON

Completely revised 1969

© 1969 Hugo's Language Institute Ltd

ISBN : 085285 008 5

5th Impression 1975

*Printed in Great Britain by
Morrison & Gibb Ltd., London and Edinburgh.*

hugo

POCKET DICTIONARY

INGLÉS

ESPANOL-INGLÉS
INGLÉS-ESPANOL

PREFACIO

Con el uso se hallará que el diccionario de bolsillo " Hugo " es un libro muy útil de referencia. Contiene, dentro de un espacio reducido, las palabras que se necesitan en la vida ordinaria. Se ha empleado el reputado sistema de pronunciación figurada " Hugo." Este método de pronunciación es tan sencillo, que cualquier persona puede usarlo inmediatamente sin la menor dificultad (véanse las páginas vi, vii, viii, y ix). *No hay claves complicadas para estudiar.*

Las palabras que tienen la misma raiz y que no aparecen en la sección Española-Inglesa se hallarán generalmente en la sección Inglesa-Española. Hemos adoptado este plan con el objeto de dejar espacio para el mayor número posible de vocablos.

PREFACE

Hugo's Spanish Dictionary will be found a most serviceable pocket reference-book. It contains in a small space the words that are needed in everyday life. Hugo's well-known system of Imitated Pronunciation has been used throughout; this method is so simple that anyone can use it at once without the slightest trouble (see pages xii–xiv). *There is no complicated key to be mastered.*

Words belonging to the same root not given in the Spanish-English section will generally be found in the English-Spanish section. This plan has been followed to provide space for the greatest possible number of words.

LA PRONUNCIACIÓN FIGURADA

Cada sílaba de la pronunciación figurada debe pronunciarse como si formara parte de una palabra española.

En la lengua inglesa hay sonidos que no existen en español. Es, por tanto, imposible imitarlos exactamente por medio de sílabas españolas. Las aclaraciones siguientes ayudarán a conseguir la exacta pronunciación de los sonidos.

VOCALES

Es muy importante distinguir las vocales largas de las breves.

Las vocales largas se muestran, en la pronunciación figurada duplicando la vocal. Por ejemplo, **cheap** (barato), chiip; **boot** (zapato), buut. En algunos casos la vocal larga va indicada por medio de un acento, como **chair** (silla), chér. Estas vocales largas se pronuncian como un **solo sonido**.

A representa un sonido breve, entre **a** y **e**. algo parecido a la **e** en 'sello.'

o*a* debe pronunciarse como la **o** en 'monte,' pero mas alargado, casi como la **oa** en 'loa.'

ŏ representa un sonido corto, y medio entre la **eu** y la **a** de las palabras francesas 'fleur' y 'lac.'

a, e, i, o, u.—Estos signos representan vocales no acentuadas, y tienen un sonido obscuro y breve, semejante a la **e** en las palabras francesas **de**, **me**, **que**, **le**, y que apenas se oye, principalmente al fin de palabra. Por ejemplo; **doctor**, doc'-ta; **partner**, part'-na. En ciertas terminaciones este sonido indistinto va indicado mediante la omisión de la vocal no acentuada:

vi

important, useful, candle, im-port'-nt, ius'-fl, kan'-dl. **El sonido verdadero de la vocal no ha de oirse.**

Es necesario tener en cuenta esta observación especialmente con respecto a las numerosas terminaciones indicadas por *a*, (en inglés *er* no acentuado), en las cuales la *a* tiene el vago e indistinto sonido sobredicho.

ei, ou.—Estas sílabas tienen respectivamente el sonido largo de la **e** y de la **o.** La **i** y la **u** deben ser pronunciadas con rapidez y tan ligeramente que apenas se oigan.

ěr como la **eu** en las palabras francesas ' peur, fleur.'

El mismo sonido, aunque pronunciado muy ligera y rapidamente, se oye también detrás de las vocales largas **ér, ír, ór, úr,** en las terminaciones **ér, ír, ór, úr,** de la pronunciación figurada.

CONSONANTES

z como en Castilla, nunca como la **s.**

D mayúscula; (Véase en la página viii).

k siempre como la **c** en ' casa,' ' como.'

j lo mismo que la **j** española, pero menos gutural.

s en letra gruesa itálica indica un sonido suave el mismo que la **s** en la palabra francesa ' chaise.'

sh como **ch** en las palabras francesas ' chat, affiche.'

CH mayúsculas representan un sonido parecido pero más suave que la **j** francesa en ' jamais.' precedido de **d.**

sh gruesas como **j** en la palabra francesa ' jamais.'

g (itálica) no suena separadamente, puesto que es un sonido nasal.

r (itálica) no se pronuncia sino muy ligeramente.

b se pronuncia siempre lo mismo que la **b** francesa, nunca como **v.**

vii

LOS DOS SONIDOS DE 'TH'

El sonido agudo ó fuerte de **th** en inglés corresponde exactamente con la pronunciación castellana de la **z** en la palabra 'vez,' ó de la **c** en 'once.' Este sonido es indicado en nuestra pronunciación figurada por medio de una **z**. Los Sud Americanos, y los naturales de otros países donde se habla español, que no suelen pronunciar la **z** de la manera castellana, deben cuidar de hacerlo cuando lean nuestra pronunciación figurada.

El sonido llano ó suave de **th** en inglés se parece al sonido agudo, precedido por una **d** débil. Si se pronuncia como la **d** española en las palabras 'padre,' 'admirar,' podrá comprenderse, aunque esta pronunciación no es absolutamente correcta. Este sonido es indicado por D (mayúscula).

El sonido llano se pronuncia también con la lengua entre los dientes, lo mismo que cuando se cecea, pero forzando del aliento para que salga fuera por **debajo** de la lengua, en lugar de por encima, como sucede en la pronunciación aguda de **th**.

LOS DOS SONIDOS DE 'S'

La **s** inglesa, así como la **s** francesa, tiene dos sonidos diferentes. Siempre es aguda, como en castellano en las palabras 'seis,' 'sobre,' al principio de una palabra; pero amenudo toma el sonido de la **z** inglesa ó francesa, especialmente entre dos vocales. La **s** suave (lo mismo que algunos españoles pronuncian la **s** in 'rosa,' 'risa,' y otras iguales) es indicado con una **s** impresa en letra itálica **gruesa**. Este sonido inglés corresponde con el de la **s** en las palabras francesas 'chose,' 'église,' 'baiser.'

'H' ASPIRADA

La letra **h** aspirada es imitada por medio de una **j**. Esta debe pronunciarse con una respiración fuerte, detrás de los dientes, y no detrás de la garganta, como sucede en la **j** gutural española, o la **g** en 'gente,' 'giro.'

' WH ' ASPIRADA

En nuestra pronunciación figurada, **ju** pronunciad muy ligeramente, y apoyando sobre la vocal que sigue, representa exactamente el sonido de **wh**. En Londres y en el Sur de Inglaterra, se aspira tan raramente* la **wh** que lo contrario parece pedante; pero en otras partes del Reino Unido, la **wh** es generalmente aspirada. Por ejemplo, en el Sur de Inglaterra, se pronuncia **when** y **what** (cuando, qué) **u**en, **u**ot; pero **ju**en, **ju**ot, es indudablemente más correcto.

*excepto en las palabras **who**, **whom**, **whose**, **whole** (quien, quien, a quien o cuyo, entero), pronunciadas **ju**u, **ju**um, **ju**us, **jo**ul, y algunas otras en las que la **w** es muda.

LA LETRA ' R '

A menos que esta letra no vaya inmediatamente seguida de una vocal, puede decirse que, al fin de una palabra o sílaba, es muda, en Londres y en casi todo el Sur de Inglaterra, o se pronuncia sólo muy ligeramente. Por ejemplo, **scholar** (escolar) y **popular** (popular) suenan casi como scol'-*a*, pop'-*iu*-l*a*. Pero la letra **r** modifica amenudo y algunas veces cambia absolutamente el sonido de la vocal precedente. Ejemplos:

español	inglés	pron. fig.
no	no	nó o n**ou**
ni	nor	n**o**r
té	tea	t**é**r
rasgar	tear	t**é**r
él	he	jí o jii
ella	her	j**e**r†
demasiado	too	tuu
puerta	door	d**ó**r

Casi en todo el resto del Reino Unido, la **r** se pronuncia más fuerte.

† pero **her aunt** (su tía) se pronuncia jĕ-ránt porque la **r** va seguida de una vocal.

ix

EL ALFABETO INGLÉS

con los nombres de las 26 letras

(Es preciso distinguir entre los NOMBRES de las letras, y su SONIDO cuando se emplean como parte de una palabra).

A	B	C	D	E	F	G	H
éi	bí	sí	dí	í	ef	CHí	éch

I	J	K	L	M	N	O	P
ai	CHéi	kéi	el	em	en	ó	pí

Q	R	S	T	U	V	W	X
kiú	ár	es	tí	iú	ví	dábl'-iu	eks

Y	Z
uai	sed

ACENTO

La señal ' indica que la sílaba precedente debe pronunciarse con más énfasis que las demás.

ADVERBIOS

El asterisco señala adjetivos a los cuales basta añadir la terminación ' ly ' para cambiarlos en adverbios. Por ejemplo: **wise**, sabio; **wisely**, sabiamente. Esta terminación ' ly ' tiene un sonide intermedio entre ' le ' y ' li.'

Advertencia—Como la pronunciación figurada en la parte Inglés-Español es unicamente para el uso de los españoles, los sonidos del inglés están representados por letras y grupos de letras de origen castellano. Debe, por lo tanto, ignorarse toda crítica procedente de extranjeros, pues éstos suelen olvidar que la pronunciación figurada no tiene por base la fonética de su propio idioma. Recíprocamente, la pronunciación figurada en la parte Español-Inglés sólo interesa a las personas de habla inglesa.

EXPLICACIÓN DE LAS ABREVIATURAS

a,	adjetivo	n.	neutro
a. pos.	adjetivo posesivo	naut.	náutico
adv.	adverbio	p.p.	participio pasado
art.	artículo	photog.	fotografía
conj.	conjunción	pl.	plural
eccl.	eclesiástico	pop.	popular
elec.	eléctrico	prep.	preposición
f.	femenino	pron.	pronombre
fam.	familiar	pron. pers.	pronombre personal
fig.	figuradamente	refl.	reflexivo
interj.	interjección	s.	substantivo
m.	masculino	s. y a.	substantivo y adjetivo
mech.	mecánica	s. & a.	
med.	médico	s. pl.	substantivo plural
mil.	militar	v.	verbo
mus.	musical	vulg.	vulgar

EL GÉNERO DE LOS SUBSTANTIVOS

Todos los substantivos ingleses son del genero neutro, excepto los que se refieren a personas.

THE IMITATED PRONUNCIATION

Our Imitated Pronunciation will always be understood by natives provided each syllable is pronounced as if it were part of an English word; but the exact sound will be still more clearly obtained if the following instructions are borne in mind:—

th must be pronounced like **th** in ' thin,' never like **th** in ' they.'

ll is to be pronounced gutturally, like the Scottish **ch** in ' loch.'

s whether represented in the imitated pronunciation by a single or a double **s**, always like the **ss** in ' missing,' never like the **s** in ' easy.'

a the Spanish **a** is pronounced like ' ah,' but shorter than in ' harm.' We imitate it by ' ah,' because the sound is never like **a** in ' hat,' but the ' ah ' must be pronounced short and sharp.

o the Spanish **o** resembles the sound of **o** in ' not,' and even slightly approaches the **aw** in ' law,' It is not so long as the **o** in ' go.'

r is rolled (on the tip of the tongue) more than in English, especially at the beginning of a word or syllable.

STRESS

The stressed syllable is indicated in our imitated pronunciation by bold type, thus: **ploo**-mah, **pah**-pel (pluma, papel).

Generally speaking, words ending in a consonant stress the last syllable; words ending in a vowel stress the last syllable but one. But the consonants (always **n** or **s**) which are merely added to form the plural do not then affect the stress, which is always the same in the plural as in the singular.

When the stress is not in accordance with rule, an acute accent is always placed over the emphasised vowel; allí (there) = ah-l'**yee**, hábil (clever) = **ah**-bil.

GENERAL HINTS ON PRONUNCIATION

You should have little trouble in pronouncing any Spanish word correctly, if you follow our system of imitated pronunciation. However, a few hints on the pronunciation of vowels and consonants, taken from our book *Spanish in Three Months*, may help to clarify any remaining problems:

VOWELS

a is pronounced like ' ah ' (**pluma** = **ploo**-mah)

e is pronounced like ' ay ' (**me** = may)

i or **y** is pronounced like ' ee ' (**prima** = **pree**-mah)

o is pronounced like ' o ' (**toro** = **to**-ro)

u is pronounced like ' oo ' (**uno** = **oo**-no)

Each vowel sound has only one sound in Spanish; this is not quite so long and broad as the English equivalent given above. The pronunciation of the vowels is shortened, as in other languages, when they occur in an unstressed syllable, or precede a consonant.

CONSONANTS

z is pronounced like **th** in ' month ' or ' thick ': **luz** (light) = looth, **zapato** (shoe) = thah-**pah**-to.

j is pronounced like the German guttural **ch**, or as in the Scottish ' loch '; it is merely the English **h** pronounced in the throat, and if you find this hard to sound, simply pronounce it like an aspirated **h**. Examples: **ojo** (eye) = **o**-Ho, **jugar** (to play) = Hoo-**gar**.

xiii

z and **j** are the only two Spanish consonants that are pronounced quite unlike their English equivalents, but there are others which differ in various lesser ways. The following points should be noted:

c before **e** or **i** is pronounced like the Spanish **z**: **cena** (supper) = **thay**-nah, **cinco** (five) = **thin**-ko.

g before **e** or **i** is pronounced like the Spanish **j**: **general** (general) = *H*ay-nay-**rahl**.

g before any other letter is like g in ' go ': **gato** (cat) = **gah**-to, **gigante** (giant) = *H*e-**gahn**-tay.

gu before **e** or **i** is like g in ' go '; before any other vowel it is like **gw** or **goo**: **guerra** (war) = **gairr**-rah, **guía** (guide) = **ghee**-ah, **guarda** (guard) = goo'**ar**-dah.

h is not pronounced at all: **hijo** (son) = ee-*H*o.

ll is pronounced early like ll in ' million ': **calle** (street) = **kah**-l'yay.

ñ is almost like ni in ' companion ': **niño** (child) = nee-n'yo, **señor** (sir) = say-n'**yor**.

qu is pronounced like **k**: **que** (that) = kay, **quince** (fifteen) = **kin**-thay.

ch is pronounced as in ' cheap ' or ' much ': **muchacha** (girl) = moo-**chah**-chah.

r is rolled on the tip of the tongue more than in English, especially at the beginning of a word or syllable: **raro** (rare) = **rrah**-ro.

s is always pronounced sharp, as in ' see ' or ' last ', never like a **z** as in ' easy ': **casa** (house) = **kah**-sah.

ACCENTS, SIGNS OF PUNCTUATION, ETC.

The acute accent (ˊ) is the only accent used in Spanish. It indicates that the stress or emphasis is to be laid on the vowel over which it is placed: **médico** (physician) = **may**-de-ko. It is also used to distinguish between words similarly spelt, but of different meaning: **te** (thee), **té** (tea), both of which are pronounced **tay**. It never alters the pronunciation of a letter.

The accent is also used in such words as **cuando** (when), **donde** (where), when they actually ask a question: ¿ **Cuándo llega el buque ?** (When does the boat arrive?), but ¿ **Sabe él cuando llega el buque ?** (Does he know when the boat arrives?).

The diaeresis (··) is placed over **u** (ü) preceded by **g**, to indicate that the **u** must be pronounced: **agüero** (omen) = ah-goo′**ay**-ro.

The tilde (~) is placed over **n** (ñ), when that letter is to be pronounced like the **ni** in 'union': **niño** (child) = **nee**-n′yo.

Question marks and exclamation marks are placed at both ends of the phrase, the first one being inverted.

ADVERBS

Spanish adverbs end generally in ' mente ' which corresponds to the English ' ly,' and are formed by adding this termination to the feminine ending ' a ' of adjectives in **o**, or to the last letter, whether the vowel ' e ' or a consonant, of the other adjectives, Ex.: **raro** (m.), **rara** (f.), **raramente; pobre, feliz** (m. & f.), **pobremente, felizmente**. Adjectives from which adverbs can thus be formed are marked with an asterisk (*).

THE SPANISH ALPHABET

with the names of the 29 letters shown by their pronunciation.

(к and w only occur in words taken from other languages)

A	**B**	**C**	**CH**	**D**	**E**	**F**
Pron. ah*	bay	thay*	chay	day	ay	eff-ay*

G	**H**	**I**	**J**	**K**	**L**
*Hay**	**ah**-chay	ee	*Ho*-tah*	kah	ell-ay

LL	**M**	**N**	**Ñ**	**O**	**P**	**Q**
ell-yay	emm-ay	enn-ay	enn-yay	o*	pay	koo

R	**S**	**T**	**U**	**V**	**W**
airr-ay	es-ay*	tay	oo	vay	**do**-blay-vay

X	**Y**	**Z**
ay-kis*	ee gre'**ay**-gah	**thay**-tah

Note—In Spanish, ch, ll and ñ represent separate letters; they therefore appear at the end of the C's, L's and N's as in other Spanish dictionaries. Similarly, where ch, ll or ñ occurs in the middle of a word, that word is to be found after -cz-, -lz- or -nz-.

VARYING PRONUNCIATIONS

The lisping pronunciation of **z**, and **c** before **e** or **i**, is usual in Castile, and as Castilian is considered the best Spanish we have used it in this dictionary. But in South and Central America, as well as in some parts of Spain, it is usual to pronounce these letters like the English ' s.' In the following examples, the Castilian pronunciation comes before the variant: **izquierdo**=ith-ke-**air**-do, iss-ke-**air**-do; **cerca**= **thair**-kah, **sair**-kah; **cielo**=the-**ay**-lo, se-**ay**-lo. The letter **ll** is pronounced in several ways; we imitate it as ' l'y . . .', but in some areas and in Latin America it has a strong guttural sound, with the ' l ' virtually disappearing. Thus **mantilla**, mahn-**tee**-l'yah, becomes mahn-**tee**-yah. In Andalusia and Argentina it is even stronger, the ' l ' sound being replaced by something like a soft ' j ' or the ' si ' in ' occasion.'

Many Spaniards pronounce a final **d** like 'th' in 'thin,' and some pronounce **d** in the middle of a word like 'th' in 'then.' It is also not unusual for them to confuse the sound of **b** with that of **v**. But you are advised to pronounce the Spanish **d**, **b**, **v**, exactly as in English, not making the final **d** too sharp and distinct.

Caution—The imitated pronunciation in the Spanish-English section, being for English people only, is framed in accordance with English 'sound-spelling' principles. Users of this Dictionary should beware of criticisms from foreigners who forget that this imitated pronunciation is not based upon their own phonetics.

Vice versa, the imitated pronunciation in the English-Spanish section is for Spanish people only.

ABBREVIATIONS
USED IN THIS DICTIONARY

a.	adjective	p.p.	past participle
adv.	adverb	pers. pron.	
art.	article		personal pronoun
conj.	conjunction	photog.	photography
eccl.	ecclesiastical	pl.	plural
elec.	electric	pop.	popular
f.	feminine	poss. adj.	
fam.	familiar		possessive adjective
fig.	figuratively	prep.	preposition
interj.	interjection	pron.	pronoun
m.	masculine	refl.	reflexive
mech.	mechanics	s.	substantive
med.	medical	s. & a. ⎰ substantive and	
mil.	military	s. y a. ⎱ adjective	
mus.	musical	s. pl.	substantive plural
n.	neuter	v.	verb
naut.	nautical	vulg.	vulgar

xvii

GEOGRAPHICAL NAMES
NOMBRES GEOGRÁFICOS

	Pronunciación figurada.		Imitated pronunciation.
Africa,	ᴀ′-fri-ka	Africa,	**ah**-fre-kah
Algeria,	Al-cʜi′-ri-*a*	Argelia,	ar-*H*ay-le-ah
America,	*a*-mer′-i-k*a*	América,	ah-**may**-re-kah
Asia,	ei′-**sha**	Asia,	ah-se-ah [l'yah
Australia,	**o**as-**trei**′-li-*a*	Australia,	ah′oos-**trah**-
Austria,	**o**as′-tri-*a*	Austria,	ah′oos-tre-ah
Belgium,	bel′cʜi-om	Bélgica,	**bel**-*H*e-kah
Brazil,	bra-**siil**′	Brasil,	brah-**seel**
Great Britain,	gre**i**t brit′-n	Gran Bretaña,	grahn bray-**tah**-n'yah
Bulgaria,	bŏl-gu**é**r′-i-*a*	Bulgaria,	bool-**gah**-re-ah
Canada,	kᴀ′-na-d*a*	Canadá	kah-nah-**dah**
China,	cha**i**′-na	China,	**chee**-nah
Denmark,	den′-maark	Dinamarca,	de-nah-**mar**-
Egypt,	**ii**′-cʜipt	Egipto,	ay-*H*eep-to
England,	ing′-gland	Inglaterra,	in-glah-**tair**-rrah
Europe,	**iu**′-rop	Europa,	ay′oo-**ro**-pah
France,	fraans	Francia,	**fran**-the-ah
Germany,	cʜ**é**r′-m*a*-ni	Alemania,	ah-lay-**mah**-ne-ah
Greece,	gri**i**s	Grecia,	**gray**-the-ah
Holland,	jol′-*a*nd	Holanda,	o-**lahn**-dah
Hungary,	jŏng′-g*a*-ri	Hungría,	oon-**gree**-ah
India,	in′-di-*a*	India,	**een**-de-ah
Ireland,	**air**′-l*a*nd	Irlanda,	eer-**lahn**-dah
Italy,	i′-tah-li	Italia,	ee-**tah**-lee-ah
Japan,	cʜ*a*-pᴀn′	Japón,	*H*ah-**pon**
Mexico,	meks′-i′-ko	Méjico,	**may**-*H*e-ko
Morocco,	m*o*-ro′-k**o**u	Marruecos,	mar-rroo′ay-kos
Netherlands,	ned**s**′-r-lands	Los Países Bajos,	los pah-**ee**-ses bah-*H*os
New Zealand,	niu **sii**′-land	Nueva Zelanda,	noo′**ay**-vah thay-**lahn**-dah

xviii

Norway, n**o**ar´-uei	Noruega, no-rroo´**ay**-gah
Portugal, p**ó**r´-tiu-gal	Portugal, p**or**-tu-gahl
Russia, rŏsh´-a	Rusia, **roo**-se-ah
Scotland, skot´-land	Escocia, ess-**ko**-the-ah
Spain, sp**ei**n	España, ess-**pahn**-yah
Sweden, su**i**d´-n	Suecia, soo´**ay**-the-ah
Switzerland, swiz´-er-land	Suiza, soo´**ee**-thah
Turkey, tĕr´-ki	Turquía, toor-**kee**-ah
(the) United Kingdom (Di) iu-nai´-ted king´-dm	El Reino Unido el rray´**ee**-no oo-**nee**-do
(the) United States (Di) iu-nai´-ted steits	Los Estados Unidos, los ess-**tah**-dos oo-**nee**-dos
Wales, u**ei**ls	(el país de) Gales, **gah**-les
American, a-mer´-i-kan	Americano, a., ah-may-re-**kah**-no
Australian, **o**as-tr**ei**´-li-an	Australiano, a., ah´oos-trah-l´**yah**-no
Belgian, bel´-CHi-an	Belga, a., **bel**-gah
British, brit´-ish	Británico, a., bre-**tah**-ne-ko
Canadian, kA-n**ei**´-di-an	Canadiense, a., kah-nah-de-**en**-say
Danish, d**ei**´-nish	Dinamarqués, a., de-nah-mar-**kess**
Dutch, dŏch	Holandés, a., o-lahn-**dess**
English, in**g**´-glish	Inglés, a., in-**gless**
French, french	Francés, a., frahn-**thess**
German, CHĕr´-man	Alemán, a., ah-lay-**mahn**
Irish, **ai**r´-ish	Irlandés, a., eer-lahn-**dess**
Italian, i-tah´-li-an	Italiano, a., ee-tah-lee-**ah**-no
Norwegian, n**o**ar-u**ii**´-CHi-an	Noruego, a., no-rroo´**ay**-go
Portuguese, p**ó**r´-tiu-g**ii**s	Portugués, a., por-too-**ghess**
Russian, rŏsh´-an	Ruso, a., **roos**-oh
Scots, skots	Escocés, a., ess-ko thess
Spanish, span´-ish	Español, a., ess-pahn-**yol**
Swedish, su**i**d´-ish	Sueco, a., soo´**ay**-koh
Swiss, suis	Suizo, a., soo´**ee**-tho
Welsh, uelsh	Galés, a., **gah**-less

Antwerp, An'tuĕrp	Amberes, ahm-**bay**-ress
Athens, az'ns	Atenas, ah-**tay**-nahs
Barcelona, baar-se-loh'-na	Barcelona, bar-thay-**loh**-nah
Berlin, bĕr-lin'	Berlín, bair-**leen**
Brussels, brŏs'-els	Bruselas, broo-**say**-lahs
Cairo, kai'-rou	Cairo, kah'**ee**-ro
Capetown, keip'-taun	Ciudad del Cabo, the-oo-**dahd** del **kah**-bo
Geneva, cʜi-nii'-va	Ginebra, He-**nay**-brah
Genoa, chen'-ou-a	Génova, Hay-no-vah
Gibraltar, cʜib-roal'-ta	Gibraltar, Heeb-rahl-**tar**
(The) Hague, (Di) jeig	La Haya, lah **ah**'e-yah
Lisbon, lisb'-on	Lisboa, liss-bo'**ah**
London, lŏn'-dn	Londres, **lon**-dress
Madrid, ma-drid	Madrid, mah-**dreed**
Marseilles, maar-sels	Marsella, mar-**say**-l'yah
New York, niuu-iork	Nueva York, noo'**ay**-vah
Orleans, oar'-li-ens	Orleans, or-lay-**ans** [york
Paris, pa'-ris	París, pah-**riss**
Rome, roum	Roma, **roh**-mah
Seville, se-vil'	Sevilla, say-**vee**-l'yah
Tangiers, tan-cʜi'-ers	Tanger, **tan**-Her
Vienna, vi-en'-a	Viena, ve-**ay**-nah
Warsaw, uoar'-soa	Varsovia, var-**so**-ve-ah
Alps, Alps	Alpes, **ahl**-pess
Black Sea, blak sii	Mar Negro, ma**r nay**-gro
Caucasus, kau'-ka-ses	Cáucaus, **kah**'oo-kah-so
Danube, dan'-iub	Danubio, dah-**noo**-be-o
Mediterranean, med-i-ter-ei'-ni-an	Mediterráneo, may-de-tair-**rrah**-nay-o
Nile, nail	Nilo, **nee**-lo
North Sea, norz sii	Mar del Norte, ma**r** del **nor**-tay
Pacific Ocean, pas-if'-ik oa'-sh'n	Océano Pacífico, o-**say**-ah-no pah-**thee**-fe-ko
Pyrenees, pi-ren-iis'	Pirineos, pe-re-**nay**-os
Seine, sein	Séna, **say**-nah
Tagus, tei'-gŏs	Tajo, **tah**-Ho
Thames, tems	Támesis, **tah**-may-siss

TABLA COMPARATIVA

Medidas   **Pesos**

MEDIDAS DE LONGITUD

1 inch (in.) = 2·54 cm.	1 furlong = 201·16 m.
1 foot (ft.) = 30·4 cm.	1 mile = 1 km, 610 m.
1 yard (yd.) = 91·4 cm.	1 fathom = 1·828 m.

1 knot = 1 km, 852 m.

MEDIDAS DE SUPERFICIE

1 square inch = 6·45 cm²	1 square yard = 8361 cm²
1 square foot = 929 cm²	1 acre = 40 áreas
1 square mile = 2·59 km² (10 sq. miles = ca. 26 km²)	

MEDIDAS DE CAPACIDAD

1 pint = 0·568 litro (8 pints = 1 gallon)
1 quart = 1·136 litro   1 gallon = 4·546 litros

PESOS (Avoirdupois)

1 ounce (oz.) = 28·35 gr. (16 oz. = 1 pound)
1 pound (lb.) = 453·59 gr. (14 lbs. = 1 stone)
1 stone = 6·35 kg. (8 stones = 1 hundredweight)
1 hundredweight (cwt.) = 50·8 kg. (20 cwt. = 1 ton)
1 ton (tonelada inglesa) = 1016 kg.

TERMÓMETRO

32° Farenheit = 0° centigrado
212° Farenheit = 100° centigrados

Por consiguiente 9° Farenheit = 5° centigrados

Para convertir grados centígrados en grados
Farenheit, multiplíquese por 9, divídase por 5, y
añadase 32.

COMPARATIVE TABLE

Measures   **Weights**

LINEAL MEASURE

1 centímetro = 0·393 inch (10 cm. = about 4 ins.)
1 metro = 39·37 ins. (10 m. = about 33 ft.)
1 hectómetro = 100 m. = 109·36 yds.
1 kilómetro = 1000 m. = 1093·63 yds.
(⅝ of a mile)

SQUARE MEASURE

1 centiárea (1 sq. metre) = 1·196 sq. yds. (10·8 sq.
1 área (100 sq. metres) = 119·6 sq. yds. [ft.]
1 hectárea (10,000 sq. metres) = 2·471 acres

CUBIC MEASURE

1 estéreo = 1·308 cu. yds.
1 litro = 1·76 pints   1 hectolitro = 22 gals.

WEIGHTS (Avoirdupois)

1 hectogramo (100 grams) = 3·527 ozs,
1 kilogramo (1000 grams) = 2·205 lbs.
1 tonelada (1000 kilograms) = 0·984 ton

THERMOMETER

0° Centigrade = 32° Farenheit
100° Centigrade = 212° Fahrenheit

5° C. are equivalent to 9° F. To convert Fahrenheit into Centigrade, subtract 32, multiply by 5, and divide by 9.

AVISOS PÚBLICOS, SEÑALES DE CARRETERA
PUBLIC NOTICES, ROAD SIGNS

Abierto	Open
¡ Alto !	Halt
Caballeros	Gentlemen
Calzada estrecha	Road narrows
Calzada irregular	Uneven surface
Calzada resbaladiza	Slippery surface
Ceda el paso	Give way
Cerrado	Closed
Cruce	Crossroads
¡ Cuidado !	Take care
Despacio	Slow
Desviación	Diversion
Dirección obligatoria	One-way traffic
Empuje	Push
Entrada	Way in
Estacionamiento	Parking
Glorieta, Redondel	Roundabout
Libre	Vacant
Obras	Road up
Ocupado	Engaged
¡ Pare !	Stop
¡ Peligro !	Danger
Pintura húmeda	Wet paint
Privado	Private
Prohibido andelantar	No overtaking
Salida	Way out
Señoras	Ladies
Se prohibe estacionar	No parking
Se prohibe fumar	No smoking
Se prohibe la entrada	No entry
Se prohibe tocar	Do not touch
Tire	Pull

SPANISH-ENGLISH DICTIONARY

a, ah, prep., at; to; in; on; by; for; as

abad, ah-**bahd**, s., abbot

abadejo, ah-bah-**day**-Ho, s., cod-fish; yellow wren

abajo, ah-**bah**-Ho, adv., below, under, underneath

abalanzar, ah-bah-lahn-**thar**, v., to balance; to dart; to rush

abalear, ah-bah-lay-**ar**, v., to winnow; to sift

abandonar, ah-bahn-do-**nar**, v., to abandon; to give up; to forsake

abandono, ah-bahn-**do**-no, s., abandonment

abanico, ah-bah-**nee**-ko, s., fan

abarca, ah-**bar**-kah, s., sandal worn by peasants

abarcar, ah-bar-**kar**, v., to embrace; to clasp

abarrotar, ah-bar-rro-**tar**, v., to stow; to overstock

abastecedor, ah-bahs-tay-thay-**dor**, s., caterer

abastecer, ah-bahs-tay-**thair**, v., to supply; to provide

abastecimiento, ah-bahs-tay-the-me-**en**-to, s., [provisions

abate, ah-**bah**-tay, s., abbé

abatido, ah-bah-**tee**-do, a., dejected; abject

abatimiento, ah-bah-te-me-**en**-to, s., depression

abatir, ah-bah-**teer**, v., to throw down; to discourage, to be depressed

abdicar, ahb-de-**kar**, v., to abdicate

abeja, ah-**bay**Hah, s., bee

abejón, ah-**bay**-Hon, s., hornet; drone

abellacado, ah-bell-yah-**kah**-do, a., mean-spirited

aberración, ah-bair-rrah-the-**on**, s., aberration

abertura, ah-bair-**too**-rah, s., opening; overture

abierto*, ah-be-**air**-to, a., open; frank

abigarrar, ah-be-gar-**rrar**, v., to variegate

abismar, ah-biss-**mar**, v., to think deeply; to [depress

abismo, ah-**biss**-mo, s., abyss

abjurar, ahb-**Hoor**-ar, v., to abjure [tening

ablandamiento, ah-blahn-dah-me-**en**-to, s., softening

ablandar, ah-blahn-**dar**, v., to mollify; to relent; [to soften

ablución, ah-bloo-the-**on**, s., ablution

abnegar, ahb-nay-**gar,** v., to renounce

abobado, ah-bo-**bah**-do, a., silly; stupid

abobamiento, ah-bo-bah-mee-**en**-to, s., stupefac-

abobar, ah-bo-**bar,** v., to stupefy   [tion

abocamiento, ah-bo-kah-me-**en**-to, s., conference

abocarse, ah-bo-**kar**-say, v., to meet; to have a
conference

abofetear, ah-bo-fay-tay-**ar,** v., to slap; to insult

abogado, ah-bo-**gah**-do, s., advocate; lawyer;
barrister

abogar, ah-bo-**gar,** v., to advocate; to plead

abohetado, ah-bo-ay-**tah**-do, a., swollen; inflated

abolengo, ah-bo-len-go, s., ancestry, lineage

abolición, ah-bo-le-the-**on,** s., abolition

abolir, ah-bo-**leer,** v., to abolish, to repeal

abollar, ah-bo-l'**yar,** v., to emboss; to dent

abominable, ah-bo-me-**nah**-blay, a., abominable

abominar, ah-bo-me-**nar,** v., to abhor; to abominate   [fit for

abonado,ah-bo-**nah**-do,s.,subscriber.a.,creditable

abonador, ah-bo-nah-**dor,** s., bail; surety

abonar, ah-bo-**nar,** v., to bail; to manure; to pay;
to credit; to subscribe

abonaré, ah-bo-nar-**ay,** s., promissory note

abono, ah-**bo**-no, s., guarantee; subscription;
receipt; manure

abordaje, ah-bor-**dah**-Hay, s., boarding a ship

abordar, ah-bor-**dar,** v., to board a ship

abordo, ah-**bor**-do, s., attack on a ship

aborrachado, ah-bor-rrah-**chah**-do, a., flushed

aborrecer, ah-bor-rray-**thair,** v., to abhor

aborrecible, ah-bor-rray-**thee**-blay, a., hateful,
abhorrent

abortivo*, ah-bor-**tee**-vo, a., abortive   [ster

aborto, ah-**bor**-to, s., miscarriage; abortion; mon-

abotonador, ah-bo-to-nah-**dor,** s., button-hook

abotonar, ah-bo-to-**nar,** v., to button

abovedado, ah-bo-vay-**dah**-do, a., vaulted

abra, ah-brah, s., bay; creek; haven

abrasamiento, ah-brah-sah-me-**en**-to, s., burning

abrasar, ah-brah-**sar,** v., to burn; to set on fire

abrazar, ah-brah-**thar,** v., to embrace; to hug

abrazo, ah-**brah**-tho, s., hug; embrace

abrelatas, ah-bray-**lah**-tahs, s., tin-opener

abreviación, ah-bray-ve-ah-the-**on**, s., abbreviation

abreviar, ah-bray-ve-**ar**, v., to abridge, cut short

abridor, ah-bre-**dor**, s., opener

abrigar, ah-bre-**gar**, v., to shelter; to cover

abrigo, ah-**bree**-go, s., shelter; overcoat

abril, ah-**breel**, s., April

abrimiento, ah-bre-me-en-to, s., opening

abrir, ah-**breer**, v., to open

abrochar, ah-bro-**char**, v., to button

abrogar, ah-bro-**gar**, v., to abrogate; to repeal

abrojo, ah-**bro**-Ho, s., thorn; thistle [eaten

abromado, ah-bro-**mah**-do, a., dark; hazy; worm

abrumado, ah-broo-**mah**-do, a., weary; overwhelmed

abrumar, ah-broo-**mar**, v., to crush; to overwhelm

abrutado, ah-broo-**tah**-do, a., brutish

absceso, ahbs-**thay**-so, s., abscess

absolución, ahb-so-loo-the-**on**, s., absolution

absoluto*, ahb-so-**loo**-to, a., absolute

absolver, ahb-sol-**vair**, v., to absolve

absorber, ahb-sor-**bair**, v., to absorb

abstemio, ahbs-**tay**-me-o, a., abstemious

abstenerse, ahbs-tay-**nair**-say, v., to abstain

abstinencia, ahbs-te-**nen**-the-ah, s., abstinence; temperance

abstinente, ahbs-te-**nen**-tay, a., abstinent

abstraer, ahbs-trah-**air**, v., to abstract

abstraido, ahbs-trah-**ee**-do, a., retired; absent-

absuelto, ahb-soo-**el**-to, a., absolved [minded

absurdo, ahb-**soor**-do, s., absurdity. a., absurd

abuela, ah-boo**'ay**-lah, s., grandmother

abuelo, ah-boo**'ay**-lo, s., grandfather

abultado, ah-bool-**tah**-do, a., bulky

abundante, ah-boon-**dahn**-tay, a., abundant

abundar, ah-boon-**dar**, v., to abound

aburrir, ah-boor-**reer**, v., to weary; to bore

abusar, ah-boo-**sar**, v., to abuse

abuso, ah-**boo**-so, s., abuse

abyección, ah-be'**ayk**-the-**on**, s., abjection

abyecto, ah-be'**ayk**-to, a., abject

acá, ah-**kah,** adv., here; hither   [worn out

acabado, ah-kah-**bah**-do, a., perfect; complete

acabamiento, ah-kah-bah-me-**en**-to, s., end; completion

acabar, ah-kah-**bar,** v., to finish; to end

academia, ah-kah-**day**-me-ah, s., academy

acaecedero, ah-kah-ay-thay-**day**-ro, a., eventual; contingent

acaecer, ah-kah-ay-**thair,** v., to happen

acaecimiento, ah-kah-ay-the-me-**en**-to, s., occurrence

acallar, ah-kah-l'**yar,** v., to quiet   [rence; event

acalorar, ah-kah-lo-**rar,** v., to warm; to inflame

acampar, ah-kahm-**pahr,** v., to camp

acanillado, ah-kah-nee-l'**yah**-do, a., ribbed (cloth)

acantilado, ah-kahn-te-**lah**-do, s., steep cliff

acantonar, ah-kahn-to-**nar,** v., to quarter (troops)

acariciar, ah-kah-re-the-**ar,** v., to fondle; to caress

acarreador, ah-kar-rray-ah-**dor,** s., porter; carrier

acarrear, ah-kar-rray-**ar,** v., to carry; to cause

acarreo, ah-kar-**rray**-o, s., cartage

acaso, ah-**kah**-so, adv., by chance.   s., chance

acceder, ahk-thay-**dair,** v., to accede; to agree

acceso, ahk-**thay**-so, s., access

accesorio, ahk-thay-**so**-re-o, a., accessory

accidentarse, ahk-the-den-**tar**-say, v., to be seized with a fit

accidente, ahk-the-**den**-tay, s., accident; sudden

acción, ahk-the-**on,** s., action; feat; battle   [fit

accionar, ahk-the-o-**nar,** v., to gesticulate

accionista, ahk-the-o-**niss**-tah, s., shareholder

acechar, ah-thay-**char,** v., to waylay; to pry

acedamente, ah-thay-dah-**men**-tay, adv., sourly

acedo, ah-**thay**-do, a., acid; sour

aceite, ah-**thay**-e-tay, s., oil

aceitería, ah-thay-e-tay-**ree**-ah, s., oil shop

aceitoso, ah-thay-e-**to**-so, a., oily; greasy

aceituna, ah-thay-e-**too**-nah, s., olive   [tion

aceleración, ah-thay-lay-rah-the-**on,** s., accelera-

acelerador, ah-thay-lay-rah-**dor,** s., accelerator

acelerar, ah-thay-lay-**rar,** v., to accelerate

acendrar, ah-then-**drar,** v., to refine metals

acento, ah-**then**-to, s., accent

acentuar, ah-then-too-**ar**, v., to accentuate

acepción, ah-thep-the-**on**, s., acceptacion; meaning

aceptable, ah-thep-**tah**-blay, a., acceptable

aceptación, ah-thep-tah-the-**on**, s., acceptation

aceptador, ah-thep-tah-**dor**, s., acceptor

aceptar, ah-thep-**tar**, v., to accept

acepto, ah-**thep**-to, a., acceptable, agreeable

acequia, ah-**thay**-ke-ah, s., canal; drain

acerado, ah-thay-**rah**-do, a., made of steel

acerbidad, ah-thair-be-**dahd**, s., acerbity; rigour

acerbo*, ah-**thair**-bo, a., harsh; cruel

acerca, ah-**thair**-kah, prep., about; relating to

acercar, ah-thair-**kar**, v., to approach

acero, ah-**thay**-ro, s., steel

acérrimo, ah-**thair**-rre-mo, a., most vigorous and　　[strong

acertado*, ah-thair-**tah**-do, a., proper; fit

acertar, ah-thair-**tar**, v., to hit the mark; to hit upon; to guess; to succeed

acertijo, ah-thair-**tee**-Ho, s, riddle

acervo, ah-**thair**-vo, s., heap

aciago, ah-the-**ah**-go, a., unfortunate; sad

acíbar, ah-**thee**-bar, s., aloes; bitterness

acicalar, ah-the-kah-**lar**, v., to polish; to dress; to　　[embellish

acidez, ah-the-**deth**, s., acidity

ácido, **ah**-the-do, a., acid; sour

acidular, ah-the-doo-**lar**, v., to acidulate

acierto, ah-the-**air**-to, s., good hit; good guess

aclamación, ah-klah-mah-the-**on**, s., acclamation

aclamar, ah-klah-**mar**, v., to acclaim; to applaud

aclaración, ah-klah-rah-thc-**on**, s., explanation

aclarar, ah-klah-**rar**, v., to explain; to clarify

aclimatar, ah-kle-mah-**tahr**, v., to acclimatize

acobardar, ah-ko-bar-**dar**, v., to daunt; to intimidate

acocear, ah-ko-thay-**ar**, v., to kick; to ill-treat

acodiciar, ah-ko-de-the-**ar**, v., to long for; to covet

acoger, ah-ko-**Hair**, v., to receive; to admit someone

acogida, acogimiento, ah-ko-**Hee**-dah, ah-ko-*He*-me-en-to, s., reception

acometedor, ah-ko-may-tay-**dor**, s., aggressor

acometer, ah-ko-may-**tair**, v., to assault; to attack

acometida, ah-ko-may-**tee**-dah, s., assault

acomodado*, ah-ko-mo-**dah**-do, a., convenient; fit; wealthy; reasonable

acomodar, ah-ko-mo-**dar**, v., to accommodate; to reconcile; to supply [lodgings

acomodo, ah-ko-**mo**-do, s., employment; situation;

acompañar, ah-kom-pah-**n'yar**, v., to accompany

acondicionado, ah-kon-de-the-o-**nah**-do, a., conditioned [to prepare

acondicionar, ah-kon-de-the-o-**nar**, v., to dispose;

acongojar, ah-kon-go-*H*ar, v., to oppress; to afflict

aconsejar, ah-kon-say-*H*ar, v., to advise

acontecer, ah-kon-tay-**thair**, v., to happen

acontecimiento, ah-kon-tay-the-me-**en**-to, s., event; happening

acopiar, ah-ko-pe-**ar**, v., to gather; to store up

acorazar, ah-ko-rah-**thah**, v., to armour

acorcharse, ah-kor-**char**-say, v., to shrivel

acordado*, ah-kor-**dah**-do, a., agreed

acordar, ah-kor-**dar**, v., to resolve; to agree; to remember

acorde, ah-**kor**-day, s., accord. a., conformable

acorrer, ah-kor-**rrair**, v., to run to; to succour

acortamiento, ah-kor-tah-me-**en**-to, s., shortening

acortar, ah-kor-**tar**, v., to shorten

acosamiento, ah-ko-sah-me-**en**-to, s., relentless persecution

acosar, ah-koh-**sar**, v., to pursue close; to harass

acostar, ah-kos-**tar**, v., to lay down; to approach

acostumbradamente, ah-kos-toom-brah-dah-**men**-tay, adv., customarily

acostumbrar, ah-kos-toom-**brar**, v., to accustom

acotación, ah-ko-tah-the-**on**, s., limit; annotation

acotar, ah-ko-**tar**, v., to delimit; to survey

acre*, ah-**kray**, a., acrid, sour

acrecentamiento, ah-kray-then-tah-me-**en**-to, s.,

acrecer, ah-kray-**thair**, v., to increase [increase

acreditar, ah-kray-de-**tar**, v., to prove; to credit

acreedor, ah-kray-ay-**dor**, s., creditor. a., deserving

acribar, ah-kre-**bar**, v., to sift

acriminar, ah-kre-me-**nar**, v., to accuse

acrimonia, ah-kre-**mo**-ne-ah, s., acrimony

acrisolar, ah-kre-so-**lar**, v., to refine; to assay

acritud, ah-kre-**tood**, s., sourness; acrimony

acta, ahk-tah, s., act; record; minutes

actitud, ahk-te-**tood**, s., attitude

activar, ahk-te-**var**, v., to push; to hurry

actividad, ahk-te-vi-**dahd**, s., activity

activo*, ahk-**tee**-vo, a., active

actor, ahk-**tor**, s., actor

actriz, ahk-**treeth**, s., actress

actuación, ahk-too-ah-the-**on**, s., proceedings at law; actuation

actual*, ahk-too-**ahl**, a., actual; present

actualidad, ahk-too-ah-le-**dahd**, s., present time

actuar, ahk-too-**ar**, v., to act, to proceed at law; to perform judicial acts

actuario, ahk-too-**ah-**re-o, s., registrar

acuarela, ah-koo'ah-**ray-**lay, s., water-colour

acuario, ah-koo-**ah-**re-o, s., aquarium

acudir, ah-koo-**deer**, v., to support; to run to; to have recourse

acueducto, ah-koo'ay-**dook-**to, s., aqueduct

ácueo, ah-koo'ay-o, a., watery   [collection

acuerdo, ah-koo'**air-**do, s., resolution; accord; re-

acumular, ah-koo-moo-**lar**, v., to accumulate

acuosidad, ah-koo'o-si-**dahd**, s., wateriness

acurrucarse, ah-koor-rroo-**kar-**say, v., to squat

acusación, ah-koo-sah-the-**on**, s., accusation

acusar, ah-koo-**sar**, v., to accuse

acusón, ah-koo-**son**, s., (fam.) sneak; tell-tale

acústica, ah-**kooss-**te-kah, s., acoustics

achacar, ah-chah-**kar**, v., to impute

achacoso, ah-chah-ko-so, a., sickly; ailing

achaparrado, ah-chah-par-**rrah-**do, a., dwarfish

achaque, ah-**chah-**kay, s., habitual indisposition

achatar, ah-chah-**tar**, v., to flatten   [humble

achicar, ah-che-**kar**, v., to diminish; to lessen; to

achicoria, ah-che-ko-re-ah, s., chicory

achispado, ah-chis-**pah-**do, a., tipsy

achuchar, ah-choo-**char**, v., to flatten; to jostle

adalid, ah-dah-**leed**, s., chief; leader

adamascado, ah-dah-mahs-**kah-**do, a., damask-like

adán, ah-**dahn,** s., Adam; (fig.) slovenly man

adaptación, ah-dahp-tah-the-on, s., adaptation.

adaptado*, ah-dahp-**tah**-do, a., adapted, fitted

adarme, ah-**dar**-may, s., half a drachm (1 gr. 79)

adecuado*, ah-day-koo'**ah**-do, a., adequate

adecuar, ah-day-koo'**ar,** v., to fit, to adapt

adefesio, ah-day-**fay**-se-o, s., extravagance; ridiculous attire   [forward

adelantado, ah-day-lahn-**tah**-do, a., anticipated

adelantar, ah-day-lahn-**tar,** v., to advance; to anticipate; to accelerate

adelante, ah-day-lahn-tay, adv., farther; forward

adelgazar, ah-del-gah-**thar,** v., to make thin

ademán, ah-day-**mahn,** s., gesture; look

además, ah-day-**mahs,** adv., moreover; further;
adentro, ah-**den**-tro, adv., within   [besides

adepto, ah-**dep**-to, a., adept, s., follower

aderezar, ah-day-ray-**thar,** v., to adorn; to dress

aderezo, ah-day-**ray**-tho, s., adorning; dressing

adestrar, ah-dess-**trar,** v., (see **adiestrar**) [(food)

adeudado, ah-day-oo-**dah**-do, a., indebted

adherentes, ah-day-**ren**-tess, s., requisites; ingre-

adherir, ah-day-**reer,** v., to adhere   [dients

adhesión, ah-day-se-**on,** s., adhesion

adición, ah-de-the-**on,** s., addition

adicto, ah-**deck**-to, a., addicted   [to train

adiestrar, ah-de-ess-**trar,** v., to guide, to teach,

adinerado, ah-de-nay-**rah**-do, a., rich; wealthy

¡ adiós ! ah-de-**os,** interj., good-bye; farewell; adieu

adivinar, ah-de-ve-**nar,** v., to foretell; to conjecture; to guess

adjetivo, ahd-**Hay**-tee-vo, s., adjective

adjudicar, ahd-Hoo-de-**kar,** v., to adjudge; to adju-

adjunta, ahd-**Hoon**-tah, s., enclosure   [dicate

adjunto, ahd-**Hoon**-to, a., enclosed

administración, ahd-me-niss-trah-the-**on,** s., administration

administrar, ahd-me-niss-**trar,** v., to manage; to
administer

admirable*, ahd-me-**rah**-blay, a., admirable

admirar, ahd-me-**rar,** v., to admire

admisible, ahd-me-**see**-blay, a., admissible

admitir, ahd-me-**teer**, v., to admit; to accept

admonición, ahd-mo-ne-the-**on**, s., admonition warning   [cook

adobar, ah-do-**bar**, v., to fertilize; to pickle; to

adocenado, ah-do-thay-**nah**-do, a., common; vul-

adoctrinar, ah-dok-tre-**nar**, v., to instruct   [gar

adolecer, ah-do-lay-**thair**, v., to be ill; to suffer

adolescencia, ah-do-less-**then**-the-ah, s., adolescence

adolescente, ah-do-less-**then**-tay, a., adolescent

adonde, ah-**don**-day, adv., whither? where?

adoptar, ah-dop-**tar**, v., to adopt

adoquín, ah-do-**keen**, s., paving stone

adorable*, ah-do-**rah**-blay, a., adorable

adorador, ah-do-rah-**dor**, s., worshipper

adorar, ah-do-**rar**, v., to adore; to worship

adormecer, ah-dor-may-**thair**, v., to cause sleep; to fall asleep; to lull

adornar, ah-dor-**nar**, v., to adorn

adquirir, ahd-ke-**reer**, v., to acquire; to get

adrede, ah-**dray**-day, adv., purposely

adscribir, ahds-kre-**beer**, v., to appoint

aduana, ah-doo-**ah**-nah, s., Custom-house; Customs

aduanero, ah-doo-ah-**nay**-ro, s., Custom-house officer

aducir, ah-doo-**theer**, v., to cite; to adduce   [cer

adueñarse, ah-doo-ay-**n'yar**-say, v., to take possession of

adulación, ah-doo-lah-the-**on**, s., adulation

adulterar, ah-dool-tay-**rar**, v., to adulterate

adulto, ah-**dool**-to, a., adult

adusto, ah-**dooss**-to, a., sullen; gloomy

advenedizo, ahd-vay-nay-**dee**-tho, a., immigrant upstart; parvenu

advenimiento, ahd-vay-ne-me-**en**-to, s., advent

adverbio, ahd-**vair**-be-o, s., adverb

adversario, ahd-vair-**sah**-re-o, s., opponent

adversidad, ahd-vair-se-**dahd**, s., adversity

advertencia, ahd-vair-**ten**-the-ah, s., warning; notice; advertence

advertido*, ahd-vair-**tee**-do, a., warned; clever

advertimiento, see **advertencia**

advertir, ahd-vair-**teer**, v., to warn; to observe

adyacente, ahdfyah-**then**-tay, a., adjacent, contiguous

aerodromo, ah-ay-ro-**dro**-mo, s., aerodrome

aeronave, ah-ay-ro-**nah**-vay, s., airship

aeroplano, ah-ay-ro-**plah**-no, s., aeroplane

aeropuerto, ah-ay-ro-poo'**air**-to, s., airport

afabilidad, ah-fah-be-le-**dahd**, s., affability

afable*, ah-**fah**-blay, a., affable

afamado, ah-fah-**mah**-do, a., celebrated; famous

afán, ah-**fahn**, s., anxiety; solicitude

afanar, ah-fah-**nar**, v., to toil; to be oversolicitous

afear, ah-fay-**ar**, v., to deface; to disfigure; to decry

afección, ah-fek-the-**on**, s., affection

afectado, ah-fek-tah-**do**, a., affected   [loving

afectuoso, ah-fek-too'**o**-so, a., affectionate; kind,

afeitar, ah-fay'e-**tar**, v., to shave; to trim

afeminado, ah-fay-me-**nah**-do, a., effeminate

aferrar, ah-fair-**rar**, v., to grasp; to grapple

afianzar, ah-fe-ahn-**thar**, v., to guarantee; to make fast; to become bail

afición, ah-fe-the-**on**, s., linking, inclination

aficionado, ah-fe-the-o-**nah**-do, s., amateur

afijo, ah-**fee**-Ho, s., affix

afilado, ah-fe-**lah**-do, a., sharpened; sharp; keen

afilar, ah-fe-**lar**, v., to sharpen; to whet

afilón, ah-fe-**lon**, s., whetstone

afín, ah-**feen**, s., relation by affinity; close by

afinar, ah-fe-**nar**, v., to complete; to polish; to tune

afincar, ah-fin-**kar**, v., to acquire real estate

afinidad, ah-fe-ne-**dahd**, s., affinity, analogy

afirmar, ah-feer-**mar**, v., to affirm; to make fast

aflicción, ah-fleck-the-**on**, s., grief; sorrow; anguish

afligir, ah-fle-**Heer**, v., to afflict; to grieve

aflojamiento, ah-flo-Hah-me-**en**-to, s., relaxation; slackening   [bilitate

aflojar, ah-flo-**Har**, v., to loosen; to relax; to deafluente,

afluente, ah-floo-**en**-tay, a., affluent; copious

afluir, ah-floo-**eer**, v., to flow into; to congregate

aforrar, ah-for-**rrar**, v., to line (clothes)   [lucky

afortunado, ah-for-too-**nah**-do, a., fortunate;

afrenta, ah-**fren**-tah, s., affront; insult

afrentar, ah-fren-**tar**, v., to affront; to insult

afuera, ah-foo'**ay**-rah, adv., abroad ; away ; outside
afueras, ah-foo'**ay**-rahs, s., environs　　[stoop
agacharse, ah-gah-char-say, v., to crouch ; to
agallas, ah-gah-l'yahs, s., glands ; gills ; galls
agarrada, ah-gar-rrah-dah, s., altercation
agarrar, ah-gar-**rrar**, v., to grasp ; to seize
agarro, ah-gar-rro, s., grasp
agasajar, ah-gah-sah-*H*ar, v., to treat kindly ; to
　regale ; to entertain
agasajo, ah-gah-**sah**-*H*o, s., kind treatment ; gift
agazaparse, ah-gah-thah-par-say, v., to hide one-
agencia, ah-*H*en-the-ah, s., agency　　　[self
agenciar, ah-*H*en-the-ar, v., to solicit ; to negotiate
agente, ah-*H*en-tay, s., agent
agigantado, ah-*H*e-gahn-**tah**-do, a., gigantic
agilidad, ah-*H*e-le-dhad, s., agility ; nimbleness
agio, agiotaje, ah-*H*e-o, ah-*H*e-o-**tah**-*H*ay, s., ex-
　change of paper money or bills for coin ; premium
agitación, ah-*H*e-tah-the-**on**, s., agitation
agitar, ah-*H*e-**tar**, v., to agitate ; to stir ; to discuss
aglomerar, ah-glo-may-**rar**, v., to agglomerate
agobiar, ah-go-be-**ar**, v., to bow ; to oppress
agobio, ah-go-be-o, s., binding down ; oppression
agolparse, ah-gol-par-say, v., to crowd ; to rush
agonía, ah-go-**nee**-ah, s., agony
agorar, ah-go-rar, v., to prognosticate
agotamiento, ah-go-tah-me-**en**-to, s., exhaustion
agotar, ah-go-tar, v., to exhaust
agraciado, ah-grah-the-**ah**-do, a., graceful ; genteel
agradable, ah-grah-**dah**-blay, a., agreeable
agradar, ah-grah-dar, v., to be pleasing ; to please
agradecer, ah-grah-day-**thair**, v., to thank for
agradecido, ah-grah-day-**thee**-do, a., thankful ;
　grateful　　　　　　　　　　　　[gratefulness
agradecimiento, ah-grah-day-thee-me-**en**-to, s.,
agrado, ah-**grah**-do, s., affability ; pleasure ; liking
agrandar, ah-grahn-**dar**, v., to enlarge
agrario, ah-**grah**-re-o, a., agrarian ; rustic
agravar, ah-grah-**var**, v., to aggravate ; to become
　grave or worse
agraviar, ah-grah-ve-**ar**, v., to offend ; to injure
agredir, ah-gray-**deer**, v., to attack ; to assault

agregación, ah-gray-gah-the-**on**, s., aggregation

agregar, ah-gray-**gar**, v., to aggregate; to gather;

agresión, ah-gray-se-**on**, s., aggression   [to heap

agreste, ah-**gress**-tay, a., rustic; rude

agriar, ah-gre-**ar**, v., to make sour; to irritate

agricultor, ah-gre-kool-**tor**, s., farmer

agrio, ah,gre-o, a., sour

agrupación, ah-groo-pah-the-on, s., cluster; group

agrupar, ah-groo-**par**, v., to cluster; to group

agua, ah,goo'ah, s., water

aguacero, ah-goo'ah-**thay**-ro, s., shower

aguado, ah-goo'ah-do, a., watered; abstemious

aguantar, ah-goo'ahn-**tar**, v., to suffer; to endure;
    to bear

aguante, ah-goo'ahn-tay, s., fortitude; firmness

aguardar, ah-goo'ar-dar, v., to expect; to wait for

aguardiente, ah-goo'ar-de-en-tay, s., brandy

aguarrás, ah-goo'ar-rrahs, s., oil of turpentine

aguazal, ah-goo'ah-thahl, s., marsh   [wit

agudeza, ah-goo-day-thah, s., acuteness; repartee;

agudo*, ah-goo-do, a., sharp; acute

agüero, ah-goo'ay-ro, s., augury; omen

aguerrir, ah-gair-rreer, v., to inure to war

águila, ah,ghee-lah, s., eagle

aguileño, ah-ghee-lay-n'yo, a., aquiline

aguinaldo, ah-ghee-**nahl**-do, s., christmas box

aguja, ah-goo-Hah, s., needle

agujerear, ah-goo-Hay-ray-ar, v., to pierce; to bore

agujero, ah-goo-Hay-ro, s., hole

aguso, ah-goo'o-so, a., aqueous

aguzar, ah-goo-thar, v., to sharpen; to whet

aherrojar, ah-air-rro-Har, v., to fetter; to chain

ahijado, ah-e-Hah-do, s., godchild

ahijar, ah-e-Har, v., to adopt

ahinco, ah-**een**-ko, s., exertion; eagerness

ahogar, ah-o-**gar**, v., smother; to choke; to drown

ahogo, ah-o-go, s., oppression; anguish; suffocation

ahondar, ah-on-dar, v., to dig; to go deep

ahora, ah-**o**-rah, adv., now

ahorcar, ah-or-kar, v., to hang

ahorrar, ah-or-rrar, v., to save; to spare

ahorro, ah-or-rro, s., economy; saving

ahuchar, ah'oo-**char**, v., to hoard up

ahuecar, ah'oo'ay-**kar**, v., to make hollow

ahumar, ah'oo-**mar**, v., to smoke; to cure in smoke

ahuyentar, ah'oo'yen-**tar**, v., to put to flight

aírado, ah'e-**rah**-do, a., irritated; angry

aire, ah'e-ray, s., air; gait; gracefulness

aislado*, ah'iss-**lah**-do, a., isolated

ajar, ah-*H*ar, v., to ruffle; to wither

ajedrez, ah-*H*ay-**dreth**, s., chess

ajeno, ah-*H*ay-no, a., another's; foreign

ajetrearse, ah-*H*ay-tray-**ar**-say, v., to tire; to fidget; to bustle about

ajo, ah-*H*o, s., garlic

ajuar, ah-*H*oo'**ar**, s., household furniture

ajuiciado, ah-*H*oo'ee-the-**ah**-do, a., judicious

ajustado*, ah-*H*oos-**tah**-do, a., exact; stingy

ajustamiento, ah-*H*oos-tah-me-**en**-to, s., agreement; settling   [to death

ajusticiar, ah-*H*oos-te-the-**ar**, v., to execute; to put

ala, ah-lah, s., wing; row; brim

alabanza, ah-lah-**bahn**-thah, s., praise

alabar, ah-lah-**bar**, v., to praise. s., boast

alabastro, ah-lah-**bahs**-tro, s., alabaster

alacena, ah-lah-**thay**-nah, s., cupboard

alacrán, ah-lah-**krahn**, s., scorpion

alado, ah-**lah**-do, a., winged

alambicar, ah-lahm-be-**kar**, v., to distil; to scru-

alambique, ah-lahm-**bee**-kay, s., still   [tinize

alambre, ah-**lahm**-bray, s., wire

alameda, ah-lah-**may**-dah, s., poplar; grove; public

álamo, ah-lah-mo, s., poplar   [walk

alarde, ah-**lar**-day, s., parade; ostentation

alardear, ah-lar-day-**ar**, v., to boast   [ing out

alargamiento, ah-lar-gah-me-**en**-to, s., lengthen-

alargar, ah-lar-**gar**, v., to lengthen; to protract; to increase

alarido, ah-lah-**ree**-do, s., outcry; howl

alarma, ah-**lar**-mah, s., alarm

alba, ahl-bah, s., dawn; daybreak

albañal, ahl-bahn-y'**ahl**, s., common sewer

albañil, ahl-bahn-y'**eel**, s., bricklayer; mason

albarda, ahl-**bar**-dah, s., pack-saddle

albaricoque, ahl-bar-re-**co**-kay, s., apricot
albedrío, ahi-bay-**dree**-o, s., free will
alberca, ahl-**bair**-kah, s., reservoir; tank
albergar, ahl-bair-**gar**, v., to lodge; to harbour
albo, ahl-bo, a., very white
albor, ahl-**bor**, s., whiteness; daybreak   [less
alborotado*, ahl-bo-ro-**tah**-do, a., turbulent; rest-
alborotar, ahl-bo-ro-**tar**, v., to disturb; to agitate
alboroto, ahl-bo-ro-to, s., tumult; riot; fuss
alborozo, abl-bo-ro-tho, s., merriment; joy
albricias, ahl-**bree**-the-ahs, s., reward for good news
albufera, ahl-boo-**fay**-rah, s., pond; lake by the sea
albur, ahl-**boor**, s., dace; risk; chance
alcachofa, ahl-kah-**cho**-fah, s., artichoke   [bawd
alcahuete, ahl-kah-oo'**ay**-tay, s., pimp; procurer;
alcalde, ahl-**kahl**-day, s., mayor; justice of the
    peace   [arm's length; ability
alcance, ahl-**kahn**-thay, s., overtaking; balance;
alcancía, ahl-kahn-**the**-ah, s., money-box
alcanfor, ahl-kahn-**for**, s., camphor
alcantarilla, ahl-kahn-tah-**ree**-l'yah, s., small
    bridge; sewer
alcanzar, ahl-kahn-**thar**, v., to catch up; to reach;
    to obtain; to comprehend; to suffice
alcaparra, ahl-kah-**par**-rrah, s., caper
alcaravea, ahl-kah-rah-**vay**-ah, s., caraway seed
alcarraza, ahl-kar-**rrah**-thath, s., water cooler
alcartaz, ahl-kar-**tath**, s., paper cornet
alcatraz, ahl-kah-**trath**, s., pelican
alcayata, ahl-kah-**yah**-tah, s., hook
alcázar, ahl-**kah**-thar, s., castle, fortress
alcoba, ahl-**ko**-bah, s., alcove
alcohol, ahl-ko-ol, s., alcohol; antimony
alcornoque, ahl-kor-**no**-kay, s., cork-tree
aldaba, ahl-**dah**-bah, s., door knocker
aldabada, ahl-dah-**bah**-dah, s., knock at the door
aldabón, ahl-dah-**bon**, s., small knocker
aldea, ahl-**day**-ah, s., small village; hamlet
aldeano, ahl-day-**ah**-no, s., villager
aldeorrio, ahl-day-**or**-rre-o, s., small unpleasant
aleación, ah-lay-ah-the-**on**, s., alloy   [village
alear, ah-lay-**ar**, v., to alloy; to flutter

alegación, ah-lay-gah-the-**on**, s., allegation

alegar, ah-lay-**gar**, v., to allege; to plead

alegoría, ah-lay-go-**ree**-ah, s., allegory

alegrar, ah-lay-**grar**, v., to make merry; to rejoice

alegre*, ah-lay-**gray**, a., merry; joyful: cheerful

alegría, ah-lay-**gree**-ah, s., merriment; mirth; joy

alejamiento, ah-lay-Hah-me-**en**-to, s., removal; strangeness

alejar, ah-lay-**Har**, v., to remove to a distance

alelarse, ah-lay-**lar**-say, v., to become stupid

alelí, ah-lay-**lee**, s., winter gilliflower

alentado, ah-len-**tah**-do, a., courageous

alentar, ah-len-**tar**, v., to breathe; to encourage;

alero, ah-**lay**-ro, s., eaves; gable-end   [to cheer

alertar, ah-lair-**tahr**, v., to alert

aleta, ah-**lay**-tah, s., small wing; fin of a fish

aleve, ah-**lay**-vay, a., treacherous

alfalfa, ahl-**fahl**-fah, s., lucern

alfarería, ah-fah-ray-**ree**-ah, s., pottery

alféizar, ahl-**fay**'e-thar, s., splay of window

alférez, ahl-**fay**-reth, s., ensign

alfiler, ahl-fe-**lair**, s., pin

alfombra, ahl-**fom**-brah, s., floor-carpet

alforja, ahl-**for**-Hah, s., saddle-bag

algarabía, ahl-gah-rah-**bee**-ah, s., arabic tongue; gibberish; din

algazara, ahl-gah-**thah**-rah, s., huzza; clamour

álgebra, **ahl**-Hay-brah, s., algebra   [aught

algo, **ahl**-go, adv., & pron., somewhat; something;

algodón, ahl-go-**don**, s., cotton

alguacil, ahl-goo'ah-**thill**, s., constable

alguien, **ahlg**-e-en, pron., someone; anyone

algún, ahl-**goon**, pron., (see **alguno**)

alguno, ahl-**goo**-no, a., some; any; somebody

alhaja, ahl-ah-**Hah**, s., jewel

alharaca, ahl-ah-**rah**-kah, s., clamour; vociferation

alhóndiga, ahl-**on**-de-gah, s., public granary; wheat exchange

alhucema, ahl-oo-**thay**-mah, s., lavender

aliado, ah-le-ah-do, a., allied

alianza, ah-le-**ahn**-thah, s., alliance

alias, ah-le-ahs, adv., otherwise; alias

alicates, ah-le-**kah**-tess, s., pincers; nippers

aliciente, ah-le-the-**en**-tay, s., attraction; induce- [ment

alienar, ah-le-ay-**nar,** (see **enajenar**)

aliento, ah-le-**en**-to, s., breath; vigour of mind

aligerar, ah-le-**Hay**-rar, v., to lighten; to alleviate

alijar, ah-le-**Har,** v., to lighten. s., stoney ground

alijo, ah-le-**Ho**, s., lightening of a ship

alimento, ah-le-**men**-to, s., nourishment; food pl.

alinear, ah-le-nay-**ar,** v., to level [alimony

aliñar, ah-lee-**n'yar,** v., to adorn; to dress; to season

aliño, ah-lee-**n'yo**, s., ornament; dress; seasoning

alisar, ah-le-**sar,** v., to plane; to polish

aliso, ah-**lee**-so, s., alder tree

alistar, ah-liss-**tar,** v., to enlist; to enrol

aliviar, ah-le-ve-**ar,** v., to ease; to soothe

alivio, ah-**lee**-ve-o, s., lightening; relief

aljaba, ahl-**Hah**-bah, s., quiver

aljibe, ahl-**Hee**-bay, s., cistern

aljofaina, ahl-Ho-fah'e-nah, s., wash-bowl, basin

alma, **ahl**-mah, s., soul; mind; human being; substance

almacén, ahl-mah-**then**, s., warehouse; storehouse

almacenaje, ahl-mah-thay-nah-**Hay**, s., ware-house rent

almacenar, ahl-mah-thay-**nar,** v., to warehouse

almacenista, ahl-mah-thay-**niss**-tah, s., ware-house owner [trees

almáciga, ahl-**mah**-the-gah, s., mastic; nursery of

almadreñas, ahl-mah-**dray**-n'yahs, s., wooden [shoes

almagre, ahl-**mah**-gray, s., red ochre

almanaque, ahl-mah-**nah**-kay, s., almanac

almeja, ah-may-**Hah**, s., mussel

almenara, ahl-may-**nah**-rah, s., beacon; channel

almendra, ahl-**men**-drah, s., almond

almendro, ahl-**men**-dro, s., almond tree

almendrado, ahl-men-**drah**-do, s., macaroon

almete, ahl-**may**-tay, s., helmet

almiar, ahl-me-**ar,** s., hay stack

almíbar, ahl-**mee**-bar, s., syrup

almidón, ahl-me-**don**, s., starch

almilla, ahl-**mee**-l'yah, s., under-waistcoat
almirante, ahl-me-**rahn**-tay, s., admiral
almirez, ahl-me-**rayth**, s., brass mortar
almizcle, ahl-**mith**-clay, s., musk [cushion
almohada, ahl-mo-**ah**-dah, s., pillow; bolster;
almohadilla, ahl-mo-ah-**dee**-l'yah, s., small pillow;
 pin-cushion
almohadón, ahl-mo-ah-**don**, s., large cushion
almoneda, ahl-mo-**nay**-dah, s., public auction
almorranas, ahl-mor-**rrah**-nahs, s., hemorrhoids;
almorzar, ahl-mor-**thar**, v., to breakfast [piles
almuerzo, ahl-moo**air**-tho, s., breakfast
alocado*, ah-lo-**kah**-do, a., foolish; wild
alocución, ah-lo-koo-the-**on**, s., allocution
alojamiento, ah-lo-Hah-me-**en**-to, s., lodging
alojar, ah-lo-**Har**, v., to lodge
alón, ah-**lon**, s., wing
alondra, ah-**lon**-drah, s., lark [lengthening
alongamiento, ah-lon-gah-me-**en**-to, s., delay;
alpaca, ahl-**pah**-kah, s., alpaca
alpargata, ahl-par-**gah**-tah, s., hempen sandal
alquería, ahl-kay-**ree**-ah, s., farmhouse [hiring
alquilamiento, ahl-ke-lah-me-**en**-to, s., letting;
alquilar, ahl-ke-**lar**, v., to let, to hire, to rent
alquiler, ahl-ke-**lair**, s., hire; fare
alquilona, ahl-ke-lo-nah, s., charwoman
alquitrán, ahl-ke-**trahn**, s., tar
alrededor, ahl-ray-**day**-dor, adv., around; about.
 s. pl., environs
altanero, ahl-tah-**nay**-ro, a., haughty
altar, ahl-**tar**, s., altar
alterable, ahl-tay-**rah**-blay, a., changeable [up
alterar, ahl-tay-**rar**, v., to alter; to change; to stir
altercado, ahl-tair-**kah**-do, s., quarrel; contest
alternar, ahl-tair-**nar**, v., to alternate
alteza, ahl-**tay**-thah, s., height; highness
altilocuente, ahl-te-lo-koo**en**-tay, a., bombastic
altivez, ahl-te-**veth**, s., haughtiness; arrogance
altivo*, ahl-**tee**-vo, a., haughty; proud
alto, ahl-to, a*., tall, lofty; high; arduous; exalted
altura, ahl-**too**-rah, s., height; altitude; summit
alubia, ah-**loo**-be-ah, s., French bean

alucinación, ah-loo-the-nah-the-**on**, s., hallucina- [tion
alud, ah-lood, s., avalanche
aludir, ah-loo-**deer**, v., to allude
alumbrar, ah-loom-**brar**, v., to light; to enlighten;
alumbre, ah-loom-bray, s., alum [to illuminate
aluminio, ah-loo-mee-ne-o, s., aluminium
alumno, ah-loom-no, s., pupil; student
alusión, ah-loo-se-**on**, s., allusion
alza, ahl-thah, s., advance in price; rise
alzada, ahl-thah-dah, s., height; stature
alzamiento, ahl-thah-me-**en**-to, s., raising up;
uprising; revolt
azar, ahl-thar, v., to raise; to erect
allá, ah-l'yah, adv., there; thither; of old
allanar, ah-l'yah-nar, v., to level; to remove diffi-
culties; to pacify
allegado, ah-l'yay-gah-do, a., near; related
allegar, ah-l'yay-gar, v., to gather; to collect
allí, ah-l'yee, adv., there
ama, ah-mah, s., mistress of the house; nurse
amable*, ah-mah-blay, a., kind
amador, ah-mah-dor, s., lover [break in
amaestrar, ah-mah-ess-trar, v., to instruct; to
amagar, ah-mah-gar, v., to threaten; to hint
amainar, ali-mah-ee-nar, v., to subside; to relax;
to lessen [to nurse
amamantar, ah-mah-mahn-tar, v., to suckle;
amancebamiento, ah-mahn-thay-bah-me-en-to,
s., concubinage [in concubinage
amancebarse, ah-mahn-thay-bar-say, v., to live
amancillar, ah-mahn-se-l'yar, v., to stain; to
defame
amanecer, ah-mah-nay-thair, v., to dawn; to
arrive at break of day [nerisms
amanerado, ah-may-nay-rah-do, a., full of man-
amansamiento, ah-mahn-sah-me-en-to-s., taming
amansar, ah-mahn-sar, v., to tame; to domesticate
amante, ah-mahn-tay, s., lover [dexterity
amaño, ah-mah-n'yo, s., skill; dexterity
amapola, ah-mah-po-lah, s., poppy
amar, ah-mar, v., to love; to like
amargar, ah-mar-gar, v., to embitter

amargo*, ah-**mar**-go, a., bitter   [ness
amargura, ah-mar-**goo**-rah, s., pain; grief; bitter-
amarillez, ah-mah-re-l'**yeth**, s., yellowness
amarillo, ah-mah-**ree**-l'yo, a., yellow
amarra, ah-**mar**-rrah, s., mooring-cable
amarradero, ah-mar-rrah-**day**-ro, s., mooring-
   berth
amarrar, ah-mar-**rrar**, v., to lie; to fasten
amartelar, ah-mar-tay-**lar**, v., to court; to woo
amasar, ah-mah-**sar**, v., to knead
amatista, ah-mah-**tiss**-tah, s., amethyst   [aspire
ambicionar, ahm-be-the-o-**nar**, v., to covet; to
ambicioso, ahm-be-the-o-so, a., ambitious; covetous
ambigüedad, ahm-be-goo'ay-**dahd**, s., ambiguity
ambos, **ahm**-bos, a., both
amedrentar, ah-may-dren-**tar**, v., to intimidate
amenazar, ah-man-nah-**thar**, v., to threaten
amenidad, ah-may-ne-**dahd**, s., amenity
ameno, ah-**may**-no, a., pleasant; agreeable
amianto, ah-me-**ahn**-to, s., asbestos
amiga, ah-**mee**-gah, s., friend; mistress; governess
amigable*, ah-me-**gah**-blay, a., friendly
amigo, ah-**mee**-go, s., friend
amilanar, ah-me-lah-**nar**, v., to frighten
amistad, ah-miss-**tahd**, s., friendship; amity
amistar, ah-miss-**tar**, v., to reconcile
amo, **ah**-mo, s., master; owner
amohinar, ah-mo-e-**nar**, v., to vex; to annoy
amojonar, ah-mo-**Ho**-nar, v., to set land-marks
amoldar, ah-mol-**dar**, v., to mould
amonedar, ah-mo-nay-**dar**, v., to coin   [warn
amonestar, ah-mo-ness-**tar**, v., to admonish; to
amontonar, ah-mon-to-**nar**, v., to heap up
amor, ah-**mor**, s., love
amoratado, ah-mo-rah-**tah**-do, a., livid
amoroso*, ah-mo-ro-so, a., loving
amortajar, ah-mor-tah-**Har**, v., to shroud   [swoon
amortecer, ah-mor-tay-**thair**, v., to deaden; to
amortiguar, ah-mor-te-goo'**ar**, v., to temper; to
amortizar, ah-mor-te-**thar**, v., to amortize   [lessen
amparar, ahm-pah-**rar**, v., to protect; to shelter
amparo, ahm-**pah**-ro, s., protection; aid; shelter

ampliación, ahm-ple-ah-the-**on**, s., amplification; enlargement
ampliar, ahm-ple-**ar**, v., to amplify; to enlarge
amplificador, ahm-ple-fe-kah-**dor**, s., amplifier
amplio*, ahm-ple-o, a., ample, large
ampolla, ahm-**po**-l'yah, s., blister; cruet
amputar, ahm-poo-**tar**, v., to amputate
amueblar, ah-moo'ay-**blar**, v., to furnish
amujerado, ah-moo-Hay-**rah**-do, a., effeminate
amuleto, ah-moo-**lay**-to, s., charm; talisman; amulet
ánade, ah-nah-day, s., duck
análisis, ah-**nah**-le-siss, s., analysis
analogía, ah-nah-lo-**Hee**-ah, s., analogy
anaquel, ah-nah-**kel**, s., shelf
anaranjado, ah-nah-rahn-**Hah**-do, a., orange-coloured
anarquía, ah-nar-**kee**-ah, s., anarchy
anca, **ahn**-kah, s., haunch
anciano, ahn-the-**ah**-no, a., aged; old (man or woman)
ancla, **ahn**-klah, s., anchor
ancho*, **ahn**-cho, a., broad; wide
anchoa, ahn-**cho**-ah, s., anchovy
anchura, ahn-**choo**-rah, s., breadth; width
andamio, ahn-**dah**-me-o, s., scaffold; platform
andar, ahn-**dar**, v., to go; to walk
andén, ahn-**den**, s., side-walk; railway platform
andrajo, ahn-**drah**-Ho, s., rag; despicable person
anegar, ah-nay-**gar**, v., to inundate
anejo, ah-**nay**-Ho, a., annexed
anexo, ah-**nek**-so, a., annexed; joined
angarillas, ahn-gah-**ree**-l'yahs, s., hand-barrow
ángel, **ahn**-Hayl, s., angel
angina, ahn-**Hee**-nah, s., quinsy
angostar, ahn-gos-**tar**, v., to narrow; to contract
angosto*, ahn-**gos**-to, a., narrow
anguila, ahn-**ghee**-lah, s., eel
ángulo, **ahn**-goo-lo, s., angle; nook
anhelar, ahn-ay-**lar**, v., to long for
anhelo, ahn-**ay**-lo, s., eagerness; longing
anillo, ah-**nee**-'yo, s., ring
animado, ah-ne-**mah**-do, a., lively; enthusiastic
animal, ah-ne-**mahl**, s., animal
animar, ah-ne-**mar**, v., to animate; to incite

ánimo, ah-ne-mo, s., courage; will; mind

animoso*, ah-ne-**mo-**so, a., brave; spirited

aniñado, ah-ne-n'yah-do, a., childish

aniquilar, ah-ne-ke-lar, v., to annihilate

anís, ah-nees, s., aniseed

anoche, ah-no-chay, adv., last night

anochecer, ah-no-chay-thair, v., to grow dark.
    al—, ahl—, at nightfall

anomalía, ah-no-mah-lee-ah, s., anomaly

anonadar, ah-no-nah-dar, v., to stun; to over-
    whelm

anónimo, ah-no-ne-mo, a., anonymous

anotar, ah-no-tar, v., to write notes; to annotate

ansia, ahn-se-ah, s., anxiety; longing

ansioso*, ahn-se-o-so, a., anxious; eager

antaño, ahn-tah-n'yo, adv., last year; long ago

ante, ahn-tay, prep., before, s., buckskin [before last

anteanoche, ahn-tay-ah-no-chay, adv., the night

anteayer, ahn-tay-ah-yair, adv., the day before
    yesterday

antebrazo, ahn-tay-brah-tho, s., forearm

antecámara, ahn-tay-kah-mah-rah, s., antecham-
    ber; hall   [dent

antecedente, ahn-tay-thay-den-tay, a., antece-

antecesores, ahn-tay-thay-sso-ress, s., predeces-

antedatar, ahn-tay-dah-tar, v., to antedate [sors

antelación, ahn-tay-lah-the-on, s., precedence
    (time)

antemano, ahn-tay-mah-no, adv., beforehand

anteojos, ahn-tay-o-Hos, s., spectacles

antepasados, ahn-tay-pah-sah-dos, s., forefathers;
    ancestors   [before

anteponer, ahn-tay-po-nair, v., to prefer; to place

anterior, ahn-tay-re-or, a., anterior   [prior to

antes, ahn-tess, adv., before; rather. prep., before

anticipar, ahn-te-the-par, v., to anticipate

anticipo, ahn-te-thee-po, s., advance payment

anticongelante, ahn-te-kon-Hay-lahn-tay, s.,
    anti-freeze

antorcha, ahn-tor-chah, s., torch

anual, ah-noo-ahl, a., yearly

anublar, ah-noo-blar, v., to cloud; to overcast

anuencia, ah-noo-en-the-ah, s., compliance; consent

anular, ah-noo-**lar,** v., to annul, a., annular

anunciar, ah-noon-the-**ar,** v., to announce

anzuelo, ahn-thoo-**ay**-lo, s., fish-hook; allurement

añadir, ah-n'yah-**deer,** v., to add

añejar, ah-n'yay-**Har,** v., to make old

añejo, ah-n'**yay**-Ho, a., old; stale

añicos, ah-n'**yee**-kos, s., small pieces; smithereens

añil, ah-n'**yeel,** s., indigo

año, ah-n'yo, s., year

añoso, ah-n'yo-so, a., aged; old   [nostalgia

añoranza, ah-n'yo-**rahn**-thah, s., home sickness;

apacentar, ah-pah-then-**tar,** v., to tend grazing cattle

apacible, ah-pah-**thee**-blay, a., gentle; placid; calm

apadrinar, ah-pah-dre-**nar,** v., to support; to patronize; to act as godfather

apagar, ah-pah-**gar,** v., to quench; to extinguish

apalabrar, ah-pah-lah-**brar,** v., to agree verbally

apalear, ah-pah-lah-**ar,** v., to beat; to cane

apañar, ah-pah-n'**yar,** v., to seize; to pilfer

aparador, ah-pah-rah-**dor,** s., sideboard   [pomp

aparato, ah-pah-**rah**-to, s., apparatus; preparation;

aparear, ah-pah-ray-**ar,** v., to match   [up

aparecer, ah-pah-ray-**thair,** v., to appear; to turn

aparejo, ah-pah-**ray**-Ho, s., harness; gear

aparente*, ah-pah-**ren**-tay, a., apparent

apariencia, ah-pah-re-**en**-the-ah, s., appearance

apartadero, ah-par-tah-**day**-ro, s., crossways; siding   [separated

apartado, ah-par-**tah**-do, s., post-office box, a.,

apartar, ah-par-**tar,** v., to separate; to remove; to dislodge

apasionado, ah-pah-se-o-**nah**-do, a., passionate

apatía, ah-pah-**tee**-ah, s., apathy

apear, ah-pay-**ar,** v., to alight; to measure land

apedrear, ah-pah-dray-**ar,** v., to stone

apegarse, ah-pay-**gar**-say, v., to attach oneself to

apelación, ah-pay-lah-the-**on,** s., appeal

apelar, ah-pay-**lar,** v., to appeal

apellido, ah-pay-l'**yee**-do, s., surname

apenas, ah-**pay**-nas, adv., scarcely

apercibir, ah-pair-the-**beer,** v., to provide; to warn

apero, ah-**pay**-ro, s., implement; tools
aperitivo, ah-pay-re-**tee**-vo, a., aperitive
apesadumbrar, ah-pay-sah-doom-**brar**, v., to vex; to afflict
apestar, ah-pess-**tar**, v., to infect; to nauseate
apetecer, ah-pah-tay-**thair**, v., to crave
apetecible, ah-pah-tay-**thee**-blay, a., desirable
apetito, ah-pah-**tee**-to, s., appetite
apiadarse, ah-pe-ah-**dar**-say, v., to pity
ápice, **ah**-pe-thay, s., apex
apilar, ah-pe-**lar**, v., to heap up
apio, **ah**-pe-o, s., celery
aplacar, ah-plah-**kar**, v., to appease; to pacify
aplanar, ah-plah-**nar**, v., to level   [to smash
aplastar, ah-plahs-**tar**, v., to flatten; to crush;
aplaudir, ah-plah'oo-**deer**, v., to applaud
aplauso, ah-**plah**'oo-so, s., applause
aplazar, ah-plah-**thar**, v., to defer; to adjourn
aplicación, ah-ple-kah-the-**on**, s., application
aplicar, ah-ple-**kar**, v., to impute; to apply
aplomar, ah-plo-**mar**, v., to overload; to plumb
apocado, ah-po-**kah**-do, a., pusillanimous
apoderado, ah-po-day-**rah**-do, s., proxy; attorney
apoderar, ah-po-day-**rar**, v., to empower; to take
apodo, ah-**po**-do, s., nickname   [possession
apolillarse, ah-po-le-**l'yar**-say, v., to be moth eaten
aportadero, ah-por-tah-**day**-ro, s., landing-place
aposentar, ah-po-sen-**tar**, v., to lodge
aposento, ah-po-**sen**-to, s., room; apartment; inn
apostar, ah-poss-**tar**, v., to bet
apostilla, ah-poss-**tee**-l'yah, s., marginal note
apóstrofe, ah-**poss**-tro-fay, s., apostrophe
apoyar, ah-po-**yar**, v., to support; to favour; to lean upon   [stay
apoyo, ah-**po**-yo, s., support; protection; prop;
apreciar, ah-pray-the-**ar**, v., to appreciate
aprehender, ah-pray-en-**dair**, v., to apprehend
apremiar, ah-pray-me-**ar**, v., to compel; to urge; to press
aprender, ah-pren-**dair**, v., to learn   [ship
aprendizaje, ah-pren-de-**thah**-Hay, s., apprentice-
aprensar, ah-pren-**sar**, v., to dress; to press

aprensión, ah-pren-se-**on**, s., apprehension

apresar, ah-pray-**sar**, v., to seize [pare

aprestar, ah-press-**tar**, v., to make ready; to pre-

apresurarse, ah-pray-soo-**rar**-say, v., to make haste; to hurry; to hasten

apretar, ah-pray-**tar**, v., to compress; to tighten

apriesa, aprisa, ah-pre-**ay**-sah, ah-**pre**-sah, adv., in haste; fast

aprieto, ah-pre-**ay**-to, s., difficulty; conflict

aprisionar, ah-pre-se-o-**nar**, v., to imprison

aprobar, ah-pro-**bar**, v., to approve

aprontar, ah-pron-**tar**, v., to prepare hastily

apropiar, ah-pro-pe-**ar**, v., to appropriate [able

aprovechable, ah-pro-vay-**chah**-blay, a., profit-

aprovechar, ah-pro-vay-**char**, v., to profit by

aproximar, ah-prok-se-**mar**, v., to approach; to fit

aptitud, ahp-te-**tood**, s., aptitude [approximate

apto*, ahp-to, a., apt; fit; convenient

apuesta, ah-poo'**ess**-tah, s., bet; wager

apuesto, ah-poo'**ess**-to, a., genteel; elegant; spruce

apuntamiento, ah-poon-tah-me-**en**-to, s., observation; abstract

apuntar, ah-poon-**tar**, v., to aim; to mark; to note

apunte, ah-**poon**-tay, s., annotation; rough sketch

apuración, ah-poo-rah-the-**on**, s., investigation; trouble

apurado, ah-poo-rah-do, a., needy; hard-up

apurar, ah-poo-**rar**, v., to worry; to fret; to exhaust

apuro, ah-**poo**-ro, s., want; affliction

aquejar, ah-kay-*H*ar, v., to afflict

aquel, aquella, aquello, ah-**kel**, ah-**kell**-yah, ah-**kell**-yo, pron., he; she; that; that-one

aquí, ah-**kee**, adv., here

aquietar, ah-ke-ay-**tar**, v., to quiet; to appease

arado, ah-**rah**-do, s., plough

arancel, ah-rahn-**thel**, s., tariff of duties

araña, ah-**rah**-n'yah, s., spider; chandelier

arañar, ah-rah-**n'yar**, v., to scratch

arar, ah-**rar**, v., to plough

arbitrar, ar-be-**trar**, v., to arbitrate

arbitrio, ar-**bee**-tre-o, s., free will; compromise

árbitro, ar-be-tro, s., arbitrator

árbol, ar-bol, s., tree
arbusto, ar-**boos**-to, s., shrub
arca, ar-kah, s., chest; safe
arcada, ar-**kah**-dah, s., arcade; nausea
arce, ar-thay, s., maple-tree
arcilla, ar-thee-l'yah, s., argil; clay
arco, ar-ko, s., arc; arch; bow
archiduque, ar-che-**doo**-kay, s., archduke
archivar, ar-che-**var**, v., to file
archivo, ar-**chee**-vo, s., archives
arder, ar-dair, v., to burn; to glow
ardid, ar-**deed**, s., stratagem; artifice
ardiente, ar-de-**en**-tay, a., ardent; burning
ardilla, ar-dee-l'yah, s., squirrel
ardor, ar-dor, s., great heat; fervour; valour
arduo, ar-doo'o, a., arduous; difficult
área, ah-ray-ah, s., area
arena, ah-**ray**-nah, s., sand; grit; arena
arenga, ah-**ren**-gah, s., harangue
arenque, ah-**ren**-kay, s., herring
argénteo, ar-**H**en-tay-o, a., silvery
argolla, ar-**go**-l'yah, s., large ring; pillory
argucia, ar-**goo**-the-ah, s., subtility, sophistry
argüir, ar-goo-**eer**, s., to argue
argumento, ar-goo-**men**-to, s., argument
aria, ah-re-ah, s., air; tune
aridez, ah-re-**deth**, s., drought, barrenness
árido, ah-re-do, a., dry, arid
arisco, ah-**riss**-ko, a., fierce, untractable   [racy
aristocracia, ah-riss-to-**krah**-the-ah, s., aristoc-
aritmética, ah-ritt-**may**-te-kah, s., arithmetic
armada, ar-**mah**-dah, s., fleet; navy
armar, ar-mar, v., to arm; to mount; to adjust
armario, ar-**mah**-re-o, s., cupboard; wardrobe
armazón, ar-mah-**thon**, s., framework, skeleton
armería, ar-may-**ree**-ah, s., armoury; arsenal
armónico, ar-**mo**-ne-ko, a., harmonic
armonio, ar-**mo**-ne-o, s., harmonium
arnés, ar-**ness**, s., harness
árnica, ar-ne-kah, s., arnica
aroma, ah-**ro**-mah, s., perfume; fragrance
arpa, ar-pah, s., hasp

arpillera, ar-pel-l'**yay**-rah, s., sack-cloth
arpón, ar-**pon,** s., harpoon
arqueología, ar-kay-o-lo-*Hee*-ah, s., archeology
arqueta, ar-**kay**-tah, s., small chest
arquitecto, ar-ke-**tek**-to, s., architect
arrabal, ar-rrah-**bahl,** s., suburb
arraigar, ar-rrah-e-**gar,** v., to root; to settle down
arraigo, ar-rrah-e-go, s., landed property
arrancar, ar-rrahn-**kar,** v., to eradicate; to pull out
arrapo, ar-**rrah**-po, s., tatter; rag; wretch
arrasar, ar-rrah-**sar,** v., to level; to raze; to demolish
arrastrar, ar-rrahs-**trar,** v., to drag along
arrastre, ar-**rrahs**-tray, s., dragging, haulage
arre, arre, ar-**rray,** interj., gee up! go on!   [pick up
arrebañar, ar-rray-bah-n'**yar,** v., to gather; to
arrebatado, ar-rray-bah-**tah**-do, a., precipitate
arrebatar, ar-rray-bah-**tar,** v., to carry off; to snatch
arrebato, ar-rray-**bah**-to, s., sudden attack; fit
arreciar, ar-rray-the-**ar,** v., to increase in strength
arrecife, ar-rray-**thee**-fay, s., reef
arredrar, ar-rray-**drar,** v., to terrify
arreglado, ar-rray-**glah**-do, a., regular; moderate
arreglar, ar-rray-**glar,** v., to arrange; to settle; to adjust
arreglo, ar-**rray**-glo, s., rule; order; arrangement
arremeter, ar-rray-may-**tair,** v., to assail
arrendar, ar-rren-**dar,** v., to rent; to hire
arrendatario, ar-rren-dah-**tah**-re-o., s., renter; lessee   [to regret
arrepentirse, ar-rray-pen-**teer**-say, v., to repent;
arrestado, ar-ess-**tah**-do, a., intrepid; daring
arrestar, ar-rress-**tar,** v., to arrest; to imprison
arresto, ar-**rress**-to, s., boldness; arrest
arriba, ar-**rree**-bah, adv., above; on high; upstairs
arribar, ar-rre-**bar,** v., to arrive; to land
arriesgar, ar-rre-ess-**gar,** v., to risk
arrimar, ar-rre-**mar,** v., to bring near; to stow; to lean against
arrinconar, ar-rrin-ko-**nar,** v., to put away

arroba, ar-rro-bah, s., weight of 25 lbs. [down

arrodillarse, ar-rro-de-l'yar-say, v., to kneel

arrogancia, ar-rro-**gahn**-the-ah, s., arrogance; haughtiness

arrojado*, ar-rro-*H*ah-do, a., rash; dashing

arrojar, ar-rro-*H*ar, v., to dart; to fling

arrollar, ar-rro-l'yar, v., to roll up; to defeat

arropar, ar-rro-par, v., to clothe; to dress

arrostrar, ar-rros-trar, v., to fight face to face

arroyo, ar-rro-yo, s., rivulet

arroz, ar-rroth, s., rice

arruga, ar-rroo-gah, s., wrinkle

arruinar, ar-rroo'e-nar, v., to ruin; to demolish

arrullo, ar-rroo-l'yo, s., lullaby; cooing

arrumar, ar-rroo-mar, v., to stow cargo

arrumbar, ar-rroom-bar, v., to put away

arte, ar-tay, s., art

arteria, ar-tay-ree-ah, s., artery; artifice; cunning

artero, ar-tay-ro, a., artful; cunning

artesano, ar-tay-sah-no, s., artisan

ártico, ar-te-ko, a., arctic

artículo, ar-tee-koo-lo, s., article

artificio, ar-te-fe-the-o, s., art; craft; artifice

artillería, ar-te-l'yay-ree-ah, s., artillery

artimaña, ar-te-mah-n'yah, s., trap; snare

arzobispo, ar-tho-biss-po, s., archbishop

as, ahs, s., ace

asa, ah-sah, s., handle

asalto, ah-sahl-to, s., assault

asar, ah-sar, v., roast [moted

ascender, ahs-then-dair, v., to ascend; to be pro-

ascenso, ahs-then-so, s., promotion

ascensor, ahs-then-sor, s., lift; hoist

asco, ahs-ko, s., disgust; loathing

asear, ah-say-ar, v., to adorn; to clean

asechar, ah-say-char, v., to waylay

asegurar, ah-say-goo-rar, v., to secure; to insure; to assert; to verify [resemble

asemejar, ah-say-may-*H*ar, v., to compare; to

asenso, ah-sen-so, s., assent

asentada, ah-sen-tah-dah, s., sitting. de una—, day-oo-nah—, at once

asentar, ah-sen-**tar**, v., to seat; to secure; to affirm; to settle; to note; to assess

asentir, ah-sen-**teer**, v., to acquiesce

aseo, ah-**say**-o, s., cleanliness   [able

asequible, ah-say-**kee**-blay, a., attainable; obtain-

aserción, ah-sair-the-on, s., assertion

aserrar, ah-sair-**rrar**, v., to saw

aserto, ah-**sair**-to (see **aserción**)

asesinar, ah-say-se-**nar**, v., to assassinate

asestar, ah-sess-**tar**, v., to aim at; to strike

así, ah-**see**, adv., so; thus;. **—que,** —kay, as soon as; so that

asidero, ah-se-**day**-ro, s., handle; pretext

asiduo, ah-se-doo'o, a., assiduous   [tract; entry

asiento, ah-se-**en**-to, s., chair; seat; stability; con-

asignar, ah-sig-**nar**, v., to assign

asilo, ah-**see**-lo, s., asylum; refuge

asimétrico, ah-se-**may**-tre-ko, a., lop-sided

asimiento, ah-se-me-**en**-to, s., grasp; attachment

asimilar, ah-se-me-**lar**, v., to assimilate

asimismo, ah-se-**miss**-mo, adv., just so; likewise

asistencia, ah-siss-**ten**-the-ah, s., actual presence; help; aid

asistenta, ah-siss-**ten**-tah, s., handmaid

asistir, ah-siss-**teer**, v., to be present; to help

asno, ahss-no, s., ass; dunce

asociar, ah-so-the-**ar**, v., to associate

asolar, ah-so-**lar**, v., to devastate; to level

asomar, ah-so-**mar**, v., to show; to begin to appear

asombrar, ah-som-**brar**, v., to astonish; to amaze

asomo, ah-**so**-mo, s., indication; conjecture; hint

asordar, ah-sor-**dar**, v., to deafen

aspa, ahs-pah, s., wings of a wind-mill

aspaviento, ahs-pah-ve-**en**-to, s., exaggerated dread; wonder

aspecto, ahs-**pek**-to, s., appearance; aspect

aspereza, ahs-pay-**ray**-thah, s., asperity; roughness

áspero*, ahs-pay-ro, a., rough; harsh

aspirar, ahs-pe-**rar**, v., to aspire; to covet

asqueroso*, ahs-kay-**ro**-so, a., filthy; loathsome

asta, ahs-tah, s., horn; staff; pole

astillar, ahs-te-l'**yar**, v.. to chip; to splinter

astillero, ahs-te-l'**yay**-ro, s., ship-yard; dockyard
astro, ahs,-tro, s., heavenly body; star
astucia, ahs-**too**-the-ah, s., craft; cunning
astuto*, ahs-**too**-to, a., astute
asumir, ah-soo-**meer**, v., to assume
asunto, ah-**soon**-to, s., subject; business; affair
asustar, ah-sooss-**tar**, v., to frighten
atacar, ah-tah-**kar**, v., to fit tight; to attack
atadero, ah-tah-**day**-ro, s., cord; rope
atado, ah-**tah**-do, s., bundle; parcel   [intercept
atajar, ah-tah-H**ar**, v., to go the shortest way; to
atañer, ah-tah-n'**yair**, v., to belong; to appertain
atar, ah-**tar**, v., to tie; to fasten; to knot
atareado, ah-tah-ray-**ah**-do, a., very busy
atasco, ah-**tahs**-ko, s., obstruction
ataúd, ah-tah-**ood**, s., coffin
atavío, ah-tah-**vee**-o, s., dress; finery   [daunt
atemorizar, ah-tay-mo-re-**thar**, v., to frighten; to
atención, ah-ten-the-**on**, s., attention
atentar, ah-ten-**tar**, v., to attempt a crime
atento, ah-**ten**-to, a., attentive
atenuar, ah-tay-noo'**ar**, v., to attenuate
aterido, ah-tay-**ree**-do, a stiff with cold
aterrar, ah-tair-**rrar**, v., to terrify
aterrorizar, ah-tair-rro-re-**thar**, v., to terrify
atestación, ah-tess-tah-the-**on**, s., attestation; affidavit
atestado, ah-tess-**tah**-do, a., attested; witnessed
atestados, ah-tess-**tah**-dos, s., testimonials
atiesar, ah-te-ay-**sar**, v., to stiffen
atisbar, ah-tiss-**bar**, v., to scrutinize; to pry
atizar, ah-te-**thar**, v., to poke the fire; to incite
atmósfera, aht-**mos**-fay-rah, s., atmosphere
atolondrado, ah-to-lon-**drah**-do, a., scatterbrained
atolondrar, ah-to-lon-**drar**, v., to confound; to amaze; to be thoughtless
atómico, ah-**to**-me-ko, a., atomic
atónito, ah-**to**-ne-to, a., astonished
atontar, ah-ton-**tar**, v., to stun; to stupefy
atormentar, ah-tor-men-**tar**, v., to torment
atornillar, ah-tor-ne-l'**yar**, v., to screw
atosigar, ah-to-se-**gar**, v., to poison; to harass

atraer, ah-trah-**air**, v., to attract
atragantarse, ah-trah-gahn-**tar**-say, v., to choke
atrancar, ah-trahn-**kar**, v., to bar a door
atrapar, ah-trah-**par**, v., to catch
atrás, ah-**trahs**, adv., backwards
atraso, ah-**trah**-so, s., backwardness. pl., arrears
atravesado, ah-trah-vay-**sah**-do, a., squint-eyed
atravesar, ah-trah-vay-**sar**, v., to place across; to cross over; to go over
atreverse, ah-tray-**vair**-say, v., to dare
atrevido, ah-tray-**vee**-do, a., bold; daring
atribuir, ah-tre-boo'**eer**, v., to attribute
atril, ah-**treel**, s., lectern; music-stand
atrio, ah-**tre**-o, s., porch; portico [knock down
atropellar, ah-tro-pay-l'**yar**, v., to trample; to
atroz, ah-**troth**, a., atrocious
atún, ah-**toon**, s., tunny fish [rattled
aturdido, ah-toor-**dee**-do, a., harebrained; giddy;
aturdir, ah-toor-**deer**, v., to bewilder; to stun
aturrullar, ah-toor-rroo-l'**yar**, v., to confound
atusar, ah-too-**sar**, v., to smooth the hair
audacia, ah'oo-**dah**-the-ah, s., audacity
audaz, ah'oo-**dath**, a., bold; audacious
auge, ah'oo-*Hay*, s., highest point; acme
augusto, ah'oo-**gooss**-to, a., august
aullar, ah-ool'**yar**, v., to howl; to yell
aullido, ah'oo-l'**yee**-do, s., howl
aumentar, ah'oo-men-**tar**, v., to increase
aún, ah'**oon**, adv., yet; still; nevertheless; even
aunque, ah'oon-**kay**, conj., though
auricular, ah'oo-re-koo-**lahr**, s., earphone
ausencia, ah'oo-**sen**-the-ah, s., absence
ausentarse, ah'oo-sen-**tar**-say, v., to absent one-
ausente, ah'oo-**sen**-tay, a., absent [self
austeridad, ah'oos-tay-re-**dahd**, s., austerity
auto, ah'**oo**-to, s., judicial decree; writ; warrant
autobús, ah'oo-to-**booss**, s., motorbus
autor, ah'oo-**tor**, s., author
autorizar, ah'oo-to-re-**thar**, v., to authorize
auxiliar, ah'ook-se-le-**ar**, v., to aid. a., assistant
auxilio, ah'ook-**see**-le-o, s., assistance; help
avalorar, ah-vah-lo-**rar**, v., to value; to estimate

avanzar, ah-vahn-**thar**, v., to advance
avariento, ah-vah-re-en-to, a., avaricious, mean
ave, ah-vay, s., bird
avejentar, ah-vay-Hen-**tar**, v., to become old
avellana, ah-vay-l'**yah**-nah, s., hazel-nut
avena, ah-**vay**-nah, s., oats
avenencia, ah-vay-**nen**-the-ah, s., agreement
avenida, ah-vay-**nee**-dah, s., avenue; flood
aventajar, ah-ven-tah-**Har**, v., to surpass; to excel
aventurar, ah-ven-too-**rar**, v., to venture
avergonzado, ah-vair-gon-**thah**-do, a., ashamed
avergonzar, ah-vair-gon-**thar**, v., to shame; to
   put to shame
avería, ah-vay-**ree**-ah, s., damage; breakdown
averiguar, ah-vair-re-goo-**ar**, v., to inquire; in-
   aversion [vestigate
aversión, ah-vair-se-**on**, s., aversion
aviación, ah-ve-ah-the-**on**, s., aviation
avidez, ah-ve-**deth**, s., avidity; greed
ávido*, ah-ve-do, a., covetous; greedy
avieso, ah-ve-**ay**-so, a., perverse; crooked
avío, ah-**vee**-o, s., preparation; provision
avión, ah-ve-**on**, s., aeroplane
avisado, ah-ve-**sah**-do, a., prudent; wise
aviso, ah-**vee**-so, s., notice; warning; advice
avispa, ah-**viss**-pah, s., wasp
avistar, ah-viss-**tar**, v., to behold from a distance
avivar, ah-ve-**var**, v., to enliven; to revive
¡ay! ah'e, interj., alas!
ayer, ah-**yair**, adv., yesterday
ayuda, ah-**yoo**-dah, s., help
ayunar, ah-yoo-**nar**, v., to fast [cipal council
ayuntamiento, ah-yoon-tah-me-**en**-to, s., muni-
azabache, ah-thah-**bah**-chay, s., jet
azada, ah-**thah**-dah, s., hoe
azafrán, ah-thah-**frahn**, s., saffron
azar, ah-**thar**, s., chance, hazard; fate
azogue, ah-**tho**-gay, s., mercury
azorar, ah-tho-**rar**, v., to confound
azotar, ah-tho-**tar**, v., to whip; to lash
azúcar, ah-**thoo**-kar, s., sugar [affable
azucarado, ah-thoo-kah-**rah**-do, a., sugared; sweet;
azucena, ah-thoo-**say**-nah, s., white lily

azufre, ah-**thoo**-fray, s., sulphur; brimstone
azul, ah-**thool,** a., blue
azulejo, ah-thoo-**lay**-Ho, s., glazed tile
azuzar, ah-thoo-**thar,** v., to set on dogs; to incite

baba, bah-bah, s., drivel; spittle
babear, bah-bay-**ar,** v., to slaver; to drivel
babia, bah-be-ah, s., **estar en—,** es-tar en—, to be absent in mind
babieca, bah-be-**ay**-kah, s., ignorant; stupid fellow
babor, bah-**bor,** s., port (side)
babosa, bah-bo-**sah,** s., slug
bacallao, bacalao, bah-kah-l'**yah**-o, bah-kah-**lah**-o, s., codfish
bacía, bah-**thee**-ah, s., metal basin
bacín, bah-**theen,** s., chamber-pot
bache, bah-chay, s., hole in the road
bachiller, bah-chil-l'**yair,** s., bachelor (degree). a., garrulous
badajo, bah-**dah**-Ho, s., bell-clapper; idle talker
bagaje, bah-**gah**-Hay, s., baggage
bagatela, bah-gah-**tay**-lah, s., trifle
bahía, bah-**Hee**-ah, s., bay; harbour
bailar, bah'e-**lar,** v., to dance
bailarín, bah'e-lah-**reen,** s., dancer
baile, bah'e-lay, s., dance; ball
baja, bah-**Hah,** s., fall of price
bajada, bah-**Hah**-dah, s., descent; slope
bajamar, bah-**Hah**-mar, s., low tide   [go down
bajar, bah-**Har,** v., to descend; to fall; to lessen; to
bajel, bah-**Hel,** s., ship; boat; vessel
bajo, bah-Ho, adv., under; below. s., sand-bank; bass. a., low; abject; humble
bajón, bah-**Hon,** s., bassoon
bala, bah-lah, s., bullet; bale
balada, bah-**lah**-dah, s., ballad
baladí, bah-lah-**dee,** a., trivial; worthless
baladrón, bah-lah-**dron,** s., boaster; bully   [sheet
balance, bah-**lahn**-thay, s., balancing; balance
balancear, bah-lahn-thay-**ar,** v., to balance; to weigh; to waver
balanza, bah-**lahn**-thah, s., scale; balance

balar, bah-lar, v., to bleat   [trade
balaustrada, bah-lah'ooss-**trah**-dah, s., balus-
balaustre, bah-lah'**ooss**-tray, s., baluster
balazo, bah-**lah**-tho, s., gunshot   [babble
balbucear, bahl-boo-thay-**ar**, v., to stutter; to
balcón, bahl-**kon**, s., balcony
baldaquino, bahl-dah-**kee**-no, s., canopy; da**l**s
baldar, bahl-**dar**, v., to cripple   [**en**—, in vain
balde, bahl-day, s., bucket. adv., **de**—, gratis;
baldío,-bahl-**dee**-o, a., untilled. s., wasteland
baldón, bahl-**don**, s., reproach; insult.
baldosa, bahl-**do**-sah, s., flat paving-stone
balido, bah-**lee**-do, s., bleating; bleat
baliza, bah-**lee**-than, s., buoy   [watering place
balneario, bahl-nay-**ah**-re-o, s., bathing resort;
balón, bah-**lon**, s., large football; large bale
balota, bah-**lo**-tah, s., ballot
balsa, bahl-sah, s., pool; pond; lake; raft
bálsamo, **bahl**-sah-mo, s., balsam; balm
baluarte, bah-loo'**ar**-tay, s., bulwark
balumba, bah-**loom**-bah, s., bulk
ballena, bah-l'**yay**-nah, s., whale
bailesta, bah-l'**yess**-tah, s., cross-bow
bamba, bahm-bah, s., chance; fluke   [to sway
bambolear, bahm-bo-lay-**ar**, v., to stagger; to swing
bambolla, bahm-**bo**-l'yah, s., ostentation
bambú, bahm-**boo**, s., bamboo
banana, bah-**nah**-nah, s., banana
banasta, bah-**nahs**-tah, s., large basket
banca, bahn-kah, s., bench; banking; washing box
bancarrota, bahn-kahr-**rro**-tah, s., bankruptcy
banco, bahn-ko, s., bench; bank
banda, bahn-dah, s., sash; band; gang; covey
bandada, bahn-**dah**-dah, s., covey
bandeja, bahn-day-_H_ah, s., tray; salver
banderilla, bahn-day-**ree**-l'yah, s., dart with a flag
    used in bullfighting
bandido, bahn-**dee**-do, s., bandit
bando, bahn-do, s., edict; faction
banquero, bahn-**kay**-ro, s., banker
banquete, bahn-**kay**-tay, s., banquet
banquillo, bahn-**kee**-l'yo, s., small stool

bañador, bah-n'yah-**dor,** s., bather
bañar, bah-n'**yar,** v., to bathe
baño, bah-n'yo, s., bath
baquetear, bah-kay-tay-**ar,** v., to vex; to beat
baraja, bah-**rah-**Hah, s., complete pack of cards
barata, bah-**rah-**tah, s., barter; bargain
baratear, bah-rah-tay-**ar,** v., to undersell
baratijas, bah-rah-**tee-**Hahs, s., trifles
baratillero, bah-rah-te-l'**yay-**ro, s., peddler
barato, bah-**rah-**to, a., cheap
baraúnda, bah-rah-**oon-**dah, s., noise; confusion
barba, **bar-**bah, s., chin; beard
barbarie, bar-**bah-**re-ay, s., barbarity; rusticity
bárbaro*, **bar-**bah-ro, a., barbarous
barbería, bar-bay-**ree-**ah, s., barber's shop or trade
barbero, bar-**bay-**ro, s., barber
barbiespeso, bar-be-ess-**pay-**so, a., thick-bearded
barbihecho, bar-be-**ay-**cho, a., fresh shaved
barbilindo, bar-be-**leen-**do, a., well shaved and trimmed
barbilucio, bar-be-**loo-**the-o, a., smooth faced
barbilla, bar-**bee-**l'yah, s., point of the chin
barbón, bar-**bon,** s., long bearded man
barbotar, bar-bo-**tar,** v., to mumble
barca, **bar-**kah, s., boat; barge
barco, **bar-**ko, s., boat; ship
barlovento, bar-lo-**ven-**to, s., windward
barniz, bar-**neeth,** s., varnish
barómetro, bah-**ro-**may-tro, s., barometer
barón, bah-**ron,** s., baron
barquero, bar-**kay-**ro, s., boatman; ferryman
barquillo, bar-kee-l'yo, s., wafer; small boat
barra, **bar-**rrah, s., bar; rod
barraca, bar-**rrah-**kah, s., hut
barragana, bar-rrah-**gah-**nah, s., concubine
barranca, bar-**rrahn-**kah, s., fissure; ravine; diffi-
barredura, bar-rray-**doo-**rah, s., sweeping [culty
barrena, bar-**rray-**nah, s., drill; gimlet
barrenar, bar-rray-**nar,** v., to pierce; to bore
barreño, bar-**rray-**n'yo, s., earthen pan; tub
barrer, bar-**rrair,** v., to sweep
barriada, bar-rree-**ah-**dah, s., district; suburb

barrica, bar-**rree**-kah, s., cask; barrel

barriga, bar-**rree**-gah, s., abdomen; belly

barril, bar-**rreel**, s., barrel

barrilla, bar-**rree**-l'yah, s., little bar; glasswort

barrio, bar-rre-o, s., ward; suburb; district

barro, bar-rro, s., clay; mud; earthenware

barrote, bar-rro-tay, s., iron bar

barruntar, bar-rroon-**tar**, v., to foresee

barrunto, bar-**rroon**-to, s., conjecture [tools

bártulos, **bar**-too-los, s., household goods; affairs;

basar, bah-**sar**, v., to establish upon a base

báscula, bahs-koo-lah, s., platform-scale

base, bah-say, s., base; basis [enough!

basta, bahs-tah, s., (needlework) basting. interj.

bastante, bahs-**tahn**-tay, adv., enough

bastardo, bahs-**tar**-do, a., bastard; spurious;
   illegitimate [carriage

bastidor, bahs-te-**dor**, s., frame; stretcher; under-

bastilla, bahs-**tee**-l'yah, s., hem

bastón, bahs-**ton**, s., cane; staff; stick

basura, bah-**soo**-rah, s., sweepings; refuse; rubbish

basurero, bah-soo-**ray**-ro, s., rubbish bin

bata, bah-tah, s., dressing-gown [from a fall

batacazo, bah-tah-**kah**-tho, s., violent contusion

batahola, bah-tah-o-lah, s., hurly-burly

batalla, bah-tah-l'yah, s., battle

batea, bah-**tay**-ah, s., painted tray; punt

batería, bah-tay-**ree**-ah, s., battery

batida, bah-**tee**-dah, s., battue; hunting party

batiente, bah-te-**en**-tay, s., jamb (of a door); leaf
   (of a door) [to stir

batir, bah-**teer**, v., to beat; to clout; to demolish

batista, bah-**tiss**-tah, s., batiste; cambric

baúl, bah'**ool**, s., trunk; chest

bautismo, bah'oo-**tiss**-mo, s., baptism

baya, bah-yah, s., berry

bayeta, bah-**yay**-tah, s., baize; rough cloth

bayo, bah-yo, a., bay; light brown

bayoneta, bah-yo-**nay**-tah, s., bayonet

bazo, bah-tho, a., yellowish brown

bazofia, bah-tho-fe-ah, s., offal; refuse; hogwash

beata, bay-**ah**-tah, s., devout woman; bigot

beatitud, bay-ah-te-**tood**, s., blessedness; holiness
beato, bay-**ah**-to, s., pious person. a., blessed
beber, bay-**bair**, v., to drink
bebida, bay-**bee**-dah, s., drink; beverage
beca, bay-kah, s., college scarf; scholarship; grant
becada, bay-**kah**-dah, s., woodcock
becerro, bay-**thair**-rro, s., yearling calf; calf-skin
bedel, bay-**del**, s., beadle
beldad, bel-**dahd**, s., beauty; belle　　　　　[like
bélico, belicoso, bay-le-ko-, bay-le-**ko**-so, a., war-
bellaco, bay-l'**yah**-ko, s., rogue. a., artful; sly;
　　cunning
bellaquería, bay-l'yah-kay-ree-ah, s., knavery
belleza, bay-l'**yay**-thah, s., beauty; handsomeness
bello*, bay-l'yo, a., beautiful; handsome
bellota, bay-l'**yo**-tah, s., acorn
bencina, ben-**thee**-nah, s., benzine
bendecir, ben-day-**theer**, v., to bless; to consecrate
bendición, ben-de-the-**on**, s., benediction; blessing
bendito, ben-**dee**-to, a., blessed; simple
beneficiar, bay-nay-fe-the-**ar**, v., to benefit; to
　　improve; to cultivate　　　　　　[tion; profit
beneficio, bay-nay-**ree**-the-o, s., benefit; benefac-
beneficioso, bay-nay-fe-the-**o**-so, a., beneficial
benemérito, bay-nay-**may**-re-to, a., meritorious;
　　deserving
beneplácito, bay-nay-**plah**-the-to, s., approbation
benévolo, bay-**nay**-vo-lo, a., benevolent
benigno*, bay-nig-no, a., benign
beodo, bay-o-do, a., drunk
berbiquí, bair-be-**kee**, s., carpenter's brace　　[plant
berenjena, bay-ren-**H**ay-nah. s., aubergine; egg-
bergante, bair-**gahn**-tay, s., ruffian
bergantín, bair-gahn-**teen**, s., brig; brigantine
bermejo, bair-may-Ho, a., bright red
bermellón, bair-mel-l'**yon**, s., vermilion
berrear, bair-rray-**ar**, v., to bellow
berrenchín, bair-rren-**cheen**, s., grunting
berrinche, bair-rreen-chay, s., anger; temper
berro, bair-rro, s., water-cress
berza, bair-thah, s., cabbage
besar, bay-**sar**, v., to kiss; to touch closely

beso, bay-so, s., kiss

bestia, bess-te-ah, s., beast; idiot; ill-bred fellow

besugo, bay-soo-go, s., sea bream

besuquear, bay-soo-kay-ar, v., to kiss repeatedly

betún, bay-toon, s., bitumen; shoe blacking

biberón, be-bay-ron, s., nursing bottle

biblia, bee-ble-ah, s., Bible

biblioteca, be-ble-o-tay-kah, s., library

bicicleta, be-the-klay-tah, s., bicycle

bicho, bee-cho, s., grub; insect

biela, be-ay-lah, s., connecting rod (mech.)

bien, be-en, adv., well; happily; very. s., good; utility; welfare

bienandanza, be-en-ahn-dahn-thah, s., prosperity

bienaventurado, be-en-ah-ven-too-rah-do, a., blessed; fortunate

bienes, be-en-ess, s., property; riches

bienestar, be-en-es-tar, s., well-being

bienhablado, be-en-ah-blah-do, a., well-spoken

bienhechor, be-en-ay-chor, s., benefactor

bienio, be-en-e-o, s., space of two years

bienmandado, be-en-mahn-dah-do, a., obedient

bienquerer, be-en-kay-rair, v., to wish the good of another; to esteem

bienvenida, be-en-vay-nee-dah, s., welcome

bifurcación, be-foor-kah-the-on, s., branch railway; junction

bigamia, be-gah-me-ah, s., bigamy

bigarro, be-gar-rro, s., periwinkle

bigote, be-go-tay, s., moustache

bilis, bee-liss, s., bile

billar, be-l'yar, s., billiards; billiard-table

billete, be-l'yay-tay, s., note; ticket

billón, be-l'yon, s., billion

bimestre, be-mess-tray, a., of two months' dura- [tion

binóculo, be-no-koo-lo, s., binocle

biografía, be-o-grah-fee-ah, s., biography

biología, be-o-lo-Hee-ah, s., biology

biombo, be-om-bo, s., screen

biplano, be-plah-no, s., biplane

birlar, beer-lar, v., to kill at one shot; to snatch [away

birlocha, beer-lo-chah, s., paper-kite

birreta, beer-**rray**-tah, s., cardinal's cap

bisabuela, be-sah-boo´**ay**-lah, s., great-grandmother

bisabuelo, be-sah-boo´**ay**-lo, s., great-grandfather

bisagra, be-**sah**-grah, s., hinge

bisecar, be-say-**kar,** v., to bisect

bisel, be-**sel,** s., bevel edge

bisojo, be-**so**-Ho, a., squint-eyed

bisonte, be-**son**-tay, s., buffalo; bison

bisoño, be-**so**-n'yo, a., undisciplined recruit; novice

bitácora, be-**tah**-ko-rah, s., binnacle

bizarría, be-thar-**rree**-ah, s., gallantry; liberality

bizarro*, be-**thar**-rro, a., gallant; generous

bizco, **beeth**-ko, a., squint-eyed

bizcocho, bith-**ko**-cho, s., biscuit

bizma, **beeth**-mah, s., poultice

blanca, **blahn**-kah, s., copper coin

blanco, **blahn**-ko, a., white; blank; target

blandear, blahn-day-**ar,** v., to soften; to yield

blandir, blahn-**deer,** v., to brandish

blando, **blahn**-do, a., soft; pliant; mild

blandujo, blahn-**doo**-Ho, a., flabby; loose [wash

blanquear, blahn-kay-**ar,** v., to bleach; to white-

blasfemar, blahs-fay-**mar,** v., to blaspheme; to

blasón, blah-**son,** s., heraldry: blazon [swear

blasonar, blah-so-**nar,** v., to boast; to praise one-

blonda, **blon**-dah, s., blond lace [self

bloque, **blo**-kay, s., block of stone

blusa, **bloo**-sah, s., blouse

boato, bo-**ah**-to, s., ostentation

bobalicón bo-bah-le-**kon,** s., great blockhead

bobería, bo-bay-**ree**-ah, s., foolish speech or action

bobo, **bo**-bo, s., simpleton; fool

boca, **bo**-kah, s., mouth

bocacalle, bo-kah-**kah**-l'yay, s., opening of a street

bocadillo, bo-kah-**dee**-l'yo, s., sandwich

bocado, bo-**kah**-do, s., morsel; mouthful

bocal, bo-**kahl,** s., pitcher; mouthpiece

bocanada, bo-kah-**nah**-dah, s., whiff; puff of

boceto, bo-**thay**-to, s., sketch [smoke

bocina, bo-**thee**-nahr, s., horn

bochorno, bo-**chor**-no, s., hot, sultry weather;

boda, bo-**dah,** s., marriage; wedding [shame

bodega, bo-**day**-gah, s., wine-vault; cellar
bodeguero, bo-day-**gay**-ro, s., tavern keeper
bodoque, bo-**do**-kay, s., pellet; dunce
bodrio, bo-dre-o, s., hodge-podge
bofetada, bo-fay-**tah**-dah, s., slap; buffet
boga, bo-gah, s., rowing
bogar, bo-**gar**, v., to row
bogavante, bo-gah-**vahn**-tay, s., big lobster
bohardilla, bo-ar-dee-l'yah, s., (see **buhardilla**)
boj, bo*H*, s., box-tree; box-wood
bola, bo-lah, s., ball; knob; fib
boleo, bo-**lay**-o, s., bowling-green
bolero, bo-**lay**-ro, s., Andalusian dance
boleta, bo-**lay**-tah, s., billet; pay order
boletín, bo-lay-**teen**, s., bulletin; official gazette
boliche, bo-lee-chay, s., jack; block
bólido, bo-le-do, s., meteorite
bolígrafo, bo-lee-grah-fo, s., ball-point pen
bolillo, bo-lee-l'yo, s., jack; bobbin
bolsa, bol-sah, s., purse; pocket; exchange
bolsillo, bol-see-l'yo, s., pocket
bollería, bo-l'yay-**ree**-ah, s., pastry shop
bollero, bo-l'**yay**-ro, s., pastry cook
bollo, bo-l'yo, s., roll; penny loaf
bomba, bom-bah, s., pump; bomb
bombero, bom-**bay**-ro, s., fireman
bombilla, bom-bee-l'yah, s., bulb (elec.), — **de flas,** — day flahs, s., flash-bulb
bombo, bom-bo, s., large drum
bombón, bom-**bon**, s., comfit; bonbon
bonanza, bo-**nahn**-thah, s., fair weather at sea; prosperity
bondad, bon-**dahd**, s., goodness; kindness
bonete, bo-**nay**-tay, s., cap
bonico*, bo-nee-ko, a., fairly good
bonificar, bo-ne-fe-**kar**, v., to improve; to credit
bonito, bo-**nee**-to, a., graceful; pretty
bono, bo-no, s., bond
boñiga, bo-n'**yee**-gah, s., cow-dung
boqueada, bo-kay-**ah**-dah, s., gasp; gasping
boquear, bo-kay-**ar**, v., to gape; to gasp
boquete, bo-**kay**-tay, s., gap; narrow entrance

boquiabierto, bo-ke-be-**air**-to, a., gaping

boquiancho, bo-ke-**ahn**-cho, a., wide-mouthed

boquihendido, bo-ke-en-**dee**-do, a., large-mouthed

boquilla, bo-**kee**-l'yah, s., little mouth; cigar-holder

boquín, bo-**keen**, s., coarse sort of baize

boquirroto, bo-keer-**rro**-to, a., loquacious

bórax, **bo**-rax, s., borax

borbollón, bor-bo-l'**yon**, s., bubbling

borbotar, bor-bo-**tar**, v., to gush out; to boil up

borceguí, bor-thay-**ghee**, s., buskin; laced shoe

borda, **bor**-dah, s., hut; cottage; gunwhale

bordar, bor-**dar**, v., to embroider   [bastard

borde, **bor**-day, s,. border; rim; hem. a., wild;

bordo, **bor**-do, a., on board

bordón, bor-**don**, s., staff; bass; burden of a song

bordonear, bor-do-nay-**ar**, v., to wander about

borla, **bor**-lah, s., tassel; lock

bornear, bor-nay-**ar**, v., to blend; to twist

borona, bo-**ro**-nah, s., millet

borrachera, bor-rrah-**cheth**, s., intoxication

borracho, bor-**rrah**-cho, a., intoxicated; drunk

borrador, bor-rrah-**dor**, s., rough draft; blotter; day-book

borrajear, bor-rrah-**Hay**-ar, v., to scribble

borrar, bor-**rrar**, v., to cross out; to blot; to erase

borrasca, bor-**rrahs**-kah, s., storm; squall; danger

borrego, bor-**rray**-go, s., lamb

borrica, bor-**rree**-kah, s., she-ass

borrico, bor-**rree**-ko, s., ass; fool

borrón, bor-**rron**, s., blot of ink; first sketch; ble-

borronear, bor-rro-nay-**ar**, v., to sketch   [mish

bosque, **bos**-kay, s., wood; forest

bosquejar, bos-kay-**Har**, v., to sketch; to plan

bosquejo, bos-**kay**-Ho, s., sketch of a painting

bosquete, bos-**kay**-tay, s., artificial grove

bostezar, bos-tay-**thar**, v., to yawn

bota, **bo**-tah, s., small leather wine bag; boot

botagueña, bo-tah-**gay**-n'yah, s., sausage made of pig's haslets

botana, bo-**tah**-nah, s., plug; plaster; scar

botar, bo-**tar**, v., to launch; to bounce

botarate, bo-tah-**rah**-tay, s., thoughtless person

botarga, bo-**tar**-gah, s., motley dress; harlequin; large sausage

bote, bo-**tay**, s., thrust; rebound; pot; boat

botella, bo-**tay**-l'yah, s., bottle

botica, bo-**tee**-kah, s., apothecary's shop

boticario, bo-te-**kah**-re-o, s., apothecary; chemist

botija, bo-**tee**-*H*ah, s., jar

botillería, bo-te-l'yay-**ree**-ah, s., ice shop

botín, bo-**teen**, s., buskin; gaiter; booty

botina, bo-**tee**;nah, s., lady's boot

botiquín, bo-te-**keen**, s., medicine chest

boto, bo-to, a., dull of understanding

botón, bo-**ton**, s., bud; button

bóveda, bo-**vay**-dah, s., arch; vault

boya, bo-yah, s., buoy

boyante, bo-**yahn**-tay, a., buoyant; prosperous

boyera, bo-**yay**-rah, s., ox-stall; cow-house

bozal, bo-**thahl**, s., muzzle

bozo, bo-tho, s., down which precedes the beard

bracear, brah-thay-**ar**, v., to swing the arms

bracero, brah-**thay**-ro, s., navvy

bragas, brah-gahs, s., breeches; knickers

braguero, brah-**gay**-ro, s., truss; bandage

bragueta, brah-**gay**-tah, s., flap of trousers

brama, brah-mah, s., rut season

bramante, brah-**mahn**-tay, s., hemp-cord; string

bramar, brah-**mar**, v., to roar; to bluster; to rage

bramido, brah-**mee**-do, s., cry uttered by wild beasts; roaring

branquia, brahn-ke-ah, s., gill of a fish

brasa, brah-sah, s., live coal; ember

bravata, brah-**vah**-tah, s., bravado

braveador, brah-vay-ah-**dor**, s., bully

bravear, brah-vay-**ar**, v., to bully   [elements

braveza, brah-**vay**-thah, s., bravery; fury of the

bravío, brah-**vee**-o, a., ferocious; wild

bravo*, brah-vo, a., brave; excellent; hectoring

bravura, brah-**voo**-rah, s., ferocity of wild beasts; courage; boast

braza, **brah**-thah, s., fathom; brace

brazalete, brah-thah-**lay**-tay, s., bracelet

brazo, brah-tho, s., arm; branch   [of beasts
brazuelo, brah-thoo'ay-lo, s., small arm; shoulder
brea, bray-ah, s., pitch; tar; sackcloth
brebaje, bray-bah-Hay, s., beverage
brécol, bray-kol, s., Brussels-sprouts
brecha, bray-chah, s., breach
brega, bray-gah, s., strife; affray; jest
breve*, bray-vay, a., brief
breviario, bray-ve-ah-re-o, s., breviary
**brezal, bray-thahl, s., heathland
brezo, bray-tho, s., heather
briba, bree-bah, s., truantship; idleness
bribón, bre-bon, s., vagrant; scoundrel; rascal
brida, bree-dah, s., bridle
brigada, bre-gah-dah, s., brigade
brillante*, bre-l'yahn-tay, a., brilliant
brillar, bre-l'yar, v., to shine
brincar, brin-kar, v., to leap; to jump
brindis, breen-diss, s., toast
brío, bree-o, s., strength; vigour; mettle
brioso*, bre-o-so, a., courageous; spirited
brisa, bree-sah, s., breeze
brizna, breeth,-nah, s., fragment; splinter; chip
broca, bro-kah, s., reel; drill; boot-nail
brocado, bro-kah-do, s., brocade
brocha, bro-chah, s., painter's brush
broche, bro-chay, s., clasp; brooch
broma, bro-mah, s., gaiety; merriment; joke
bromear, bro-may-ar, v., to make fun; to jest
bromista, bro-miss-tah, s., practical joker
bromo, bro-mo, s., bromine
bronca, bron-kah, s., practical joke; quarrel
bronce, bron-thay, s., bronze; brass
bronco, bron-ko, a., rough; rude; hard; harsh
bronquedad, bron-kay-dahd, s., harshness; rude-
bronquio, bron-ke-o, s., bronchus   [ness
bronquitis, bron-kee-tiss, s., bronchitis
broquel, bro-kel, s., shield
brotar, bro-tar, v., to bud; to gush
broza, bro-thah, s., brushwood; farrago
bruces, (a or de), ah, day **broo-**thess, adv., with
    the mouth downwards

bruja, broo-*H*ah, s., witch

brujería, broo-*H*ay-ree-ah, s., witchcraft

brújula, broo-*H*oo-lah, s., sea compass

bruma, broo-mah, s., sea-fog; haziness

bruno, broo-no, s., black plum; plum tree

bruñido, broo-n'**yee**-do, a., polished

bruñir, broo-n'**yeer**, v., to polish

brusco, broo*ss*-ko, a., rude; rough; abrupt

brusquedad, broo*ss*-kay-**dahd**, s., abruptness

brutal, broo-tahl, a., brutal [tality

brutalidad, broo-tah-le-**dahd**, s., roughness; bru-

bruto, broo-to, s., brute, a., coarse; rough

bruza, broo-thah, s., brush

bubón, boo-**bon**, s., morbid tumour; bubo

bucarán, boo-kah-**rahn**, s., buckram

bucear, boo-thay-**ar**, v., to dive

bucle, boo-klay, s., curl; ringlet [mouthful

buche, boo-chay, s., crop; craw; maw; stomach

buen, bueno*, boo'en, boo'**ay**-no, a., good

buenaventura, boo'ay-nah-ven-**too**-rah, s., good

buey, boo-ay'e, s., ox [luck

búfalo, boo-fah-lo, s., buffalo

bufanda, boo-fahn-dah, s., muffler, scarf

bufar, boo-**far**, v., to puff with anger; to snort

bufete, boo-**fay**-tay, s., desk; writing-table

bufido, boo-fee-do, s., snorting

bufo, boo-fo, s., buffoon; mimic; jester

bufonada, boo-fo-**nah**-dah, s., buffoonery

buhardilla, boo'ar-dee-l'yah, s., small garret;

buharda, [*sic*] [attic

buhonería, boo'o-nay-ree-ah, s., peddler's wares

buhonero, boo'o-**nay**-ro s., peddler; hawker

buitre, boo'ee-tray, s., vulture

bujería, boo-*H*ay-**ree**-ah, s., bauble; knick-knack

bujía, boo-*H*ee-ah, s., spark plug; wax candle

bula, boo-lah, s., papal bull

bulbo, bool-bo, s., bulb [confusedly

bulto, bool-to, s., bulk; bundle; package. **a—, ah—,**

bulla, boo-l'yah, s., noise; bustle; crowd

bullanga, boo-l'**yahn**-gah, s., tumult; riot

bullicio, boo-l'**yee**-the-o, s., bustle; noise

bullir, boo-l'**yeer**, v., to boil; to bustle; to fluster

buñuelo, boo-n'yoo-**ay**-lo, s., fritter
buque, boo-kay, s., vessel; ship
burbuja, boor-boo-*H*ah, s., bubble
burdel, boor-**del**, s., brothel
burdo, boor-do, a., coarse; common
buril, boo-**reel**, s., engraving tool
burilar, boo-re-**lar**, v., to engrave
burla, boor-lah, s., scoff; mockery; jest; jeer
burlar, boor-lar, v., to ridicule; to mock; to hoax
burlería, boor-lay-ree-ah, s., fun; artifice; drollery; [illusion
burlesco, boor-**less**-ko, a., burlesque
burlón, boor-lon, s., jester; scoffer
burra, boor-rrah, s., she-ass
burrada, boor-rrah-dah, s., stupid action
burrero, boor-**rray**-ro, s., ass-keeper
burro, boor-rro, s., ass; donkey
burujón, boo-roo-*H*on, s., bump
busca, booss-kah, s., search; research
buscada, booss-**kah**-dah, s., search; inquiry
buscar, booss-**kar**, v., to seek; to search
buscón, booss-**kon**, s., searcher; pilferer
busto, booss-to, s., bust
butaca, boo-**tah**-kah, s., large arm-chair
buzo, boo-tho, s., diver
buzon, boo-**thon**, s., letter-box; conduit

cabal, kah-**bahl**, a., exact; perfect; full
cabalgada, kah-bahl-**gah**-dah, s., cavalcade
caballar, kah-bah-l'**yar**, a., equine
caballeresco, kah-bah-bah-l'yay-**ress**-ko, a., chivalrous
caballería, kah-bah-l'yay-**ree**-ah, s., riding beast; [stud
    cavalry
caballeriza, kah-bah-l'yay-**ree**-thah, s., stable; stud
caballero, kah-bah-l'**yay**-ro, s., gentleman; knight; [easel
    horseman
caballete, kah-bah-l'**yay**-tay, s., ridge; trestle
caballo, kah-bah-l'yo, s., horse; (chess) knight
cabaña, kah-**bah**-n'yah, s., hut; cottage
cabecear, kah-bay-thay-**ar**, v., to nod; to shake
    the head in disapprobation
cabeceo, kah-bay-**thay**-o, s., nod; shake of the head

cabecera, kah-bay-**thay**-rah, s., head of a table, etc.; upper end

cabellera, kah-bay-l'**yay**-rah, s., long hair

cabello, kah-**bay**-l'yo, s., hair

cabelludo, kah-bay-l'**yoo**-do, a., hairy

caber, kah-**bair**, v., to contain; to be contained

cabestrillo, kah-bess-**tree**-l'yo, s., sling [ning

cabeza, kah-**bay**-thah, s., head; chief; top; begin-

cabezada, kah-bay-**thah**-dah, s., headshake; stroke with the head; nod; halter

cabezal, kah-bay-**thahl**, s., bolster

cabezo, kah-**bay**-tho, s., summit of a hill

cabezudo, kah-bay-**thoo**-do, a., obstinate; stubborn

cabezuela, kah-bay-thoo-**ay**-lah, s., dolt; bran; rosebud

cabida, kah-**bee**-dah, s., content; capacity

cabildo, kah-**beel**-do, s., chapter of a cathedral

cabilla, kah-**bee**-l'yah, s., tree-nail

cabizbaio, kah-bith-**bah**-Ho, a., crestfallen; [thoughtful

cable, kah-blay, s., cable

cabo, kah-bo, s., extremity; cape; chief; rope

cabotaje, kah-bo-**tah**-Hay, s., coasting trade

cabra, kah-brah, s., she-goat

cabrerizo, kah-bray-**ree**-tho, s., goatherd

cabrestante, kah-bress-**tahn**-tay, s., capstan

cabria, kah-bre-ah, s., crane; axle-free

cabriola, kah-bre-o-lah, s., caper; gambol; jump

cabrito, kah-**bree**-to, s., kid

cabrón, kah-**bron**, s., goat

caca, kah-kah, s., excrements of a child

cacahuete, kah-kah-oo'**ay**-tay, s., pea-nut

cacao, kah-kah-o, s., cocoa-tree; cocoa

cacarear, kah-kah-ray-**ar**, v., to cackle; to brag

cacera, kay-**thay**-rah, s., canal; channel

cacería, kah-thay-**ree**-ah, s., hunting party

cacerola, kah-thay-**ro**-lah, s., stew-pan; saucepan

cacto, kahk-to, s., cactus

cacha, kah-chah, s., handle of a knife

cachar, kah-**char**, v., to break in pieces

cacharro, kah-**char**-rro, s., earthen pot

cachete, kah-**chay**-tay, s., cheek; slap in the face

cachetero, kah-chay-**tay**-ro, s., dagger

cachetudo, kah-chay-**too**-do, a., chubby
cachidiablo, kah-che-de-**ah**-blo, s., hobgoblin
cachifollar, kah-che-fo-l'**yar**, v.. to snub
cachipolla, kah-che-po-l'yah, s., day-fly
cachiporra, kah-che-por-rrah, s., club; cudgel
cachivache, kah-che-**vah**-chay, s., broken crockery; worthless fellow
cacho, '**kah**-cho, s., slice; small piece
cachondo, kah-**chon**-do, a., rutting
cachorrillo, kah-chor-**rree**-l'yo, s., pocket pistol
cachorro, kah-**chor**-rro, s., puppy; cub
cachucha, kah-**choo**-chah, s., man's fur cap; Spanish dance
cachupín, kah-choo-**peen**, s., Spanish colonist in Mexico and Central America
cada, kah-dah, a., every; each
cadalso, kah-**dahl**-eo, s., scaffold
cadáver, kah-**dah**-vair, s., corpse
cadejo, kah-**day**-Ho, s., entangled hair; skein
cadena, kah-**day**-nah, s., chain; series
cadencia, kah-**den**-the-ah, s., cadence
cadeneta, kah-day-**nay**-tah, s., lace; chain-stich
cadenilla, kah-day-**nee**-l'yah, s., small chain
cadente, kah-**den**-tay, a., rhythmical
cadera, kah-**day**-rah, s., hip
cadete, kah-**day**-tay, s., cadet
caduco*, kah-**doo**-ko, a., worn out; decrepit
caedizo, kah-ay-**dee**-tho, a., tottering
caer, kah-**air**, v.. to fall; to fall due; to happen to; to decline; to die
café, kah-**fay**, s., coffee; coffee-house
cafetera, kah-fay-**tay**-rah, s., coffee-pot
cafetero, kah-fay-**tay**-ro, s., coffee-house keeper
caída, kah-ee-dah, s., fall; downfall; declivity
caído, kah-**ee**-do, a., languid; downfallen
caimiento, kah'e-me-**en**-to, s., languidness; dejec-   [tion
cairel, kah'e-**rel**, s., fringe; trimmings
caja, kah Hah, s., box; chest; cash; desk; coffin
cajero, kah'e-Hay-ro, s., cashier   [rettes]
cajetilla, kah-Hay-**tee**-l'yah, s., package (of cigacajón,** kah-**Hon**, s., box; chest; drawer; till
cal, kahl, s., lime

cala, kah-lah, s., creek; cove

calabaza, kah-lah-**bah**-thah, s., pumpkin

calabazada, kah-lah-bah-**thah**-dah, s., knock with the head

calabobos, kah-lah-**bo**-bos, s., drizzle

calabozo, kah-lah-**bo**-tho, s., dungeon

calafatear, kah-lah-fah-tay-**ar**, v., to calk

calamar, kah-lah-**mar**, s., squid

calambre, kah-**lahm**-bray, s., cramp

calamidad, kah-lah-me-**dahd**, s., calamity

calamitoso, kah-lah-me-**to**-so, s., calamitous

cálamo, kah-lah-mo, s., sweet-flag; pen; flute

calamorra, kah-lah-**mor**-rrah, s., (fam.) head

calandria, kah-**lahn**-dre-ah, s., calender; mangle

calaña, kah-lah-n'yah, s., pattern; character

calar, kah-**lar**, v., to penetrate; to permeate; to discover; to pierce; to put; to sink

calavera, kah-lah-**vay**-rah, s., skull; madcap

calcañal, kahl-kah-n'**yahl**, s., heel

calcar, kahl-**kar**, v., to trace; to copy

calce, kahl-thay, s., tyre of a wheel

calceta, kahl-**thay**-tah, s., stocking; fetters

calcetería, kahl-thay-tay-**ree**-ah, s., hosier's shop

calcetín, kahl-thay-**teen**, s., sock [or trade

calcina, kahl-**thee**-nah, s., mortar

calcinar, kahl-the-**nar**, v., to calcine

calcio, kahl-**the**-o, s., calcium

calco, kahl-ko, s., tracing

calculador, kahl-koo-lah-**dor**, s., computer

cálculo, kahl-koo-lo, s., calculation; calculus

calda, kah.-dah, s., warming; heating

caldear, kahl-day-**ar**, v., to heat; to weld iron

caldera, kahl-**day**-rah, s., boiler; caldron

calderilla, kahl-day-**ree**-l'yah, s., copper coin; small change

caldillo, kahl-**dee**-l'yo, s., sauce; broth

caldo, kahl-do, s., broth; sauce; gravy

calefacción, kah-lay-fahk-the-**on**, s., heating

calendario, kah-len-**dah**-re-o, s., calendar

calentador, kah-len-tah-**dor**, s., warming-pan

calentar, kah-len-**tar**, v., to heat

calentura, kah-len-**too**-rah, s., fever; temperature

calenturiento, kah-len-too-re-**en**-to, a., feverish

calesa, kah-**lay**-sah, s., gig; chaise

caleta, kah-**lay**-tah, s., cove; creek

caletre, kah-**lay**-tray, s., understanding; discernment; acumen

calibrar, kah-le-**brar,** v., to gauge; to calibrate

calibre, kah-**lee**-bray, s., calibre

calicó, kah-le-**ko,** s., calico

calidad, kah-le-**dahd,** s., quality; rank; condition

cálido, kah-le-do, a., hot

caliente, kah-le-**en**-tay, a., warm; feverish. **en—,** en—, immediately

calificar, kah-le-fe-**kar,** v., to qualify; to rate; to class; to attest   [ness

calígine, kah-**lee**-He-nay, s., mist; obscurity; dim-

cáliz, kah-lith, s., chalice; calyx

calizo, kah-**lee**-tho, a., calcareous

calma, kahl-mah, s., calm   [anodyne

calmante, kahl-**mahn**-tay, a., soothing; sedative;

calmar, kahl-**mar,** v., to calm; to allay; to soothe

calmo, kahl-mo, a., treeless; barren

calmoso, kahl-**mo**-so, a., tranquil; slow

caló, kah-lo, s., slang   [ment

calor, kah-**lor,** s., heat; warmth; glow; excite-

caloría, kah-lo-**ree**-ah, s., calory

calorífero, kah-lo-ree-**fay**-ro, s., heater; radiator

calumnia, kah-**loom**-ne-ah, s., slander

calumniador, kah-loom-ne-ah-**dor,** s., slander

calumniar, kah-loom-ne-**ar,** v., to slander

caluroso, kah-loo-**ro**-so, a., warm; hot; vehement

calva, kahl-vah, s., bald head

calvicie, kahl-**vee**-the-ay, s., baldness

calvo, kahl-vo, a., bald

calza, kahl-thah, s., trousers; hose

calzada, kahl-**thah**-dah, s., causeway; high-road

calzado, kahl-**thah**-do, s., footwear

calzador, kahl-thah-**dor,** s., shoe-horn

calzar, kahl-**thar,** v., to pull on shoes. &c.

calzoncillos, kahl-thon-**thee**-l'yoss, s., drawers

calzones, kahl-**tho**-ness, s., trousers

callado*, kah-l'**yah**-do, a., silent; discreet; reserved

callar, kah-l'**yar,** v., to keep silence; to hush up

calle, kah-l'yay, s., street; lane; alley

calleja, kah-l'yay-Hah, (see **callejuela**)   [age

callejuela, kah-l'yay-Hoo'ay-lah, s., narrow pass-

callo, kah-l'yo, s., corn (on the feet); wen; tripe

cama, kah-mah, s., bed; couch; bedstead; litter

camafeo, kah-mah-fay-o, s., cameo

cámara, kah-mah-rah, s., hall; cabin. —**de aire,**   —day ah'e-ray, s., inner tube (of tyre)

camarada, kah-mah-**rah**-dah, s., comrade   [attic

camaranchón, kah-mah-rahn-**chon**, s., garret;

camarera, kah-mah-**ray**-rah, s., waitress

camarilla, kah-mah-**ree**-l'yah, s., small room; clique

camarón, kah-mah-**ron**, s., shrimp; prawn

camarote, kah-mah-**ro**-tay, s., berth

cambalachear, kahm-bah-lah-chay-**ar**, v., to barter

cambiar, kahm-be-**ar**, v., to barter; to exchange;   to change

cambio, kahm-be-o, s., barter; rate of exchange

cambista, kahm-**biss**-tah, s., banker; changer

camelar, kah-may-**lar**, v., to flirt; to woo; to seduce

camello, kah-**may**-l'yo, s., camel

camero, kah-**may**-ro, s., upholsterer

camilla, kah-**mee**-l'yah, s., small bed; dressing-   room; stretcher

caminante, kah-me-**nahn**-tay, s., traveller; walker

caminar, kah-me-**nar**, v., to travel; to walk; to   move along   [sion

caminata, kah-me-**nah**-tah, s., long walk; excur-

camino, kah-**mee**-no, s., high road; way; journey

camión, kah-me-**on**, s., truck   [calling

camisa, kah-**mee**-sah, s., shirt; chemise   [dasher

camisero, kah-me-**say**-ro, s., shirt-maker; haber-

camiseta, kah-me-**say**-tah, s., undershirt; vest

camisola, kah-me-**so**-lah, s., ruffled shirt; dicky

camomila, kah-moh-**mee**-lah, s., camomile

camorra, kah-**mor**-rrah, s., quarrel   [person

camorrista, kah-mor-**rriss**-tah, s., quarrelsome

campana, kahm-**pah**-nah, s., bell

campanada, kahm-pah-**nah**-dah, s., stroke of a bell

campanario, kahm-pah-**nah**-re-o, s., belfry

campanear, kahm-pah-nay-**ar**, v., to ring the bell   frequently

campaña, kahm-**pah**-n'yah, s., campaign; level country

campar, kahm-**par**, v., to excel; to encamp

campeón, kahm-pay-**on**, s., champion

campesino, kah-pay-**see**-no, a., rural; rustic

campiña, kahm-**pee**-n'yah, s., campaign; field

campo, kahm-po, s., country; field. **—santo, — sahn-**to, burial-ground

camuflaje, kah-moo-**flah**-*H*ay, s., camouflage

camuza, kah-**moo**-thah, s., chamois

can, kahn, s., dog

canal, kah-**nahl**, s., channel; canal; drinking-[trough

canalón, kah-nah-**lon**, s., large gutter; spout

canalla, kah-**nah**-l'yah, s., mob; rabble

canapé, kah-nah-**pay**, s., couch; settee [zounds!

canario, kah-**nah**-re-o, s., canary bird. interj.

canasta, kah-**nahs**-tah, s., basket; hamper; crate

cancela, kahn-**thay**-lah, s., front-door grating

cancelar, kahn-thay-**lar**, v., to cancel; to annul

cancelaría, kahn-thay-lah-**ree**-ah, s., papal chan-[cery

cáncer, kahn-thair, s., cancer

cancilla, kahn-**thee**-l'yah, s., wicker-door

canciller, kahn-thee-**l'yair**, s., chancellor

canción, kahn-the-**on**, s., song; ballad

candado, kahn-**dah**-do, s., padlock

candar, kahn-**dar**, v., to lock; to shut

candela, kahn-**day**-lah, s., candle [delabrum

candelabro, kahn-day-**lah**-bro, s., chandelier; can-

candente, kahn-**den**-tay, a., red-hot

candidato, kahn-de-**dah**-to, s., candidate

candidez, kahn-de-**deth**, s., candour; simplicity

cándido, kahn-de-do, a., candid; simple; white

candiotera, kahn-de-o-**tay**-rah, s., wine-cellar

candonga, kahn-**don**-gah, s., artful flattery; play-ful trick [practical jokes

candonguear, kahn-don-gay-**ar**, v., to jeer; to play

candor, kahn-**dor**, s., candour; ingenuousness

candoroso, kahn-do-**ro**-so, a., candid; sincere

canela, kah-**nay**-lah, s., cinnamon

canelón, kah-nay-**lon**, s., icicle; cinnamon candy

cangrejo, kahn-**gray**-*H*o, s., crab; crawfish

canguro, kahn-**goo**-ro, s., kangaroo

canicie, kah-**nee**-the ay, s., whiteness of the hair

canijo, kah-**nee**-*H*o, a., weak; sickly; infirm

canilla, kah-**nee**-l'yah, s., shin-bone; arm-bone

canino, kah-**nee**-no, a., canine

canje, kahn-*H*ay, s., exchange

cano, kah-no, a., hoary; grey-haired

canoa, kah-**no**-ah, s., canoe

canon, kah-non, s., canon; rule

canónigo, kah-**no**-ne-go, s., canon or prebendary

cansado*, kahn-**sah**-do, a., tired; tedious; worn out

cansar, kahn-**sar**, v., to weary; to tire; to bore

cantar, kahn-**tar**, v., to sing. s., song [to molest

cántara, kahn-tah-rah, s., pitcher; wine-measure (32 pint)

cantarillo, kahn-tah-**ree**-l'yo, s., small pitcher

cantatriz, kahn-tah-**treeth**, s., (woman) singer

cantera, kahn-**tay**-rah, s., stone quarry; talent

cantidad, kahn-te-**dahd**, s., quantity; measure; portion; number; sum of money

cantilena, kahn-te-**lay**-nah, s., ballad; irksome repetition of a subject

cantimplora, kahn-tim-**plo**-rah, s., water-bottle

cantina, kahn-**tee**-nah, s., cellar; canteen

cantinero, kahn-te-**nay**-ro, s., butler; sutler

canto, kahn-to, s., singing; edge; point; stone

cantón, kahn-**ton**, s., corner; region

cantor, kahn-**tot**, s., singer; minstrel

cantueso, kahn-too'**ay**-so, s., French lavender

canuto, kah-**noo**-to, s., small tube

caña, kah-n'yah, s., cane; reed; stalk

cañada, kah-n'**yah**-dah, s., glen; dale; glade

cañamazo, kah-n'yah-**mah**-tho, s., coarse canvas

cáñamo, kah-n'yah-mo, s., hemp [main

cañería, kah-n'**yay**-ree-ah, s., aqueduct; water-

caño, kah-n'yo, s., tube; pipe; sewer; conduit

cañón, kah-n'**yon**, s., tube; down; quill; cannon; gallery; gorge

cañonazo, kah-n'yo-**nah**-tho, s., cannon-shot

cañonero, kah-n'yo-**nay**-ro, s., gunboat

caoba, kah-o-bah, s., mahogany

caolín, kah-o-**leen**, s., china clay

caos, kah-oss, s., chaos

caótico, kah-o-te-ko, chaotic

capa, ⊠kah-pah, s., cloak; mantle; layer; cover; pretence; hinder; wrapper; coat of paint

capacidad, kah-pah-the-**dahd**, s., capacity; extent

capacha, kah-**pah**-chah, s., frail; hamper

capar, kah-**par**, v., to geld

caparazón, kah-pah-rah-**thon**, s., caparison; carcass of a fowl; feed-bag

caparrosa, kah-par-**rro**-sah, s., copperas

capataz, kah-pah-**tahth**, s., overseer; superintendent; foreman

capaz, kah-**path**, a., capable; competent; spacious

capazo, kah-**pah**-tho, s., large frail; hamper

capcioso, kahp-the-o-so, a., captious

capear, kah-pay-**ar**, v., to challenge a bull with a cloak; to deceive

capellán, kah-pay-l'**yahn**, s., chaplain

capilla, kah-**pee**-l'yah, s., hood; cowl; chapel; choir; chapter; proof-sheet

capirote, kah-pe-**ro**-tay, s., hood

capital, kah-pe-**tahl**, s., capital (money, town), a.,* capital; essential

capitán, kah-pe-**tahn**, s., captain [tainry

capitanía, kah-pe-tah-**nee**-ah, s., captainship; cap-

capitel, kah-pe-**tel**, s., capital of a column

capitulación, kah-pe-too-lah-the-**on**, s., capitulation. pl., articles of a marriage contract

capitular, kah-pe-too-**lar**, v., to conclude an agreement; to capitulate. s., member of a chapter, a., capitulary [chapter of a book

capítulo, kah-**pee**-too-lo, s., chapter of a cathedral

capón, kah-**pon**, s., capon; gelding

caponera, kah-po-**nay**-rah, s., coop

capote, kah-**po**-tay, s., sort of cloak

capricho, kah-**pree**-cho, s., caprice, whim, mood

caprichoso*, kah-pre-**cho**-so, a., capricious

cápsula, kahp-soo-lah, s., capsule; percussion cap

captar, kahp-**tar**, v., to captivate [rest

capturar, kahp-too-**rar**, v., to apprehend; to ar-

capucha, kah-**poo**-chah, s., hood

capuchina, kah-poo-**chee**-nah, s., nasturtium

capucho, kah-**poo**-cho, s., cowl; hood

capullo, kah-**poo**-l'yo, s., cocoon; bud of flowers
cara, kah-rah, s., face; mien; front; surface
carabela, kah-rah-**bay**-lah, s., caravel
carabina, kah-rah-**bee**-nah, s., carbine
carabinero, kah-rah-be-**nay**-ro, s., carabineer
caracol, kah-rah-**kol**, s., snail; prancing of a horse
caracolear, kah-rah-ko-lay-**ar**, v., to caracole; to twist   [writing; type
carácter, kah-**rahk**-tair, s., character; hand-
carado, kah-**rah**-do, a., faced. **bien —,** be-**en —,** pretty-faced; **mal —,** mahl —, ill-faced
; caramba ! kah-**rahm**-bah, interj., hah ! strange !
carambola, kah-rah-**bo**-lah, s., (billiards) cannon; trick to deceive
caramelo, kah-rah-**may**-lo, s., caramel   [ceedingly
caramente, kah-rah-**men**-tay, adv., dearly; ex-
caramillo, kah-rah-**mee**-l'yo, s., flageolet; flute
carantoñero, kah-rahn-to-n'**yay**-ro, s., cajoler; flatterer
carátula, kah-**rah**-too-lah, s., pasteboard mask
caravana, kah-rah-**vah**-nah, s., caravan
carbón, kar-**bon**, s., charcoal; coal; cinder
carbonada, kar-bo-**nah**-dah, s., broiled steak or
carbonato, kar-bo-**nah**-to, s., carbonate   [chop
carboncillo, kar-bon-**thee**-l'yo, s., small coal; black crayon   [pit
carbonera, kar-bo-**nay**-rah, s., coal-celler; coal-
carbonero, kar-bo-**nay**-ro, s., charcoal maker;
carbono, kar-**bo**-no, s., carbon   [coal-merchant
carbunco, carbunclo, carbúnculo, kar-**boon**-ko, kar-**boon**-klo, kar-**boon**-koo-lo, s., carbuncle
carcajada, kar-kah-**H**ah-dah, s., loud laughter
cárcel, kar-thel, s., prison; jail
carcelería, kar-thay-lay-**ree**-ah, s., imprisonment
carcelero, kar-thay-**lay**-ro, s., jailer
carcoma, kar-ko-mah, s., woodlouse; anxious concern; dry rot
carcomer, kar-ko-**mair**, v., to gnaw; to consume
carda, kar-dah, s., carding; card   [by degrees
cardar, kar-dar, v., to card wool
cardenal, kar-day-**nahl**, s., cardinal
cardencha, kar-den-chah, s., teasel

cardenillo, kar-day-**nee**-l'yo, s., verdigris

cárdeno, kar-day-no, a., livid

cardinal, kar-de-**nahl**, a., principal; fundamental

cardo, kar-do, s., thistle

carear, kah-ray-**ar**, v., to confront (criminals)

carecer, kah-ray-**thair**, v., to need; to lack

carena, kah-**ray**-nah, s., careening

carencia, kah-**ren**-the-ah, s., want; need; lack

careo, kah-**ray**-o, s., confrontation

carestía, kah-ress-**tee**-ah, s., scarcity; famine

careta, kah-**ray**-tah, s., mask of pasteboard

carga, kar-gah, s., load; freight; burden; weight; cargo; charge; tax   [are loaded

cargadero, kar-gah-**day**-ro, s., place where goods

cargador, kar-gah-**dor**, s., charger; freighter

cargamento, kar-gah-**men**-to, s., cargo

cargar, kar-**gar**, v., to load; to freight; to charge; to book

cargazón, kar-gah-**thon**, s., cargo   [obligation

cargo, kar-go, s., burden; loading; office; charge;

cari . . . , kah-re, prefix meaning "faced"

cariancho, kar-re-**ahn**-cho, a., broad-faced

cariarse, kah-re-**ar**-say, v., to grow carious

caribe, kah-ree-bay, s., cannibal; savage

caricia, kah-**ree**-the-ah, s., caress

caridad, kah-re-**dahd**, s., charity

caridoliente, kah-re-do-le-**en**-tay, a., sad looking

caries, kah-re-ess, s., caries

carigordo, kah-re-**gor**-do, a., plump-faced

carilargo, kah-re-**lar**-go, a., long-visaged

carilucio, kah-re-**loo**-thee-o, a., bright-faced

carinegro, kah-re-**nay**-gro, a., of a swarthy complexion

cariño, kah-**ree**-n'yo, s., love; tenderness; affection

cariñoso, kah-re-n'**yo**-so, a., affectionate; loving

carirredondo, kah-re-rray-**don**-do, a., round-faced

caritativo, kah-re-tah-**tee**-vo, a., charitable

cariz, kah-**reeth**, s., aspect (of weather); prospect

carmen, kar-men, s., country-house and garden

carmesí, kar-may-**see**, a., crimson

carmín, kar-**meen**, s., carmine

carnada, kar-**nah**-dah, s., bait

carnaval, kar-nah-**vahl,** s., carnival

carne, kar-nay, s., flesh; meat; pap; kin

carnero, kar-**nay**-ro, s., sheep; mutton

carnicería, kar-ne-thay-**ree**-ah, s., shambles; slaughter; butcher's shop

carnicero, kar-ne-**thay**-ro, s., butcher. a., carni-

carnoso, kar-**no**-so, a., fleshy [vorous

carnuza, kar-**noo**-than, s., excess of meat producing loathing

caro, kah-ro, adv., dearly, a., dear; costly

carozo, kah-**ro**-tho, s., core of an apple

carpa, kar-pah, s., carp (fish) [docket

carpeta, kar-**pay**-tah, s., table-cover; portfolio;

carpintero, kar-pin-**tay**-ro, s., carpenter

carpo, kar-po, s., carpus; wrist

carraco, kar-**rrah**-ko, a., old; withered; decrepit

carral, kar-**rrahl,** s., barrel

carralero, kar-rrah-**lay**-ro, s., cooper

carraspera, kar-rrahs-**pay**-rah, s., hoarseness

carrera, kar-**rray**-rah, s., race; course; high-road

carreta, kar-**rray**-tah, s., long narrow cart [career

carretada, kar-rray-**tah**-dah, s., careful

carretaje, kar-rray-**tah**-Hay, s., cartage

carretear, kar-rray-tay-**ar,** v., to cart

carretera, kar-rray-**tay**-rah, s., high-road [carter

carretero, kar-rray-**tay**-ro, s., cartwright; carman;

carretilla, kar-rray-**tee**-l'yah, s., wheel-barrow

carril, kar-**rreel,** s., rut; (railway) rail

carrillo, kar-**rree**-l'yo, s., cheek

carro, kar-rro, s., cart

carrocero, kar-rro-**thay**-ro, s., carriage-builder

carroña, kar-**rro**-n'yah, s., carrion

carroza, kar-**rro**-thah, s., large coach

carruaje, kar-rroo'**ah**-Hay, s., vehicle of any kind

carta, kar-tah, s., letter; map; ordinance; card for playing

cartabón, kartah-**bon,** s., square; rule

cartapacio, kar-tah-**pah**-the-o, s., satchel; portfolio [letter

cartearse, kar-tay-**ar**-say, v., to correspond by

cartel, kar-**tel,** s., placard; poster; cartel

cartera, kar-**tay**-rah, s., portfolio; letter-case.

cartero, kar-**tay**-ro, s., postman   [pocket-book

cartilla, kar-tee-l'yah, s., primer; certificate

cartón, kar-ton, s., pasteboard; cartoon; cardboard

cartuchera, kar-too-**chay**-rah, s., cartridge-box

cartucho, kar-**too**-cho, s., cartridge

cartulina, kar-too-lee-nah, s., bristol-board

carvallo, kar-vah-l'yo, s., oak

casa, kah-sah, s., house; home; household

casaca, kah-**sah**-kah, s., coat

casación, kah-sah-the-**on**, s., cassation

casadero, kah-sah-**day**-ro, a., fit for marriage

casamiento, kah-sah-me-**en**-to, s., marriage

casar, kah-**sar**, v., to marry

casarse, kah-**sar**-say, v., to get married

cascabel, kahs-kah-**bel**, s., hawk-bell; jingle

cascada, kahs-**kah**-dah, s., cascade; waterfall

cascadura, kahs-kah-**doo**-rah, s., bursting or break-

cascajo, kahs-kah-Ho, s., gravel   [ing asunder

cascanueces, kahs-kah-noo-**ay**-thess, s., nut-cracker

cascar, kahs-**kar**, v., to crack, burst, break

cáscara, kahs-kah-rah, s., rind; peel; husk; bark

¡cáscaras!, kahs-kah-rahs, interj., (expressing surprise or admiration) wonderful!

cascarón, kahs-kah-**ron**, s., egg-shell

cascarrón, kahs-kar-**rron**, a., rough; rude; harsh

casco, kahs-ko, s., helmet; cask; hull (of a ship);

cascote, kahs-**ko**-tay, s., rubbish; débris   [hoof

casería, kah-say-ree-ah, s., messuage

caserío, kah-say-**ree**-o, s., village; hamlet

casero, kah-**say**-ro, s., landlord; house agent. a., domestic; homely

caseta, kah-**say**-tah, s., small house; cottage

casi, kah-se, adv., almost   [lodge; pigeon-hole

casilla, kah-**see**-l'yah, s., ticket-office; keeper's

casimir, kah-se-**meer**, s., kerseymere

caso, kah-so, s., event; case; occurrence; accident; opportunity

caspa, kahs-pah, s., dandruff; scurf

¡cáspita!, kahs-pe-tah, interj., gracious!

casquete, kahs-**kay**-tay, s., helmet; skull-cap

casquijo, kahs-kee-Ho., s., gravel

casquillo, kahs-**kee**-l'yo, s., tip; ferrule; socket; iron arrow-head [caste

casta, kahs-tah, s., race; breed; kindred; kind;

castaña, kahs-tah-n'yah, s., chestnut

castañeta, kahs-tah-n'**yay**-tah, s., snapping of the fingers; castenet

castaño, kahs-tah-n'yo, s., chestnut-tree, a., hazel

castidad, kahs-te-**dahd**, s., chastity

castigar, kahs-te-**gar**, v., to chastise; to punish

castigo, kahs-**tee**-go, s., chastisement; punishment

castillejo, kahs-te-l'**yay**-Ho, s., small castle; go-

castillo, kahs-**tee**-l'yo, s., castle [cart; scaffolding

castizo, kahs-**tee**-tho, a., pure-blooded; (language)

casto*, kahs-to, a., chaste [pure

castor, kah-**tor**, s., beaver

castrar, kahs-**trar**, v., to geld; to castrate

casual*, kah-soo-**ahl**, a., casual; accidental

casualidad, kah-soo-ah-le-**dahd**, s., chance; accident [wretched cottage or hut

casuca, casucha, kah-**soo**-kah, kah-**soo**-chah, s.,

cata, kah-tah, s., trying by taste; sample

catador, kah-tah-**dor**, s., taster; sampler

catalejo, kah-tah-**lay**-Ho, s., telescope

catalogar, kah-tah-lo-**gar**, v., to catalogue

catálogo, kah-**tah**-lo-go s., catalogue

cataplasma, kah-tah-**plahs**-mah, s., poultice

catar, kah-**tar**, v., to taste; to sample

catarata, kah-tah-**rah**-tah, s., waterfall; cataract

catarro, kah-**tar**-rro, s., catarrh

catastro, kah-**tahs**-tro, s., land-register

catástrofe, kah-**tahs**-tro-fay, s., catastrophe

cataviento, kah-tah-ve-**en**-to, s., weather-cock

cátedra, kah-tay-drah, s., chair of a professor; professorship

catedral, kah-tay-**drahl**, s., cathedral

catedrático, kah-tay-**drah**-te-ko, s., professor

categórico, kah-tay-**go**-re-ko, a., categorical

catequismo, kah-tay-**kiss**-mo, s., catechism

caterva, kah-**tair**-vah, s., multitude; throng; swarm

católico, kah-**to**-le-ko, a., catholic

catorce, kah-**tor**-thay, s., & a., fourteen

catorceno, kah-tor-**thay**-no, a., fourteenth

catre, kah-tray, s., small bedstead; cot
cauce, kah'oo-thay, s., bed of a river; ditch
caución, kah'oo-the-on, s., caution; security; surety
caucionar, kah'oo-the-o-nar, v., to guard against;
caucho, kah'oo-cho, s., india-rubber [to bail
caudal, kah'oo-dahl, s., fortune; health; volume
of water [water; abundant; rich
caudaloso, kah'oo-dah-lo-so, a., carrying much
caudillo, kah'oo-dee-l'yo, s., chief; leader
causa, kah'oo-sah, s., cause; motive; lawsuit
causante, kah'oo-sahn-tay, s., causer; constituent
causar, kah'oo-sar, v., to cause; to originate; to use
cáustico, kah'ooss-te-ko, a., caustic
cautela, kah'oo-tay-lah, s., caution; prudence; heed
cauteloso, kah'oo-tay-lo-so, a., cautious
cauterio, kah'oo-tay-re-o, s., cautery [vate
cautivar, kah'oo-te-var, v., to imprison; to capti-
cautiverio, kah'oo-te-vay-re-o, s., captivity
cautivo, kah'oo-te-vo, a., a captive
cauto, kah'oo-to, a., cautious, wary
cava, kah-vah, s., digging; wine-cellar
cavador, kah-vah-dor, s., digger
cavar, kah-var, v., to dig
cavidad, kah-ve-dahd, s., cavity
cavilación, kah-ve-lah-the-on, s., cavilling
cavilar, kah-ve-lar, v., to cavil
caviloso*, kah-ve-lo-so, a., captious
cayada, kah-yah-dah, s., shepherd's hook; crozier
cayo, kah-yo, s., rock; shoal; islet; reef
caz, kath, s., canal for irrigation; flume
caza, kah-thah, s., hunt; game
cazador, kah-thah-dor, s., hunter
cazar, kah-thar, v., to chase; to hunt
cazo, kah-tho, s., saucepan; ladle; glue pot
cazón, kah-thon, s., dog-fish
cazuela, kah-thoo'ay-lah, s., stew-pan
cazurro, kah-thoor-rro, a., taciturn; sullen; sulky
¡**ce!**, thay, interj., here!
ceba, thay-bah, s., fattening of animals
cebada, thay-bah-dah, s., barley
cebar, thay-bar, v., to fatten annimals
cebo, thay-bo, s., food; fodder; fattening; bait

cebolla, thay-**bo**-l'yah, s., onion

cebón, thay-**bon**, s., fat bullock or hog

cebra, thay, thay-brah, s., zebra [as ' th ')

cecear, thay-thay-**ar**, v., to lisp (to pronounce 's'

cecina, thay-**the**-nah, s., dried beef

cedazo, thay-**dah**-tho, s., sieve; strainer

ceder, thay-**dair**, v., to grant; to transfer; to submit; to abate

cedro, thay-dro, s., cedar

cédula, thay-doo-lah, s., slip of paper; order; bill; decree; warrant; identity card

céfiro, thay-fe-ro, s., zephyr

cegar, thay-**gar**, v., to blind

cegato, thay-**gah**-to, a., (fam,) short-sighted

ceguedad, thay-gay-**dahd**, s., blindness

ceguera, thay-gay-rah, s., blindness

ceja, thay-Ha, s., eyebrow

cejar, thay-Har, v., to relax; to slacken; to give up

celada, thay-**lah**-dah, s., helmet; ambush

celador, thay-lah-**dor**, s., curator; warden

celar, thay-**lar**, v., to fulfil duties carefully; to watch; to conceal; to engrave

celda, thel-dah, s., cell

celebérrimo, thay-lay-**bair**-rre-mo, a., most celebrated

celebrar, thay-lay-**brar**, v., to celebrate; to praise

célebre,* thay-lay-bray, a., celebrated; famous

celeridad, thay-lay-re-**dahd**, s., celerity

celeste, thay-**less**-tay, a., celestial; heavenly; per-

celibato, thay-le-**bah**-to, s., celibacy [fect

célibe, thay-le-bay, s., bachelor

celo, thay-lo, s., zeal; rut. pl., jealousy

celosía, thay-lo-**see**-ah, s., Venetian blind; lattice;

celoso, thay-lo-so, a., zealous; jealous [jealousy

célula, thay-loo-lah, s., cellule; cell

cementar, thay-men-**tar**, v., to cement

cementerio, thay-men-**tay**-re-o, s., cemetery

cemento, thay-men-to, s., cement

cena, thay-nah, s., supper

cenador, thay-nah-**dor**, s., arbor; bower

cenagal, thay-nah-**gahl**, s., quagmire; slough; bog

cenar, thay-**nar**, v., to sup

cencerro, then-**thair**-rro, s., bell worn by the leading wether or cow

cendal, then-**dahl,** s,. crape ; gauze

cenefa, thay-**nay**-fah, s., border ; fringe

cenicero, thay-ne-**thay**-ro, s., ash-pan ; ash-hole

cenit, thay-**neet,** s., zenith

ceniza, thay-**nee**-thah, s., ashes

cenizo, thay-**nee**-tho, a., ash-coloured

censo, then-so, s., census ; poll-tax ; annuity

censurar, then-soo-**rar,** v., to criticize ; to censure ; to blame

centavo, then-**tah**-vo, s., hundredth part ; cent

centella, then-**tay**-l'yah, s., lightning ; spark

centena, then-**tay**-nah, s., hundred   [rye field

centenar, then-tay-**nar,** s., hundred ; centenary ;

centeno, then-**tay**-no, s., rye. a., hundredth

centésimo, then-**tay**-se-mo, a., hundredth

céntimo, then-te-mo, s., centime

centinela, then-te-**nay**-lah, s., sentinel

central, then-**trahl,** a., central

centro, then-tro, s., centre ; headquarters ; club

céntuplo, then-too-plo, a., hundredfold

ceñido, thay-**n'yee**-do, a., close fitting   [abbreviate

ceñir, thay-**n'yeer,** v., to gird ; to hem in ; to

ceño, thay-n'yo, s., frown ; ferrule

cepa, thay-pah, s., stump ; stock ; vine-stock

cepillo, thay-**pee**-l'yo, s., plane ; clothes-brush ; poor-box

cepo, thay-po, s., anvil-block ; stocks ; snare

cera, thay-rah, s., wax

cerafolio, thay-rah-**fo**-le-o, s., chervil

cerato, thay-rah-to, s., cerate

cerca, thair-kah, adv., close by ; near. s., fence

cercado, thair-**kah**-do, s., inclosure   [nearly

cercanamente, thair-kah-nah-**men**-tay,adv.,nigh ;

cercanía, thair-kah-**nee**-ah, s., proximity ; neighbourhood

cercano, thair-**kah**-no, a., near ; close by

cercar, thair-**kar,** v., to inclose ; to hedge ; to hem

cercenar, thair-thay-**nar,** v., to pare ; to clip ; to curtail

cerceta, thair-**thay**-tah, s., widgeon

cerciorar, thair-the-o-**rar,** v., to assure; to affirm; to ascertain

cerco, thair-ko, s., hoop; ring; circle; blockade

cerda, thair-dah, s., horse-hair; bristle

cerdo, thair-do, s., hog; pig

cerdoso, thair-**do-**so, a., bristly

cerebro, thay-**ray-**bro, s., cerebrum; brain

cerero, thay-**ray-**ro, s., wax-chandler

cereza, thay-**ray-**thah, s., cherry

cerilla, thay-**ree-**l'yah, s., wax taper; vesta; car-wax

cerner, thair-**nair,** v., to sift; to blossom; to hover

cernidillo, thair-ne-**dee-**l'yo, s., drizzle; mizzle

cernidura, thair-ne-**doo-**rah, s., sifting

cero, thay-ro, s., zero; cipher; naught

cerote, thay-**ro-**tay, s., shoemaker's wax

cerquita, thair-**kee-**tah, adv., very near. s., small inclosure

cerradero, thair-rrah-**day-**ro, s., bolt staple

cerrado, thair-**rrah-**do, a., reserved; obscure; obstinate

cerrador, thair-rrah-**dor,** s., shutter; fastener

cerradura, thair-rrah-**doo-**rah, s., lock; closure; locking-up

cerrajero, thair-rrah-*H*ay-ro, s., locksmith

cerramiento, thair-rrah-me-**en-**to, s., closure; shutting-up   [to fasten; to stop up

cerrar, thair-**rrar,** v., to close; to shut; to lock

cerril, thair-**rreel,** a., mountainous; rough; wild

cerro, thair-rro, s., hill; neck; back-bone

cerrojo, thair-rro-*H*o, s., bolt; latch

certamen, thair-**tah-**men, s., literary controversy

certeza, certidumbre, thair-**tay-**thah, thair-te-**doom-**bray, s., certainty

certificado, thair-te-fe-**kah-**do, s., certificate

certificar, thair-te-fe-**kar,** v., to certify. — **una carta,** — oo-nah-**kar-**tah, to register a letter

cerval, thair-**vahl,** a., belonging to a deer

cervato, thair-**vah-**to, s., fawn   [house

cervecería, thair-vay-thay-**ree-**ah, s., brewery; ale-

cerveza, thair-**vay-**thah, s., beer

cervicabra, thair-ve-**kah-**brah, s., gazelle

cerviguillo, cerviz, thair-ve-**ghee**-l'yo, thair-**veeth,** s., nape; cervix

cesación, thay-sah-the-**on,** s., cessation; stopping

cesar, thay-**sar,** v., to cease; to leave off; to stop

cesible, thay-**see**-blay, a., transferable

cesión, thay-se-**on,** s., cession; transfer; assignment

cesionario, thay-se-o-**na**-re-o, s., transferee

cesionista, thay-se-o-**niss**-tah, s., transferrer

césped, thess-payd, s., turf; sod; lawn

cesta, thess-tah, s., basket

cesto, thess-to, s., hand-basket

cestón, thess-**ton,** s., large basket; gabion

cetrería, thay-tray-**ree**-ah, s., falconry

cetrino, thay-**tree**-no, a., citrine; jaundiced;

cetro, thay-tro, s., sceptre; reign [melancholy

ciática, the-**ah**-te-kah, s., sciatica

cicatería, the-kah-tay-**ree**-ah, s., niggardliness; stinginess

cicatero, the-kah-**tay**-ro, a., niggardly; stingy

cicatriz, the-kah-**treeth,** s., cicatrice; scar

ciclo, thee-klo, s., cycle

ciclón, the-**klon,** s., cyclone

cidra, thee-drah, s., citron

ciego*, the-**ay**-go, a., blind; (passage) shut up

cielo, the-**ay**-lo, s., heaven; sky; climate

cien, the-**en,** a., (used before nouns), one hundred

ciénaga, the-**en**-ah-gah, s., marsh

ciencia, the-**en**-the-ah, s., science; knowledge

cieno, the-**en**-o, s., mud; slough

ciento, the-**en**-to, s. & a., one hundred

cierne, the-**air**-nay, **estar en —,** es-tar en —, to

cierro, the-**air**-rro, s., inclosure [be in blossom

cierto, the-**air**-to, a., certain

cierva, the-**air**-vah, s., hind

ciervo, the-**air**-vo, s., deer

cierzo, the-**air**-tho, s., cold northerly wind

cifra, thee-frah, s., cipher; abbreviation; sum total

cigarra, the-**gar**-rrah, s., cicada

cigarrera, the-gar-**rray**-rah, s., cigar-case

cigarrillo, the-gar-**rree**-l'yo, s., cigarette

cigarro, the-**gar**-rro, s., cigar

ciguatera, the-goo'ah-**tay**-rah, s., jaundice

cigüeña, the-goo**'ay**-n'yah, s., white stork
cilindro, the-**leen**-dro, s., cylinder
cima, thee-mah, s., summit; crest; top
cimarrón, the-mar-**rron,** a., wild; unruly
címbalo, theem-bah-lo, s., cymbal
cimborio, thim-**bo**-re-o, s., cupola; dome
cimbrar, thim-**brar,** v., to brandish; to vibrate
cimbreño, thim-**bray**-n'yo, a., pliant; flexible
cimentar, the-men-**tar,** v., to found
cimiento, the-me-**en**-to, s., foundation; basis;
cinc, think, s., zink   [origin
cincel, thin-**thel,** s., chisel
cincelar, thin-thay-**lar,** v., to chisel; to engrave
cinco, thin-ko, s. & a., five
cincuenta, thin-kov'en-tah, s & a., fifty
cincha, thin-chah, s., girth; belt
cine, thee-nay, s., cinema
cíngaro, thin-gah-ro, s., gipsy
cíngulo, thin-goo-lo, s., girdle
cinta, thin-tah, s., ribbon; tape; sash
cinteado, thin-tay-**ah**-do, a., adorned with ribbons
cinto, thin-to, s., belt
cintura, thin-**too**-rah, s., waist
cinturón, thin-too-**ron,** s., broad belt
ciprés, the-**press,** s., cypress-tree
circo, theer-ko, s., circus
circuir, theer-koo**'eer,** v., to surround
circuito, theer-koo**'ee**-to, s., circuit
circular, theer-koo-**lar,** v., to circulate
círculo, theer-koo-lo, s., circle
circuncidar, theer-koon-the-**dar,** v., to circumcise
circundar, theer-koon-**dar,** v., to surround
circunflejo, theer-koon-**flay**-Ho, a., circumflex
circunloquio, theer-koon-**lo**-ke-o,s.,circumlocution
circunspecto, theer-koons-**pek**-to, a., circumspect;
cautious   [cumstance
circunstancia, theer-koons-**tahn**-the-ah, s., cir-
circunstante, theer-koons-**tahn**-tay,a.,surround-
ing. pl., bystanders
circunvecino, theer-koon-**vay**-the-no, a., neigh-
cirio, thee-re-o, s., wax candle   [bouring
cirro, theer-rro, s., schirrus; cirrus

ciruela, the-roo'**ay**-lah, s., plum

cirugía, the-roo-*Hee*-ah, s., surgery

cirujano, the-roo-*H*ah-no, s., surgeon

ciscar, thiss-**kar,** v., to besmear;

cisco, thiss-ko, s., coal-dust; quarrel

cisma, thiss-mah, s., schism; discord

cisne, thiss-nay, s., swan

cita, thee-tah, s., quotation; summons; rendezvous

citación, the-tah-the-**on,** s., citation; quotation; summons

citar, the-**tar,** v., to convoke; to summon; to quote

cítara, thee-tah-ra, s., zither

citerior, the-tay-re-**or,** a., hither; toward this side

ciudad, the'oo-**dahd,** s., city; town corporation

ciudadano, the'oo-dah-**dah**-no, s., citizen

ciudadela, the'oo-dah-**day**-lah, s., citadel

civilidad, the-ve-le-**dahd,** s., civility; urbanity

civismo, the-**viss**-mo, s., patriotism

cizalla, the-**thah**-l'yah, s., shears; filings

cizaña, the-**thah**-n'yah, s., darnel; tare; discord

clac, klahk, s., opera-hat

clamar, klah-**mar,** v., to cry out; to clamour; to want; to demand

clamor, klah-**mor,** s., clamour; outcry

clamorear, klah-mo-ray-**ar,** v., to clamour; to implore assistance; to toll

clandestino, klahn-dess-**tee**-no, a., clandestine

clara, klah-rah, s., white of an egg

claraboya, klah-rah-**bo**-yah, s., sky-light

clarear, klah-ray-**ar,** v., to dawn

clarete, klah-**ray**-tay, s., claret [distinctness

claridad, klah-re-**dahd,** s., clearness; brightness;

clarificar, klah-re-fe-**kar,** v., to clarify

clarín, klah-**reen,** s., trumpet; bugle

clarinete, klah-re-**nay**-tay, s., clarinet

clarividencia, klah-re-ve-**den**-the-ah, s., clairvoyance [light; manifest; open

claro*, klah-ro, a., clear; transparent; lucid; thin;

claroscuro, klah-ros-**koo**-ro, s., chiaroscuro; light and shade [cription

clase, klah-say, s., class; rank; order; kind; des-

clásico, klah-se-ko, a., classical; classic

claudicar, klah'oo-de-**kar**, v., to halt; to limp; to claudicate

claustro, klah'ooss-tro, s., cloister [lation

cláusula, klah'oo-soo-lah, s., clause; article; stipu-

clausular, klah'oo-soo-**lar**, v., to close a period

clausura, klah'oo-**soo-**rah, s., closure; confinement

clava, klah'-vah, s., club; cudgel

clavado, klah-**vah-**do, a., nailed; exact; precise

clavar, klah-**var**, v., to nail; to fasten with nails

clave, klah-vay, s., key; code; clue

clavel, klah-vel, s., carnation

clavicordio, klah-ve-**kor**-de-o, s., harpsichord

clavícula, klah-**vee-**koo-lah, s., clavicle; collar bone

clavija, klah-**vee-***H*ah, s., pin; peg; nog

clavillo, klah-**vee-**l'yo, s., small nail; tack

clavo, klah-vo, s., nail; corn (on the feet); clove

clemencia, klay-**men-**the-ah, s., clemency

clemente*, klay-**men-**tay, a., clement

clerecía, klay-ray-**thee**-ah, s., clergy

clérigo, klay-re-go, s., cleric; priest; clergyman

clero, klay-ro, s., clergy

cliente, kle-**en**-tay, s., client

clientela, kle-en-**tay-**lah, s., clientele

clima, klee-mah, s., climate

clínica, klee-ne-kah, s., clinic

clisado, kle-**sah-**do, s., stereotyping

clisé, kle-**say,** s., stereotype plate; cliché

clistel, kliss-**tel**, s., clyster

cloaca, klo-**ah-**kah, s., sewer

cloquear, klo-kay-**ar**, v., to cluck; to cackle

cloral, klo-**rahl**, s., chloral

cloro, klo-ro, s., chlorine

cloruro, klo-**roo**-ro, s., chloride

club, kloob, s., club; association

coacción, ko-ahk-the-**on**, s., compulsion; coercion

coadyuvar, ko-ahd-yoo-**var**, v., to help; to assist

coagular, ko-ah-goo-**lar**, v., to coagulate

coalición, ko-ah-le-the-**on**, s., coalition

coartada, ko-ar-**tah-**dah, s., alibi

coartar, ko-ar-**tar**, v., to limit; to restrain

coba, ko-bah, s., (fam.) humbug

cobarde, ko-**bar-**day, a., coward; faint-hearted

cobardía, ko-bar-dee-ah, s., cowardice
cobertera, ko-bair-**tay**-rah, s., pot-lid; cover
cobertizo, ko-bair-tee-tho, s., shed; hut
cobijar, ko-be-*H*ar, v., to cover; to shelter
cobijo, ko-bee-*H*o, s., shelter; lodge
cobrador, ko-brah-dor, s., collector of rents; railway conductor [of money
cobranza, ko-**brahn**-thah, s., collection or recovery
cobrar, ko-**brar**, v., to recover; to collect; to recuperate
cobre, ko-bray, s., copper
cobrizo, ko-**bree**-tho, a., coppery
cobro, ko-bro, (see **cobranza**)
cocción, kok-the-**on**, s., coction
cocear, ko-thay-ar, v., to kick
cocer, ko-**thair**, v., to cook; to boil; to dress victuals
cocido, ko-**thee**-do, s., boiled meat and vegetables. a., boiled; baked; cooked
cocina, ko-**thee**-nah, s., kitchen
cocinero, ko-the-**nay**-ro, s., cook
coco, ko-ko, s., cocoa-tree; cocoa-nut
cocodrilo, ko-ko-**dree**-lo, s., crocodile
cócora, ko-ko-rah, s., bore é
cochambre, ko-**chahm**-kray, s., (fam.) greasy, stinking thing
coche, ko-chay, s., coach
cochero, ko-**chay**-ro, s., coachman
cochina, ko-**chee**-nah, s., sow
cochinamente, ko-che-nah-**men**-tay, adv., foully; filthily; basely
cochinería, ko-che-nay-**ree**-ah, s., filthiness, foulness
cochura, ko-**choo**-rah, s., coction; boiling [ness
codazo, ko-**dah**-tho, s., push with the elbow
codear, ko-day-ar, v., to elbow
codeso, ko-**day**-so, s., hairy cytisus
códice, ko-de-thay, s., codex; old manuscript
codicia, ko-**dee**-the-ah, s., covetousness; cupidity
codiciar, ko-de-the-**ar**, v., to covet
codicioso, ko-de-the-**o**-so, a., covetous
código, ko-de-go, s., code (of laws)
codillo, ko-**dee**-l'yo, s., knee; angle; bend; stirrup
codo, ko-do, s., elbow; cubit
codorniz, ko-dor-**neeth**, s., quail

coercer, ko-air-**thair**, v., to coerce
coerción, ko-air-the-**on**, s., coercion
coetáneo, ko-ay-**tah**-nay-o, s., contemporary
coexistir, ko-ek-siss-**teer**, v., to coexist
cofia, ko-fe-ah, s., head-gear; colf; net
cofre, ko-fray, s., trunk; boot (of car)
cogedor, ko-Hay-**dor**, s., collector; dust-box
coger, ko-**H**air, v., to catch; to gather; to grasp;
to contain
cogitabundo, ko-He-tah-**boon**-do, a., thoughtful
cogote, ko-**go**-tay, s., occiput
cohabitar, ko-ha-be-**tar**, v., to cohabit
cohechar, ko-ay-**char**, v., to bribe
cohecho, ko-**ay**-cho, s., bribery
coherente, ko-ay-**ren**-tay, a., coherent
cohesivo, ko-ay-**see**-vo, a., cohesive
cohete, ko-**ay**-tay, s., rocket
cohibición, ko-e-be-the-**on**, s., prohibition; restraint
cohibir, ko-e-**beer**, v., to prohibit; to restrain
cohonestar, ko-o-ness-**tar**, v., to give an honest
appearance to an action
cohorte, ko-**or**-tay, s., cohort
coincidir, ko-in-the-**deer**, v., to coincide
cojear, ko-Hay-**ar**, v., to limp; to deviate from virtue
cojera, ko-Hay-rah, s., lameness; limping
cojinete, ko-He-**nay**-tay, s., small cushion; pad
cojo, ko-Ho, s. & a., lame; cripple
cok, kok, s., cloke
col, kol, s., cabbage
cola, ko-lah, s., tail; train; trail; glue
colaborar, ko-lah-bo-**rar**, v., to collaborate
colación, ko-lah-the-**on**, s., critical comparison;
[collation
colada, ko-lah-dah, s., wash
colador, ko-lah-**dor**, s., colander; blunder
coladura, ko-lah-**doo**-rah, s., straining
colapez, ko-lah-**peth**, s., isinglass
colapso, ko-lah-**p**-so, s., collapse [stealthily
colar, ko-**lar**, v., to strain; to collate; to enter
colcha, kol-chah, s., coverlet; bedspread
colchón, kol-**chon**, s., mattress
colear, ko-lay-**ar**, v., to wag the tail
colección, ko-lek-the-**on**, s., collection

colectar, ko-lek-**tar**, v., to collect (taxes)
colector, ko-lek-**tor**, s., collector; gatherer
colega, ko-**lay**-gah, s., colleague
colegatario, ko-lay-gah-**tah**-re-o, s., colegatee
colegial, ko-lay-*He*-**ahl**, s., collegian. a., collegial
colegiatura, ko-lay-*He*-ah-**too**-rah, s., fellowship in a college
colegio, ko-**lay**-*He*-o, s., college
colegir, ko-lay-*Heer*, v., to collect; to infer
cólera, **ko**-lay-rah, s., cholera; fury; rage
colérico, ko-**lay**-re-ko, a., choleric; irascible
coleta, ko-**lay**-tah, s., queue of the hair; postscript
colgadero, kol-gah-**day**-ro, s., hat rack
colgadizo, kol-gah-**dee**-tho, s., shed. a., pendent
colgadura, kol-gah-**doo**-rah, s., tapestry; hangings; bunting
colgar, kol-**gar**, v., to hang up; to adorn with
cólico, **ko**-le-ko, s., colic [hangings
coliflor, ko-le-**flor**, s., cauliflower
coligarse, ko-le-**gar**-say, v., to unite; to confeder-
colina, ko-**lee**-nah, s., hillock [ate
colindante, ko-lin-**dahn**-tay, a., contiguous
coliseo, ko-le-**say**-o, s., theatre; playhouse
colmar, kol-**mar**, v., to heap up; to make up
colmena, kol-**may**-nah, s., bee-hive
colmillo, kol-**mee**-l'vo, s., canine tooth; fang; tusk
colmo, **kol**-mo, s., heap; completion; height
colocación, ko-lo-kah-the-**on**, s., situation; employment
colocar, ko-lo-**kar**, v., to arrange; to place; to locate
colonia, ko-**lo**-ne-ah, s., colony
colonizar, ko-lo-ne-**thar**, v., to colonize
colono, ko-**lo**-no, s., colonist; settler
coloquio, ko-**lo**-ke-o, s., colloquy; talk
color, ko-**lor**, s., colour; dye; pretext
coloración, ko-lo-rah-the-**on**, s., colouring
colorado, ko-lo-**rah**-do, a., ruddy; red
colorar, ko-lo-**rar**, v., to colour; to blush
colorear, ko-lo-ray-**ar**, v., to palliate; to excuse; [to redden
colorete, ko-lo-**ray**-tay, s., rouge
colorín, ko-lo-**reen**, s., linnet; loud colour
colorir, ko-lo-**reer**, v., to colour

coloso, ko-**lo**-so, s., colossus   [tance; to guess
columbrar, ko-loom-**brar**, v., to discern at a dis-
columna, ko-**loom**-nah, s., column; pillar
columnata, ko-loom-**nah**-tah, s., colonnade
columpiar, ko-loom-pe-**ar**, v., to swing
colusorio, ko-lo-**so**-re-o, a., collusive
collado, ko-l'**yah**-do, s., hill; hillock; fell
collar, ko-l'**yar**, s., necklace; collar
coma, ko-mah, s., comma
comadre, ko-**mah**-dray, s., midwife; gossip
comadrear, ko-mah-dray-**ar**, v., to gossip
comadrón, ko-mah-**dron**, s., accoucheur
comadrona, ko-mah-**dro**-nah, s., midwife
comandar, ko-mahn-**dar**, v., to command
comandita, ko-mahn-**dee**-tah, s., partnership
comarca, ko-**mar**-kah, s., territory; district;
   boundary
comarcano, ko-mar-**kah**-no, a., neighbouring
comba, komba, kom-bah, s., curvature; bend; convexity
combadura, kom-bah-**doo**-rah, s., curvature; war-
   ping
combar, kom-**bar**, v., to curve; to bend; to warp
combate, kom-**bah**-tay, s., combat; fight; battle
combatir, kom-bah-**teer**, v., to fight; to combat;
   to contradict
combinar, kom-be-**nar**, v., to combine   [eatable
comedero, ko-may-**day**-ro, s., dining-room.; a.,
comediante, ko-may-de-**ahn**-tay, s., actor; comedian   [gentle
comedido, ko-may-**dee**-do, a., polite; courteous;
comedirse, ko-may-**deer**-say, v., to govern oneself
comedor, ko-may-**dor**, s., eater; dining-room
comendador, ko-men-dah-**dor**, s., knight comman-
   der of a military order
comentar, ko-men-**tar**, v., to comment
comentario, ko-men-**tah**-re-o, s., commentary
comento, ko-**men**-to, s., comment; explanation
comenzar, ko-men-**thar**, v., to begin
comer, ko-**mair**, v., to eat; to dine   [trader
comerciante, ko-mair-the-**ahn**-tay, s., merchant;
comercio, ko-**mair**-the-o, s., trade; commerce
cometa, ko-**may**-tah, s., comet; kite

cometer, ko-may-**tair**, v., to commit; to entrust; to perpetrate

cometido, ko-may-**tee**-do, s., commission; trust

comezón, ko-may-**thon**, s., itching; longing

cómico, **ko**-me-ko, s., comedian. a., comical

comida, ko-**mee**-dah, s., food; dinner; fare

comidilla, ko-me-**dee**-l'yah, s., light repast; hobby

comido, ko-**mee**-do, a., fed; satiate

comienzo, ko-me-**en**-tho, s., beginning; origin

comilón, ko-me-**lon**, s., great eater; glutton

comillas, ko-**mee**-l'yahs, s., inverted commas

comisar, ko-me-**sar**, v., to confiscate; to attach

comisario, ko-me-**sah**-re-o, s., commissary

comisión, ko-me-se-**on**, s., commission; trust; mandate

comisionar, ko-me-se-o-**nar**, v., to commission

comisionista, ko-me-se-o-**niss**-tah, s., commission [agent

comiso, ko-**mee**-so, s., confiscation

comitiva, ko-me-**tee**-vah, s., suite; retinue

commutador, kom-moo-tah-**dor**, s., commuter

como, **ko**-mo, adv., how; in what manner; like;

cómoda, **ko**-mo-dah, s., chest of drawers [as; why

comodidad, ko-mo-de-**dahd**, s., comfort; convenience; ease; profit

cómodo, **ko**-mo-do, a., convenient; handy; suitable

compacto, kom-**pak**-to, a., compact

compadecer, kom-pah-**day**-thair, v., to pity

compadre, kom-**pah**-dray, s., godfather; friend

compaginar, kom-pah-n'**nar**, v., to arrange; to compare [comrade; associate

compañero, kom-pah-n'**yay**-ro, s., companion;

compañía, kom-pah-n'**yee**-ah, s., company

comparación, kom-pah-rah-the-**on**, s., comparison

comparar, kom-pah-**rar**, v., to compare; to confront

comparecencia, kom-pah-ray-**then**-the-ah, s., (Courts) appearance [appear

comparecer, kom-pah-ray-**thair**, v., (Courts) to

comparición, kom-pah-re-the-**on**, s., (Courts) appearance [merary

comparsa, kom-**par**-sah, s., (theatre) supernu-

compartimiento, kom-par-te-me-**en**-to, s., compartment

compartir, kom-par-**teer,** v., to divide into equal parts; to share

compás, kom-**pahs,** s., pair of compasses

compasar, kom-pah-**sar,** v., to measure; to regulate

compasivo, kom-pah-**see**-vo, a., compassionate

compeler, kom-pay-**lair,** v., to compel; to force

compendiar, kom-pen-de-**ar,** v., to epitomize

compendio, kom-**pen**-de-o, s., compendium

compendioso, kom-pen-de-**o**-so, a., abridged; concise [balance

compensar, kom-pen-**sar,** v., to compensate; to

competencia, kom-pay-**ten**-the-ah, s., competition; competence; aptitude [adequate

competente, kom-pay-**ten**-tay, a., competent; apt;

competir, kom-pay-**teer,** v., to compete; to contest

compinche, kom-**peen**-chay, s., comrade; chum; pal [complacency

complacencia, kom-plah-**then**-the-ah, s., pleasure;

complacer, kom-plah-**thair,** v., to please; to be pleased [agreeable

complaciente, kom-plah-the-**en**-tay, a., pleasing;

completar, kom-play-**tar,** v., to complete

completo*, kom-**play**-to, a., complete; finished

complicar, kom-ple-**kar,** v., to complicate

cómplice, kom-**ple**-thay, s., accomplice

complot, kom-**plot,** s., plot; conspiracy

componedor, kom-po-nay-**dor,** s., mender; compositor; arbitrator

componer, kom-po-**nair,** v., to compose; to construct; to advise; to restore; to reconcile

componible, kom-po-**nee**-blay, a., accommodable; mendable

comportable, kom-por-**tah**-blay, a., endurable

comportar, kom-por-**tar,** v., to suffer; to tolerate

comportarse, kom-por-**tar**-say, v., to behave oneself

comporte, kom-**por**-tay, s., conduct; manner

composición, kom-po-se-the-**on,** s., composition; mending; cleanliness; compact; modesty

compota, kom-**po**-tah, s., compote; jam

compra, kom-**prah,** s., purchase; shopping

comprador, kom-prah-**dor,** s., purchaser; buyer

comprar, kom-**prar,** v., to buy; to purchase

comprender, kom-pren-**dair**, v., to understand; to comprise
comprensible, kom-pren-**see**-blay, a., comprehen-[sible
comprensión, kom-pren-se-**on**, s., comprehension; understanding [restrain
comprimir, kom-pre-**meer**, v., to compress; to
comprobar, kom-pro-**bar**, v., to verify; to prove
comprometer, kom-pro-may-**tair**, v., to compromise; to jeopardize; to bind
compromisario, kom-pro-me-**sah**-re-o, s., arbitra-
compuerta, kom-poo-**air**-tah, s., lock; sluice [tor
compuesto, kom-poo-**ess**-to, s. & a., compound
compunción, kom-poon-the-**on**, s., compunction; repentance [punction
compungirse, kom-poon-_Heer_-say, v., to feel com-
compungivo, kom-poon-_Hee_-vo, a., pricking
computar, kom-poo-**tar**, v., to compute; to reckon
comulgar, ko-mool-**gar**, v., to administer or receive the sacrament
común, ko-**moon**, a., common; customary; vulgar
comunal, ko-moo-**nahl**, s., commonalty, a., common
comunero, ko-moo-**nay**-ro, s., commoner, a., popular
comunicado, ko-moo-ne-**kah**-do, s., statement
comunicar, ko-moo-ne-**kar**, v., to communicate; to impart [community
comunidad, ko-moo-ne-**dahd**, s., commonness; community
comúnmente, ko-**moon**-men-tay, adv., commonly
con, kon, prep., with; by; for; in; among
conato, ko-**nah**-to, s., effort; endeavour; attempt
concadenar, kon-kah-day-**nar**, v., to link together
cóncavo, con-kah-vo, a., concave [stand
concebir, kon-thay-**beer**, v., to conceive; to under-
conceder, kon-thay-**dair**, v., to give; to grant; to concede
concejal, kon-thay-_Hahl_, s., municipal councillor
concejo, kon-thay-_Ho_, s., municipal council
concentrar, kon-then-**trar**, v., to concentrate
concepto, kon-**thep**-to, s., thought; opinion; concept
conceptuar, kon-thep-too-**ar**, v., to conceive; to judge [pertain
concernir, kon-thair-**neer**, v., to concern; to ap-

concertar, kon-thair-tar, v., to concert; to regulate; to agree

concesionario, kon-thess-e-o-nah-re-o, s., grantee

conciencia, kon-the-en-the-ah, s., conscience

concienzudo, kon-the-en-thoo-do, a., conscientious

concierto, kon-the-air-to, s., agreement; accommodation; concert [cile

conciliar, kon-the-le-ar, v., to conciliate; to reconcilio, kon-thee-le-o, s., council

concisión, kon-the-se-on, s., conciseness

conciso*, kon-thee-so, a., concise

concitar, kon-the-tar, v., to stir up; to agitate

conciudadano, kon-the-oo-dah-dah-no, s., fellow-citizen [to end

concluir, kon-kloo'eer, v., to conclude; to infer;

concluyente*, kon-kloo-yen-tay, a., conclusive

concordar, kon-kor-dar, v., to accord; to conform

concorde, kon-kor-day, a., concordant [crete

concretar, kon-kray-tar, v., to sum up; to con-

concurrir, kon-koor-rreer, v., to concur; to assist; to contribute

concursar, kon-koor-sar, v., to declare insolvent

concurso, kon-koor-so, s., concourse; aid; com-

concha, kon-chah, s., shell [petition

conchabar, kon-chah-bar, v., to join; to conspire

conchado, kon-chah-do, a., scaly

conchudo, kon-choo-do, a., shelly; cunning

condado, kon-dah-do, s., county; earldom

conde, kon-day, s., count; earl

condecorar, kon-day-ko-rar, v., to decorate; to honour; to reward

condena, kon-day-nah, s., sentence

condenación, kon-day-nah-the-on, s., condemnation; conviction (of a criminal) [tence

condenar, kon-day-nar, v., to condemn; to sen-

condensar, kon-den-sar, v., to condense

condesa, kon-day-sah, s., countess [cend

condescender, kon-dess-then-dair, v., to condes-

condestable, kon-dess-tah-blay, s., constable

condicionar, kon-de-the-o-nar, v., to agree; to condition

condigno*, kon-dig-no, a., condign; deserved

condimentar, kon-de-**men**-tar, v., to dress or season victuals [fellow

condiscípulo, kon-diss-**thee**-poo-lo, s., school-

condolerse, kon-do-**lair**-say, v., to condole ; to be sorry for

condominio, kon-do-mee-ne-o, s., joint ownership

condonación, kon-do-nah-the-**on**, s., forgiving

condonar, kon-do-**nar**, v., to pardon ; to remit

conducción, kon-dook-the-**on**, s., conveyance ; cartage ; conduct [to guide

conducir, kon-doo-**theer**, v., to drive ; to conduct ;

conducta, kon-**dook**-tah, s., behaviour ; conveyance

conducto, kon-**dook**-to, s., conduit [ance

conductor, kon-dook-**tor**, s., conductor

conectar, ko-nek-**tar**, v., to connect

conejo, ko-**nay**-Ho, s., rabbit

conexionar, ko-nek-se-o-**nar**, v., to connect

conexo, ko-**nek**-so, a., connected [ary

confección, kon-fek-the-**on**, s., confection ; electu-

confeccionar, kon-fek-the-o-**nar**, v., to make ; to compound

conferencia, kon-fay-**ren**-the-ah, s., conference ; lecture [to bestow

conferir, kon-fay-**reer**, v., to confer ; to compare ;

confesado, kon-fay-**sah**-do, a., confessed ; penitent

confesar, kon-fay-**sar**, v., to confess [ional

confesionario, kon-fay-se-o-nah-re-o, s., confess-

confiado, kon-fe-**ah**-do, a., trusting

confianza, kon-fe-**ahn**-thah, s., confidence [in

confiar, kon-fe-**ar**, v., to confide ; to hope ; to trust

confidencia, kon-fe-den-the-ah, s., confidence ; secret information [trusty

confidente, kon-fe-**den**-tay, s., confidant. a*.,

confín, kon-**feen**, s., limit ; boundary ; confine

confinar, kon-fe-**nar**, v., to banish ; to border upon

confirmar, kon-feer-**mar**, v., to confirm

confite, kon-**fe**-tay, s., comfit ; sugar-plum

confitera, kon-fe-**tay**-rah, s., sweatmeat-box

confitería, kon-fe-tay-**ree**-ah, s., confectioner's [shop

confitero, kon-fe-**tay**-ro, s., confectioner

confitura, kon-fe-**too**-rah, s., jam ; confection

conflicto, kon-**fleek**-to, s., conflict

confluir, kon-floo'**eer**, v., to meet (of rivers)

conformar, kon-for-**mar**, v., to conform; to suit; to fit; to comply [formable; congruent

conforme, kon-**for**-may, adv., agreeably. a., con-

confortar, kon-for-**tar**, v., to comfort

confraternidad, kon-frah-tair-ne-**dahd**, s., confraternity [front

confrontar, kon-fron-**tar**, v., to compare; to con-

confundir, kon-foon-**deer**, v., to confound; to confuse; to confute

confuso, kon-**foo**-so, a., confused; obscure; per-

confutar, kon-foo-**tar**, v., to confute [plexed

congelar, kon-**Hay**-lar, v., to congeal; to freeze

congénito, kon-**Hay**-ne-to, a., congenital

conglomerarse, kon-glo-may-**rar**-say, v., to conglomerate

congoja, kon-go-**Hah**, s., anguish; heartbreaking

congojoso, kon-go-**Ho**-so, a., painful; distressing

congraciamiento, kon-grah-the-ah-me-**en**-to, s., obsequiousness; flattery

congraciarse, kon-grah-the-**ar**-say, v., to ingratiate oneself [to compliment

congratular, kon-grah-too-**lar**, v., to congratulate; to gratify

congregar, kon-gray-**gar**, v., to assemble; to gather

congreso, kon-**gray**-so, s., congress

congrio, kon-**gre**-o, s., conger-eel [consistency

congruencia, kon-groo-en-the-ah, s., congruence;

conjetura, kon-**Hay**-too-rah, s., conjecture; guess

conjunción, kon-**Hoon**-the-**on**, s., conjunction

conjunto*, kon-**Hoon**-to, a., united; conjunct

conjurado, kon-**Hoo**-rah-do, s., conspirator

conjurador, kon-**Hoo**-rah-**dor**, s., conjurer

conjurar, kon-**Hoo**-**rar**, v., to conspire; to exercise; to entreat

conjuro, kon-**Hoo**-ro, s., conjuration; exorcism

conmemorar, kon-may-mo-**rar**, v., to commemorate

conmigo, kon-**mee**-go, pron., with me [mination

conminación, kon-me-nah-the-**on**, s., threat; com-

conmutar, kon-moo-**tar**, v., to commute

connatural, kon-nah-too-**rahl**, a., inborn

connaturalizarse, kon-nah-too-rah-le-**thar**-say, v., to accustom oneself to labour, climate of food

connotar, kon-no-**tar**, v., to connote, to imply

cono, ko-no, s., cone

conocedor, ko-no-thay-**dor**, s., connoisseur; expert

conocer, ko-no-**thair**, v., to know; to be acquainted with; to understand

conocible, ko-no-**thee**-blay, a., knowable [known

conocido, ko-no-**thee**-do, s., acquaintance. a.,

conocimiento, ko-no-the-me-en-to, s., knowledge; acquaintance; bill of lading; voucher

conquista, kon-**kiss**-tah, s., conquest

conquistador, kon-kiss-tah-**dor**, s., conqueror

conquistar, kon-kiss-**tar**, v., to conquer [tion

consabido, kon-sah-**bee**-do, a., aforesaid; in ques-

consagrar, kon-sah-**grar**, v., to consecrate

consciente, kons-the-en-tay, a., conscious

consecución, kon-say-koo-the-**on**, s., attainment

consecuencia, kon-say-koo'**en**-the-ah, s., consequence

consecuente, kon-say-koo'**en**-tay, a., consequent

conseguir, kon-say-**gheer**, v., to attain; to get

conseja, kon-**say**-Hah, s., fable; tale

consejero, kon-say-**Hay**-ro, s., adviser; counsellor

consejo, kon-**say**-Ho, s., counsel; advice; council

consenso, kon-**sen**-so, s., consensus

consentimiento, kon-sen-te-me-en-to, s., consent

consentir, kon-sen-**teer**, v., to consent

conserje, kon-**sair**-Hay, s., doorkeeper

conserva, kon-**sair**-vah, s., preserve [to keep

conservar, kon-sair-**var**, v., to preserve; to candy

considerado*, kon-se-day-**rah**-do, a., prudent; considerate

considerar, kon-se-day-**rar**, v., to consider; to meditate; to think over [office

consigna, kon-**sig**-nah, s., watchword; luggage

consignación, kon-sig-nah-the-**on**, s., consignation; consignment

consignador, kon-sig-nah-**dor**, s., consigner

consignar, kon-sig-**nar**, v., to consign; to make over; to deposit in trust [trustee

consignatario, kon-sig-nah-**tah**-re-o, s., consignee;

consigo, kon-**see**-go, pron., with oneself

consiguiente, kon-se-ghee-**en**-tay, a., consequent

consistencia, kon-siss-**ten**-the-ah, s., consistence;
consistir, kon-siss-**teer**, v., to consist   [stability
consola, kon-**so**-lah, s., console
consolar, kon-so-**lar**, v., to console; to cheer
consonante, kon-so-**nahn**-tay, a., concordant;
  consonant   [to agree
consonar, kon-so-**nar**, v., to harmonize; to rhyme;
consorcio, kon-**sor**-the-o, s., partnership; friendly
  intercourse
consorte, kon-**sor**-tay, s., consort; accomplice
conspirar, kons-pe-**rar**, v., to conspire; to plot
constancia, kons-**tahn**-the-ah, s., constancy;
  steadiness
constar, kons-**tar**, v., to be evident; to consist of
consternar, kons-tair-**nar**, v., to terrify
constipación, kons-te-pah-the-**on**, s., constipation
constiparse, kons-te-**par**-say, v., to catch a cold
constituir, kons-te-too-**eer**, v., to constitute
construir, kons-troo-**eer**, v., to construct
consuelo, kon-soo'**ay**-lo, s., consolation; joy
cónsul, kon-sool, s., consul
consulado, kon-soo-**lah**-do, s., consulate
consulta, kon-**sool**-tah, s., consultation; question
consultar, kon-sool-**tar**, v., to consult
consultivo, kon-sool-**tee**-vo, a., advisory
consultor, kon-sool-**tor**, s., adviser   [mation
consumación, kon-soo-mah-the-**on**, s., consum-
consumado, kon-soo-**mah**-do, a., consummate;
  complete
consumir, kon-soo-**meer**, v., to consume
consumo, kon-**soo**-mo, s., consumption (of provisions and merchandise); excise tax
consunción, kon-soon-the-**on**, s., consumption [ing
contabilidad, kon-tah-be-le-**dahd**, s., bookkeep-
contacto, kon-**tak**-to, s., contact
contado, kon-**tah**-do, a., scarce; rare. **de**—, day
  —, instantly. **al** —, ahl —, for cash
contador, kon-tah-**dor**, s., accountant; counter
contagiar, kon-tah-He-**ar**, v., to infect
contaminar, kon-tah-me-**nar**, v., to contaminate
contante, kon-**tahn**-tay, s., ready money; cash
contar, kon-**tar**, v., to count; to look upon; to rely

contemplar, kon-tem-**plar**, v., to contemplate

contemporáneo, kon-tem-po-re-**rah**-nay-o, a., contemporary [porize

contemporizar, kon-tem-po-re-**thar**, v., tem-

contención, kon-ten-the-**on**, s., contention; emulation

contendiente, kon-ten-de-**en**-tay, s., litigant

contener, kon-tay-**nair**, v., to contain; to hold

contenido, kon-tay-**nee**-␣o, s., content, a., moderate

contentar, kon-ten-**tar**, v., to content; to please

contentible, kon-ten-**tee**-blay, a., contemptible

contestación, kon-tess-tah-the-**on**, s., reply; answer [agree

contestar, kon-tess-**tar**, v., to reply; to attest; to

contienda, kon-te-**en**-dah, s., contest; conflict

contigo, kon-**tee**-go, pron., with you

contiguo, kon-**tee**-goo'o, a., contiguous

continente, kon-te-**nen**-tay, s., continent; countenance. a., continent [emergency

contingencia, kon-tin-*H*en-the-ah, s., contingency

continuar, kon-te-noo'**ar**, v., to continue

continuo*, kon-**tee**-noo'o, a., continuous

contonearse, kon-to-nay-**ar**-say, v., to strut

contorno, kon-**tor**-no, s., environs; outline

contra, kon-trah, prep., against; opposite to

contrabando, kon-trah-**bahn**-do, s., contraband; smuggling [cotillon

contradanza, kon-trah-**dahn**-thah, s., quardrille;

contradecir, kon-trah-day-**theer**, v., to contradict; to gainsay

contraer, kon-trah-**air**, v., to contract [to forge

contrahacer, kon-trah-ah-**thair**, v., to counterfeit;

contralor, kon-trah-**lor**, s., comptroller

contraluz, kon-trah-**looth**, s., counterlight

contramandar, kon-trah-mahn-**dar**, v., to countermand

contraorden, kon-trah-**or**-den, s., countermand

contrapelo, kon-trah-**pay**-lo, adv., against the grain

contraponer, kon-trah-po-**nair**, v., to compare; to oppose

contraprueba, kon-trah-proo'**ay**-bah, s., counter-proof

contrariar, kon-trah-re-**ar**. v., to contradict; to thwart; to disappoint [trariety

contrariedad, kon-trah-re-ay-**dahd**, s., con-**contrario**[1], kon-**trah**-re-o, a., contrary; adverse

contrarrestar, kon-trah-rress-**tar**, v., to check; to counteract [watchword

contraseña, kon-trah-**say**-n'yah, s., countersign;

contrastar, kon-trahs-**tar**, v., to contrast; to oppose

contraste, kon-**trahs**-tay, s., opposition; contrast

contrata, kon-**trah**-tah, s., contract

contratante, kon-trah-**tahn**-tay, s., contractor

contratar, kon-trah-**tar**, v., to contract; to trade

contratista, kon-trah-**tiss**-tah, s., contractor

contrato, kon-**trah**-to, s., contract; agreement

contraveneno, kon-trah-vay-**nay**-no, s., anitdote

contravenir, kon-trah-vay-**neer**, v., to contravene

contraventana, kon-trah-ven-**tah**-nah, s., outside window-shutter [contribution

contribución, kon-tre-boo-the-**on**, s., tax; duty:

contribuir, kon-tre-boo'**eer**, v., to contribute

contrincante, kon-trin-**kahn**-tay, s., rival

contristar, kon-triss-**tar**, v., to sadden; to grieve

contrito, kon-**tree**-to, a., penitent [contractor

controvertir, kon-tro-vair-**teer**, v., to controvert;

contundente, kon-toon-**den**-tay, a., producing a contusion

conturbar, kon-toor-**bar**, v., to disturb; to disquiet

convalecer, kon-vah-lay-**thair**, v., to regain health

convecino, kon-vay-**thee**-no, a., neighbouring

convencer, kon-ven-**thair**, v., to convince

convencimiento, kon-ven-the-me-**en**-to, s., con-viction [cile

convenible, kon-vay-**nee**-blay, a., compliant; do-**conveniencia,** kon-vay-ne-**en**-the-ah, s., utility; convenience [venient

conveniente, kon-vay-ne-**en**-tay, a., useful; con-**convenio,** kon-**vay**-ne-o, s., agreement; pact

convenir, kon-vay-**neer**, v., to agree; to corres-pond; to convene

convento, kon-**ven**-to, s., convent

convergir, kon-vair-*Heer*, v., to converge
conversable, kon-vair-*sah*-blay, a., sociable
conversar, kon-vair-*sar*, v., to converse; to talk; [to chat
converso, kon-vair-so, s., convert
convertir, kon-vair-*teer*, v., convert
conyexo, kon-vek-so, a., convex
convicto, kon-*veek*-to, a., convicted; guilty
convidada, kon-ve-*dah*-dah, s., invitation to drink; treat
convidar, kon-ve-*dar*, v., to invite; to treat
convincente, kon-vin-*then*-tay, a., convincing
convite, kon-*vee*-tay, s., invitation
convocar, kon-vo-*kar*, v., to convoke; to convene
conyugal, kon-yoo-*gahl*, a., conjugal
cónyuges, kon-yoo-*Hess*, s., husband and wife
cooperar, ko-o-pay-*rar*, v., to co-operate
cooperario, ko-o-pay-*rah*-re-o, s., co-operator
coopositor, ko-o-po-se-*tor*, s., competitor
coordenado, ko-or-day-*nah*-do, a., co-ordinate
coordinar, ko-or-de-*nar*, v., to co-ordinate
copa, ko-pah, s., cup; goblet. pl., hearts (at cards)
copera, ko-*pay*-rah, s., cupboard
copete, ko-*pay*-tay, s., toupee; tuft
copia, ko-pe-ah, s., abundance; copy
copiar, ko-pe-*ar*, v., to copy; to draw from life
copioso, ko-pe-o-so, a., copious; plentiful
copla, ko-plah, s., couplet; lampoon; ballad
copo, ko-po, s., snowflake
copón, ko-pon, s., cibary; ciborium
cópula, ko-poo-lah, s., coupling; sexual union
coqueta, ko-*kay*-tah, s., coquette; flirt [flirtation
coquetería, ko-kay-tay-*ree*-ah, s., coquetry;
coracero, ko-rah-*thay*-ro, s., cuirassier [passion
coraje, ko-*rah*-Hay, s., courage; bravery; anger;
coraza, ko-*rah*-thah, s., cuirass
corazón, ko-rah-*thon*, s., heart; core
corbata, kor-*bah*-tah, s., cravat; tie [crooked
corcovado, kor-ko-*vah*-do, a., humpbacked;
corcovar, kor-ko-*var*, v., to crook
corche, kor-chay, s., cork-soled sandel
corchete, kor-*chay*-tay, s., clasp; crotch
corcho, kor-cho, s., cork

cordaje, kor-**dah**-Hay, s., cordage

cordel, kor-**del**, s., cord; rope

cordero, kor-**day**-ro, s., lamb; dressed lambskin

cordillera, kor-de-l'**yay**-rah, s., chain of mountains

cordón, kor-**don**, s., cord; twisted lace; military cordon   [maker

cordonero, kor-do-**nay**-ro, s., lace-maker; rope

cordura, kor-**doo**-rah, s., prudence; judgment

corea, ko-**ray**-ah, s., dance accompanied with a chorus; St Vitus's dance

coriáceo, ko-re-**ah**-thay-o, a., leathery

cornada, kor-**nah**-dah, s., thrust with a horn

corneja, kor-**nay**-Hah, s., crow; fetlock

corneta, kor-**nay**-tah, s., cornet; horn

cornijal, kor-ne-**Hahl**, s., corner; angle

cornudo, kor-**noo**-do, a., horned

coro, **ko**-ro, s., choir; chorus

corona, ko-**ro**-nah, s., crown; coronet; tonsure; halo; regal power

coronar, ko-ro-**nar**, v., to crown; to complete

coronel, ko-ro-**nel**, s., colonel

coronilla, ko-ro-nee-l'yah, s., small crown; top of the head   [or carcass

corpanchón, kor-pahn-**chon**, s., very big body

corpiño, kor-**pee**-n'yo, s., waist; corset-cover

corporal, kor-po-**rahl**, a., corporal; bodily

corpóreo, 'kor-**por**-ray-o, a., corporeal

corral, kor-**rrahl**, s., yard; pen; fold; fish-pond

correa, kor-**rray**-ah, s., leather strap; leash; leather

correcto*, kor-**rrek**-to, a., correct   [belt

corredera, kor-rray-**day**-rah, s., slide; cockroach

corredor, kor-rray-**dor**, s., runner; race-horse broker; corridor

corregidor, kor-rray-He-**dor**, s., corregidor (mayor of a town); corrector   [to mitigate

corregir, kor-rray-**Heer**, v., to correct; to temper;

correntío, kor-rren-**tee**-o, a., current; running

correo, kor-**rray**-o, s., post; postman; post-office

correr, kor-**rrair**, v., to run; to flow; to expand to be current; to flourish

correspondencia, kor-rres-pon-**den**-the-ah, s., correspondence

corresponder, kor-rress-pon-**dair**, v., to return a favour; to correspond; to regard   [dent; agent

corresponsal, kor-rress-pon-**sahl**, s., correspondent

corretaje, kor-rray-**tah**-Hay, s., brokerage

corretear, kor-rray-tay-**ar**, v., to rove; to ramble

corretero, kor-rray-**tay**-ro, s., gadder

corrida, kor-**rree**-dah, s., course; race

corrido, kor-**rree**-do, a., experienced; abashed

corriente, kor-rre-**en**-tay, s., current; flow; course. a., running

corrillo, kor-**rree**-l'yo, s., group of gossipers

corrimiento, kor-rre-me-**en**-to, s., running sore

corro, kor-rro, (see corrillo)

corroborar, kor-rro-bo-**rar**, v., to corroborate

corroer, kor-rro-**air**, v., to corrode

corromper, kor-rrom-**pair**, v., to corrupt

corruptela, kor-rrop-**tay**-lah, s., corruption

corruptor, kor-rrop-**tor**, s., corrupter

corsario, kor-sah-re-o, s., corsair

corsé, kor-say, s., corset

corta, kor-tah, s., felling of wood; cutting

cortabolsas, kor-tah-**bol**-sahs, s., pickpocket

cortado, kor-**tah**-do, a., adapted; proportioned;

cortafrío, kor-tah-**free**-o, s., cold-chisel   [exact

cortar, kor-tar, v., to cut; to curtail; to chop

corte, kor-tay, s., cutting edge; cut. s.f., Court; retinue; levee; yard

cortedad, kor-tay-**dahd**, s., smallness; dulness; timidity   [escort

cortejar, kor-tay-Har, v., to court; to woo; to

cortejo, kor-**tay**-Ho, s., courtship; homage

cortés, kor-tess, a., courteous; polite

cortesana, kor-tay-**sah**-nah, s., courtesan

cortesanía, kor-tay-sah-**nee**-ah, s., courtesy

cortesano, kor-tay-**sah**-no, a., court-like; courteous; courtier

cortesía, kor-tay-**see**-ah, s., courtesy; compliment

corteza, kor-**tay**-thah, s., bark; rind; crust;

corto*, kor-to, a., short; small   [rusticity

cortocircuito, korr-to-theer-koo'ee-to, s., short-circuit

corvadura, kor-vah-**doo**-rah, s., curvature

corvo, kor-vo, a., bent; crooked

cosa, koh-sah, s., thing; substance; object

cosecha, ko-say-chah, s., harvest; crop

cosechar, ko-say-char, v., to reap; to gather

coselete, ko-say-lay-tay, s., corselet

coser, ko-sair, v., to sew

cosido, ko-see-do, s., sewing; needlework

cosquilloso, kos-ke-l'yo-so, a., ticklish

costa, kos-tah, s., cost; charge; coast

costado, kos-tah-do, s., side

costal, kos-tahl, s., sack. a., costal

costanero, kos-tah-nay-ro, a., sloping　　　　[loss

costar, kos-tar, v., to cost; to cause deteriment or

coste, ko-stay, s., cost; expense　　　　[the coast

costear, kos-tay-ar, v., to pay the cost; to sail along

costilla, kos-tee-l'yah, s., rib; cutlet; stave

costo, kos-to, s., cost; price; charge

costoso*, kos-to-so, a., costly; difficult

costra, kos-trah, s., crust; scab

costumbre, kos-toom-bray, s., custom

costura, kos-too-rah, s., seam; needlework

costurera, kos-too-ray-rah, s., seamstress

costurero, kos-too-ray-ro, s., lady's work-box

costurón, kos-too-ron, s., coarse suture; large scar

cota, ko-tah, s., coat of mail

cotejar, ko-tay-Har, v., to compare; to confront

cotejo, ko-tay-Ho, s., comparison; collation

cotidiano, ko-te-de-ah-no, a., daily

cotilla, ko-tee-l'yah, s., stays　　　　[current

cotización, ko-te-thah-the-on, s., quotation; price-

cotizar, ko-te-thar, v., to quote prices

coto, ko-to, s., inclosure; district; landmark

cotón, ko-ton, s., printed cotton　　　　[woman

cotorra, ko-tor-rrah, s., small parrot; loquacious

covacha, ko-vah-chah, s., small cave　　　　[portunity

coyuntura, ko-yoon-too-rah, s., articulation; op-

coz, koth, s., kick; drawback; recoil

cráneo, krah-nay-o, s., skull

crápula, krah-poo-lah, s., intoxication; debauchery

crasitud, krah-se-tood, s., fatness; stupidity

craso*, krah-so, a., fat; greasy; thick　　　　[originator

creador, kray-ah-dor, s., the Creator; creator;

crear, kray-**ar,** v., to create; to establish

crecer, kray-**thair,** v., to grow; to increase

creces, kray-thess, s., increase; excess

crecida, kray-**thee**-dah, s., swell of rivers; freshet

crecido, kray-**thee**-do, a., increased; large; grown

creciente, kray-the-**en**-tay, s., swell; leaven; crescent; flood-tide. a., growing   [growth

crecimiento,   kray-the-me-**en**-to, s., increase;

crédito, kray-de-to, s., credit

credulidad, kray-doo-le-**dahd,** s., credulity

crédulo, kray-doo-lo, a., credulous

creedero, kray-ay-**day**-ro, a., credible

creedor, kray-ay-**dor,** (see **crédulo**)

creencia, kray-**en**-the-ah, s., belief; creed

creer, kray-**air,** v., to believe

creíble, kray-**ee**-blay, a., credible

crema, kray-mah, s., cream; diæresis

cremallera, kray-mah-l'**yay**-rah, s., zip-fastener

crepúsculo, kray-**pooss**-koo-lo, s., twilight

crespo, kress-po, a., crisp; curled

crespón, kress-**pon,** s., crape

cresta, kress-tah, s., cockscomb; top; crest

creta, kray-tah, s., chalk

creyente, kray-**yen**-tay, s., believer

cría, kree-ah, s., brood of animals; breeding

criada, kre-ah-dah, s., maid-servant   [young trees

criadero, kre-ah-**day**-ro, s., nursery; plantation of

criado, kre-**ah**-do, s., servant

criador, kre-ah-**dor,** s., breeder; creator. a., fecund

crianza, kre-**ahn**-thah, s., breeding; education. nursery

criar, kre-**ar,** v., to breed; to rear

criatura, kre-ah-**too**-rah, s., creature

criba, kree-bah, s., sieve; riddle

cribar, kre-**bar,** v., to sift

crimen, kree-men, s., crime

criminar, kre-me-**nar,** v., to incriminate

criminoso, kre-me-**no**-so, a., criminal

crin, kreen, s., mane; horse-hair

crillo, kre-o-l'yo, s., creole

cripta, kreep-tah, s., crypt

crisis, kree-sis, s., crisis

crisol, kre-**sol**, s., crucible

crispar, kriss-**par**, v., to cause a convulsive contraction of the muscles

crispatura, kriss-pah-**too**-rah, s., spasmodic contraction

cristal, kriss-**tahl**, s., crystal; looking-glass

Cristiandad, kriss-te-ahn-**dahd**, s., Christianity; [Christendom

Cristo, kriss-to, s., Christ

criterio, kre-**tay**-re-o, s., criterion

crítica, **kree**-te-kah, s., criticism; critique; censure

criticar, kre-te-**kar**, v., to criticize; to find fault

criticón, kre-te-**kon**, s., would-be critic

croar, kro-**ar**, v., to croak

crónico, **kro**-ne-ko-a, chronic

cronicón, kro-ne-**kon**, s., brief chronicle

cronómetro, kro-**no**-may-tro, s., chronometer

croqueta, kro-**kay**-tah, s., croquette; fritter

cruce, **kroo**-thay, s., cross-roads

crucero, kroo-**thay**-ro, s., transept; cross-bearer; [cruiser

cruceta, kroo-**thay**-tah, s., cross-piece

crucificar, kroo-the-fe-**kar**, v., to crucify

crucifijo, kroo-the-**fee**-Ho, s., crucifix

crudeza, kroo-**day**-thah, s., crudity; rudeness

crudo*, **kroo**-do, a., raw; crude

cruel*, kroo'**el**, a., cruel

crueldad, kroo'el-**dahd**, s., cruelty

cruento, kroo'**en**-to, a., bloody; cruel

crujía, kroo-**Hee**-ah, s., gangway

crujido, kroo-**Hee**-do, s., crack; creak; clash; crackling; rustle

crujir, kroo-**Heer**, v., to crackle; to rustle

cruz, krooth, s., cross [crossed

cruzado, kroo-**thah**-do, s., crusader. a., crosswise;

cruzar, kroo-**thar**, v., to cross; to cruise

cuaderna, koo'ah-**dair**-nah, s., fourth part

cuadernillo, koo'ah-dair-**nee**-l'yo, s., quire of paper

cuaderno, koo'ah-**dair**-no, s., writing-book

cuadra, koo'**ah**-drah, s., stable; hall; block of houses

cuadrado, koo'ah-**drah**-do, a., square

cuadragésimo, koo'ah-drah-**Hay**-se-mo, a., fortieth

cuadrante, koo'ah-**drahn**-tay, s., quadrant; sun dial; clock face

cuadrar, koo'ah-**drar**, v., to square; to fit; to adjust to accomodate

cuadrilongo, koo'ah-dre-**lon**-go, a., oblong

cuadrilla, koo'ah-**dree**-l'yah, s., gang; crew; band

cuádruplo, koo'ah-droo-plo, a., fourfold

cuajar, koo'ah-Har, v., to coagulate; to curd

cual, koo'ahl, adv., as. pron., which

caulidad, koo'ah-le-dahd, s., quality

cualquiera, koo'ahl-ke-ay-rah, pron., any one;

cuan, koo'ahn, adv., how; as   [whoever

cuando, koo'ahn-do, adv., when; if; although; even

cuantía, koo'ahn-tee-ah, s., amount; quality

cuantioso, koo'ahn-te-o-so, a., numerous; copious; rich

cuanto, koo'ahn-to, adv., respecting; whilst. a., how much; how many; as much as; the more.
—**antes,** —**ahn**-tess, immediately; —**más,** —mahs, moreover

cuarenta, koo'ah-**ren**-tah, s, & a., forty

cuarentena, koo'ah-ren-**tay**-nah, s., forty days, months or years; Lent; quarantine

cuaresma, koo'ah-**ress**-mah, s., Lent

cuarta, koo'ar-tah, s., fourth; quarter

cuartear, koo'ar-tay-ar, v., to divide into four parts

cuartel, koo'ar-**tel**, s., quarter; district; ward; barracks

cuarterón, koo'ar-tay-ron, s., quarter of a pound

cuarteto, koo'ar-**tay**-to, s., quartet   [of paper

cuartilla, koo'ar-**tee**-l'yah, s., fourth part; sheet

cuarto, koo'ar-to, s., fourth; quarter; room; apartment

cuartos, koo'ar-tos, s., cash; money

cuatro, koo'ah-tro, s. & a., four

cuba, koo-bah, s., cask; tub

cubeta, koo-bay-tah, s., small cask

cúbico, koo-be-ko, a., cubic; cubical

cubierto, koo-be-air-to, s., cover (part of a table service); shed; dinner course   [goblet

cubilete, koo-be-lay-tay, s., copper pan; pastry;

cubo, koo, bo, s., cube; wooden pail

cubrir, koo-breer, v., to cover; to screen

cucaracha, koo-kah-rah-chah, s., cockroach

cuclillas, koo-clee-l'yahs, adv., **en—**, en—, in a cowering manner

cuclillo, koo-klee-l'yo, s., cuckoo; cuckold

cuco, koo-ko, s., cuckoo. a., dainty; cunning; crafty

cucurucho, koo-koo-**roo**-cho, s., paper cornet

cuchara, koo-**chah**-rah, s., spoon

cucharón, koo-chah-**ron**, s., large spoon; ladle

cuchichear, koo-che-chay-**ar**, v., to whisper

cuchilla, koo-**chee**-l'yah, s., large kitchen knife

cuchillero, koo-che-l'**yay**-ro, s., cutler

cuchillo, koo-**chee**-l'yo, s., knife

cuchitril, koo-che-**treel**, s., very small room; den

cuchufleta, koo-choo-**flay**-tah, s., joke; jest; fun

cuelga, koo'**el**-gah, s., cluster of dried fruit

cuello, koo'**ay**-l'yo, s., neck; collar of garments

cuenca, koo'**en**-kah, s., wooden bowl; river basin

cuenta, koo'**en**-tah, s., reckoning; account; bill; reason; report [former

cuentista, koo'en-**tiss**-tah, s., table-bearer; in-

cuento, koo'**en**-to, s., relation; tale; fairy tale; fable

cuerda, koo'**air**-dah, s., cord; rope; string; chain

cuerdo, koo'**air**-do, a., prudent; discreet; wise

cuerna, koo'**air**-nah, s., horn vessel

cuerno, koo'**air**-no, s., horn; feeler

cuero, koo'**ay**-ro, s., pelt; hide; leather

cuerpo, koo'**air**-po, s., body; the trunk

cuervo, koo'**air**-vo, s., raven; crow

cuesco, koo'**ess**-ko, s., kernel

cuesta, koo'**ess**-tah, s., hill; slope [blem

cuestión, koo'ess-te-**on**, s., question; dispute; pro-

cuestionar, koo'ess-te-o-**nar**, v., to question; to

cueva, koo'**ay**-vah, s., cave; cellar [dispute

cuévano, koo'**ay**-vah-no, s., basket; hamper

cuidado, koo'e-**dah**-do, s., care; custody; anxiety

cuidadoso, koo'e-dah-**do**-so, a., careful; mindful

cuidar, koo'e-**dar**, v., to heed; to care

cuita, koo'**ee**-tah, s., grief; affliction

cuitado, koo'e-**tah**-do, a., anxious; wretched; timid

culata, koo-lah-tah, s., breech of a gun; butt-end

culebra, koo-lay-brah, s., snake

culebrear, koo-lay-bray-**ar**, v., to move along like a snake

culero, koo-**lay**-ro, s., clout. a., slothful
culminar, kool-me-**nar,** v., to culminate
culo, koo-lo, s., rump; bottom; socket
culpa, kool-pah, s., fault; sin; guilt
culpable, kool-**pah**-blay, a., guilty
culpado, kool-**pah**-do, a., accused
culpar, kool-**par,** v., to impeach; to reproach; to accuse [accuse
cultivar, kool-te-**var,** v., to cultivate
culto, kool-to, s., worship; religion; cult. a*., elegant; affected; polished
cultura, kool-**too**-rah, s., culture
cumbre, koom-bray, s., top, summit [order
cúmplase, koom-plah-say, v., countersign of an
cumpleaños, koom-play-**ah**-n'yos, s., birthday
cumplido, koom-**plee**-do, s., compliment. a*., large; plentiful
cumplimiento, koom-ple-me-**en**-to, s., compliment; completion [to fulfil
cumplir, koom-**pleer,** v., to discharge; to perform;
cúmulo, koo-moo-lo, s., heap; pile
cuna, koo-nah, s., cradle; source; origin
cundir, koon-**deer,** v., to spread (liquids or news)
cunear, koo-nay-**ar,** v., to rock a cradle
cuña, koo-n'yah, s., wedge; quoin
cuñado, koo-n'yah-do, s., brother-in-law
cuñada, koo-n'yah-dah, s., sister-in-law
cuño, koo-n'yo, s., die; coin
cuota, koo'o-tah, s., quota; share
cupón, koo-pon, s., coupon
cúpula, koo-poo-lah, s., cupola; dome; vault
cura, koo-rah, s., parson
curación, koo-rah-the-**on,** s., cure; healing
curador, koo-rah-**dor,** s., curator
curar, koo-rar, v., to cure; to preserve; to heal
curia, koo-re-ah, s., ecclesiastical court
curiosear, koo-re-o-say-**ar,** v., to pry into others affairs [ness; rarity
curiosidad, koo-re-o-se-**dahd,** s., curiosity; neat-
cursado, koor-**sah**-do, a., skilled; accustomed
cursar, koor-sar, v., to frequent a place; to do a thing frequently; to study
curso, koor-so, s., course; series; route

curtido, koor-**tee**-do, a., expert; weather-beaten.

curtidos, koor-**tee**-dos, s., tanned leather [tanned

curtir, koor-**teer**, v., to tan; to harden

curva, koor-vah, s., curve; bend

curvo, koor, koor-yo, a., curved; crooked

cúspide, kooss-pe-day, s., summit; apex; top

custodia, kooss-**to**-de-ah, s., custody; guardianship

custodio, kooss-**to**-de-o, s., custodian [guard

cutis, koo-tiss, s., skin [which, of whom, whose

cuyo, cuya, koo-yo, **koo**-yah, pron. poss., of

chabacanería, chah-bah-kah-nay-**ree**-ah, s., coarseness

chabacano, chah-bah-**kah**-no, a., coarse

chacota, chah-**ko**-tah, s., noisy mirth [mirth

chacotear, chah-ko-tay-**ar**, v., to indulge in noisy

cháchara, chah-chah-rah, s., prattle, chit-chat

chafallar, chah-fah-l'**yar**, v., to botch

chafallón, chah-fah-l'**yon**, s., botcher

chaflán, chah-**flahn**, s., bevel; chamfer

chal, chahl, s., shawl

chalán, chah-**lahn**, s., hawker; horse-dealer

chalanear, chah-lah-nay-**ar**, v., to buy or sell dexterously; to deal in horses [selling and buying

chalanería, chah-lah-nay-**ree**-ah, s., cunning in

chaleco, chah-**lay**-ko, s., waistcoat

chalina, chah-**lee**-nah, s., necktie; scarf

chalote, chah-**lo**-tay, s., shallot

chalupa, chah-**loo**-pah, s., sloop

chamarasca, chah-mah-**rahs**-kah, s., brushwood fire [old furniture

chamarillero, chah-mah-re-l'**yay**-ro, s., dealer in

chambelán, chahm-bay-**lan**, s., chamberlain

chambón, cham-**bon**, a., awkward

chambra, chahm-brah, s., matinée

chamorro, chah-**mor**-rro, a., shorn

chamuscar, chah-mooss-**kar**, v., to singe; to scorch

canciller, chahn-the-l'**yair**, s., chancellor

chancla, chahn-klah, s., old shoe

chancleta, chahn-**klay**-tah, s., slipper

chanclo, chahn-klo, s., patten; galosh

chanflón, chahn-**flon**, a., awkward; clumsy

chanza, chahn-thah, s., joke; jest; fun

chapa, chah-pah, s., thin metal plate [rain

chaparrón, chah-par-**rron**, s., violent shower of

chapear, chah-pay-**ar**, v., to cover with metal plates

chápiro, chah-pe-ro, word used only in: **¡voto al chápiro! ¡por vida del chápiro!** good gracious!

chapitel, chah-pe-**tel**, s., capital of a pillar; spire

chapodar, chah-po-**dar**, v., to lop trees

chapón, chah-**pon**, s., blot of ink

chapotear, chah-po-tay-**ar**, v., to wet with a sponge; to dabble [bungle

chapucear, chah-poo-thay-**ar**, v., to botch; to

chapucero, chah-poo-**thay**-ro, s., blacksmith; botcher. a., clumsy; bungling

chapurrar, chah-poor-**rrar**, v., to talk gibberish

chapuz, chah-**pooth**, s., ducking

chapuzar, chah-poo-**thar**, v., to duck; to dive

chaqueta, chah-**kay**-tah, s., jacket

charanga, chah-**rahn**-gah, s., fanfare [puddle

charca, charco, char-kah, **char**-ko, s., pool;

charla, char-lah, s., prattle; garrulity

charlar, char-**lar**, v., to chatter; to prate

charlatán, char-lah-**tahn**, s., idle talker; quack

charolar, chah-ro-**lar**, v., to varnish [action

charrada, char-**rrah**-dah, s., coarse speech or

charretera, char-rray-**tay**-rah, s., epaulet

charro, char-rro, a., tawdry; gaudy

chasco, chahs-ko, s., fun; jest; trick [to fool

chasquear, chahs-kay-**ar**, v., to crack with a whip;

chato, chah-to, a., flat; flat-nosed

chaveta, chah-vay-tah, s., bolt; forelock; key

chelín, chay-**leen**, s., shilling

chico, chee-ko, s., little boy. a., little; small

chicolear, che-ko-lay-**ar**, v., to pay compliments (to a woman)

chicote, che-**ko**-tay, s., fat boy

chicuelo, che-koo**'ay**-lo, s., little boy; urchin

chichón, che-**chon**, s., bump on the head

chifla, chee-flah, s., whistle; paring-knife

chiflar, che-**flar**, v., to whistle; become insane

chillar, che-l'**yar**, v., to scream; to shriek

chillido, che-l'**yee**-go, s., shriek; scream
chillón, che-l'**yon**, a., shrill; showy; tawdry
chimenea, che-may-**nay**-ah, s., chimney
chimpancé, chim-pahn-**thay**, s., chimpanzee
china, chee-nah, s., pebble; china-ware
chinche, cheen-chay, s., bug; thumb-tack
chinchoso, chin-**cho**-so, a., tiresome
chinela, che-**nay**-lah, s., slipper
chinero, che-**nay**-ro, s., china cupboard
chiquirritín, che-keer-rre-**teen**, s., infant
chirigota, che-re-**go**-tah, s., jest; joke
chirimía, che-re-**mee**-ah, s., clarion
chiripa, che-**ree**-pah, s., (billiards) fluke; lucky hit
chirivía, che-re-**vee**-ah, s., parsnip
chirlar, cheer-**lar**, v., to prattle
chirle, cheer-lay, a., (fam.) insipid; tasteless
chirlo, cheer-lo, s., large wound on the face
chirriar, cheer-rre-**ar**, v., to hiss; to creak; to chirp
chirrido, cheer-**rree**-do, s., chirping; chattering
chirrión, cheer-rre-on, s., tumbrel
¡chis! chiss, interj., hush!
chisme, chiss-may, s., misreport; lumber
chismear, chiss-may-**ar**, v., to tattle; to tell tales
chispa, chiss-pah, s., spark; very small diamond;
  acumen [sparks; to hiss
chisporrotear, chiss-por-rro-tay-**ar**, v., to sputter
chistar, chiss-**tar**, v., to mutter; to mumble
chiste, chiss-tay, s., witticism; joke
chistoso, chiss-**to**-so, a., gay; facetious
chiticalla, che-te-kah-l'yah, s., discreet person
¡chitón! ¡chitón! chee-to-che-**ton**, interj., hush!
chivo, chee-vo, s., kid; he-goat
chocar, cho-**kar**, v., to collide; to clash; to fight;
  to digest
chocarrería, cho-kar-rray-**ree**-ah, s., buffoonery;
  coarse jest
chocolate, cho-co-**jah**-tay, s., chocolate
chochear, cho-chay-**ar**, v., to dote; to grow feeble
chofeta, cho-**fay**-tah, s., chafing-dish [dispute
choque, cho-**kay**, s., shock; collision; skirmish
chocería, cho-re-thay-**ree**-ah, s., sausage shop
chorrera, chorr-**rray**-rah, s., spout; shirt frill

chorro, chor-rro, s., jet; spurt. **a chorros,** ah **chor**-rros, abundantly

choza, cho-thah, s., hut; hovel; shanty

chozno, choth-no, s., great-grandson

chubasco, choo-**bahs**-ko, s., squall; shower

chuchería, choo-chay-**ree**-ah, s., bauble; trinket

chufar, choo-**far,** v., to mock

chufletear, choo-flay-tay-**ar,** v., to sneer; to taunt

chulada, choo-**lah**-dah, s., droll speech or action; breach of manners

chulear, choo-lay-**ar,** v., to sneer; to boast

chulería, choo-lay-**ree**-ah, s., pleasing manner

chuleta, choo-**lay**-tah, s., chop; cutlet

chulo, choo-lo, s., punster; artful person

chunga, choon-gah, s., jest; joke   [gibe

chunguearse, choon-gay-**ar**-say, v., to chaff; to

chupa, choo-pah, s., waistcoat   [to fool

chupar, choo-**par,** v., to suck; to sponge upon;

chupón, choo-**pon,** s., parasite

churro, choor-rro, s., sort of fritter. a., coarse-woolled

chuscada, chooss-**kah**-dah, s., buffoonery

chusco, chooss-ko, a., pleasant; droll

chusma, chooss-mah, s., rabble; mob

chuzo, choo-tho, s., pike. **llover a chuzos,** l'yo-**vair** ah **choo**-thos, to rain heavily

dable, dah-blay, a., practical, feasible   [writer

dactilógrafo, dahk-te-**lo**-grah-fo, s., typist; type-

dádiva, dah-de-vah, s., gift

dadivoso, dah-de-**vo**-so, a., generous

dado, dah-do, s., die. a., given, — **que,** — kay, provided; assuming that   [of a bill

dador, dah-**dor,** s., giver; bearer of a letter; drawer

daga, dah-gah, s., dagger

¡dale! dah-lay, interjection expressing displeasure at obstinacy

dama, dah-mah, s., lady; (draughts) queen

damajuana, dah-mah-Hoo'**ah**-nah, s., demijohn

damasco, dah-**mahs**-ko, s., damask; damson

damería, dah-may-**ree**-ah, s., prudery

damisela, dah-me-**say**-lah, s., young lady

damnificar, dahm-ne-fe-**kar**, v., to hurt; to damage

danta, dahn-tah, s., tapir

danzar, dahn-**thar**, v., to dance

dañar, dah-n'**yar**, v., to hurt; to damage

daño, dah-n'yo, s., damage; harm; prejudice; loss

dañoso*, dah-n'**yo**-so, a., hurtful; injurious

dar, dar, v., to give; to bestow; to supply; to impart; to yield. — **a,** — ah, to be situated; — **con,** — kon, to find; — **de,** — day, to fall down; — **en,** — en, to fall into; to find; — **que,** — kay, to cause

dársena, dar-say-nah, s., dry-dock, basin

data, dah-tah, s., date; item

datar, dah-**tar**, v., to date

dátil, dah-til, s., date (fruit)

dato, dah-to, s., datum

de, day, prep., of; from; for; by

deán, day-**ahn**, s., dean

debajo, day-**bah**-Ho, adv., under; beneath.—**de,**—day, prep., under

debate, day-**bah**-tay, s., debate

debatir, day-bah-**teer**, v., to debate

debe, day-bay, s., debtor side of an account; debit

deber, day-**bair**, v., to owe; to be obliged to. s., duty; obligation; debt

debido*, day-**bee**-do, a., due

débil, day-bil, a., feeble; weak; frail; pusillanimous

debilidad, day-be-le-**dahd**, s., debility; weakness

debilitar, day-be-le-**tar**, v., to debilitate; to weaken

débito, day-be-to, s., debt; duty

década, day-kah-dah, s., decade

decadencia, day-kah-**den**-the-ah, s., decay; decline

decaer, day-kah-**air**, v., to decline; to decay; to [fade

decano, day-kah-no, s., senior; dean

decantación, day-kahn-tah-the-**on**, s., decanting

decantar, day-kahn-**tar**, v., to exaggerate; to decant

decapitar, day-kah-pe-**tar**, v., to behead

decenal, day-thay-**nahl**, a., decennial

decencia, day-**then**-the-ah, s., decency; modesty

decenio, day-**thay**-ne-o, s., space of ten years; decennium

deceno, day-**thay**-no, a., tenth

decente, day-**then**-tay, a., decent; honest; decor-
decidido*, day-the-**dee**-do, a., decided   [ous
decidir, day-the-**deer**, v., to decide
decidor, day-the-**dor**, s., fluent speaker
décimo, **day**-the-mo, a., tenth
decir, day-**theer**, v., to say; to tell; to speak; to
   state; to name; to denote
decisión, day-the-se-**on**, s., decision; judgement;
decisivo, day-the-se-vo, a., decisive   [verdict
declamar, day-klah-**mar**, v., to declaim; to recite
declarar, day-klah-**rar**, v., to declare; to expound
declinar, day-kle-**nar**, v., to decline; to decay; to
declive, day-**klee**-vay, s., declivity; slope   [sink
decorar, day-ko-**rar**, v., to decorate
decoro, day-**ko**-ro, s., honour; circumspection;
   integrity; decorum
decoroso, day-ko-**ro**-so, a., decorous; decent
decrecer, day-kray-**thair**, v., to decrease
decrépito, day-**kray**-pe-to, a., decrepit
decretar, day-kray-**tar**, v., to decree; to resolve
decreto, day-**kray**-to, s., decree; decision
décuplo, **day**-koo-plo, a., tenfold
decurso, day-**koor**-so, s., course of time
dechado, day-**chah**-do, s., sample; pattern; model
dedal, day-**dahl**, s., thimble; finger-stall
dedicar, day-de-**kar**, v., to dedicate
dedicatoria, day-de-kah-**to**-re-ah, s., dedication
dedillo, day-dee-l'yo, s., little finger
dedo, **day**-do, s., finger; toe   [to deduct
deducir, day-doo-**theer**, v., to deduce; to infer;
defecto, day-**fek**-to, s., defect; fault
defectuoso*, day-fek-too'o-so, a., defective
defender, day-fen-**dair**, v., to defend; to protect
defendible, day-fen-dee-blay, a., defensible
defensa, day-**fen**-sah, s., defence; vindication
defensor, day-fen-**sor**, s., defender; supporter
deferente, day-fay-**ren**-tay, a., deferential; defer-
   ring   [yield
deferir, day-fay-**reer**, v., to defer; to submit; to
deficiente, day-fe-the-**en**-tay, a., deficient; defec-
definible, day-fe-nee-blay, a., definable   [tive
definir, day-fe-**neer**, v., to define; to determine

deformar, day-for-**mar,** v., to deform

deforme, day-**for**-may, a., disfigured; ugly

defraudación, day-frah'oo-dah-the-**on,** s., fraud; deceit

defraudar, day-frah'oo-**dar,** v., to defraud; to cheat

defunción, day-foon-the-**on,** s., decease [eracy

degeneración, day-**Hay**-nay-rah-the-**on,** s., degen-

degenerar, day-**Hay**-nay-**rar,** v., to degenerate

degollar, day-go-l'**yar,** v., to behead; to ruin; to annihilate

degradar, day-grah-**dar,** v., to degrade

degüello, day-goo'ay-l'yo, s., decollation

dehesa, day-**ay**-sah, s., pasture-ground

deidad, day-e-**dahd,** s., deity; divinity

dejación, day-Hah-the-**on,** s., abandonment; relinquishment

dejadez, day-Hah-**deth,** s., slovenliness; neglect

dejado, day-**Hah**-do, a., indolent; dejected

dejar, day-**Har,** v., to leave; to omit; to forsake; to yield; to allow

delación, day-lah-the-**on,** s., denunciation

delantal, day-lahn-**tahl,** s., apron

delante, day-**lahn**-tay, adv., before. prep., in front of; facing [advantage

delantera, day-lahn-**tay**-rah, s., front; forefront

delantero, day-lahn-**tay**-ro, s., leader. a., foremost

delatar, day-lah-**tar,** v., to denounce

delator, day-lah-**tor,** s., informer; denouncer

delegado, day-lay-**gah**-do, s. & a., delegate; deputy

delegar, day-lay-**gar,** v., to delegate

deleitable, day-lay'e-**tah**-blay, a., delectable

deleite, day-**lay**'e-tay, s., delight

deletéreo, day-lay-**tay**-ray-o, a., deleterious

deletrear, day-lay-tray-**ar,** v., to spell

deleznable, day-leth-**nah**-blay, a., brittle; fragile; frail; perishable

delfín, del-**feen,** s., dolphin; dauphin

delgadez, del-gah-**deth,** s., thinness; slenderness

delgado, del-**gah**-do, a., thin; slim

deliberación, day-le-bay-rah-the-**on,** s., deliberation; reflection

deliberar, day-le-bay-**rar**, v., to deliberate

delicadez, day-le-kah-**deth**, s., delicacy; weakness

delicadeza, day-le-kah-**day**-thah, s., delicateness; fineness; subtlety

delicado*, day-le-**kah**-do, a., delicate; weak; exquisite; thin

delicia, day-lee-the-ah, s., delight

delicioso*, day-le-the-**o**-so, a., delicious [offender

delincuente, day-lin-koo'**en**-tay, a., delinquent;

delinear, day-le-nay-**ar**, v., to sketch

delinquir, day-lin-**keer**, v., to transgress the law

deliquio, day-lee-ke'o, s., swoon; ecstasy

delirar, day-le-**rar**, v., to rave; to talk wildly

delirio, day-lee-re-o, s., delirium

delito, day-lee-to, s., transgression; delinquency

delusorio*, day-loo-**so**-re-o, a., deceitful

demacrado, day-mah-**krah**-do, a., emaciated

demanda, day-**mahn**-dah, s., demand; claim; request

demandador, day-mahn-dah-**dor**, s., (law) plain-

demandar, day-mahn-**dar**, v., to demand [tiff

demarcar, day-mar-**kar**, v., to mark out limits

demás, day-**mahs**, adv., besides; moreover, **lo, la, los, las—**, lo, lah, los, lahs—, the rest

demasía, day-mah-**see**-ah, s., excess; surplus

demasiado, day-mah-se-**ah**-do, adv., excessively, a., excessive

demencia, day-**men**-the-ah, s., dementia

dementar, day-men-**tar**, v., to drive mad

demente, day-**men**-tay, a., demented; mad; insane

demérito, day-**may**-re-to, s., demerit

demisión, day-me-se-**on**, s., submission; humility

democrático, day-mo-**krah**-te-ko, a., democratic

demoler, day-mo-**lair**, v., to demolish

demonio, day-**mo**-ne-o, s., demon

demora, day-**mo**-rah, s., delay [tarry

demorar, day-mo-**rar**, v., to delay; to remain; to

demostrar, day-mos-**trar**, v., to demonstrate; to prove

denegar, day-nay-**gar**, v., to deny

dengue, **den**-gay, s., prudery; affection; short veil; dengue

denigración, day-ne-grah-the-**on**, s., denigration; defamation

denigrar, day-ne-**grar**, v., to revile; to defame

denodado, day-no-**dah**-do, a., intrepid; daring

denominar, day-no-me-**nar**, v., to denominate; to give name to

denotar, day-no-**tar**, v., to denote; to signify

densidad, den-se-**dahd**, s., density

denso, den-so, a., dense; thick; compact

dentado, den-**tah**-do, a., indented; serrated

dentadura, den-tah-**doo**-rah, s., set of teeth

dentellear, den-tel-l'yay-**ar**, v., to bite

dentista, den-**tiss**-tah, s., dentist

dentro, den-tro, adv., inside; within

denuedo, day-noo'**ay**-do, s., boldness; intrepidity

denuesto, day-noo'**ess**-to, s., affront; insult

denunciador, day-noon-the'ah-**dorr**, s., informant

denunciar, day-noon-the-**ar**, v., to denounce; to betray; to accuse

deparar, day-pah-**rar**, v., to offer; to furnish

departamento, day-par-tah-**men**-to, s., department

departir, day-par-**teer**, v., to converse [ment

dependencia, day-pen-**den**-the-ah, s., dependence; business; staff

depender, day-pen-**dair**, v., to depend

dependiente, day-pen-de-**en**-tay, s., dependent; employee

deplorar, day-plo-**rar**, v., to deplore

deponer, day-po-**nair**, v., to depose; to attest

deportar, day-por-**tar**, v., to banish; to exile

deporte, day-**por**-tay, s., amusement; diversion; sport

deposición, day-po-se-the-**on**, s., deposition; declaration; degradation

depositador, day-po-se-tah-**dor**, s., depositor

depositar, day-po-se-**tar**, v., to deposit

depositario, day-po-se-**tah**-re-o, s., depositary; trustee; receiver [sediment

depósito, day-**po**-se-to, s., deposit; warehouse;

depravar, day-prah-**var**, v., to deprave [prayer

deprecación, day-pray-kah-the-**on**, s., petition;

deprecar, day-pray-**kar**, v., to implore; to pray

depreciar, day-pray-the-**ar,** v., to depreciate ; to undervalue

depredar, day-pray-**dar,** v., to rob ; to pillage

deprimir, day-pre-**meer,** v., to depress ; to humble

depuesto, day-poo'**ess-**to, a., deposited ; deprived

depurar, day-poo-**rar,** v., to depurate ; to cleanse

derecha, day-ray-chah, s., right hand ; right side

derechera, day-ray-**chay-**rah, s., direct road

derecho, day-ray-cho, s., right ; justice ; law ; tax ; duty, a., right ; straight   [straightness

derechura, day-ray-**choo-**rah, s., right way

derivar, day-re-**var,** v., to derive ; to deflect

derogatorio, day-ro-gah-**tor-**re-o, a., derogatory

derogar, day-ro-**gar,** v., to derogate ; to annul ; to reform

derramamiento, dair-rrah-mah-me-**en-**to, s., overflow ; shedding ; effusion ; scattering

derramar, dair-rrah-**rar,** v., to pour ; to spill ; to spread ; to waste

derrame, dair-rrah-may, s., leakage ; overflow

derredor, dair-rray-**dor,** s., circumference, **en—,** en—, about   [sprained

derrengado, dair-rren-**gah-**do, a., crooked ;

derrengar, dair-rren-**gar,** v., to sprain ; to wrench

derretir, dair-rray-**teer,** v., to dissolve ; to consume ; to melt ; to fuse   [to throw down

derribar, dair-rre-**bar,** v., to demolish ; to ruin ;

derribo, dair-**rree-**bo, s., demolition

derrocar, dair-rro-**kar,** v., to pull down   [squander

derrochar, dair-rro-**char,** v., to dissipate ; to

derrota, dair-**rro-**tah, s., ship's course ; road ; defeat of an army   [defeat

derrotar, dair-rro-**tar,** v., to destroy ; to rout ; to

derruir, dair-rroo'**eer,** v., to demolish   [crumble

derrumbar, dair-rroom-**bar,** v., to precipitate ; to

desabonarse, day-sah-bo-**nar-**say, v., to cancel a subscription

desabotonar, day-sah-bo-to-**nar,** v., to unbutton ; to blossom

desabrido, day-sah-**bree-**do, a., tasteless ; peevish

desabrigar, day-sah-bre-**gar,** v., to uncover

desabrigo, day-sah-**bree-**go, s., nudity ; destitution

desabrir, day-sah-**breer**, v., to vex; to harass

desabrochar, day-sah-bro-**char**, v., to unclasp; to unfasten [the fresh air

desacalorarse, dess-ah-kah-lo-**rar**-say, v., to take

desacato, day-sah-**kah**-to, s., disrespect

desacertar, day-sah-thair-**tar**, v., to commit a mistake; to err

desacierto, day-sah-the-**air**-to, s., mistake; blunder

desacomodado, day-sah-ko-mo-**dah**-do, a., destitute; out of employment

desacomodar, day-sah-ko-mo-**dar**, v., to incommode; to molest

desaconsejar, day-sah-kon-say-**Har**, v., to dis-

desacordar, day-sah-kor-**dar**, v., to untune [suade

desacorde, day-sah-**kor**-day, a., discordant

desacostumbrado, day-sah-kos-toom-**brah**-do, a., unusual

desacreditar, day-sah-kray-de-**tar**, v., to discredit

desacuerdo, day-sah-koo**-air**-do, s., disagreement; mistake [disaffected

desafecto, day-sah-**fek**-to, s., disaffection, a.,

desafiar, day-sah-fe-**ar**, v., to challenge

desafición, day-sah-fe-the-**on**, s., disaffection

desafío, day-sah-**fee**-o, s., challenge; contest

desaforado, day-sah-fo-**rah**-do, a., lawless; huge

desafortunado, day-sah-for-too-**nah**-do, a., unfortunate; unlucky [outrage

desafuero, day-sah-foo**-ay**-ro, s., act of injustice

desagarrar, day-sah-gar-**rrar**, v., to release

desagradable, day-sah-grah-**dah**-blay, a., disagreeable; unpleasant

desagradar, day-sah-grah-**dar**, v., to displease

desagradecer, day-sah-grah-day-**thair**, v., to be ungrateful

desagrado, day-sah-**grah**-do, s., displeasure

desagraviar, day-sah-grah-ve-**ar**, v., to make amends

desaguadero, day-sah-goo**'ah**-**day**-ro, s., drain

desaguar, day-sah-goo**'ar**, v., to drain

desahogado, day-sah-o-**gah**-do, a., impudent; unencumbered; well-to-do [recover

desahogar, day-sah-o-**gar**, v., to ease pain; to

desahogo, day-sah-**o**-go, s., alleviation; easing; release [give up

desahuciar, day-sah-oo-the-**ar**, v., to despair; to

desahumado, day-sah-oo-**mah**-do, a., faded; vapid

desairado, day-sah'e-**rah**-do, a., disregarded; slighted; rejected

desairar, day-sah'e-**rar**, v., to disregard; to rebuff

desaire, day-**sah**'e-ray, s., rebuff; disdain

desalentar, day sah-len-**tar**, v., to discourage

desaliento, day-sah-le-**en**-to, s., dismay; dejection

desaliño, day-sah-lee-n'yo, s., slovenliness

desalmado, day-sahl-**mah**-do, a., soulless; inhuman

desalojar, day-sah-lo-*H*ar, v., to dislodge; to move

desalterar, day-sahl-tay-**rar**, v., to allay

desamistarse, day-sah-miss-**tar**-say, v., to fall out

desamoldar, day-sah-mol-**dar**, v., to disfigure

desamparar, day-sahm-pah-**rar**, v., to forsake; to abandon [nish

desamueblar, day-sah-moo'ay-**blar**, v., to unfur-

desandrajado, day-sahn-drah-*H*a-do, a., ragged

desangrar, day-sahn-**grar**, v., to bleed to excess

desanimar, day-sah-ne-**mar**, v., to dishearten; to discourage

desánimo, day-**sah**-ne-mo, s., discouragement

desanudar, day-sah-noo-**dar**, v., to untie; to disentangle [able

desapacible, day-sah-pah-**thee**-blay, a., disagree-

desaparecer, day-sah-pah-ray-**thair**, v., to disappear [tion

desapego, day-sah-**pay**-go, s., alienation of affec-

desapercibido, day-sah-pair-the-**bee**-do, a., unprepared; unawares

desapiadado, day-sah-pe-ah-**dah**-do, a., merciless

desapoderado, day-sah-po-day-**rah**-do, a., impetuous

desapreciar, day-sah-pray-the-**ar**, v., to depreciate

desaprender, day-sah-pren-**dair**, v., to unlearn

desapretar, day-sah-pray-**tar**, v., to slacken; to loosen

desaprisionar, day-sah-pre-se-o-**nar**, v., to set free

desaprobar, day-sah-pro-**bar**, v., to disapprove

desaprovechar, day-sah-pro-vay-**char**, v., to turn

desarmar, day-sar-**mar**, v., to disarm [to bad use

desarraigar, day-sar-rrah'e-**gar**, v., to root out; to eradicate

desarrapado, day-sar-rrah-**pah**-do, a., ragged

desarreglo, day-sar-**rray**-glo, s., disorder; confusion

desarrimar, day-sar-rre-**mar**, v., to remove

desarrollar, day-sar-rro-l'**yar**, v., to develop; to promote; to expand

desaseado, day-sah-say-**ah**-do, a., slovenly; untidy

desaseo, day-sah-**say**-o, s., slovenliness; untidiness

desasir, day-sah-**seer**, v., to loosen

desasosiego, day-sah-so-se-**ay**-go, s., restlessness

desastrado, day-sahs-**trah**-do, a., ragged; slovenly

desatacar, day-sah-tah-**kar**, v., to loosen; to untie

desatar, day-sah-**tar**, v., to untie; to undo; to unfasten; to loose

desatavío, day-sah-tah-**vee**-o, s., disarray

desatención, day-sah-ten-the-**on**, s., inattention; incivility

desatender, day-sah-ten-**dair**, v., to disregard

desatentar, day-sah-ten-**tar**, v., to perplex

desatento, day-sah-**ten**-to, a., inattentive; discourteous   [wild

desatinado, day-sah-te-**nah**-do, a., extravagant;

desatino, day-sah-**tee**-no, s., extravagance; nonsense; folly

desatracar, day-sah-trah-**kar**, v., to sheer off

desatrancar, day-sah-trahn-**kar**, v., to unbar

desautorizado, day-sah'oo-to-re-**thah**-do, a., unauthorized   [diate; to disown

desautorizar, day-sah'oo-to-re-**thar**, v., to repu-

desavenencia, day-sah-vay-**nen**-the-ah, s., discord   [profitable; inferior

desaventajado, day-sah-ven-tah-*H*ah-do, a., un-

desaviar, day-sah-ve-**ar**, v., to go astray; to deprive of necessaries

desayunarse, day-sah-yoo-**nar**-say, v., to breakfast

desayuno, day-sah-**yoo**-no, s., breakfast

desazón, day-sah-**thon,** s., insipidity; disgust; restlessness

desbandarse, dess-bahn-**dar**-say, v., to disband

desbarajuste, dess-bah-rah-**H**oos**s**-tay, s., disorder; confusion   [smash

desbaratar, dess-bah-rah-**tar,** v., to destroy; to

desbarrar, dess-bar-**rrar,** v., to slip; to talk nonsense

desbastar, dess-bahs-**tar,** v., to smooth; to waste

desbocado, dess-bo-**kah**-do, a., runaway (horse)

desbordar, dess-bor-**dar,** v., to overflow

desbravar, dess-brah-**var,** v., to tame; to break in (horse); to abate

desbroce, dess-**bro**-thay, s., clearing

descabellado, dess-kah-bay-l'**yah**-do, a., dishevelled, preposterous · absurd

descabezar, dess-kah-bay-**thar,** v., to behead

descaecer, dess-kah-ay-**thair,** v., to decline

descalabro, dess-kah-**lah**-bro, s., misfortune; considerable loss

descalificar, dess-kah-le-fe-**kar,** v., to disqualify

descalzar, dess-kahl-**thar,** v., to pull off shoes and stockings   [to misguide

descaminar, dess-kah-me-**nar,** v., to lead astray;

descampado, dess-kahm-**pah**-do, a., free, clear

descansar, dess-kahn-**sar,** v., to rest; to pause

descanso, dess-**kahn**-so, s., rest; repose

descarado, dess-kah-**rah**-do, a., impudent [lently

descararse, dess-kah-**rar**-say, v., to behave inso-

descarbonizar, dess-kah**r**-bo-ne-**thar,** v., to decarbonize

descarga, dess-**kar**-gah, s., unloading

descargadero, dess-kar-gah-**day**-ro, s., wharf

descargar, dess-kar-**gar,** v., to unload; to discharge

descargo, dess-**kar**-go, s., unloading; acquittal

descariño, dess-kah-**ree**-n'yo, s., loss of affection

descaro, dess-**kah**-ro, s., impudence; effrontery

descarriar, dess-kar-rre-**ar,** v., to misguide; mislead

descarrío, dess-kar-**rree**-o, s., losing one's way

descartar, dess-kar-**tar,** v., to discard; to dismiss

descasar, dess-kah-**sar,** v., to divorce

descascarar, dess-kahs-kah-**rar**, v., to decorticate

descastado, dess-kahs-**tah**-do, a., degenerate

descender, dess-then-**dair**, v., to descend; to get

descenso, dess-**then**-so, s., descent [down

descifrar, dess-the-**frar**, v., to decipher

desclavar, dess-klah-**var**, v., to unnail

descocarse, dess-ko-**kar**-say, v., to be impudent

descoco, dess-**ko**-ko, s., impudence

descoger, dess-ko-**Hair**, v., to unfold; to expand

descolgar, dess-kol-**gar**, v., to unhang

descollar, dess-ko-l'**yar**, v., to surpass

descombrar, dess-kom-**brar**, v., to disencumber

descomedido, dess-ko-may-**dee**-do, a., insolent; excessive; rude [portionate

descompasado, dess-kom-pah-**sah**-do, a., dispro-

descomponer, dess-kom-po-**nair**, v., to discompose; to decompose; to disturb; to upset

descompuesto, dess-kom-poo'**ess**-to, a., out of order; insolent

descomunal, dess-ko-moo-**nahl**, a., uncommon; huge; colossal [baffle

desconcertar, dess-kon-thair-**tar**, v., to disturb; to

desconfiar, dess-kon-fe-**ar**, v., to distrust

desconocer, dess-ko-no-**thair**, v., to disregard; to ignore; to disown

desconocido, dess-ko-no-**thee**-do, a., unknown

desconsiderado, dess-kon-se-day-**rah**-do, a., inconsiderate [dejected

desconsolado, dess-kon-so-**lah**-do, a., disconsolate;

desconsuelo, dess-kon-soo'**ay**-lo, s., affliction

descontar, dess-kon-**tar**, v., to discount; to take for granted

descontento, dess-kon-**ten**-to, s., discontent

descontinuo, dess-kon-**tee**-noo'o, a., disjoined

desconvenir, dess-kon-vay-**neer**, v., to disagree

descorazonar, dess-ko-rah-tho-**nar**, v., to dishearten

descorrer, dess-kor-**rrair**, v., to draw (a curtain)

descortés, dess-kor-**tess**, a., unpolite; discourteous

descortesía, dess-kor-tay-**see**-ah, s., incivility

descoser, dess-ko-**sair**, v., to unstitch; to disjoin; to unseam

descosido, dess-ko-**see**-do, s., tear; rip; idle talker

descoyuntar, dess-ko-yoon-**tar,** v., to disjoint; to derange

descrédito, dess-**kray**-de-to, s., discredit [credit

descreer, dess-kray-**air,** v., to disbelieve; to dis-

describir, dess-kre-**beer,** v., to describe

descripción, dess-krip-the-**on,** s., description

descuartizar, dess-koo-ar-te-**thar,** v., to quarter; to carve

descubierto, dess-koo-be-**air**-to, a., bareheaded; uncovered; discovered

descubrir, dess-koo-**breer,** v., to discover

descuello, dess-koo-**ay**-l'yo, s., excessive height; pre-eminence; haughtiness

descuento, dess-koo-**en**-to, s., discount

descuidar, dess-koo-e-**dar,** v., to neglect [gence

descuido, dess-koo-**ee**-do, s., carelessness; negli-

desde, dess-day, prep., from; since

desdén, des-**den,** s., disdain; contempt

desdentado, dess-den-**tah**-do, a., toothless

desdeñar, dess-day-n'**yar,** v., to disdain

desdeñoso, dess-day-n'**yo**-so, a., disdainful

desdicha, dess-dee-chah, s., misfortune

desdoblar, dess-do-**blar,** v., to unfold

deseable, day-say-**ah**-blay, a., desirable

desear, day-say-**ar,** v., to desire; to wish

desecar, day-say-**kar,** v., to dry; to desiccate

desechar, day-say-**char,** v., to depreciate; to reject; to cast off

desecho, day-say-cho, s., residue; refuse; disregard

desembalar, day-sem-bah-**lar,** v., to unpack

desembarazar, day-sem-bah-rah-**thar,** v., to clear; to free; to ease [disembark

desembarcar, day-sem-bar-**kar,** v., to land; to

desembarco, day-sem-**bar**-ko, s., landing; unshipment

desembolsar, day-sem-bol-**sar,** v., to disburse

desembragar, dess-em-brah-**garr,** v., to declutch

desembrollar, day-sem-bro-l'**yar,** v., to disentangle

desemejante, day-say-may-*H*ahn-tay, a., dissimilar

desemejanza, day-say-may-*H*ahn-thah, s., dissimilarity

desempapelar, day-sem-pah-pay-lar, v., to unwrap [pack

desempaquetar, day-sem-pah-kay-tar, v., to un-

desempeñar, day-sem-pay-n'yar, v., to redeem; to clear from debt; to fulfil

desempeño, day-sem-pay-n'yo, s., redeeming a pledge; fulfilment [disconnect

desencajar, day-sen-kah-*H*ar, v., to disjoint; to

desencantar, day-sen-kahn-tar, v., to disenchant

desenconar, day-sen-ko-nar, v., to allay an inflammation

desenfadar, day-sen-fah-dar, v., to appease

desenfado, day-sen-fah-do, s., freedom; ease; relaxation [tiousness

desenfreno, day-sen-fray-no, s., looseness; licen-

desenganchar, day-sen-gahn-char, v., to unhook; to unfasten [to disappoint

desengañar, day-sen-gah-n'yar, v., to undeceive;

desenlace, day-sen-lah-thay, s., denouement

desenmarañar, day-sen-mah-rah-n'yar, v., to disentangle [mask

desenmascarar, day-sen-mahs-kah-rar, v., to un-

desenojar, day-say-no-*H*ar, v., to appease anger

desenredar, day-sen-ray-dar, v., to disentangle; to extricate

desenrollar, day-sen-ro-l'yar, v., to unroll

desensortijado, day-sen-sor-te-*H*ah-do, a., displaced

desentenderse, day-sen-ten-dair-say, v., to feign ignorance; to take no notice

desenterrar, day-sen-tair-rrar, v., to unearth

desentono, day-sen-to-no, s., disharmony

desentrañar, day-sen-trah-n'yar, v., to gut; to penetrate into difficult matters

desenvainar, day-sen-vah'e-nar, v., to unsheathe

desenvoltura, day-sen-vol-too-rah, s., effrontery; sprightliness

desenvolver, day-sen-vol-vair, v., to unroll

desenvuelto, day-sen-voo'el-to, a., free; easy; [sprightly

deseo, day-say-o, s., desire [sprightly

deseoso, day-say-**o**-so, a., desirous

desertar, day-sair-**tar**, v., to desert

desesperación, day-sess-pay-rah-the-**on**,s.,despair

desesperado, day-sess-pay-**rah**-do, a., desperate

desesperanzar, day-sess-pay-rahn-**thar**, v., to deprive of hope; to discourage [less

desfachatado, dess-fah-chah-**tah**-do, a., shame-

desfalcar, dess-fahl-**kar**, v., to cut off; to embezzle

desfallecer, dess-fah-l'yay-**thair**, v., to pine away; to faint [able

desfavorable, dess-fah-vo-**rah**-blay, a., unfavour-

desfavorecer, dess-fah-vo-ray-**thair**, v., to discountenance

desfigurar, dess-fe-goo-**rar**, v., to disfigure

desfiladero, dess-fe-lah-**day**-ro, s., defile; gorge

desflorar, dess-flo-**rar**, v., to tarnish; to sully

desgajar, dess-gah-*Har*, v., to lop; to break in pieces [appetite

desgana, dess-**gah**-nah, s., reluctance; lack of

desgarbado, dess-gar-**bah**-do, a., uncouth; gawky

desgarrado, dess-gar-**rrah**-do, a., dissolute

desgarrar, dess-gar-**rrar**, v., to rend; to tear

desgastar, dess-gahs-**tar**, v., to consume; to wear away [management

desgobierno, dess-go-be-air-no, s., misrule; mis-

desgracia, dess-**grah**-the-ah, s., misfortune; disgrace

desgraciadamente, dess-grah-the-ah-dah-**men**-tay, adv., unfortunately

desgraciar, dess-grah-the-**ar**, v., to displease

desgranar, dess-grah-**nar**, v., to thrash grain; to shell (as peas)

desgrasar, dess-grah-**sar**, v., to remove the grease

desguarnecer, dess-goo'ar-nay-**thair**, v., to strip of ornaments; to disgarnish

deshabitado, day-sah-be-**tah**-do, a., uninhabited

deshabituar, day-sah-be-too'**ar**, v., to disaccustom

deshacer, day-sah-**thair**, v., to undo; to destroy; to liquefy; to cancel [part with

deshacerse, day-sah-**thair**-say, v., to get rid; to

desharrapado, day-sar-rrah-**pah**-do, a., shabby

deshelar, day-say-**lar**, v., to thaw

desheredar, day-say-ray-**dar,** v., to disinherit

deshielo, day-se-**ay**-lo, s., thaw

deshilar, day-se-**lar,** v., to ravel

deshincar, day-sin-**kar,** v., to draw out ; to remove

deshoje, day-**so**-Hay, s., fall of leaves [sweep

deshollinador, day-so-l'yee-nah-**dor,** s., chimney-

deshonestidad, day-so-ness-te-**dahd,** s., dishonesty

deshonesto*, day-so-**ness**-to, a., dishonest

deshonorar, day-so-no-**rar,** v., to dishonour ; to deprive of office [affront

deshonra, day-**sonn**-rah, s., dishonour ; disgrace

deshonrar, day-sonn-**rar,** v., to defame ; to disgrace ; to insult

deshora, day-so-rah, s., unseasonable time [bones

deshuesar, day-soo'ay-**sar,** v., to take out the

desidia, day-**see**-de-ah, s., idleness ; laziness

desierto, day-se-**air**-to, a., deserted

designar, day-sig-**nar,** v., to purpose ; to appoint ; to designate

designio, day-**seeg**-ne-o, s., design ; intention

desigual, day-se-goo'**ahl,** a., unequal ; uneven

desinterés, day-sin-tay-**ress,** s., disinterestedness

desistir, day-siss-**teer,** v., to desist ; to give up

desjuntar, dess-Hoon-**tar,** v., to disjoint ; to separate

deslavado, dess-lah-**vah**-do, a., barefaced [rate

desleal, dess-lay-**ahl,** a., disloyal

desleír, dess-lay-**eer,** v., to dilute

deslenguado, dess-len-goo'**ah**-do, a., foul-mouthed

desliar, dess-le-**ar,** v., to untie [tangle

desligar, dess-le-**gar,** v., to loose ; to untie ; to disentangle

deslindar, dess-lin-**dar,** v., to set land marks

deslinde, dess-**leen**-day, s., demarcation

desliz, dess-**leeth,** s., false step ; slip ; fault

deslizadizo, dess-le-thah-**dee**-tho, a., slippery

deslizar, dess-le-**thar,** v., to slip

deslucir, dess-loo-**theer,** v., to tarnish

deslumbrar, dess-loom-**brar,** v., to dazzle

deslustrar, dess-looss-**trar,** v., to tarnish ; to dim

desmadejar, dess-mah-day-**Har,** v., to enervate

desmán, dess-**mahn,** s., misbehaviour

desmandar, dess-mahn-**dar,** v., to countermand ; to transgress

desmanotado, dess-mah-no-**tah**-do, a., awkward

desmaña, dess-**mah**-n'yah, s., clumsiness

desmarañar, dess-mah-rah-n'**yar,** v., to disentangle

desmayar, dess-mah-**yar,** v., to dismay; to be dispirited; to faint

desmayo, dess-**mah**-yo, s., swoon; dismay

desmedido, dess-may-**dee**-do, a., out of proportion

desmejora, dess-may-**Ho**-rah, s., deterioration

desmejorar, dess-may-**Ho**-rar, v., to debase; to impair

desmembrar, dess-mem-**brar,** v., to dismember

desmentir, dess-men-**teer,** v., to give the lie to; to contradict [to break in bits

desmenuzar, dess-may-noo-**thar,** v., to crumble

desmerecer, dess-may-ray-**thair,** v., to become unworthy of; to deteriorate

desmesurado, dess-may-soo-**rah**-do, a., immeasurable; excessive

desmigar, dess-me-**gar,** v., to crumble bread

desmochar, dess-mo-**char,** v., to lop; to mutilate

desmontar, dess-mon-**tar,** v., to fell wood; to dismount; to take apart

desmoralizar, dess-mo-rah-le-**thar,** v., to demoralize

desnatar, dess-nah-**tar,** v., to skim milk [ralize

desnivel, dess-ne-**vel,** s., unevenness

desnudar, dess-noo-**dar,** v., to denude; to undress

desnudo, dess-**noo**-do, a., naked; bare

desnutrición, dess-noo-tre-the-**on,** s., malnutrition

desobedecer, day-so-bay-day-**thair,** v., to disobey

desobediencia, day-so-bay-de-**en**-the-ah, s., disobedience

desobligar, day-so-ble-**gar,** v., to relieve from an obligation; to disoblige [empty

desocupado, day-so-koo-**pah**-do, a., disengaged;

desoír, day-so-**eer,** v., not to heed

desolado, day-so-**lah**-do, a., desolate

desollado, day-so-l'**yah**-do, a., impudent

desollar, day-so-l'**yar,** v., to flay; to skin

desorden, day-**sor**-den, s., disorder; confusion; disturbance [disarrange

desordenar, day-sor-day-**nar,** v., to disturb; to

desorejado, day-so-ray-*Hah*-do, a., degraded

desorganizar, day-sor-gah-ne-*thar*, v., to disorganize

desorientar, day-so-re-en-*tar*, v., to bewilder; to

desosar, day-so-*sar*, v., to bone   [disconcert

despabilar, dess-pah-be-*lar*, v., to snuff a candle

despacio, dess-*pah*-the-o, adv., slowly; gently

despacito, dess-pah-*thee*-to, adv., very gently

despachar, dess-pah-*char*, v., to forward; to expedite

despacho, dess-*pah*-cho, s., dispatch; expedient; custom; counting-house; office

desparejar, dess-pah-ray-*Har*, v., to make uneven

despavorido, dess-pah-vo-*ree*-do, a., terrified

despechar, dess-pay-*char*, v., to enrage; to excite indignation; to fret

despedida, dess-pay-*dee*-dah, s., leave-taking

despedir, dess-pay-*deer*, v., to discharge; to dismiss

despedirse, dess-pay-*deer*-say, v., to take leave

despegado, dess-pay-*gah*-do, a., unglued; harsh; unaffectionate

despego, dess-*pay*-go, s., asperity; indifference

despejado, dess-pay-*Hah*-do, a., sprightly; dexterous

despejar, dess-pay-*Har*, v., to clear away obstructions; to become bright

despejo, dess-*pay*-*Ho*, s., clearing; sprightliness

despenar, dess-pay-*nar*, v., to relieve from pain

despender, dess-pen-*dair*, v., to spend; to squander

despensa, dess-*pen*-sah, s., pantry   [der

despensero, dess-pen-*say*-ro, s., butler; steward

despeñadero, dess-pay-n'yah-*day*-ro, s., precipice

despeñar, dess-pay-*n'yar*, v., to precipitate

desperdiciar, dess-pair-de-the-*ar*, v., to squander; to waste   [scatter

desperdigar, dess-pair-de-*gar*, v., to separate; to

desperezarse, dess-pay-ray-*thar*-say, v., to stretch one's limbs   [rioration

desperfecto, dess-pair-*fek*-to, s., blemish; deteri-

despernado, dess-pair-*nah*-do, a., weary

despertar, dess-pair-*tar*, v., to awake

despiadado, dess-ah-**dah**-do, a., unmerciful
despierto, dess-pe-**air**-to, a., awake
despilfarrar, dess-pil-far-**rrar**, v., to squander
despintar, dess-pin-**tar**, v., to efface; to blot; to fade [displeasure
desplacer, dess-plah-**thair**, v., to displease. s.,
desplegar, dess-play-**gar**, v., to unfold; to display
desplomarse, dess-plo-**mar**-say, v., to fall to the ground; to collapse [pluck
desplumar, dess-ploo-**mar**, v., to deplume; to
despoblar, dess-po-**blar**, v., to depopulate
despojar, dess-po-**Har**, v., to despoil
despojo, dess-po-**Ho**, s., spoliation. pl., giblets
desposado, dess-po-**sah**-do, a., newly married
desposar, dess-po-**sar**, v., to marry; to betroth
desposeer, dess-po-say-**air**, v., to dispossess
desposorios, dess-po-**so**-re-os, s., betrothal
déspota, dess-po-tah, s., despot
despreciable, dess-pray-the-**ah**-blay, a., despicable; contemptable
despreciar, dess-pray-the-**ar**, v., to despise
desprecio, dess-**pray**-the-o, s., scorn; contempt
desprender, dess-pren-**dair**, v., to unfasten; to separate [interestedness] landslide
desprendimiento, dess-pren-de-me-**en**-to, s., dis-
desprevención, dess-pray-ven-the-**on**, s., improvidence [vided] unprepared
desprevenido, dess-pray-vay-**nee**-do a., unpro-
desproporción, dess-pro-por-the-**on**, s., dispropor-
despropósito, dess-pro-**po**-se-to, s., absudity [tion
desprovisto, dess-pro-**viss**-to, a., unprovided
después, dess-poo'**ess**, adv., after; afterwards, next
despuntar, dess-poon-**tar**, v., to blunt; to bud
desquitar, dess-ke-**tar**, v., to retrieve a loss; to retaliate [venge
desquite, dess-**kee**-tay, s., recovery of a loss; re-
destacamento, dess-tah-kah-**men**-to, s., detach-
destacar, dess-tah-**kar**, v., to detach [ment
destajo, dess-**tah**-Ho, s., piece-work
destapar, dess-tah-**par**, v., to uncover
destello, dess-**tay**-l'yo, s., sparkle; flash
desteñir, dess-**tay**-n'yeer, v., to discolour

desterrar, dess-tair-**rrar**, to exile; to banish

destiempo, dess-te-**em**-po, adv., **a —**, ah —, unseasonably

destierro, dess-te-**air**-rro, s., exile; banishment

destilar, dess-te-**lar**, v., to distil

destinar, dess-te-**nar**, v., to destine

destino, dess-**tee**-no, s., destiny; fate; profession

destituir, dess-te-too-**eer**, v., to deprive; to dis-

destorcer, dess-tor-**thair**, v., to untwist   [miss

destornillado, dess-tor-ne-l'**yah**-do, a., heedless

destornillador, dess-tor-ne-l'**yah**-dor, s., screw-
driver   [act or speak rashly

destornillar, dess-tor-ne-l'**yar**, v., to unscrew; to

destrabar, dess-trah-**bar**, v., to unfasten; to sepa-

destramar, dess-trah-**mar**, v., to unweave   [rate

destreza, dess-**tray**-thah, s., dexterity; skill

destripar, dess-tre-**par**, v., to eviscerate; to crush

destrozar, dess-tro-**thar**, v., to destroy; to break
into pieces

destrucción, dess-trook-the-**on**, s., destruction

destruir, dess-troo-**eer**, v., to destroy; to waste

desunir, day-soo-**neer**, v., to separate

desusar, day-soo-**sar**, v., to disuse

desvaído, dess-vah-**ee**-do, a., pallid

desválido, dess-vah-**lee**-do, a., helpless; destitute

desván, dess-**vahn**, s., garret; loft

desvanecer, dess-vah-nay-**thair**, v., to disintegrate; to cause to evanesce; to vanish

desvanecimiento, dess-vah-nay-the-me-**en**-to, s.,
giddiness; dizziness   [delirious

desvariar, dess-vah-re-**ar**, v., to rave; to be

desvarío, dess-vah-**ree**-o, s., delirium; caprice

desvelar, dess-vay-**lar**, v., to keep awake

desvencijado, dess-ven-the-**H**ah-do, a., rickety;
shaky

desventaja, dess-ven-**tah**-Hah, s., disadvantage

desventajoso, dess-ven-tah-**H**o-so, a., disadvantageous

desventura, dess-ven-**too**-rah, s., misfortune

desventurado, dess-ven-too-**rah**-do, a., unfortunate   [dent; shameless

desvergonzado, dess-vair-gon-**thah**-do, a., impu-

desvergüenza, dess-vair-goo'**en**-thah, s., shamelessness; effrontery [track

desvío, dess-**vee**-o, s., deviation; aversion; side-

detallar, day-tah-l'**yar**, v., to detail; to relate

detalle, day-tah-l'yay, s., detail [minutely

detallista, day-tah-l'**yiss**-tah, s., retailer

detener, day-tay-**nair**, v., to detain; to tarry

detenido, day-tay-nee-do, a., niggardly; irresolute

detentar, day-ten-**tar**, v., to keep unlawfully

detergente, day-tair-*H*en-tay, s., detergent

deteriorar, day-tay-re-o-**rar**, v., to deteriorate

determinar, day-tair-me-**nar**, v., to determine

detersión, day-tair-se-on, s., cleansing a sore

detersivo, day-tair-see-yo, s., detergent

detestar, day-tess-**tar**, v., to detest

detractar, day-trak-**tar**, v., to detract

detraer, day-trah-**air**, v., to take away; to defame

detrás, day-**trahs**, adv., behind; after

detrimento, day-tre-**men**-to, s., detriment

deuda, day'oo-dah, s., debt

deudo, day'oo-do, s., parent

deudor, day'oo-**dor**, s., debtor

devanar, day-vah-**nar**, v., to reel; to spool

devanear, day-vah-nay-**ar**, v., to rave

devastar, day-vahs-**tar**, v., to devastate; to ravage

devengar, day-ven-**gar**, v., to earn

devoción, day-vo-the-**on**, s., devotion; piety

devolver, day-vol-**vair**, v., to return; to restore

devorar, day-vo-**rar**, v., to devour

devoto, day-**vo**-to, a., devout; devoted

devuelto, day-voo'**el**-to, a., returned

día, dee-**ah**, s., day, — **de años,** — day ah-n'yos, birthday, — **útil,** — oo-til, working day

diablo, de-**ah**-blo, s., devil

diáfano, de-ah-fah-no, a., transparent

dialéctica, de-ah-**lek**-te-kah, s., dialectics

diálogo, de-**ah**-lo-go, s., dialogue

diamante, de-ah-**mahn**-tay, s., diamond

diario, de-ah-re-o, s., daily paper; diary. a., daily

diarrea, de-ar-**rray**-ah, s., diarrhœa [sketch

dibujar, de-boo-*H*ar, v., to draw; to design; to

diccionario, dik-the-o-**nah**-re-o, s., dictionary

diciembre, de-the-**em**-bray, s., December

dictado, dik-**tah**-do, s., dictation

dictamen, dik-**tah**-men, s., opinion; judgment

dictar, dik-**tar**, v., to dictate

dicho, dee-cho, s., saying; sentence. a., said

dichoso, de-cho-so, a., happy

diecinueve, de-eth-e-noo'**ay**-vay, s., & a., nineteen

diente, de-**en**-tay, s., tooth; fang

diestra, de-**ess**-trah, s., right hand

diestro*, de-**ess**-tro, a., right; dexterous; skilful

dieta, de-**ay**-tah, s., diet

dietario, de-ay-**tah**-re-o, s., record book

diez, de-**eth**, s. & a., ten

diezmo, de-**eth**-mo, s., tithe; tenth part

difamar, de-fah-**mar**, v., to defame

diferente*, de-fay-**ren**-tay, a., different

diferir, de-fay-**reer**, v., to delay; to differ

difícil, de-**fee**-thil, a., difficult; hard

dificultad, de-fe-kool-**tahd**, s., difficulty

dificultoso, de-fe-kool-**to**-so, a., difficult

difidente, de-fe-**den**-tay, a., diffident; distrustful

difundir, de-foon-**deer**, v., to diffuse; to divulge

difunto, de-**foon**-to, a., defunct; late

difuso, de-**foo**-so, a., diffuse

digerible, de-**H**ay-**ree**-blay, a., digestible

digerir, de-**H**ay-**reer**, v., to digest

digital, de-**H**e-**tahl**, s., foxglove. a., digital

dígito, dee-**H**e-to, s., digit

dignarse, dig-**nar**-say, v., to deign

dignidad, dig-ne-**dahd**, s., dignity

dignificar, dig-ne-fe-**kar**, v., to dignify

digno, dig-no, a., worthy; deserving

dije, dee-**H**ay, s., relic; child's trinkets. pl., toys

dilacerar, de-lah-thay-**rar**, v., to dilacerate

dilación, de-lah-the-**on**, s., delay

dilapidar, de-lah-pe-**dar**, v., to dilapidate

dilatar, de-lah-**tar**, v., to dilate; to protract

dilección, de-lek-the-**on**, s., affection; love

dilecto, de-**lek**-to, a., loved; beloved

diligente*, de-le-**H**en-tay, a., diligent

dilogía, de-lo-**H**ee-ah, s., ambiguity

diluir, de-loo'**eer**, v., to dilute

diluviar, de-loo-ve-**ar**, v., to rain like a deluge
diluvio, de-**loo**-ve-o, s., deluge; flood
dimanación, de-mah-nah-the-**on**, s., issuing from
dimanar, de-mah-**nar**, v., to emanate; to spring
diminuir, de-me-noo-**eer**, v., to diminish [from
diminuto*, de-me-**noo**-to, a., very small
dimisión, de-me-se-**on**, s., resignation
dimitir, de-me-**teer**, v., to resign
dinero, de-**nay**-ro, s., coin; money; coinage
dintel, din-**tel**, s., lintel
diócesis, de-**o**-thay-siss, s., diocese
Dios, de-**os**, s., God
diosa, de-**o**-sah, s., goddess
diplomático, de-plo-**mah**-te-ko, a., diplomatic
diputado, de-poo-**tah**-do, s., deputy; assignee;
M.P.
diputar, de-poo-**tar**, v., to depute; to constitute
dique, dee-kay, s., dike
dirección, de-rek-the-**on**, s., direction; guidance;
address
directo, de-**rek**-to, a., straight; direct [age
dirigir, de-re-**Heer**, v., to direct; to guide; to man-
dirimir, de-re-**meer**, v., to dissolve; to annul
discernimiento, diss-thair-ne-me-**en**-to, s., discernment
discernir, diss-thair-**neer**, v., to discern; to discriminate
disciplina, diss-the-**plee**-nah, s., discipline; in-
discípulo, diss-**thee**-poo-lo, s., disciple [struction
disco, **diss**-ko, s., disk
discordar, diss-kor-**dar**, v., to disagree; to discard
discorde, diss-**kor**-day, a., discordant
discrecional, diss-kray-the-o-**nahl**, a., optional
discrepar, diss-kray-**par**, v., to differ
disculpa, diss-**kool**-pah, s., excuse; apology
disculpar, diss-kool-**par**, v., exculpate; to apologize
discurrir, diss-koor-**rreer**, v., to ramble about;
to discuss; to contrive
discursar, diss-koor-**sar**, v., to discourse
discurso, diss-**koor**-so, s., discourse; space of time
discutible, diss-koo-**tee**-blay, a., controvertible;
disputable

discutir, diss-koo-**teer**, v., to discuss

disecar, de-say-**kar**, v., to dissect

diseminar, de-say-me-**nar**, v., disseminate

disensión, de-sen-se-**on**, s., dissension

disentería, de-sen-tay-**ree**-ah, s., dysentery

disentimiento, de-sen-te-me-**en**-to, s., dissent

diseñar, de-say-n'**yar**, v., to sketch; to outline

diseño, de-**say**-n'yo, s., drawing; design; sketch

disertar, de-sair-**tar**, v., discourse; to debate; to argue

diserto, de-**sair**-to, s., eloquent; fluent [ed

disforme, diss-**for**-may, a., hideous; huge; deform-

disfraz, diss-**frath**, s., mask; disguise; dissimula-

disfrute, diss-**froo**-tay, s., use; enjoyment [tion

disgustar, diss-gooss-**tar**, v., to disgust; to displease; to dislike

disgusto, diss-**goos**-to, s., disgust; displeasure

disidente, de-se-**den**-tay, s. & a., dissent; dissenter

disimular, de-se-moo-**lar**, v., to dissemble; to over-

disipar, de-se-**par**, v., to dissipate [look

dislocar, diss-lo-**kar**, v., to dislocate

disoluto, de-so-**loo**-to, a., dissolute

disolver, de-sol-**vair**, v., to dissolve; to melt

disparado*, diss-pah-**rah**-do, a., precipitate

disparar, diss-pah-**rar**, v., to shoot; to fire [ish

disparatado, diss-pah-rah-**tah**-do, a., absurd; fool-

disparatar, diss-pah-rah-**tar**, v., to act or talk absurdly; to blunder

disparate, diss-pah-**rah**-tay, s., nonsense; absurdity; blunder

disparidad, diss-pah-re-**dahd**, s., disparity

disparo, diss-**pah**-ro, s., discharge; nonsense

dispendioso, diss-pen-de-**o**-so, a., expensive

dispensa, diss-**pen**-sah, s., exemption; dispensation

dispensar, diss-pen-**sar**, v., to dispense; to dispense with; to deal out

dispersar, diss-pair-**sar**, v., to scatter; to rout

disperso, diss-**pair**-so, a., dispersed; scattered

displicencia, diss-ple-**then**-the-ah, s., displeasure

displicente, diss-ple-**then**-tay, a., displeasing; peevish; fretful

disponer, diss-po-**nair**, v., to dispose; to arrange; to prepare; to distribute; to regulate

disponible, diss-po-**nee**-blay, a., disposable

dispuesto, diss-poo-**ess**-to, a., disposed; ready; comely

disputa, diss-**poo**-tah, s., dispute; controversy

disputar, diss-poo-**tar**, v., to dispute; to argue

distancia, diss-**tahn**-the-ah, s., distance

distar, diss-**tar**, v., to be distant; to be different

distinción, diss-tin-the-**on**, s., distinction

distinguir, diss-tin-**gheer**, v., to distinguish

distinto*, diss-**teen**-to, a., distinct

distraer, diss-trah-**air**, v., to distract; to amuse

distraído, diss-trah'**ee**-do, a., absent-minded; heedless

distribuir, diss-tre-boo'**eer**, v., to distribute; to sort

distrito, diss-**tree**-to, s., district [sort

disturbio, diss-**toor**-be-o, s., disturbance

disuadir, de-soo'ah-**deer**, v., to dissuade

diurno, dee'**oor**-no, a., diurnal

divagar, de-vah-**gar**, v., to ramble; to digress

divergente, de-vair-**Hen**-tay, a., divergent

divergir, de-vair-**Heer**, v., to diverge

diversidad, de-vair-se-**dahd**, s., diversity

diversión, de-vair-se-**on**, s., diversion; recreation

diverso, de-**vair**-so, a., diverse; different

diversos, de-**vair**-sos, a., several; sundry

divertir, de-vair-**teer**, v., to divert; to amuse

dividendo, de-ve-**den**-do, s., dividend

dividir, de-ve-**deer**, v., to divide; to separate

divieso, de-ve-**ay**-so, s., furuncle; boil

divino, de-**vee**-no, a., divine

divisa, de-**vee**-sah, s., badge; motto; mark

divisar, de-ve-**sar**, v., to perceive indistinctly

divorciar, de-vor-the-**ar**, v., to divorce

divocio, de-**vor**-the-o, s., divorce; disunion

divulgar, de-vool-**gar**, v., to divulge

dobladillo, do-blah-**dee**-l'yo, s., hem

doblado, do-**blah**-do, a., thick-set; deceitful

dobladura, do-blah-**doo**-rah, s., fold; crease

doblar*, do-**blar**, v., to double

doble*, do-**blay**, a., double; thick-set; artful

doblez, do-**bleth**, s., fold; crease; duplicity
doblón, do-**blon**, s., doubloon (ancient Spanish [gold coin]
doce, do-**thay**, s. & a., twelve
docena, do-**thay**-nah, s., dozen
doceno, do-**thay**-no, a., twelfth
dócil, do-**thil**, a., docile
docto, **dok**-to, a., learned
doctor, dok-**tor**, s., doctor; physician
doctrina, dok-**tree**-nah, s., doctrine
doctrinar, dok-tre-**nar**, v., to teach; to instruct
doctrinero, dok-tre-**nay**-ro, s., catechist
documento, do-koo-**men**-to, s., document
dogo, **do**-go, s., terrier; bulldog
dolar, do-**lar**, v., to plane; to smooth
dolencia, do-**len**-the-ah, s., affliction; ailment
doler, do-**lair**, v., to ache; to hurt [complain
dolerse, do-**lair**-say, v., to repent; to feel for; to
doliente, do-le-**en**-tay, a., suffering: sorrowful
dolor, do-**lor**, s., pain; aching; grief
dolorido, do-lo-**ree**-do, a., doleful
doloroso, do-lo-**ro**-so, a., sorrowful; painful
doloso, do-**lo**-so, a., deceitful
domador, do-mah-**dor**, s., tamer; horse-breaker
domar, do-**mar**, v., to tame; to subdue
domeñar, do-may-n'**yar**, v., to reclaim; to master
domesticar, do-mess-te-**kar**, v., to domesticate
doméstico, do-**mess**-te-ko, s., domestic servant.
  a., domestic
domiciliarse, do-me-the-le-**ar**-say, v., to take up
  residence
domicilio, do-me-**thee**-le-o, s., domicile
dominar, do-me-**nar**, v., to domineer; to sway
domingo, do-**meen**-go, s., Sunday [estate
dominio, do-**mee**-ne-o, s., dominion; territory;
dominó, do-me-**no**, s., domino
don, don, s., title for a gentleman; equivalent to
  Mr., but used only before Christian names
donador, do-nah-**dor**, s., donor; giver
donaire, do-**nah**'e-ray, s., grace; elegance
donatario, do-nah-**tee**-re-o, s., grantee
donativo, do-nah-**tee**-vo, s., free contribution; gift
doncella, don-**thel**-l'yah, s., maid; virgin; lass

doncellez, don-thel-l'**yeth,** s., maidenhood
donde, don-day, adv., where, **de—,** day—, from what place? **—quiera,** — ke-**ay**-rah, anywhere
dondiego, don-de-ay-go, s., jalap; marvel of Peru
donoso, do-**no**-so, a., graceful; pleasant
doña, do-n'yah, s., lady; Mrs. (used only before a Christian name)
dorado, do-**rah**-do, a., gilt; gilded
dorar, do-**rar,** v., to gild; to palliate
dormidero, dor-me-**day**-ro, a., sleepy; narcotic
dormir, dor-**meer,** v., to sleep
dormitar, dor-me-**tar,** v., to doze
dormitorio, dor-me-**to**-re-o, s., dormitory; bed-room [room
dorso, dor-so, s., back part
dos, doss, s. & a., two
dosel, do-**sel,** s., canopy
dosis, do-siss, s., dose
dotar, do-**tar,** v., to endow
dote, do-tay, s., dowry. pl., talents
draga, draga, drah-gah, s., dredge
dragón, drah-**gon,** s., dragon; dragoon
dramático, drah-**mah**-te-ko, a., dramatical
drástico, drahs-te-ko, a., drastic
drenaje, dray-**nah**-Hay, s., draining; drainage
droga, dro-gah, s., drug
droguería, dro-gay-**ree**-ah, s., drug store or trade
droguero, dro-**gay**-ro, s., druggist
dual, doo-**ahl,** a., dual
dualidad, doo-ah-le-**dahd,** s., duality
dubitativo, doo-be-tah-**tee**-vo, a., doubtful
ducado, doo-**kah**-do, s., duchy; dukedom; ducat
ducéntesimo, doo-**then**-tay-se-mo, a., two hundredth
dúctil, dook-til, a., ductile [dredth
ducha, doo-chah, s., shower-bath
duda, doo-dah, s., doubt; suspense
dudable, doo-**dah**-blay, a., dubious; doubtful
dudar, doo-**dar,** v., to doubt
dudoso, doo-**do**-so, a., doubtful; uncertain
duelo, doo'ay-lo, s., duel; sorrow; mourning
duende, doo'**enn**-day, s., elf; hobgoblin; ghost
dueña, doo'**ay**-n'yah, s., duenna; married lady; proprietress

dueño, doo-**ay**-n'yo, s., owner; master
dueto, doo-**ay**-to, s., duet
dulce*, dool-thay, a., sweet; mild; gentle
dulcedumbre, doo-thay-**doom**-bray, s., sweetness
dulzura, dool-**thoo**-rah, s., sweetness; gentleness;
duna, doo-nah, s., dune   [graciousness
dúo, doo'o, s., duet
duodécimo, doo'o-**day**-the-mo, a., twelfth
duplicado, doo-ple-**kah**-do, s., duplicate
duplicar, doo-ple-**kar**, v., to double; to duplicate;
    to repeat
duplicidad, doo-ple-the-**dahd**, s., duplicity
duplo, doo-plo, a., double; duplicate
duque, doo-kay, s., duke
duquesa, doo-**kay**-sah, s., duchess
durable, doo-rah-blay, a., lasting; durable
duración, doo-rah-the-**on**, s., duration
duradero, doo-rah-**day**-ro, a., lasting
durante, doo-**rahn**-tay, adv., while; during
durar, doo-**rar**, v., to last; to endure
durazno, doo-**rath**-no s., peach   [losity
dureza, doo-**ray**-thah, s., hardness; obstinacy; cal-
durmiente, door-me-**en**-tay, a., dormant; s.,
    (railways) sleeper
duro, doo-ro, s., dollar. a*., hard; harsh

!ea! ay-ah, interj., come now!
ebanista, ay-bah-**niss**-tah, s., cabinet-maker
ébano, ay-bah-no, s., ebony
ebrio, ay-bre-o, a., intoxicated
eclipse, ay-**kleep**-say, s., eclipse
eco, ay-ko, s., echo
economía, ay-ko-no-**mee**-ah, s., economy
económo, ay-ko-no-mo, s., curator; trustee
ecuador, ay-koo'ah-**dor**, s., equator   [mity
ecuanimidad, ay-koo'ah-ne-me-**dahd**, s., equani-
ecuestre, ay-koo-**ess**-tray, a., equestrian
echada, ay-**chah**-dah, s., cast; throw
echar, ay-**char**, v., to cast; to throw; to cast away
edad, ay-**dahd**, s., age
edición, ay-de-the-**on**, s., edition; issue
edicto, ay-**deek**-to, s., edict

edificar, ay-de-fe-**kar**, v., to build; to edify
edificio, ay-de-**fee**-the-o, s., edifice, building
editor, ay-de-**tor**, s., publisher; editor
educación, ay-doo-kah-the-**on**, s., education
educar, ay-doo-**kar**, v., to educate
educir, ay-doo-**theer**, v., to educe; to bring out
efectivo, ay-fek-**tee**-vo, a., effective
efecto, ay-**fek**-to, s., effect
efectos, ay-**fek**-tos, s., effects; goods
efectuar, ay-fek-too′**ar**, v., to execute; to effect
efemérides, ay-fay-**may**-re-dess, s., ephemeris
eficacia, ay-fe-**kah**-the-ah, s., efficacy
eficaz, ay-fe-**kath**, a., efficacious
eficiencia, ay-fe-the-**en**-the-ah, s., efficiency
eficiente*, ay-fe-the-**en**-tay, a., efficient
efímero, ay-**fee**-may-ro, a., ephemeral
egoísmo, ay-go-**iss**-mo, s., selfishness
egregio, ay-**gray**-He-o, a., egregious; eminent
egreso, ay-**gray**-so, s., expense; debit
eje, ay-**Hay**, s., axis; axle-tree   [formance
ejecución, ay-**Hay**-koo-the-**on**, s., execution; per-
ejecutar, ay-**Hay**-koo-**tar**, v., to execute; to per-
     form
ejecutor, ay-**Hay**-koo-**tor**, s., executor; executioner
ejemplar, ay-**Hem**-**plar**, s., exemplar; copy; pat-
     tern. a., exemplary
ejemplo, ay-**Hem**-plo, s., example; pattern
ejercer, ay-**Hair**-**thair**, v., to exercise; to practise
ejercicio, ay-**Hair**-**thee**-the-o, s., exercise; office
ejercitar, ay-**Hair**-the-**tar**, v., to exercise
ejército, ay-**Hair**-the-to, s., army
ejido, ay-**Hee**-do, s., common; public land
el, ell, masculine article, the
elaborar, ay-lah-bo-**rar**, v., to elaborate
elación, ay-lah-the-**on**, s., elation
elástico, ay-**lahs**-te-ko, a., elastic
elección, ay-lek-the-**on**, s., election; choice
electo, ay-**lek**-to, s., elect. a., chosen; elect
electricidad, ay-lek-tre-the-**dahd**, s., electricity
eléctrico, ay-**lek**-tre-ko, a., electric
electrónico, ay-lek-**tro**-ne-ko, a., electronic
elefante, ay-lay-**fahn**-tay, s., elephant

elegancia, ay-lay-**gahn**-the-ah, s., elegance; neatness

elegante, ay-lay-**gahn**-tay, a., elegant; graceful

elegible, ay-lay-**Hee**-blay, a., eligible

elegir, ay-lay-**Heer**, v., to elect; to select

elemento, ay-lay-**men**-to, s., element

elenco, ay-len-ko, s., catalogue; index; list [rise

elevación, ay-lay-vah-the-**on**, s., elevation; height;

elevado, ay-lay-vah-do, a., elevated; exalted

elevar, ay-lay-**var**, v., to raise; to lift; to exalt

elocución, ay-lo-koo-the-**on**, s., elocution

elocuente, ay-lo-koo'**en**-tay, a., eloquent

elogiar, ay-lo-**He-ar**, v., to praise

elogio, ay-lo-**He**-o, s., eulogy; praise

elucidar, ay-loo-the-**dar**, v., to elucidate

eludir, ay-loo-**deer**, v., to elude

ella, ell-yah, pron., she

ello, ell-yo, pron., it

emanar, ay-mah-**nar**, v., to emanate

embadurnar, em-bah-door-**nar**, v., to besmear

embaimiento, em-bah'e-me-en-to, s., delusion; imposture

embajada, em-bah-**Hah**-dah, s., embassy

embajador, em8bah-**Hah**-dor, s., ambassador

embalaje, em-bah-**lah**-Hay, s., packing; package

embalar, em-bah-**lar**, v., to pack [perfume

embalsamar, em-bahl-sah-**mar**, v., to embalm; to

embarazada, em-bah-rah-**thah**-dah, a., pregnant

embarazar, em-bah-rah-**thar**, v., to embarrass

embarazo, em-bah-rah-tho, s., embarrassment; pregnancy [tangled; embarrassing

embarazoso, em-bah-rah-**tho**-so, a., difficult; en-

embarcación, em-bar-kah-the-**on**, s., embarkation; craft; ship [wharf

embarcadero, em-bar-kah-**day**-ro, s., quay;

embarcar, em-bar-**kar**, v., to embark

embargador, em-bar-gah-**dor**, s., sequestrator

embargar, em-bar-**gar**, v., to sieze; to restrain

embargo, em-**bar**-go, s., embargo; sequestration

embarnizar, em-bar-ne-**thar**, v., to varnish

embarque, em-**bar**-kay, s., shipment [aground

embarrancarse, em-bar-rrahn-**kar**-say, v., to run

embarrar, em-bar-**rrar,** v., to plaster; to debauch
embastar, em-bahs-**tar,** v., to baste; to stitch
embate, em-**bah**-tay, s., dashing of the waves
embaucar, em-bah'oo-**kar,** v., to impose upon;
embaular, em-bah'oo-**lar,** v., to cram [to trick
embeber, em-bay-**bair,** v., to imbibe; to contain
embelecar, em-bay-lay-**kar,** v., to deceive
embeleco, em-bay-**lay**-ko, s., fraud [cinate
embelesar, em-bay-ay-**sar,** v., to charm; to fas-
embellecer, em-bay-l'yay-**thair,** v., to embellish
embellecimiento, em-bay-l'yay-the-me-**en**-to, s.,
  adornment
embestida, em-bess-**tee**-dah, s., assault, charge
embestir, em-bess-**teer,** v., to assail
embobado, em-bo-**bah**-do, a., spell-bound
embobar, em-bo-**bar,** b., to amuse
embobarse, em-bo-**bar**-say, v., to stand gaping
embocadura, em-bo-kah-**doo**-rah, s., mouth-piece
embolsar, em-bol-**sar,** v., to put money in a purse;
  to imburse
emborrachar, em-bor-rrah-**char,** v., to intoxicate
emboscada, em-boss-**kah** dah, s., ambuscade; am-
embotado, em-bo-**tah**-do, a., blunt, dull [bush
embotar, em-bo-**tar,** v., to blunt
embotellamiento, em-bo-tay-l'yah-me-**en**-to, s.,
  traffic jam
embotellar, em-bo-tay-l'**yar,** v., to bottle
embozo, em-bo-tho, s., muffler
embragar, em-brah-**gar,** v., to clutch
embravecer, em-brah-vay-**thair,** v., to irritate
embriagar, em-bre-ah-**gar,** v., to intoxicate; to
embridar, em-bre-**dar,** v., to bridle [enrapture
embrocar, em-bro-**kar,** v., to decant
embrollar, em-bro-l'**yar,** v., to embroil
embrollo, em-**bro**-l'yo, s., trickery; tangle
embromado, em-bro-**mah**-do, a., misty; hazy;
  vexed
embromar, em-bro-**mar,** v., to wheedle; to chaff
embrujar, em-broo-Har, v., to bewitch
embrutecer, em-broo-tay-**thair,** v., to stupefy
embuchado, em-boo-**chah**-do, s., large pork saus-
embudo, em-**boo**-do, s., funnel [age

embuste, em-**booss**-tay, s., artful tale; lie
embustero, em-booss-**tay**-ro, s., liar; cheat
embutido, em-boo-**tee**-do, s., sausage
emergencia, ay-mair-_H_en-the-ah, s., emergency
emigrar, ay-me-**grar**, v., to emigrate
eminencia, ay-me-**nen**-the-ah, s., eminence
eminente*, ay-me-**nen**-tay, a., eminent
emisario, ay-me-**sah**-re-o, s., emissary
emisión, ay-me-se-**on**, s., emission; issue
emitir, ay-me-**teer**, v., to emit; to issue
emoción, ay-mo-the-**on**, s., emotion
empacar, em-pah-**kar**, v., to pack up
empachar, em-pah-**char**, v., to embarrass; to cram
empacho, em-**pah**-cho, s., bashfulness; embarrassment   [payers
empadronar, em-pah-dro-**nar**, v., to register tax
empalagar, em-pah-lah-**gar**, v., to cloy; to surfeit
empalagoso, em-pah-lah-**go**-so, a., cloying; annoy-
empalar, em-pah-**lar**, v., to impale   [ing
empalizada, em-pah-le-**thah**-dah, s., palisade
empalmar, em-pahl-**mar**, v., to dovetail; to couple
empalme, em-**pahl**-may, s., (railway) branch-line; junction
empanada, em-pah-**nah**-dah, s., meat-pie
empañar, em-pah-**n'yar**, v., to blur
empapar, em-pah-**par**, v., to imbibe; to soak
empapelar, em-pah-pay-**lar**, v., to wrap in paper
empaque, em-**pah**-kay, s., packing; appearance
empaquetar, em-pah-kay-**tar**, v., to pack   [mure
emparedar, em-pah-ray-**dar**, v., to confine; to im-
emparejar, em-pah-ray-_H_ar, v., to level; to match;
emparrado, em-par-**rrah**-do, s., bower   [to equal
empastar, em-pahs-**tar**, v., to paste; to impaste
empatar, em-pah-**tar**, v., to equal; to tie; to draw
empate, em-**pah**-tay, s., equality of votes; suspension
empedernir, em-pay-dair-**neer**, v., to harden
empedrado, em-pay-**drah**-do, s., stone pavement
empedrar, em-pay-**drar**, v., to pave
empegado, em-pay-**gah**-do, s., tarpaulin
empegar, em-pay-**gar**, v., to pitch

empeine, em-**pay**'e-nay, s., groin; instep; hoof

empellón, em-pay-l'**yon,** s., push; heavy blow

empeñado, em-pay-n'**yah**-do, a., in debt

empeñar, em-pay-n'**yar,** v., to pawn; to oblige

empeño, em-**pay**-n'yo, s., pledge; engagement; determination

empeorar, em-pay-o-**rar,** v., to impair; to grow [worse

emperador, em-pay-rah-**dor,** s., emperor

emperatriz, em-pay-rah-**treeth,** s., empress

empero, em-**pay**-ro, conj., yet; however

emperrarse, em-pair-**rrar**-say, v., to persist obstinately in

empezar, em-pay-**thar,** v., to begin

empinar, em-pe-**nar,** v., to raise; to drink much

emplastar, em-plahs-**tar,** v., to plaster; to obstruct

emplazar, em-plah-**thar,** v., to summon

empleado, em-play-**ah**-do, s., employee

emplear, em-play-**ar,** v., to employ; to invest

empleo, em-**play**-o, s., employment; investment

emplomador, em-plo-mah-**dor,** s., plumber

emplomar, em-plo-**mar,** v., to plumb

empobrecer, em-po-bray-**thair,** v., to impoverish

empolvar, em-pol-**var,** v., to powder

emponzoñamiento, em-pom-tho-n'yah-me-**en**-to, s., poisoning

emponzoñar, em-pon-tho-n'**yar,** v., to poison

emporcar, em-por-**kar,** v., to soil; to foul

emporio, em-**po**-re-o, s., emporium

emprender, em-pren-**dair,** v., to undertake

empresa, em-**pray**-sah, s., undertaking; firm

empresario, em-pray-**sah**-re-o, s., manager (of a theatre)

empréstito, em-**press**-te-to, s., loan

empujar, em-poo-**Har,** v., to push; to impel

empuje, em-poo-**Hay,** s., impulsion; push

empujón, em-poo-**Hon,** s., violent shove; push

empuñar, em-poo-n'**yar,** v., to grasp; to grip with [the fist

emular, ay-moo-**lar,** v., to emulate

émulo, **ay**-moo-lo, s., competitor; rival

emulsión, ay-mool-se-**on,** s., emulsion

en, en, prep., in; for; on; upon; at; into

enaguas, ay-**nah**-goo'ahs, s., under-skirt

enajenación, ay-nah-*Hay*-nah-the-*on*, s., alienation; absence of mind; insanity

enajenar, ay-nah-*Hay*-**nar**, v., to alienate

enamorado*, ay-nah-mo-**rah**-do, a., in love

enamorar, ay-nah-mo-**rar**, v., to inspire love

enano, ay-**nah**-no, s., dwarf. a., dwarfish

enarbolar, ay-nar-bo-**lar**, v., to hoist

enardecer, ay-nar-day-**thair**, v., to inflame

encabezamiento, en-kah-bay-thah-me-**en**-to, s., heading; title; tax-roll

encabezar, en-kah-bay-**thar**, v., to put a heading or title; to lead

encabritarse, en-kah-bre-**tar**-say, v., to rear up

encadenar, en-kah-day-**nar**, v., to chain; to link; to shackle

encajar, en-kah-*Har*, v., to incase

encaje, en-kah-*Hay*, s., incasing; lace; inlaid work

encajonar, en-kah-*Ho*-**nar**, v., to pack in a box

encandilar, en-kahn-de-**lar**, v., to dazzle

encantador, en-kahn-tah-**dor**, s., enchanter. a., charming

encantar, en-kahn-**tar**, v., to enchant; to delight

encanto, en-**kahn**-to, s., enchantment; delight

encañonar, en-kah-n'yo-**nar**, v., to put in a tube; to plait

encapotar, en-kah-po-**tar**, v., to cloak; to become cloudy

encapricharse, en-kah-pre-**char**-say, v., to be infatuated [hood

encapuchar, en-kah-poo-**char**, v., to cover with a

encarado, en-kah-**rah**-do, a., faced. **bien,mal**—, be-**en**, mahl—, good looking, ill looking

encaramar, en-kah-rah-**mar**, v., to climb

encarar, en-kah-**rar**, v., to face [onment

encarcelación, en-kar-thay-lah-the-**on**, s., imprisonment

encarcelar, en-kar-thay-**lar**, v., to imprison

encarecer, en-kah-ray-**thair**, v., to raise the price; to extol [hancement

encarecimiento, en-kah-ray-the-me-**en**-to, s., enhancement

encargado, de negocios, en-kar-**gah**-do day nay-**go**-the-os, s., chargé d'affaires; agent

encargar, en-kar-**gar**, v., to commission

encargo, en-kar-go, s., charge; commission
encariñarse, en-kah-re-n'yar-say, v., to become fond of [coloured]
encarnado, en-kar-nah-do, a., incarnate; flesh-
encarnecer, en-kar-nay-thair, v., to grow fat
encarnizar, en-kar-ne-thar, v., to irritate
encarrilar, en-kar-rre-lar, v., to direct; to set right
encartar, en-kar-tar, v., to proscribe; to summon
encastrar, en-kahs-trar, v., to enchase
encenagarse, en-thay-nah-gar-say, v., to wallow in mire
encender, en-then-dair, v., to kindle; to light
encendido, en-then-dee-do, a., inflamed; red
encendimiento, en-then-de-me-en-to, s., conflagration
encerado, en-thay-rah-do, s., oil-cloth; blackboard
encerrar, en-thair-rrar, v., to lock or shut up; to contain
enchufar, en-choo-far, v., to plug in
encía, en-thee-ah, s., gum (of the teeth)
encierro, en-the-air-rro, s., confinement; prison
encima, en-thee-mah, adv., above; over
encina, en-thee-nah, s., evergreen oak
enclavar, en-klah-var, v., to nail; to embed
enclavijar, en-klah-ve-Har, v., to peg
encoger, en-ko-Hair, v., to contract; to shrink
encogido*, en-ko-Hee-do, a., pusillanimous
encojar, en-ko-Har, v., to cripple
encolar, en-ko-lar, v., to glue
encolerizar, en-ko-lay-re-thar, v., to anger
encomendable, en-ko-men-dah-blay, a., commendable [entrust]
encomendar, en-ko-men-dar, v., to commend; to
encomiar, en-ko-me-ar, v., to praise
encomienda, en-ko-me-en-dah, s., commission; patronage. pl., compliments
enconar, en-ko-nar, v., to inflame; to irritate
encontrar, en-kon-trar, v., to meet; to encounter
encopetado, en-ko-pay-tah-do, a., boastful
encorvar, en-kor-var, v., to bend; to curve
encovar, en-ko-var, v., to put in a cellar; to conceal
encrespar, en-kress-par, v., to curl; to ruffle

encrucijada, en-kroo-the-*H*ah-'ah, s., crossway
encrudecer, en-kroo-day-**thair**, v., to exasperate
encuadernar, en-koo'ah-dair-**nar**, v., to bind
encubierto*, en-koo-be-**air**-to, a., hidden [books
encubrir, en-koo-**breer**, v., to hide; to cloak
encuentro, en-koo'en-tro, s., encounter; collision
encumbrado, en-ko-m-**brah**-do, a., elevated; lofty
encurtidos, en-koor-**tee**-dos, s., pickles
endeble, en-**day**-blay, a., feeble; weak
endemoniado, en-day-mo-ne-**ah**-do, a., devilish
enderezado,* en-day-ray-**thah**-do, a., fit; appropriate
enderezar, en-day-ray-**thar**, v., to straighten
endiablado, en-de-ah-**blah**-do, a., devilish
endibia, en-dee-be-ah, s., endive
endiosamiento, en-de-o-sah-me-**en**-to, s., haughtiness; ecstasy
endosador, en-do-sah-**dor**, s., endorser
endoso, en-**do**-so, s., endorsement
endulzar, en-dool-**thar**, v., to sweeten; to soften
endurecer, en-doo-ray-**thair**, v., to indurate; to
enebro, ay-nay-bro, s., juniper [harden
enemiga, ay-nay-**mee**-gah, s., enmity; ill-will
enemigo, ay-nay-**mee**-go, s., enemy, a., inimical
enemistad, ay-nay-miss-**tahd**, s., enmity
energía, ay-nair-*H*ee-ah, s., energy
enérgico, ay-nair-*H*e-ko, a., energetic
enero, ay-**nay**-ro, s., January
enervar, ay-nair-**var**, v., to enervate
enfadar, eh-fah-**dar**, v., to vex; to molest; to in-
enfado, en-**fah**-do, s., vexation; trouble [cense
enfadoso, en-fah-**do**-so, a., troublesome; vexatious
énfasis, **en**-fah-siss, s., emphasis
enfermar, en-fair-**mar**, v., to fall ill
enfermedad, en-fair-may-**dahd**, s., illness
enfermo, en-**fair**-mo, a., ill; sick; infirm
enfilar, en-fe-**lar**, v., to place in a line
enflaquecer, en-flah-kay-**thair**, v., to weaken; to become thin
enfrenar, en-fray-**nar**, v., to bridle; to curb
enfrente, en-**fren**-tay, adv., opposite
enfriar, en-fre-**ar**, v., to cool

enfurecer, en-foo-ray-**thair**, v., to make furious

engalanar, en-gah-lah-**nar**, v., to adorn

engallado, en-gah-l'**yah**-do, a., erect; upright; haughty

enganchar, en-gahn-**char**, v., to hook; to ensnare; [to enlist

engañabobos, en-gah-n'yah-**bo**-bos, s., impostor;

engañador, en-gah-n'yah-**dor**, s., cheat [foottrap

engañar, en-gah-n'**yar**, v., to cheat; to fool

engaño, en-**gah**-n'yo, s., mistake; deceit; hoax

engaste, en-**gahs**-tay s., enchasing

engendrar, en-Hen-**drar**, v., to engender

engolfado, en-gol-**fah**-do, a., engrossed; absorbed

engolosinar, en-go-lo-se-**nar**, v., to inspire a longing for; to allure

engomar, en-go-**mar**, v., to gum; to size

engordar, en-gor-**dar**, v., to fatten

engorro, en-**gor**-rro, s., embarrassment

engranaje, en-grah-**nah**-Hay, s., gear; gearing

engranar, en-grah-**nar**, v., to gear

engrandecer, en-grahn-day-**thair**, v., to enlarge

engrasar, en-grah-**sar**, v., to grease; to lubricate

engreimiento, en-gray'e-me-en-to, s., conceit

engullir, en-goo-l'**yeer**, v., to swallow

enharinar, en-ah-re-**nar**, v., to cover with flour

enhestar, en-ess-**tar**, v., to set upright

enhilar, en-e-**lar**, v., to thread; to direct

enhorabuena, en-o-rah-boo'**ay**-nah, adv., well and good. s., congratulation [hour

enhoramala, en-o-rah-**mah**-lah, adv., in an evil

enigmático, ay-nig-**mah**-te-ko, a., enigmatical

enjabonar, en-Hah-bo-**nar**, v., to soap [swarm

enjambrar, en-Ham-**brar**, v., to hive bees; to

enjaular, en-Hah'oo-**lar**, v., to cage; to imprison

enjoyar, en-Ho-**yar**, v., to adorn with jewels

enjuagar, en-Hoo'ah-**gar**, v., to rinse

enjugador, en-Hoo-gah-**dor**, s., clothes-horse

enjutar, en-Hoo-**tar**, v., to dry

enjuto, en-Hoo-to, a., dried; lean [link; affinity

enlace, en-**lah**-thay, s., connection; coherence;

enladrillado, en-lah-dre-l'**yah**-do, s., brick pavement [lace

enlazar, en-lah-**thar**, v., to unite; to bind; to

enlodar, en-lo-**dar**, v., to bemire; to stain

enloquecer, en-lo-kay-**thair**, v., to madden

enlucido, en-loo-**thee**-do, s., colour-wash

enlutar, en-loo-**tar**, v., to put into mourning

enmaderación, en-mah-day-rah-the-**on**, s., wood-work

enmarañar, en-mah-rah-n'**yar**, v., to entangle

enmascarar, en-mahs-kah-**rar**, v., to mask

enmendación, en-men-dah-the-**on**, s., emendation

enmendar, en-men-**dar**, v., to amend; to correct; to improve   [ward

enmienda, en-me-**en**-dah, s., amendment; re-

enmohecer, en-mo-ay-**thair**, v., to mould

enmudecer, en-moo-day-**thair**, v., to be silent

ennegrecer, en-nay-gray-**thair**, v., to blacken

enojadizo, ay-no-Hah-**dee**-tho, a., fretful; peevish

enojar, ay-no-**Har**, v., to anger; to tease

enojoso, ay-no-Ho-so, a., vexatious

enorme,* ay-**nor**-may, a., enormous

enormidad, ay-nor-me-**dahd**, s., enormity

enranciarse, en-rahn-the-**ar**-say, v., to grow rancid

enrarecer, en-rah-ray-**thair**, v., to rarefy

enrayar, en-rah-**yar**, v., to fix spokes in a wheel

enredar, en-ray-**dar**, v., to entangle; to ensnare; to puzzle

enredo, en-**ray**-do, s., entanglement; intricacy

enrejado, en-ray-Hah-do, s., trellis; railing

enriquecer, en-re-kay-**thair**, v., to enrich

enriscado, en-riss-kah-do, a., craggy

enrizar, en-re-**thar**, v., to curl

enrojecer, en-ro-Hay-**thair**, v., to make red-hot; to redden; to blush

enrollar, en-ro-l'**yar**, v., to roll; to wind; to coil

enronquecer, en-ron-kay-**thair**, v., to make hoarse

enroscar, en-ros-**kar**, v., to twist; to coil

ensalada, en-sah-**lah**-dah, s., salad; hodge-podge

ensaladera, en-sah-lah-**day**-rah, s., salad bowl

ensalmar, en-sahl-**mar**, v., to set bones

ensamblador, en-sahm-blah-**dor**, s., joiner   [gore

ensanche, en-**sahn**-chay, s., dilatation; widening;

ensañar, en-sah-n'**yar**, v., to irritate; to enrage

ensartar, en-sar-**tar**, v., to string; to thread

ensayar, en-sah-**yar**, v., to assay; to test; to rehearse

ensenada, en-say-**nah**-dah, s., creek

enseña, en-**say**-n'yah, s., standard; colours

enseñanza, en-say-n'**yahn**-thah, s., teaching

enseñar, en-say-n'**yar**, v., to teach

enseñorearse, en-say-n'yo-ray-**ar**-say, v., to possess oneself of [furniture

enseres, en-**say**-ress, s., chattels; implements;

ensillar, en-se-l'**yar**, v., to saddle

ensogar, en-so-**gar**, v., to fasten with a rope

ensopar, en-so-**par**, v., to steep bread in wine

ensordecer, en-sor-day-**thair**, v., to deafen

ensuciar, en-soo-the-**ar**, v., to defile; to pollute

entablar, en-tah-**blar**, v., to cover with boards; to start a negotiation; to initiate

entallador, en-tah-l'yah-**dor**, s., sculptor; engraver

entallar, en-tah-l'**yar**, v., to engrave

entallecer, en-tah-l'yay-**thair**, v., to shoot; to sprout

entapizar, en-tah-pe-**thar**, v., to hang with tapestry

ente, en-tay, s., being; entity

entendederas, en-ten-day-**day**-rahs, s., (fam.) understanding

entender, en-ten-**dair**, v., to understand; to judge

entendido, en-ten-**dee**-do, a., wise; learned

entendimiento, en-ten-de-me-**en**-to, s., understanding; knowledge

enterar, en-tay-**rar**, v., to inform; to instruct

entereza, en-tay-**ray**-thah, s., entireness; rectitude; perfection

enterizo, en-tay-**ree**-tho, a., entire; whole

enternecer, en-tair-nay-**thair**, v., to move to commiseration [passion

entero, en-tay-ro, a., entire; sound

enterramiento, en-tair-rrah-me-**en**-to, s., interment; burial

enterrar, en-tair-**rrar**, v., to inter; to bury

entibiar, en-te-be-**ar**, v., to make lukewarm

entidad, en-te-**dahd**, s., entity

entierro, en-te-**air**-rro, s., funeral; burial

entiznar, en-tith-**nar**, v., to revile; to stain

entoldar, en-tol-**dar**, v., to cover with awnings

entonación, en-to-nah-the-**on**, s., intonation

entonar, en-to-**nar**, v., to intone; to intonate

entonces, en-**ton**-thess, adv., then

entono, en-**to**-no, s., intonation; arrogance

entontecer, en-ton-tay-**thair**, v., to make foolish

entornar, en-tor-**nar**, v., to set ajar

entorpecer, en-tor-pay-**thair**, v., to stupefy; to [benumb

entrada, en-**trah**-dah, s., entrance

entrambos, en-**trahm**-bos, pron., both

entrampar, en-trahm-**par**, v., to entrap; to ensnare

entrañable, en-trahn-**yah**-blay, a., intimate; affectionate

entrañas, en-**trah**-n'yahs, s., bowels; entrails

entrar, en-**trar**, v., to enter

entre, en-tray, prep., between; among; amongst

entreabierto, en-tray-ah-be-**air**-to, a., ajar

entrecejo, en-tray-**thay**-Ho, s., space between the eyebrows; frown

entreclaro, en-tray-**klah**-ro, a., dim [tercept

entrecoger, en-tray-ko-**Hair**, v., to catch; to in-

entrecortar, en-tray-kor-**tar**, v., to cut without dividing [tween decks

entrecubiertas, en-tray-koo-be-**air**-tahs, s., be-

entredicho, en-tray-**dee**-cho, s., interdiction

entrefino, en-tray-**fee**-no, a., middling fine

entrega, en-**tray**-gah, s., delivery

entregar, en-tray-**gar**, v., to deliver; to pay

entrelazar, en-tray-lah-**thar**, v., to interlace

entremedias, en-tray-**may**-de-ahs, adv., in the meantime

entremés, en-tray-**mess**, s., interlude; side-dish

entremeter, en-tray-may-**tair**, v., to insert.—**se,** — say, to intrude; to meddle; to interfere

entremetido, en-tray-may-**tee**-do, s., meddler

entrepaño, en-tray-**pah**-n'yo, s., panel

entresacar, en-tray-sah-**kar**, v., to choose; to sift

entresuelo, en-tray-soo'**ay**-lo, s., mezzanine

entretanto, en-tray-**tahn**-to, adv., meanwhile

entretela, en-tray-**tay**-lah, s., buckrain

entretener, en-tray-tay-**nair**, v., to amuse

entretenido, en-tray-tay-**nee**-do, a., amusing

entretenimiento, en-tray-tay-ne-me-**en**-to, s., entertainment [tumn

entretiempo, en-tray-te-**em**-po, s., spring or au-

entrever, en-tray-**vair**, v., to have a glimpse of

entrevista, en-tray-**viss**-tah, s., interview

entristecer, en-triss-tay-**thair**, v., to sadden

entronque, en-**tron**-kay, s., cognation; railway junction

entumecer, en-too-may-**thair**, v., to benumb

entumirse, en-too-**meer**-say, v., to become torpid

entupir, en-too-**peer**, v., to obstruct

enturbiar, en-toor-be-**ar**, v., to make turbid; to muddle

entusiasmar, en-too-se-ahs-**mar**, v., to enrapture

enumerar, ay-noo-may-**rar**, v., to enumerate

enunciar, ay-noon-the-**ar**, v., to enunciate

envanecer, en-vah-nay-**thair**, v., to make vain

envasador, en-vah-sah-**dor**, s., funnel

envase, en-**vah**-say, s., cask; container [old

envejecer, en-vay-*H*ay-**thair**, v., to make or grow

envenenar, en-vay-nay-**nar**, v., to poison

envés, en-**vess**, s., wrong side

enviado, en-ve-**ah**-do, s., envoy; messenger

enviar, en-ve-**ar**, v,. to send; to remit

envidia, en-**vee**-de-ah, s., envy; spite

envidiar, en-ve-de-**ar**, v., to envy; to grudge

envilecer, en-ve-lay-**thair**, v., to vilify

envío, en-**vee**-o, s., remittance; shipment

envoltura, en-vol-**too**-rah, s., wrapper; covering

envolver, en-vol-**vair**, v., to involve; to wrap up

envuelto, en-voo-**el**-to, s., wrapper. a., wrapped

enyesar, en-yay-**sar**, v., to whitewash

épico, **ay**-pe-ko, a., epic

epidémico, ay-pe-**day**-me-ko, a., epidemic

epilogar, ay-pe-lo-**gar**, v., to sum up

episódico, ay-pe-**so**-de-ko, a., episodical

epístola, ay-**piss**-to-lah, s., epistle; letter

epíteto, ay-**pee**-tay-to, s., epithet

epitomar, ay-pe-to-**mar**, v., to epitomize

época, **ay**-po-kah, s., epoch; period; time

equilibrio, ay-ke-lee-**bre**-o, s., equilibrium [crew

equipaje, ay-ke-**pah**-*H*ay, s., baggage; equipment;

equipo, ay-kee-po, s., outfit; equipment

equivaler, ay-ke-vah-**lair**, v., to be equivalent

equivocación, ay-ke-vo-kah-the-**on**, s., mistake

equivocado, ay-ke-vo-**kah**-do, a., mistaken

equivocar, ay-ke-vo-**kar**, v., to mistake

equívoco, ay-**kee**-vo-ko, s., quibble, a., ambiguous

era, ay-rah, s., era; period

erario, ay-rah-re-o, s., exchequer

erección, ay-rek-the-**on**, s., erection; foundation

erguir, air-**gheer**, v., to raise up straight

erigir, ay-re-**H**eer, v., to erect

erizado, air-re-**thah**-do, a., bristly

erizo, ay-**ree**-tho, s., hedgehog

erradizo, air-rrah-**dee**-tho, a., wandering

errar, air-**rrar**, v., to err; to mistake; to roam

error, air-**rror**, s., error; mistake; fault

esbelto, ess-**bel**-to, a., tall; well shaped

esbozo, ess-**bo**-tho, s., sketch; outline

escabeche, ess-kah-**bay**-chay, s., souse; pickle; pickled fish

escabroso, ess-kah-**bro**-so, a., rough; rugged

escabullirse, ess-kah-boo-l'**yeer**-say, v., to slip [away

escala, ess-**kah**-lah, s., ladder; scale

escalada, ess-kah-**lah**-dah, s., storming a place

escaldar, ess-kahl-**dar**, v., to scald

escalera, ess-kah-**lay**-rah, s., staircase

escalfador, ess-kahl-fah-**dor**, s., chafing-dish

escalfar, ess-kahl-**far**, v., to boil eggs; to scorch

escalón, ess-kah-**lon**, s., step; grade

escama, ess-**kah**-mah, s., scale (of fishes) [palm

escamotear, ess-kah-mo-tay-**ar**, v., (jugglery) to

escándalo, ess-**kahn**-dah-lo, s., scandal

escaño, ess-**kah**-n'yo, s., bench with a back

escapada, ess-kah-**pah**-dah, s., flight; escapade

escapar, ess-kah-**par**, v., to escape; to flee

escaparate, ess-kah-pah-**rah**-tay, s., glass-case; shop-window

escape, ess-**kah**-pay, s., escape; evasion

escapulario, ess-kah-poo-**lah**-re-o, s., scapulary

escaramuza, ess-kah-rah-**moo**-thah, s., skirmish

escarapela, ess-kah-rah-**pay**-lah, s., cockade

escarcha, ess-**kar**-chah, s., white frost

escardar, ess-kar-**dar,** v., to weed

escarlata, ess-kar-**lah**-tah, s., scarlet colour

escarlatina, ess-kar-lah-**tee**-nah, s., scarlet fever

escarmentar, ess-kar-men-**tar,** v., to be warned by experience

escarnecer, ess-kar-nay-**thair,** v., to scoff; to

escarnio, ess-**kar**-ne-o, s., scoff; jeer [ridicule

escarola, ess-kah-**ro**-lah, s., endive

escarpado, ess-kar-**pah**-do, a., steep; craggy

escaso*, ess-**kah**-so, a., short; niggardly; scarce; scanty

escatimar, ess-kah-te-**mar,** v., to curtail

escena, ess-**thay**-nah, s., stage; scene; sight

escéptico, ess-**thep**-te-ko, a., sceptical

esclarecer, ess-klah-ray-**thair,** v., to lighten; to illustrate

esclarecido, ess-klah-ray-**thee**-do, a., illustrious

esclavina, ess-klah-**vee**-nah, s., pilgrim's cloak

esclavitud, ess-klah-ve-**tood,** s., slavery

esclavo, ess-**klah**-vo, s., slave

esclusa, ess-**kloo**-sah, s., lock; sluice

escoba, ess-**ko**-bah, s., broom

escobilla, ess-ko-**bee**-l'yah, s., brush

escocer, ess-ko-**thair,** v., to cause or feel a sharp pain; to smart

escofina, ess-ko-**fee**-nah, s., rasp

escoger, ess-ko-**Hair,** v., to select; to pick out

escogimiento, ess-ko-He-me-**en**-to, s., selection

escolar, ess-ko-**lar,** s., scholar; student

escolta, ess-**kol**-tah, s., escort; guard

escollera, ess-ko-l'**yay**-rah, s., breakwater; jetty

escombro, ess-**kom**-bro, s., rubbish

esconder, ess-kon-**dair,** v., to conceal

escondite, ess-kon-**dee**-tay, s., concealment; hid-[ing-place

escopeta, ess-ko-**pay**-tah, s., shotgun

escopeteo, ess-ko-pay-**tay**-o, s., discharge of guns

escoplear, ess-ko-play-**ar,** v., to chisel

escoplo, ess-**ko**-plo, s., chisel

escorbuto, ess-kor-**boo**-to, s., scurvy [thing

escoria, ess-**ko**-re-ah, s., dross; scoria; worthless

escoriar, ess-ko-re-**ar,** v., (see **excoriar**)

escorpión, ess-kor-pe-**on,** s., scorpion

escotar, ess-ko-**tar**, v., to cut out; to contribute

escote, ess-**ko**-tay, s., low necked dress; tucker; share; quota; scot

escotilla, ess-ko-tee-l'yah, s., hatchway

escozor, ess-ko-**thor**, s., pungent pain

escribanía, ess-kre-bih-**nee**-ah, s., notary's office; writing-desk

escribano, ess-kre-**bah**-no, s., notary public

escribiente, ess-kre-be-**en**-tay, s., clerk

escribir, ess-kre-**beer**, v., to write   [tion

escrito, ess-**kree**-to, s., writing; literary composi-

escritor, ess-kre-**tor**, s., writer; author

escritorio, ess-kre-**to**-re-o, s., writing-desk; office

escritura, ess-kre-**too**-rah, s., writing; deed

escrúpulo, ess-**kroo**-poo-lo, s., doubt; scruple

escrutar, ess-kroo-**tar**, v., to scrutinize

escucha, ess-**koo**-chah, s., sentinel

escuchar, ess-koo-**char**, v., to listen; to heed

escudar, ess-koo-**dar**, v., to shield

escudo, ess-**koo**-do, s., shield; coat of arms; coin

escuela, ess-koo′**ay**-lah, s., school

escueto, ess-koo′**ay**-to, a., bare; clean

esculpir, ess-kool-**peer**, v., to sculpture

escultura, ess-kool-**too**-rah, s., sculpture

escupidera, ess-koo-pe-**day**-rah, s., spittoon

escupir, ess-koo-**peer**, to spit

escurrir, ess-koor-**rrer**, v., to drain; to wring

ese, esa, ay-say, ay-sah, demonstr. adj., that

ése, ésa, ay-say, ay-sah, pron., that

esencia, ay-**sen**-the-ah, s., essence

esfera, ess-**fay**-rah, s., sphere

esfinge, ess-**fin**-Hay, s., sphinx

esforzado, ess-for-**thah**-do, a., strong; valiant

esforzar, ess-for-**thar**, v., to strengthen. — **se**, — say, to make efforts

esfuerzo, ess-foo′**air**-tho, s., courage; effort

esgrima, ess-**gree**-mah, s., fencing

esgrimir, ess-gre-**meer**, v., to fence

eslabón, ess-lah-**bon**, s., link of a chain; steel for striking fire

esmalte, ess-**mahl**-tay, s., enamel

esmerado, ess-may-**rah**-do, a., highly finished

esmeril, ess-may-**reel,** s., emery
esmero, ess-**may**-ro, s., careful attention
eso, ay-so, pron., that
esotro, ay-so-tro, pron., this or that other
espaciar, ess-pah-the-**ar,** v., to extend; to spread; to space
espacio, ess-**pah**-the-o, s., space; distance; slowness
espada, ess-**pah**-dah, s., sword   [ness
espalda, ess-**pahl**-dah, s., shoulder
espaldar, ess-pahl-**dar,** s., back of a seat; espalier
espaldilla, ess-pahl-**dee**-l'yah, s., shoulder-blade
espantadizo, ess-pahn-tah-**dee**-tho, a., timid; shy
espantajo, ess-pahn-**tah**-Ho, s., scarecrow
espantar, ess-pahn-**tar,** v., to frighten; to terrify
espantoso, ess-pahn-**to**-so, a., frightful
esparadrapo, ess-pah-rah-**drah**-po, s., court-plaster; sticking plaster
esparcido, ess-par-**the**-do, a., scattered
esparcir, ess-par-**theer,** v., to scatter; to spread
espárrago, ess-**par**-rrah-go, s., asparagus   [abroad
esparto, ess-**par**-to, s., esparto grass
espasmo, ess-**pahs**-mo, s., spasm
espátula, ess-**pah**-too-lah, s., spatula
especia, ess-**pay**-the-ah, s., spice
especial, ess-pay-the-**ahl,** a., special
especie, ess-**pay**-the-ay, s., kind; sort
especiería, ess-pay-the-ay-**ree**-ah, s., grocery
especiero, ess-pay-the-**ay**-ro, s., grocer
especificar, ess-pay-the-fe-**kar,** v., to specify
espectáculo, ess-pek-**tah**-koo-lo, s., spectacle
espectador, ess-pek-tah-**dor,** s., spectator   [show
espectro, ess-**pek**-tro, s., spectre; spectrum
especular, ess-pay-koo-**lar,** v., to speculate
espéculo, ess-**pay**-koo-lo, s., speculum
espejo, ess-**pay**-Ho, s., looking-glass; mirror
espera, ess-**pay**-rah, s., expectation; wait; respite
esperanza, ess-pay-**rahn**-thah, s., hope
esperar, ess-pay-**rar,** v., to hope; to wait for
espesar, ess-pay-**sar,** v., to thicken
espeso, ess-**pay**-so, a., thick; dense
espetera, ess-pay-**tay**-rah, s., kitchen rack
espía, ess-**pee**-ah, s., spy

espiga, ess-**pee**-gah, s., ear of corn

espigar, ess-pe-**gar**, v., to glean

espina, ess-**pee**-nah, s., thorn; fish-bone; spine

espinaca, ess-pe-**nah**-kah, s., spinach

espinar, ess-pe-**nar**, v., to prick with thorns

espinazo, ess-pe-**nah**-tho, s., back-bone

espino, ess-**pee**-no, s., hair-thorn

espinoso, ess-pe-**no**-so, a., thorny; arduous

espiral, ess-pe-**rahl**, a., spiral

espirar, ess-pe-**rar**, v., to expire

espíritu, ess-**pee**-re-too, s., spirit; soul; genius; ardour; courage; life; alcohol

espiritual, ess-pe-re-too-**ahl**, a., spiritual; ghostly

espirituoso, ess-pe-re-too-**o**-so, a., spirituous; spirited

esplendidez, ess-plen-de-**deth**, s., splendour

espléndido, ess-**plen**-de-do, a., splendid

esplendor, ess-plen-**dor**, s., splendour

espliego, ess-ple-**ay**-go, s., lavender

espolada, ess-po-**lah**-dah, s., prick with a spur

espolón, ess-po-**lon**, s., cock's spur

esponja, ess-pon-Hah, s., sponge

esponjar, ess-pon-Har, v., to sponge

esponsales, ess-pon-**sah**-less, s., betrothal

espontáneo*, ess-pon-**tah**-nay-o, a., spontaneous

esposa, ess-**po**-sah, s., wife. pl., handcuffs

esposo, ess-**po**-so, s., husband

espuela, ess-poo-**ay**-lah, s., spur; stimulus

espuerta, ess-poo-**air**-tah, s., basket; frail

espuma, ess-**poo**-mah, s., froth; lather; foam; scum   [the mouth

espumajear, ess-poo-mah-Hay-**ar**, v., to foam at

espumar, ess-poo-**mar**, v., to skim; to scum; to

espumoso, ess-poo-**mo**-so, a., frothy, foamy [foam

espurio, ess-**poo**-re-o, a., a spurious

esputo, ess-**poo**-to, s., spittle; sputum

esquela, ess-**kay**-lah, s., billet; note

esqueleto, ess-kay-**lay**-to, s., skeleton

esquema, ess-**kay**-mah, s., scheme; plan

esquilar, ess-ke-**lar**, v., to shear; to clip; to fleece

esquilmar, ess-kil-**mar**, v., to harvest; to impo-

esquina, ess-**kee**-nah, s., corner; angle   [verish

esquivar, ess-ke-**var**, v., to shun ; to avoid ; to elude

esquivo, ess-**kee**-vo, a., elusive ; shy ; reserved

estabilidad, ess-tah-be-le-**dahd**, s., stability

estable*, ess-**tah**-blay, a., stable

establecer, ess-tah-blay-**thair**, v., to establish

establecido, ess-tah-blay-**thee**-do, a., established

establo, ess-**tah**-blo, s., stable   [in business

estaca, ess-**tah**-kah, s., stake ; stick ; cudgel

estacada, ess-tah-**kah**-dah, s., palisade ; fence

estacazo, ess-tah-**kah**-tho, s., blow with a stake

estación, ess-tah-the-**on**, s., condition ; season ;
time ; station   [stationary

estacionarse, ess-tah-the-o-**nar**-say, v., to remain

estadista, ess-tah-**diss**-tah, s., statesman

estadístico, ess-tah-**diss**-te-ko, a., statistical

estadizo, ess-tah-**dee**-tho, a., stagnant

estado, ess-**tah**-do, s., state ; condition ; rank

estafa, ess-**tah**-fah, s., swindle ; theft

estafador, ess-tah-fah-**dor**, s., swindler

estafar, ess-tah-**far**, v., to swindle

estafeta, ess-tah-**fay**-tah, s., post-office branch

estallar, ess-tah-l'**yar**, v., to burst ; to explode

estallido, ess-tah-l'**yee**-do, s., crack ; explosion

estambre, ess-**tahm**-bray, s., worsted ; stamen

estameña, ess-tah-**may**-n'yah, s., serge

estampa, ess-**tahm**-pah, s., print ; stamp ; pattern

estampar, ess-tahm-**par**, v., to print ; to stamp

estampido, ess-tahn-pee-do, s., report of a gun ;
crash   [signet

estampilla, ess-tahm-**pee**-l'yah, s., rubber stamp

estancación, ess-tahn-kah-the-**on**, s., stagnation

estancar, ess-tahn-**kar**, v., to stem a current ; to
be stagnant

estancia, ess-**tahn**-the-ah, s., stay ; dwelling

estanco, ess-**tahn**-ko, s., tobacco shop

estandarte, ess-tahn-**dar**-tay, s., banner ; standard

estanque, ess-**tahn**-kay, s., pond ; reservoir

estante, ess-**tahn**-tay, s., stand ; shelf

estaño, ess-**tah**-n'yo, s., tin   [condition

estar, ess-**tar**, v., to be ; to be in a place, state or

estatua, ess-tah-**too**'ah, s., statue

estatuto, ess-tah-**too**-to, s., statute ; law

este, ess-tay, s., east

este, esta, estos, estas, ess-tay, **ess**-tah, **ess**-tos, **ess**-tahs, demonstr. adj., this; these

éste, ésta, ess-tay, **ess**-tah, pron., this

estela, ess-tay-lah, s., track of a ship

estera, ess-tay-rah, s., mat

estercolar, ess-tair-ko-**lar**, v., to dung; to manure

estereofónico, ess-tair-re'o-**fo**-ne-ko, a., stereophonic

estéril, ess-tay-ril, a., barren; fruitless

esterlina, ess-tair-**lee**-nah, s., pound sterling

esternón, ess-tair-**non**, s., sternum

estero, ess-tay-ro, s., estuary; matting

estertor, ess-tair-**tor**, s., death rattle

estética, ess-tay-te-kah, s., æsthetics

estiaje, ess-te-**ah**-Hay, s., low-water mark

estibador, ess-te-bah-**dor**, s., stevedore

estiércol, ess-te-**air**-kol, s., dung; manure

estigma, ess-tig-mah, s., stigma

estilar, ess-te-**lar**, v., to use; to be accustomed

estilo, ess-tee-lo, s., style; custom   [pen

estilográfica, ess-te-lo-**grah**-fe-kah, s., fountain

estimar, ess-te-**mar**, v., to estimate; to esteem;

estímulo, ess-tee-moo-lo, s., stimulus   [to judge

estío, ess-tee-o, s., summer

estipendio, ess-te-**pen**-de-o, s., stipend

estipular, ess-te-poo-**lar**, v., to stipulate

estirar, ess-te-**rar**, v., to stretch; to pull

estirón, ess-te-**ron**, s., pulling; stretching

estirpe, ess-teer-pay, s., race; origin

esto, ess-to, pron., this

estocada, ess-to-**kah**-dah, s., stab; thrust

estofa, ess-to-fah, s., quilted stuff; quality

estofado, ess-to-**fah**-do, s., stew. a., ornamented; stewed

estofar, ess-to-**far**, v., to quilt; to stew

estoico, ess-to-e-ko, a., stoic

estólido, ess-to-le-do, a., stupid

estómago, ess-to-mah-go, s., stomach

estoque, ess-to-kay, s., rapier

estorbo, ess-tor-bo, s., impediment; obstruction

estornino, ess-tor-**nee**-no, s., starling

estornudar, ess-tor-noo-**dar**, v., to sneeze
estrada, ess-**trah**-dah, s., causeway
estrado, ess-**trah**-do, s., drawing-room; dais
estrambótico, ess-trahm-**bo**-te-ko, a., eccentric; queer
estrangular, ess-trahn-goo-**lar**, v., to strangle
estratégico, ess-trah-**tay**-He-ko, a., strategical
estrato, ess-**trah**-to, s., stratum; layer
estraza, ess-**trah**-thah, s., rag   [to compress
estrechar, ess-tray-**char**, v., to tighten; to contract;
estrecho*, ess-**tray**-cho, s., straight. a., narrow; close; tight; intimate; penurious
estregadura, ess-tray-gah-**doo**-rah, s., friction
estregar, ess-tray-**gar**, v., to rub; to scratch
estrella, ess-**tray**-l'yah, s., star
estrellado, ess-tray-l'yah-do, a., starry
estrellar, ess-tray-l'yar, v., to shatter
estremecer, ess-tray-may-**thair**, v., to shake; to tremble; to shudder   [gurate
estrenar, ess-tray-**nar**, v., to handsel; to inau-
estreno, ess-**tray**-no, s., first use; first performance
estreñir, ess-tray-n'**yeer**, v., to tie close; to constipate
estrépito, ess-**tray**-pe-to, s., din; clangour; crash
estribar, ess-tre-**bar**, v., to rest upon
estribillo, ess-tre-bee-l'yo, s., burden of a song
estribo, ess-**tree**-bo, s., stirrup; buttress
estricto*, ess-**treek**-to, a., strict; accurate; severe
estropear, ess-tro-pay-**ar**, v., to maim; to cripple
estructura, ess-trook-**too**-rah, s., structure
estruendo, ess-troo'**en**-do, s., clamour; turmoil
estrujar, ess-troo-Har, v., to press; to squeeze
estuario, ess-too-**ah**-re-o, s., estuary; inlet
estuco, ess-**too**-ko, s., stucco
estuche, ess-**too**-chay, s., case (for jewelry, scissors, &c.)
estudiante, ess-too-de-**ahn**-tay, s., student
estudiar, ess-too-de-**ar**, v., to study
estudio, ess-**too**-de-o, s., study; library; studio
estudioso, ess-too-de-o-so, a., studious
estufa, ess-**too**-fah, s., stove; heater
estufador, ess-too-fah-**dor**, s., stew-pan

estupefacto, ess-too-pay-**fahk**-to, a., stupefied
estupendo, ess-too-**pen**-do, a., stupendous
estupidez, ess-too-pe-**deth**, s., stupidity
estúpido, ess-**too**-pe-do, a., stupid
estupor, ess-too-**por**, s., stupor; amazement
esturión, ess-too-re-**on**, s., sturgeon
etapa, ay-**tah**-pah, s., station; stop
éter, ay-**tair**, s., ether
eternizar, ay-tair-ne-**thar**, v., to perpetuate
eterno, ay-**tair**-no, a., eternal
ética, ay-te-kah, s., ethics
ético, ay-te-ko, a., ethical
etiqueta, ay-te-**kay**-tah, s., etiquette; label
etnólogo, et-**no**-lo-go, s., ethnologist
eucalipto, ay'oo-kah-**leep**-to, s., eucalyptus
eucaristía, ay'oo-kah-riss-**tee**-ah, s., Eucharist
eufónico, ay'oo-**fo**-ne-ko, a., euphonic
evacuar, ay-vah-koo'**ar**, v., to evacuate
evadir, ay-vah-**deer**, v., to evade
evaluación, ay-vah-loo'ah-the-**on**, s., valuation
evaluar, ay-vah-loo'**ar**, v., to estimate
evaporar, ay-vah-po-**rar**, v., to evaporate
evasión, ay-vah-se-**on**, s., evasion; subterfuge
evento, ay-**ven**-to, s., event
evidente, ay-ve-**den**-tay, a., evident
evitable, ay-ve-**tah**-blay, a., avoidable
evitar, ay-ve-**tar**, v., to avoid
evocar, ay-vo-**kar**, v., to evoke
exacción, ek-sahk-the-**on**, s., exaction
exacerbar, ek-sah-thair-**bar**, v., to exasperate
exactitud, ek-sahk-te-**tood**, s., exactness; accuracy
exacto*, ek-**sahk**-to, a., exact; punctual
exagerar, ek-sah-Hay-**rar**, v., to exaggerate
exaltar, ek-sahl-**tar**, v., to exalt; to extol
examen, ek-**sah**-men, s., examination
examinador, ek-sah-me-nah-**dor**, s., examiner
examinando, ek-sah-me-**nahn**-do, s., candidate
exangüe, ek-**sahn**-goo'ay, a., bloodless; anæmic
exánime, ek-**sah**-ne-may, a., spiritless; weak; lifeless
exasperar, ek-sahs-pay-**rar**, v., to exasperate
excavar, eks-kah-**var**, v., to excavate

excedente, eks-thay-**den**-tay, s., excess. a., excessive; exceeding

exceder, eks-thay-**dair**, v., to exceed; to excel

excelente*, eks-thay-**len**-tay, a., excellent

excelsitud, eks-thel-se-**tood**, s., loftiness

excelso, eks-**thel**-so, a., sublime; elevated; lofty

excéntrico, eks-**then**-tre-ko, a., eccentric

excepción, eks-thep-the-**on**, s., exception

excepto, eks-**thep**-to, adv., except that; excepting

exceptuar, eks-thep-too'**ar**, v., to except; to exempt

excesivo, eks-thay-**see**-vo, a., excessive

exceso, eks-**thay**-so, s., excess

excitar, eks-the-**tar**, v., to excite

exclamar, eks-klah-**mar**, v., to exclaim

excluir, eks-kloo'**eer**, v., to exclude [cate

excomulgar, eks-ko-mool'**gar**, v., to excommuni-

excoriar, eks-ko-re-**ar**, v., to flay; to excoriate

excreción, eks-kray-the-**on**, s., excretion

excremento, eks-kray-**men**-to, s., excrement

excursión, eks-koor-se-**on**, s., excursion

excusa, eks-**koo**-sah, s., excuse

excusar, eks-koo-**sar**, v., to excuse

exento, ek-**sen**-to, a., exempt; free

exequias, ek-**say**-ke-ahs, s., obsequies

exhalar, ek-sah-**lar**, v., to exhale

exhausto, ek-**sah'**ooss-to, a., exhausted

exhibir, ek-se-**beer**, v., to exhibit

exhortar, ek-sor-**tar**, v., to exhort

exhorto, ek-**sor**-to, s., letters requisitorial

exhumar, ek-soo-**mar**, v., to disinter

exigente, ek-se-*H*en-tay, a., exacting

exigible, ek-se-*H*ee-blay, a., demandable

exigir, ek-se-*H*eer, v., to demand; to exact

exigüidad, ek-se-goo'e-**dahd**, s., exiguity

exiguo, ek-**see**-goo'o, a., exiguous

eximio, ek-**see**-me-o, a., very eminent

eximir, ek-se-**meer**, v., to exempt

existencia, ek-siss-**ten**-the-ah, s., existence. pl., stock in hand

existente, ek-siss-**ten**-tay, a., existing

existir, ek-siss-**teer**, v., to exist

éxito, ek-se-to, s., issue; result; end; success

exonerar, ek-so-nay-**rar**, v., to exonerate
exorbitante, ek-sor-be-**tahn**-tay, a., exorbitant
exótico, ek-**so**-te-ko, a., exotic
expansión, eks-pahn-se-**on**, s., expansion
expatriarse, eks-pah-tre-**ar**-say, v., to emigrate
expectativa, eks-pek-tah-**tee**-vah, s., expectancy; hope
expectorar, eks-pek-to-**rar**, v., to expectorate
expedición, eks-pay-de-the-**on**, s., expedition; dispatch [agent
expedidor, eks-pay-de-**dor**, s., sender; shipper;
expediente, eks-pay-de-**en**-tay, s., (law) proceedings; expedient; resource; provision; pretext; file of papers
expedir, eks-pay-**deer**, v., to expedite
expedito, eks-pay-**dee**-to, a., expeditious; prompt
expeler, eks-pay-**lair**, v., to expel
expendeduría, eks-pen-day-doo-**ree**-ah, s., tobacco shop
expensas, eks-**pen**-sahs, s., expenses; costs [trial
experiencia, eks-pay-re-**en**-the-ah, s., experience;
experimento, eks-pay-re-**men**-to, s., experiment
experto, eks-**pair**-to, a., expert
expiación, eks-pe-ah-the-**on**, s., expiation
expirar, eks-pe-**rar**, v., to expire; to die
explanación, eks-plah-nah-the-**on**, s., explanation
explanar, eks-plah-**nar**, v., to explain; to level
explayar, eks-plah-**yar**, v., to extend; to dilate
explicar, eks-ple-**kar**, v., to explain
explícito*, eks-**plee**-the-to, a., explicit
explorar, eks-plo-**rar**, v., to explore
explosión, eks-plo-se-**on**, s., explosion
explotar, eks-plo-**tar**, v., to work mines, lands, &c.; to exploit
expoliar, eks-po-le-**ar**, v., to despoil [to hazard
exponer, eks-po-**nair**, v., to expose; to expound;
exportar, eks-por-**tar**, v., to export
expósito, eks-**po**-se-to, s., foundling
expresar, eks-pray-**sar**, v., to express
expreso, eks-**pray**-so, s., express train, a., express
exprimir, eks-pre-**meer**, v., to squeeze out
ex-profeso, eks-pro-**fay**-so, adv., on purpose

expulsar, eks-pool-**sar,** v., to expel

expurgar, eks-poor-**gar,** v., to expurgate

exquisito, eks-ke-**see**-to, a., exquisite

éxtasis, eks-tah-siss, s., ecstasy

extender, eks-ten-**dair,** v., to extend; to expand [to enlarge

extenso, eks-**ten**-so, a., extensive

extenuar, eks-tay-noo-**ar,** v., to extenuate; to debilitate

exterior, eks-tay-re-**or,** s. & a., exterior; external

exterminio, eks-tair-**mee**-ne-o, s., extermination; expulsion [foreign

externo, eks-**tair**-no, a., external; outward

extinguir, eks-tin-**gheer,** v., to extinguish

extintor, eks-tin-**tor,** s., extinguisher

extirpar, eks-teer-**par,** v., to extirpate

extra, eks-trah, prep., out; without; besides

extracción, eks-trahk-the-**on,** s., extraction

extractar, eks-trahk-**tar,** v., to extract

extracto, eks-**trahk**-to, v., to extract

extraer, eks-trah-**air,** v., to extract; to remove

extranjero, eks-trahn-**Hay**-ro, s., foreigner; stranger. a., foreign [wonder

extrañar, eks-trah-n'**yar,** v., to alienate; to

extrañeza, eks-trah-n'**yay**-thah, s., oddity; wonderment; estrangement

extraño, eks-**trah**-n'yo, a., strange; foreign; rare

extraviado, eks-trah-ve-**ah**-do, a., mislaid; missing

extraviar, eks-trah-ve-**ar,** v., to mislead

extremado, eks-tray-**mah**-do, a., extreme

extremar, eks-tray-**mar,** v., to carry to an extreme; to complete [extreme unction

extremaunción, eks-tray-mah'oon-the-**on,** s.,

extremo, eks-**tray**-mo, a., extreme, last

extremoso, eks-tray-**mo**-so, a., extreme; excessive

extrínseco, eks-**treen**-say-ko, a., extrinsic

fábrica, **fah**-bre-kah, s., fabrication; factory

fabricante, fah-bre-**kahn**-tay, s., manufacturer

fabriquero, fah-bre-**kay**-ro, s., manufacturer; churchwarden; artisan

fábula, fah-boo-lah, s., fable; story

fabuloso, fah-boo-**lo**-so, a., fabulous

facción, fahk-the-**on**, s., faction ; feature
fácil, fah-thil, a., easy ; facile
facilitar, fah-the-le-**tar**, v., to facilitate
facineroso, fah-the-nay-**ro**-so, a., extremely wicked
factible, fahk-**tee**-blay, a., feasible
factor, fahk-**tor**, s., factor
factoría, fahk-to-**ree**-ah, s., factory
factura, fahk-**too**-rah, s., invoice
facturar, fahk-too-**rar**, v., to invoice
facultad, fah-kool-**tahd**, s., faculty
facultar, fah-kool-**tar**, v., to empower ; to authorize
facultativo, fah-kool-tah-**tee**-vo, s., practitioner.
   a., optional
facundo, fah-**koon**-do, a., eloquent ; fluent
facha, fah-chah, s., appearance ; look
fachada, fah-**chah**-dah, s., façade ; frontage
fachenda, fah-**chen**-dah, s., conceit
faena, fah-**ay**-na, s., work ; chore ; task
faisán, fah'e-**sahn**, s., pheasant
faja, fah-*H*ah, s., band ; sash ; girdle
fajardo, fah-*H*ar-do, s., vol-au-vent, meat-pie
fajo, fah-*H*o, s., bundle
falacia, fah-**lah**-the-ah, s., fallacy
falange, fah-lahn-*H*ay, s., phalanx
falaz, fah-**lahth**, a., deceitful
falda, fahl-dah, s., skirt ; lap ; slope
faldellín, fahl-day-l'**yeen**, s., underskirt
faldón, fahl-**don**, s., long flowing skirt
falible, fah-lee-blay, a., fallible
falsario, fahl-**sah**-re-o, s., forger
falsear, fahl-say-**ar**, v., to falsify ; to forge
falsedad, fahl-say-**dahd**, s., falsehood ; untruth
falsete, fahl-**say**-tay, s., spigot ; falsetto voice
falso*, fahl-so, a., false ; counterfeit
falta, fahl-tah, s., fault ; offence ; want ; flaw
faltar, fahl-**tar**, v., to be wanting ; to fail ; to need
faltriquera, fahl-tre-**kay**-rah, s., pocket
fallar, fah-l'**yar**, v., to give sentence ; to miss ; to
fallecer, fahl-'yay-**thair**, v., to die   [fail
fallecimiento, fah-l'yay-the-me-**en**-to, s., death
fallido, fah-l'**yee**-do, a., frustrated ; bankrupt
fallo, fah-l'yo, s., judgment

fama, fah-mah, s., fame ; name ; glory

familia, fah-**mee**-le-ah, s., family

familiar, fah-me-le-**ar**, s., college servant. a., familiar ; domestic ; frequent

famoso, fah-**mo**-so, a., famous

fámulo, fah-moo-lo, s., college servant

fanal, fah-**nahl**, s., lighthouse ; lantern

fanatismo, fah-nah-**tiss**-mo, s., fanaticism

fandango, fahn-**dahn**-go, s., fandango, Spanish dance

fanfarrón, fahn-far-**rron**, s., hector ; braggart

fangal, fahn-**gahl**, s., slough ; quagmire

fango, fahn-go, s., mire ; mud

fantasía, fahn-tah-**see**-ah, s., fancy ; caprice

farándula, fah-**rahn**-doo-lah, s., profession of a low comedian

farda, far-dah, s., bundle of clothing

fardel, far-**del**, s., bag ; knapsack

fardo, far-do, s., bale of goods ; parcel

farfante, far-**fahn**-tay, s., boasting babbler

farfullar, far-foo-l'**yar**, v., to jabber

faringe, fah-**reen**-Hay, s., pharynx

farmacéutico, far-mah-**thay**'oo-te-ko, s., chemist;

farmacia, far-mah-the-ah, s., pharmacy [druggist

faro, fah-ro, s., lighthouse

farol, fah-**rol**, s., lantern

faroléar, fah-ro-lay-**ar**, v., to strut

farsa, far-sah, s., farce ; company of players

farsante, far-**sahn**-tay, s., actor ; player ; humbug

fas (por — o por nefas), fahs (por — o por **nay**-fahs), adv., justly or unjustly

fascinar, fahs-the-**nar**, v., to fascinate

fase, fah-say, s., phase

fastidiar, fahs-te-de-**ar**, v., to excite disgust ; to

fastidio, fahs-**tee**-de-o, s., disgust ; loathing [bore

fastidioso, fahs-te-de-o-**o**-so, a., squeamish

fastuoso, fahs-too'o-so, a., ostentatious

fatalidad, fah-tah-le-**dahd**, s., fatality ; ill-fortune

fatídico, fah-**tee**-de-ko, a., ominous ; fatidical

fatiga, fah-**tee**-gah, s., fatigue ; weariness

fatigar, fah-te-**gar**, v., to tire

fatigoso, fah-te-**go**-so, a., tiresome

fatuidad, fah-too'e-**dahd,** s., fatuity

fatuo, fah-too'o, a., fatuous

fauces, fah'oo-thess, s., fauces; gullet

fausto, fah'ooss-to, s., splendour; pomp. a., happy; fortunate

fautor, fah'oo-**tor,** s., abetter; favourer

favor, fah-**vor,** s., favour

favorable*, fah-vo-**rah**-blay, s., favourable [tect

favorecer, fah-vo-ray-**thair,** v., to favour; to pro-

favorito, fah-vo-**ree**-to, s. & a., favourite

faz, fath, s., face

fe, fay, s., faith; certificate

fealdad, fay-ahl-**dahd,** s., ugliness

febrero, fay-**bray**-ro, s., February

febril, fay-**breel,** a., feverish

fecal, fay-**kahl,** a., feculent; fæcal [tilize

fecundar, fay-koon-**dar,** v., to fecundate; to fer-

fecundo, fay-**koon**-do, a., fruitful; prolific

fecha, fay-chah, s., date (of a letter, &c.)

fechar, fay-**char,** v., to date

fechoría, fay-cho-**ree**-ah, s., misdeed

felicidad, fay-le-the-**dahd,** s., felicity; bliss

felicitar, fay-le-the-**tar,** v., to congratulate

feligrés, fay-le-**gress,** s., parishioner

feliz, fay-**leeth,** a., happy; fortunate

felonía, fay-lo-**nee**-ah, s., felony; treachery

felpudo, fel-poo-do, s., door-mat. a., shaggy

femenino, fay-may-**nee**-no, a., feminine

fementido, fay-men-**tee**-do, a., false; unfaithful

fenda, fen-dah, s., fissure; crack

fenecer, fay-nay-**thair,** v., to finish; to die [tion

fenecimiento, fay-nay-the-me-**en**-to, s., termina-

fenómeno, fay-**no**-may-no, s., phenomenon

feo*, fay-o, a., ugly; deformed

feracidad, fay-rah-the-**dahd,** s., fertility

feraz, fay-**rath,** a., fertile

féretro, fay-ray-tro, s., bier; coffin; hearse

feria, fay-re-ah, s., fair

feriar, fay-re-**ar,** v., to buy; to sell; to barter

fermento, fair-men-to, s., leaven

ferocidad, fay-ro-the-**dahd,** s., ferocity

feroz, fay-**roth,** a., ferocious

ferrería, fair-rray-**ree**-ah, s., foundry
ferretería, fair-rray-tay-**ree**-ah, s., hardware-shop
ferrocarril, fair-rro-kar-**rreel**, s., railway
fértil, fair-til, a., fertile
férula, fay-roo-lah, s., ferrule; yoke; authority
ferviente, fair-ve-**en**-tay, a., fervent
fervor, fair-**vor**, s., fervour; ardour
festejar, fess-tay-*H*ar, v., to feast; to woo
festejo, fess-**tay**-*H*o, s., feast; courtship
festín, fess-**teen**, s., feast; banquet
festivo*, fess-**tee**-vo, a., festive; merry
festón, fess-**ton**, s., festoon; wreath
fetidez, fay-te-**deth**, s., fetidity
fétido, fay-te-do, a., fetid
feudo, fay'oo-do, s., fief; feud
fiado, (al), ah-l fe'**ah**-do, adv., on credit
fiador, fe'ah-**dor**, s., surety; bail
fiambre, fe'**ahm**-bray, a., cold served (victuals)
fianza, fe'**ahn**-thah, s., security; bail
fiar, fe'**ar**, v., to guarantee; to bail; to give credit
fibra, fee-brah, s., fibre   [to entrust
ficción, fik-the-**on**, s., fiction; tale
ficticio, fik-**tee**-the-o, a., fictitious
ficha, fee-chah, s., marker; index card
fidedigno, fe-day-**dig**-no, a., trustworthy
fideicomisario, fe-day'e-ko-me-**sah**-re-o, s., trus-
fideicomiso, fe-day'e-ko-**mee**-so, s., trust   [tee
fidelidad, fe-day-le-**dahd**, s., fidelity
fideos, fe-**day**-os, s., vermicelli
fiebre, fe'**ay**-bray, s., fever
fiel, fe'**ell**, a., faithful
fieltro, fe'**ell**-tro, s., felt
fiera, fe'**ay**-rah, s., wild beast
fiereza, fe'ay-**ray**-thah, s., fierceness; cruelty
fiero*, fe'**ay**-ro, a., fierce; ferocious; cruel
fiesta, fe'**ess**-tah, s., feast; holiday
figón, fe-**gon**, s., eating-house
figonero, fe-go-**nay**-ro, s., eating-house keeper
figura, fe-**goo**-rah, s., figure; shape; face; picture
figurar, fe-goo-**rar**, v., to shape; to figure; to sketch
figurilla, fe-goo-**ree**-l'yah, s., little insignificant
   person

FIG 149 **FIS**

figurón, fe-goo-**ron**, s., pretentious nobody
fija, fee-*H*ah, s., door-hinge
fijar, fe-*H*ar, v., to fix; to fasten
fijeza, fe-*H*ay-thah, s., firmness; fixedness
fijo*, fee-*H*o, a., firm; fixed; secure; settled
fila, fee-lah, s., row; line; tier; rank
filamento, fe-lah-**men**-to, s., filament; fibre
filatura, fe-lah-**too**-rah, s., spinning
filete, fe-**lay**-tay, s., fillet; hem
filetear, fe-lay-tay-**ar**, v., to fillet; to crease
filiación, fe-le'ah-the-**on**, s., filiation; register
filigrana, fe-le-**grah**-nah, s., filigree
filo, fee-lo, s., cutting edge
filón, fe-**lon**, s., vein; lode
filosofía, fe-lo-so-**fee**-ah, s., philosophy
filtrador, fil-trah-**dor**, s., filter
filtro, **feel**-tro, s., filter; love-potion
fin, feen, s., end; conclusion
finado, fe-**nah**-do, a., defunct; deceased
final*, fe-**nahl**, a., final
finca, **feen**-kah, s., real estate
fineza, fe-**nay**-thah, s., fineness; delicacy
fingidor, fin-*H*e-**dor**, s., dissembler; feigner
fingimiento, fin-*H*e-me-**en**-to, s., simulation
fingir, fin-*H*eer, v., to feign; to dissemble
finiquito, fe-ne-**kee**-to, s., close of an account;
finito, fe-**nee**-to, a., finite   [quittance
fino*, **fee**-no, a., fine; pure; delicate; acute; sagacious
finura, fe-**noo**-rah, s., fineness; purity; delicacy
firma, **feer**-mah, s., signature
firmar, feer-**mar**, v., to sign   [resolute
firme*, **feer**-may, a., firm; stable; secure; constant;
fiscal, fiss-**kahl**, s., attorney-general. a., fiscal
fisco, **fiss**-ko, s., exchequer
fisga, **fiss**-gah, s., banter; chaff; raillery
fisgar, fiss-**gar**, v., to pry; to peep
física, **fiss**-se-kah, s., physics   [physical
físico, **fee**-se-ko, s., naturalist; physician; face. a.,
fisonomía, fe-so-no-**mee**-ah, s., physiognomy
fístula, **fiss**-too-lah, s., water-pipe; fistula
fisura, fe-**soo**-rah, s., fissure

flaco, flah-ko, a., lean; lank; feeble

flacura, flah-**koo**-rah, s., meagreness; weakness

flagrante, flah-**grahn**-tay, a., flagrant. **en**—, en—, in the act

flamante, flah-**mahn**-tay, a., flaming; quite new

flanco, flahn-ko, s., flank [dismay

flaquear, flah-kay-**ar**, v., to flag; to slacken; to

flaqueza, flah-**kay**-thah, s., leanness; feebleness

flato, flah-to, s., flatulency

flatulento, flah-too-**len**-to, a., flatulent

flauta, flah'oo-tah, s., flute

flautín, flah'oo-**teen**, s., piccolo

flautista, flah'oo-**tiss**-tah, s., flute player

fleco, flay-ko, s., fringe; flounce

flecha, flay-chah, s., arrow

flechero, flay-**chay**-ro, s., archer

fleje, flay-Hay, s., iron strap or hoop

flema, flay-mah, s., phlegm

flemático, flay-**mah**-te-ko, a., phlegmatic

flemudo, flay-**moo**-do, a., sluggish; slow

fletador, flay-tah-**dor**, s., freighter; character

fletamento, flay-tah-**men**-to, s., freighting; char-

fletar, flay-tar, v., to freight; to charter [tering

flete, flay-tay, s., freight

flexión, flek-se-**on**, s., flexion [ziness; sloth

flojedad, flo-Hay-**dahd**, s., weakness; laxity; la-

flojo, flo-Ho, a., slack; feeble; flexible

flor, flor, s., flower

florear, flo-ray-**ar**, v., to adorn with flowers

florecer, flo-ray-**thair**, v., to blossom

florera, flo-**ray**-rah, s., flower girl

florero, flo-**ray**-ro, s., flower-pot

floresta, flo-**ress**-tah, s., forest; thicket

florete, flo-**ray**-tay, s., fencing foil

florido, flo-ree-do, a., florid; flowery

florón, flo-ron, s., large flower

flota, flo-tah, s., fleet

flotante, flo-**tahn**-tay, a., floating

flotar, flo-tar, v., to float

flote, flo-tay, s., floating, **a**—, ah—, afloat

flotilla, flo-tee-l'yah, s., small fleet

fluctuar, flook-too'**ar**, v., fluctuate

fluidez, floo'e-**deth**, s., fluidity; fluency
flúido, floo'e-do, a., fluid; fluent
fluir, floo'eer, v., to flow; to run
flujo, floo-Ho, s., flux; flow
foca, fo-kah, s., seal
foco, foh-ko, s., focus; source; foresail
fofo, fo-fo, a., spongy; soft
fogata, fo-gah-tah, s., blaze; bonfire
fogón, fo-gon, s., hearth; cooking place
fogoso, fo-go-so, a., impetuous; vehement
foliar, fo-le-ar, v., to foliate
folio, fo-le-o, s., folio; leaf
follaje, fo-l'yah-Hay, s., foliage [paper
folletín, fo-l'yay-teen, s., serial story in a news-
folletista, fo-l'yay-tiss-tah, s., pamphleteer
folleto, fo-l'yay-to, s., pamphlet; tract
follón, fo-l'yon, s. & a., lazy
fomentar, fo-men-tar, v., to foment; to promote
fomento, fo-men-to, s., promotion; fomentation
fonda, fon-dah, s., inn; hotel
fondista, fon-diss-tah, s., innkeeper
fondo, fon-do, s., bottom; depth; stock
fondos, fon-dos, s., funds; stocks
fonética, fo-nay-te-kah, s., phonetics
fónico, fo-ne-ko, a., acoustic; phonic
fonógrafo, fo-no-grah-fo, s., phonograph
fontanal, fon-tah-nahl, s., spring of water
forajido, fo-rah-Hee-do, s., outlaw
foráneo, fo-rah-nay-o, a., foreign; strange
forastero, fo-rahs-tay-ro, a., strange; exotic
forcejear, for-thay-Hay-ar, v., to struggle; to strive
forcejo, for-thay-Ho, s., struggle
forense, fo-ren-say, a., forensic
forja, for-Hah, s., forge; smithy
forjador, for-Hah-dor, s., forger; blacksmith
forjadura, for-Hah-doo-rah, s., forging
forma, for-mah, s., form; shape; manner
formalidad, for-mah-le-dahd, s., formality; requisite; requirement [plete; to legalize
formalizar, for-mah-le-thar, v., to make com-
formón, for-mon, s., chisel
fórmula, for-moo-lah, s., formula; recipe

fornicario, for-ne-**kah**-re-o, s., fornicator
fornido, for-**nee**-do, a., robust; stout
foro, fo-ro, s., court of justice; bar
forraje, for-**rrah**-Hay, s., fodder
forrar, for-**rrar**, v., to line; to cover
fortachón, for-tah-**chon**, a., very strong
fortalecer, for-tah-lay-**thair**, v., to strengthen;
  to encourage   [vigour; fortress
fortaleza, for-tah-**lay**-thah, s., fortitude; courage;
fortificar, for-te-fe-**kar**, v., to fortify
fortín, for-**teen**, s., small fort
fortuito*, for-**too**'e-to, a., foruitous
fortuna, for-**too**-nah, s., fortune; chance; fate
forzadamente, for-thah-dah-**men**-tay, adv., force-
forzado, for-**thah**-do, s., convict   [fully
forzador, for-thah-**dor**, s., ravisher
forzamiento, for-thah-me-**en**-to, s., forcing
forzoso, for-**tho**-so, a., unavoidable; compulsory
forzudo, for-**thoo**-do, a., strong
fosa, fo-sah, s., grave; pit
fosco, fos-ko, a., frowning; cross
fosforera, fos-fo-**ray**-rah, s., match-box
fósforo, fos-fo-ro, s., phosphorus; match
fósil, fo-sil, s. & a., fossil
foso, fo-so, pit; moat; ditch
fotografía, fo-to-grah-**fee**-ah, s., photography
fotógrafo, fo-**to**-grah-fo, s., photographer
frac, frahk, s., dress-coat
fracasar, frah-kah-**sar**, v., to fail
fracaso, frah-**kah**-so, s., downfall; ruin; failure
fracturar, frahk-too-**rar**, v., to fracture; to break
fragancia, frah-**gahn**-the-ah, s., fragrance; scent
fragata, frah-**gah**-tah, s., frigate
frágil, frah-Hil, a., fragile; brittle; frail
fragmento, frag-**men**-to, s., fragment
fragoso, frah-go-so, a., craggy; rough; eneven
fragua, frah-goo'ah, s., forge
fraguar, frah-goo'**ar**, v., to forge; to contrive
fraile, frah'e-lay, friar
frambuesa, frahm-boo'**ay**-sah, s., raspberry
francachela, frahn-kah-**chay**-lah, s., luxurious
  repast

franco, frahn-ko, s., franc. a., frank; open; free
franela, frah-nay-lah, s., flannel
franja, frahn-H**ah**, s., fringe   [to disengage
franquear, frahn-kay-ar, v., to exempt; to prepay;
franqueo, frahn-kay-o, s., postage
franqueza, frahn-kay-thah, s., freedom; frankness
franquicia, frahn-kee-the-ah, s., exemption from
frasco, frahs-ko, s., flask   [taxes
frase, frah-say, s., phrase
frasquera, frahs-kay-rah, s., liquor-case
fraude, frah'oo-day, s., fraud
fraudulento, frah'oo-doo-len-to, a., fraudulent
fray, frah'e, s., friar
frecuentar, fray-koo'en-tar, v., to frequent
frecuente*, fray-koo'en-tay, a., frequent
fregadero, fray-gah-day-ro, s., scullery
fregar, fray-gar, v., to rub; to scour; to scrub
fregona, fray-go-nah, s., scullery-maid
freidura, fray'e-doo-rah, s., frying
freir, fray-eer, v., to fry
frenesí, fray'nay-see, s., frenzy
frenético, fray-nay-te-ko, a., mad; frantic
freno, fray-no, s., bridle; brake   [posite
frente, fren-tay, s., front; face. **en—**, en—, op-
fresa, fray-sah, s., strawberry   [looking
frescachón, fress-kah-chon, a., stout; good-
fresco, fress-ko, a., fresh; cool; recent
frescura, fress-koo-rah, s., freshness; frankness;
fresno fress-no, s., ash-tree   [tranquillity; cheek
frialdad, fre-ahl-dahd, s., coldness
fricción, frik-the-on, s., friction
friega, fre'ay-gah, s., rubbing with flesh-brush,
frigidez, fre-H**e-deth**, s., frigidity   [flannel, etc.
frígido, fre-H**e-do**, a., frigid
frigorífico, fre-go-ree-fe-ko, s., refrigerator
frío, free-o, a., cold; indifferent
friolento, fre-o-len-to, a., very sensitive to cold
frisar, fre-sar, v., to frizzle; to resemble; to ap-
        proach   [dish of fried fish
fritada, fritura, fre-tah-dah, fre-**too**-rah, s.,
frito, free-to, a., fried
frívolo, free-vo-lo, a., frivolous

frondoso, fron-**do**-so, a., leafy
frontal, fron-**tahl**, s., altar hanging. a., frontal
frontera, fron-**tay**-rah, s., frontier
fronterizo, fron-tay-**ree**-tho, a., bordering upon
frontis, fron-tiss, s., frontispiece
frotación, fro-tah-the-**on**, s., rubbing; friction
frotar, fro-**tar**, v., to rub
fructuoso, frook-too-**o**-so, a., fruitful; profitable
frugal, froo-**gahl**, a., frugal; sparing
fruición, froo'e-the-**on**, s., fruition; enjoyment
fruncir, froon-**theer**, v., to pucker; to frown
fruslería, frooss-lay-**ree**-ah, s., trifle; futility
fruslero, frooss-lay-ro, a., frivolous; futile
frustrar, frooss-**trar**, v., to frustrate
fruta, froo-tah, s., fruit
frutera, froo-**tay**-rah, s., fruit-dish
frutero, froo-**tay**-ro, s., fruiterer; fruit-dish
fruto, froo-to, s., fruit; profit; benefice
¡fu! foo, interj., phew! **ni — ni fa,** ne — ne fah, (fam.) neither the one nor the other
fuego, foo'ay-go, s., fire
fuente, foo'en-tay, s., fountain; source; dish
fuera, foo'ay-rah, adv., from outward. interj., out of the way!
fuero, foo'ay-ro, s., statute-law; jurisdiction
fuerte, foo'air-tay, adv., strongly. a., vigorous; strong
fuerza, foo'air-thah, s., strength; force
fuga, foo-gah, s., flight; escape
fugarse, foo-gar-say, v., to escape; to fly
fugaz, foo-**gath**, a., fugacious; fleeting
fugitivo, foo-He-tee-vo, a., fugitive; runaway
fulano, foo-lah-no, s., such a one. **—, sutano y mengano,** —, soo-**tah**-no e men-**gah**-no, Tom, Dick and Harry
fulgente, fool-Hen-tay, a., refulgent
fulgor, fool-gor, s., resplendence
fuliginoso, foo-le-He-no-so, a., dark; obscure
fulminante, fool-me-nahn-tay, s., cap. a., fulminating; explosive
fullería, fool-l'yay-ree-ah, s., cheating at play
fullero, foo-l'yay-ro, s., sharper; cheater at play

fumadero, foo-mah-**day**-ro, s., smoking-room

fumador, foo-mah-**dor,** s., smoker

fumar, foo-**mar,** v., to smoke

fumarada, foo-mah-**rah**-dah, s., puff; whiff; pipeful of tobacco

función, foon-the-**on** s., function; festival; performance

funcionar, foon-the-o-**nar,** v., to work; to operate

funcionario, foon-the-o-**nah**-re-o, s., official

funda, foon-dah, s., case; sheath; cover; envelope

fundador, foon-dah-**dor,** s., founder

fundamento, foon-dah-**men**-to, s., foundation

fundar, foon-**dar,** v., to found; to ground

fundible, foon-**dee**-blay, a., fusible

fundición, foon-de-the-**on,** s., fusion; foundry

fundir, foon-**deer,** v., to melt metals

fúnebre, foo-nay-bray, a., mournful; sad

funesto, foo-**ness**-to, a., fatal; disastrous

furgón, foor-**gon,** s., van; waggon

furia, foo-re-ah, s., fury

furibundo, foo-re-**boon**-do, a., furious, frantic

furioso, foo-re-o-so, a., furious; raging

furor, foo-**ror,** s., fury

furtivo, foor-**tee**-vo, a., furtive

fuselaje, foo-say-**lah**-Hay, s., fuselage

fusil, foo-**seel,** s., rifle; gun; musket

fusilero, foo-se-**lay**-ro, s., fusileer   [tion

fusión, foo-se-**on,** s., fusion; alliance; amalgama-

fusta, fooss-tah, s., whiplash

fustán, fooss-**tahn,** s., fustian

fustigar, fooss-te-**gar,** v., to cudgel; to fustigate

fútil, foo-til, a., futile

futilidad, foo-te-le-**dahd,** s., futility

futuro, foo-**too**-ro, a., future

gabán, gah-**bahn,** s., overcoat

gabardina, gah-bar-**dee**-nah, s., gabardine

gabarra, gah-**bar**-rrah, s., lighter; barge

gabarro, gah-**bar**-rro, s., defect in cloth; error accounts

gabela, gah-**bay**-lah, s., gabel; duty; excise

gabinete, gah-be-**nay**-tay, s., cabinet; study

gaceta, gah-**thay**-tah, s., gazette
gachas, gah-chahs, s., porridge; pap
gacho, gah-cho, a., curvated; bent downwards
gafa, gah-fah, s., hook. pl., spectacles
gafetes, gah-**fay**-tess, s., hooks and eyes; clasp
gaita, gah'e-tah, s., bagpipe; flageolet
gaitería, gah'e-tay-**ree**-ah, s., gay and gaudy dress
gaje, gah-*Hay*, s., salary; wages; fee
gajo, gah-*Ho*, s., branch; bunch of grapes
gala, gah-lah, s., gala; full dress
galán, gah-**lahn**, s., gallant; wooer; actor
galano, gah-**lah**-no, a., genteel; elegant
galante*, gah-**lahn**-tay, a., gallant; courtly
galantear, gah-lahn-tay-**ar**, v., to court; to woo
galanteo, gah-lahn-**tay**-o, s., courtship; wooing
galantería, gah-lahn-tay-**ree**-ah, s., gallantry
galanura, gah-lah-**noo**-rah, s., showiness; gracefulness
galápago, gah-**lah**-pah-go, s., fresh-water tortoise
galardón, gah-lar-**don**, s., reward
galardonar, gah-lar-do-**nar**, v., to recompense
galbana, gahl-**bah**-nah, s., laziness
galbanero, gahl-bah-**nay**-ro, a., lazy; indolent
galeote, gah-lay-o-tay, s., galley-slave
galera, gah-**lay**-rah, s., galley; wagon
galería, gah-lay-**ree**-ah, s., gallery
galgo, gahl-go, s., greyhound
gálico, gah-le-ko, s., syphilis
galimatías, gah-le-mah-**tee**-ahs, s., gibberish
galocha, gah-**lo**-chah, s., galoche; clog
galón, gah-**lon**, s., lace; braid; trimming
galonear, gah-lo-nay-**ar**, v., to trim with lace
galopar, gah-lo-**par**, v., to gallop
galope, gah-**lo**-pay, s., gallop
galopín, gah-lo-**peen**, s., urchin; rogue
galladura, gah-l'yah-**doo**-rah, s., tread of an egg
gallarda, gah-l'yar-dah, s., Spanish dance
gallardear, gah-l'yar-day-**ar**, v., to act with grace
gallardía, gah-l'yar-**dee**-ah, s., gracefulness
gallardo*, gah-l'yar-do, a., gay; graceful; gallant
gallareta, gah-l'yah-**ray**-tah, s., widgeon
gallarón, gah-l'yah-**ron**, s., bustard

gallear, gah-l'yay-**ar**, v., to tread (as birds); to assume an air of importance

galleta, gah-l'**yay**-tah, s., biscuit

gallina, gah-l'**yee**-nah, s., hen

gallinero, gah-l'yee-**nay**-ro, s., hen-coop

gallineta, gah-l'yee-**nay**-tah, s., sand-piper

gallito, gah-l'**yee**-to, s., beau; coxcomb

gallo, gah-l'yo, s., cock

gama, gah-mah, s., gamut

gambeta, gahm-**bay**-tah, s., cross-caper

gamella, gah-**may**-l'yah, s., wooden-trough

gamo, gah-mo, s., buck of the fallow-deer

gamón, gah-**mon**, s., asphodel   [leather

gamuza, gah-**moo**-thah, s., chamois; chamois

gana, gah-nah, s., appetite; inclination; desire

ganable, gah-nah-blay, a., obtainable   [dealer

ganadero, gah-nah-**day**-ro, s., cattle owner, cattle

ganado, gah-**nah**-do, s., cattle; herd; drove

ganancia, gah-**nahn**-the-ah, s., gain; profit

ganar, gah-**nar**, v., to gain; to win

gancho, gahn-cho, s., hook

ganga, gahn-gah, s., grouse; gangue; bargain

gangoso, gahn-**go**-so, a., snuffling

ganguear, gahn-gay-**ar**, v., to snuffle

ganoso, gah-**no**-so, a., desirous

gansada, gahn-**sah**-dah, s., stupidity

ganso, gansa, gahn-so, **gahn**-sah, s., gander; goose; silly person

ganzúa, gahn-**thoo**-ah, s., picklock

gañán, gah-n'**yahn**, s., day labourer

garabatear, gah-rah-bah-tay-**ar**, v., to hook; to scrawl; to scribble

garabato, gah-rah-**bah**-to, s., hook; scribble

garante, gah-**rahn**-tay, s., guarantor

garantía, gah-rahn-**tee**-ah, s., security; bond

garantizar, gah-rahn-te-**thar**, v., to guarantee

garañón, gah-rah-n'**yon**, s., jackass

garapiña, gah-rah-**pee**-n'yah, s., congealed particles of a liquid

garbanzo, gar-**bahn**-tho, s., chick-pea

garbear, gar-bay-**ar**, v., to affect an air of dignity

garbillar, gar-be-l'**yar**, v., to sift; to garble

garbillo, gar-**bee**-l'yo, s., sieve
garbo, gar-bo, s., gracefulness; elegance
garboso, gar-**bo**-so, a., graceful; gallant
garfio, gar-fe-o, s., hook; gaff
gargajear, gar-gah-Hay-ar, v., to expectorate
garganta, gar-gahn-tah, s., throat; ravine
gargantilla, gar-gahn-tee-l'yah, s., necklace
gárgara, gar-gah-rah, s., gargle
gargarismo, gar-gay-riss-mo, s., gargle
gárgola, gar-go-lah, s., gargoyle
garguero, gar-gay-ro, s., windpipe
garita, gah-ree-tah, s., sentry-box; porter's lodge
garito, gah-ree-to, s., gambling den
garlar, gar-lar, v., to chatter
garlito, gar-lee-to, s., snare; trap
garra, gar-rrah, s., claw; talon
garrafa, gar-rrah-fah, s., decanter; carafe
garrafal, gar-rrah-fahl, s., great; huge
garrafón, gar-rrah-fon, s., large carafe
garrapata, gar-rrah-pah-tah, s., tick (insect)
garrapatear, gar-rrah-pah-tay-ar, v., to scribble
garrocha, gar-rro-chah, s., dart; goad-stick
garrote, gar-rro-tay, s., club; truncheon; garrote (strangulation)
garrotillo, gar-rro-tee-l'yo, s., quinsy; croup
garrucha, gar-rroo-chah, s., pulley [rulous
gárrulo, gar-rroo-lo, a., chirping; prattling; gar-
garulla, gah-roo-l'yah, s., (fam.) rabble
garza, gar-thah, s., heron
garzo, gar-tho, a., blue-eyed
garzón, gar-thon, s., lad; boy
gas, gahs, s., gas
gasa, gah-sah, s., gauze
gastador, gahs-tah-dor, s., spendthrift; pioneer
gastar, gahs-tar, v., to expend; to waste; to use
gata, gah-tah, s., she-cat
gatear, gah-tay-ar, v., to climb up; to clamber
gatesco, gah-tess-ko, a., feline
gato, gah-to, s., cat
gatuno, gah-too-no, (see **gatesco**)
gaveta, gah-vay-tah, s., drawer; till; locker
gavilán, gah-ve-lahn, s., sparrow-hawk

gavilla, gah-**vee**-l'yah, s., sheaf of corn-stalk
gavión, gah-ve-**on**, s., gabion
gaviota, gah-ve-o-tah, s., sea-gull
gavota, gah-**vo**-tah, s., gavotte
gayo, gay, gah-yo, a., gay; merry
gazapo, gah-**thah**-po, s., young rabbit
gazmoñería, gath-mo-n'yay-**ree**-ah, s., prudery; [hypocrisy
gaznate, gath-**nah**-tay, s., windpipe
gazuza, gah-**thoo**-thah, s., violent hunger
gema, *H*ay-mah, s., gem
gemelo, *H*ay-**may**-lo, s., twin. m. pl., binocular
gemido, *H*ay-**mee**-do, s., groan; moan
gemir, *H*ay-**meer**, v., to moan
genciana, *H*en-the-**ah**-nah, s., gentian
generador, *H*ay-nay-rah-**dor**, s., generator
general, *H*ay-nay-**rahl**, s., general. a., general
generala, *H*ay-nay-**rah**-lah, s., general (beat of the
    drum)
genérico, *H*ay-**nay**-re-ko, a., generic
género, *H*ay-nay-ro, s., genus; class; kind. —
    humano, — oo-mah-no, mankind
generoso*, *H*ay-nay-**ro**-so, a., generous [ning
génesis, *H*ay-nay-siss, s., genesis; origin; begin-
genio, *H*ay-ne-o, s., genius; disposition; temper
gente, *H*en-tay, s., people; folk; nation; family
gentecilla, *H*en-tay-**thee**-l'yah, s., people
gentil, *H*en-**teel**, s., heathen. a., genteel; elegant
gentileza, *H*en-te-**lay**-thah, s., gentility; refinement
gentilhombre, *H*en-til-**om**-bray, s., aristocrat
gentilidad, *H*en-te-le-**dahd**, s., heathendom
gentío, *H*en-**tee**-o, s., crowd
genuino, *H*ay-noo'ee-no, a., genuine
geografía, *H*ay-o-grah-**fee**-ah, s., geography
geométrico, *H*ay-o-**may**-tre-ko, a., geometrical;
    geometric
gerencia, *H*ay-**ren**-the-ah, s., management
gerente, *H*ay-**ren**-tay, s., manager
germen, *H*air-men, s., germ; origin
germinar, *H*air-me-**nar**, v., to germinate; to sprout
gestear, *H*ess-tay-**ar**, v., to make grimaces
gesticular, *H*ess-te-koo-**lar**, v., to gesticulate
gestión, *H*ess-te-**on**, s., management; negotiation

gestionar, *H*ess-te-o-**nar,** v., to procure; to deal;
gesto, *H*ess-to, s., face; gesture   [to manage
gestor, *H*ess-**tor,** s., manager; promoter; proxy
giba, *H*ee-bah, s., hump; hunch
gibado, *H*e-**bah**-do, a., humpbacked
gigante, *H*e-**gahn**-tay, s., giant. a., gigantic
gimotear, *H*e-mo-tay-**ar,** v., to whine
ginebra, *H*e-**nay**-brah, s., gin
gira, *H*ee-rah, s., tour; excursion
girada, *H*e-**rah**-dah, s., pirouette; gyration
girado, *H*e-**rah**-do, s., drawee
girador, *H*e-rah-**dor,** s., drawer (of bills)
girante, *H*e-**rahn**-tay, s., drawer (of bills)
girar, *H*e-**rar,** v., to turn round; to draw (bills)
girasol, *H*e-rah-**sol,** s., sun-flower   [(of bills)
giro, *H*ee-ro, s., turning round; draft; circulation
gitanear, *H*e-tah-nay-**ar,** v., to flatter; to wheedle
gitano, *H*e-**tah**-no, s., gipsy
glacial, glah-the-**al,** a., icy
glándula, **glahn**-doo-lah, s., gland
glasé, glah-**say,** s., glacé silk
globo, **glo**-bo, s., globe; sphere; balloon
gloria, **glo**-re-ah, s., glory
gloriarse, glo-re-**ar**-say, v., to glory; to boast in
glorieta, glo-re-**ay**-tah, s., arbour; bower
glorificar, glo-re-fe-**kar,** v., to glorify
glorioso, glo-re-**o**-so, a., glorious
glosa, **glo**-sah, s., gloss; commentary
glosario, glo-**sah**-re-o, s., glossary
glotón, glo-**ton,** s., glutton
glotonería, glo-to-nay-**ree**-ah, s., gluttony
glutinoso, gloo-te-**no**-so, a., glutinous; viscous
gobernación, go-bair-nah-the-**on,** s., government
gobernador, go-bair-nah-**dor,** s., governor; ruler
gobernar, go-bair-**nar,** v., to govern
gobierno, go-be-**air**-no, s., government
gobio, **go**-be-o, s., gudgeon
goce, **go**-thay, s., enjoyment
gola, **go**-lah, s., gullet; throat; gorge
goleta, go-**lay**-tah, s., schooner
golfo, golf-fo, s., gulf; bay
golondrina, go-lon-**dree**-nah, s., swallow

golosina, go-lo-*see*-nah, s., titbit; dainty sweet

golpe, **gol**-pay, s., blow; stroke; hit; knock; dent

golpeador, gol-pay-ah-*dor*, s., striker; knocker

golpear, gol-pay-*ar*, v., to beat; to strike; to knock;

golpeo, gol-*pay*-o, s., beating; striking   [to bruise

goma, *go*-mah, s., gum

gondolero, gon-do-*lay*-ro, s., gondolier

gordal, gor-*dahl*, a., fat; fleshy; big

gordo, **gor**-do, a., fat; corpulent

gordura, gor-*doo*-rah, s., grease; fatness; corpu-   [lence

gorgorito, gor-go-*ree*-to, s., quiver of the voice

gorila, go-*ree*-lah, s., gorilla

gorjeo, gor-*Hay*-o, s., trilling, quaver

gorra, **gor**-rrah, s., cap; bonnet

gorrión, gor-rre-*on*, s., sparrow

gorrista, gor-*rriss*-tah, s., parasite; sponger

gorro, **gor**-rro, s., night-cap

gorrón, gor-*rron*, s., parasite; debauchee; spindle

gota, **go**-tah, s., drop; gout

gotear, go-tay-*ar*, v., to drop; to dribble; to drip

gotera, go-*tay*-rah, s., gutter; leakage

gotoso, go-**to**-so, a., gouty

gozar, go-*thar*, v., to enjoy

gozo, **go**-tho, s., joy; pleasure

gozoso, go-**tho**-so, a., joyful

grabador, grah-bah-*dor*, s., engraver

grabar, grah-**bar**, v., to engrave

gracia, **grah**-the-ah, s., grace; favour

grácil, **grah**-thil, a., slender; gracile

gracioso, grah-the-**o**-so, a., graceful

grada, **grah**-dah, s., step of a staircase; grading   harrow

gradar, grah-**dar**, v., to harrow   [steps

gradería, grah-day-**ree**-ah, s., series of seats or

grado, **grah**-do, s., step; degree; will; pleasure

graduado, grah-doo-**ah**-do, s., graduate. a., gra-   duated

graduando, grah-doo-*ahn*-do, s., undergraduate

graduar, grah-doo-*ar*, v., to grade; to divide into   degrees; to graduate

gráfico, **grah**-fe-ko, a., graphic; graphical

grafito, grah-**fee**-to, s., graphite

grajo, grah-*H*o, s., jackdaw

gramática, grah-**mah**-te-kah, s., grammar

gramo, grah-mo, s., gramme

gramófono, grah-**mo**-fo-no, s., gramophone

gran, grahn, a., (used only before substantives in the singular. See **grande**)

grana, grah-nah, s., grain; cochineal; scarlet

granada, grah-**nah**-dah, s., pomegranate; shell

granado, grah-**nah**-do, a., notable; select; pome-

granar, grah-**nar**, v., to seed [granate tree

grande, grahn-day, s., grandee. a., great; large; big; grand [grandeeship

grandeza, grahn-**day**-thah, s., greatness; grandeur;

grandioso, grahn-de-o-so, a., grand; splendid

grandor, grahn-**dor**, s., size; tallness [in bulk

granel, grah-nel, s., heap of grain. **a —,** ah —,

granero, grah-**nay**-ro, s., granary; barn

granito, grah-nee-to, s., granite

granizada, grah-ne-**thah**-dah, s., hailstorm

granizar, grah-ne-**thar**, v., to hail

granja, grahn-*H*ah, s., grange; farm [profit

granjear, grahn-*H*ay-**ar**, v., to gain; to earn; to

granjería, grahn-*H*ay-**ree**-ah, s., gain; profit

grano, grah-no, s., grain

granuja, grah-noo-*H*ah, s., rogue

grapa, grah-pah, s., clamp; clasp

grasa, grah-sah, s., grease; suet; fat

grasera, grah-**say**-rah, s., dripping-pan

grasiento, grah-se-en-to, a., greasy; filthy; oily

graso, grah-so, a., fat; oily

gratificar, grah-te-fe-**kar**, v., to reward; to tip;

gratitud, grah-te-**tood**, s., gratitude [to gratify

grato*, grah-to, a., pleasant; acceptable; grateful

gratuito, grah-too-**ee**-to, a., gratuitous

gravamen, grah-vah-men, s., charge; obligation;

gravar, grah-**var**, v., to burden [mortgage

grave, grah-vay, a., weighty; grave; important; serious [seriousness

gravedad, grah-vay-**dahd**, s., gravity; heaviness;

gravoso, grah-**vo**-so, a., onerous; unbearable

graznar, grath-**nar**, v., to croak; to cackle

greda, gray-dah, s., chalk; marl; clay

gregal, gray-**gahl**, s., north-east wind. a., grega-
greguería, gray-gay-**ree**-ah, s., outcry   [rious
gremio, gray-me-o, s., society ; corporation
greña, gray-n'yah, s., long entangled hair
greñudo, gray-n'**yoo**-do, a., dishevelled
gresca, gress-kah, s., clatter ; tumult ; wrangle
grey, gray'e, s., flock ; herd   [confusion
grieta, gre-ay-tah, s., crevice ; crack ; flaw
grietarse, gre-ay-**tar**-say, v., to crack ; to split
grifo, gree-fo, s., griffin ; tap
grifón, gre-**fon**, s., water-cock
grillete, gre-l'**yay**-tay, s., shackles, fetters
grillo, gree-l'yo, s., cricket (an insect). pl., fetters
grima, gree-mah, s., fright ; astonishment ; disgust
gris, griss, a., grizzled ; gray
grita, gree-tah, s., uproar ; halloo   [to shriek
gritar, gre-**tar**, v., to shout ; to bawl ; to cry up
gritería, gre-tay-**ree**-ah, s., outcry ; shouting
grito, gree-to, s., cry ; scream ; shout
grosella, gro-say-'lyah, s., red currant
grosería, gro-say-**ree**-ah, s., rudeness ; ill-breeding
grosero, gro-**say**-ro, a., coarse, rude
grosura, gro-**soo**-rah, s., suet ; tallow ; fat
grúa, groo'ah, s., crane (machine)
gruesa, groo'**ay**-sah, s., gross (twelve dozen)
grueso, groo'**ay**-so, s., corpulence. a., bulky ; gross
grulla, groo-l'yah, s., crane (bird)   [large ; coarse
grumete, groo-**may**-tay, s., cabin-boy
grumo, groo-mo, s., grume ; curd ; cluster ; pith
gruñido, groo-n'**yee**-do, s., grunt ; growl
gruñir, groo-n'**yeer**, v., to grunt ; to creak
grupa, groo-pah, s., croup
grupo, groo-po, s., group
gruta, groo-tah, s., grotto ; cavern
guadaña, goo'ah-**dah**-n'yah, s., scythe
guadañar, goo'ah-dah-n'**yar**, v., to mow
guantada, goo'ahn-**tah**-dah, s., slap with the open
guante, goo'ahn-tay, s., glove   [hand
guantería, goo'ahn-tay-**ree**-ah, s., glover's shop
guantero, goo'ahn-**tay**-ro, s., glover   [in dress
guapeza, goo'ah-**pay**-thah, s., courage ; ostentation
guapo, goo'**ah**-po, a., handsome ; valiant ; spruce

guarda, goo'**ar**-dah, s., guard; keeper; custody

guardabosque, goo'ar-dah-**bos**-kay, s., forester; gamekeeper

guardabrisa, goo'ar-dah-**bree**-sah, s., lamp shade

guardacantón, goo'ar-dah-kahn-**ton**, s., corner-stone [cutter

guardacostas, goo'ar-dah-**kos**-tahs, s., revenue

guardafuegos, goo'ar-dah-foo'**ay**-gos, s., fender

guardar, goo'ar-**dar**, v., to keep; to guard

guardarropa, goo'ar-dah-**rro**-pah, s., wardrobe

guardia, goo'**ar**-de-ah, s., guard; watch

guardián, goo'ar-de-**ahn**, s., keeper; guardian

guardilla, goo'ar-**dee**-l'yah, s., garret; attic

guardoso, goo'ar-**do**-so, a., stingy

guarecer, goo'ah-ray-**thair**, v., to shelter; to assist; to aid; to cure

guarida, goo'ah-**ree**-dah, s., den; haunt; shelter

guarismo, goo'ah-**riss**-mo, s., cipher; figure

guarnecer, goo'ar-nay-**thair**, v., to garnish; to set; to adorn

guarnición, goo'ar-ne-the-**on**, s., garniture; setting; garrison

guarnir, goo'ar-**neer**, (see **guarnecer**)

guarro, goo'**ar**-rro, s., pig

guasa, goo'**ah**-sah, s., jest; irony

guasón, goo'ah-**son**, a., joking; dull

¡**guay!** goo'**ah**'e, interj., alas!

gubia, goo-be-ah, s., gouge

guedeja, gay-**day**-Hah, s., lion's mane; lock of hair

guerra, gair-rrah, s., war; warfare; hostility

guerrero, gair-**rray**-ro, s., warrior. a., warlike

guerrilla, gair-**rree**-l'yah, s., guerrilla; skirmish

guerrillero, gair-rree-l'**yay**-ro, s., partisan; guerrilla fighter

guía, ghee-ah, s., guide-book

guiar, ghee-**ar**, v., to guide

guija, ghee-Hah, s., pebble

guijarro, ghee-**Har**-rro, s., pebble; stone

guinda, gheen-dah, s., cherry

guindilla, gheen-**dee**-l'yah, s., red pepper

guiñada, ghee-n'**yah**-dah, s., wink

guiñapo, ghee-n'**yah**-po, s., tatter; rag

guiñar, ghee-n**'yar,** v., to wink

guión, ghee-**on,** s., standard ; banner ; hyphen

guirnalda, gheer-**nahl**-dah, s., garland

guisado, ghee-**sah**-do, s., stew

guisandero, ghee-sahn-**day**-ro, s., cook

guisante, ghee-**sahn**-tay, s., pea

guisar, ghee-**sar,** v., to cook ; to dress

guiso, ghee-so, s., seasoning ; cooked dish

guita, ghee-tah, s., thread ; twine

guitarra, ghee-**tar**-rrah, s., guitar

gula, goo-lah, s., gluttony

gusano, goo-**sah**-no, s., caterpillar ; maggot ; worm

gustar, gooss-**tar,** v., to taste ; to like ; to enjoy

gusto, gooss-to, s., taste ; pleasure

gustoso*, gooss-**to**-so, a., tasty ; pleasing

gutural, goo-too-**rahl,** a., a guttural

haba, ah-bah, s., bean

habanera, ah-bah-**nay**-rah, s., Cuban dance

habano, ah-**bah**-no, s., Havana cigar

haber, ah-**bair,** v., to have, — **de,** — day, to have to... s., property ; assets

habichuela, ah-be-choo**'ay**-lah, s., French bean

hábil*, ah-bil, a., capable ; skilful

habilidad, ah-be-le-**dahd,** s., ability ; skill

habilitado, ah-be-le-**tah**-do, s., paymaster. a., qualified

habitante, ah-be-**tahn**-tay, s., inhabitant

hábito, ah-be-to, s., dress ; habit ; custom

habituar, ah-be-too**'ar,** v., to accustom

habla, ah-blah, s., speech ; language

hablador, ah-blah-**dor,** s., prattler

habladuría, ah-blah-doo-**ree**-ah, s., gossip ; slanderous talk

hablar, ah-**blar,** v., to speak ; to talk

hablista, ah-**bliss**-tah, s., purist

hacecillo, ah-thay-**thee**-l'yo, s., small sheaf

hacedero, ah-thay-**day**-ro, a., feasible

hacedor, ah-thay-**dor,** s., maker ; author

hacendado, ah-then-**dah**-do, s., landholder

hacendista, ah-then-**diss**-tah, s., financier ; economist

hacer, ah-**thair**, v., to make; to do; to perform; to produce

hacia, ah-the-ah, adv., towards; above [wealth

hacienda, ah-the-**en**-dah, s., landed property;

hacinar, ah-the-**nar**, v., to pile up

hacha, ah-chah, s., large taper; axe

hachear, ah-chay-ar, v., to hew

hacho, ah-cho, s., torch

halagar, ah-lah-**gar**, v., to cajole; to flatter

halago, ah-**lah**-go, s., cajolery; caress [luring

halagüeño, ah-lah-goo'**ay**-n'yo, a., flattering; al-

halar, ah-**lar**, v., to haul; to pull on

halcón, ahl-**kon**, s., falcon

hálito, **ah**-le-to, s., breath; vapour

hallar, ah-l'**yar**, v., to find; to meet with

hallazgo, ah-l'**yath**-go, s., find; reward for finding

hamaca, ah-**mah**-kah, s., hammock

hambre, **ahm**-bray, s., hunger; famine; longing

hambrear, ahm-bray-**ar**, v., to starve; to be hungry

hambriento, ahm-bre-**en**-to, a., hungry; eager

haragán, ah-rah-**gahn**, s., idler; loiterer

harapo, ah-**rah**-po, s., rag; tatter

harina, ah-**ree**-nah, s., flour; meal

harinoso, ah-re-**no**-so, a., mealy

hartar, ar-**tar**, v., to cloy; to satiate; to disgust

harto, ar-to, adv., enough. a., satiated; sufficient

hartura, ar-**too**-rah, s., satiety [far as

hasta, **ahs**-tah, prep., until; up to; down to; as

hastío, ahs-**tee**-o, s., loathing; tedium

hato, **ah**-to, s., flock; herd

haya, **ah**-yah, s., beech tree

haz, ath, s., fagot; bundle; sheaf [deed

hazaña, ah-**thah**-n'yah, s., feat; exploit; heroic

hazañería, ah-thah-n'yay-**ree**-ah, s., affectation

hazañero, ah-thah-n'**yay**-ro, a., affected; prudish

hazañoso, ah-thah-n'**yo**-so, a., valiant; heroic

hazmerreir, ath-mair-rray-**eer**, s., laughing-stock

hebilla, ay-bee-l'yah, s., buckle; clasp

hebra, **ay**-brah, s., needful; thread; fibre

hechicero, ay-che-**thay**-ro, s., charmer. a., be-witching

hechizar, ay-che-**thar**, v., to enchant; to bewitch

hechizo, ay-**chee**-tho, s., enchantment

hecho, ay-cho, s., action; feat; point in litigation. a., made; ready-made; done

hechura, ay-**choo**-rah, s., form; shape; make; workmanship

heder, ay-**dair**, v., to stink

hedor, ay-**dor**, s., stench; stink

helada, ay-**lah**-dah, s., frost; nip

helado, ay-**lah**-do, s., ice-cream. a., frozen

helar, ay-**lar**, v., to freeze; to congeal

hélice, ay-le-thay, s., helix; propeller

helicóptero, ay-le-**kop**-tay-ro, s., helicopter

hembra, em-brah, s., female

hemorragia, ay-mor-**rrah**-*H*ee-ah, s., hemorrhage

hemorroide, ay-mor-**rro**-e-day, s., hemorrhoids;

henchir, en-**cheer**, v., to fill up; to stuff   [piles

hendedura, en-day-**doo**-rah, s., crack; chink; cranny

hender, en-**dair**, v., to crack; to cleave; to split

heno, ay-no, s., hay

heraldo, ay-**rahl**-do, s., herald

herbaje, air-bah-*H*ay, s., herbage; pasture

herborizar, air-bo-re-**thar**, v., to herborize

heredad, ay-ray-**dahd**, s., farm; property

heredar, ay-ray-**dar**, v., to inherit

heredero, ay-ray-**day**-ro, s., heir

hereje, ay-ray-*H*ay, s., heretic

herejía, ay-ray-*H*ee-ah, s., heresy

herencia, ay-**ren**-the-ah, s., inheritance

herida, ay-**ree**-dah, s., wound

herir, ay-**reer**, v., to wound; to strike; to offend

hermana, air-**mah**-nah, s., sister   [to fraternize

hermanar, air-mah-**nar**, v., to match; to suit;

hermandad, air-mahn-**dahd**, s., fraternity; conformity; brotherhood

hermano, air-**mah**-no, s., brother

hermoso, air-**mo**-so, a., beautiful; handsome

hermosura, air-mo-**soo**-rah, s., beauty

héroe, ay-ro-ay, s., hero

heroína, ay-ro-ee-nah, s., heroine

herrador, air-rrah-**dor**, s., farrier

herradura, air-rrah-**doo**-rah, s., horse-shoe
herramental, air-rrah-men-**tahl**, s., tool-bag
herrar, air-**rrar**, v., to shoe horses
herrero, air-**rray**-ro, s., smith
herrumbre, air-**rroom**-bray, s., rust
hervir, air-**veer**, v., to boil
hervor, air-**vor**, s., ebullition
hético, **ay**-te-ko, a., hectic　　　　　[excrements
hez, eth, s., lee; dross; dregs. pl., **heces, ay**-thess,
hidalgo, e-**dahl**-go, s., hidalgo; nobleman
hidalguía, e-dahl-**ghee**-ah, s., nobility
hiedra, e-**ay**-drah s., ivy
hiel, e-**ell**, s., gall; bile
hielo, e-**ay**-lo, s., frost; ice
hiena, e-**ay**-nah, s., hyena
hierba, e-**air**-bah, s., grass; weed; herb
hierro, e-**air**-rro, s., iron tool
higa, ee-gah, s., amulet
hígado, **ee**-gah-do, s., liver
higo, ee-go, s., fig
higuera, e-**gay**-rah, s., fig-tree
hijo, ee-**H**o, s., son
hija, ee-**H**ah, s., daughter　　　　　[daughter
hijuela, e-**H**oo'**ay**-lah, s., patch; mattress; little
hila, ee-lah, s., row; line
hilacha, e-**lah**-chah, s., filament
hilado, e-**lah**-do, s., spun material; yarn. a., spun
hilador, e-lah-**dor**, s., spinner
hilar, e-**lar**, v., to spin
hilaridad, e-lah-re-**dahd**, s., hilarity
hilera, e-**lay**-rah, s., row; line; file
hilo, ee-lo, s., thread
hilván, il-**vahn**, s., basting
hilvanar, il-vah-**nar**, v., to tack; to baste; to
　stitch
himeneo, e-may-**nay**-o, s., marriage
himno, **eem**-no, s., hymn
hincapié, in-kah-pe-**ay**, s., insistence; strong effort
hincar, in-**kar**, v., to thrust in　　　　[vain
hinchado, in-**chah**-do, a., swollen; arrogant;
hinchar, in-**char**, v., to inflate; to swell
hinchazón, in-chah-**thon**, s., swelling; inflation

hinojo, in-o-*Ho*, s., fennel; knee

hipar, e-*par*, v., to hiccough; to pant

hipo, ee-po, s., hiccough, desire; anger

hipocresía, e-po-cray-*see*-ah, s., hypocrisy

hipoteca, e-po-*tay*-kah, s., mortgage

hipótesis, e-po-tay-siss, s., hypothesis

histerismo, iss-tay-*riss*-mo, s., hysterics

historia, iss-*to*-re-ah, s., history

histórico, iss-*to*-re-ko, a., historical

historieta, iss-to-re-*ay*-tah, s., short story

hita, ee-tah, s., brad; wire-nail

hito, ee-to, s., landmark; post; mile-stone

hocicar, o-the-*kar*, v., to fall face downwards

hocico, o-*thee*-ko, s., snout. (fam.) face

hogaño, o-gah-n'yo, adv., this year

hogar, o-gar, s., hearth; home

hoguera, o-*gay*-rah, s., bonfire

hoja, o-*Hah*, s., leaf; sheet; blade

hojalata, o-Hah-*lah*-tah, s., tin plate

hojalatero, o-Hah-lah-*tay*-ro, s., tinsmith

hojaldre, o-*Hahl*-dray, s., puff-pastry

hojear, o-*Hay*-*ar*, v., to turn the leaves of a book

holgado, ol-*gah*-do, a., loose; large; at leisure; well off

holgar, ol-gar, v., to rest; to be at ease; to take pleasure in

holgazán, ol-gah-*than*, s., idler; loiterer

holgura, ol-*goo*-rah, s., ease; width

hollar, o-l'yar, v., to trample

hollejo, o-l'yay-*Ho*, s., peel; rind; pellicle

hollín, o-l'yeen, s., soot

hombrada, om-*brah*-dah, s., manly action

hombre, om-bray, s., man

hombría de bien, om-*bree*-ah day be-*en*, s., probity [probity]

hombro, om-bro, s., shoulder

hombruno, om-*broo*-no, a., virile; manly

homenaje, o-may-*nah*-Hay, s., homage

homónimo, o-*mo*-ne-mo, a., namesake

honda, on-dah, s., sling

hondo*, on-do, a., profound; deep

hondón, on-don, s., bottom

hondura, on-*doo*-rah, s., depth; profundity

honesto*, o-**ness**-to, a., honest

hongo, on-go, s., fungus; mushroom

honor, o-**nor**, s., honour   [women]

honra, on-**rah**, s., honour; reputation; chastity (in

honrado, on-rah-do, a., honest; honourable

honrar, on-**rar**, v., to honour; to praise; to credit

honrilla, on-ree-l'yah, s., nice point of honour

honroso, on-ro-so, a., honourable

hopo, o-po, s., bushy tail

hora, o-rah, s., hour

horadar, o-rah-**dar**, v., to bore; to pierce

horado, o-rah-do, s., cavern; grotto

horca, or-kah, s., pitchfork; gallows

horcado, or-kah-do, a., forked

horcajadas (a), ah-or-kah-*H* ah-dahs, adv., astride

horchata, or-chah-tah, s., orgeat

horda, or-dah, s., horde; clan; tribe

horizonte, o-re-**thon**-tay, s., horizon

horma, or-**mah**, s., mould

hormiga, or-**mee**-gah, s., ant

hormigón, or-me-gon, s., concrete

hormiguero, or-me-**gay**-ro, s., ant-hill

hornero, or-**nay**-ro, s., baker

hornillo, or-nee-l'yo, s., small stove

horno, o-rno, s., oven

horquilla, or-kee-l'yah, s., forked stick; hair-pin

horrendo, or-**ren**-do, a., dreadful; awful

horro, or-rro, a., enfranchised; free

horror, or-**rror**, s., horror; consternation

horrorizar, or-rro-re-**thar**, v., to cause horror

horroroso, or-rro-ro-so, a., horrid; hideous

hortaliza, or-tah-lee-thah, s., garden stuff; vegetables

hortelano, or-tay-lah-no, s., gardener; ortolan

hortera, or-tay-rah, s., wooden bowl

hosco, os-ko, a., dark-coloured; sullen

hospedaje, os-pay-**dah**-*H*ay, s., hospitality; lodg-

hospedar, os-pay-**dar**, v., to lodge   [ing

hospedería, os-pay-day-**ree**-ah, s., hospice; hostelry

hospedero, os-pay-**day**-ro, s., host; inn-keeper

hospicio, os-**pee**-the-o, s., hospice; orphanage

hospital, os-pe-**tahl**, s., hospital
hostelero, os-tay-**lay**-ro, s., inn-keeper
hostería, os-tay-**ree**-ah, s., inn; tavern; hostelry
hostia, os-te-ah, s., host
hostigar, os-te-**gar**, v., to harass; to scourge
hostil, os-**teel**, a., hostile
hoy, o'e, adv., to-day
hoya, hoyo, o-yah, o-yo, s., hole; pit; grave
hoyoso, o-yo-so, a., full of holes
hoz, oth, s., sickle
hucha, oo-chah, s., money-box
hueco, oo-**ay**-ko, a., hollow; empty
huelga, oo-**ell**-gah, s., rest; recreation; strike
huelgo, oo-**ell**-go, s., breath; respiration
huella, oo'**ay**-l'yah, s., track; footprint
huérfano, oo'**air**-fah-no, s., orphan
huero, oo'**ay**-ro, a., empty; addle
huerta, oo'**air**-tah, s., vegetable garden
huerto, oo'**air**-to, s., orchard
hueso, oo'**ay**-so, s., bone; stone; core
huésped, oo'**ess**-ped, s., guest; inn-keeper; host
hueste, oo'**ess**-tay, s., army in campaign
hueva, oo'**ay**-vah, s., spawn; roe
huevo, oo'**ay**-vo, s., egg
huida, oo'**ee**-dah, s., flight; escape
huir, oo'**eer**, v., to fly; to escape
hulla, oo'-l'yah, s., pit-coal
humano*, oo-**mah**-no, a., human; humane
humazo, oo-**mah**-tho, s., dense smoke
humear, oo-may-**ar**, v., to smoke
humedad, oo-may-**dahd**, s., humidity; moisture
humedecer, oo-may-day-**thair**, v., to moisten;
to wet; to soak
húmedo, oo-**may**-do, a., humid; wet
humero, oo-**may**-ro, s., funnel; shaft
húmero, oo-**may**-ro, s., shoulder-blade
humildad, oo-mil-**dahd**, s., humility
humilde, oo-**meel**-day, a., humble; meek
humillar, oo-me-l'**yar**, v., to humiliate; to subdue
humo, oo-mo, s., smoke; fume
humor, oo-**mor**, s., humour; disposition; temper
humorada, oo-mo-**rah**-dah, s., sprightliness

humorista, oo-mo-**rees**-tah, s., humourist
humoso, oo-**mo**-so, a., smoky   [lapse
hundimiento, oon-de-me-**en**-to, s., sinking; col-
hundir, oon-**deer**, v., to submerge; to sink; to
huracán, oo-rah-**kahn**, s., hurricane   [crush
hurgar, oor-**gar**, v., to stir; to excite; to poke
hurgón, oor-**gon**, s., poker
hurón, oo-**ron**, s., ferret   [stealth
hurtadillas (a), ah-oor-tah-dee-l'yahs, adv., by
hurtar, oor-**tar**, v., to steal; to rob
hurto, oor-to, s., theft; robbery
húsar, oo-sar, s., hussar   [to pry
husma, (andar a la) ahn-dar ah lah **ooss**-mah,
husmear, ooss-may-**ar**, v., to scent; to pry; to peep
husmo, ooss-mo, s., smell of tainted meat
huso, oo-so, s., spindle
huta, oo-tah, s., hut

ictericia, ik-tay-ree-the-ah, s., jaundice
ida, ee-dah, s., departure; sally
idea, e-**day**-ah, s., idea; scheme
ideal, e-day-**ahl**, s. & a., ideal
idear, e-day-**ar**, v., to form an idea; to plan
idéntico, e-**den**-te-ko, a., identical
idilio, e-**dee**-le-o, s., idyl
idioma, e-de-o-mah, s., idiom
idiota, e-de-o-tah, s., idiot. a., idiotic
ídolo, ee-do-lo, s., idol
idoneidad, e-do-nay'e-**dahd**, s., fitness; capacity
idóneo, e-do-nay-o, a., qualified; competent
iglesia, e-**glay**-se-ah, s., church
ígneo, **ig**-nay-o, a., igneous
ignífugo, ig-nee-foo-go, a., fireproof
ignorancia, ig-no-**rahn**-the-ah, s., ignorance
ignoto, ig-no-to, a., unknown
igual, e-goo'**ahl**, a., equal
igualar, e-goo'ah-**lar**, v., to equalize
igualdad, e-goo'ahl-**dahd**, s., equality
ilación, e-lah-the-**on**, s., inference
ilegal, e-lay-**gahl**, a., illegal; unlawful
ilegible, e-lay-_Hee_-blay, a., illegible
ileso, e-lay-so, a., unhurt

ilimitado, e-le-me-**tah**-do, a., unlimited
iluminar, e-loo-me-**nar**, v., to illuminate; to enlighten
ilusión, e-loo-se-**on**, s., illusion
iluso, e-**loo**-so, a., deceived; deluded
ilustrar, e-looss-**trar**, v., to illustrate
ilustre, e-**looss**-tray, a., illustrious
imagen, e-**mah**-Hen, s., image
imaginar, e-mah-He-**nar**, v., to imagine [tiveness
imaginativa, e-mah-He-nah-tee-vah, s., imagina-
imaginería, e-mah-He-nay-**ree**-ah, s., fancy embroidery in colours
imán, e-**mahn**. s., magnet
imantar, e-mahn-**tar**, v., to magnetize
imbécil, im-**bay**-thil, a., imbecile
imberbe, im-**bair**-bay, s., beardless youth
imbuir, im-boo'eer, v., to imbue
imitado, e-me-**tah**-do, a., imitated; similar
imitar, e-me-**tar**, v., to imitate
impaciencia, im-pah-the-**en**-the-ah, s., impatience
impacientar, im-pah-the-en-**tar**, v., to make impatient; to irritate
impaciente, im-pah-the-**en**-tay, a., impatient
impacto, im-**pahk**-to, a., impact
impar, im-**par**, a., odd; uneven
imparcial, im-par-the-**ahl**, a., impartial
impartible, im-par-**tee**-blay, a., indivisible
impartir, im-par-**teer**, v., to impart
impávido, im-**pah**-ve-do, a., intrepid; calm [less
impecable, im-pay-**kah**-blay, a., impeccable; fault-
impedir, im-pay-**deer**, v., to impede; to obstruct
impeler, im-pay-**lair**, v., to impel; to spur
impensado, im-pen-**sah**-do, a., unexpected
imperar, im-pay-**rar**, v., to rule [donable
imperdonable, im-pair-do-**nah**-blay, a., unpar-
imperecedero, im-pay-ray-thay-**day**-ro, a., imper-
imperfecto, im-pair-**fek**-to, a., imperfect [ishable
impericia, im-pay-**ree**-the-ah, s., unskilfulness
imperio, im-**pay**-re-o, s., empire
imperioso, im-pay-re-**o**-so, a., imperious
imperito, im-pay-**ree**-to, a., unskilled
impertérrito, im-pair-**tair**-rre-to, a., dauntless

imperturbable, im-pair-toor-**bah**-blay, a., unmoved

ímpetu, eem-pay-too, s., impetus; impulse

impío, im-**pee**-o, a., impious

implicar, im-ple-**kar**, v., to implicate

implorar, im-plo-**rar**, v., to implore; to entreat

impolítica, im-po-**lee**-te-kah, s., discourtesy

impolítico, im-po-lee-te-ko, a., impolitic; impolite

imponer, im-po-**nair**, v., to impose; to charge upon falsely; to instruct

importar, im-por-**tar**, v., to import; to concern

importe, im-**por**-tay, s., amount; value

importunar, im-por-too-**nar**, v., to importune

imposibilitar, im-po-se-be-le-**tar**, v., to render impossible; to disable

imposible, im-po-**see**-blay, a., impossible

imposta, im-**pos**-tah, s., impost; springer

impostura, im-pos-**too**-rah, s., false imputation imposture

imprenta, im-**pren**-tah, s., printing; printing-office

impresión, im-pray-se-**on**, s., impression; stamp; edition

impresionar, im-pray-se-o-**nar**, v., to imprint; to impress

impreso, im-pray-so, s., printed matter [impress

impresor, im-pray-**sor**, s., printer

imprevisión, im-pray-ve-se-**on**, s., improvidence

imprevisto, im-pray-**viss**-to, a., unforeseen

imprimir, im-pre-**meer**, v., to print; to stamp

improbo, eem-pro-bo, a., dishonest; laborious

improperio, im-pro-**pay**-re-o, s., reproach; insult

impropiedad, im-pro-pe-ay-**dahd**, s., impropriety; unsuitability

impropio, im-**pro**-pe-o, a., improper; unfit

improvisar, im-pro-ve-**sar**, v., to extemporize

improviso, im-pro-**vee**-so, a., unforeseen; unexpected

impúdico, im-**poo**-de-ko, a., unchaste; impudent

impuesto, im-poo'**ess**-to, s., tax; duty. a., informed

impugnación, im-poog-nah-the-**on**, s., opposition

impugnar, im-poog-**nar**, v., to impugn

impulsar, im-pool-**sar**, v., to impel; to prompt

impulsor, im-pool-**sor**, s., impeller; driver

impune, im-**poo**-nay, a., unpunished

impureza, im-poo-**ray**-thah, s., impurity

imputar, im-poo-**tar**, v., to impute; to accuse

inacabable, in-ah-kah-**bah**-blay, a., interminable

inacción, in-ahk-the-**on**, s., inaction [able

inaceptable, in-ah-thep-**tah**-blay, a., unaccept-

inadecuado, in-ah-day-koo'**ah**-do, a., inadequate

inadvertido, in-ahd-vair-**tee**-do, a., unnoticed; unobserved

inagotable, in-ah-goh-**tah**-blay, a., inexhaustible

inaguantable, in-ah-goo'ahn-**tah**-blay, a., insupportable; unbearable

inajenable, in-ah-*H*ay-**nah**-blay, a., inalienable

inalterable, in-ahl-tay-**rah**-do, a., unchanged

inamovible, in-ah-mo-**vee**-blay, a., immovable

inapagable, in-ah-pah-**gah**-blay, a., unquenchable [tite

inapetente, in-ah-pay-**ten**-tay, a., without appe-

inasequible, in-ah-say-**kee**-blay, a., unattainable

inaudito, in-ah'oo-dee-to, a., unheard of

inaugurar, in-ah'oo-goo-**rar**, v., to inaugurate

incalificable, in-kah-le-fe-**kah**-blay, a., unqualifiable

incansable, in-kahn-**sah**-blay, a., indefatigable

incapacitar, in-kah-pah-the-**tar**, v., to incapacitate; to disable

incapaz, in-kah-**path**, a., unable; incapable

incauto, in-**kah**'oo-to, a., incautious

incendio, in-**then**-de-o, s., conflagration; fire

incertidumbre, in-thair-te-**doom**-bray, s., uncertainty

incesante*, in-thay-**sahn**-tay, a., unceasing

incidencia, in-the-**den**-the-ah, s., incidence; incidente

incidente, in-the-**den**-tay, s. & a., incident [cident

incidir, in-the-**deer**, v., to fall into or upon

incienso, in-the-**en**-so, s., incense

incierto, in-the-**air**-to, a., uncertain

incinerar, in-the-nay-**rar**, v., to cremate

inciso, in-**thee**-so, clause (in a long sentence)

incitación, in-the-tah-the-**on**, s., incitement

incitar, in-the-**tar**, v., to incite; to instigate

incivilidad, in-the-ve-le-**dahd**, s., incivility
inclemencia, in-klay-**men**-the-ah, s., inclemency
inclinado, in-kle-**nah**-do, a., a slanting; sloping
inclinar, in-kle-**nar**, v., to incline; to slope
incluir, in-kloo′eer, v., to include
inclusa, in-**kloo**-sah, s., foundling hospital
incluso, in-**kloo**-so, a., enclosed
incoar, in-ko-ar, v., to begin; to inchoate
incobrable, in-ko-**brah**-blay, a., irrecoverable; irretrievable
incógnito, in-**kog**-ne-to, a., unknown [retrievable
incoherencia, in-ko-ay-**ren**-the-ah, s., incoherence
incoloro, in-ko-**lo**-ro, a., colourless
incólume, in-ko-loo-may, a., sound; safe
incomodar, in-ko-mo-**dar**, v., to inconvenience; to disturb [fortable
incómodo, in-**ko**-mo-do, a., inconvenient; uncom-
incompasivo, in-kom-pah-**see**-vo, a., pitiless
incomplexo, in-kom-**plek**-so, a., simple
incomprensible, in-kom-pren-**see**-blay, a., incomprehensible [pressible
incomprimible, in-kom-pre-**mee**-blay, a., incom-
incomunicar, in-ko-moo-ne-**kar**, v., to isolate
inconcebible, in-kon-thay-**bee**-blay, a., inconceivable
inconexo, in-**kó**-nek-so, a., unconnected
inconfeso, in-kon-**fay**-so, a., who has not admitted his guilt [querable
inconquistable, in-kon-kiss-**tah**-blay, a., uncon-
inconsciente, in-kons-the-**en**-tay, a., unconscious
incontable, in-kon-**tah**-blay, a., uncountable
incontrastable, in-kon-trahs-**tah**-blay, a., insurmountable [nient
inconvenible, in-kon-vay-**nee**-blay, a., inconve-
incorrección, in-kor-rrek-the-**on**, s., inaccuracy; impropriety
incorregible, in-kor-rray-*H*ee-blay, a., incorrigible
incrédulo, in-**kray**-doo-lo, a., incredulous
increíble, in-kray-ee-blay, a., incredible
increpación, in-kray-pah-the-**on**, s., reprehension
increpar, in-kray-par, v., to reprehend; to rebuke
incriminar, in-kre-me-**nar**, v., to incriminate
incubar, in-koo-**bar**, v., to hatch

inculpar, in-**kool**-par, v., to inculpate
inculto, in-**kool**-to, a., uncultivated; uncultured
incultura, in-kool-**too**-rah, s., want of culture
incuria, in-**koo**-re-ah, s., carelessness; neglect
incurioso, in-koo-re-o-so, a., negligent
incurrir, in-koor-**rreer,** v., to incur
indagación, in dah-gah-the-**on,** s., investigation
indagar, in-dah-**gar,** v., to investigate
indebido, in-day-**bee**-do, a., undue; unlawful
indecente, in-day-**then**-tay, a., indecent
indecible*, in-day-**thee**-blay, a., inexpressible
indeciso*, in-day-**thée**-so, a., irresolute; undecided
indecoroso*, in-day-ko-**ro**-so, a., indecorous
indefectible, in-day-fek-**tee**-blay, a., unfailing
indefenso, in-day-**fen**-so, a., defenceless
indeleble, in-day-**lay**-blay, a., indelible
indeliberación, in-day-le-bay-rah-the-**on,** s., in-[*advertency*
indemne, in-**dem**-nay, a., unhurt
indemnizar, in-dem-ne-**thar,** v., to indemnify
independiente, in-day-pen-de-**en**-tay, a., independent [*pherable*
indescifrable, in-dess-the-**frah**-blay, a., indeci-
indescriptible, in-dess-krip-**tee**-blay, a., indescribable [*terminate; irresolute*
indeterminado, in-day-tair-me-**nah**-do, a., inde-
indicación, in-de-kah-the-**on,** s., indication
indicar, in-de-**kar,** v., to indicate; to suggest
indicción, in-dik-the-**on,** s., convocation
índice, in-de-thay, s., index; forefinger
indiciado, in-de-the-**ah**-do, a., suspected
indiciar, in-de-the-**ar,** v., to give reasons to sus-[*pect*
indicio, in-**dee**-the-o, s., indication; sign
indígena, in-**dee**-*H*ay-nah, s. & a., indigene; indigenous; native
indigesto, in-de-*H*ess-to, a., indigestible [*dignant*
indignar, in-dig-**nar,** v., to irritate; to make in-
indigno, in-**dig**-no, a., unworthy
indirecta, in-de-**rek**-tah, s., innuendo
indirecto*, in-de-**rek**-to, a., indirect [*sable*
indisculpable, in-diss-kool-**pah**-blay, a., inexcu-
indisponer, in-diss-po-**nair,** v., to disable; to indispose

indispuesto, in-diss-poo'**ess**-to, a., indisposed
indistinguible, in-diss-tin-**ghee**-blay, a., un-distinguishable
individuo, in-de-vee-doo'o, s., individual
indiviso, in-de-vee-so, a., undivided
indocto, in-**dok**-to, a., ignorant
índole, een-do-lay, s., disposition; temper; humour
indomable, in-do-**mah**-blay, a., untamable
indómito, in-do-me-to, a., untamed
inducción, in-dook-the-**on**, s., inducement
inducir, in-doo-**theer**, v., to induce; to persuade
indudable, in-doo-**dah**-blay, a., indubitable
indulgente, in-dool-**H**en-tay, a., indulgent
indulto, in-**dool**-to, s., pardon; reprieve
industria, in-**dooss**-tre-ah, s., industry
inédito, in-**ay**-de-to, a., unpublished
ineficaz, in-ay-fe-**kahth**, a., inefficacious
ineludible, in-ay-loo-dee-blay, a., unavoidable
ineptitud, in-ep-te-**tood**, s., ineptitude
inerme, in-**air**-may, a., disarmed; defenceless
inerte, in-**air**-tay, a., inert; sluggish
inesperado, in-ess-pay-**rah**-do, a., unexpected
inexhausto, in-ek-**sah**'ooss-to, a., unexhausted
inexperto, in-eks-**pair**-to, a., inexperienced
inextinguible, in-eks-tin-**ghee**-blay, a., inextinguishable
infamación, in-fah-mah-the-**on**, s., defamation
infamar, in-fah-**mar**, v., to defame
infame, in-**fah**-may, a., infamous
infanta, in-**fahn**-tah, s., infanta; female infant
infantil, in-fahn-**teel**, a., childlike
infatigable, in-fah-te-**gah**-blay, a., indefatigable
infausto, in-fah'**ooss**-to, a., unlucky; unhappy
infecto, in-**fek**-to, a., infected
infecundo, in-fay-**koon**-do, a., barren; sterile
infelicidad, in-fay-le-the-**dahd**, s., misfortune
infeliz, in-fay-**lith**, a., unhappy
inferioridad, in-fay-re-o-re-**dahd**, s., inferiority
inferir, in-fay-**reer**, v., to infer; to deduce
inficionar, in-fe-the-o-**nar**, v., to infect
infiel, in-fe-**ell**, a., unfaithful; disloyal
infierno, in-fe-**air**-no, s., hell

infiltrar, in-fil-**trar**, v., to infiltrate
ínfimo, een-fe-mo, a., lowest; vilest
inflamar, in-flah-**mar**, v., to inflame
inflar, in-**flar**, v., to swell   [able
inflexible, in-flek-**see**-blay, a., inflexible; inexor-
infligir, in-fle-**Heer**, v., to inflict
influir, in-floo'**eer**, v., to influence
influjo, in-**floo**Ho, s., influx; influence
influyente, in-floo-**yen**-tay, a., influential
informante, in-for-**man**-tay, s., informant
informar, in-for-**mar**, v., to inform   [shapeless
informe, in-**for**-may, s., information; report. a.,
infortunio, in-for-**too**-nee-o, s., misfortune
infractor, in-frahk-**tor**, s., infringer; transgressor
infrascrito, in-frah-**skree**-to, a., undersigned
infringir, in-frin-**Heer**, v., to infringe
infructuoso, in-frook-too'**o**-so, a., fruitless
ínfulas, een-foo-lahs, s., presumption; conceit
infundado, in-foon-**dah**-do, a., groundless
infundir, in-foon-**deer**, v., to infuse
ingeniar, in-Hay-ne-**ar**, v., to conceive; to devise
ingeniero, in-Hay-ne-**ay**-ro, s., engineer
ingeniería, in-Hay-ne-ay-**ree**-ah, s., engineering
ingenio, in-**Hay**-ne-o, s., genius; cleverness
ingénito, in-**Hay**-ne-to, a., inborn [ness; candour
ingenuidad, n-Hay-noo'e-**dahd**, s., ingenuous-
ingerir, in-Hay-**reer**, v., to swallow
ingle, een-glay, s., groin
inglete, in-**glay**-tay, s., diagonal
ingrato, in-**grah**-to, a., ungrateful; unpleasant
ingresar, in-gray-**sar**, v., to enter
ingreso, in-**gray**-so, s., ingress; entry
inhábil, in-**ah**-bil, a., incapable; unqualified
inhabitado, in-ah-be-**tah**-do, a., uninhabited
inhalar, in-ha-**lar**, v., to inhale
inhibición, in-e-be-the-**on**, s., inhibition
inhibir, in-e-**beer**, v., to inhibit; to prohibit
inhumación, in-oo-mah-the-**on**, s., burial
inhumano, in-oo-**mah**-no, a., inhuman
inicial, in-e-the-**al**, a., initial
iniciar, in-e-the-**ar**, v., to initiate
inicuo, in-ee-**koo'o**, a., iniquitous

injertar, in-*H*air-**tar**, v., to graft [wrong

injuriar, in-*H*oo-re-**ar**, v., to injure; to insult; to

inmaculado*, in-mah-koo-**lah**-do, a., pure; spotless

inmanejable, in-mah-nay-*H*ah-blay, a., unruly

inmediato*, in-may-de-ah-to, a., immediate

inmenso, in-**men**-so, a., immense; boundless

inmerecido, in-may-ray-**thee**-do, a., undeserved

inmergir, in-mair-*H*eer, v., to immerse [interfere

inmiscuir, in-miss-koo'**eer**, v., to meddle with; to

inmoral, in-mo-**rahl**, a., immoral; licentious

inmortal, in-mo-**tahl**, a., immortal; everlasting

inmóvil, in-**mo**-vil, a., motionless

inmovilizar, in-mo-vil-e-**thar**, v., to immobilize

inmueble, in-moo'**ay**-blay, s., immovable property

inmundo, in-**moon**-do, a., filthy; obscene

inmune, in-**moo**-nay, a., immune

inmutar, in-moo-**tar**, v., to change; to alter

innato, in-**nah**-to, a., inborn

innegable, in-nay-**gah**-blay, a., undeniable

innoble, in-**no**-blay, a., ignoble; of obscure birth

inobediente, in-o-bay-de-**en**-tay, a., disobedient

inobservancia, in-ob-sair-vahn-**the**-ah, s., inad-

inodoro, in-o-do-ro, a., odourless [vertency

inquietar, in-ke-ay-**tar**, v., to disquiet

inquietud, in-ke-ay-**tood**, s., inquietude; restless-

inquilino, in-ke-**lee**-no, s., tenant; lodger [ness

inquina, in-**kee**-nah, s., aversion; hatred

inquirir, in-ke-**reer**, v., to enquire; to search

insaciable, in-sah-the-**ah**-blay, a., insatiable

insalubre, in-sah-**loo**-bray, a., unhealthy

insano, in-**sah**-no, a., insane; mad [to enrol

inscribir, ins-kre-**beer**, v., to inscribe; to register;

insecto, in-**sek**-to, s., insect

inseguro, in-say-**goo**-ro, a., unsafe; uncertain

insensatez, in-sen-sah-**teth**, s., stupidity

insensible, in-sen-**see**-blay, a., senseless; insensi-

insepulto, in-say-**pool**-to, a., unburied [tive

inservible, in-sair-**vee**-blay, a., unserviceable;

insidioso, in-se-de-**oh**-so, a., insidious [useless

insigne, in-**sig**-nay, a., notable; noted

insignia, in-**sig**-ne-ah, s., decoration; badge

insinuar, in-se-noo'**ar**, v., to insinuate; to suggest

insipidez, in-se-pe-**deth**, s., insipidity
insistir, in-sis-**teer**, v., to insist; to dwell upon
insociable, in-so-the-**ah**-blay, a., unsociable
insolación, in-so-lah-the-**on**, s., sun-stroke
insolente, in-so-**len**-tay, a., insolent
insólito, in-**so**-le-to, a., unwonted; unusual
insomnio, in-**som**-ne-o, s., sleeplessness
insoportable, in-so-por-**tah**-blay, a., intolerable; unbearable
insostenible, in-sos-tay-**nee**-blay, a., indefensible
inspeccionar, ins-pek-the-o-**nar**, v., to inspect; to oversee
inspirar, ins-pe-**rar**, v., to inspire; to induce
instante, ins-**tahn**-tay, s., instant. a., instant
instar, ins-**tar**, v., to press; to urge   [pressing
instaurar, ins-tah'oo-**rar**, v., to restore; to re-es-
instituir, ins-te-too-**eer**, v., to institute   [tablish
institutriz, ins-te-too-**treeth**, s., governess
instruir, ins-troo-**eer**, v., to instruct; to inform; to drill
insubordinar, in-soo-bor-de-**nar**, v., to rebel
insufrible, in-soo-**free**-blay, a., insufferable
insulso, in-**sool**-so, a., tasteless; dull
insulto, in-**sool**-to, s., insult   [tial
insustancial, in-sooss-tahn-the-**al**, a., unsubstan-
intacto, in-**tahk**-to, a., untouched; intact
integración, in-te-grah-the-**on**, s., integration
integrar, in-te-**grar**, v., to integrate
intemperie, in-tem-**pay**-re-ay, s., bad weather.
a la —, ah lah —, outdoors   [ill-timed
intempestivo, in-tem-pes-**tee**-vo, a., unseasonable;
intencionado, in-ten-the-o-**nah**-do, a., inclined;
intento, in-**ten**-to, s., intent; design   [disposed
interceder, in-tair-thay-**dair**, v., to intercede
interdecir, in-tair-day-**theer**, v., to prohibit
interés, in-tay-**ress**, s., interest; profit; share;
ínterin, een-tay-rin, adv., meanwhile   [concern
interino, in-tay-**ree**-no, a., provisional
interior, in-tay-re-or, a., interior
internar, in-tair-**nar**, v., to penetrate inland
interpelar, in-tair-pay-**lar**, v., to appeal to; to interpellate

interponer, in-tair-po-**nair**, v., to interpose

intérprete, in-**tair**-pray-tay, s., interpreter

interrogar, in-tair-rro-**gar**, v., to interrogate; to question

interrumpir, in-tair-rroom-**peer**, v., to interrupt

intervalo, in-tair-**vah**-lo, s., interval

intervenir, in-tair-vay-**neer**, v., to intervene

interventor, in-tair-ven-**tor**, s., comptroller; inspector

intestino, in-tess-**tee**-no, s., intestine

intimidar, in-te-me-**dar**, v., to intimidate

íntimo, **een**-te-mo, a., innermost; intimate

intraducible, in-trah-doo-**thee**-blay, a., untranslatable [promising

intransigente, in-trahn-se-**Hen**-tay, a., uncom-

intransitable, in-trahn-se-**tah**-blay, a., impassable

intratable, in-trah-**tah**-blay, a., intractable

intrépido, in-**tray**-pe-do, a., fearless; dauntless

intrigar, in-tre-**gar**, v., to intrigue; to plot

intrincar, in-trin-**kar**, v., to entangle; to involve

introducir, in-tro-doo-**theer**, v., to introduce

intruso, in-**troo**-so, s., intruder. a., intrusive

inundar, in-oon-**dar**, v., to inundate; to flood

inusitado, in-oo-se-**tah**-do, a., unusual

inútil, in-**oo**-til, a., useless

inutilizar, in-oo-te-le-**thar**, v., to render useless

invadir, in-vah-**deer**, v., to invade

inválido, in-**vah**-le-do, a., weak; invalid; null

invasor, in-vah-**sor**, s., invader

invencible, in-ven-**thee**-blay, a., unconquerable

invendible, in-ven-**dee**-blay, a., unsalable

inventario, in-ven-**tah**-re-o, s., inventory

inventiva, in-ven-**tee**-vah, s., faculty of invention

invernáculo, in-vair-**nah**-koo-lo, s., hot-house

invernada, in-vair-**nah**-dah, s., winter season

invernal, in-vair-**nahl**, a., wintry

inverosímil, in-vay-ro-**see**-mil, a., unlikely

invertir, in-vair-**teer**, v., to invert; to invest

investigar, in-vess-te-**gar**, v., to investigate

inveterado, in-vay-tay-**rah**-do, a., old; chronic; obstinate

invicto, in-**veek**-to, a., unconquerable; invincible

invierno, in-ve-**air**-no, s., winter
invitación, in-ve-tah-the-**on**, s., invitation
invitar, in-ve-**tar**, v., to invite; to treat
invocar, in-vo-**kar**, v., to invoke
involuntario, in-vo-loon-**tah**-re-o, a., involuntary
inyectar, in-yek-**tar**, v., to inject
ir, eer, v., to go; to fit
ira, ee-rah, s., anger; wrath
iracundo, e-rah-**koon**-do, a., enraged; furious
iris, ee-riss, s., rainbow; iris
ironía, e-ro-**nee**-ah, s., irony   [able
irrazonable, ir-rrah-tho-**nah**-blay, a., unreason-
irrecuperable, ir-rray-koo-pay-**rah**-blay, a., irrecoverable
irrecusable, ir-rray-koo-**sah**-blay, a., unimpeachable; incontrovertible
irredimible, ir-rray-de-**mee**-blay, a., irredeemable
irreflexión, ir-rray-flek-the-**on**, s., rashness
irrefragable, ir-rray-frah-**gah**-blay, a., irrefutable
irregular, ir-rray-goo-**lar**, a., abnormal; irregular
irremediable, ir-rray-may-de-**ah**-blay, a., incurable; helpless   [proachable
irreprensible, ir-rray-pren-**see**-blay, a., irre-
irresoluble, ir-rray-so-**loo**-blay, a., irresolute
irresponsable, ir-rress-pon-**sah**-blay, a., irrespon-
irrigar, ir-rre-**gar**, v., to irrigate   [sible
irrisible, ir-rre-**see**-blay, a., risible
irritar, ir-rre-**tar**, v., to irritate
isla, eess-lah, s., isle; island
isleño, iss-**lay**-n'yo, s., islander
islote, iss-lo-tay, s., small barren island
istmo, eest-mo, s., isthmus
itinerario, e-te-nay-**rah**-re-o, s., itinerary; time-
izar, e-**thar**, v., to hoist; to have   [table
izquierdear, ith-ke-air-day-**ar**, v., to go wrong
izquierdo, ith-ke-**air**-do, a., left-handed; left

jabalí, Hah-bah-**lee**, s., wild boar
jabalina, Hah-bah-**lee**-nah, s., wild sow; javelin
jabón, Hah-bon, s., soap
jabonado, Hah-bo-**nah**-do, s., washing
jabonar, Hah-bo-**nar**, v., to soap

jabonería, *H*ah-bo-nay-**ree**-ah, s., soap manufac-
jaca, *H*ah-kah, s., nag; pony   [tory
jacinto, *H*ah-**theen**-to, s., hyacinth
jaco, *H*ah-ko, s., nag; pony
jactancia, Hahk-**tahn**-the-ah, s., boasting
jactarse, Hahk-**tar**-say, v., to boast
jadear, Hah-day-**ar**, v., to pant; to palpitate
jaez, *H*ah-**eth**, s., harness; kind; quality
jalea, *H*ah-**lay**-ah, s., jelly
jalear, Hah-lay-**ar**, v., to shout; to halloo
jaletina, Hah-lay-**tee**-nah, s., calf's foot jelly
jalón, Hah-**lon**, s., levelling pole
jamás, *H*ah-**mahs**, s., adv., never
jamba, *H***ahm**-bah, s., door-jamb
jamón, Hah-**mon**, s., gammon; ham
jaque, *H*ah-kay, s., check at chess; move
jaqueca, Hah-**kay**-kah, s., megrim; headache
jarabe, Hah-**rah**-bay, s., syrup
jardín, Har-**deen**, s., garden
jardinería, Har-de-nay-**ree**-ah, s., gardening
jardinero, Har-de-**nay**-ro, s., gardener
jarra, *H***ar**-rrah, s., jug; jar; pitcher
jarrete, Har-**rray**-tay, s., ham; hock
jarretera, Har-rray-**tay**-rah, s., garter
jarro, *H***ar**-rro, s., jug
jaula, *H*ah'oo-lah, s., cage; coop; cell
jayán, *H*ah-**yahn**, s., tall, robust person
jazmín, *H*ath-**meen**, s., jasmine
jefe, *H*ay-fay, s., chief; head; leader
jengibre, Hen-**hee**-bray, s., ginger
jerarquía, Hay-rar-**kee**-ah, s., hierarchy
jerez, *H*ay-**reth**, s., sherry
jerga, *H*air-gah, s., coarse cloth; jargon
jergón, Hair-**gon**, s., straw mattress
jerigonza, Hay-re-**gon**-thah, s., gibberish
jeringa, Hay-**reen**-gah, s., syringe
jibia, *H*ee-be-ah, s., cuttle-fish
jícara, *H*ee-kah-rah, s., chocolate-cup
jigote, He-**go**-tay, s., mince meat
jilguero, *H*il-**gay**-ro, s., linnet
jinete, He-**nay**-tay, s., horseman
jira, *H*ee-rah, s., tour; picnic; strip of cloth

jirafa, *He-***rah**-fah, s., giraffe
jirón, *He-***ron** s., rag; pennant
jocoso*, *Do-***ko**-so, a., waggish; jocular
jornada, *Hor-***nah**-dah, s., journey; expedition; day's work
jornal, *Hor-***nahl**, s., day-work; day-wages
joroba, *Ho-***ro**-bah, s., hump; importunity
jorobado, *Ho-ro-***bah**-do, s., hunchback
jorobar, *Ho-ro-***bar**, v., to importune; to tease
jota, *Ho-*tah, s., iota; jot; Spanish dance
joven, *Ho*-ven, s., youth; young man or woman.
jovial, *Ho-ve-***ahl**, a., jovial [a., young
joya, *Ho*-yah, s., jewel; present
joyería, *Ho-yay-***ree**-ah, s., jewellery; jeweller's [shop
joyero, *Ho-yay*-ro, s., jeweller
juanete, *Hoo'ah-***nay**-tay, s., cheek-bone; bunion
jubilación, *Hoo-be-lah-the-***on**, s., superannuation
jubilar, *Hoo-be-***lar**, v., to pension off
júbilo, *Hoo*-be-lo, s., merriment; rejoicing
jubón, *Hoo-***bon**, s., doublet; jacket
judas, *Hoo*-dahs, s., traitor
judía, *Hoo-***dee**-ah, s., French bean
judicial, *Doo-de-the-***ahl**, a., judicial; juridical
judío, *Hoo-***dee**-o, s & a., Jew; Jewish
juego, *Hoo'***ay**-go, s., play; game; set
jueves, *Hoo'***ay**-vess, s., Thursday
juez, *Hoo-***eth**, s., judge
jugada, *Hoo-***gah**-dah, s., play; move [to mock
jugar, *Hoo-***gar**, v., to play; to gamble; to trifle;
jugo, *Hoo*-go, s., sap; juice
jugoso, *Hoo-***go**-so, a., juicy; succulent
juguete, *Hoo-***gay**-tay, s., toy; trinket; joke
juguetear, *Hoo-gay-tay-***ar**, v., to trifle; to fool
juguetón, *Hoo-gay-***ton**, a., playful
juicio, *Hoo'***ee**-the-o, s., judgment
juicioso, *Hoo'e-***the-o**-so, a., judicious
julio, *Hoo*-le-o, s., July
jumento, *Hoo-***men**-to, s., ass; stupid person
juncal, *Hoon-***kahl**, s., ground full of rushes
junco, *Hoon*-ko, s., rush
junio, *Hoo*-ne-o, s., June
junta, *Hoon*-tah, s., assembly; council

juntar, *H*oon-**tar,** v., to join
junto, *H*oon-to, adv., near; close to; at hand
juntura, *H*oon-**too**-rah, s., juncture; joint
jurado, *H*oo-**rah**-do, s., jury; juryman. a., sworn
juramento, *H*oo-rah-**men**-to, s., oath
jurar, *H*oo-**rar,** v., to swear; to make oath
jurista, *H*oo-**riss**-tah, s., jurist; lawyer
justa, *H*ooss-tah, s., joust; tournament
justicia, *H*ooss-**tee**-the-ah, s., justice; equity
justificado, *H*ooss-te-fe-**kah**-do, a., justified
justificar, *H*ooss-te-fe-**kar,** v., to justify
justipreciar, *H*ooss-te-pray-the-**ar,** v., to estimate;
    to appraise   [lawful; correct
justo*, *H*ooss-to, adv., justly; tightly. a., just;
juvenil, *H*oo-vay-**neel,** a., juvenile
juventud, *H*oo-ven-**tood,** s., youthfulness; youth
juzgado, *H*ooth-**gah**-do, s., tribunal; judicature
juzgar, *H*ooth-**gar,** v., to judge

kilogramo, ke-lo-**grah**-mo, s., kilogramme
kilómetro, ke-**lo**-may-tro, s., kilometre
kiosco, ke-**os**-ko, kiosk

la, lah feminine article, the. pron., her, it
laberinto, lah-bay-**reen**-to, s., maze'
labio, **lah**-be-o, s., lip
labor, lah-**bor,** s., labour; task; work; toil; tillage
laborioso*, lah-bo-re-o-so, a., laborious; industrious
labrado, lah-**brah**-do, s., cultivated land. a., worked
labrador, lah-brah-**dor,** s., labourer; farmer;
    peasant
labrar, lah-**brar,** v., to plough; to till; to carve
labriego, lah-bre-**ay**-go, s., peasant
laca, **lah**-kah, s., lac; lacquer
lacayo, lah-**kah**-yo, s., lackey; groom
lacerar, lah-thay-**rar,** v., to tear in pieces; to hurt
lacio, **lah**-the-o, a., languid; straight (hair)
lacra, **lah**-krah, s., scar; fault
lacrar, lah-**krar,** v., to seal with sealing wax
lacre, **lah**-kray, s., sealing-wax
lácteo, **lahk**-tay-o, a., milky
ladear, lah-day-**ar,** v., to tilt; to incline on one side

ladera, lah-**day**-rah, s., declivity
ladilla, lah-**dee**-l'yah, s., crab-louse; barley
ladino, lah-**dee**-no, a., sagacious; cunning
lado, lah-do, s., side
ladrar, lah-**drar**, v., to bark
ladrillo, lah-**dree**-l'yo, s., brick
ladrón, lah-**dron**, s., thief
ladronera, lah-dro-**nay**-rah, s., den of thieves
lagarto, lah-**gar**-to, s., lizard; artful person
lago, lah-go, s., lake
lagotear, lah-go-tay-**ar**, v., to flatter; to cajole
lágrima, lah-gre-mah, s., tear; drop
laguna, lah-**goo**-nah, s., lagoon; pond; gap
lagunoso, lah-goo-**no**-so, a., marshy
lama, lah-mah, s., mud; slime; ooze
lamedor, lah-may-**dor**, s., licker; allurement
lamentar, lah-men-**tar**, v., to lament
lamento, lah-**men**-to, s., lamentation
lamer, lah-**mair**, v., to lick; to lap
lámina, lah-me-nah, s., plate; sheet
laminar, lah-me-**nar**, v., to roll metal into sheets
lámpara, lahm-pah-rah, s., lamp
lamparero, lahm-pah-**ray**-ro, s., lamp-lighter
lamparilla, lahm-pah-**ree**-l'yah, s., small lamp
lampiño, lahm-**pee**-n'yo, a., beardless
lana, lah-nah, s., wool
lanar, lah-**nar**, a., woolly
lance, lahn-thay, s., cast; occurrence
lancear, lahn-thay-**ar**, v., to wound with a lance
lancero, lahn-**thay**-ro, s., lancer
lancha, lahn-chah, s., barge; lighter; launch
lanero, lah-**nay**-ro, s., dealer in wool. a., woollen
langosta, lahn-**gos**-tah, s., lobster
langostín, lahn-gos-**teen**, s., crawfish
languidecer, lahn-ghe-day-**thair**, v., to languish
lanilla, lah-**nee**-l'yah, s., fine flannel
lanoso, lah-**no**-so, a., woolly
lanza, lahn-thah, s., lance; spear
lanzadera, lahn-thah-**day**-rah, s., shuttle
lanzar, lahn-**thar**, v., to throw; to dart; to fling
laña, lah-n'yah, s., cramp-iron
lapa, lah-pah, s., scum

lápida, lah-pe-dah, s., memorial stone
lápiz, lah-pith, s., pencil
lardar, lar-dar, v., to baste with lard
lardo, lar-do, s., lard
larga, lar-gah, s., delay. **a la —,** ah lah —, slowly
largamente, lar-gah-**men**-tay, adv., largely; for a
largar, lar-gar, v., to loosen [long time
largo, lar-go, a., long; protracted; liberal
largor, lar-gor, s., length
largueza, lar-gay-thah, s., liberality
largura, lar-goo-rah, s., length
laringe, lah-reen-Hay, s., larynx
lascivia, lahs-thee-ve-ah, s., lasciviousness
laso, lah-so, a., weary; lax [ject
lástima, lahs-te-mah, s., compassion; pitiful ob-
lastimar, lahs-te-mar, v., to wound; to offend
lastimero, lahs-te-**may**-ro, a., sad; doleful
lastrar, lahs-trar, v., to ballast a ship
lastre, lahs-tray, s., ballast
lata, lah-tah, s., tin-plate; lath; can
latente, lah-ten-tay, a., latent
latido, lah-tee-do, s., panting; throbbing
látigo, lah-te-go, s., whip
latir, lah-teer, v., to palpitate
lato, lah-to, a., large; extensive
latón, lah-ton, s., brass
latrocinio, lah-tro-thee-ne,.-o., s., larceny; theft
laúd, lah'ood, s., lute
láudano, lah'oo-dah-no, s., laudanum
laudo, lah'oo-do, s., award, finding (of a tribunal,
laurel, lah'oo-**rel**, s., laurel [etc.]
lauro, lah'oo-ro, s., glory; honour; triumph
lavadero, lah-vah-**day**-ro, s., laundry
lavadura, lah-vah-**doo**-rah, s., wash; washing
lavamanos, lah-vah-**mah**-nos, s., washing-stand
lavandera, lah-vahn-**day**-rah, s., laundress;
washerwoman
lavar, lah-var, v., to wash
lavatorio, lah-vah-to-re-o, s., washing; lavatory
laxante, lahk-sahn-tay, s., laxative
laxar, lahk-sar, v., to loosen; to soften
laxitud, lahk-se-**tood**, s., laxity

laxo, lahk-so, a., lax; slack

laya, lah-yah, s., quality; kind; class; spade

lazada, lah-thah-dah, s., bow-knot

lazo, lah-tho, s., slip-knot; snare

le, lay, pers. pron., to him; to her; him; her

leal, lay-**ahl**, a., loyal

lealtad, lay-ahl-**tahd**, s., loyalty

lebrato, lay-**brah**-to, s., leveret

lebrel, lay-**brel**, s., greyhound

lebrillo, lay-**bree**-l'yo, s., earthenware tub

lección, lek-the-**on**, s., lesson; reading; reprimand

lectura, lek-**too**-rah, s., reading; lecture

lecha, lay-chah, s., roe

leche, lay-chay, s., milk

lechería, lay-chay-**ree**-ah, s., dairy

lecho, lay-cho, s., bed; litter; layer

lechón, lay-**chon**, s., sucking pig

lechuga, lay-**choo**-gah, s., lettuce

lechuza, lay-**choo**-thah, s., owl

leer, lay-**air**, v., to read; to lecture

legado, lay-**gah**-do, s., deputy; legacy

legajo, lay-**gah**-Ho, s., file; bundle of papers

légamo, lay-gah-mo, s., slime; mud

legaña, lay-**gah**-n'yah, s., blearedness

legar, lay-**gar**, v., to depute; to bequeath

legatario, lay-gah-**tah**-re-o, s., legatee

legislar, lay-Hiss-**lar**, v., to legislate   [genuine

legítimo*, lay-**Hee**-te-mo, a., legitimate; lawful;

lego, lay-go, s., layman; lay-brother. a., lay; ignorant

legua, lay-goo'ah, s., league

legumbre, lay-**goom**-bray, s., vegetables

leído, lay-ee-do, a., well-read

lejano, lay-Hah-no, a., distant; remote

lejos, lay-Hos, adv., far-off. s., perspective

lelo, lay-lo, a., stupid

lema, lay-mah, s., theme; text; motto

lencería, len-thay-**ree**-ah, s., draper's shop

lencero, len-**thay**-ro, s., linen-draper

lengua, len-goo'ah, s., tongue; language; idiom

lenguado, len-goo'**ah**-do, s., sole (fish)

lenguaje, len-goo'**ah**-Hay, s., language; speech

lenguaz, len-goo'*ath*, a., talkative
lengüeta, len-goo'*ay*-tah, s., small tongue; epiglottis; needle of a balance
lenidad, lay-ne-**dahd**, s., lenity
lente, len-tay, s., lens
lenteja, len-tay-*H*ah, s., lentil
lentitud, len-te-**tood**, s., slowness
lento, len-to, a., slow
leña, lay-n'yah, s., fire-wood
leñador, lay-n'yah-**dor**, s., woodman; woodcutter
leñero, lay-n'**yay**-ro, s., timber-merchant
leño, lay-n'yo, s., block; log; dull person
león, lay-**on**, s., lion
leona, lay-**o**-nah, s., lioness
lepra, lay-prah, s., leprosy
lerdo, lair-do, a., slow; dull; obtuse
lesión, lay-se-**on**, s., wound; injury
letanía, lay-tah-**nee**-ah, s., litany
letargo, lay-**tar**-go, s., lethargy
letra, lay-trah, s., letter; type; inscription
letrado, lay-**trah**-do, s., lawyer. a., learned
letrero, lay-**tray**-ro, s., label; lettering; inscription; notice; poster
letrina, lay-**tree**-nah, s., privy
leva, lay-vah, s., act of weighing anchor; levy; lever
levadizo, lay-vah-**dee**-tho, a., that can be lifted
levadura, lay-vah-**doo**-rah, s., leaven; yeast
levantado, lay-vahn-**tah**-do, a., raised; lofty
levantamiento, lay-vahn-tah-me-**en**-to, s., elevation; uprising
levantar, lay-vahn-**tar**, v., to raise; to lift
levante, lay-**vahn**-tay, s., east; east wind
levar, lay-**var**, v., to weigh anchor
leve, lay-vay, a., light; trifling
levedad, lay-vay-**dahd**, s., levity
ley, lay'e, s., law
leyenda, lay-**yen**-dah, s., legend; story
liar, le-**ar**, v., to tie; to bind
libar, le-**bar**, v., to sip; to suck
libelo, le-**bay**-lo, s., lampoon; libel; petition
libertad, le-bair-**tahd**, s., liberty

libertador, le-bair-tah-**dor**, s., deliverer

libertar, le-bair-**tar**, v., to free; to deliver

libertinaje, le-bair-te-**nah**-Hay, s., licentiousness

libidinoso*, le-be-de-**no**-so, a., lustful

libra, lee-brah, s., pound

librado, le-**brah**-do, s., drawee

librador, le-**brah**-dor, s., deliverer; drawer

libramiento, le-brah-me-**en**-to, s., warrant; order of payment [draft

librancista, le-brahn-**thiss**-tah, s., holder of a

libranza, le-**brahn**-thah, s., draft; bill; cheque

librar, le-**brar**, v., to free; to deliver; to exempt; to draw

libre, lee-bray, a., free; clear; licentious

librea, le-**bray**-ah, s., livery

librejo, le-**bray**-Ho, s., little book; worthless book

librería, le-bray-**ree**-ah, s., bookshop; library

librero, le-**bray**-ro, s., bookseller

libreta, le-**bray**-tah, s., note-book

librete, le-**bray**-tay, s., small book; foot-warmer

libro, lee-bro, s., book

licenciar, le-then-the-**ar**, v., to permit; to allow; to license; to discharge

licitar, le-the-**tar**, v., to bid at auction

lícito, lee-the-to, a., lawful; licit

licor, le-**kor**, s., liquor

licorista, le-ko-**riss**-tah, s., liquor dealer

licuación, le-koo'ah-the-**on**, s., liquefaction

licuar, le-koo'**ar**, v., to liquefy

lidiar, le-de-**ar**, v., to fight; to oppose; to contend

liebre, le-**ay**-bray, s., hare

lienzo, le-**en**-tho, s., linen; canvas

liga, lee-gah, s., garter; bird lime; league; alloy

ligadura, le-gah-**doo**-rah, s., ligature; binding

ligar, le-**gar**, v., to bind; to alloy

ligazón, le-gah-**thon**, s., tie; fastening

ligereza, le-Hay-**ray**-thah, s., lightness; levity

ligero, le-**Hay**-ro, a., light; swift; trifling

lijar, le-**Har**, v., to smooth; to polish

lila, lee-lah, s., lilac tree or flower

lima, lee-mah, s., lime-tree; file

limadura, le-mah-**doo**-rah, s., filings

limar, le-**mar**, v., to file; to polish
limbo, leem-bo, s., limbo [strain
limitar, le-me-**tar**, v., to limit; to bound; to re-
límite, lee-me-tay, s., limit; boundary
limítrofe, le-mee-tro-fay, a., conterminous
limo, lee-mo, s., slime; mud
limón, le-**mon**, s., lemon
limosna, le-**mos**-nah, s., alms [table
limosnero, le-mos-**nay**-ro, s., almoner, a., chari-
limoso, le-**mo**-so, a., slimy; muddy
limpia, limpiadura, leem-pe-ah lim-pe-ah-**doo**-
rah, s., cleaning
limpiar, lim-pe-**ar**, v., to clean; to scour
limpieza, lim-pe-**ay**-thah, s., cleanliness; purity
limpio, leem-pe-o, a., clean; pure; clear
linaje, le-**nah**-Hay, s., lineage
linaza, le-**nah**-thah, s., linseed
lince, leen-thay, s., lynx
lindante, lin-**dahn**-tay, a., bordering
lindar, lin-**dar**, v., to be contiguous
lindero, lin-**day**-ro, a., bordering
lindeza, lin-**day**-thah, s., elegance; prettiness
lindo, leen-do, a., pretty; fine
línea, lee-nay-ah, s., line; boundary
lingote, lin-**go**-tay, s., ingot
lino, lee-no, s., flax; linen; canvas
linterna, lin-**tair**-nah, s., lantern
lío, lee-o, s., bundle; parcel
liquen, lee-ken, s., lichen
liquidar, le-ke-**dar**, v., to liquefy; to liquidate
líquido, lee-ke-do, s., balance, a., liquid; clear
lira, lee-ra, s., lyre
lirio, lee-re-o, s., lily
lirón, le-**ron**, s., dormouse
lis, leess, s., flower-de-luce
lisiar, le-se-**ar**, v., to lame; to cripple; to hurt
liso, lee-so, a., plain; even; flat
lisonja, le-**son**-Hah, s., adulation
lisonjear, le-son-Hay-**ar**, v., to flatter; to wheedle
lisonjero, le-son-**Hay**-ro, s., flatterer
lista, liss-tah, s., slip of paper; strip; catalogue
listar, liss-**tar**, v., to stripe

listo, liss-to, a., ready; active; prompt; clever
listón, liss-ton, s., ribbon; tape; strip; lath
lisura, le-**soo**-rah, s., smoothness; evenness; sin-
litera, le-**tay**-rah, s., litter; berth [cerity
literato, le-tay-**rah**-to, s., writer. a., literary
literatura, le-tay-rah-**too**-rah, s., literature
litigar, le-te-**gar**, v., to litigate; to dispute
litigio, te-**tee**-He-o, s., litigation; contest
litografía, le-to-grah-**fe**-ah, s., lithography
litoral, le-to-**rahl,** s., littoral; coast; shore
litro, **lee**-tro, s., litre
liviano, le-ve-**ah**-no, a., light; fickle; lewd
lividez, le-ve-**deth,** s., lividity
lizo, **lee**-tho, s., wrap-thread
lo, neuter art., the. pers. pron., him; it
loa, lo-ah, s., praise
loable, lo-**ah**-blay, a., praiseworthy
loar, lo-**ar,** v., to praise
loba, lo-bah, s., she-wolf
lobado, lo-**bah**-do, s., (horses) tumour
lobato, lo-**bah**-to, s., wolf cub
lobo, lo-bo, s., wolf
lóbrego, lo-**bray**-go, a., murky; gloomy
lóbulo, lo-**boo**-lo, s., lobe
local, lo-**kahl,** s., premises. a., local
localidad, lo-kah-le-**dahd,** s., locality
loco, lo-ko, a., mad; crazy
locuaz, lo-koo'**ahth,** a., loquacious
locura, lo-**koo**-rah, s., madness; folly
locutorio, lo-koo-**to**-re-o, s., parlour in monasteries
lodo, lo-do, a., mud; mire
lógica, lo-**He**-kah, s., logic
lograr, lo-**grar,** v., to gain; to get
logro, lo-gro, s., gain; profit; interest
loma, lo-mah, s., hillock
lomo, lo-mo, s., back; loin
lona, lo-nah, s., canvas
longevo, lon-**Hay**-vo, a., long-lived
longitud, lon-He-**tood,** s., length; longitude
lonja, lon-Hah, s., exchange; warehouse; slice of
lonjista, lon-**Hiss**-tah, s., grocer [meat
lontananza, lon-tah-**nahn**-thah, s., distance

loquear, lo-kay-**ar**, v., to play the fool
loro, lo-ro, s., parrot
los, los, plur. art., the. pron., them
losa, lo-sah, s., flag-stone; slab
lote, lo-tay, s., lot; share; part
lotería, lo-tay-**ree**-ah, s., lottery
loza, lo-thah, s., chinaware; crockery
lozanía, lo-thah-nee-ah, s., luxuriance; freshness
lozano, lo-**than**-no, a., luxuriant; sprightly
lúbrico, loo-bre-ko, a., slippery; lewd
lucerna, loo-**thair**-nah, s., glow-worm
lúcido*, loo-the-do, a., lucid; brilliant
lucir, loo-**theer**, v., to shine; to exceed; to dress well
lucrativo, loo-krah-**tee**-vo, a., lucrative
lucro, loo-kro, s., gain; profit; lucre
luctuoso, look-too-**o**-so, a., sad; mournful
lucha, loo-chah, s., struggle; strife; fight [debate
luchar, loo-**char**, v., to wrestle; to struggle; to
luego, loo**'ay**-go, adv., immediately; presently
lugar, loo-**gar**, s., place; spot; town; village;
    space; occasion; motive
lugareño, loo-gah-**ray**-n'yo, s., villager
lugarteniente, loo-**gar**-tay-ne-**en**-tay, s., deputy;
    lieutenant
lúgubre, loo-goo-bray, a., sad; lugubrious
lujo, loo-Ho, s., luxury
lujuria, loo-Hoo-re-ah, s., lewdness; lust
lujurioso*, loo-Hoo-re-**o**-so, a., lustful
limbre, loom-bray, s., fire; spark; brightness
luminar, loo-me-**nar**, s., luminary
luminaria, loo-me-**nah**-re-ah, s., illumination
luna, loo-nah, s., moon; mirror-plate
lunar, loo-**nar**, s., mole; blemish. a., lunar
lunes, loo-ness, s., Monday
luneta, loo-**nay**-tah, s., orchestra stall
lustrar, looss-**trar**, v., to purify; to lustrate
lustro, looss-tro, s., lustre; gloss; period of five
luto, loo-to, s., mourning; sorrow   [years
luz, looth, s., light

llaga, l'yah-gah, s., sore; wound; crack
llagar, l'yah-**gar**, v., to wound; to hurt

llama, l'**yah**-mah, s., flame ; blaze
llamada, l'yah-**mah**-dah, s., call ; marginal note
llamar, l'yah-**mar**, v., to call ; to name ; to invoke
llamarada, l'yah-mah-**rah**-dah, s., blaze
llana, l'**yah**-nah, s., trowel ; plain
llaneza, l'yah-**nay**-thah, s., plainness ; simplicity
llano*, l'**yah**-no, a., plain ; level ; even ; simple
llanta, l'**yahn**-tah, s., tyre
llanto, l'**yahn**-to, s., flood of tears
llanura, l'yah-**noo**-rah, s., evenness ; prairie
llave, l'**yah**-vay, s., key ; lock (of a gun)
llavero, l'yah-**vay**-ro, s., key-ring
llavín, l'yah-**veen**, s., latch-key
llegada, l'yay-**gah**-dah, s., arrival
llegar, l'yay-**gar**, v., to arrive ; to amount to
llegarse, l'yay-**gar**-say, v., to go to a neighbouring place ; to join
llenar, l'yay-**nar**, v., to fill ; to occupy ; to satisfy
lleno, l'**yay**-no, a., full
llevadero, l'yay-vah-**day**-ro, a., tolerable
llevar, l'yay-**var**, v., to carry ; to convey ; to bear ; to lead ; to endure
llorar, l'yo-**rar**, v., to weep ; to mourn
lloro, l'**yo**-ro, s., weeping
lloroso, l'yo-**ro**-so, a., mournful ; tearful
llovediza, l'yo-vay-**dee**-thah, s., rain-water
llover, l'yo-**vair**, v., to rain ; to shower
llovizna, l'yo-vith-**nar**, v., to drizzle
lluvia, l'**yoo**-ve-ah, s., rain
lluvioso, l'yoo-ve-o-so, a., rainy ; showery

maca, mah-kah, s., bruise (in fruit) ; stain
macarrones, mah-kar-**rro**-ness, s., macaroni
macarse, mah-**kar**-say, v., (fruit) to rot
maceta, mah-**thay**-tah, s., flower-pot
macizo, mah-**thee**-tho, a., solid ; massive
machacar, mah-chah-**kar**, v., to crush ; to harp (on a subject)
machacón, mah-chah-**kon**, a., importunate
machete, mah-**chay**-tay, s., cutless
macho, mah-cho, s., male animal
machorra, mah-**chor**-rrah, s., barren woman

madeja, mah-**day**-*H*ah, s., skein; lock of hair
madera, mah-**day**-rah, s., timber; wood [work
maderaje, mah-day-**rah**-*H*ay, s., timber; wood-
madero, mah-**day**-ro, s., beam; log
madrastra, mah-**drahs**-trah, s., step-mother
madraza, mah-**drah**-thah, s., indulgent mother
madre, mah-dray, s., mother; matrix; bed of a
river
madreselva, mah-dray-**sel**-vah, s., honeysuckle
madriguera, mah-dre-**gay**-rah, s., burrow; den
madrina, mah-**dree**-nah, s., godmother
madrugada, mah-droo-**gah**-dah, s., dawn
madrugar, mah-droo-**gar**, v., to rise early
madurar, mah-doo-**rar**, v., to ripen
madurez, mah-doo-**reth**, s., maturity
maduro, mah-**doo**-ro, a., mature; ripe; judicious
maestra, mah-**ess**-trah, s., school mistress
maestre, mah-**ess**-tray, s., grand master of a military order [waiter
maestresala, mah-ess-tray-**sah**-lah, s., head
maestría, mah-ess-**tree**-ah, s., mastery; master-
maestro, mah-**ess**-tro, s., master [ship
mágico, mah-*H*e-ko, a., magic
magistrado, mah-*H*iss-**trah**-do, s., magistrate
magnánimo, mahg-**nah**-'ne-mo, a., magnanimous
magnesia, mahg-**nay**-se-ah, s., magnesia
magnético, mahg-**nay**-te-ko, a., magnetical
magnífico, mahg-**nee**-fe-ko, a., magnificent
magno, mahg-no, a., great
mago, mah-go, s., magician
magra, mah-grah, s., slice of bacon; rasher
magro, mah-gro, a., lean; meagre
magullar, mah-goo-l'**yar**, v., to bruise; to mangle
maíz, mah-**eeth**, s., maize
majada, mah-*H*ah-dah, s., sheep-fold
majadería, mah-*H*ah-day-**ree**-ah, s., foolishness
majador, mah-*H*ah-dor, s., pounder; pestle
majestad, mah-*H*ess-**tahd**, s., majesty
majo, mah-*H*o, a., gallant; spruce
majuelo, mah-*H*oo'**ay**-lo, s., hawthorn
mal, mahl, adv., badly. s., evil; illness. a., ill; bad
malbaratar, mahl-bah-rah-**tar**, v., to squander

malcontento, mahl-con-**ten**-to, a., discontented

malcriado, mahl-kre-**ah**-do, a., ill-bred

maldad, mahl-**dahd**, s., wickedness

maldecir, mahl-day-**theer**, v., to curse; to defame

maldición, mahl-de-the-**on**, s., curse; damnation

maldito, mahl-**dee**-to, a., cursed; wicked; perversed

malecón, mah-lay-**kon**, s., embankment; mole; dike [der

maledicencia, mah-lay-de-**then**-the-ah, s., slan-

maleficio, mah-lay-**fee**-the-o, s., witchcraft; charm

maléfico, mah-**lay**-fe-ko, a., mischievous

malestar, mah-less-**tar**, s., uneasiness

maleta, mah-**lay**-tah, s., portmanteau; valise

malévolo, mah-**lay**-vo-lo, a., malevolent

maleza, mah-lay-thah, s., brambles; thicket of weeds

malgastar, mahl-gahs-**tar**, v., to misspend; to waste

malhablado, mahl-ah-**blah**-do, a., foul-mouthed

malhecho, mahl-ay-cho, s., evil deed, a., ill-shaped

malhechor, mahl-ay-**chor**, s., malefactor

maliciar, mah-le-the-**ar**, v., to suspect; to corrupt

maligno, mah-**leeg**-no, a., malignant

malintencionado, mahl-in-ten-the-o-**nah**-do, a., ill disposed

malmandado, mahl-mahn-**dah**-do, a., disobedient

malo, **mah**-lo, a., bad; evil

malograr, mah-lo-**grar**, v., to lose (an opportunity); to miss; to spoil

malogro, mah-**lo**-gro, s., miscarriage; failure

malparado, mah-pah-**rah**-do, a., impaired

malparto, mahl-**par**-to, s., abortion; miscarriage

malquerer, mahl-kay-**rair**, v., to bear ill-will

malquistar, mahl-kiss-**tar**, v., to cause quarrels

malsano, mahl-**sah**-no, a., unwholesome; unhealthy

maltratar, mahl-trah-**tar**, v., to treat ill; to abuse

malva, **mahl**-vah, s., mallow

malvado, mahl-**vah**-do, a., wicked

malversar, mahl-vair-**sar**, v., to embezzle

malla, **mah**-l'yah, s., mesh of a net

mamar, mah-**mar**, v., to suck

mampara, mahm-**pah**-rah, s., screen
mamparo, mahm-**pah**-ro, s., bulkhead; partition
manada, mah-**nah**-dah, s., herd; flock
manadero, mah-nah-**day**-ro, s., spring; source; shepherd
manantial, mah-nahn-te-**ahl**, s., source; spring
manar, mah-**nar**, v., to spring from
mancamiento, mahn-kah-me-**en**-to, s., deficiency
mancar, mahn-**kar**, v., to maim
manceba, mahn-**thay**-bah, s., concubine
mancebo, mahn-**thay**-bo, s., youth; apprentice
mancillar, mahn-the-l'**yar**, v., to stain
manco, **mahn**-ko, s., handless; armless
mancomún, mahn-ko-**moon**, adv., jointly
mancha, **mahn**-chah, s., stain; blot   [file
manchar, mahn-**char**, v., to stain; to soil; to de-
manda, **mahn**-dah, s., legacy   [ger
mandadero, mahn-dah-**day**-ro, s., porter; messen-
mandado, mahn-**dah**-do, s., mandate; message; errand   [precept
mandamiento, mahn-dah-me-**en**-to, s., command;
mandante, mahn-**dahn**-tay, s., chief; constituent
mandar, mahn-**dar**, v., to command; to order; to transmit
mandatario, mahn-dah-**tah**-re-o, s., agent; proxy
mandato, mahn-**dah**-to, s., mandate
mandil, mahn-**deel**, s., coarse apron
mando, **mahn**-do, s., order; authority
mandón, mahn-**don**, a., domineering
mandril, mahn-**dreel**, s., mandrel
manear, mah-nay-**ar**, v., to hobble
manecilla, mah-nay-**thee**-l'yah, s., small hand
manejar, mah-nay-H**ar**, v., to manage
manejo, mah-**nay**Ho, s., management; intrigue
manera, mah-**nay**-rah, s., manner
manga, **mahn**-gah, s., sleeve; water-spout
mango, **mahn**-go, s., handle; haft
mangueta, mahn-**gay**-tah, s., syringe
manguito, mahn-**ghee**-to, s., muff
manía, mah-**nee**-ah, s., mania
maniatar, mah-ne-ah-**tar**, v., to handcuff
manicomio, mah-ne-**ko**-me-o, s., lunatic asylum

manifestar, mah-ne-fess-**tar,** v., to manifest; to declare [a., plain; obvious

manifiesto, mah-ne-fe-**ess**-to, s., (ship) manifest.

manija, mah-**nee**-Hah, s., handle

manilargo, mah-ne-**lat**-go, a., long-handed; liberal

manilla, mah-**nee**-l'yah, s., bracelet; manacle

maniobra, mah-ne-o-brah, s., manœuvre

maniobrar, mah-ne-o-**brar,** v., to manœuvre

manipular, mah-ne-poo-**lar,** v., to manipulate

maniquí, mah-ne-kee, s., manikin [tender

manir, mah-**neer,** v., to keep meat till it grows

manirroto, mah-neer-**rro**-to, a., extravagant

manivela, mah-ne-**vay**-lah, s., crank, crankshaft

manjar, mahn-Har, s., food; victuals

mano, man-no, s., hand; quire of paper

manojo, mah-**no**-Ho, s., bunch; bundle

manosear, mah-no-say-**ar,** v., to handle [culate

manotear, mah-no-tay-**ar,** v., to buffet; to gesti-

mansedumbre, mahn-say-**doom**-bray, s., meek-

mansión, mahn-se-**on,** s., abode; sojourn [ness

manso, mahn-so, a., meek; gentle; tame

manta, mahn-tah, s., blanket; travelling rug

manteca, mahn-**tay**-kah, s., butter; lard; fat

mantecada, mahn-tay-**kah**-dah, s., buttered toast

mantel, mahn-**tel,** s., table-cloth

mantelería, mahn-tay-lay-**ree**-ah, s., table-linen

mantequera, mahn-tay-**kay**-rah, s., churn; butter-

mantequilla, mahn-tay-kee-lyah, s., butter [dish

mantilla, mahn-**tee**-l'yah, s., mantilla; head-shawl

mantillo, mahn-**tee**-l'yo, s., vegetable earth

manto, mahn-to, s., cloak; mantle

manubrio, mah-**noo**-bre-o, s., handle; crank

manufactura, mah-noo-fahk-**too**-rah, s., manu-

facture [ance

manutención, mah-noo-ten-the-**on,** s., mainten-

manzana, mahn-**thah**-nah, s., apple; block of

houses

manzanilla, mahn-thah-**nee**-l'yah, s., camomile

maña, mah-n'yah, s., skill; dexterity; knack

mañana, mah-n'**yah**-nah, adv., to-morrow. s., morning; morrow. **— por la —, — por lah —,** to-morrow morning

mañear, mah-n'yay-**ar**, v., to manage with cleverness

mañoso, mah-n'**yo**-so, a., dexterous; handy; crafty

mapa, mah, mah-pah, s., map

máquina, mah-ke-nah, s., machine

maquinaria, mah-ke-**nah**-re-ah, s., machinery

maquinismo, mah-ke-**niss**-mo, s., mechanization

manquinista, mah-ke-**niss**-tah, s., engineer; [mechanic

mar, mar, s., sea

maraña, mah-**rah**-n'yah, s., tangle [gold

maravilla, mah-rah-**vee**-l'yah, s., wonder; mari-

maravillar, mah-rah-ve-l'**yar**, v., to admire; to marvel

maravilloso, mah-rah-ve-l'**yo**-so, a., wonderful

marca, mar-kah, s., mark; stamp; sign; label; brand [to note

marcar, mar-**kar**, v., to mark; to stamp; to label;

marcialidad, mar-the-ah-le-**dahd**, s., martialness;

marco, mar-ko, s., frame; mark [frankness

marcha, mar-chah, s., march [goods

marchamo, mar-**chah**-mo, s., customs' mark on

marchante, mar-**chahn**-tay, s., dealer; customer

marchapié, mar-chah-pe-**ay**, s., foot-board

marchitable, mar-che-**tah**-blay, a., perishable

marchitar, mar-che-**tar**, v., to wither

marea, mah-**ray**-ah, s., tide

mareo, mah-**ray**-o, s., sea-sickness

marfil, mar-**feel**, s., ivory

marga, mar-gah, s., loam; ticking

margarita, mar-gah-**ree**-tah, s., periwinkle; daisy

margen, mar-Hen, s., margin; edge; fringe

marginar, mar-He-**nar**, v., to make marginal notes

marica, mah-**ree**-kah, s., magpie

maridable, mah-re-**dah**-blay, a., conjugal

marido, mah-**ree**-do, s., husband

marimacho, mah-re-**mah**-cho, s., virago

marimorena, mah-re-mo-**ray**-nah, s., (fam.) quarrel

marina, mah-**ree**-nah, s., shore; navy; seamanship

marinaje, mah-re-**nah**-Hay, s., seamanship; sailors

marinar, mah-re-**nar**, v., to salt fish [seaworthy

marinero, mah-re-**nay**-ro, s., mariner; sailor. a.,

marino, mah-**ree**-no, s., mariner. a., marine

mariposa, mah-re-**po**-sah, s., butterfly
marquita, mah-re-**kee**-tah, s., lady-bird
mariscal, mah-riss-**kahl**, s., marshal; farrier
marisma, mah-**riss**-mah, s., marsh
marmita, mar-**mee**-tah, s., kettle; pot
maroma, mah-**ro**-mah, s., rope; cable
marqués, mar-**kess**, s., marquis
marquesa, mar-**kay**-sah, s., marchioness
marquesina, mar-kay-see-nah, s., marquee
marquetería, mar-kay-tay-**ree**-ah, s., marquetry;
marrana, mar-**rrah**-nah, s., sow   [inlaid work
marrar, mar-**rrar**, v., to deviate; to err
marras, mar-rrahs, adv., long ago
marro, mar-rro, s., quoits; miss; failure
marroquí, mar-rro-**kee**, s., morocco (leather)
marrullero, mah-rroo-l'**yay**-ro, a., cunning; deceit-
marsellés, mar-say-l'**yess**, s., short jacket   [ful
marsopla, mar-**so**-plah, s., porpoise
martes, martes, mar-tess, s., Tuesday
martillo, mar-tee-l'yo, s., hammer
martinete, mar-te-**nay**-tay, s., swift; drop-ham-
mártir, martir, mar-teer, s., martyr   [mer
martirio, mar-tee-re-o, s., martyrdom
marzo, marzo, mar-tho, s., March
mas, mas, mahs, conj., but; yet
más, mahs, adv., more; moreover; besides
masa, mah-sah, s., dough; mortar; mass; crowd
masada, mah-**sah**-dah, s., farm-house and stock
mascar, mahs-**kar**, v., to masticate
máscara, mahs-kah-rah, s., mask; subterfuge
mascarada, mahs-kah-**rah**-dah, s., masquerade
mascarón, mahs-kah-**ron**, s., grotesque face;
 figure-head
mascullar, mahs-koo-l'**yar**, v., to mumble
masilla, mah-**see**-l'yah, s., putty; mastic
masón, mah-**son**, s., Freemason
masonería, mah-so-nay-**ree**-ah, s., Freemasonry
masticar, mahs-te-**kar**, v., to masticate
mástil, mahs-til, s., mast
mastín, mahs-**teen**, s., mastiff
mastranzo, mahs-**trahn**-tho, s., mint
mastuerzo, mahs-too'**air**-tho, s., common cress

mata, mah-tah, s., shrub; sprig; copse; lock of hair
matadero, mah-tah-**day**-ro, s., slaughter-house
matador, mah-tah-**dor**, s., killer
matanza, mah-tahn-thah, s., slaughter
matar, mah-tar, v., to kill; to murder; to worry
matasanos, mah-tah-**sah**-nos, s., quack; charlatan
mate, mah-tay, s., checkmate [stuff
materia, mah-**tay**-re-ah, s., material; substance;
maternidad, mah-tair-ne-**dahd**, s., maternity
matiz, mah-**teeth**, s., shade of colours
matón, mah-ton, s., bully
matorral, mah-tor-**rrahl**, s., thicket; copse
matoso, mah-**to**-so, a., bushy
matraquear, mah-trah-kay-**ar**, v., to jest; to scoff
matricular, mah-tre-koo-**lar**, v., to matriculate
matrimonio, mah-tre-**mo**-ne-o, s., marriage
matriz, mah-**treeth**, s., womb; female screw;
mould. a., principal
matrona, mah-**tro**-nah, s., matron; midwife
matutino, mah-too-**tee**-no, a., matutinal; early
maulería, mah'oo-lay-**ree**-ah, s., frippery
maullar, mah'oo-l'**yar**, v., to mew [principally
máximamente, mahk-se-mah-men-tay, adv.,
máxime, mahk-se-may (see **maximamente**)
máximo, mahk-se-mo, a., chief; principal; very
maya, mah-yah, s., daisy [great
mayo, mah-yo, s., May
mayonesa, mah-yo-**nay**-sah, s., mayonnaise
mayor, mah-**yor**, s., superior; chief. a., greater;
bigger; elder. **por —, por —,** by wholesale
mayordomo, mah-yor-**do**-mo, s., steward
mayoría, mah-yo-**ree**-ah, s., majority; greater
part; full age
maza, mah-thah, s., club
mazo, mah-tho, s., mallet; bundle; importunate
me, may, pers. pron., me; to me [person
mear, may-**ar**, v., to make water
mecánico, may-**kah**-ne-ko, s., mechanic. a.,
mechanical [anization
mecanización, may-kah-ne-thah-the-**on**, s., mech-
mecedora, may-thay-**dor**-rah, s., rocking chair
mecer, may-**thair**, v., to rock

mecha, may-chah, s., wick; bundle of fibres; roll
mechero, may-chay-ro, s., cigarette-lighter [of lint
medalla, may-dah-l'yah, s., medal
media, may-de-ah, s., stocking; hose [mediatory
medianero, may-de-ah-nay-ro, s., mediator, a.,
**medianía, may-de-ah-nee-ah, s., mediocrity
**mediante, may-de-ahn-tay, adv., by means of
**mediar, may-de-ar, v., to mediate; to be in the
**mediato, may-de-ah-to, a., mediate [middle
**medicina, may-de-thee-nah, s., medicine
**medición, may-de-the-on, s., measurement
**médico, may-de-ko, s., physician. a., medical
**medida, may-dee-dah, s., measure
**mediero, may-de-ay-ro, s., hosier
**medio, may-de-o, s., middle; midway. a., half
**mediocre, may-de-o-kray, a., mediocre
**mediodía, may-de-o-dee-ah, s., noon
**medir, may-deer, v., to measure
**meditar, may-de-tar, v., to meditate
**medrar, may-drar, v., to thrive; to improve
**medro, may-dro, s., progress; improvement
**medroso, may-dro-so, a., timorous; fearful
**médula, may-doo-lah, s., marrow; pith
**mégano, may-gah-no, s., down; dune
**mejor, may-Hor, adv., & a., better
**mejora, may-Ho-rah, s., improvement; increase
**mejorar, may-Ho-rar, v., to improve; to enhance;
    to recover from illness or calamity
**mejunje, may-Hoon-Hay, s., mixed beverage
**melado, may-lah-do, a., honey-coloured
**melancólico, may-lahn-ko-le-ko, a., sad; gloomy
**melena, may-lay-nah, s., dishevelled hair; mane
**melocotón, may-lo-ko-ton, s., peach
**melodioso, may-lo-de-o-so, a., melodious
**melón, may-lon, s., melon
**meloso, may-lo-so, a., honeyed; mellow
**melote, may-lo-tay, s., treacle
**mellado, may-l'yah-do, a., notched; toothless
**mellar, may-l'yar, v., to notch; to injure
**mellizo, may-l'yee-tho, a., twin [heading
**membrete, mem-bray-tay, s., note; address;
**membrillo, mem-bree-l'yo, s., quince; quince-tree

memo, may-mo, a., silly   [reminder
memoria, may-**mo**-re-ah, s., memory; memorial
memorial, may-mo-re-**ahl**, s., memorandum-book
menaje, may-**nah**-**H**ay, s., household furniture
mención, men-the-**on**, s., mention
mendigar, men-de-gar, v., to beg
mendigo, men-**dee**-go, s., beggar
menear, may-nay-**ar**, v., to move; to stir
meneo, may-**nay**-o, s., waddling motion of the body
menester, may-ness-**tair**, s., necessity; want; need. pl., natural necessities
menestra, may-**ness**-trah, s., vegetable soup
menestral, may-ness-**trahl**, s., artisan; mechanic
mengano, men-**gah**-no, s., (used after **fulano**) such a one
mengua, men-goo'ah, s., diminution; disgrace
menguado, men-goo'**ah**-do, s., poltroon; wretch; decrease. a., cowardly; impaired
menguante, men-goo'**ahn**-tay, s., ebb-tide; decline
menguar, men-goo'**ar**, v., to decay; to wane
menor, may-**nor**, s., under age. a., less; smaller
menoría, may-no-**ree**-ah, s., nonage; inferiority
menos, may-nos, adv., less   [lessen
menoscabar, may-nos-kah-**bar**, v., to impair; to
menospreciar, may-nos-pray-the-**ar**, v., to under-rate; to despise
mensaje, men-**sah**-H́ay, s., message; errand
mensajería, men-sah-H́ay-**ree**-ah, s., steamship line; forwarding agency
mensajero, men-sah-H́ay-ro, s., messenger
menstruo, mens-troo'o, s., courses; menses
mensual, men-soo'**ahl**, a., monthly   [salary
mensualidad, men-soo'ah-le-**dahd**, s., monthly
menta, men-tah, s., mint; peppermint
mentar, men-**tar**, v., to mention
mente, men-tay, s., mind; understanding; will
mentecato, men-tay-**kah**-to, a., silly; crack-brained
mentir, men-**teer**, v., to lie; to deceive; to feign
mentira, men-**tee**-rah, a., s., lie; fib
mentís, men-**teess**, interj., you lie!
menudear, may-noo-day-**ar**, v., to repeat; to
menudillos, may-noo-**dee**-l'yos, s., giblets   [retail

menudo*, may-**noo**-do, a., minute; small. **a —,** ah —, repeatedly; frequently

meñique, may-n'**yee**-kay, s., little finger

meollo, may-o-l'yo, s., marrow; understanding;

meple, may-play, s., maple [substance

mequetrefe, may-kay-**tray**-fay, s., coxcomb

meramente, may-rah-**men**-tay, adv., merely

merca, mair-kah, s., (fam.) purchase

mercachifle, mair-kah-**chee**-flay, s., peddler; hawker [dise; commodity

mercadería, mair-kah-day-**ree**-ah, s., merchan-

mercado, mair-**kah**-do, s., market; mart

mercancía, mair-kahn-**thee**-ah, s., goods; wares

mercante, mair-**kahn**-tay, s. & a., dealer; mer-

mercar, mair-**kar**, v., to buy [cantile

merced, mair-**thed**, s., gift; grace; mercy

mercería, mair-thay-**ree**-ah, s., haberdashery

mercero, mair-**thay**-ro, s., haberdasher

merecedor, may-ray-thay-**dor**, a., deserving

merecer, may-ray-**thair**, v., to deserve

merecimiento, may-ray-the-me-**en**-to, s., merit

merendar, may-ren-**dar**, v., to have an afternoon meal between mid-day dinner and supper

meridiano, may-re-de-**ah**-no, s., meridian. a., me-ridional

merienda, may-re-**en**-dah, s., light afternoon meal

merino, may-**ree**-no, s., merino; judge; shepherd

mérito, may-re-to, s., merit; desert

merluza, mair-**loo**-thah, s., cod; hake

merma, mair-mah, s., leakage; diminution

merodear, may-ro-day-**ar**, v., to maraud

mes, mess, s., month

mesa, may-sah, s., table

mesar, may-**sar**, v., to pluck off the hair

meseta, may-**say**-tah, s., landing of a staircase;

mesilla, may-**see**-l'yah, s., small table [plateau

mesón, may-**son**, s., inn; hostelry

mesonero, may-so-**nay**-ro, s., inn-keeper

mestizo, mess-**tee**-tho, s., a mongrel; half-breed

mesura, may-**soo**-rah, s., moderation; gravity

mesurado, may-soo-**rah**-do, a., moderate; circum-

meta, may-tah, s., boundary; goal [spect

metáfora, may-**tah**-fo-rah, s., metaphor
metal, may-**tahl**, s., metal
metálico, may-**tah**-le-ko, a., metallic
meteoro, may-tay-o-ro, s., meteor
meter, may-**tair**, v., to put; to insert
método, may-to-do, s., method
metralla, may-trah-l'yah, s., grape-shot
metro, may-tro, s., metre (measure and verse)
mezcla, meth-klah, s., mixture
mezclador, meth-klah-**dorr**, s., mixer
mezclar, meth-**klar**, v., to mix; to blend
mezquino, meth-**kee**-no, a., mean; petty
mezquita, meth-kee-tah, s., mosque
mi, me, poss. a., my. s., (music, E)
mí, me, pers. pron., me
miaja, me-ah-Hah, s., crumb; bit
mico, mee-ko, s., monkey
microbio, me-**kro**-be-o, s., microbe
micrófono, me-kro-fo-no, s., microphone
miedo, me-**ay**-do, s., fear
miel, me-**ell**, s., honey
miembro, me-**em**-bro, s., member
mientras, me-**en**-trahs, adv., meanwhile
miera, me-**ay**-rah, s., juniper oil; resin
miércoles, me-**air**-ko-less, s., Wednesday
mies, me-**ess**, s., ripe wheat; harvest; harvest-time
miga, mee-gah, s., crumb; bit
mijo, mee-Ho, s., millet
mil, meel, s., one thousand
milagro, me-**lah**-gro, s., miracle; wonder
milano, me-**lah**-no, s., kite
milésimo, me-**lay**-se-mo, a., thousandth [inch
milímetro, me-lee-**may**-tro, s., millimetre (0.039
militar, me-le-**tar**, v., to serve in the army. s.
milla, mee-l'yah, s., mile [soldier. a., military
millar, mel-l'**yar**, s., thousand; a great number
millón, mel-**yon**, s., million
millonésimo, me-l'yo-**nay**-se-mo, a., millionth
mimar, me-**mar**, v., to spoil; to pet
mimbre, meem-bray, s., wicker
mímica, mee-me-kah, s., mimicry
mimo, mee-mo, s., caress; petting

mimoso, me-**mo**-so, a., delicate, soft
mina, mee-nah, s., mine; conduit; source
minar, me-**nar**, v., to mine; to sap; to ruin
minería, me-nay-**ree**-ah, s., mine work; mining
minero, me-**nay**-ro, s., miner
mingo, meen-go, s., (billiards) red ball
mínimo, mee-ne-mo, s., minimum. a., the smallest
ministerio, me-niss-**tay**-re-o, s., ministry; office
ministrar, me-niss-**trar**, v., to minister; to supply
ministro, me-**niss**-tro, s., minister
minorar, me-no-**rar**, v., to lessen; to reduce
minorativo, me-no-rah-**tee**-vo, a., lessening
minoría, me-no-**ree**-ah, s., minority
minucia, me-**noo**-the-ah, s., minuteness; trifle
minucioso, me-noo-the-o-so, a., minutely precise
minué, me-noo-**ay**, s., minuet
minutario, me-noo-**tah**-re-o, s., minute-book
minuto, me-**noo**-to, s., minute
mío, mee-o, poss. pron., my; mine
miope, mee-o-pay, a., short-sighted [purpose
mira, mee-rah, s., aim of a gun; care; vigilance;
mirada, me-**rah**-dah, s., glance; gaze; look
mirado, me-**rah**-do, a., considerate; prudent
mirador, me-rah-**dor**, s., observatory; balcony
mirar, me-**rar**, v., to look; to observe
mirilla, me-**ree**-l'yah, s., peep-hole
mirlo, meer-lo, s., blackbird
mirón, me-ron, s., looker-on
mirto, meer-to, s., myrtle
misa, mee-sah, s., mass
misántropo, me-**sahn**-tro-po, s., misanthropist
miscelánea, miss-thay-**lah**-nay-ah, s., medley
miseria, me-**say**-re-ah, s., misery; meanness
misericordia, me-say-re-**kor**-de-ah, s., merciful-
misionero, me-se-o-**nay**-ro, s., missionary [ness
misiva, me-**see**-vah, s., missive
mismo, **miss**-mo, a., same; similar; equal
misterio, miss-**tay**-re-o, s., mystery
mitad, me-**tahd**, s., half
mitigar, me-te-**gar**, v., to mitigate
mito, mee-to, s., myth
mitón, me-ton, s., mitten

mixto, meeks-to, a., mixed; composite; cross-
mixturar, miks-too-**rar**, v., to mix [breed
mobiliario, mo-be-le-**a**-re-o, s., furniture
moblar, mo-**blar,** v., to provide with furniture
mocedad, mo-thay-**dahd,** s., juvenility
mocetón, mo-thay-**ton,** s., robust youth
mochuelo, mo-choo'**ay**-lo, s., red owl
moda, mo-dah, s., fashion; mode [exemplar
modelo, mo-**day**-lo, s., model; pattern; standard;
moderar, mo-day-**rar,** v., to moderate
modesto, mo-**dess**-to, a., modest
módico, mo-de-ko, a., moderate in price
modificar, mo-de-fe-**kar,** v., to modify
modismo, mo-**diss**-mo, s., idiom
modista, mo-**diss**-tah, s., dressmaker; milliner
modo, mo-do, s., mode; method; moderation;
modorra, mo-**dor**-rrah, s., drowsiness [civility
modoso, mo-**do**-so, a., temperate; well-behaved
módulo, mo-doo-lo, s., modulation; module
mofa, mo-fah, s., mockery; jeer
mofarse, mo-**far**-say, v., to mock
mofeta, mo-**fay**-tah, s., gas spring; skunk
mogollón, mo-go-l'**yon,** s., parasite
mogote, mo-**go**-tay, s., hillock
mohatra, mo-**ah**-trah, s., sham sale
mohina, mo-ee-nah, s., sadness; mournfulness
mohíno, mo-ee-no, a., fretful; peevish
moho, mo-o, s., moss; mould; rust
mohoso, mo-o-so, a., mouldy; rusty
mojada, mo-*H*ah-dah, s., wetting; sop
mojama, mo-*H*ah-mah, s., salt tunny fish
mojar, mo-*H*ar, v., to wet; to damp [fist
mojicón, mo-*H*e-**kon,** s., punch; blow with clenched
mojiganga, mo-*H*e-**gahn**-gah, s., masquerade
mojigato, mo-*H*e-**gah**-to, a., hypocritical; prudish
mojón, mo-*H*on, s., landmark; milestone
molde, mol-day, s., mould; pattern
moldear, mol-day-**ar,** v., to mould; to cast
moldura, mol-**doo**-rah, s., moulding
mole, mo-lay, s., mass; bulk
molécula, mo-lay-**koo**-lah, s., molecule
moledor, mo-lay-**dor,** s., miller; grinder; bore

moler, mo-**lair**, v., to grind; to mill
molestar, mo-less-**tar**, v., to molest; to annoy
molestia, mo-**less**-te-ah, s., molestation; annoyance; bother; inconvenience
molicie, mo-lee-the-ay, softness; effeminacy
molienda, mo-le-**en**-dah, s., grinding; weariness
molinero, mo-le-**nay**-ro, s., miller; grinder
molinete, mo-le-**nay**-tay, s., windlass; turnstile
mollar, mo-l'**yar**, a., soft; lean; boneless; credulous
molleja, mo-l'**yay**-Hah, s., gizzard; sweetbread
mollera, mo-l'**yay**-rah, s., crown of the head
mollete, mo-l'**yay**-tay, s., plump cheek
momento, mo-**men**-to, s., moment
momia, mo-me-ah, s., mummy
momio, mo-me-o, a., lean; meagre. **de —, day —,** [gratis
monada, mo-**nah**-dah, s., grimace
monaguillo, mo-nah-**ghee**-l'yo, s., acolyte
monarca, mo-**nar**-kah, s., monarch
monarquía, mo-nar-**kee**-ah, s., monarchy; kingdom
monasterio, mo-nahs-**tay**-re-o, s., monastery
monda, mon-dah, s., pruning
mondadientes, mon-dah-de-**en**-tess, s., toothpick
mondadura, mon-dah-**doo**-rah, s., cleaning; peel
mondar, mon-**dar**, v., to trim; to peel
mondongo, mon-**don**-go, s., tripe
monear, mo-nay-**ar**, v., to monkey
moneda, mo-**nay**-dah, s., money; coin; currency
monería, mo-nay-**ree**-ah, s., mimicry; bauble
monigote, mo-ne-**go**-tay, a., ignorant
monja, mon-Hah, s., nun
monje, mon-Hay, s., monk
mono, mo-no, s., monkey, a., neat; pretty
monóculo, mo-**no**-koo-lo, s., monocle
monótono, mo-**no**-to-no, a., monotonous
monseñor, mon-say-n'**yor**, s., monseigneur
monstruo, mons-troo'o, s., monster
monta, mon-tah, s., amount; worth [amount
montante, mon-**tahn**-tay, s., upright; standard;
montaña, mon-tah-n'yah, s., mountain
montar, mon-tar, v., to mount; to amount to
montaraz, mon-tah-**rahth**, a., mountainous; wild

montear, mon-tay-**ar**, v., to hunt; to make a working drawing

montera, mon-**tay**-rah, s., cloth cap; hunting cap

montero, mon-**tay**-ro, s., hunter

montés, mon-**tess**, a., wild

montículo, mon-**tee**-koo-lo, s., mound

monto, **mon**-to, s., amount; sum

montón, mon-**tone**, s., heap; pile

montuoso, mon-too'**o**-so, a., mountainous

montura, mon-**too**-rah, s., saddle; mount; (jewellery) setting

monzón, mon-**thon**, s., monsoon

moña, **mo**-n'yah, s., ornament of ribbons; badge on a bull's neck in the ring; drunkenness

moño, **mo**-n'yo, s., chignon; tuft

moñudo, mo-n'**yoo**-do, a., crested

moquear, mo-kay-**ar**, v., to snivel

mora, **mo**-rah, s., blackberry

morada, mo-**rah**-dah, s., residence; abode

morado, mo-**rah**-do, a., violet; mulberry-coloured

morador, mo-rah-**dor**, s., inhabitant; lodger

moral*, mo-**rahl**, s., morality. a., moral

moraleja, mo-rah-**lay**-*H*ah, s., moral maxim

morar, mo-**rar**, v., to inhabit; to lodge; to live

morbidez, mor-be-**deth**, s., softness; mellowness; morbidity

mórbido, **mor**-be-do, a., morbid; mellow

morbo, **mor**-bo, s., disease; illness

morcilla, mor-**thee**-l'yah, s., black pudding

morcillero, mor-thee-l'**yay**-ro, s., pork butcher

mordaz, mor-**dath**, a., sarcastic; biting

mordedura, mor-day-**doo**-rah, s., bite

morder, mor-**dair**, v., to bite; to gnaw

mordiente, mor-de-en-**tay**, s., mordant

mordiscar, mor-diss-**kar**, v., to gnaw

morena, mo-**ray**-nah, s., lamprey; brown bread

moreno, mo-**ray**-no, a., brown; tawny

morera, mo-**ray**-rah, s., mulberry-tree

moribundo, mo-re-**boon**-do, a., dying

morigerar, mo-re-*H*ay-**rar**, v., to moderate

morir, mo-**reer**, v., to die

morlaco, mor-**lah**-ko, a., affecting ignorance

moro, mo-ro, a., (fam.) undiluted (wine)

moroso, mo-ro-so, a., slow; tardy

morral, mor-rrahl, s., nose-bag

morralla, mor-rrah-l'yah, s., small fry; rubbish

morriña, mor-rree-n'yah, s., melancholy; home-sickness

morsa, mor-sah, s., walrus; morse [sickness

mortaja, mor-tah-Hah, s., shroud; mortise

mortal, mor-tahl, s. & a., mortal

mortecino, mor-tay-thee-no, a., dying; pale

mortero, mor-tay-ro, s., mortar; cement

mortífero, mor-tee-fay-ro, a., deadly [torment

mortificar, mor-te-fe-kar, v., to mortify; to

mortuorio, mor-too-o-re-o, s., burial. a., mortuary

mosaico, mo-sah'e-ko, a., mosaic; marquetry

mosca, moss-kah, s., fly

moscatel, moss-kah-tel, s., muscatel

moscón, moss-kon, s., large fly

mosquete, moss-kay-tay, s., musket

mosquitero, moss-ke-tay-ro, s., mosquito net

mosquito, moss-kee-to, s., mosquito

mostacera, moss-tah-thay-rah, s., mustard pot

mostacho, moss-tah-cho, s., moustache

mostaza, moss-tah-thah, s., mustard

mosto, moss-to, s., must; new wine

mostrado, moss-trah-do, a., accustomed; inured

mostrar, moss-trar, v., to show; to prove

mostrenco, moss-tren-ko, a., stray; vagabond

mota, mo-tah, s., mote; speck; burl in cloth

mote, mo-tay, s., motto; nickname

motín, mo-teen, s., mutiny

motivar, mo-te-var, v., to assign a motive

motivo, mo-tee-vo, s., motive; cause; reason

motocicleta, mo-to-the-klay-tah, s., motor-cycle

motón, mo-ton, s., pulley

motor, mo-tor, s., motor

movedizo, mo-vay-dee-tho, a., movable; shifting

movedor, mo-vay-dor, s., mover

mover, mo-vair, v., to move; to drive

móvil, mo-vil, a., movable

movilizar, mo-ve-le-thar, v., to mobilize

movimiento, mo-ve-me-en-to, s., movement; motion; sedition; working

moza, mo-thah, s., girl ; lass ; maid-servant

mozalbete, mo-thahl-**bay**-tay, s., lad ; youth

mozo, mo-tho, s., youth ; man-servant. a., young

muchacha, moo-**chah**-chah, s., girl ; lass

muchacho, moo-**chah**-cho, s., boy ; lad

muchedumbre, moo-chay-**doom**-bray, s., multitude ; abundance

mucho, moo-cho, adv., much. a., much ; plenty

muda, moo-dah, s., change ; alteration ; moulting

mudable, moo-**dah**-blay, a., changeable ; fickle

mudanza, moo-**dahn**-thah, s., change ; inconstancy ; removal

mudar, moo-**dar**, v., to change ; to moult ; to change one's residence

mudez, moo-**deth**, s., dumbness

mudo, moo-do, a., dumb

mueblaje, moo'ay-**blah**-Hay, s., household furniture   [movable

mueble, moo'**ay**-blay, s., piece of furniture. a.,

mueca, moo'**ay**-kah, s., grimace

muela, moo'**ay**-lah, s., millstone ; grindstone ; molar teeth

muelle, moo'**ay**-l'yay, s., mole ; jetty. a., tender ;

muellaje, moo'ay-l'**yah**-Hay, s., wharfage   [soft

muérdago, moo'**air**-dah-go, s., mistletoe

muerte, moo'**air**-tay, s., death

muerto, moo'**air**-to, s., corpse. a., dead

muesca, moo'**ess**-kah, s., notch ; groove

muestra, moo'**ess**-trah, s., pattern ; sample

muestrario, moo'ess-**trah**-re-o, s., set of samples

mugido, moo-**Hee**-do, s., lowing

mugir, moo-**Heer**, v., to low ; to bellow

mugre, moo-gray, s., dirt ; grime

mujer, moo-**Hair**, s., woman ; wife

mujeril, mo-**Hay**-reel, a., womanish ; womanly

mula, moo-lay, s., she-mule

muladar, moo-lah-**dar**, s., dung-hill

mulatero, moo-lah-**tay**-ro, s., muleteer

mulato, moo-**lah**-to, s., mulatto

muleta, moo-**lay**-tah, s., crutch ; prop

multa, mool-tah, s., fine ; penalty ; forfeit

multar, mool-**tar**, v., to fine ; to mulct

múltiple, mool-té-play, a., multiple   [multiply

multiplicar, mool-te-ple-**kar**, v., to increase; to

multitud, mool-te-**tood**, s., multitude

mullir, mool-l'**yeer**, v., to make soft; to mollify

mundo, moon-do, s., world

munición, moo-ne-the-**on**, s., ammunition

municionar, moo-ne-the-o-**nar**, v., to store; to supply with ammunition

municipio, moo-ne-**thee**-pe-o, s., municipality

munífico, moo-**nee**-fe-ko, a., munificent

muñeca, moo-n'**yay**-kah, s., wrist; doll

muñeco, moo-n'**yay**-ko, s., puppet

muñón, moo-n'**yon**, s., stump of an amputated limb

muralla, moo-**rah**-l'yah, s., rampart; wall

murciélago, moor-the-**ay**-lah-go, s., (animal) bat

murga, moor-gah, s., band of street musicians

murmurar, moor-moo-*H*ay-**ar**, v., to mutter

murmurio, moor-**moo**-re-o, s., murmur

muro, moo-ro, s., wall; rampart

murrio, moor-rre-o, a., sad; melancholy

murtilla, moor-**tee**-l'yah, s., myrtle

musaraña, moo-sah-**rah**-n'yah, s., shrew-mouse

músculo, mooss-koo-lo, s., muscle

muselina, moo-say-**lee**-nah, s., muslin

museo, moo-**say**-o, s., museum

musgo, mooss-go, s., moss

música, moo-se-kah, s., music

músico, moo-se-ko, s., musician. a., musical

musitar, moo-se-**tar**, v., to mumble; to mutter

muslo, mooss-lo, s., thigh

mustio, mooss-te-o, a., withered; sad

mutilar, moo-te-**lar**, v., to mutilate; to maim

mutuamente, moo-too'ah-**men**-tay, adv., mutu-

mutuo, moo-too'o, a., mutual   [ally

muy, moo'e, adv., greatly; very

nabo, nah-bo, s., rape; turnip

nácar, nah-kar, s., mother-of-pearl; nacre

nacer, nah-**thair**, v., to be born

nacido, nah-**thee**-do, a., proper; apt; fit

nacimiento, nah-the-me-**en**-to, s., birth; origin

nación, nah-the-**on**, s., nation

nada, nah-dah, s., nothing
nadadero, nah-dah-**day**-ro, s., swimming-place
nadador, nah-dah-**dor**, s., swimmer
nadar, nah-**dar**, v., to swim
nadie, nah-de-ay, pron., nobody
nado, (a) ah nah-do, adv., afloat
naipe, nah'e-pay, s., playing-card
nalgá, nalh-gah, s., buttock, rump
nao, na-o, s., ship
naranja, nah-**rahn**-Hah, s., orange
naranjado, nah-rahn-**Hah**-do, a., orange-coloured
narciso, nar-**thee**-so, s., daffodil; narcissus
nardo, nar-do, s., spikenard; tuberose
narigón, nah-re-**gon**, a., large-nosed
nariz, nah-**reeth**, s., nose; nostril
narrar, nar-**rrar**, v., to narrate; to relate
nasa, nah-sah, s., fish-trap
nata, nah-tah, s., cream
natalicio, nah-tah-lee-the-o, s., birthday
natátil, nah-**tah**-til, a., able to swim
natillas, nah-**tee**-l'yahs, s., custard
nato, nah-to, a., born
natural, nah-too-**rahl**, a., natural; native
naturaleza, nah-too-rah-**lay**-thah, s., nature
naufragar, nah'oo-frah-**gar**, v., to be shipwrecked
naufragio, nah'oo-frah-**He**-o, s., shipwreck
náufrago, nah'oo-frah-go, a., shipwrecked
nauseabundo, nah'oo-say-ah-**boon**-do, a., naus-
nausear, nah'oo-say-**ar**, v., to nauseate   [eous
náutica, nah'oo-te-kah, s., navigation
navaja, nah-vah-Hah, s., razor; clasp-knife
navajada, navajazo, nah-vah-Hah-dah, nah-
   vah-Hah-tho, s., gash with a razor or knife
nave, nah-vay, s., ship; nave
navegar, nah-vay-**gar**, v., to nivagate
navidad, nah-ve-**dahd**, s., Christmas-day
naviero, nah-ve-**ay**-ro, s., ship-owner
navío, nah-vee-o, s., ship
neblina, nay-**blee**-nah, s., mist, fog
nebuloso, nay-boo-**lo**-so, a., misty; foggy; cloudy
necedad, nay-thay-**dahd**, s., gross ignorance;
   stupidity

necesaria, nay-thay-**sah**-re-ah, s., water-closet
necesario*, nay-thay-**sah**-re-o, a., necessary ; need-
neceser, nay-thay-**sair**, s., toilet-case　　[ful
necesidad, nay-thay-se-**dahd**, s., necessity
necesitado, nay-thay-se-**tah**-do, a., necessitous ;
　　needy　　[need
necesitar, nay-thay-se-**tar**, v., to necessitate ; to
necio*, nay-the-o, a., ignorant ; foolish ; imprudent
nefasto, nay-**fahs**-to, a., ominous ; unlucky
negable, nay-**gah**-blay, a., deniable
negado, nay-**gah**-do, a., incapable ; inapt
negar, nay-**gar**, v., to deny ; to refuse ; to forbid
negligente, nay-gle-**H**en-tay, a., negligent ; heed-
　　less
negociado, nay-go-the-**ah**-do, s., department ; bu-
　　reau ; business　　[dealer
negociante, nay-go-the-**ahn**-tay, s., merchant ;
negociar, nay-go-the-**ar**, v., to trade ; to negotiate
negocio, nay-**go**-the-o, s., occupation ; business ;
　　transaction
negrear, nay-gray-**ar**, v., to grow or appear black
negro, nay-gro, a., black ; dark
negrura, nay-**groo**-rah, s., blackness
nervio, nair-ve-o, s., nerve
nervioso, nair-ve-o-so, a., nervous
nervudo, nair-**voo**-do, a., vigorous
neto, nay-to, a., neat ; pure ; net
neumático, nay'oo-**mah**-te-ko, a., pneumatic
neutral, neutro, nay'oo-**trahl,** nay'**oo**-tro, a.,
　　neutral ; neuter
nevada, nay-**vah**-dah, s., snowfall
nevar, nay-**var**, v., to snow
nevería, nay-vay-**ree**-ah, s., ice-house
ni, ne, conj., neither ; nor
nicho, nee-cho, s., niche ; recess in a wall
nido, nee-do, s., nest
niebla, ne-**ay**-blah, s., fog ; mist ; haze
nieto, ne-**ay**-to, s., grandson
nieve, ne-**ay**-vay, s., snow　　[minute
nimio*, nee-me-o, a., excessively careful ; prolix;
ningún, ninguno, nin-**goon,** nin-**goo**-no, a.,
　　none ; not one

niña, nee-n'yah, s., girl; pupil of the eye
niñera, ne-n'**yay**-rah, s., nursery-maid
niñería, ne-n'yay-**ree**-ah, s., puerility; childish
niñez, ne-n'**yeth,** s., childhood [action
niño, nee-n'yo, s., child; infabt. a., childish
níquel, nee-kel, s., nickel
níspero, niss-pay-ro, s., medlar-tree
nítido, nee-te-do, a., bright; shining
nitrato, ne-trah-to, s., nitrate
nitro, nee-tro, s., saltpetre
nivel, ne-vel, s., level
no, no, adv., no, not
nobiliario, no-be-le-**ah**-re-o, a., nobiliary
noble, no-blay, s., nobleman, a*., noble
nobleza, no-**blay**-thah, s., nobleness; nobility
noción, no-the-**on,** s., notion
nocivo, no-**thee**-vo, a., noxious
nocturno, nok-**toor**-no, a., nocturnal
noche, no-chay, s., night
nochebuena, no-chay-boo'**ay**-nah, s., Christmas-
nodriza, no-**dree**-thah, s., wet-nurse [eve
nogal, no-**gahl,** s., walnut-tree
nombradía, nom-brah-**dee**-ah, s., fame; reputation
nombrar, nom-**brar,** v., to name; to appoint
nombre, nom-bray, s., name; title; reputation;
noun
nómina, no-me-nah, s., list; catalogue; pay-roll
non, non, a., odd; uneven
nonada, no-**nah**-dah, s., trifle
nonagésimo, no-nah-*H*ay-se-mo, a., ninetieth
nono, no-no, a., ninth
no obstante, no-obs-**tahn**-tay, adv., nevertheless
nordeste, nor-**dess**-tay, s., north-east
noria, no-re-ah, s., draw-well; noria
norte, nor-tay, s., north
nos, nos, pron., us
nosotros, nos-o-tros, pron., we; us; ourselves
nota, no-tah, s., note; mark; remark; censure;
renown; bill
notar, no-tar, v., to note; to heed; to censure
notario, no-**tah**-re-o, s., notary

noticia, no-**tee**-the-ah, s., news; notice; knowledge;
noticiar, no-te-the-**ar**, v., to give notice　[advice
noticioso, no-te-the-**ay**-ro, s., reporter
noticioso, no-te-the-o-so, a., informed; learned
notificar, no-te-fe-**kar**, v., to notify
notorio, no-**to**-re-o, a., notorious
novedad, no-vay-**dahd**, s., novelty; newness
novela, no-**vay**-lah, s., novel; tale
noveno, no-**vay**-no, a., ninth
noventa, no-**ven**-tah, s. & a., ninety
novia, no-ve-ah, s., bride
novicio, no-**vee**-the-o, s., novice
noviembre, no-ve-**em**-bray, s., November
novilla, no-**vee**-l'yah, s., heifer
novillo, no-**vee**-l'yo, s., young bull; steer
novio, no-ve-o, s., bridegroom
novísimo, no-**vee**-se-mo, a., newest; latest
nubada, noo-**bah**-dah, s., shower of rain; abun-
nubarrón, noo-bar-**rron**, s., large cloud　[dance
nube, noo-bay, s., cloud
nublado, noo-**blah**-do, a., cloudy
nuca, noo-kah, s., nape of the neck
núcleo, noo-klay-o, s., nucleus
nudillo, noo-**dee**-l'yo, s., knuckle
nuera, noo'**ay**-rah, s., daughter-in-law
nuestro, noo'**ess**-tro, poss. pron., our
nueve, noo'**ay**-vay, s. & a., nine
nuevo*, noo'**ay**-vo, a., new; novel; fresh
nuez, noo'**eth**, s., walnut
nulidad, noo-le-**dahd**, s., nullity; insignificance;
nulo, noo-lo, a., null; void　[nobody
numerar, noo-may-**rar**, v., to number; to enumerate; to count; to page
número, noo-may-ro, s., number; figure
nunca, noon-kah, adv., never
nuncio, noon-the-o, s., messenger; nuncio
nupcias, noop-the-ahs, s., nuptials; wedding
nutria, noo-tre-ah, s., otter
nutricio, noo-**tree**-the-o, a., nutritious
nutrición, noo-tre-the-**on**, s., nutrition
nutrimento, noo-tre-**men**-to, s., food; nourish-
nutrir, noo-**treer**, v., to nourish　[ment; nutrition

ñagaza, n'yah-**gah**-thah, s., bird-call; decoy
ñame, n'**yah**-may, s., yam
ñaque, n'yah-kay, s., heap of useless trifles
ñoclo, n'**yo**-klo, s., macaroon
ñoñería, n'yo-n'yay-**ree**-ah, s., dotage
ñoño, n'**yo**-n'yo, a., decrepit

o, o, conj., or; either   [obfuscate
obcecar, ob-thay-**kar**, v., to blind; to obscure; to
obedecer, o-bay-day-**thair**, v., to obey
obediente, o-bay-de-**en**-tay, a., obedient
obertura, o-bair-**too**-rah, s., (music) overture
obesidad, o-bay-se-**dahd**, s., obesity
óbice, o-be-thay, s., obstacle
obispo, o-**biss**-po, s., bishop
óbito, o-be-to, s., decease; death
objeción, ob-Hay-the-**on**, s., objection
objetar, ob-Hay-**tar**, v., to object
objeto, ob-**Hay**-to, s., object
oblea, o-**blay**-ah, s., wafer
oblicuo, -**oblee**-koo'o, a., oblique; slanting; inclined
obligación, o-ble-gah-the-**on**, s., obligation; duty;
    bond; debenture   [strain
obligar, o-ble-**gar**, v., to compel; to bind; to con-
obligatorio, o-ble-gah-**to**-re-o, a., binding; obliga-
    tory
obra, o-brah, s., work; book; writings; power; toil
obrador, o-brah-**dor**, s., workshop
obraje, o-brah-**Hay**, s., manufacture
obrar, o-**brar**, v., to work; to operate; to perform
obrero, o-**bray**-ro, s., workman; labourer   [darken
obscurecer, obs-koo-ray-**thair**, v., to obscure; to
obscuridad, obs-koo-re-**dahd**, s., obscurity; dark-
    ness
obscuro*, obs-**koo**-ro, a., obscure; dark; gloomy
obsequiar, ob-say-ke-**ar**, v., to court; to pay at-
    tentions; to serve
obsequioso, ob-say-ke-**o**-so, a., obsequious
observar, ob-sair-**var**, v., to observe
obsesión, ob-say-se-**on**, s., obsession
obstáculo, obs-**tah**-koo-lo, s., obstacle
obstinarse, obs-te-**nar**-say, v., to be obstinate

obstruir, obs-troo'*eer*, v., to obstruct
obtención, ob-ten-the-*on*, s., attainment
obtener, ob-tay-*nair*, v., to obtain ; to attain
obturador, ob-too-rrah-*dorr*, s., gasket (mech.)
obtuso, ob-*too*-so, a., obtuse ; blunt
obviar, ob-ve-*ar*, v., to obviate
obvio, *ob*-ve-o, a., obvious
oca, o-kah, s., goose
ocasionar, o-kah-se-o-*nar*, v., to cause ; to occasion
ocaso, o-*kah*-so, occident ; sunset
océano, o-*thay*-ah-no, s., ocean
ocio, o-the-o, s., leisure ; pastime
ociosidad, o-the-o-se-*dahd*, s., idleness ; leisure
ocioso, o-the-*o*-so, a., idle ; fruitless
octavo, ok-*tah*-vo, a., eighth
octogésimo, ok-to-*Hay*-se-mo, a., eightieth
octubre, ok-*too*-bray, s., October
oculista, o-koo-*liss*-tah, s., oculist
ocultación, o-kool-tah-the-*on*, s., concealment
ocultar, o-kool-*tar*, v., to hide ; to mask ; to keep secret
oculto, o-*kool*-to, a., hidden ; secret
ocupante, o-koo-*pahn*-tay, s., occupier
ocupar, o-koo-*par*, v., to occupy ; to fill ; to employ
ocurrir, o-koor-*rreer*, v., to happen ; to occur ; to take place
ochavado, o-chah-*vah*-do, a., octagonal
ochavo, o-*chah*-vo, s., small brass coin
ochenta, o-*chen*-tah, s. & a., eighty
ocho, o-cho, s. & a., eight
odio, o-de-o, s., hatred
odioso, o-de-*o*-so, a., odious ; hateful
odorífero, o-do-*ree*-fay-ro, a., odoriferous ; fragrant
odre, o-dray, s., leather bag for wine   [grant
oeste, o'*ess*-tay, s., west ; west wind
ofender, o-fen-*dair*, v., to offend
ofensa, o-*fen*-sah, s., offence
ofensor, o-fen-*sor*, s., offender
oferta, o-*fair*-tah, s., offer ; tender
oficial, o-fe-the-*ahl*, s., workman ; workmaster ; clerk. a., official
oficiar, o-fe-the-*ar*, v., to officiate

oficina, o-fe-**thee**-nah, s., workshop ; office

oficio, o-**fee**-the-o, s., office ; occupation

oficioso, o-fe-the-**o**-so, a., officious ; meddling

ofrecer, o-fray-**thair**, v., to offer ; to present ; to bid   [mise

ofrecimiento, o-fray-the-me-**en**-to, s., offer ; pro-

ofuscación, o-fooss-kah-the-**on**, s., dimness of the sight ; obfuscation   [obfuscate

ofuscar, o-fooss-**kar**, v., to darken ; to dazzle ; to

oible, o'**ee**-blay, a., audible

oido, o'**ee**-do, s., hearing ; ear. p.p., heard   [Court

oidor, o'e-**dor**, s., hearer ; judge of the Supreme

oir, o'**eer**, v., to hear ; to listen

¡ojalá! o-Hah-**lah**, interj., would to God !

ojeada, o-Hay-**ah**-dah, s., glance ; glimpse

ojear, o-Hay-**ar**, v., to eye ; to glance

ojeriza, o-Hay-**ree**-thah, s., spite ; grudge ; ill-will

ojete, o-**Hay**-tay, s., eyelet

ojinegro, o-He-**nay**-gro, a., black-eyed

ojiva, o-**Hee**-vah, s., ogive

ojo, o-**Ho**, s., eye

ola, o-lah, s., wave ; billow

oleada, o-lay-**ah**-dah, s., surge

óleo, o-**lay**-o, s., oil

oleoso, o-lay-**o**-so, a., oily

oler, o-**lair**, v., to smell ; to scent

olfato, ol-**fah**-to, s., sense of smell

oliscar, o-liss-**kar**, v., to smell ; to scent

oliva, o-**lee**-vah, s., olive

olmo, **ol**-mo, s., elm-tree

olor, o-**lor**, s., smell ; odour

oloroso, o-lo-**ro**-so, (see **odorífero**)

olvidadizo, ol-ve-dah-**dee**-tho, a., forgetful

olvidar, ol-ve-**dar**, v., to forget

olvido, ol-**vee**-do, s., forgetfulness, oblivion

olla, o-**l'yah**, s., stew-pot. — **podrida**, — po-**dree**-dah, stew

ollería, o-l'yay-**ree**-ah, s., pottery ; crockery-shop

ombligo, om-**blee**-go, s., navel

ominoso, o-me-**no**-so, a., ominous

omisión, o-me-se-**on**, s., omission ; negligence

omiso, o-**mee**-so, a., neglectful ; remiss

omitir, o-me-**teer**, v., to omit; to leave out
omnipotente, om-ne-po-**ten**-tay, a., omnipotent; almighty
omnisciente, om-niss-thee-**en**-tay, a., omniscient
once, **on**-thay, s. & a., eleven
onda, **on**-dah, s., wave
ondear, on-day-**ar**, v., to undulate
onza, **on**-thah, s., ounce
opaco, o-**pah**-ko, a., opaque; dark
opción, op-the-**on**, s., option
operar, o-pay-**rar**, v., to operate
operario, o-pay-**rah**-re-o, s., working-man
ópimo, o-pe-mo, a., rich; fruitful
opinar, o-pe-**nar**, v., to opine; to consider
opíparo, o-**pe**-pah-ro, a., sumptuous
oponer, o-po-**nair**, v., to oppose [able
oportuno*, o-por-**too**-no, a., opportune; season-
opositor, o-po-se-**tor**, s., opponent
opresor, o-pray-**sor**, s., oppressor
oprimir, o-pre-**meer**, v., to oppress
oprobio, o-**pro**-be-o, s., opprobrium; ignominy
optar, op-**tar**, v., to choose; to select
óptico, **op**-te-ko, a., optical; visual
óptimo, **op**-te-mo, a., best
opuesto, o-poo'**ess**-to, a., opposite; contrary; adverse
opugnar, o-poog-**nar**, v., to impugn; to resist
opulento, o-poo-**len**-to, a., opulent
opúsculo, o-**pooss**-koo-lo, s., booklet; tract; short [treatise
oquedad, o-kay-**dahd**, s., cavity
ora, **o**-ra, conj., now; then; either; whether
orador, o-rah-**dor**, s., orator; public speaker
orar, o-**rar**, v., to harangue; to pray
orbe, **or**-bay, s., sphere, orb
órbita, **orr**-be-tah, s., orbit
orden, **or**-den, s., order (in all its significations)
ordenación, or-day-nah-the-**on**, s., arrangement; ordination [nance; orderly
ordenanza, or-day-**nahn**-thah, s., order; ordi-
ordenar, or-day-**nar**, v., to put in order; to order; to command; to confer holy orders
ordeñar, or-day-n'**yar**, v., to milk

ordinarió, or-de-**nah**-re-o, s., ordinary fare. a., ordinary ; customary

orear, o-ray-**ar**, v., to air ; to ventilate

oreja, o-ray-**H**ah, s., auricle ; ear

orejudo, o-ray-**H**oo-do, a., long-eared

orfandad, or-fahn-**dahd**, s., orphanage [work

orfebrería, or-fay-bray-**ree**-ah, s., gold an silver

organizar, or-gah-ne-**thar**, v., to organize

órgano, or-gah-no, s., organ

orgía, or-**H**ee-ah, s., orgy ; frantic revel

orgullo, or-**goo**-l'yo, s., pride ; haughtiness

orgulloso, or-goo-l'yo-so, a., proud ; haughty

oriente, o-re-en-tay, s., Orient ; east

orífice, o-**ree**-fe-thay, s., goldsmith

orificio, o-ree-**fee**-the-o, s., orifice ; aperture

origen, o-**ree**-Hen, s., origin ; source ; lineage

originar, o-re-He-**nar**, v., to originate [shore

orilla, o-**ree**-l'yah, s., limit ; border ; margin ; edge ;

orillar, o-re-l'**yar**, v., to arrange ; to conclude ; to

orillo, o-**ree**-l'yo, s., selvage [border

orín, o-**reen**, s., rust of iron ; pl., urine

orina, o-**ree**-nah, s., urine

orinal, o-re-**nahl**, s., urinal

orla, or-lah, s., list ; selvage ; border ; fringe

orlar, or-**lar**, v., to border

ornar, or-**nar**, v., to adorn

oro, o-ro, s., gold

orondo, o-**ron**-do, a., pompous ; hollow

oropel, o-ro-**pel**, s., tinsel

orquesta, or-**kess**-tah, s., orchestra

ortiga, or-**tee**-gah, s., nettle

orto, or-to, s., rising of the sun or a star

oruga, o-**roo**-gah, s., caterpillar

orujo, o-**roo**-Ho, s., peel of pressed grapes or olives

orza, or-thah, s., gallipot

orzuelo, or-thoo-**ay**-lo, s., sty (tumour on the eyelids) ; snare ; trap

os, os, pron., you ; ye

osa, o-sah, s., she-bear

osadía, o-sah-**dee**-ah, s., daring ; intrepidity

osado*, o-**sah**-do, a., bold ; audacious

osar, o-**sar**, v., to dare ; to venture

osario, o-**sah**-re-o, s., charnel house

oscilar, os-the-**lar**, v., to oscillate

ósculo, os-**koo**-lo, s., kiss

oscurecer, os-koo-ray-**thair**, (see **obscurecer**)

oscuro, os-**koo**-ro, (see **obscuro**)

óseo, o-**say**-o, a., bony

oso, o-so, s., bear   [boast

ostentar, os-ten-**tar**, v., to show; to exhibit; to

ostra, os-trah, s., oyster

osudo, o-**soo**-do, a., bony

otear, o-tay-**ar**, v., to watch from a high point;
     to examine

otoñada, o-to-n'**yah**-dah, s., autumn season

otoñal, o-to-n'**yahl**, a., autumnal

otoño, o-to-n'yo, s., autumn   [licence

otorgamiento, o-tor-gah-me-**en**-to, s., grant;

otorgar, o-tor-**gar**, v., to consent; to agree; to
     covenant; to execute

otro, o-tro, a., other; another

otrosí, o-tro-**see**, adv., moreover; besides

ovación, o-vah-the-**on**, s., ovation

óvalo, o-**vah**-lo, s., oval

ovar, o-var, v., to lay eggs

ovario, o-**vah**-re-o, s., ovary

oveja, o-**vay**-*H*ah, s., ewe

ovillo, o-**vee**-l'yo, s., clew; ball

óvulo, o-**voo**-lo, s., ovule

óxido, **ok**-se-do, s., oxide

oyente, o-**yen**-tay, s., auditor; hearer

ozono, o-**tho**-no, s., ozone

pabellón, pah-bay-l'**yon**, s., pavilion; arbour;
     flag

pábilo, **pah**-be-lo, s., wick; snuff of a candle

paca, **pah**-kah, s., package

pacato, pah-**kah**-to, a., pacific; gentle

pacer, pah-**thair**, v., to pasture; to feed

paciencia, pah-the-en-the-ah, s., patience

pacífico*, pah-**thee**-fe-ko, a., peaceful

pacotilla, pah-ko-tee-l'yah, s., venture goods

pactar, pahk-**tar**, v., to convenant; to contract

pacto, **pahk**-to, s., contract; agreement; pact

pachón, pah-**chon**, s., phlegmatic man; pointer (dog) [ness

pachorra, pah-**chor**-rrah, s., slowness; sluggish-

padecer, pah-day-**thair**, v., to suffer; to bear

padecimiento, pah-day-the-me-**en**-to, s., suffering

padrastro, pah-**drahs**-tro, s., step-father

padre, pah-dray, s., father

padrino, pah-**dree**-no, s., god-father

padrón, pah-**dron**, s., poll; note of infamy

paga, pah-gah, s., payment; fee; wages

pagadero, pah-gah-**day**-ro, a., payable [office

pagaduría, pah-gah-doo-**ree**-ah, s., paymaster's

pagamento, pah-gah-**men**-to, s., payment

pagano, pah-**gah**-no, s. & a., heathen; pagan

pagar, pah-**gar**, v., to pay

pagaré, pah-gah-**ray**, s., promissory note

página, pah-He-nah, s., page (of a book)

pago, pah-go, s., payment

país, pah**'iss**, s., country; region; landscape

paisaje, pah'e-**sah**-Hay, s., landscape

paisano, pah'e-**sah**-no, s., countryman

paja, pah-Hah, s., straw

pájaro, pah-**Hah**-ro, s., bird; sly fellow (fam.)

pajarota, pah-**Hah**-**ro**-tah, s., false report

paje, pah-Hay, s., page (boy)

pala, pah-lah, s., shovel; blade; spade

palabra, pah-**lah**-brah, s., word

palabrero, pah-lah-**bray**-ro, a., loquacious

palabrita, pah-lah-**bree**-tah, s., short word; word full of meaning

palaciego, pah-lah-the-**ay**-go, s., courtier. a., per-taining to a palace

palacio, pah-**lah**-the-o, s., palace

paladar, pah-lah-**dar**, s., palate; taste; relish

paladear, pah-lah-day-**ar**, v., to relish [public

paladino, pah-lah-**dee**-no, a., manifest; evident;

palafrenero, pah-lah-fray-**nay**-ro, s., groom

palanca, pah-**lahn**-kah, s., lever; crowbar

palanquín, pah-lahn-**keen**, s., public porter; covered litter

palco, pahl-ko, s., (theatre) box

paleto, pah-**lay**-to, s., fallow-deer; rustic

paliar, pah-le-**ar**, v., to palliate

palidecer, pah-le-day-**thair**, v., to grow pale

palidez, pah-le-**deth**, s., paleness ; wanness

pálido, pah-le-do, a., pallid ; pale

palio, pah-le-o, s., cloak ; pall

palique, pah-lee-kay, s., small talk

palizada, pah-le-**thah**-dah, s., palisade

palma, pahl-mah, s., palm-tree ; palm-leaf ; palm of the hand

palmada, pahl-**mah**-dah, s., slap ; applause

palmear, pahl-may-**ar**, v., to clap hands

palmera, pahl-**may**-rah, s., palm-tree

palmo, pahl-mo, s., span ; palm (8 inches)

palo, pah-lo, s., stick ; cudgel ; mast ; blow with a stick

paloma, pah-**lo**-mah, s., pigeon ; dove

palomar, pah-lo-**mar**, s., dove-cot

palomera, pah-lo-**may**-rah, s., dove-cot

palpar, pahl-**par**, v., to feel ; to touch ; to grope

palurdo, pah-**loor**-do, s. & a., rustic

pamplina, pahm-**plee**-nah, s., duck-weed ; futility

pan, pan, s., bread ; loaf ; food

panadería, pah-nah-day-**ree**-ah, s., bakery

panal, pah-**nahl**, s., honey-comb

pandear, pahn-day-**ar**, v., to bend ; to bulge out

pandereta, pahn-day-**ray**-tah, s., tambourine

pandilla, pahn-**dee**-l'yah, s., party ; gang

panecillo, pah-nay-**thee**-l'yo, s., small loaf ; French [roll

panela, pah-**nay**-lah, s., small biscuit

pánfilo, pahn-fe-lo, a., slow ; sluggish   [protégé

paniaguado, pah-ne-ah-goo'**ah**-do, s., servant ;

pánico, pah-ne-ko, s. & a., panic

pantalón, pahn-tah-**lon**, s., trousers

pantalla, pahn-**tah**-l'yah, s., screen ; lamp shade

pantano, pahn-**tah**-no, s., swamp ; marsh ; bog ; reservoir ; dam

panteón, pahn-tay-**on**, s., pantheon ; mausoleum

pantera, pahn-**tay**-rah, s., panther   [dumb show

pantomima, pahn-to-**mee**-mah, s., pantomime ;

pantorrilla, pahn-tor-**rree**-l'yah, s., calf of the leg

pantuflo, pahn-**too**-flo, s., slipper

panza, pahn-thah, s., paunch ; belly

pañal, pah-n'**yahl**, s., swaddling-clout
pañería, pah-n'yay-**ree**-ah, s., draper's shop
pañero, pah-n'**yay**-ro, s., draper
paño, **pah**-n'yo, s., cloth; drapery
pañol, pah-n'**yol**, s., store-room (in a ship)
pañuelo, pah-n'yoo-**ay**-lo, s., handkerchief
papa, **pah**-pah, s., Pope; fib. pl., potatoes
papada, pah-**pah**-dah, s., double chin
papagayo, pah-pah-**gah**-yo, s., parrot
papanatas, pah-pah-**nah**-tahs, s., simpleton
páparo, **pah**-pah-ro, s., rustic; churl   [ument
papel, pah-**pel**, s., paper; writing; part; role; doc-
papelera, pah-pay-**lay**-rah, s., writing-desk
papelería, pah-pay-lay-**ree**-ah, s., stationery
papelero, pah-pay-**lay**-ro, s., stationer   [paper-bag
papeleta, pah-pay-**lay**-tah s., slip of paper; card;
papilla, pah-**pee**-l'yah, s., pap; guile; deceit
paquebote, pah-kay-**bo**-tay, s., packet-boat
paquete, pah-**kay**-tay, s., parcel; package
par, par, s., pair; peer. a., equal; even
para, **pah**-rah, prep., for; to; in order to; toward
parabién, pah-rah-be-**en**, s., congratulation
parabrisas, pah-rah-**bree**-sahs, s., windscreen
parábola, pah-**rah**-bo-lah, s., parable; parabola
paracaídas, pah-rah-kah-ee-dahs, s., parachute
parada, pah-**rah**-dah, s., halt; pause; stall
paradera, pah-rah-**day**-rah, s., sluice
paradero, pah-rah-**day**-ro, s., halting-place; end
parado, pah-**rah**-do, a., remiss; inactive; indolent
paraguas, pah-rah-**goo**'ahs, s., umbrella
paragüero, pah-rah-goo'**ay**-ro, s., umbrella-stand
paraíso, pah-rah-ee-so, s., paradise
paraje, pah-**rah**-Hay, s., place
paralelo, pah-rah-**lay**-lo, s., comparison. a., par-
parálisis, pah-**rah**-le-siss, s., paralysis   [allel
paramento, pah-rah-**men**-to, s., ornament
páramo, **pah**-rah-mo, s., wilderness; paramo
parangón, pah-rahn-**gon**, s., paragon; model;
   comparison
parar, pah-**rar**, v., to stop; to halt; to detain
pararrayos, pah-rar-**rrah**-yos, s., lightning-rod or
   conductor

parcela, par-**thay**-lah, s., plot of land
parcial*, par-the-**ahl**, a., partial
parco*, par-ko, a., sober; sparing; moderate
parche, par-chay, s., plaster; sticking-plaster
pardal, par-**dahl**, s., sparrow; leopard. a., rustic
pardear, par-day-**ar**, v., to become grey [word!
¡pardiez! par-de-**eth**, interj., by Jove! upon my
pardo, par-do, a., brown; dark grey
parear, pah-ray-**ar**, v., to match; to couple
parecer, pah-ray-**thair**, v., to appear; to seem.
   s., opinion; look
parecido, pah-ray-**thee**-do, a., like; similar; look-
pared, pah-**red**, s., wall [ing
paredón, pah-ray-**don**, s., thick wall
pareja, pah-**ray**-Hah, s., pair; match; coupling
parejo, pah-**ray**-Ho, a., equal; similar; even
parentela, pah-ren-**tay**-lah, s., parentage
pareo, pah-**ray**-o, s., coupling; matching
paridad, pah-re-**dahd**, s., parity
pariente, parienta, pah-re-en-tay, pah-re-en-
   tah, s. & a., kinsman; kinswoman
parihuela, pah-re-oo-**ay**-lah, s., barrow; stretcher
parir, pah-**reer**, v., to give birth
parla, par-lah, s., loquacity; talk
parlamentar, par-lah-men-**tar**, v., to parley
parlamento, par-lah-**men**-to, s., parliament;
   speech
parlar, par-**lar**, v., to speak with ease; to chatter
parlón, a., talkative
parodia, pah-ro-de-ah, s., parody
parpadear, par-pah-day-**ar**, v., to wink
párpado, par-pah-do, s., eye-lid
parque, par-kay, s., park; paddock
parra, par-rrah, s., vine on stakes or on a wall
párrafo, pah-rrahf-o, s., paragraph
parrilla, par-rree-l'yah, s., gridiron; grate
párroco, par-rro-ko, s., parson; rector
parroquia, par-rro-ke-ah, s., parish
parte, par-tay, s., part; share; place; interest;
partera, par-tay-rah, s., midwife [party
partible, par-tee-blay, a., divisible [distribution
partición, par-te-the-**on**, s., partition; division;

participar, par-te-the-**par**, v., to inform; to participate

partícipe, par-**tee**-the-pay, s., partner. a., sharing

partícula, par-**tee**-koo-lah, s., particle

partida, par-**tee**-dah, s., departure; item; entry; parcel; stakes; game. pl., talents

partidario, par-te-**dah**-re-o, s., partisan

partido, par-**tee**-do, s., party; district; utility; game. a., divided

partir, par-**teer**, v., to part; to divide; to depart

parto, par-to, s., childbirth

párvulo, par-voo-lo, s., child. a., innocent; humble   [ble

pasa, pah-sah, s., raisin

pasada, pah-**sah**-dah, s., passage

pasadero, pass-ah-**day**-ro, a., supportable; passable   [able

pasadizo, pah-sah-**dee**-tho, s., passage

pasador, pah-sah-**dor**, s., bolt; pin; peg

pasaje, pah-**sah**-*Hay*, s., passage

pasajero, pah-sah-*H*ay-ro, s., passenger. a., transitory   [sitory

pasamano, pah-sah-**mah**-no, s., balustrade

pasaporte, pah-sah-**por**-tay, s., passport

pasar, pah-**sar**, v., to pass; to convey; to exceed   **— a, —** ah, to proceed to

pasatiempo, pah-sah-te-**em**-po, s., pastime

pascua, pahs-koo'ah, s., Easter

pase, pah-say, s., pass; passport

pasear, pah-say-ar, v., to walk; to take a walk

paseo, pah-**say**-o, s., walk; promenade; drive

pasillo, pah-**see**-l'yo, s., passage; corridor

pasión, pah-se-**on**, s., passion

pasivo, pah-**see**-vo, s., liabilities. a., passive

pasmar, pahs-**mar**, v., to astound; to wonder

pasmo, pahs-mo, s., amazement

pasmoso, pahs-**mo**-so, a., wonderful

paso, pah-so, s., pace; step; passage

pasta, pahs-tah, s., paste

pastar, pahs-**tar**, v., to graze; to pasture

pastel, pahs-**tel**, s., pie; cake; pastel

pastelero, pahs-tay-**lay**-ro, s., pastrycook

pasto, pahs-to, s., pasture; food

pastor, pahs-**tor**, s., shepherd; pastor; clergyman

pastoso, pahs-**to**-so, a., pasty

pastura, pahs-**too**-rah, s., pasturage
pata, pah-tah, s., foot, leg (of beasts)
patada, pah-**tah**-dah, s., kick
patalear, pah-tah-lay-**ar**, v., to kick about violently
patán, pah-**tahn**, s., rustic ; churl
patata, pah-**tah**-tah, s., potato
patatús, pah-tah-**tooss**, s., swoon [evident
patente, pah-**ten**-tay, s., patent. a*., manifest ;
patentizar, pah-ten-te-**thar**, v., to make evident
paternal, pah-**tair**-nahl, a., fatherly
pateta, pah-**tay**-tah, s., lame person
patético, pah-**tay**-te-ko, a., pathetic
patíbulo, pah-**tee**-boo-lo, s., gallows
patillas, pah-**tee**-l'yahs, s., whiskers
patín, pah-**teen**, s., skate
patinar, pah-te-**nar**, v., to skate
patio, pah-te-o, s., courtyard ; (theatre) pit
patizambo, pah-te-**thahm**-bo, a., bandy-legged
pato, pah-to, s., duck ; drake [sense
patochada, pah-to-**chah**-dah, s., blunder ; non-
patraña, pah-**trah**-n'yah, s., fabulous story
patria, pah-tre-ah, s., native country
patrio, pah-tre-o, a., native
patrocinio, pah-tro-**thee**-ne-o, s., patronage [tern
patrón, pah-**tron**, s., patron ; host ; landlord ; pat-
patrono, pah-**tro**-no, s., patron ; protector ; lord of the manor ; employer
patrulla, pah-**troo**-l'yah, s., patrol
patudo, pah-**too**-do, a., club-footed
paupérrimo, pah'oo-**pair**-rre-mo, a., very poor
pausa, pah'oo-sah, s., pause ; rest
pausado, pah'oo-**sah**-do, adv., slowly. a., slow
pausar, pah'oo-**sar**, v., to pause ; to rest
pauta, pah'oo-tah, s., paper-ruler ; standard ; model
pava, pah-vah, s., turkey-hen
pavimento, pah-ve-**men**-to, s., pavement
pavo, pah-vo, s., turkey
pavón, pah-**von**, s., peacock
pavonada, pah-vo-**nah**-dah, s., strut ; short walk
pavonear, pah-vo-nay-**ar**, v., to strut
pavor, pah-**vor**, s., dread ; terror
pavoroso, pah-vo-**ro**-so, a., frightful ; awful

pavura, pah-**voo**-rah, s., fright; terror
payaso, pah-**yah**-so, s., clown
payo, pah-yo, s., churl
paz, path, s., peace
pazguato, path-goo'**ah**-to, s., simpleton
pe, pay, s., the letter P. **de — a pa,** day — ah pah, from beginning to end
peaje, pay-ah-Hay, s., bridge-toll
peana, pay-**ah**-nah, s., pedestal; foot-stool
peatón, pay-ah-**ton**, s., pedestrian
peca, pay-kah, s., freckle; speck
pecado, pay-**kah**-do, s., sin
pecador, pay-kah-**dor**, s., sinner
pecar, pay-**kar**, v., to sin
pecera, pay-**thay**-rah, s., fish-globe; aquarium
pécora, pay-ko-rah, s., sheep's head; shrewd woman
pecoso, pay-**ko**-so, a., freckled
peculiar', pay-koo-le-**ar**, a., peculiar
peculio, pay-**koo**-le-o, s., private purse or property
pecunia, pay-koo-ne-ah, s., money
pecuniario, pay-koo-ne-**ah**-re-o, a., pecuniary; monetary
pechera, pay-**chay**-rah, s., shirt-front
pechero, pay-**chay**-ro, s., bib. a., commoner
pecho, pay-cho, s., chest; breast; gradient
pechuga, pay-**choo**-gah, s., breast of a fowl
pedazo, pay-**dah**-tho, s., piece; bit; fragment
pedernal, pay-dair-**nahl**, s., flint
pedicular, pay-de-koo-**lar**, a., lousy
pediduro, pay-de-**koo**-ro, s., chiropodist
pedido, pay-**dee**-do, s., order; goods for sale
pedigüeño, pay-de-goo'**ay**-n'yo, s., beggar
pedir, pay-**deer**, v., to ask; to beg; to demand; [to order (goods)]
pedo, pay-do, s., flatulence
pedrada, pay-**drah**-dah, s., stoning
pedregoso, pay-dray-**go**-so, a., stony; afflicted with gravel
pedrera, pay-**dray**-rah, s., quarry
pedrería, pay-dray-**ree**-ah, s., jewellery
peer, pay-**air**, v., to break wind
pega, pay-gah, s., gluing; pitch; practical joke
pegar, pay-**gar**, v., to join; to glue; to beat

pegote, pay-**go**-tay, s., sticking-plaster

peinador, pay'e-nah-**dor**, s., hairdresser

peinar, pay'e-**nar**, v., to comb

peine, pay'e-nay, s., comb

pejiguera, pay-*H*e-**gay**-rah, s., (fam.) bother

peladilla, pay-lah-**dee**-l'yah, s., sugar-almond

pelaje, pay-**lah**-*H*ay, s., pelage ; quality of the hair or the wool

pelar, pay-**lar**, v., to skin ; to pluck

peldaño, pel-**dah**-n'yo, s., every step of a flight of stairs

pelea, pay-**lay**-ah, s., battle ; fight ; quarrel

pelear, pay-lay-**ar**, v., to fight ; to quarrel

pelele, pay-**lay**-lay, s., man of straw

peletería, pay-lay-tay-**ree**-ah, s., furrier's trade or shop

peliagudo, pay-le-ah-**goo**-do, a., difficult ; skilful

pelicano, pay-le-**kah**-no, a., grey-haired

pelícano, pay-lee-kah-no, s., pelican

película, pay-lee-koo-lah, s., film

peligrar, pay-le-**grar**, v., to be in danger

peligro, pay-**lee**-gro, s., peril ; danger

peligroso*, pay-le-**gro**-so, a., dangerous

pelillo, pay-**lee**-l'yo, s., short hair ; trifle

pelo, pay-lo, s., hair ; down ; flaw

peloso, pay-**lo**-so, a., hairy

pelota, pay-**lo**-tah, s., ball ; Spanish ball game

pelote, pay-**lo**-tay, s., goat's hair

pelotear, pay-lo-tay-**ar**, v., to play at ball ; to argue

pelotera, pay-lo-**tay**-rah, s., quarrel

peltre, pell,-tray, s., pewter

peluca, pay-**loo**-kah, s., wig

peludo, pay-**loo**-do, a., hairy ; shaggy

peluquero, pay-loo-**kay**-ro, s., hair-dresser

pelusa, pay-**loo**-sah, s., down of plants or fruit

pella, pay-l'yah, s., pellet ; fleece ; lump of molten metal ; lard ; heron

pellejo, pay-l'**yay**-*H*o, s., skin ; hide ; peel ; wine-skin

pelliza, pay-l'**yee**-thah, s., pelisse ; tippler

pellizcar, pay-l'yeeth-**kar**, v., to pinch

pena, pay-nah, s., punishment ; pain

penado, pay-**nah**-do, a., punished ; painful [grieve

penar, pay-**nar**, v., to chastise ; to suffer pain ; to

pendencia, pen-**den**-the-ah, s., dispute; quarrel
pendenciero, pen-den-the-**ay**-ro, a., quarrelsome
pender, pen-**dair**, v., to hang; to depend
pendiente, pen-de-**en**-tay, s., ear-ring; slope. a., hanging; pendent
péndola, **pen**-do-lah, s., pendulum; quill
pendón, pen-**don**, s., standard; pennon
péndulo, **pen**-doo-lo, a., pendulum. a., hanging
penetrar, pay-nay-**trar**, v., to penetrate
penique, pay-**nee**-kay, s., penny   [ance
penitenciar, pay-ne-ten-the-**ar**, v., to impose pen-
penoso*, pay-**no**-so, a., painful   [—, purposely
pensado, pen-**sah**-do, a., deliberate. **de —**, day
pensamiento, pen-sah-me-**en**-to, s., thought
pensar, pen-**sar**, v., to think
pensativo, pen-sah-**tee**-vo, a., pensive; thoughtful
pensión, pen-se-**on**, s., pension; boarding-house
pensionista, pen-se-o-**niss**-tah, s., pensioner
penúltimo, pay-**nool**-te-mo, a., penultimate
penuria, pay-**noo**-re-ah, s., penury
peña, **pay**-n'yah, s., rock; large stone
peñasco, pay-n'**yahss**-ko, s., large-rock
peón, pay-**on**, s., day-labourer; foot soldier; spinning top
peonada, pay-o-**nah**-dah, s., day's work
peor, pay-**or**, adv. & a., worse
pepino, pay-**pee**-no, s., cucumber
pepita, pay-**pee**-tah, s., kernel; pip
pequeñez, pay-kay-n'**yeth**, s., smallness
pequeño, pay-**kay**-n'yo, a., little; small; young
pera, **pay**-rah, s., pear
percance, pair-**kahn**-thay, s., mishap
percibir, pair-the-**beer**, v., to receive; to collect; to perceive
percutir, pair-koo-**teer**, v., to strike; to percuss
percha, **pair**-chah, s., pole; perch (fish)
perder, pair-**dair**, v., to lose
pérdida, **pair**-de-dah, s., loss, waste
perdiz, pair-**deeth**, s., partridge
perdón, pair-**don**, s., pardon   [excuse
perdonar, pair-do-**nar**, v., to forgive; to remit; to
perdurable, pair-doo-**rah**-blay, a., lasting

perecedero, pay-ray-thay-**day**-ro, a., perishable
perecer, pay-ray-**thair**, v., to perish
peregrino, pay-ray-**gree**-no, s., pilgrim. a., strange
perejil, pay-ray-**Heel**, s., parsley
perendengue, pay-ren-**den**-gay, s., ear-ring; cheap ornament
perentorio, pay-ren-**to**-re-o, a., peremptory
pereza, pay-**ray**-thah, s., laziness; slowness
perezoso, pay-ray-**tho**-so, a., lazy; idle; indolent
perfeccionamiento, pair-fek-the-o-nah-me-**en**-to, s., improvement
perfecto*, pair-**fek**-to, a., perfect; complete
pérfido, pair-fe-do, a., perfidious
perfil, pair-**feel**, s., profile; side view
perfilar, pair-fe-lar, v., to outline
perforar, pair-fo-**rar**, v., to perforate
perfume, pair-**foo**-may, s., perfume
pergamino, pair-gah-**mee**-no, s., parchment
pericia, pay-**ree**-the-ah, s., skill; expertness
perifollo, pay-re-**fo**-l'yo, s., chervil. pl., women's ornaments   [tour
perímetro, pay-**ree**-may-tro, s., perimeter; con-
periódico, pay-re-o-de-ko, s., newspaper. a., periodical
peripuesto, pay-re-poo-**ess**-to, a., very spruce
periquito, pay-re-**kee**-to, s., parrakeet
perito, pay-**ree**-to, a., skilful; experienced [injure
perjudicar, pair-*H*oo-de-**kar**, v., to prejudice; to
perjuicio, pair-*H*oo-ee-the-o, s., prejudice
perjurio, pair-*H*oo-re-o, s., perjury
perjuro, pair-*H*oo-ro, s., perjurer. a., forsworn
perla, pair-lah, s., pearl
permanecer, pair-mah-nay-**thair**, v., to remain; to stay
permanente*, pair-mah-**nen**-tay, a., permanent
permeable, pair-may-**ah**-blay, a., permeable
permiso, pair-**mee**-so, a., permission; leave; licence
permitir, pair-me-**teer**, v., to permit; to allow
permutar, pair-moo-**tar**, v., to exchange; to permute
pernear, pair-nay-**ar**, v., to kick; to shake the legs
pernetas (en), en pair-**nay**-tahs, adv., bare-legged

pernicioso, pair-ne-the-**o**-so, a., pernicious
pernil, pair-**neel**, s., hock; ham
pernio, pair-ne-o, s., door or window hinge
pernoctar, pair-nok-**tar**, v., to pass the night
pero, pay-ro, conj., but; yet
perogrullada, pay-ro-groo-l'**yah**-dah, s., obvious and commonplace truth
perol, pay-**rol**, s., boiler; kettle
peroné, pay-ro-**nay**, s., fibula
peroración, pay-ro-rah-the-**on**, s., peroration
perorata, pay-ro-**rah**-tah, s., harangue; speech
perpetrar, pair-pay-**trar**, v., to perpetrate
perpetuo*, pair-pay-too'o, a., perpetual
perplejo*, pair-**play**-Ho, a., perplexed
perra, pair-rrah, s., bitch. — **gorda, — gor**-dah, 10 céntimos piece. — **chica, — chee**-kah, 5 céntimos piece
perramente, pair-rrah-**men**-tay, adv., very badly
perrería, pair-rray-**ree**-ah, s., pack of dogs; vexation
perro, pair-rro, s., dog
perruno, pair-**rroo**-no, a., canine
perseguir, pair-say-**gheer**, v., to pursue; to harrass
perseverar, pair-say-vay-**rar**, v., to persevere
persiana, pair-se-ah-nah, s., window-blind; shutter [of the cross
persignarse, pair-sig-**nar**-say, v., to make the sign
persistir, pair-siss-**teer**, v., to persist
persona, pair-so-nah, s., person
personaje, pair-so-nah-Hay, s., personage
perspectiva, pair-spek-**tee**-vah, s., perspective; view; prospect
perspicacia, pair-spe-**kah**-the-ah, s., perspicacity
perspicaz, pair-spe-**kath**, a., perspicacious
perspicuo*, pair-**spee**-koo'o, a., perspicuous
persuadir, pair-soo'ah-**deer**, v., to persuade
pertenecer, pair-tay-nay-**thair**, v., to belong to; to appertain
pértiga, pair-te-gah, s., pole; rod
pertiguero, pair-te-**gay**-ro, s., verger
pertinaz*, pair-te-**nath**, a., pertinacious
pertrechos, pair-**tray**-chos, s., stores; ammunition; tools

perturbar, pair-toor-**bar,** v., to perturb

perverso, pair-**vair**-so, a., perverse

pesa, pay-sah, s., weight   [ed

pesada, pay-**sah**-dah, s., weighing ; quantity weigh-

pesadez, pay-sah-**deth,** s., heaviness ; gravity ;
    slowness ; drowsiness

pesado*, pay-**sah**-do, a., heavy ; cumbrous ; slug-
    gish ; vexatious

pesadumbre,   pay-sah-**doom**-bray,   s.,   grief ;
    sorrow

pésame, pay-sah-may, s., expression of condolence

pesantez, pay-sahn-**teth,** s., gravity ; heaviness

pesar, pay-**sar,** v., to weigh ; to cause regret ; to
    ponder.   s., sorrow ; regret.   **a — de,** ah — day,
    in spite of

pesaroso, pay-sah-**ro**-so, a., sorrowful ; repentant

pesca, pesca, pess-kah, s., fishing ; catch

pescado, pess-**kah**-do, s., fish

pescador, pess-kah-**dor,** s., fisherman

pescante, pess-**kahn**-tay, s., coach-box

pescar, pess-**kar,** v., to fish

pescuezo, pess-koo**'ay**-tho, s., neck

pesebre, pay-**say**-bray, s., crib ; manger

peseta, pay-**say**-tah, s., Spanish monetary unit

pésimo*, pesi-se-mo, a., very bad

peso, pay-so, weight ; load

pesquería, pess-kay-**ree**-ah, s., fishing ; fishery

pesquisa, pess-**kee**-sah, s., enquiry ; search

pestaña, pess-**tah**-n'yah, s., eye-lash ; flange

pestañear, pess-tah-n'yay-**ar,** v., to blink ; to wink

peste, pess-tay, s., pest ; pestilence

pestillo, pess-**tee**-l'yo, s., bolt

petaca, pay-**tah**-kah, s., tobacco-pouch

petardear, pay-tar-day-**ar,** v., to cheat

petardista, pay-tar-**diss**-tah, s., cheat ; swindler

petardo, pay-**tar**-do, s., petard

petimetre, pay-te-**may**-tray, s., coxcomb

peto, pay-to, s., breast ; stomacher

pez, peth, s., fish

pezón, pay-**thon,** s., nipple

pezuña, pay-thoo-n'yah, s., hoof

piadoso, pe-ah-**do**-so, a., pious ; merciful

pian, piano, pe-**ahn,** pe-**ah**-no, adv gently;
softly; slowly

piano, pe-**ah**-no, s., pianoforte

piar, pe-**ar,** v., to chirp

piara, pe-**ah**-rah, s., herd of swine

pica, pee-kah, s., pike; spear

picada, pe-**kah**-dah, s., puncture

picadero, pe-kah-**day**-ro, s., riding-school

picador, pe-kah-**dor,** s., riding-master; (bull-fights)
pricker

picadura, pe-kah-**doo**-rah, s., (insect) bite, sting

picante, pe-**kahn**-tay, s., piquancy. a., piquant;
stinging

picaporte, pe-kah-**por**-tay, s., spring-latch; latch-
key; door-knocker

picar, pe-**kar,** v., to prick; to sting; to nibble;
to peck; to itch

picardía, pe-kar-**dee**-ah, s., mischief

picaresco, pe-kah-**ress**-ko, a., roguish

pícaro, pee-kah-ro, a., knavish; mischievous

picatoste, pe-kah-**tos**-tay, s., buttered toast

picazón, pe-kah-**thon,** s., itching; displeasure

pico, pee-ko, s., beak; bill; nib; peak; garrulity

picón, pe-**kon,** s., lampoon; very small charcoal

picota, pe-**ko**-tah, s., pillory; top

picotear, pe-ko-tay-**ar,** v., to strike with the bill;
to wrangle

pictórico, pik-**to**-re-ko, a., pictorial

pichón, pe-**chon,** s., young pigeon

pie, pe-**ay,** s., foot; basis; trunk; foundation;
motive. **a—firme,** ah — **feer**-may, steadfastly

piedad, pe-ay-**dahd,** s., piety; mercy; pity

piedra, pe-ay-drah, s., stone; hail

piel, pe-**ell,** s., skin; hide; peel

pierna, pe-**air**-nah, s., leg; leg of mutton; limb

pieza, pe-**ay**-thah, s., piece; coin

pifia, pee-fe-ah, s., (billiards) miss   [tle

pila, pee-lah, s., pile; heap; font; trough for cat-

pilar, pe-**lar,** s., basin of a fountain; column;

píldora, peel-do-rah, s., pill   [pillar

pilón, pe-**lon,** s., basin of a fountain; cattle trough

piloto, pe-**lo**-to, s., pilot

pillada, pe-l'**yah**-dah, s., knavish trick
pillar, pe-l'**yar,** v., to plunder
pillo, pee-l'yo, s., rogue; thief. a., roguish
pimentón, pe-men-**ton,** s., red pepper
pimienta, pe-me-**en**-tah, s., pepper
pimpollar, pim-po-l'**yar,** s., (plants) nursery
pimpollo, pim-**po**-l'yo, s., sprout; shoot; lively
pina, pee-nah, s., conical mound; jaunt   [youth
pinar, pe-**nar,** s., pine-grove
pincel, pin-**thell,** s., painter's brush
pincelar, pin-thay-**lar,** v., to paint
pinchar, pin-**char,** v., to prick; to puncture
pineda, pe-**nay**-dah, s., pine-grove
pingajo, pin-**gah**-Ho, s., rag; tatter
pingüe, peen-goo'ay, a., abundant; rich (profit)
pino, pee-no, s., pine-tree. a., steep
pinocha, pe-**no**-chah, s., pine-cone
pinta, peen-tah, s., spot; stain; pint   [exact
pintado, pin-**tah**-do, a., painted; mottled; just;
pintar, pin-**tar,** v., to paint
pintiparado, pin-te-pah-**rah**-do, a., perfectly like
pintor, pin-**tor,** s., painter
pintoresco, pin-to-**ress**-ko, a., picturesque
pintorrear, pin-tor-rray-**ar,** v., to daub
pintura, pin-**too**-rah, s., painting; picture
pinzas, pin-thahs, s., nippers; tweezers
pinzón, pin-**thon,** s., chaffinch   [apple
piña, pee-n'yah, s., cone of the pine-tree; pine-
pío, pee-o, s., longing; puling of chickens. a., pious;
piojo, pe-o-Ho, s., louse   [merciful
pipa, pee-pah, s., cask; tobacco pipe
pipote, pe-**po**-tay, s., keg
pique, pee-kay, s., pique. **a —,** ah —, on the point
   of. **echar a —,** ay-**char** a —, to sink (a ship).
   irse a —, eer-say ah —, to founder (ship)
piquete, pe-**kay**-tay, s., small wound; small hole;
pira, pee-rah, s., funeral pile   [picket
pirata, pe-**rah**-tah, s., pirate
piratería, pe-rah-tay-**ree**-ah, s., piracy
piropo, pe-**ro**-po, s., compliment; flattery
pirueta, pe-roo'**ay**-tah, s., pirouette
pisada, pe-**sah**-dah, s., footstep; footprint

pisar, pe-**sar,** v., to tread; to trample

pisaverde, pe-sah-**vair**-day, s., (fam.) fop   [tank

piscina, piss-**thee**-nah, s., fish-pond; swimming

piso, pe-so, s., floor; story; flat; apartment

pisotear, pe-so-tay-**ar,** v., to trample

pista, piss-tah, s., track; trail; scent; trace

pisto, piss-to, s., thick broth

pistola, piss-**to**-lah, s., pistol

pistolete, piss-to-**lay**-tay, s., pocket-pistol   [cap

pistón, piss-ton, s., piston; embolus; percussion

pitada, pe-tah-dah, s., blow of a whistle

pitanza, pe-**tahn**-thah, s., pittance; daily allow-

pitillo, pe-tee-l'yo, s., cigarette   [ance

pito, pee-to, s., whistle

pitón, pe-ton, s., tenderling; sprig; nozzle; horn

pizarra, pe-**thar**-rrah, s., slate

pizca, pith-kah, s., bit; jot

pizpireta, pith-pe-**ray**-tah, s., lively (woman)

placa, **plah**-kah, s., plate; insignia of an order of
knighthood

pláceme, **plah**-thay-may, s., congratulation

placentero, plah-then-**tay**-ro, a., pleasant; joyful;
mirthful

placer, plah-**thair,** v., to please. s., pleasure;

placidez, plah-the-**deth,** s., placidity   [consent

plácido, **plah**-the-do, a., placid

plaga, **plah**-gah, s., plague; pestilence

plagar, plah-**gar,** v., to plague; to infest

plagio, **plah**-*H*e-o, s., plagiarism

plan, plahn, s., plan; design; scheme; plot

plana, **plah**-nah, s., trowel; (book) page; plain

plancha, **plahn**-chah, s., plate; (clothes) iron;
— **de vapour,** day vah-**porr,** s., steam-iron

planchar, plahn-**char,** v., to iron (clothes); to press

planicie, plah-nee-**the**-ay, s., plain

plano, **plah**-no, s., plan; map; chart. a., plain;
level; flat

planta, **plahn**-tah, s., sole of the foot; plant;
plan of a building   [to jilt

plantar, plahn-**tar,** v., to plant; to fix upright;

plantear, plahn-tay-**ar,** v., to plan; to trace

plantel, plahn-**tell,** s., nursery-garden

plantilla, plahn-**tee**-l'yah, s., young plant; pattern; inner sole of a shoe

plantón, plahn-**ton**, s., sprout; sentry

plañidero, plah-n'yee-**day**-ro, a., mournful

plañido, plah-n'yee-do, s., moan; lamentation

plasmar, plahs-**mar**, v., to mould

plástico, plahs-te-ko, a., plastic

plata, plah-tah, s., silver; money (fam.)

plátano, plah-tah-no, s., banana; plane-tree

platea, plah-**tay**-ah, s., (theatre) orchestra; pit

platear, plah-tay-**ar**, v., to plate

platería, plah-tay-**ree**-ah, s., silversmith's shop or [trade

platero, plah-**tay**-ro, s., silversmith

plática, plah-te-kah, s., discourse; conversation

platillo, plah-**tee**-l'yo, s., small dish; saucer [chat

platino, plah-**tee**-no, s., platinum

plato, plah-to, s., dish; plate; daily fare

playa, plah-yah, s., shore; beach

plaza, plah-thah, s., square; market-place; fortified town; employment

plazo, plah-tho, s., term; date; instalment

pleamar, play-ah-**mar**, s., high-water

plebe, play-bay, s., common people; plebs

plebeyo, play-**bay**-yo, a., plebeian

plegable, play-gah-blay, a., pliable

plegar, play-**gar**, v., to fold; to plait; to double

plegaria, play-gah-**ree**-ah, s., prayer

pleitear, play'e-tay-**ar**, v., to plead; to litigate

pleito, play'e-to, s., lawsuit proceedings

plenilunio, play-ne-**loo**-ne-o, s., full moon

plenitud, play-ne-**tood**, s., fulness

pliego, ple-**ay**-go, s., sheet of paper

pliegue, ple-**ay**-gay, s., fold; plait; crease

plomada, plo-**mah**-dah, s., plumb-bob

plomero, plo-**may**-ro, s., plumber

plomizo, plo-**mee**-tho, a., leaden

plomo, plo-mo, s., lead

pluma, **ploo**-mah, s., feather; pen

plumero, ploo-**may**-ro, s., plume; feather-duster

plumón, ploo-**mon**, s., down; feather-bed

pluvial, ploo-ve-**ahl**, a., rainy; pluvial

población, po-blah-the-**on**, s., population

poblado, po-**blah**-do, s., town; village; place inhabited   [cupy; to stock; to settle

poblar, po-**blar**, v., to people; to found; to oc-

pobre*, po-bray, a., poor

pobreza, po-**bray**-thah, s., poverty

pocilga, po-**theel**-gah, s., pig-sty

pócima, po-the-mah, s., potion; brew

poco, po-ko, adv., a little. s., small quantity. a.,

poda, po-dah, s., pruning   [little; scanty; few

poder, po-**dair**, v., to be able. s., power; authority; force

poderdante, po-dair-**dahn**-tay, s., constituent

poderío, po-day-**ree**-o, s., power; might; dominion

poderoso, po-day-**ro**-so, a., powerful; efficacious

podre, po-dray, s., pus; matter

podredumbre, po-dray-**doom**-bray, s., putrid matter; corruption

podrir, po-**dreer**, (see **pudrir**)

poesía, po-ay-**see**-ah, s., poetry

polaina, po-lah'**ee**-nah, s., legging; gaiter

polea, po-**lay**-ah, s., pulley

policía, po-le-**thee**-ah, s., police

poligloto, po-le-**glo**-to, s., linguist

polígono, po-**lee**-go-no, s., polygon. a., polygonal

polilla, po-**lee**-l'yah, s., moth

política, po-**lee**-te-kah, s., politics

póliza, po-**lee**-thah, s., policy; scrip

polizonte, po-le-**thon**-tay, s., (fam.) detective

polo, po-lo, s., pole

poltrón, pol-**tron**, a., idle; lazy

poltrona, pol-**tro**-nah, s., easy chair

polvareda, pol-vah-**ray**-dah, s., cloud of dust

polvo, pol-vo, s., dust; powder

pólvora, pol-vo-rah, s., gun-powder

polvorear, pol-vo-ray-**ar**, v., to powder

polla, po-l'yah, s., pullet

pollada, po-l'yah-dah, s., hatch; covey

pollero, po-l'**yay**-ro, s., poulterer

pollino, po-l'**yee**-no, s., donkey; ass; stupid fellow

pollo, po-l'yo, s., chicken; nestling; young man

polluelo, po-l'yoo'**ay**-lo, s., small chicken

pomada, po-**mah**-dah, s., pomatum ; pomade
pomar, po-**mar**, s., orchard
pómez, po-meth, s., pumice-stone
pomo, po-mo, s., fruit ; apple ; pommel ; flagon
pompa, pom-pah, s., pomp ; pageant
pomponearse, pom-po-nay-**ar**-say, v., to strut
ponche, pon-chay, s., punch
ponderación, pon-day-rah-the-**on**, s., consideration ; weighing   [gerate
ponderar, pon-day-**rar**, v., to ponder ; to exag-
ponderoso, pon-day-**ro**-so, a., ponderous ; grave
ponedero, po-nay-**day**-ro, a., egg-laying
poner, po-**nair**, v., to put ; to place ; to lay eggs ; to
contribute
ponerse, po-**nair**-say, v., to set about
poniente, po-ne-**en**-tay, s., west ; west-wind
pontífice, pon-**tee**-fe-thay, s., Pope ; pontiff
pontón, pon-**ton**, s., pontoon
pontonero, pon-to-**nay**-ro, s., pontooner
ponzoña, pon-**tho**-n'yah, s., poison
popa, po-pah, s., poop ; stern
populacho, po-poo-**lah**-cho, s., populace ; mob
poquedad, po-kay-**dahd**, s., paucity ; cowardice
poquito, po-kee-to, a., very little   [trifle
por, por, prep., for ; by ; about ; through ; by means
of ; on account of   [ware
porcelana, por-**thay**-lah-nah, s., porcelain ; china-
porcino, por-**thee**-no, a., hoggish ; swinish
porción, por-the-**on**, s., part ; portion ; lot
porcuno, por-**koo**-no, a., porcine ; hoggish
porche, por-**chay**, s., porch ; covered walk
pordiosero, por-de-o-**say**-ro, s., beggar
porfía, por-**fee**-ah, s., obstinacy ; stubbornness ;
insistence
porfiado, por-fe-**ah**-do, a., obstinate ; insistent
porfiar, por-fe-**ar**, v., to wrangle ; to persist ; to
pormenor, por-may-**nor**, s., detail   [insist
poro, po-ro, s., pore
porque, por-kay, conj., because
¿por qué? por **kay**, conj., why?
porquería, por-kay-**ree**-ah, s., nastiness ; filth
porrillo (a), ah por-**rree**-l'yo, adv., copiously

porrón, por-**rron**, s., pitcher
portada, por-**tah**-dah, s., portal; frontispiece
portador, por-tah-**dor**, s., carrier; bearer; tray
portaequipajes, por-tah-ay-ke-**pah**-Hayss, s., luggage-rack
portal, por-**tahl**, s., porch; portico
portamonedas, por-tah-mo-**nay**-dahs, s., purse
portarse, por-**tar**-say, v., to behave
portátil, por-**tah**-til, a., portable
portazgo, por-**tahth**-go, s., toll; turnpike duty
porte, **por**-tay, s., porterage; postage; carriage; conduct
portear, por-tay-**ar**, v., to convey
portento, por-**ten**-to, s., portent
portero, por-**tay**-ro, s., janitor; doorkeeper
portillo, por-**tee**-l'yo, s., aperture; gap; breach
portón, por-**ton**, s., inner door of a house
porvenir, por-vay-**neer**, s., future
pos (en), en **pos**, adv., after; behind; in pursuit of
posada, po-**sah**-dah, s., lodging house; inn
posadero, po-sah-**day**-ro, s., innkeeper; host
poseedor, po-say-ay-**dor**, s., possessor
poseer, po-say-**air**, v., to hold; to possess; to own
poseído, po-say-ee-do, a., possessed with the devil
posibilitar, po-se-be-le-**tar**, v., to render possible
posible*, po-**see**-blay, a., possible. s., pl., wealth; means
posición, po-se-the-**on**, s., position; posture; pose; attitude; situation
positivo, po-se-**tee**-vo, a., positive; true; certain
poso, **po**-so, s., sediment; dregs
posponer, pos-po-**nair**, v., to postpone
posta, **pos**-tah, s., post stage; relay
poste, **pos**-tay, s., post; pillar
postema, pos-**tay**-mah, s., abscess; tumour
postergar, pos-tair-**gar**, v., to leave behind; to delay
posterior*, pos-tay-re-**or**, a., posterior; hinder
postigo, pos-**tee**-go, s., wicket; postern; shutter
postilla, pos-**tee**-l'yah, s., scab on wounds
postilloso, pos-te-l'**yo**-so, a., scabby
postizo, pos-**tee**-tho, a., artificial; false

postor, pos-**tor**, s., bidder

postrar, pos-**trar**, v., to prostrate

postre, pos-**tray**, s., dessert. a., last in order

postremo, pos-**tray**-mo, a., last

postrer, pos-**trair**, a., last ; hindermost

postulado, pos-too-**lah**-do, s., postulate

póstumo, pos-too-mo, a., posthumous

postura, pos-**too**-rah, s., posture ; bet ; wager ; agreement

potable, po-**tah**-blay, a., drinkable

potaje, po-**tah**-Hay, s., pottage ; medley

potasa, po-**tah**-sah, s., potash

pote, po-tay, s., pot ; jar ; standard measure or weight

potencia, po-**ten**-the-ah, s., power ; potency

potencial, po-ten-the-**ahl**, a., potential ; virtual

potente, po-**ten**-tay, a., potent

potestad, po-tess-**tahd**, s., power

potra, po-trah, s,. hernia ; filly

potro, po-tro, s., colt ; foal ; rack

poyo, po-yo, s., stone bench

poza, po-**thah**, s., puddle

pozal, po-**thahl**, s., bucket ; pail ; coping of a well

pozo, po-tho, s., well

practicante, prahk-te-**kahn**-tay, s., practitioner

practicar, prahk-te-**kar**, v., to practise ; to exercise

pradera, pradería, prah-**day**-rah, prah-day-ree-ah, s., meadow

prado, prah-do, s., lawn ; meadow

pre, pray, s., daily pay allowed to soldiers

preboste, pray-**bos**-tay, s., provost

precaver, pray-kah-**vair**, v., to provide against

precavido*, pray-kah-**vee**-do, a., cautious

preceder, pray-thay-**dair**, v., to precede

precepto, pray-**thep**-to, s., precept ; order ; man-

preces, pray-thess, s., prayers   [date

preciado, pray-the-**ah**-do, a., valued ; prized

preciarse, pray-the-**ar**-say, v., to boast ; to take a price in

precio, pray-the-o, s., price ; coat ; value ; reward

precipitar, pray-the-pe-**tar**, v., to precipitate ; to rush

precisar, pray-the-**sar**, v., to fix with precision; to compel; to need

precisión, pray-the-se-**on**, s., necessity; compulsion; preciseness   [cise

preciso, pray-**thee**-so, a., necessary; precise; con-

preclaro, pray-**klah**-ro, a., illustrious   [proclaim

preconizar, pray-ko-ne-**thar**, v., to eulogize; to

preconocer, pray-ko-no-**thair**, v., to foreknow

precoz, pray-**koth**, a., precocious

precursor, pray-koor-**sor**, s., harbinger; forerunner

predecir, pray-day-**theer**, v., to foretell

prédica, pray-de-kah, s., sermon

predicador, pray-de-kah-**dor**, s., preacher

predicar, pray-de-**kar**, v., to publish; to preach

predilecto, pray-de-**lek**-to, a., favourite

predio, pray-de-o, s., landed property; farm

predisponer, pray-diss-po-**nair**, v., to predispose

predominio, pray-do-**mee**-ne-o, s., predominance

prefacio, pray-**fah**-the-o, s., preface

preferible, pray-fay-ree-blay, a., preferable

preferir, pray-fay-**reer**, v., to prefer

prefijo, pray-**fee**-Ho, s., prefix

pregonar, pray-go-**nar**, v., to proclaim; to cry out

pregonero, pray-go-**nay**-ro, s., town crier; auctioneer

pregunta, pray-**goon**-tah, s., question; enquiry

preguntar, pray-goon-**tar**, v., to ask; to question; to enquire

preguntón, pray-goon-**ton**, a., inquisitive

prejuzgar, pray-*Hooth*-**gar**, v., to prejudge

prelado, pray-**lah**-do, s., prelate

premiar, pray-me-**ar**, v., to reward; to remunerate

premio, pray-me-o, s., reward; premium

premioso*, pray-me-o-so, a., tight; troublesome; rigid

premura, pray-**moo**-rah, s., urgency

prenda, pren-dah, s., pledge; token; garment; person or object dearly loved. pl., talents

prender, pren-**dair**, v., to seize; to imprison

prendería, pren-day-**ree**-ah, s., pawnbroker's shop

prensa, pren-sah, s., press; printing press

prensar, pren-**sar**, v., to press

preñado, pray-n'**yah**-do, s., pregnancy. a., preg-

preparar, pray-pah-**rar**, v., to prepare [nant

preponderar, pray-pon-day-**rar**, v., to preponder-

prepotente, pray-po-**ten**-tay, a., a prepotent [ate

presa, pray-sah, s., capture; seizure; prey; dam

presagiar, pray-sah-He-**ar**, v., to presage; to forebode

presbiterio, press-be-**tay**-re-o, s., parsonage;

presbítero, pray-**bee**-tay-ro, s., priest [chancel

precindir, press-thin-**deer**, v., to prescind; to
cut off; to do without

prescribir, press-kre-**beer**, v., to prescribe

presenciar, pray-sen-the-**ar**, v., to be present;
to witness

presentar, pray-sen-**tar**, v., to present; to exhibit;
to give

presente, pray-**sen**-tay, s., present; gift. a*.,
present; actual

presentir, pray-sen-**teer**, v., to have a presenti-

preservar, pray-sair-**var**, v., to preserve [ment

presidiario, pray-se-de-ah-re-o, s., convict

presidio, pray-**see**-de-o, s., garrison; fortress;
penitentiary

presidir, pray-se-**deer**, v., to preside

presilla, pray-**see**-l'yah, s., noose; loop

presión, pray-se-on, s., pressure

preso, pray-so, s., prisoner

prestación, press-tah-the-on, s., lending

prestamista, press-tah-**miss**-tah, s., lender; pawn-

préstamo, press-tah-mo, s., loan [broker

prestar, press-**tar**, v., to lend [speed

presteza, press-tay-thah, s., quickness; haste;

prestigio, press-tee-He-o, s., prestige; sleight of
hand [ready

presto, press-to, adv., quickly. a., quick; prompt;

presumible, pray-soo-**mee**-blay, a., presumable

presumido, pray-soo-**mee**-do, a., presumptuous;
arrogant [jecture

presumir, pray-soo-**meer**, v., to presume; to con-

presunción, pray-soon-the-on, s., presumption;
conjecture

presuntivo, pray-soon-**tee**-vo, a., presumptive

presuntuoso,* pray-soon-too'**o**-so, a., presumptuous

presuponer, pray-soo-po-**nair**, v., to presuppose

presupuesto, pray-soo-poo'**ess**-to, s., estimate; budget

presuroso*, pray-soo-**ro**-so, a., hasty; prompt

pretender, pray-ten-**dair**, v., to pretend; to claim; to endeavour

pretenso, pray-**ten**-so, a., pretended [omission

preterición, pray-tay-re-the-**on**, s., preterition;

pretérito, pray-**tay**-re-to, a., preterit; past

pretextar, pray-teks-**tar**, v., to use a pretext

pretil, pray-**teel**, s., breast-work; parapet

pretina, pray-**tee**-nah, s., girdle; waistband; belt

prevalecer, pray-vah-lay-**thair**, v., to prevail; to surpass

prevaricar, pray-vah-re-**kar**, v., to prevaricate

prevención, pray-ven-the-**on**, s., foresight; warning; prevention

prevenido, pray-vay-**nee**-do, a., prepared; provided; cautious

prevenir, pray-vay-**neer**, v., to foresee; to prevent; to advise

prever, pray-**vair**, v., to foresee; to forecast

previo*, pray-ve-o, previous

prieto, pre-**ay**-to, a., very black; compressed; tight

prima, pree-mah, s., premium; female cousin

primavera, pre-mah-**vay**-rah, s., spring season; primrose

primero, pre-**may**-ro, adv., first; rather; sooner. a., first; principal; former

primo, pre-mo, s., male cousin. a., first

primogénito, pre-mo-**H**ay-ne-to, s. & a., first born

primor, pre-**mor**, s., beauty; dexterity; nicety

primoroso, pre-mo-**ro**-so, a., neat; elegant; exquisite

princesa, prin-**thay**-sah, s., princess [site

principal, prin-the-**pahl**, s., capital. a., principal

príncipe, **prin**-the-pay, s., prince

principiar, prin-the-pe-**ar**, v., to begin

principio, prin-**thee**-pe-o, s., beginning; principle

pringar, prin-**gar**, v., to baste; to grease; to slander

pringue, **preen**-gay, s., grease; lard; greasiness

prior, pre-**or,** s., prior. a., prior; precedent

prisa, pree-sah, s., hurry

prisión, pre-se-**on,** s., seizure; prison; fetters

prisionero, pre-se-o-**nay**-ro, s., prisoner

prisma, priss-mah, s., prism

privada, pre-**vah**-dah, s., water-closet

privado, pre-**vah**-do, s., favourite. a., private

privar, pre-**var,** v., to deprive; to despoil; to pro-

privilegio, pre-ve-**lay**-He-o, s., privilege   [hibit

pro, pro, s., m. & f., profit; benefit; advantage
    en —, en —, in favour of

probanza, pro-**bahn**-thah, s., proof; evidence

probar, pro-**bar,** v., to try; to prove; to taste

probatura, pro-bah-**too**-rah, s., trial; test; tasting

probeta, pro-**bay**-tah, s., test-tube

probidad, pro-be-**dahd,** s., honesty; integrity

procacidad, pro-kah-the-**dahd,** s., petulance; sau-
    ciness; impudence

procaz, pro-**kahth,** a., bold; insolent

procedencia, pro-thay-**den**-the-ah, s., origin

proceder, pro-thay-**dair,** v., to proceed; to emanate

procedimiento, pro-thay-de-me-**en**-to, s., pro-
    ceeding; procedure

proceloso, pro-thay-**lo**-so, a., tempestuous

prócer, pro-thair, a., lofty; eminent

procesar, pro-thay-**sar,** v., to prosecute; to indict

proceso, pro-**thay**-so, s., process; lawsuit

proclama, pro-**klah**-mah, s., proclamation

proclividad, pro-kle-ve-**dahd,** s., proclivity

procura, pro-**koo**-rah, s., power of attorney

procurador, pro-koo-rah-**dorr,** s., solicitor;
    attorney

prodigar, pro-de-**gar,** v., to lavish

prodigio, pro-dee-He-o, s., prodigy

pródigo*, pro-de-go, a., prodigal

producir, pro-doo-**theer,** v., to produce

producto, pro-**dook**-to, s., product

proeza, pro-**ay**-thah, s., prowess; bravery

profano, pro-**fah**-no, a., profane

proferir, pro-fay-**reer,** v., to pronounce; to ex-
    press; to utter

profesar, pro-fay-**sar,** v., to profess

profesor, pro-fay-**sor**, s., professor; teacher
profeta, pro-**fay**-tah, s., prophet
profético, pro-**fay**-te-ko, a., prophetic
profetizar, pro-fay-te-**thar**, v., to prophesy; to
    predict; to foretell
prófugo, pro-**foo**-go, a., fugitive
profundo*, pro-**foon**-do, a., profound; deep
progenitura, pro-Hay-ne-**too**-rah, s., progeny
programa, pro-**grah**-mah, s., programme
programador, pro-grah-mah-**dorr**, s., programmer
progreso, pro-**gray**-so, s., progress; advancement
prohibir, pro-e-**beer**, v., to prohibit; to forbid
prohijar, pro-e-**Har**, v., to adopt
prohombre, pro-**om**-bray, s., headman; leader
prójimo, pro-**He**-mo, s., fellow-creature
prole, pro-lay, s., issue; offspring; race
prolijo, pro-lee-**Ho**, a., prolix
prólogo, pro-lo-go, s., prologue; preface
prolongadamente   pro-lon-gah-dah-**men**-tay,
    adv., protractedly
prolongar, pro-lon-**gar**, v., to prolong
promedio, pro-**may**-de-o, s., middle; average
promesa, pro-**may**-sah, s., promise; pious vow
prometer, pro-may-**tair**, v., to promise
prometido, pro-may-**tee**-do, s., betrothed; fiancé(e)
prominencia, pro-me-**nen**-the-ah, s., prominence;
    protuberance
promiscuo, pro-**miss**-koo'o, a., promiscuous
promover, pro-mo-**vair**, v., to promote; to forward
pronombre, pro-**nom**-bray, s., pronoun
prontitud, pron-te-**tood**, s., promptitude
pronto, **pron**-to, adv., promptly. s., sudden im-
    pulse. a., prompt   [book
prontuario, pron-too'**ah**-re-o, s., memorandum-
pronunciamiento, pro-noon-the-ah-me-**en**-to, s.,
    insurrection   [to rebel
pronunciar, pro-noon-the-**ar**, v., to pronounce;
propalar, pro-pah-**lar**, v., to divulge
propasar, pro-pah-**sar**, v., to go beyond; to trans-
propender, pro-pen-**dair**, v., to incline   [gress
propenso, pro-**pen**-so, a., inclined; prone
propicio*, pro-**pee**-the-o, a., propitious

propiedad, pro-pe-ay-**dahd**, s., ownership; property; dominion

propina, pro-**pee**-nah, s., fee; gratuity; tip

propincuo, pro-**peen**-koo'o, a., near; contiguous

propio, pro-pe-o, s., messenger. a.,* private; proper; fit; natural

proponer, pro-po-**nair**, v., to propose; to resolve

proporcionar, pro-por-the-o-**nar**, v., to proportion; to adjust; to afford

propósito, pro-**po**-se-to, s., purpose; purport

propuesta, pro-poo'**ess**-tah, s., proposal; tender

propulsión, pro-pool-se-**on**, s., propulsion

propulsor, pro-pool-**sor**, s., propeller

prorrata, pror-**rrah**-tah, s., quota

prórroga, pror-rro-gah, s., prorogation; extension; renewal

prorrumpir, pror-rroom-**peer**, v., to break forth

prosa, pro-sah, s., prose

proscribir, pros-kre-**beer**, v., to proscribe [secute

proseguir, pro-say-**gheer**, v., to pursue; to pro-

prosélito, pro-**say**-le-to, s., proselyte; convert

prospecto, pros-**pek**-to, s., prospectus·

próspero*, pros-pay-ro, a., prosperous [oneself

prosternarse, pros-tair-**nar**-say, v., to prostrate

prostituir, pros-te-too'**eer**, v., to prostitute

prostituta, pros-te-**too**-tah, s., prostitute

proteger, pro-tay-**H**air, v., to protect

protervo, pro-**tair**-vo, a., perverse

protestar, pro-tess-**tar**, v., to protest [tage

provecho, pro-**vay**-cho, s., profit; benefit; advan-

provechoso*, pro-vay-**cho**-so, a., profitable

proveeduría, pro-vay-ay-doo-**ree**-ah, s., storehouse; purveyor's office

proveer, pro-vay-**air**, v., to provide; to supply with

proveído, pro-vay'**ee**-do, s., judgment; sentence

proveimiento, pro-vay'e-me-**en**-to, s., supply

provenir, pro-vay-**neer**, v., to proceed from

próvido, pro-ve-do, a., provident

provocar, pro-vo-**kar**, v., to provoke

próximo, prok-se-mo, a., next

proyecto, pro-**yek**-to, s., project; scheme; design

prudente*, proo-**den**-tay, a., prudent

prueba, proo′ay-bah, s., proof; test; experiment
prurito, proo-ree-to, s., itching; yearning
psiquiatría, psee-kee-ah-tree-ah, s., psychiatry
púa, poo′ah, s., prickle; prong; graft
pubertad, poo-bair-tad, s., adolescence
publicar, poo-ble-kar, v., to publish; to proclaim
público*, poo-ble-ko, a., public   [to reveal
puchero, poo-chay-ro, s., earthen pot; stew
púdico, poo-de-ko, a., chaste; modest
pudiente, poo-de-en-tay, a., rich; opulent
pudor, poo-dor, s., modesty; bashfulness
pudrir, poo-dreer, v., to rot
pueblo, poo′ay-blo, s., town; village; population
puente, poo′en-tay, s., bridge
puerca, poo′air-kah, s., sow
puerco, poo′air-ko, s., pig. a., filthy; coarse
pueril, poo′ay-reel, a., puerile; childish
puerro, poo′air-rro, s., leek
puerta, poo′air-tah, s., door
puerto, poo′air-to, s., port; haven; harbour
pues, poo′ess, conj., then; therefore; since. interj.,
       well then!
puesta, poo′ess-tah, s., setting; sunset
puesto, poo′ess-to, s., place; spot; stand; em-
       ployment. **— que,** — kay, although; inas-
púgil, poo-Hil, s., boxer; pugilist   [much as
pugna, poog-nah, s., combat; conflict; struggle
pugnar, poog-nar, v., to fight; to struggle
puja, poo-Hah, s., outbidding at auction sale
pujante, poo-Hahn-tay, a., powerful; strong
pujanza, poo-Hahn-thah, s., might; strength
pujar, poo-Har, v., to outbid
pulcritud, pool-kre-tood, s., neatness; tidiness
pulcro, pool-kro, a., tidy; neat
pulga, pool-gah, s., flea
pulgada, pool-gah-dah, s., inch
pulgar, pool-gar, s., thumb
pulido, poo-lee-do, a., neat; cleanly; polished
pulimento, poo-le-men-to, s., polish
pulir, poo-leer, v., to polish; to burnish
pulmón, pool-mon, s., lung
pulmonía, pool-mo-nee-ah, s., pneumonia

pulpa, pool-**pah,** s., pulp

pulpo, pool-**po,** s., octopus

pulsar, pool-**sar,** v., to feel the pulse

pulso, pool-**so,** s., pulse

pulla, poo-l'yah, s., loose expression; repartee

pundonor, poon-do-**nor,** s., point of honour

punta, poon-tah, s., point

puntada, poon-**tah-**dah, s., stitch

puntal, poon-**tahl,** s., prop

puntapié, poon-tah-pe-**ay,** s., kick   [to dot

puntear, poon-tay-**ar,** v., to play upon the guitar;

puntería, poon-tay-ree-ah, s., aim

puntilla, poon-**tee-**l'yah, s., narrow lace edging.
  de **—s,** day **—s,** on tiptoe

punto, poon-to, s., point; dot; aim; stitch; spot;
  gist   [exact

puntual*, poon-too'**ahl,** a., punctual; prompt;

punzada, poon-**thah-**dah, s., prick; sting; com-

punzar, poon-**thar,** v., to prick; to sting [punction

punzón, poon-**thon,** s., punch; awl

puñado, poo-n'**yah-**do, s., handful; a few

puñal, poo-n'**yahl,** s., poniard; dagger

puño, poo-n'yo, s., fist; cuff

pupa, poo-pah, s., pimple

pupilaje, poo-pe-**lah-**Hay, s., boarding-school

pupilo, poo-**pee-**lo, s., pupil; scholar

pupitre, poo-**pee-**tray, s., writing-case; writing-desk

pureza, poo-**ray-**thah, s., purity; innocence

purga, poor-gah, s., purge

purificar, poo-re-fe-**kar,** v., to purify

puro*, poo-ro, a., pure; mere; genuine; incorrupt

púrpura, poor-poo-rah, s., purple

pusilánime*, poo-se-**lah-**ne-may, a., pusillanimous

putrefacto, poo-tray-**fahk-**to, a., rotten, putrid

pútrido, poo-tree-do, a., putrid

puya, poo-yah, s., goad

que, kay, pron., that; who; which; what

quebrada, kay-**brah-**dah, s., broken ground; ravine

quebradizo, kay-brah-**dee-**tho, a., brittle; frail

quebradura, kay-brah-**doo-**rah, s., fracture;
  rupture

quebrantamiento, kay-brahn-tah-me-*en*-to, s., fracture; weariness; breaking a prison; violation of the law   [to violate; to fatigue
quebrantar, kay-brahn-*tar,* v., to break; to grind;
quebrar, kay-*brar,* v., to break
quedar, kay-*dar,* v., to stay; to resolve; to agree
quedo, kay-do, adv., gently; softly
quehacer, kay-ah-*thair,* s., business; occupation
queja, *kay-H*ah, s., complaint; grudge
quejarse, kay-*H*ar-say, v., to complain
quejido, kay-*Hee*-do, s., complaint; moan
quejoso, kay-*H*o-so, a., querulous
quema, *kay*-mah, s., combustion
quemadura, kay-mah-*doo*-rah, s., burn
quemar, kay-*mar,* v., to burn
quemazón, kay-mah-*thon,* s., burning
querella, kay-ray-l'yah, s., complaint; plaint; quarrel; dispute   [complain
querellarse, kay-ray-l'*yar*-say, v., to lament; to
querencia, kay-*ren*-the-ah, s., affection
querer, kay-*rair,* v., to wish; to desire; to will
quesera, kay-*say*-rah, s., dairy; cheese dish
queso, *kay*-so, s., cheese   [ruptcy
quiebra, ke-*ay*-brah, s., crack; fracture; bank-
quiebro, kay-*bro,* s., trill; inclination of the body
quien, ke-*en,* pron., who; whom; which
quienquiera, ke-en-ke-*ay*-rah, pron., whoever
quieto,* ke-*ay*-to, a., quiet; still; peaceable
quietud, ke-ay-*tood,* s., quietude; peace
quijada, ke-*H*ah-dah, s., jaw; jaw-bone
quijotada, ke-*H*o-*tah*-dah, s., quixotic action
quijote, ke-*H*o-tay, s., thigh guard; quixotic person
quilate, ke-*lah*-tay, s., carat
quimera, ke-*may*-rah, s., chimera; illusion
química, *kee*-me-kah, s., chemistry
quincalla, kin-*kah*-l'yah, s., hardware
quince, *keen*-thay, s. & a., fifteen
quinceno, kin-*thay*-no, a., fifteenth
quincuagésimo, kin-koo'ah-*H*ay'se-mo, a., fiftieth
quinientos, ke-ne-*en*-tos, a., five hundred
quinqué, kin-*kay,* s., oil table-lamp
quinta, *keen*-tah, s., country house; cottage

quintañón, kin-tah-n'**yon,** s. centenarian
quintar, kin-**tar,** v., to draw one out of five
quinto, keen-to, s., one fifth; conscript
quisquilloso, kiss-ke-l'**yo**-so, a., fastidious; peevish
¡quita!kee-tah, interj., God forbid!
quitar, ke-**tar,** v., to remove; to rob
quito, kee-to, a., free; quits
quizá, quizás, ke-**thah,** ke-**thahs,** adv., perhaps

rabadilla, rrah-bah-**dee**-l'yah, s., rump; coccyx
rábano, rrah-bah-no, s., radish
rabia, rrah-be-ah, s., rabies; rage; fury
rabieta, rrah-be-**ay**-tah, s., fretting; impatience
rabioso, rrah-be-**o**-so, tabid; furious
rabo, rrah-bo, s., tail
racimo, rrah-**thee**-mo, s., bunch of grapes
racionar, rrah-the-o-the-**nar,** v., to reason; to [argue
ración, rrah-the-**on,** s., ration; prebend
racha, rrah-chah, s., gust of wind
rada, rrah-dah, s., roadstead
radiación, rah-de-ah-the-**on,** s., radiation
radiador, rah-de-ah-**dorr,** s., radiator
radiar, rrah-de-**ar,** v., to radiate
radio, rrah-de-o, s., radius; ray; radio; **—activi-
    dad,** —ahk-te-ve-**dahd,** s., radio-activity;
    —activo, —ahk-te-vo, a., radioactive;
    —difusión, —de-foo-se-**on,** s., broadcasting
raedura, rrah-ay-**doo**-rah, s., erasure; scrapings
raer, rrah-**air,** v., to scrape; to erase
ráfaga, rrah-fah-gah, s., violent squall of wind
raído, rrah**ee**-do, a., scraped; worn out
raigón, rrah**e**-**gon,** s., stump
raimiento, rrah**e**-me-**en**-to, s., scraping; erasure
raíz, rrah**eeth,** s., root; base; basin; origin
raja, rrah Hah, s., crack; cranny
rajadura, rrah-Hah-**doo**-rah, s., cleft; rent; split
rajar, rrah-Har, v., to split; to rend; to cleave
ralea, rrah-**lay**-ah, s., race; breed; species
rallar, rrah-l'**yar,** v., to grate
rama, rrah-mah, s., branch
ramaje, rrah-mah-Hay, s., mass of branches
rambla, rrahm-blah, s., sandy beach

ramilla, rrah-**mee**-l'yah, s., twig; sprig

ramillete, rrah-me-l'**yay**-tay, s., nosegay　[ness

ramo, rrah-mo, s., branch; cluster; line of busi-

rampa, rrahm-pah, s., slope

ramplón, rrahm-**plon,** a., rude; unpolished

rana, rrah-nah, s., frog

rancio, rrahn-the-o, a., rancid; rank　[camp

ranchería, rrahn-chay-**ree**-ah, s., mess; horde;

ranchero, rrahn-**chay**-ro, s., mess steward; ranch
owner

rancho, rrahn-cho, s., mess; mess-room; ranch

rango, rrahn-go, s., rank; quality

ranura, rrah-**noo**-rah, s., groove; slot

rapacejo, rrah-pah-**thay**-Ho, s., fringe; border;
child; urchin

rapacería, rrah-pah-thay-**ree**-ah, s., childish action

rapadura, rrah-pah-**doo**-rah, s., shaving; hair-cut

rapar, rrah-**par,** v., to shave; to rob

rapaz, rrah-**path,** s., young boy. a., rapacious

rapaza, rrah-**pah**-thah, s., young girl

rapidez, rrah-pe-**deth,** s., rapidity

rápido*, rrah-pe-do, a., rapid

rapiña, rrah-**pee**-n'yah, s., plunder

raposa, rrah-**po**-sah, s., vixen; cunning person

raposo, rrah-**po**-so, s., fox　[abduction

rapto, rrahp-to, s., rape; rapine; ecstasy; rapture

raptor, rrahp-**tor,** s., ravisher; abductor

raqueta, rrah-**kay**-tah, s., racket

raquítico, rrah-**kee**-te-ko, a., rickety; feeble

rareza, rrah-**ray**-thah, s., rarity; rareness

raro*, rrah-ro, adv., rarely. a., rare; scarce; queer;

ras, rrahs, s., level; even surface　[odd

rasar, rrah-**sar,** v., to level with a strickle; to graze

rascacielos, rrahs-kah-the-**ay**-lohs, s., skyscraper

rascadura, rrahs-kah-**doo**-rah, s., scratching;
scraping

rascapiés, rrahs-kah-pe-**ess,** s., door-scraper

rascar, rrahs-**kar,** v., to scratch; to scrape

rascazón, rrahs-kah-**thon,** s., pricking; itching

rasero, rrah-**say**-ro, s., strickle

rasgar, rrahs-**gar,** v., to tear; to rend

rasgón, rrahs-**gon,** s., rent; rag; tatter

rasguñar, rrahs-goo-n'**yar,** v., to scratch ; to scrape
raso, rrah-so, a., plain ; flat ; clear   [rasp
raspar, rrahs-**par,** v., to rub off ; to scrape ; to
rastra, rrahs-trah, s., sledge ; train ; track [rake
rastrear, rrahs-tray-**ar,** v., to trace ; to track ; to
rastrero, rrahs-**tray**-ro, a., creeping ; grovelling ;
          low ; cringing
rastro, rrahs-tro, s., track ; trail ; rake
rasurar, rrah-soo-**rar,** v., to shave
rata, rrah-tah, s., rat
ratear, rrah-tay-**ar,** v., to apportion ; to filch
ratero, rrah-**tay**-ro, s., pickpocket. a., creeping
rato, rrah-to, s., short time
ratón, rrah-**ton,** s., mouse   [hole
ratonera, rrah-to-**nay**-rah, s., mouse-trap ; mouse-
raudal, rrah'oo-**dahl,** s., torrent   [skate
raya, rrah-yah, s., stroke ; line ; boundary ; (fish)
rayano, rrah-**yah**-no, a., neighbouring ; contiguous
raza, rrah-thah, s., race ; lineage ; breed   [firm
razón, rrah-**thon,** s., reason ; motive ; account ;
razonar, rrah-tho-**nar,** v., to reason ; to discourse
reacio, rray-**ah**-the-o, a., stubborn
reagudo, rray-ah-**goo**-do, a., very acute
real, rray-**ahl,** a., real ; true ; royal
realce, rray-**ahl**-thay, s., embossment ; highlight
realzar, rray-ahl-**thar,** v., to elevate ; to emboss
reasumir, rray-ah-soo-**meer,** v., to resume
rebaja, rray-bah-**H**ah, s., abatement ; rebate
rebajar, rray-bah-**H**ar, v., to abate ; to lessen
rebalsar, rray-bahl-**sar,** v., to dam water
rebanar, rray-bah-**nar,** v., to slice
rebaño, rray-bah-n'yo, s., flock ; herd
rebasar, rray-bah-**sar,** v., to sail past ; to go be-
          yond ; to overflow
rebatir, rray-bah-**teer,** v., to resist ; to repel ; to
rebato, rray-bah-to, s., alarm   [refute
rebelde, rray-**bell**-day, s., rebel. a., rebellious
reblandecer, rray-blahn-day-**thair,** v., to soften
rebolludo, rray-bo-l'**yoo**-do, a., thick-set ; (dia-
          mond) rough   [to abound
rebosar, rray-bo-**sar,** v., to run over ; to overflow ;
rebotar, rray-bo-**tar,** v., to rebound ; to clinch

rebozo, rray-**bo**-tho, s., muffler

rebullir, rray-boo-l'**yeer**, v., to begin to move

reburujar, rray-boo-roo-**H**ar, v., to wrap up

rebusca, rray-**booss**-kah, s., research ; gleaning

rebuznar, rray-booth-**nar**, v., to bray

recabar, rray-kah-**bar**, v., to obtain by entreaty

recado, rray-**kah**-do, s., message ; greetings ; outfit

recaer, rray-kah-**air**, v., to fall back ; to devolve

recaída, rray-kah-**ee**-dah, s., relapse

recalar, rray-kah-**lar**, v., to soak ; to reach land

recalcar, rray-kahl-**kar**, v., to squeeze in ; to harp upon ; to emphasize [sist

recalcitrar, rray-kahl-the-**trar**, v., to wince ; to re-

recalentar, rray-kah-len-**tar**, v., to heat again

recámara, rray-**kah**-mah-rah, s., dressing room ; breech of a gun

recambio, rray-**kahm**-be-o, s., spare part

recapacitar, rray-kah-pah-the-**tar**, v., to recall to [mind

recargo, rray-**kar**-go, s., surcharge

recatado*, rray-kah-**tah**-do, a., circumspect ; shy

recatar, rray-kah-**tar**, v., to conceal ; to take care

recaudar, rray-kah'oo-**dar**, v., to collect taxes

recaudo, rray-**kah**'oo-do, s., collection ; surety

recelar, rray-thay-**lar**, v., to fear ; to distrust

receloso, rray-thay-**lo**-so, a., distrustful

receta, rray-**thay**-tah, s., recipe ; prescription

recetar, rray-thay-**tar**, v., to prescribe medicines

recibimiento, rray-the-be-me-**en**-to, s., reception ; receipt

recibir, rray-the-**beer**, v., to receive ; to admit

recibo, rray-**thee**-bo, s., receipt

recién, rray-the-**en**, adv., recently

reciente*, rray-the-**en**-tay, a., recent

recinto, rray-**theen**-to, s., enclosure ; precinct

recio, rray-the-o, adv., stoutly. a., strong ; coarse

reclamar, rray-klah-**mar**, v., to claim ; to demand

reclamo, rray-**klah**-mo, s., call ; decoy-bird

reclinar, rray-kle-**nar**, v., to lean on or upon

reclinatorio, rray-kle-nah-**to**-re-o, s., couch ; pray-ing-desk

recluir, rray-kloo'**eer**, v., to shut up

reclutar, rray-kloo-**tar**, v., to recruit

recobrar, rray-ko-**brar**, v., to recover

recodo, rray-**ko**-do, s., corner; turn

recoger, rray-ko-**Hair**, v., to collect; to shelter

recogida, rray-ko-**Hee**-dah, s., gathering; harvesting

recogimiento, rray-ko-He-me-**en**-to, s., concentration

recomendar, rray-ko-men-**dar**, v., to recommend

recompensa, rray-kom-**pen**-sah, s., compensation; reward

recóndito, rray-**kon**-de-to, a., recondite

reconocer, rray-ko-no-**thair**, v., to examine; to recognize

reconocido, rray-ko-no-**thee**-do, a., grateful

reconocimiento, rray-ko-no-the-me-**en**-to, s., gratitude; inspection

recontar, rray-kon-**tar**, v., to recount [nation

reconvención, rray-kon-ven-the-**on**, s., recrimi-

reconvenir, rray-kon-vay-**neer**, v., to recriminate

recopilar, rray-ko-pe-**lar**, v., to compile

recordar, rray-kor-**dar**, v., to remind; to remember

recorrer, rray-kor-**rrair**, v., to run over; to per-

recortar, rray-kor-**tar**, v., to cut away [use

recorte, rray-**kor**-tay, s., outline; cutting

recoser, rray-ko-**sair**, v., to sew again

recostar, rray-kos-**tar**, v., to lean against

recrear, rray-kray-**ar**, v., to amuse

recreo, rray-**kray**-o, s., recreation

rectificar, rrek-te-fe-**kar**, v., to rectify

recto*, rrek-to, a., straight; right; just; honest

recuento, rray-koo'**en**-to, s., inventory; recount

recuerdo, rray-koo'**air**-do, s., remembrance; me-

recuesto, rray-koo'**ess**-to, s., declivity [mory

recular, rray-koo-**lar**, v., to fall back; to recoil

recuperar, rray-koo-pay-**rar**, v., to regain

recurrir, rray-koor-**rreer**, v., to resort; to recur

recurso, rray-**koor**-so, s., recourse

rechazar, rray-chah-**thar**, v., to repel; to repulse;

rechazo, rray-**chah**-tho, s., rebound [to reject

rechiflar, rray-che-**flar**, v., to mock; to ridicule

rechinar, rray-che-**nar**, v., to creak; to squeak; to gnash the teeth

rechoncho, rray-**chon**-cho, a., chubby

red, rred, s., net; netting

redacción, rray-dak-the-**on**, s., wording; editing; editorial rooms or staff

redactor, rray-dak-**tor**, s., editor; journalist

redada, rray-**dah**-dah, s., catch; haul

rededor, rray-day-**dor**, s., environs. **al —**, ahl —, round about

redentor, rray-den-**tor**, s., redeemer

redil, rray-**deel**, s., sheep cot

redimir, rray-de-**meer**, v., to redeem; to ransom

rédito, **rray**-de-to, s., revenue; rent; interest

redituar, rray-de-too'**ar**, v., to yield [yield]

redoblar, rray-do-**blar**, v., to redouble; to rivet

redoma, rray-**do**-mah, s., phial

redonda, rray-**don**-dah, s., district; pasture ground

redondel, rray-don-**dell**, s., circle; roundabout

redondo, rray-**don**-do, a., round

redopelo, rray-do-**pay**-lo, s., rubbing against the grain; scuffle

reducir, rray-doo-**theer**, v., to reduce

reducto, rray-**dook**-to, s., redoubt

redundar, rray-doon-**dar**, v., to be redundant; to overflow; to redound

reelegir, rray-ay-lay-**Heer**, v., to re-elect

reembolsar, rray-em-bol-**sar**, v., to re-imburse

reemplazar, rray-em-plah-**thar**, v., to replace; to restore

reencuentro, rray-en-koo'**en**-tro, s., encounter

refacción, rray-fahk-the-**on**, s., refection; repast

referir, rray-fay-**reer**, v., to relate; to refer; to refine [report]

refinado, rray-fe-**nah**-do, a., refined [report]

refinar, rray-fe-**nar**, v., to refine [flected; reflex]

reflejo, rray-**flay**-Ho, s., reflected light. a., re-

reflexión, rray-flek-the-**on**, s., reflection

refluir, rray-floo'**eer**, v., to flow back [inforce]

reforzar, rray-for-**thar**, v., to strengthen; to re-

refrán, rray-**frahn**, s., proverb [another]

refregar, rray-fray-**gar**, v., to rub one thing against

refrenar, rray-fray-**nar**, v., to restrain; to curb

refrendar, rray-fren-**dar**, v., to countersign

refresco, rray-**fress**-ko, s., refreshment

refriega, rray-fre-**ay**-gah, s., affray; skirmish

refrigerio, rray-fre-*Hay*-re-o, s., refreshment
refuerzo, rray-foo'air-tho, s., reinforcement
refugiar, rray-foo-*He*-ar, v., to shelter; to take refuge
refundir, rray-foon-*deer*, v., to recast; to rearrange
refunfuñar, rray-foon-fon-n'*yar*, v., to grumble
refutar, rray-foo-*tar*, v., to refute   [to growl
regadera, rray-gah-*day*-rah, s., watering-pot
regalado, rray-gah-*lah*-do, a., delicate; dainty
regalo, rráy-*gah*-lo, s., present; gift; keepsake
regalón, rray-gah-*lon*, a., pampered
regañar, rray-gah-n'*yar*, v., to snarl; to growl; to quarrel
regar, rray-*gar*, v., to water; to irrigate
regata, rray-*gah*-tah, s., small water channel; regatta; boat-race
regate, rray-*gah*-tay, s., dodging
regatear, rray-gah-tay-*ar*, v., to haggle
regazo, rray-*gah*-tho, s., lap
regentar, rray-*Hen*-tar, v., to rule; to govern
regidor, rray-*He*-dor, s., alderman. a., governing
régimen, *rray*-*He*-men, s., rule; management; government of verbs
regimiento, rray-*He*-me-*en*-to, s., administration; government; regiment
regio*, *rray*-*He*-o, a., royal
región, rray-*He*-on, region; district
regir, rray-*Heer*, v., to rule; to control
registrador, rray-*Hiss*-trah-*dor*, s., registrar; recorder; — **de cinta magnetofónica,** day **thin**-tah mag-nay-to-*fo*-ne-kah, s., tape-recorder   [mine; to register
registrar, rray-*Hiss*-*trar*, v., to search; to exa-
registro, rray-*Hiss*-tro, s., search; registry; en-
regla, **rray**-glah, s., rule; statute   [rolment
reglado*, rray-*glah*-do, a., regulated; temperate
reglamento, rray-glah-*men*-to, s., regulation; ordinance; by-law
reglar, rray-*glar*, v., to regulate. a., regular
regocijar, rray-go-the-*Har*, v., to rejoice
regocijo, rray-go-*thee*-Ho, s., joy; merriment
regodeo, rray-go-*day*-o, s., joy; mirth   [pleasure

regordete, rray-gor-**day**-tay, a., chubby ; plump

regresar, rray-gray-**sar,** v., to return ; to regress

regreso, rray-**gray**-so, s., return ; regression

regüeldo, rray-goo'**ell**-do, s., eructation

reguera, rray-**gay**-rah, s., irrigation canal

reguero, rray-**gay**-ro, s., rivulet ; gutter ; drain

regular, rray-goo-**lar,** v., to regulate. a.,* regular

régulo, **rray**-goo-lo, s., chief of a petty state ;
basilisk   [regurgitate

regurgitar, rray-goor-*H*e-**tar,** v., to overflow ; to

rehacer, rray-ah-**thair,** v., to make again ; to
mend ; to revive

rehecho, rray-**ay**-cho, a., remade

rehén, rray-**en,** s., hostage

rehilete, rray'e-**lay**-tay, s., shuttlecock

rehusar, rray'oo-**sar,** v., to refuse ; to decline

reidero, rray'e-**day**-ro, a., laughable

reina, rray'**ee**-nah, s., queen

reinado, rray'e-**nah**-do, s., reign

reinar, rray'e-**nar,** v., to reign

reincidir, rray-in-the-**deer,** v., to relapse

reintegrar, rray-in-tay-**grar,** v., to restore ; to

reír, rray'**eer,** v., to laugh   [refund

reja, rray-*H*ah, s., plough-share ; grate ; railing

rejón, rray-*H*on, s., dagger ; poniard ; spear

rejuvenecer, rray-*H*oo-vay-nay-**thair,** v., to make
or grow young again

relacionar, rray-lah-the-o-**nar,** v., to relate ; to
connect

relajación, rray-lah-*H*ah-the-**on,** s., relaxation ;
laxity   [remit

relajar, rray-lah-*H*ar, v., to relax ; to slacken ; to

relamido, rray-lah-**mee**-do, a., overnice in dress

relámpago, rray-**lahm**-pah-go, s., flash of lightning

relance, rray-**lahn**-thay, s., fortuitous event

relapso, rray-**lahp**-so, a., relapsed

relatar, rray-lah-**tar,** v., to relate

relato, rray-**lah**-to, s., narrative

releer, rray-lay-**air,** v., to read over again

relente, rray-**len**-tay, s., night dew

relevación, rray-lay-vah-the-**on,** s., liberation ;
relief ; remission

relevante, rray-lay-**vahn**-tay, a., excellent; great; eminent

relevar, rray-lay-**var**, v., to emboss; to exonerate; to relieve

relevo, rray-**lay**-vo, s., relief

relieve, rray-le-**ay**-vay, s., raised work; relief

religar, rray-le-**gar**, v., to bind more tightly

religión, rray-le-*He*-on, s., religion

relinchar, rray-lin-**char**, v., to neigh

relindo, rray-**leen**-do, a., very neat

reliquia, rray-**lee**-ke-ah, s., residue; remains; re-

reloj, rray-lo*H*, s., clock; watch   [lics

relojero, rray-lo-*H*ay-ro, s., watchmaker

relucir, rray-loo-**theer**, v., to shine; to excel

relumbrar, rray-loom-**brar**, v., to sparkle; to glisten

rellano, rray-l'yah-no, s., landing place of a stair-

rellenar, rray-l'yay-**nar**, v., to refill; to stuff   [case

relleno, rray-l'yay-no, s., stuffing. a., satiated

remachar, rray-mah-**char**, v., to rivet; to clinch

remanente, rray-mah-**nen**-tay, s., remainder

remar, rray-**mar**, v., to row; to paddle

rematar, rray-mah-**tar**, v., to finish

remate, rray-**mah**-tay, s., conclusion

remedio, rray-**may**-de-o, s., remedy

rememorar, rray-may-mo-**rar**, v., to recall to mind

remendar, rray-men-**dar**, v., to patch; to repair

remendón, rray-men-**don**, s., cobbler

remero, rray-**may**-ro, s., rower; oarsman

remesa, rray-**may**-sah, s., shipment

remiendo, rray-me-**en**-do, s., patch; clout   [ous

remilgado, rray-mil-**gah**-do, a., affected; fastidi-

remirado, rray-me-**rah**-do, a., prudent; cautious

remirar, rray-me-**rar**, v., to revise; to act with care

remisión, rray-me-se-**on**, s., pardon; forgiveness

remiso*, rray-**mee**-so, a., remiss; slack

remitir, rray-me-**teer**, v., to remit; to forgive; to defer

remo, rray-mo, s., oar; hard work   [to defer

remoción, rray-mo-the-on, s., removal

remojar, rray-mo-*H*ar, v., to steep; to soak

remolacha, rray-mo-**lah**-chah, s., beetroot

remolcador, rray-mol-kah-**dor**, s., tow boat

remolcar, rray-mol-**kar**, v., to tow
remolinar, rray-mo-le-**nar**, v., to whirl
remolino, rray-mo-**lee**-no, s., whirl; whirlpool
remolque, rray-**mol**-kay, s., towing
remontar, rray-mon-**tar**, v., to soar; to go up (river)
remorder, rray-mor-**dair**, v., to cause remorse;
to fret   [morse
remordimiento, rray-mor-de-me-**en**-to, s., re-
remoto*, rray-**mo**-to, a., remote
remover, rray-mo-**vair**, v., to remove; to stir up
removimiento, rray-mo-ve-me-**en**-to, s., removal
remozar, rray-mo-**thar**, v., to make or look young
remunerar, rray-moo-nay-**rar**, v., to reward; to
remunerate
renacer, rray-nah-**thair**, v., to be born again
renacimiento, rray-nah-the-me-**en**-to, s., new
birth; renaissance
renacuajo, rray-nah-koo'**ah**-Ho, s., tadpole
rencilla, rren-**thee**-l'yah, s., grudge; discard; feud
rencor, rren-**kor**, s., rancour
rendición, rren-de-the-**on**, s., surrender; yield
rendidamente, rren-de-dah-**men**-tay, adv.,
humbly
rendija, rren-dee-Hah, s., crevice; crack
rendimiento, rren-de-me-**en**-to, s., income; yield
rendir, rren-**deer**, v., to subdue; to surrender; to
yield
renegar, rray-nay-**gar**, v., to disown; to swear
renglón, rren-**glon**, s., line
reniego, rray-ne-**ay**-go, s., blasphemy
reno, rray-no, s., reindeer
renombre, rray-nom-bray, s., renown
renovar, rray-no-**var**, v., to renovate; to renew
renta, rren-tah, s., income; rent
rentero, rren-**tay**-ro, s., farmer; lessee   [means
rentista, rren-**tiss**-tah, s., person with independent
renuencia, rray-noo'en-thah, s., reluctance
renuevo, rray-noo'**ay**-vo, s., sprout; renewal
renunciar, rray-noon-the-**ar**, v., to renounce
reñir, rray-n'**yeer**, v., to quarrel; to scold
reo, rray-o, s., offender; culprit; defendant
reojo, rray-o-Ho, adv., **de —,** day —, askance

reparar, rray-pah-**rar**, v., to repair; to notice

reparo, rray-**pah**-ro, s., repair; consideration; doubt; objection

repartir, rray-par-**teer**, v., to distribute

repasar, rray-pah-**sar**, v., to repass; to revise

repecho, rray-**pay**-cho, s., declivity [reject

repeler, rray-pay-**lair**, v., to repel; to refute; to

repeloso, rray-pay-**lo**-so, a., touchy; peevish

repente, rray-**pen**-tay, adv., **de—**, day—, suddenly

repercutir, rray-pair-koo-**teer**, v., to reflect; to reverberate; to rebound

repetir, rray-pay-**teer**, v., to repeat

repicar, rray-pe-**kar**, v., to chime

repique, rray-**pee**-kay, s., chime

repisa, rray-**pee**-sah, s., bracket

replegar, rray-play-**gar**, v., to refold

repleto, rray-**play**-to, a., replete

réplica, rray-ple-kah, s., reply; retort

repliegue, rray-ple'**ay**-gay, s., doubling; fold

reponer, rray-po-**nair**, v., to replace; to restore

reponerse, rray-po-**nair**-say, v., to recover lost health

reportar, rray-por-**tar**, v., to refrain; to carry

reposo, rray-**po**-so, s., rest; repose

repostería, rray-pos-tay-**ree**-ah, s., confectionery; pantry; larder

represa, rray-**pray**-sah, s., dam; sluice; lock

represar, rray-pray-**sar**, v., to recapture; to retain

representar, rray-pray-sen-**tar**, v., to represent; to perform; to act

reprimir, rray-pre-**meer**, v., to repress

reprobable, rray-pro-bah-blay, a., reprehensible

reprobar, rray-pro-**bar**, v., to reprove; to rebuke

réprobo, rray-pro-bo, s. & a., reprobate [blame

reprochar, rray-pro-**char**, v., to reproach; to

reproducir, rray-pro-doo-**theer**, v., to reproduce

reptil, rep-**teel**, s., reptile

república, rray-**poo**-ble-kah, s., republic [claim

repudiar, rray-poo-de-**ar**, v., to repudiate; to dis-

repuestos, rray-poo'**ess**-tos, s. pl., spare parts

repulsa, rray-**pool**-sah, s., refusal; repulse

repulsar, rray-pool-**sar**, v., to reject; to decline

reputar, rray-poo-**tar**, v., to repute ; to estimate

requerir, rray-kay-**reer**, v., to request ; to require

requesón, rray-kay-**son**, s., curd

requiebro, rray-ke-**ay**-bro, s., endearing expression

res, ress, s., head of cattle ; beast

resabiar, rray-sah-be-**ar**, v., to become vicious

resabio, rray-**sah**-be-o, s., unpleasant ; taste ; viciousness

resaca, rray-**sah**-kah, s., surge ; surf ; redraft

resaltar, rray-sahl-**tar**, v., to jut out ; to be evident

resarcimiento, rray-sar-the-me-**en**-to, s., compensation

resarcir, rray-sar-**theer**, v., to compensate

resbalar, rress-bah-**lar**, v., to slip ; to slide

rescatar, ress-kah-**tar**, v., to redeem ; to recover

rescate, rress-**kah**-tay, s., ransom   [tion

rescisión, rress-the-se-**on**, s., recission ; cancella-

rescoldo, rress-**kol**-do, s., embers   [to resent

resentirse, rray-sen-**teer**-say, v., to grow weak ;

reseña, rray-**say**-n'yah, s., review ; brief description

reservar, rray-sair-**var**, v., to reserve ; to save

resfriado, rress-fre-**ah**-do, s., cold

resguardar, rress-goo'ar-**dar**, v., to preserve ; to defend

resguardo, rress-goo'**ar**-do, s., guard ; security

residencia, rray-se-**den**-the-ah, s., abode ; domicile ; residence

residenciar, rray-se-den-the-**ar**, v., to impeach

residir, rray-se-**deer**, v., to reside

residuo, rray-**see**-doo'o, s., residue ; remnant

resignar, rray-sig-**nar**, v., to resign ; to give up

resistente, rray-siss-ten-tay, a., tough ; resisting

resma, rress-mah, s., ream of paper

resoluto, rray-so-**loo**-to, a., resolute ; bold

resolver, rray-sol-**vair**, v., to resolve

resollar, rray-so-l'**yar**, v., to breath heavily

resonar, rray-so-**nar**, v., to resound ; to echo

resoplar, rray-so-**plar**, v., to breath audibly ; to snort

resorte, rray-**sor**-tay, s., spring ; resiliency

respaldar, rress-pahl-**dar**, v., to endorse

respaldarse, rress-pahl-**dar**-say, v., to lean back

respaldo, rress-**pahl**-do, s., back; endorsement
respetar, rress-pay-**tar,** v., to respect; to honour
respeto, rress-**pay**-to, s., respect; regard
respigar, rress-pe-**gar,** v., to glean
respirar, rress-pe-**rar,** v., to breathe; to live
respiro, rress-**pee**-ro, s., breathing; respite
resplandecer, rress-plahn-day-**thair,** v., to shine;
  to glitter [responsible for
responder, rress-pon-**dair,** v., to answer; to be
respuesta, rress-poo'**ess**-tah, s., answer; reply
resquebrar, rress-kay-**brar,** v., to crack; to split;
  to burst [tongue
resquemar, rress-kay-**mar,** v., to burn or sting the
resquicio, rress-kee-the-o, s., chink; crack
resta, rress-tah, s., rest; remainder
restablecer, rress-tah-blay-**thair,** v., to re-estab-
  lish; to reinstate
restante, rress-**tahn**-tay, s., remainder
restañar, rress-tah-n'**yar,** v., to stanch; to re-tin
restar, rress-**tar,** v., to subtract [pair
restaurar, rress-tah'oo-**rar,** v., to restore; to re-
restituir, rress-te-too'**eer,** v., to give back; to refund
resto, rress-to, s., residue; balance. pl., remains
restregar, rress-tray-**gar,** v., to scrub
restringir, rress-trin-Heer, v., to restrain; to re-
resuelto, rray-soo'**ell**-to, a., resolute [strict
resuello, rray-soo'**ay**-l'yo, s., breathing; panting
resulta, rray-**sool**-tah, s., consequence; result
resultado, rray-sool-**tah**-do, s., result [tion
resumen, rray-**soo**-men, s., summary; recapitula-
resumir, rray-soo-**meer,** v., to abridge; to sum up
retal, rray-**tahl,** s., remnant; clipping
retallo, rray-**tah**-l'yo, s., new shoot
retama, rray-**tah**-mah, s., broom; furze
retar, rray-**tar,** v., to challenge
retardar, rray-tar-**dar,** v., to retard; to delay
retazo, rray-**tah**-tho, s., remnant; piece; cutting
retemblar, rray-tem-**blar,** v., to tremble; to vibrate
retén, rray-**ten,** s., store; stock; reserve
retener, rray-tay-**nair,** v., to retain
retentiva, rray-ten-**tee**-vah, s., retentiveness

reticencia, rray-te-**then**-the-ah, s., reticence

retina, rray-**tee**-nah, s., retina

retintín, rray-tin-**teen**, s., tinkling; jingle

retinto, rray-**teen**-to, a., dark; obscure [privy

retirada, rray-te-**rah**-dah, s., retreat; retirement;

retirar, rray-te-**rar**, v., to withdraw; to retire

retiro, rray-**tee**-ro, s., retreat; retirement

reto, rray-to, s., challenge

retocar, rray-to-**kar**, v., to retouch; to finish

retoñar, rray-to-n'**yar**, v., to sprout; to reappear

retoque, rray-to-kay, s., finishing stroke

retorcer, rray-tor-**thair**, v., to twist; to distort

retornar, rray-tor-**nar**, v., to come back; to give
back

retorno, rray-**tor**-no, s., return; exchange

retorsión, rray-tor-se-**on**, s., retort; rejoinder

retozo, rray-**tho**, s., friskiness

retractar, rray-trahk-**tar**, v., to retract; to recant

retraer, rray-trah-**air**, v., to dissuade. — **se,** to
retire; to shun

retraído, rray-trah-ee-do, s., lover of solitude

retraimiento, rray-trah-e-me-en-to, s., retreat;

retrasar, rray-trah-**sar**, v., to defer [refuge

retraso, rray-trah-so, s., delay

retratar, rray-trah-**tar**, v., to portray

retrato, rray-trah-to, s., portrait

retrechero, rray-tray-**chay**-ro, a., flattering; win-

retreta, rray-**tray**-tah, s., tattoo [some

retrete, rray-**tray**-tay, s., closet; privy

retribuir, rray-tre-boo'**eer**, v., to retribute; to
recompense; to reward

retroceso, rray-tro-**thay**-so, s., retrocession

retrógrado, rray-**tro**-grah-do, a., retrograde

retronar, rray-tro-**nar**, v., to thunder again

retumbar, rray-toom-**bar**, v., to resound

reuma, rray'**oo**-mah, s., rheum

reunir, rray'oo-**neer**, v., to reunite

revalidación, rray-vah-le-dah-the-**on**, s., confirma-

revalidar, rray-vah-le-**dar**, v., to ratify [tion

revejecer, rray-vay-Hay-**thair**, v., to grow old
prematurely

revender, rray-ven-**dair**, v., to retail; to resell

revenirse, rray-vay-**neer**-say, v., to grow sour; to shrink

reventar, rray-ven-**tar,** v., to burst; to molest

rever, rray-**vair,** v., to review; to revise [lamp

reverbero, rray-vair-**bay**-ro, s., reflector; street-

reverenciar, rray-vay-ren-the-**ar,** v., to revere

reverendo, rray-vay-**ren**-do, a., reverend

reverente, rray-vay-**ren**-tay, a., respectful

reverso, rray-**vair**-so, s., reverse side

reverter, nay-vair-**tair,** v., to overflow

revés, rray-**vess,** s., back side; wrong side

revestir, rray-vess-**teer,** v., to dress; to clothe

revisar, rray-ve-**sar,** v., to revise; to review

revisor, rray-ve-**sor,** s., revisor; ticket-collector

revista, rray-**viss**-tah, s., review

revivir, rray-ve-**veer,** v., to revive

revocar, rray-vo-**kar,** v., to revoke

revolcarse, rray-vol-**kar**-say, v., to wallow

revoloteo, rray-vo-lo-**tay**-o, s., fluttering; hovering

revoltillo, rray-vol-**tee**-l'yo, s., medley; jumble

revoltoso, rray-vol-**to**-so, a., turbulent [tionize

revolucionar, rray-vo-loo-the-o-**nar,** v., to revolu-

revolvedor, rray-vol-vay-**dor,** s., disturber

revolver, rray-vol-**vair,** v., to revolve; to stir

revólver, rray-**vol**-vair, s., revolver (pistol)

revoque, rray-**vo**-kay, s., whitewashing

revuelta, rray-voo'**ell**-tah, s., revolt

revuelto, rray-voo'**ell**-to, a., restless; intricate

rey, rray'e, s., king

reyerta, rray-**yair**-tah, s., dispute; wrangle

rezago, rray-**thah**-go, s., remainder

rezar, rray-**thar,** v., to pray

rezongar, rray-thon-**gar,** v., to grumble

rezumarse, rray-thoo-**mar**-say, v., to ooze

ría, rree-ah, s., mouth of a river

riada, rre-ah-**dàh,** s., overflow; inundation

ribazo, rre-**bah**-tho, s., sloping bank

ribera, rre-**bay**-rah, s., shore; beach

ribete, rre-**bay**-tay, s., ribbon; seam; bordc1

ricacho, rre-**kah**-cho, a., very rich

ricino, rre-**thee**-no, s., castor-oil plant

rico*,* rree-ko, a., rich; wealthy

ridiculez, rre-de-koo-**leth**, s., ridiculous action
ridículo, rre-**dee**-koo-lo, a., ridiculous
riego, rre-**ay**-go, s., irrigation
rienda, rre-**en**-dah, s., rein; bridle; restraint
riesgo, rre-**ess**-go, s., risk; danger
rifa, rifa, rree-fah, s., raffle
rígido, rígido, rree-*He*-do, a., rigid; severe
rigor, rre-**gor**, s., rigour
rimbombar, rrim-bom-**bar**, v., to resound
rimero, rre-**may**-ro, s., heap; pile
rincón, rrin-**kon**, s., corner; nook
ringlera, rrin-**glay**-rah, s., row; file
riña, riña, rree-n'yah, s., dispute; quarrel
riñón, riñón, rre-n'yon, s., kidney
río, río, rree-o, s., river; stream
riqueza, rre-**kay**-thah, s., riches; wealth
risa, risa, rree-sah, s., laugh; laughter; laughing-stock
risada, rre-**sah**-dah, s., horse-laugh
risco, rriss-ko, s., crag; cliff
risueño, rre-soo'**ay**-n'yo, a., smiling; pleasing
rival, rre-**vahl**, s., rival; competitor
rivalidad, rre-vah-le-**dahd**, s., rivalry; emulation
rizo, rree-tho, s., ringlet; curl
robar, rro-**bar**, v., to rob; to plunder; to steal
roble, roble, rro-blay, s., oak
roblón, rro-**blon**, s., rivet
robo, rro-bo, s., robbery; theft; spoliation
robusto*, rro-**booss**-to, a., robust
roca, rro-kah, s., rock; cliff; stone
rocalla, rro-kah-l'yah, s., talus of rocks
roce, rro-thay, s., friction; familiarity
rociar, rro-the-**ar**, v., to sprinkle
rocín, rocinante, rro-**theen**, rro-the-**nahn**-tay, s., hack; jade
rocío, rocío, rro-**thee**-o, s., dew; slight shower
rodada, rro-**dah**-dah, s., rut; wheel track
rodar, rro-**dar**, v., to roll; to wander about
rodear, rro-day-**ar**, v., to surround; to encompass
rodeo, rro-**day**-o, s., turning; winding; delay; eva-
rodilla, rodilla, rro-dee-l'yah, s., knee; clout [sion
rodillo, rro-dee-l'yo, s., roller
roedor, rro-ay-**dor**, s., rodent

roer, rro-**air**, v., to gnaw
rogación, rro-gah-the-**on**, s., petition; supplication
rogar, rro-**gar**, v., to implore; to pray
rojear, rro-**Hay-ar**, v., to redden
rojo, rro-Ho, a., red
rol, rrol, s., list; roll; catalogue
rollizo, rro-l'**yee**-tho, a., plump; round; robust
rollo, rro-l'yo, s., roll; roller
romana, rro-**mah**-nah, s., steelyard
romance, rro-**mahn**-thay, s., Spanish language
romería, rro-may-**ree**-ah, s., pilgrimage; picnic
romero, rro-**may**-ro, s,. pilgrim; rosemary
rompedero, rrom-pay-**day**-ro, a., brittle; fragile
romper, rrom-**pair**, v., to break; to wear out
ron, rron, s., rum
ronca, rron-kah, s., threat; boast; braggadocio
roncar, rron-**kar**, v., to snore
roncería, rron-thay-**ree**-ah, s., sloth; cajolery
roncero, rron-**thay**-ro, a., slow; lazy
ronco, rron-ko, a., hoarse; husky
roncha, rron-chah, s., wheal; fraud
ronda, rron-dah, s., night patrol; round
rondar, rron-**dar**, v., to partol; to serenade
ronquera, rron-**kay**-rah, s., hoarseness
ronquido, rron-**kee**-do, s., snore; harsh sound
roña, rro-n'yah, s., scab; filth
roñería, rro-n'yay-**ree**-ah, s., cunning; stinginess
roñoso, rro-n'**yo**-so, a., scabby; stingy; filthy
ropa, rro-pah, s., cloth; material; wearing apparel
ropería, rro-pay-**ree**-ah, s., old clothes trade or shop
ropón, rro-**pon**, s., loose gown worn over the clothes
roquete, rro-**kay**-tay, s., rochet
rosa, rro-sah, s., rose
rosca, rros-kah, s., screw; worm; spiral
rosetón, rro-say-**ton**, s., rose-window
rostro, rros-tro, s., feature; human face; beak
rota, rro-tah, s., rout; course; rattan
rotar, rro-**tar**, v., to rotate
roto, rro-to, a., broken; leaky; ragged; lewd
rotular, rro-too-**lar**, v., to label; to ticket; to endorse
rótulo, rro-too-lo, s., label; lettering; title

rotura, rro-**too**-rah, s., rupture; breakage; cleft
roya, rro-yah, s., rust; mildew; red blight [rasion
rozadura, rro-thah-**doo**-rah, s., friction; gall; ab-
rozamiento, rro-thah-me-**en**-to, s., friction; rub-
rozar, rro-**thar**, v., to brush against [bing
rozo, rro-tho, s., weeding
rubí, rroo-bee, s., ruby
rubia, rroo-be-ah, s., madder
rubio, rroo-be-o, a., golden; fair (hair); blonde
rubor, rroo-**bor**, s., blush; flush; shamefulness
rubro, rroo-bro, a., red; reddish
rucio, rroo-the-o, a., silver grey
ruda, rroo-dah, s., rue
rudeza, rroo-**day**-thah, s., roughness; rudeness
rudo*, rroo-do, a., rude; rough
rueda, rroo'**ay**-dah, s., wheel; turn; circle
ruedo, rroo'**ay**-do, s., rotation; border; mat
ruego, rroo'**ay**-go, s., request; entreaty
rugido, rroo-**Hee**-do, s., roar
rugir, rroo-**Heer**, v., to roar; to bellow
rugoso, rroo-go-so, a., wrinkled
ruibarbo, rroo'e-**bar**-bo, s., rhubarb
ruido, rroo'ee-do, s., noise; tumult
ruidoso*, rroo'e-**do**-so, a., noisy
ruin, rroo'een, a., vile; mean; base
ruina, rroo'ee-nah, s., ruin
ruindad, rroo'een-**dah**t, s., meanness; baseness
ruinoso, rroo'e-no-so, a., ruinous
ruiseñor, rroo'e-say-n'**yor**, s., nightingale
ruleta, rroo-**lay**-tah, s., roulette
rumbo, room-bo, s., bearing; course; route
rumbón, rroom-**bon**, a., pompous; liberal
rumiar, rroo-me-**ar**, v., to ruminate
rumor, rroo-**mor**, s., rumour
runrún, rroon-**rroon**, s., rumour; report
rústico*, rrooss-te-ko, a., rustic
ruta, rroo-tah, s., route; itinerary
rutina, rroo-ree-nah, s., routine; custom

sábado, sah-bah-do, s., Saturday
sábana, sah-bah-nah, s., bed-sheet
sabañón, sah-bah-n'**yon**, s., chilblain

sabedor, sah-bay-**dor**, s., well informed person
saber, sah-**bair**, v., to know
sabido, sah-**bee**-do, a., learned   [knowledge
sabiduría, sah-be-doo-**ree**-ah, s., learning; wisdom;
sabio*, saber-be-o, a., wise; learned
sable, sah-blay, s., sabre; cutlass
sabor, sah-**bor**, s., relish; taste; savour
saborear, sah-bo-ray-**ar**, v., to relish; to taste; to
sabroso*, sah-**bro**-so, a., savoury; tasty   [enjoy
sabueso, sah-boo'**ay**-so, s., bloodhound
saca, sah-kah, s., exportation; sack
sacacorchos, sah-kah-**kor**-chos, s., corkscrew
sacadineros, sah-kah-de-**nay**-ros, s., catchpenny
sacamuelas, sah-kah-moo'**ay**-lahs, s., dentist
sacar, sah-**kar**, v., to draw out; to extort; to remove; to take out
sacerdote, sah-thair-**do**-tay, s., priest
saciar, sah-the-**ar**, v., to satiate
saciedad, sah-the-ay-**dahd**, s., satiety
saco, sah-ko, s., sack; bag
sacro, sah-kro, a., holy; sacred
sacudida, sah-koo-**dee**-dah, s., shake; jerk
sacudido*, sah-koo-**dee**-do, a., harsh; intractable
sacudir, sah-koo-**deer**, v., to shake; to jerk; to
saeta, sah-**ay**-tah, s., arrow; dart   [beat
sagaz*, sah-**gath**, a., sagacious
sagrado*, sah-**grah**-do, a., sacred; consecrated
sagrario, sah-**grah**-re-o, s., tabernacle; ciborium
sagú, sah-**goo**, s., sago
sahumar, sah-oo-**mar**, v., to fumigate
saín, sah-**een**, s., grease; fat; dirt
sainete, sah'e-**nay**tay, s., one act farce
sajar, sah-_H_ar, v., to scarify
sal, sahl, s., salt
sala, sah-lah, s., hall; saloon
salado, sah-**lah**-do, a., salted; witty; winsome
saladura, sah-lah-**doo**-rah, s., salting; salted pro-
salar, sah-**lar**, v., to salt   [visions
salazón, sah-lah-**thon**, s., salted meal
salchicha, sahl-**chee**-chah, s., sausage
saldar, sahl-**dar**, v., to liquidate; to settle
salero, sah-**lay**-ro, s., salt-cellar; (fam.) wit

saleroso, sah-lay-**ro**-so, a., graceful; witty

saleta, sah-**lay**-tah, s., small hall

salida, sah-**lee**-dah, s., departure; outlet; exit

salina, sah-**lee**-nah, s., salt-pit

salir, sah-**leer**, v., to go out; to appear

salitre, sah-**lee**-tray, s., saltpetre

saliva, sah-**lee**-vah, s , saliva; spittle

salmón, sahl-**mon**, s., salmon

salmuera, sahl-moo-**ay**-rah, s., brine

salobre, sah-**lo**-bray, a., brackish; briny

salón, sah-**lon**, s., saloon; hall

salpicar, sahl-pe-**kar**, v., to bespatter; to splash

salpimentar, sahl-pe-men-**tar**, v., to season with pepper and salt

salsa, **sahl**-sah, s., sauce; gravy

salsera, sahl-**say**-rah, s., sauce-boat

saltar, sahl-**tar**, v., to leap; to spring; to rebound

saltarín, sahl-tah-**reen**, s., dancer; restless young rake

saltear, sahl-tay-**ar**, v., to rob on the highway

salteo, sahl-**tay**-o, s., assault on the highway

salterio, sahl-**tay**-re-o, s., psalter

salto, **sahl**-to, s., leap; jump

saltón, sahl-**ton**, s., grasshopper. **ojos saltones**, o-**H**os sahl-**to**-ness, goggle-eyes

salubre, sah-**loo**-bray, a., healthful

salud, sah-**lood**, s., health

saludar, sah-loo-**dar**, v., to greet; to salute

saludo, sah-**loo**-do, s., salutation; bow; greeting

salva, **sahl**-vah, s., salvo; salver

salvado, sahl-**vah**-do, s., bran

salvador, sahl-vah-**dor**, s., saviour

salvaguardia, sahl-vah-goo'**ar**-de-ah, s., safeguard

salvaje*, sahl-**vah**-**H**ay, a., savage

salvajería, sahl-vah-**H**ay-ree-ah, s., savageness; brutal action

salvamento, sahl-vah-**men**-to, s., salvage

salvar, sahl-**var**, v., to save

salvavidas, sahl-vah-**vee**-dahs, s., life-preserver

¡ salve ! sahl-vay, interj., hail!

salvia, **sahl**-ve-ah, s., sage (plant)

salvilla, sahl-**vee**-l'yah, s., salver

salvo, salvo, sahl-vo, adv., excepting a*., safe [duct
salvoconducto, sahl-vo-kon-**dook**-to, s., safe-con-san, sahn, a., (abbrev. of **santo**) saint
sanar, sah-**nar**, v., to heal
sanativo, sah-nah-**tee**-vo, a., curative
sanción, sahn-the-**on**, s., sanction
sandez, sahn-**deth**, s., folly; stupidity
sandía, sahn-**dee**-ah, s., water-melon
sandio, sahn-de-o, a., foolish; nonsensical
saneamiento, sah-nay-ah-me-**en**-to, s., indemni-fication; drainage
sanear, sah-nay-**ar**, v., to indemnify; to drain
sangrar, sahn-**grar**, v., to bleed
sangre, sahn-gray, s., blood; race
sangría, sahn-**gree**-ah, s., bleeding
sangriento*, sahn-gre-**en**-to, a., bloody; gory
sanguijuela, sahn-ghee-*Hoo'ay*-lah, s., leech
sanidad, sah-ne-**dahd**, s., soundness; health
sano*, **sah**-no, a., sound; sane
santiamén, sahn-te-ah-**men**, s., moment; twink-ling of an eye
santidad, sahn-te-**dahd**, s., sanctity; holiness
santiguar, sahn-te-goo'**ar**, v., to make the sign of the Cross
santo*, sahn-to, a., saint; holy; sacred
saña, sah-n'yah, s., anger; passion; rage
sañudo, sah-n'**yoo**-do, a., furious
sapo, sah-po, s., large toad
saquear, sah-kay-**ar**, v., to ransack; to plunder
saqueo, sah-**kay**-o, s., pillage
sarampión, sah-rahm-pe-**on**, s., measles
sarao, sah-**rah**-o, s., ball; dance
sardina, sar-**dee**-nah, s., anchovy; sardine
sarga, sar-**gah**, s., serge
sargento, sar-*H*en-to, s., sergeant
sarmiento, sar-me-en-to, s., vine-shoot
sarna, sar-nah, s., itch; mange
sarracina, sar-rrah-**thee**-nah, s., tumultuous con-**sarro,** sar-rro, s., incrustation of the tongue [test
sarta, sar-tah, s., string of beads; line; row; series
sartén, sar-**ten**, s., frying-pan
sastre, sahs-tray, s., tailor

sastrería, sahs-tray-**ree**-ah, s., tailor's shop

satélite, sah-**tay**-le-tay, s., satellite; bailiff

sátira, **sah**-te-rah, s., satire   [atone

satisfacer, sah-tiss-fah-**thair**, v., to satisfy; to

satisfecho, sah-tiss-**fay**-cho, a., satisfied; conceited

sauce, sah'oo-thay, s., willow

saúco, sah'oo-ko, s., elder-tree

savia, **sah**-ve-ah, s., sap

saya, **sah**-yah, s., upper petticoat

sayo, **sah**-yo, s., smock-coat

sayón, sah-**yon**, s., corpulent, ugly-looking fellow

sazón, sah-**thon**, ş., maturity; season; flavour

sazonar, sah-tho-**nar**, v., to season; to mature

se, say, pron., himself; herself; itself; themselves;
    oneself; to him; to her

sebo, **say**-bo, s., fat; suet; tallow

secador, say-kah-**dor**, s., drier

secar, say-**kar**, v., to dry

seco*, **say**-ko, a., dry; parched; barren; bare

secreta, say-**kray**-tah, s., water-closet

secretear, say-kray-tay-**ar**, v., to talk privately

secreto*, say-**kray**-to, s., secrecy. a*., secret

secuela, say-koo'**ay**-lah, s., sequel; continuation

secuestro, say-koo'**ess**-tro, s., sequestration

secundar, say-koon-**dar**, v., to second; to aid

sed, sed., thirst; eagerness

seda, **say**-dah, s., silk

sede, **say**-day, s., see

sedería, say-day-**ree**-ah, s., silk stuff

sedoso, say-**do**-so, a., silken; silky

seducir, say-doo-**theer**, v., to seduce; to entice

segadora, say-gah-**do**-rah, s., mowing machine;

segar, say-**gar**, v., to reap; to mow   [mower

segregar, say-gray-**gar**, v., to segregate

seguida, say-**ghee**-dah, s., succession; followers

seguido*, say-**ghee**-do, a., continued; successive

seguir, say-**gheer**, v., to follow; to pursue

según, say-**goon**, prep., according to   [cond

segundo, say-**goon**-do, s., (time) second. a., se-

seguro, say-**goo**-ro, s., assurance; insurance. a*.,

seis, say'iss, s., six   [secure; sure; certain

selva, **sel**-vah, s., forest

sellar, say-l'**yar**, v., to seal; to stamp; to conclude
sello, say-l'yo, s., seal; stamp
semana, say-**mah-**nah, s., week
semanal, say-mah-**nahl**, a., weekly
sembrar, sem-**brar**, v., to sow; to scatter; to seed
semejante, say-may-_H_**ahn-**tay, a., similar; like
semejanza, say-may-_H_**ahn**-thah, s., resemblance
semestre, say-**mess-**tray, s., semester, a., half
semi, say-me, prefix, semi; half   [yearly
semidiós, say-me-de'**os**, s., demigod
semilla, say-**mee-**l'yah, s., seed; origin
seminario, say-me-**nah-**re-o, s., seminary (a school)
sémola, say-mo-lah, s., semolina
senado, say-**nah-**do, s., senate
sencillez, sen-the-l'**yeth**, s., simplicity; artlessness
sencillo*, sen-**thee-**l'yo, a., simple; guileless
senda, sen-dah, s., path; footpath
senil, say-neel, a., senile
seno, say-no, s., breast; bosom
sensato, sen-**sah-**to, a., judicious; prudent
sensible, sen-**see-**blay, a., sensible; perceptible;
    painful
sensual*, sen-soo'**ahl**, a., sensuous; sensual
sentado, sen-**tah-**do, a., sedate; judicious
sentar, sen-**tar**, v., to fit; to set up; to seat; to
    suit   [press an opinion
sentenciar, sen-ten-the-**ar**, v., to sentence; to ex-
sentido, sen-**tee-**do, s., sense; reason; meaning.
    a*., sensible
sentimiento, sente-me-**en-**to, s., sentiment; grief;
sentina, sen-**tee-**nah, s., sink; drain   [opinion
sentir, sen-**teer**, v., to feel; to perceive; to suffer;
    to regret
seña, say-n'yah, s., sign; token; signal; pass-word
señal, say-n'**yahl**, s., sign; signal; token; land-
señalado*, say-n'yah-lah-do, a., famous   [mark
señalar, say-n'yah-**lar**, v., to stamp; to mark; to
señor, say-n'**yor**, s., sir; mister; lord   [signalise
señora, say-n'**yo-**rah, s., lady; mistress; madam
señorear, say-n'yo-ray-**ar**, v., to domineer; to excel
separado*, say-pah-**rah-**do, a., separated; separate
separar, say-pah-**rar**, v., to separate

sepelio, say-**pay**-le-o, s., burial

septiembre, sep-te-**em**-bray, s., September

séptimo, sep-te-mo, a., seventh

sepulcro, say-**pool**-kro, s., sepulchre; grave

sepultar, say-pool-**tar**, v., to bury

sequedad, say-kay-**dahd**, s., dryness; barrenness

sequía, say-**kee**-ah, s., dryness; drought

séquito, say-ke-to, s., retinue; train; suite

ser, sair, v., to be; to exist; to happen; to belong; to become   [to pacify

serenar, say-ray-**nar**, v., to clear up; to settle;

sereno, say-**ray**-no, s., night watchman.   a*.,

serie, say-re-ay, s., series   [serene; cloudless

seriedad, say-re-ay-**dahd**, s., seriousness; sincer-

serio*, say-re-o, a., serious; severe   [ity

sermonear, sair-mo-nay-**ar**, v., to reprimand

serpiente, sair-pe-**en**-tay, s., serpent

serranía, sair-rrah-**nee**-ah, s., ridge of mountains

serrano, sair-**rrah**-no, s., mountaineer

serrar, sair-**rrar**, v., to saw

serrín, sair-**rreen**, s., sawdust

servible, sair-vee-blay, a., serviceable

servicial, sair-ve-the-**ahl**, a., obsequious; obliging

servicio, sair-**vee**-the-o, s., service

servidero, sair-ve-**day**-ro, a., fit for service

servidumbre, sair-ve-**doom**-bray, s., servitude

servil, sair-**veel**, a., servile; grovelling

servilleta, sair-ve-l'**yay**-tah, s., napkin

servir, sair-**veer**, v., to serve; to wait at table
— **se,** to deign; to please

sesenta, say-**sen**-tah, s. & a., sixty

sesentón, say-sen-**ton**, s. & a., sexagenarian

sesgado*, sess-**gah**-do, a., slanting

sesgar, sess-**gar**, v., to slope; to bevel

sesgo, sess-go, s., bias; slope. a., sloped; biassed

seso, say-so, s., brain; intelligence

sesudo*, say-**soo**-do, a., judicious; discreet; wise

seta, say-tah, s., mushroom

setenta, say-**ten**-tah, s. & a., seventy

setentón, say-ten-**ton**, s. & a., septuagenarian

seto, say-to, s., fence; enclosure

seudónimo, say'oo-**do**-ne-mo, s., pseudonym

severidad, say-vay-re-**dahd**, s., severity

severo*, say-**vay**-ro, a., severe

sexagésimo, sek-sah-*Hay*-se-mo, a., sixtieth

sexo, sek-so, s., sex

sexto, seks-to, a., sixth

sí, see, adv., yes. pron., himself; herself, &c.

si, see, conj., if

sibilante, se-be-**lahn**-tay, a., hissing

sidra, see-drah, s., cider

siega, se-**ay**-gah, s., reaping; harvest time

siempre, se-**em**-pray, adv., always. — **jamás,** — *Hah*-**mahs**, for ever and ever

sien, se-**en**, s., temple (of the head)

sierpe, se-**air**-pay, s., serpent; snake

sierra, se-**air**-rrah, s., saw; ridge of mountains

siervo, se-**air**-vo, s., serf; slave; servant

siesta, se-**ess**-tah, s., afternoon nap

siete, se-**ay**-tay, s., & a. seven

sifón, se-**fon**, s., syphon

sigilar, se-*He*-**lar**, v., to seal; to conceal

sigilo, se-*Hee*-lo, s., secret; secrecy

sigiloso, se-*He*-lo-so, a., reserved; silent

siglo, see-glo, s., century

signar, sig-**nar**, v., to sign. — **se,** to make the sign of the Cross

significar, sig-ne-fe-**kar**, v., to signify; to mean

signo, seeg-no, sign; mark

siguiente, se-ghee-**en**-tay, a., following

silbar, sil-**bar**, v., to whistle

silbato, sil-**bah**-to, s., whistle

silbido, sil-**bee**-do, s., hiss; whistling

silencio, se-**len**-the-o, s., silence

silicio, se-**lee**-the'o, s., silicon

silueta, se-loo'**ay**-tah, s., silhouette

silvestre, sil-**vess**-tray, a., wild; rustic

silla, see-l'yah, s., chair; see; saddle; seat

sillar, se-l'**yar**, s., ashlar; horseback

sillero, se-l'**yay**-ro, s., saddler

sillón, se-l'**yon**, s., easy-chair; arm-chair

símbolo, seem-bo-lo, s., symbol; sign

simiente, se-me-**en**-tay, s., seed

símil, see-mil, s., simile. a., similar

simio, see-me-o, s., male ape
simpatía, sim-pah-**tee**-ah, s., sympathy
simpleza, sim-**play**-thah, s., silliness; rusticity
simplificar, sim-ple-fe-**kar**, v., to simplify
simulado, se-moo-**lah**-do, a., sham
sin, sin, prep., without. — **embargo,** — em-**bar**-go, notwithstanding
sincerar, sin-thay-**rar**, v., to exculpate; to justify
sincero*, sin-**thay**-ro, a., sincere
sincopa, seen-ko-pah, s., fainting-fit
sindicado, sin-de-**kah**-do, s., syndicate
síndico, seen-de-ko, s., trustee; receiver
singlar, sin-glar, v., to sail over a course
singularizar, sin-goo-lah-re-**thar**, v., to distinguish; to single out
siniestra, se-ne'**ess**-trah, s., left hand
siniestro, se-ne'**ess**-tro, s., disaster. a*., sinister
sino, see-no, conj., if not; except; only; but
sinónimo, se-**no**-ne-mo, a., synonymous
sinrazón, sin-rah-**thon**, s., wrong; injustice
sinsabor, sib-sah-**bor**, s., displeasure; disgust
sintaxis, sin-**tahk**-siss, s., syntax
sintético, sin-**tay**-te-ko, a., synthetic
síntoma, seen-to-mah, s., symptom
sinuoso, se-noo'o-so, a., sinuous
siquiera, se-ke'**ay**-rah, conj., at least. **ni —,** ne —, not even
sirena, se-**ray**-nah, s., siren
sirgár, seer-gar, v., to tow
sirvienta, seer-ve-en-tah, s., maidservant
sisa, see-sah, s., petty theft
sisar, se-**sar**, v., to pilfer; to size for gilding
sisón, se-son, s., pilferer
sitial, se-te-**ahl**, s., seat of honour; stool
sitiar, se-te-**ar**, v., to besiege
sitio, see-te-o, s., place; site; siege
sito, see-to, a., situated
situado, se-too'**ah**-do, a., placed; situate
situar, se-too'**ar**, v., to place
so, so, prep., under; below
soba, **so**-bah, s., softening; beating; rubbing
sobaco, so-bah-ko, s., armpit

sobar, so-**bar,** v., to handle; to soften; to pummel

soberanía, so-bay-rah-**nee**-ah, s., sovereignty; dominion

soberano, so-bay-**rah**-no, s. & a., sovereign

soberbia, so-**bair**-be-ah, s., pride; haughtiness

soberbio*, so-**bair**-be-o, a., proud; superb

sobornar, so-bor-**nar,** v., to suborn; to bribe

sobra, so-**brah,** s., surplus; excess; offence. pl., offals

sobradillo, so-brah-**dee**-l'yo, s., penthouse

sobrado, so-**brah**-do, s., garret; attic. a., wealthy

sobrante, so-**brahn**-tay, s., residue; surplus

sobrar, so-**brar,** v., to have more than necessary; to be left

sobre, so-bray, prep., above; over. s., envelope

sobrecama, so-bray-**kah**-mah, s., quilt

sobrecargar, so-bray-kar-**gar,** v., to overload; to overcharge

sobrecargo, so-bray-**kar**-go, s., supercargo; purser

sobrecejo, so-bray-**thay**-Ho, s., frown

sobrecoger, so-bray-ko-**Hair,** v., to surprise

sobredicho, so-bray-**dee**-cho, a., aforesaid

sobredorar, so-bray-do-**rar,** v., to gild; to palliate

sobrehumano, so-bray'oo-**mah**-no, a., superhuman

sobrellevar, so-bray-l'yay-**var,** v., to endure; to undergo; to bear [lively

sobremanera, so-bray-mah-**nay**-rah, adv., excess-

sobremesa, so-bray-**may**-sah, s., table-cloth; des-

sobrenadar, so-bray-nah-**dar,** v., to float [sert

sobrenatural*, so-bray-nah-too-**rahl,** a., super-natural [nickname

sobrenombre, so-bray-**nom**-bray, s., surname;

sobrentender, so-bren-ten-**dair,** v., to understand

sobrepaga, so-bray-**pah**-gah, s., extra pay

sobrepeso, so-bray-**pay**-so, s., overweight

sobreponer, so-bray-po-**nair,** v., to put over; to overcome

sobreprecio, so-bray-**pray**-the-o, s., extra price

sobrepujar, so-bray-poo-**Har,** v., to surpass; to excel; to exceed [outvie

sobresalir, so-bray-sah-**leer,** v., to surpass; to

sobresaltar, so-bray-sahl-**tar**, v., to startle
sobrescrito, so-bress-**kree**-to, s., address of a letter
sobreseer, so-bray-say-**air**, v., to desist [risk
sobreseguro, so-bray-say-**goo**-ro, adv., without
sobreseimiento, so-bray-say'e-me-**en**-to, s., suspension; (law) stay of proceedings [foreman
sobrestante, so-bress-**tahn**-tay, s., overseer
sobretarde, so-bray-**tar**-day, s., close of the evening
sobretodo, so-bray-**to**-do, s., overcoat
sobreveedor, so-bray-vay-ay-**dor**, s., supervisor
sobrevenir, so-bray-vay-**neer**, v., to supervene;
 to happen [outlive
sobrevivir, so-bray-ve-**veer**, v., to survive; to
sobrina, so-**bree**-nah, s., niece
sobrino, so-**bree**-no, s., nephew
sobrio*, so-bre-o, a., sober; frugal
socaliñar, so-kah-le-n'**yar**, v., to extort by trickery
socapa, so-**kah**-pah, s., pretext; pretence
socarrar, so-kar-**rrar**, v., to half roast
socarrón, so-kar-**rron**, a., cunning; crafty
socavar, so-kah-**var**, v., to undermine
sociedad, so-the'ay-**dahd**, s., society
socio, so-the-o, s., associate; partner
socolor, so-ko-**lor**, s., pretext; pretence
socorrido, so-kor-**rree**-do, a., supplied
socorro, so-**kor**-rro, s., help; aid; succour
sodio, so-de-o, s., sodium
soez, so-**eth**, a., mean; vile; coarse
sofocar, so-fo-**kar**, v., to suffocate; to quench
soga, so-gah, s., rope; halter
sojuzgar, so-Hooth-**gar**, v., to subdue
sol, sol, s., sun
solana, so-**lah**-nah, s., sunny place
solano, so-**lah**-no, s., easterly wind
solapa, so-**lah**-pah, s., lapel; pretext
solapado, so-lah-**pah**-do, a., cunning; artful
solapar, so-lah-**par**, v., to button up; to conceal
solar, so-**lar**, s., ground-plot, a., solar
solaz, so-**lath**, s., solace; consolation
solazar, so-lah-**thar**, v., to console; to comfort;
solazo, so-**lah**-tho, s., scorching sun [to cheer
soldada, sol-**dah**-dah, s., wages

soldadesco, sol-dah-**dess**-ko, a., soldierly

soldado, sol-**dah**-do, s., soldier; private

soldadura, sol-dah-**doo**-rah, s., soldering

soldar, sol-**dar**, v., to solder; to weld; to mend

soledad, so-lay-**dahd**, s., solitude; loneliness; desert

solemne*, so-**lem**-nay, a., solemn; grand

soler, so-**lair**, v., to use to; to be accustomed to

solera, so-**lay**-rah, s., beam

solería, so-lay-**ree**-ah, s., pavement; sole-leather

solicitar, so-le-the-**tar**, v., to solicit

solícito*, so-**lee**-the-to, a., solicitous

solicitud, so-le-the-**tood**, s., solicitude; application

solidaridad, so-le-dah-rre-**dahd**, s., solidarity

solidez, so-le-**deth**, s., solidity

sólido*, so-**le**-do, a., solid

solio, so-**le**-o, s., canopied throne

solitario, so-le-**tah**-re-o, a., solitary; lonely

sólito, so-**le**-to, a., accustomed

soliviar, so-le-ve-**ar**, v., to lift up

solo, so-lo, a., alone; lonely

sólo, so-lo, adv., only. [loin

solomillo, solomo, so-lo-**mee**-l'yo, so-**lo**-mo, s.,

soltar, sol-**tar**, v., to untie; to loosen

soltería, sol-tay-**ree**-ah, s., celibacy [married

soltero, sol-**tay**-ro, s., bachelor. a., single; un-

soltura, sol-**too**-rah, s., agility; ease; skill

solución, so-loo-the-**on**, s., solution

solvencia, sol-**ven**-the-ah, s., solvency

sollozar, so-l'yo-**thar**, v., to sob

somanta, so-**mahn**-tah, s., beating

sombra, **som**-brah, s., shade; shadow

sombrerera, som-bray-**ray**-rah, s., hat-box

sombrero, som-**bray**-ro, s., hat

sombrío, som-**bree**-o, a., shady; sombre; dark

sombrilla, som-**bree**-l'yah, s., parasol; sunshade

someter, so-may-**tair**, v., to subject; to subdue

sometimiento, so-may-te-me-**en**-to, s., submission

son, son, s., sound; report

sonado, so-**nah**-do, a., celebrated

sonar, so-**nar**, v., (music) to play; to sound; to blow the nose

sonda, son-dah, s., plummet; sounding

sondar, sondear, son-dar, son-day-**ar**, v., to sound; to gauge

soneto, so-nay-to, s., sonnet

sonido, so-nee-do, s., sound

sonreírse, son-ray-eer-say, v., to smile

sonrisa, son-ree-sah, s., smile

sonrojo, son-ro-Ho, s., blush

sonsacar, son-sah-kar, v., to draw one out

soñar, so-n'yar, v., to dream

soñoliento, so-n'yo-le-en-to, a., sleepy; drowsy; [lazy

sopa, so-pah, s., sop; soup

sopapo, so-pah-po, s., slap; blow

sopera, so-pay-rah, s., soup-tureen

soplar, so-plar, v., to blow; to steal artfully; [prompt

soplete, so-play-tay, s., blow-pipe

soplón, so-plon, s., informer

sopor, so-por, s., drowsiness; sleepiness

soportar, so-por-tar, v., to suffer; to tolerate; to

soporte, so-por-tay, s., support; base [endure

sor, sor, s., (nun) sister

sorber, sor-bair, v., to sip; to suck

sorbete, sor-bay-tay, s., sherbet [ness

sordera, sordez, sor-day-rah, sor-**deth**, s., deaf-

sordidez, sor-de-deth, s., sordidness; nastiness; covetousness

sórdido*, sor-dee-do, a., sordid; nasty; licentious

sordo, sor-do, a., deaf; noiseless; muffled

sorna, sor-nah, s., irony

sorprender, sor-pren-dair, v., to surprise

sorpresa, sor-pray-sah, s., surprise

sortija, sor-tee-Hah, s., finger-ring; hoop

sosa, so-sah, s., glasswort; soda

sosegado, so-say-gah-do, a., quiet; peaceful

sosegar, so-say-gar, v., to appease; to rest

sosería, so-say-ree-ah, s., insipidity

sosiego, so-se-ay-go, s., tranquillity; calmness

soslayar, sos-lah-yar, v., to do or place obliquely

soso*, so-so, a., tasteless

sospecha, sos-pay-chah, s., suspicion

sospechar, sos-pay-char, v., to suspect

sospesar, sos-pay-sar, v., to suspend; to lift

sostén, sos-**ten,** s., support

sostener, sos-tay-**nair,** v., to sustain; to prop

sota, so-tah, s., (cards) knave

sotabanco, so-tah-**bahn**-ko, s., garret

sotana, so-**tah**-nah, s., cassock

sótano, so-tah-no, s., underground cellar; basement

sotavento, so-tah-**ven**-to, s., leeward; lee

sotechado, so-tay-**chah**-do, s., shed

soto, so-to, s., grove; thicket

su, soo, pron., his; her; its; their; one's

suave*, soo'**ah**-vay, a., smooth; soft; gentle

suavizar, soo'ah-ve-**thar,** v., to soften

subarrendar, soob-ar-rren-**dar,** v., to sublet; to sublease

subasta, soo-**bahs**-tah, s., auction　　　[sublease

súbdito, soob-de-to, s. & a., subject

subida, soo-**bee**-dah, s., mounting; ascent; increase

subir, soo-**beer,** v., to ascend; to mount; to increase

súbito, soo-be-to, adv., suddenly; unexpectedly.　—a*., sudden; unforseen

sublevar, soo-blay-**var,** v., to excite rebellion

sublime*, soo-**blee**-may, a., sublime

subrayar, soob-rrah-**yar,** v., to underline

subrepción, soob-rrep-the-**on,** s., underhand action

subrogar, soob-rro-**gar,** v., to surrogate

subsanar, soob-sah-**nar,** v., to excuse; to repair

subscribir, soobs-kre-**beer,** v., to subscribe

subsidiar, soob-se-de-**ar,** v., to subsidize

subsiguiente, soob-se-ghee-**en**-tay, a., subsequent

subsistencia, soob-siss-**ten**-the-ah, s., subsistence;　[livelihood

subsistir, soob-siss-**teer,** v., to subsist

substancia, soobs-**tahn**-the-ah, s., substance; aliment; nature of things　　　[replace

substituir, soobs-te-too-**eer,** v., to substitute; to

substraer, soobs-trah-**air,** v., to subtract. —**se,** to withdraw

subteniente, soob-tay-ne-**en**-tay, s., second lieutenant

suburbio, soo-**boor**-be-o, s., suburb　　　[tenant

subvenir, soob-vay-**neer,** v., to aid; to assist; to subvene

subversivo, soob-vair-**see**-vo, a., subversive

subyugar, soob-yoo-**gar,** v., to subdue

suceder, soo-thay-**dair**, v., to succeed; to inherit; to follow; to happen

suceso, soo-**thay**-so, s., success; occurrence; issue

sucio*, soo-the-o, a., dirty; nasty; filthy

suco, soo-ko, s., juice; sap

sucumbir, soo-koom-**beer**, v., to succumb

sucursal, soo-koor-**sahl**, s., branch office

sudar, soo-**dar**, v., to sweat; to perspire; to toil

sudeste, soo-**dess**-tay, s., south-east

sudoeste, soo-do-**ess**-tay, s., south-west

suegra, soo'**ay**-grah, s., mother-in-law

suegro, soo'**ay**-gro, s., father-in-law

suela, soo'**ay**-lah, s., sole of the shoe

sueldo, soo'**ell**-do, s., wages; pay

suelo, soo'**ay**-lo, s., soil; ground; floor

suelto, soo'**ell**-to, a., loose; swift; free; easy

sueño, soo'**ay**-n'yo, s., sleep; dream; vision

suero, soo'**ay**-ro, s., whey; serum

suerte, soo'**air**-tay, s., chance; fortune; luck; fate; kind; manner

suficiente*, soo-fe-the-**en**-tay, a., sufficient; apt;

sufragar, soo-frah-**gar**, v., to defray   [fit

sufrible, soo-**free**-blay, a., bearable

sufridor, soo-fre-**dor**, s. & a., long-suffering

sufrimiento, soo-fre-me-en-to, s., sufferance

sufrir, soo-**freer**, v., to suffer; to tolerate; to

sugerir, soo-Hay-**reer**, v., to suggest   [undergo

sujeción, soo-Hay-the-**on**, s., subjection

sujetar, soo-Hay-**tar**, v., to subdue; to subject; to fasten   [ject; liable

sujeto, soo-Hay-to, s., subject; matter. a., sub-

suma, soo-mah, s., sum; amount; addition

sumar, soo-**mar**, v., to sum; to add

sumario, soo-**mah**-re-o, s. & a., summary

sumergir, soo-mair-**Heer**, v., to submerge; to immerse; to plunge

sumidero, soo-me-**day**-ro, s., sewer; drain

suministrar, soo-me-niss-**trar**, v., to supply; to

sumir, soo-**meer**, v., to sink; to depress   [provide

sumiso, soo-**mee**-so, a., submissive

sumo*, soo-mo, a., highest; greatest

suntuoso*, soon-**too**'o-so, a., sumptuous

supeditar, soo-pay-de-**tar,** v., to subdue; to subject

superar, soo-pay-**rar,** v., to overcome; to surpass

superávit, soo-pay-**rah**-vit, s., surplus

superchería, soo-pair-chay-**ree**-ah, s., fraud; cheat

superficie, soo-pair-fee-the-ay, s., surface [val

supervivencia, soo-pair-ve-**ven**-the-ah, s., survi-

superviviente, soo-pair-ve-ve-**en**-tay, s. & a., survivor [falsify a writing

suplantar, soo-plahn-**tar,** v., to supplant; to

suplemento, soo-play-**men**-to, s., supply; supple- [ment

súplica, **soo**-ple-kah, s., petition

suplicar, soo-p.e-**kar,** v., to implore; to entreat; to appeal

suplicio, soo-**plee**-the-o, s., torture [fill up

suplir, soo-**pleer,** v., to supply; to furnish; to

suponer, soo-po-**nair,** v., to suppose; to assume

suprimir, soo-pre-**meer,** v., to suppress [posed

supuesto, soo-poo-**ess**-to, s., supposition. a., sup-

sur, soor, s., south

surco, **soor**-ko, s., furrow; line

surgir, soor-*Heer,* v., to emerge

surtido, soor-**tee**-do, s., assortment

surtidor, soor-te-**dor,** s., jet of water

surtir, soor-**teer,** v., to provide; to supply

suscitar, sooss-the-**tar,** v., to excite; to promote

suspender, sooss-pen-**dair,** v., to suspend

suspicaz*, sooss-pe-**kath,** a., suspicious

suspirar, sooss-pe-**rar,** v., to sigh; to long for

sustancia, sooss-**tahn**-the-ah, s., (see **substancia**)

sustentable, sooss-ten-**tah**-blay, a., defensible; sustainable [support

sustentáculo, sooss-ten-**tah**-koo-lo, s., prop;

sustentar, sooss-ten-**tar,** v., to sustain; to nourish

sustento, sooss-**ten**-to, s., food; sustenance

sustituir, sooss-te-too'**eer,** v., to substitute

susto, **sooss**-toh, s., scare; fright; shock [mur

susurrar, soo-soor-**rrar,** v., to whisper; to mur-

sutil*, soo-**teel,** a., subtle; keen; flimsy

sutleza, soo-te-**lay**-thah, s., subtlety; acumen

suyo, **soo**-yo, pron., his; hers; theirs. pl., family friends; servants

TAB 286 TAL

taba, tah-bah, s., small bone
tabaco, tah-bah-ko, s., tobacco
tábano, tah-bah-no, s., hornet
tabaquero, tah-bah-**kay**-ro, s., tobacconist
tabardillo, tah-bar-**dee**-l'yo, s., burning fever
taberna, tah-bair-nah, s., tavern
tabernero, tah-bair-**nay**-ro, s., tavern-keeper
tabicar, tah-be-**kar,** v., to wall up
tabique, tah-**bee**-kay, s., partition wall
tabla, tah-blah, s., board; table; index; list
tablado, tah-**blah**-do, s., scaffold; stage
tablazón, tah-blah-**thon,** s., platform; planks
tableta, tah-**blay**-tah, s., tablet
tablilla, tah-**blee**-l'yah, s., notice board; tablet
tablón, tah-**blon,** s., plank; thick board
taburete, tah-boo-**ray**-tay, s., stool; (theatre) stall
tacañería, tah-kah-n'yay-**ree**-ah, s., meanness
tacaño, tah-**kah**-n'yo, a., stingy
tácito*, tah-the-to, a., tacit; implied
taco, tah-ko, s., stopper; wad; billiard cue
tacón, tah-**kon,** s., heel-piece
taconear, tah-ko-nay-**ar,** v., to walk loftily on the heels
tacha, tah-chah, s., fault; defect
tachar, tah-**char,** v., to find fault with
tacto, tahk-to, s., touch; tact
tafetán, tah-fay-**tahn,** s., taffeta
tafilete, tah-fe-**lay**-tay, s., morocco leather
tahona, tah-**o**-nah, s., bakehouse
tahonero, tah-o-**nay**-ro, s., baker
tahur, tah**-oor,** s., gambler; cheat
taimado, tah'e-**mah**-do, a., sly; crafty
taja, tah-Hah, s., cut; dissection; tally
tajadura, tah-Hah-**doo**-rah, s., cut; notch; section
tajamar, tah-Hah-**mar,** s., cutwater
tajar, tah-Har, v., to cut; to chop; to hew
tajo, tah-Ho, s., cut; incision
tal, tahl, a., such; so; as; similar; equal
tala, tah-lah, s., felling of trees; devastation
taladrar, tah-lah-**drar,** v., to bore; to drill; to pierce
taladro, tah-**lah**-dro, s., bit; borer; drill
talar, tah-**lar,** v., to fell trees; to lay waste

talega, tah-**lay**-gah, s., bag; sack; bagful

talento, tah-**len**-to, s., talent

talión, tah-le-**on**, s., retaliation

talismán, tah-liss-**mahn**, s., talisman; amulet

talmente, tahl-**men**-tay, adv., in the same manner

talón, tah-**lon**, s., heel; counterfoil

talud, tah-**lood**, s., talus; slope; ramp

talla, tah-l'yah, s., raised work; sculpture

tallar, tah-l'yar, v., to cut; to carve in wood

talle, tah-l'yay, s., shape; size; waist

taller, tah-l'yair, s., workshop; laboratory

tallista, tah-l'yeess-tah, s., carver in wood

tallo, tah-l'yo, s., shoot; sprout; stem

tamaño, tah-mah-n'yo, s., size. a., as large; so   [large

tambalear, tahm-bah-lay-ar, v., to stagger; to   waver

también, tahm-be-**en**, adv., & conj. also; as well

tambor, tahm-bor, s., drum; drummer

tamboril, tahm-bo-**reel**, s., tabour; tabouret

tamiz, tah-**meeth**, s., fine sieve

tamo, tah-mo, fluff; dust

tampoco, tahm-**po**-ko, adv., neither

tan, tahn, adv., so; so much. s., sound of the drum

tanda, tahn-dah, s., turn; task; gang; batch

tanganillo, tahn-gah-nee-l'yo, s., small prop

tantear, tahn-tay-ar, v., to measure; to proportion;   to examine

tanteo, tahn-**tay**-o, s., calculation; computation

tanto, tahn-to, adv., so. s., quantity. a., so much

tañedor, tah-n'yay-**dor**, s., player on a musical

tañer, tah-n'yair, (see **tocar**)   [instrument

tapa, tah-pah, s., lid; cover

tapar, tah-par, v., to cover; to conceal

tapete, tah-**pay**-tay, s., small carpet; rug; table

tapiar, tah-pe-ar, v., to wall up   [cover

tapicería, tah-pe-thay-**ree**-ah, s., tapestry

tapiz, tah-**peeth**, s., tapestry

tapón, tah-**pon**, s., cork; plug; bung

taquigrafía, tah-ke-grah-**fee**-ah, s., shorthand

taquígrafo, tah-**kee**-grah-fo, s., stenographer;   shorthand-typist   [file

taquilla, tah-kee-l'yah, s., booking-office; letter-

tara, tah-rah, s., tare

tardanza, tar-dahn-than, s., slowness; delay

tardar, tar-dar, v., to delay; to put off; to tarry

tarde, tar-day, adv., late. — s., afternoon; evening

tardiamente, tar-de-ah-men-tay, adv., too late

tardío, tar-dee-o, a., late; too late

tardo, tar-do, a., slow; sluggish; tardy

tarea, tah-ray-ah, s., task; day's work

tarifa, tah-ree-fah, s., tariff

tarima, tah-ree-mah, s., stand; daïs

tarjeta, tar-Hay-tah, s., card. — **postal,** — postarro, tar-rro, s., jar [tahl, postcard

tartajear, tar-tah-Hay-ar, v., to stutter; to stammer

tartamudear, tar-tah-moo-day-ar, v., to stutter; to stammer

tartamundo, tar-tah-moo-do, s., stutterer; stam-

tártaro, tar-tah-ro, s., tartar; hell [merer

tarugo, tah-roo-go, s., wooden peg or pin

tasa, tah-sah, s., rate; price; valuation

tasación, tar-sah-the-on, s., appraisement

tasar, tah-sar, v., to appraise; to value

tatarabuelo, tah-tah-rah-boo'ay-lo, s., great-great-

¡tate! tah-tay, interj., beware! [grandfather

taza, tah-thah, s., cup; bowl; basin of a fountain

té, tay, s., tea

te, tay, pron., thee

tea, tay-ah, s., torch

teatro, tay-ah-tro, s., theatre; play-house

tecla, tay-klah, s., key of a piano or organ

teclado, tay-klah-do, s., keyboard

técnica, tek-ne-kah, s., technique

tecnología, tek-no-lo-Hee'ah, s., technology

techo, tay-cho, s., roof; ceiling

techumbre, tay-choom-bray, s., vaulted roof

tedio, tay-de-o, s., loathing; tediousness

teja, tay-Hah, s., roof-tile

tejedor, tay-Hay-dor, s., weaver

tejer, tay-Hair, v., to weave

tejido, tay-Hee-do, s., texture; fabric; web

tela, tay-lah, s., cloth

telar, tay-lar, s., loom

telaraña, tay-lah-rah-n'yah, s., cobweb

telefonear, tay-lay-fo-nay-ar, v., to telephone

teléfono, tay-**lay**-fo-no, s., telephone

telegrafiar, tay-lay-grah-fe-**ar,** v., to telegraph; [to wire

telégrafo, tay-lay-grah-fo, s., telegraph

telegrama, tay-lay-**grah**-mah, s., telegram

telémetro, tay-**lay**-may-tro, s., range-finder

telescopio, tay-less-**ko**-pe-o, s., telescope [camera

televisión, tay-lay-ve-se-**on,** s., television

telón, tay-**lon,** s., (theatre) curtain

tema, tay-mah, s., theme

temblar, tem-**blar,** v., to tremble; to shake; to

temblón, tem-**blon,** a., tremulous [quiver

temblor, tem-**blor,** s., trembling

temer, tem-mair, v., to fear; to doubt

temerario*, tay-may-**rah**-re-o, a., rash; imprudent

temeroso*, tay-may-ro-so, a., timid; timorous

temible, tay-**mee**-blay, a., terrible; frightful

temor, tay-**mor,** s., dread; fear

témpano, tem-pah-no, s., iceberg; big piece of ice

tempestad, tem-pess-**tahd,** s., tempest; storm

templado, tem-**plah**-do, a., temperate

templador, tem-plah-**dor,** s., tuner

templar, tem-**plar,** v., to temper; to tune

temple, tem-play, s., temper (metal)

templo, tem-plo, s., temple

temporada, tem-po-**rah**-dah, s., spell; season

temporal, tem-po-**rahl,** s., tempest; season. a.,
  temporary; temporal

temprano, tem-**prah**-no, adv., early. a., precocious

tenacillas, tay-nah-**thee**-l'yahs, s., tweezers

tenaz*, tay-**nath,** a., tenacious

tenazas, tay-**nah**-thahs, s., tongs; pincers

tenca, ten-kah, s., tench

tender, ten-**dair,** v., to stretch out; to expand

tendero, ten-**day**-ro, s., shopkeeper; haberdasher

tendido, ten-**dee**-do, s., row of seats in a circus

tenebroso*, tay-nay-**bro**-so, a., dark; obscure

tenedor, tay-nay-**dor,** s., holder; fork [tenancy

tenencia, tay-**nen**-the-ah, s., possession; lieu-

tener, tay-**nair,** v., to have; to hold; to possess;
  to contain; to retain

teniente, tay-ne-**en**-tay, s., deputy; lieutenant

tenor, tay-**nor,** s., tenor, purport; (singer) tenor

tentar, ten-**tar**, v., to touch ; to try ; to tempt
tentativa, ten-tah-**tee**-vah, s., attempt ; trial
tenue*, tay-noo'ay, a., thin ; slender
tenuidad, tay-noo'e-**dahd**, s., tenuity ; weakness
teñir, tay-n'**yeer**, v., to tinge ; to dye
teoría, tay-o-**ree**-ah, s., theory
tercer, tercero, tair-**thair**, tair-**thay**-ro, a., third
tercería, tair-thay-**ree**-ah, s., mediation
tercero, tair-**thay**-ro, s., third person
terciado, tair-the-**ah**-do, s., cutlass   [mediate
terciar, tair-the-**ar**, v., to divide in three parts ; to
tercio, tair-the-o, s., third part ; half a load
terciopelo, tair-the-o-**pay**-lo, s., velvet
terco, tair-ko, a., pertinacious ; obstinate
tergiversar, tair-*He*-vair-**sar**, v., to tergiversate ;
          to misrepresent   [condition
término, tair-me-no, s., term ; end ; boundary ;
termómetro, tair-mo-**may**-tro, s., thermometer
termos, tair-mos, s., vacuum flask
termostato, tair-mo-**stah**-to, s., thermostat
ternero, tair-**nay**-ro, s., calf ; bullock
terneza, tair-**nay**-thah, s., softness ; tenderness
terno, tair-no, s., suit, ternary number
ternura, tair-**noo**-rah, s., tenderness
terquedad, tair-kay-**dahd**, s., stubbornness
terrado, tair-**rrah**-do, s., terrace
terraplén, tair-rrah-**plen**, s., embankment
terremoto, tair-rray-**mo**-to, s., earthquake
terrenal, terreno, tair-rray-**nahl**, tair-**rray**-no,
          a., terrestrial
terrible*, tair-**rree**-blay, a., terrible
terrón, tair-**rron**, s., cold ; mound ; lump
terror, tair-**rror**, s., terror ; dread
terso, tair-so, a., smooth ; glossy
tersura, tair-**soo**-rah, s., smoothness
tertulia, tair-**too**-le-ah, s., evening party ; circle ;
tesón, tay-**son**, s., tenacity   [assembly
tesoro, tay-**so**-ro, s., treasure ; treasury
testa, tess-tah, s., head
testador, tess-tah-**dor**, s., testator
testamento, tess-tah-**men**-to, s., will ; testament
testar, tess-**tar**, v., to make a will

testarudo, tess-tah-**roo**-do, a., obstinate

testificación, tess-te-fe-kah-the-**on**, s., attestation

testigo, tess-**tee**-go, s., witness [attest

testimoniar, tes-te-mo-ne-**ar**, v., to testify; to

testimonio, tess-te-**mo**-ne-o, s., testimony; attes-

tesura, tay-**soo**-rah, s., stiffness [tation

teta, tay-tah, s., teat; udder; breast

tetera, tay-**tay**-rah, s., tea-pot

tétrico, tay-tre-ko, a., gloomy; sullen

tez, teth, s., complexion

ti, tee, pron., thee

tía, tee-ah, s., aunt

tibieza, te-be-**ay**-thah, s., lukewarmness

tibio, tee-be-o, a., lukewarm

tiburón, te-boo-**ron**, s., shark [weather; while

tiempo, te-**em**-po, s., time; term; occasion; season;

tienda, te-en-dah, s., tent; awning; tilt; shop

tienta, te-en-tah, s., probe; sagacity

tiento, te-en-to, s., touch; tact; blow. **a —,** ah **—,** gropingly

tierno*, te-**air**-no, a., tender [country

tierra, te-**air**-rrah, s., earth; land; ground; native

tieso, te-**ay**-so, a., stiff; hard; rigid

tifus, tee-fooss, s., typhus

tigre, tee-gray, s., tiger

tijeras, te-*H*ay-rahs, s., scissors; shears

tildar, til-**dar**, v., to brand

tilde, teel-day, s., sign of the letter **ñ**; iota; very small thing

tilo, tee-lo, s., lime-tree

timbrar, tim-**brar**, v., to stamp

timbre, teem-bray, s., stamp; (voice) timbre

timidez, te-me-**deth**, s., timidity

tímido,* tee-me-do, a., timid

timón, te-**mon**, s., helm; rudder

tina, tee-nah, s., vat; tub

tinaja, te-**nah**-*H*ah, s., large earthen jar

tinglado, tin-**glah**-do, s., shed; cart-house

tinieblas, te-ne'ay-blahs, s., darkness

tino, tee-no, s., skill in touch; knack; judgment

tinta, teen-tah, s., ink; tint

tinte, teen-tay, s., tint; dye

tintero, tin-**tay**-ro, s., inkstand
tinto, teen-to, a., dyed; red (wine)
tintura, tin-**too**-rah, s., tincture; dye; rouge
tiña, tee-n'yah, s., scab
tío, tee-o, s., uncle
típico, tee-pe-ko, a., typical
tipo, tee-po, s., type; pattern; standard
tira, tee-rah, s., stripe; list; band
tirabuzón, te-rah-boo-**thon**, s., corkscrew
tirada, te-**rah**-dah, s., cast; throw; distance
tiranía, te-rah-**nee**-ah, s., tyranny
tirano, te-**rah**-no, s., tyrant; despot
tirante, te-**rahn**-tay, s., joist; gear; trace. a., drawn; tight   [draw; to shoot; to aim at
tirar, te-**rar**, v., to throw; to cast; to pull; to
tiritar, te-re-**tar**, v., to shiver
tiro, tee-ro, s., cast; throw; shot; fling; prank
tirón, te-**ron**, s., pull; haul; tyro
tirria, teer-rre-ah, s., aversion; dislike
tisana, te-**sah**-nah, s., ptisan
tisis, tee-siss, s., phthisis; consumption
tisú, te-**soo**, s., gold and silver tissue   [Judy show
títere, tee-tay-ray, s., puppet. pl., Punch and
titubear, te-too-bay-**ar**, v., to vacillate; to doubt;
título, tee-too-lo, s., title   [to hesitate
tiza, tee-thah, s., chalk; clay
tiznar, tith-**nar**, v., to smut; to tarnish
tizne, teeth-nay, s., soot; coal smut
tizón, te-**thon**, s., firebrand
toalla, to'**ah**-l'yah, s., towel
tobillo, to-bee-**l'**yo, s., ankle
toca, to-kah, s., head-dress; thin fabric
tocadiscos, to-kah-**dess**-koss, s., record-player
tocador, to-kah-**dor,** s., (music) player; toilet table; boundoir   [tive
tocante, to-**kahn**-tay, prep., relating to. a., rela-
tocar, to-**kar,** v., to touch; to play on; to concern.
— **se,** to put one's hat on
tocayo, to-**kah**-yo, s., namesake
tocinero, to-the-**nay**-ro, s., pork-butcher
tocino, to-**thee**-no, s., bacon; salt pork
tocón, to-**kon**, s., stump

tocho, to-cho, a., boorish; unpolished

todavía, to-dah-**vee**-ah, adv., yet; still; even

todo, to-do, s., whole. a., all; entire

toldo, tol-do, s., awning

tolerancia, to-lay-**rahn**-the-ah, s., toleration;

tolerar, to-lay-**rar**, v., to tolerate [tolerance

toma, to-mah, s., taking; grasp; capture; dose

tomar, to-**mar**, v., to take; to seize; to gasp

tomate, to-**mah**-tay, s., tomato

tomillo, to-mee-l'yo, s., thyme

tomo, to-mo, s., bulk; tome; volume

ton, ton, s., tone. sin — ni son, sin — ne son,
without rhyme or reason

tonada, to-**nah**-dah, s., tune; song

tonel, to-nell, s., cask; barrel

tonelada, to-nay-**lah**-dah, s., ton

tonelaje, to-nay-**lah**-Hay, s., tonnage; capacity

tono, to-no, s., tone; tune

tontada, ton-**tah**-dah, s., nonsense

tontear, ton-tay-**ar**, v., to fool

tonto*, ton-to, a., foolish; stupid

topar, to-par, v., to collide

tope, to-pay, s., butt; top

topera, to-**pay**-rah, s., mole-hole

topetar, to-pay-**tar**, v., to butt

tópico, to-pe-ko, s., topic; subject. a., topical

topo, to-po, s., mole

toque, to-kay, v., touch; ringing of bells

torbellino, tor-bay-l'**yee**-no, s., whirlwind

torcer, tor-**thair**, v., to twist; to bend; to distort

torcido*, tor-**thee**-do, a., tortuous; twisted

tordo, tor-do, s., thrush. a., speckled; dappled

toreo, to-**ray**-o, s., bull-fighting

torero, to-**ray**-ro, s., bull-fighter

tormenta, tor-**men**-tah, s., storm [ture

tormento, tor-**men**-to, s., torment; anguish; tor-

torna, tor-nah, s., restitution; return

tornar, tor-**nar**, v., to return; to restore

tornasol, tor-nah-**sol**, s., sunflower

tornear, tor-nay-**ar**, v., to turn on a lathe

tornillo, tor-nee-l'yo, s., male screw; clamp

torno, tor-no, s., lathe; gyration

toro, to-ro, s., bull

toronja, to-ron-*H*ah, s., shaddock; grape-fruit

torpe, tor-pay, a., slow; dull; obscene

torpeza, tor-pay-thah, s., heaviness; dulness; [lewdness

torre, tor-rray, s., tower

torrente, tor-**rren**-tay, s., torrent

torreón, tor-rray-**on**, s., fortified tower

torrero, tor-**rray**-roh, s., lighthouse-keeper

torrezno, tor-**rreth**-no, s., rasher of bacon

tórrido, tor-rre-do, a., torrid; parched; hot

torsión, tor-se-**on**, s., twist

torso, tor-so, s., trunk of a statue; bust

torta, tor-tah, s., round cake; pie

tortilla, tor-**tee**-l'yah, s., omelet

tórtola, tor-to-lah, s., turtle-dove

tortuga, tor-**too**-gah, s., turtle; tortoise

tortuoso, tor-too-**o**-soh, a., winding; sinuous

tortura, tor-**too**-rah, s., torsion; torture

torvo, tor-vo, a., stern; grim; severe

torzal, tor-**thahl**, s., cord; twist

tos, toss, s., cough

tosco*, toss-ko, a., coarse; uncouth; ill-bred

toser, to-**sair**, v., to cough

tosquedad, toss-kay-**dahd**, s., roughness; coarse- [ness

tostada, toss-**tah**-dah, s., toast

tostar, toss-**tar**, v., to toast; to roast

total, to-**tahl**, s. & a., whole; total

tozudo, to-**thoo**-do, a., obstinate [mel

traba, trah-bah, s., tie; ligament; obstacle; tram- [ship

trabajar, trah-bah-*H*ar, v., to work

trabajo, trah-**bah**-*H*o, s., work; difficulty; hard-

trabar, trah-**bar**, v., to join; to fasten; to fetter

trabilla, trah-bee-l'yah, s., stitch; strap

tracción, trah-the-**on**, s., traction

traducción, trah-dook-the-**on**, s., translation

traducir, trah-doo-**theer**, v., to translate

traductor, trah-dook-**tor**, s., translator [to attract

traer, trah-**air**, v., to bring; to carry; to wear

tráfago, trah-fah-go, s., traffic; business

traficar, trah-fe-**kar**, v., to trade

tráfico, trah-fe-ko, s., traffic; business; commerce

tragaluz, trah-gah-**looth**, s., sky-light

tragantón, trah-gahn-**ton,** a., gluttonous   [lously

tragar, trah-**gar,** v., to swallow; to believe credu-

trago, trah-go, s., draught of liquor

tragón, trah-**gon,** a., gluttonous

traición, trah'e-the-**on,** s., treason

traido, trah'ee-do, a., worn out

traidor, trah'e-**dor,** s., traitor. a., treacherous

traílla, trah'ee-l'yah, s., leash; lash

traje, trah-*H*ay, s., costume; dress

trajinar, trah-*H*ee-**nar,** v., to convey goods

trama, trah-mah, s., plot; conspiracy

tramar, trah-**mar,** v., to weave; to plot

trámite, trah-me-tay, s., business transaction

tramo, trah-mo, s., plot of ground; flight of stairs

tramoya, trah-mo-yah, s., (theatre) trick; wile

tramoyista, trah-mo-**yiss-**tah, s., stage-machinist
    or carpenter; scene-shifter

trampa, trahm-pah, s., trap; snare; trap-door

trampear, trahm-pay-**ar,** v., to swindle

trampista, trahm-**piss-**tah, s., swindler

tramposo, trahm-**po-**so, a., deceitful; swindling

trancar, trahn-**kar,** v., to barricade; to bar a door

trance, trahn-thay, s., danger; critical moment

tranco, trahn-ko, s., long step or stride

tranquilo*, trahn-**kee-**lo, a,. tranquil; calm; quiet

transacción, trahn-sahk-the-**on,** s., compromise;
    negotiation; transaction

transbordar, trahns-bor-**dar,** v., to transship

transcribir, trahns-kre-**beer,** v., to transcribe;
    to copy

transcurrir, trahns-koor-**rreer,** v., to elapse

transcurso, trahns-**koor-**so, s., lapse of time

transeúnte, trahn-say-**oon-**tay, s., passer-by. a.,
    transitory

transferir, trahns-fay-**reer,** v., to transfer

transfigurar, trahns-fe-goo-**rar,** v., to transfigure;
    to transform

transformar, trahns-for-**mar,** v., to transform

tránsfuga, trahns-foo-gah, s., deserter; runaway

transgredir, trahns-gray-**deer,** v., to transgress

transigir, trahn-se-*H*eer, v., to compound; to
    compromise

transitar, trahns-se-**tar**, v., to travel; to pass by

tránsito, **trahn**-se-to, s., transit

transmitir, trahns-me-**teer**, v., to transmit

transpirar, trahns-pe-**rar**, v., to transpire; to perspire

transportar, trahns-por-**tar**, v., to transport; to convey

tranvía, trahn-**vee**-ah, s., tramway [convey

trapacería, trah-pah-thay-**ree**-ah, s., fraud; cheat

trapacero, trah-pah-**thay**-ro, s., deceitful

trápala, **trah**-pah-lah, s., stamping with the feet; garrulity

trapecio, trah-**pay**-the-o, s., swing; trapeze

trapero, trah-**pay**-ro, s., dealer in rags

trapisonda, trah-pe-**son**-dah, s., noise; bustle

trapo, **trah**-po, s., rag; tatter

tras, trahs., after; behind

trascender, trahs-then-**dair**, v., to transcend; to exhale a strong scent

trasegar, trah-say-**gar**, v., to overset; to decant

trasera, trah-**say**-rah, s., back part; croup

trasero, trah-**say**-ro, s., buttock; a hind

trasgo, **trahs**-go, s., hobgoblin; bogey-man

trasiego, trah-se-**ay**-go, s., decanting

traslación, trahs-lah-the-**on**, s., transfer; adjournment; translation

trasladar, trahs-lah-**dar**, v., to transport; to translate; to copy [removal

traslado, trahs-**lah**-do, s., transcript; transfer

traslúcido, trahs-**loo**-thee-do, a., transparent

traslumbrarse, trahs-loom-**brar**-say, v., to be dazzled; to vanish [parent body

trasluz, trahs-**looth**, s., light seen through a transparent

trasnochar, trahs-no-**char**, v., to sit up all night

traspapelarse, trahs-pah-pay-**lar**-say, v., to be mislaid among other papers

traspasar, trahs-pah-**sar**, v., to go beyond; to pass over; to transfer; to trespass

traspaso, trahs-**pah**-so, s., conveyance; trespass

traspié, trahs-pe-**ay**, s., trip; stumble [clip

trasquilar, trahs-ke-**lar**, v., to shear; to lop; to

trastienda, trahs-te-**en**-dah, s., back-room behind a shop

trasto, trahs-to, s., old furniture; lumber; rubbish

trastornar, trahs-tor-**nar**, v., to overthrow; to disturb; to confuse [confusion

trastorno, trahs-**tor**-no, s., overthrow; disorder;

trastrocar, trahs-tro-**kar**, v., to invert the order of things [abridge

trasuntar, trah-soon-**tar**, v., to transcribe; to

trasunto, trah-**soon**-to, s., copy; likeness

trata, trah-tah, s., slave-trade

tratable, trah-**tah**-blay, a., tractable

tratado, trah-**tah**-do, s., treaty; treatise

tratamiento, trah-tah-me-**en**-to, s., treatment

tratante, trah-**tahn**-tay, s., dealer in provisions

tratar, trah-**tar**, v., to treat (a subject); to trade; to use

través, trah-**vess**, s., bias; misfortune. **al —,** ahl —, across

travesía, trah-vay-**see**-ah, s., passage; crossing

travesura, trah-vay-**soo**-rah, s., prank; frolic

travieso, trah-ve-**ay**-so, a., lively; frolicsome

traza, trah-thah, s., first sketch; outline

trazado, trah-**thah**-do, s., layout

trazar, trah-**thar**, v., to plan out

trébol, tray-bol, s., clover

trece, tray-thay, s. & a., thirteen

trecho, tray-cho, s., space; distance

tregua, tray-goo'ah, s., truce

treinta, tray-in-tah, s. & a., thirty [dable

tremendo, tray-**men**-do, a., tremendous; formi-

trementina, tray-men-**tee**-nah, s., turpentine

trémulo, tray-moo-lo, a., trembling

tren, tren, s., train; equipage; retinue

trencilla, tren-**thee**-l'yah, s., braid

treno, tray-no, s., lamentation

trenza, tren-thah, s., braided hair

trepar, tray-**par**, v., to climb; to crawl

trepidar, tray-pe-**dar**, v., to shake; to quake

tres, tres, s. & a., three

triaca, tre-**ah**-kah, s., theriac

tribunal, tre-boo-**nahl**, s., tribunal; court of jus-

triciclo, tre-**thee**-klo, s., tricycle [tice

trigésimo, tre-**Hay**-se-mo, a., thirtieth

trigo, tree-go, s., wheat

trigueño, tre-gay-n'yo, a., swarthy

trillado, tre-l'yah-do, a., thrashed; beaten; trite

trillar, tre-l'yar, v., to thrash; to beat

trimestre, tre-mess-tray, s., three months; quarter

trincar, trin-kar, v., to break into small pieces

trinchar, trin-char, v., to carve

trino, tree-no, s., trill. a., containing three things

tripa, tree-pah, s., tripe

tripe, tree-pay, s., plush; shag

tripudo, tre-poo-do, a., big-bellied

tripulación, tre-poo-lah-the-on, s., crew of a ship

tripular, tre-poo-lar, v., to man a ship

triscar, triss-kar, v., to stamp the feet; to frisk

triste*, triss-tay, a., sad

tristeza, triss-tay-thah, s., sadness; sorrow

triturar, tre-too-rar, v., to grind; to pound

triunfar, tre-oon-far, v., to triumph

trocar, tro-kar, v., barter; to exchange

trofeo, tro-fay-o, s., trophy

tromba, trom-bah, s., water-spout

trompa, trom-pah, s., horn; wind instrument; trunk of an elephant

trompeta, trom-pay-tah, s., trumpet

tronada, tro-nah-dah, s., thunder-strom

troncar, tron-kar, v., to mutilate

tronco, tron-ko, s., trunk

troncho, tron-cho, s., sprig; stem; stalk

trono, tro-no, s., throne

tropa, tro-pah, s., troop

tropel, tro-pell, s., rush; bustle; crowd

tropezar, tro-pay-thar, v., to stumble; to meet by chance

troquel, tro-kell, s., die; stamp

trotar, tro-tar, v., to trot

trozo, tro-tho, s., piece; fragment

trucha, troo-chah, s., trout

trueno, troo'ay-no, s., thunder-clap

trueque, troo'ay-kay, s., exchange; barter

trufa, troo-fah, s., truffle

truhán, troo'an, s., rascal; scoundrel

truncar, troon-kar, v., to truncate; to maim

tú, too, pron., thou

tu, too, a., thy ; thine
tubérculo, too-**bair**-koo-lo, s., tuber ; tubercle
tubo, too-bo, s., pipe ; tube
tuerca, too'**air**-kah, s., female screw
tuerto, too'**air**-to, a., squint-eyed ; one-eyed
tuétano, too'**ay**-tah-no, s., marrow
tufo, too-fo, s., fume ; strong and offensive smell
tul, tool, s., tulle
tulipán too-le-**pahn**, s., tulip
tullido, too-l'**yee**-do, a., crippled ; maimed
tumbar, toom-bar, v., to throw down ; to tumble
tumor, too-**mor**, s., tumour   [ment
túmulo, too-moo-lo, s., tomb ; sepulchral monu-
tumulto, too-mool-to, s., tumult ; uproar
tunante, too-**nahn**-tay, s., rake. a., cunning
túnel, too-nel, s., tunnel
túnica, too-ne-kah, s., tunic
tuno, too-no, s., truant
tupir, too-**peer**, v., to press close. —**se,** to glut
turba, toor-bah, s., crowd ; rabble   [oneself
turbación, toor-bah-the-**on**, s., perturbation
turbar, toor-**bar**, v., to disturb ; to trouble
turbio*, turbo*, toor-be-o, a., muddy ; troubled ; obscure
turbión, toor-be-**on**, s., heavy shower
turbulento*, toor-boo-**len**-to, a., turbid ; disor-
turnar, toor-nar, v., to alternate   [derly
turno, toor-no, s., turn ; alternate order
turquesa, toor-**kay**-sah, s., turquoise
turquí, toor-kee, s., deep blue colour
turrón, toor-**rron**, s., nougat
¡tús! tooss, interj., word used for calling dogs
tutear, too-tay-**ar**, v., to thou
tutela, too-**tay**-lah, s., guardianship ; tutelage
tutor, too-**tor**, s., tutor ; instructor
tuyo, tuya, too-yo, too-yah, a., thine

ubre, oo-bray, s., teat ; udder
ufanarse, oo-fah-**nar**-say, v., to boast
ufano*, oo-**fah**-no, a., arrogant ; cheerful
ujier, oo-**He**-air, s., usher
úlcera, ool-thay-rah, s., ulcer
ultimar, ool-te-**mar**, v., to end ; to finish

ultimo*, ool-te-mo, a., last; latest; final
ultrajar, ool-trah-*Har*, v., to outrage
ultraje, ool-trah-*Hay*, s., outrage
umbral, oom-**brahl**, s., threshold
un, oon, a., (for **uno**), one, a, an
unánime*, oo-**nah**-ne-may, a., unanimous
unción, oon-the-**on**, s., unction
ungüento, oon-goo'**en**-to, s., ointment
único*, oo-ne-ko, a., unique; sole; singular
unidad, oo-ne-**dahd**, s., unity
uniforme, oo-ne-**for**-may, s. & a., uniform
unión, oo-ne-**on**, s., union; joint; fusion; conso-
   lidation   [blend. **—se**, to associate
unir, oo-neer, v., to unite; to join; to blind; to
universidad, oo-ne-vair-se-**dahd**, s., university
universo, oo-en-vair-so, s., universe
uno, oo-no, a., one; sole; only
untar, oon-tar, v., to anoint; to grease
untuoso, oon-too'o-so, a., unctuous
uña, oo-n'yah, s., nail; hoof; claw; talon
uñada, oo-n'yah-dah, s., scratch with the nail
urbano*, oor-**bah**-no, a., urban; urbane
urdir, oor-deer, v., to warp; to contrive
urgente*, oor-*Hen*-tay, a., urgent
urgir, oor-*Heer*, v., to be urgent; to urge
urraca, oor-**rrah**-kah, s., magpie
usado, oo-**sah**-do, a., used; worn out; second-hand
usanza, oo-**sahn**-thah, s., usage; custom; use
usar, oo-**sar**, v., to use; to accustom
uso, oo-so, s., use; service; custom; fashion
usted, oos-**ted**, pron., you (contraction of Vuestra
   Merced, lit., "your Honour")
utensilio, oo-ten-**see**-le-o, s., utensil; tool; imple-
útero, oo-tay-ro, s., uterus; womb   [ment
útil*, oo-til, a., useful
uva, oo-vah, s., grape

vaca, vah-kah, s., cow; beef
vacaciones, vah-kah-the-**o**-ness, s., holidays
vacada, vah-**kah**-dah, s., drove of cows
vacante, vah-**kahn**-tay, s., vacancy. a., vacant
vacar, vah-kar, v., to vacate; to be vacant

vaciar, vah-the-**ar**, v., to empty ; to hollow
vacío, vah-**thee**-o, s., vacuum. a., empty
vacunar, vah-koo-**nar**, v., to vaccinate
vadeable, vah-day-**ah**-blay, a., fordable
vagabundo, vah-gah-**boon**-do, a., vagabond
vagancia, vah-**gahn**-the-ah, s., vagrancy
vago, vah-go, s., vagabond. a., vagrant ; vague
vagón, vah-**gon**, s., wagon ; van
vaguear, vah-gay-**ar**, v., to loiter ; to rove
vaguedad, vah-gay-**dahd**, s., vagueness
vaina, vah**'**e-nah, s., scabbard ; pod ; husk
vainilla, vah**'**e-**nee**-l'yah, s., vanilla
vaivén, vah**'**e-**ven**, s., swaying ; oscillation
vajilla, vah-Hee-l'yah, s., dinner-set
vale, vah-lay, s., promissory note ; voucher
valedero, vah-lay-**day**-ro, a., valid ; available
valedor, vah-lay-**dor**, s., protector ; defender
valentía, vah-len-**tee**-ah, s., valour ; courage
valer, vah-**lair**, v., to protect ; to be worth
valeroso*, vah-lay-**ro**-so, a., valiant ; brave
valía, vah-**lee**-ah, s., valuation ; credit ; value
válido*, val\.vah-le-do, a., valid ; binding   [esteemed
valido, vah-**lee**-do, s., favourite. a., favoured
valiente, vah-le-**en**-tay, a., valiant ; brave
valija, vah-**lee**-Hah, s., valise ; mail-bag ; post
valijero, vah-le-**Hay**-ro, s., postman
valimiento, vah-le-me-**en**-to, s., use ; benefit ;   [favour
valor, vah-**lor**, s., value ; valour
valorar, vah-lo-**rar**, v., to value ; to appraise
vals, vals, s., waltz
vallado, vah-l'**yah**-do, s., stockade ; fence
valle, vah-l'yay, s., valley
vanagloria, vah-nah-**glo**-re-ah, s., vainglory
vanidad, vah-ne-**dahd**, s., vanity
vanidoso, vah-ne-**do**-so, a., vain ; showy
vano*, vah-no, a., vain ; useless ; conceited
vapor, vah-**por**, s., vapour ; steam ; steamboat
vapul(e)ar, vap-poo-**lar** (-lay-**ar**), v., to flog ; to   [beat
vaquería, vah-kay-**ree**-ah, s., herd of cattle ; dairy
vara, vah-rah, s., rod ; pole ; shaft ; ell
varar, vah-**rar**, v., to launch a ship ; to be stranded

variar, vah-re-**ar,** v., to vary; to change; to alter

varilla, vah-**ree**-l'yah, s., rod; spindle

vario*, vah-re-o, a., various; variable. pl., some;

varón, vah-**ron,** s., man (male human being) [several

varonil, vah-ro-**neel,** a., manly; vigorous

vasar, vah-**sar,** s., shelf in a kitchen

vasija, vah-see-*H*ah, s., vessel for liquids

vaso, vah-so, s., vase; vessel; tumbler

vástago, vahs-tah-go, s., stem; bud; shoot; off-

vasto, vahs-to, a., vast; huge [spring

vaticinio, vah-te-**thee**-ne-o, s., prediction

vaya, vah-yah, s., scoff; jest

vecindad, vay-thin-**dahd,** s., neighbourhood; vicinity [bouring

vecino, vay-**thee**-no, s., neighbour. a., neigh-

veda, vay-dah, s., time when hunting or fishing is forbidden

vedar, vay-**dar,** v., to forbid; to impede

vega, vay-gah, s., open country; plain

vehículo, vay-ee-koo-lo, s., vehicle

veinte, vay-in-tay, s. & a., twenty

vejación, vay-*H*ah-the-**on,** s., vexation

vejar, vay-*H*ar, v., to vex

vejez, vay-*H*eth, s., old age; decay

vejiga, vay-*H*ee-gah, s., bladder

vela, vay-lah, s., vigil; watch; candle; sail; awning

velar, vay-lar, v., to watch; to be awake; to keep vigil; to work at night

veleidad, vay-lay'e-**dahd,** s., velleity; faint desire;

veleta, vay-lay-tah, s., vane [levity

velo, vay-lo, s., veil

velocímetro, vay-lo-**thee**-may-tro, s., speedometer

veloz*, vay-loth, a., swift; fast

vello, vay-l'yo, s., down; nap

vellón, vay-l'yon, s., fleece; lock of wool

velludo, vay-l'yoo-do, s., velvet. a., woolly; downy;

vena, vay-nah, s., vein; seam (geol.) [hairy

venado, vay-nah-do, s., deer; stag

vencedor, ven-thay-**dor,** s., victor; winner

vencejo, ven-thay-*H*o, s., string; band; martinet

vencer, ven-**thair,** v., to vanquish; to conquer; to win

vencido, ven-**thee**-do, a., conquered; matured; payable

vencimiento, ven-the-me-**en**-to, s., maturity (of [bill]

venda, ven-dah, s., bandage; fillet

vendar, ven-**dar,** v., to bandage; to hoodwink

vendaval, ven-dah-**vahl,** s., strong south wind;

vendedor, ven-day-**dor,** s., vendor; seller [gale

vender, ven-**dair,** v., to sell; to betray

vendimia, ven-**dee**-me-ah, s., vintage; grape [harvest

veneno, vay-**nay**-no, s., venom; poison

venero, vay-**nay**-ro, s., vein of metal; source

venganza, ven-**gahn**-thah, s., vengeance

vengar, ven-**gar,** v., to revenge. — **se,** to be revenged on

venia, vay-ne-ah, s., pardon; leave; bow with the head

venida, vay-**nee**-dah, s., arrival

venidero, vay-ne-**day**-ro, a., future

venir, vay-**neer,** v., to come; to spring from

venta, ven-tah, s., sale; roadside inn

ventaja, ven-**tah**-Hah, s., advantage; commodity

ventajoso*, ven-tah-Ho-so, a., advantageous

ventana, ven-**tah**-nah, s., window

ventear, ven-tay-**ar,** v., (wind) to blow; to scent; to investigate

ventisca, ven-**tiss**-kah, s., snow-storm [town

ventorrillo, ven-to-**rree**-l'yo, s., petty inn near a

ventosa, ven-**to**-sah, s., vent; cupping; air-hole

ventrudo, ven-**troo**-do, a., big-bellied

ventura, ven-**too**-rah, s., luck; venture; risk

venturoso*, ven-too-**ro**-so, a., fortunate

ver, vair, v., to see; to look; to observe

vera, vay-rah, s., edge

verano, vay-**rah**-no, s., summer season

veras, vay-rahs, s., truth. **de —,** day —, in truth

veraz, vay-**rath,** a., veracious

verbo, vair-bo, s., word; verb

verdad, vair-**dahd,** s., truth

verdadero, vair-dah-**day**-ro, a., true; real; genverde, **vair**-day, a., green; immature [uine

verdín, vair-**deen**, s., mould

verdugo, vair-**doo**-go, s., hangman; executioner

verdura, vair-**doo**-rah, s., verdure; greens

vereda, vay-**ray**-dah, s., path; footpath

vergel, vair-**Hell**, s., orchard [ful

vergonzoso*, vair-gon-**tho**-so, a., bashful; shame-

vergüenza, vair-goo'**en**-thah, s., shame; bashful-

verídico, vay-**ree**-de-ko, a., truthful [ness

verja, vair-*H*ah, s., grate; railing

vernáculo, vair-**nah**-koo-lo, a., native; vernacular

verosímil, vay-ro-**see**-mil, a., likely; credible

verruga, vair-**rroo**-gah, s., wart; pimple

versado, vair-**sah**-do, a., versed; conversant

versar, vair-**sar**, v., to be conversant

vertedor, vair-tay-**dor**, s., nightman; sewer

verter, vair-**tair**, v., to spill; to empty; to translate

vértice, vair-**te**-thay, s., top; apex; vertex

vertiente, vair-te-en-tay, s., water-shed; slope

vespertino, vess-pair-**tee**-no, a., of the evening

vestido, vess-**tee**-do, s., dress; clothes; garment

vestir, vess-**teer**, v., to clothe; to dress; to adorn;
to cloak

vestuario, vess-too'**ah**-re-o, s., clothes; wardrobe;
uniform; vestry

veta, vay-tah, s., vein; lode

vez, veth, s., turn; time

vía, vee'ah, s., way; road; track

viajar, ve'ah-*H*ar, v., to travel

viaje, ve'ah-*H*ay, s., journey; travel; voyage

viajero, ve'ah-*H*ay-ro, s., traveller; passenger

víbora, vee-bo-rah, s., viper

vibrar, ve-brar, v., to vibrate

vicario, ve-kah-re-o, s., vicar. a., vicarious

viciar, ve-the-ar, v., to vitiate; to adulterate

vicio, vee-the-o, s., vice

vid, vid, s., vine

vida, vee-dah, s., life

vidrio, vee-dre-o, s., glass

viejo, ve-ay-*H*o, a., old; ancient

viento, ve-en-to, s., wind

vientre, ve-en-tray, s., belly

viernes, ve-air-ness, s., Friday

viga, vee-gah, s., beam

vigente, ve-*H*en-tay, a., in force

vigésimo, ve-**Hay**-se-mo, a., twentieth
vigilar, ve-He-lar, v., to watch over; to invigilate
vigorar, ve-go-rar, v., to strengthen
vihuela, ve-oo'ay-lah, s., guitar
vil*, veel, a., vile
vileza, ve-lay-thah, s., vileness
vilipendiar, ve-le-pen-de-ar, v., to revile
villa, ve-l'yah, s., town; municipality
villanaje, ve-l'yah-nah-Hay, s., peasantry
villano, ve-l'yah-no, s., rustic. a*., villainous
vinagre, ve-nah-gray, s., vinegar
vinatero, ve-nah-tay-ro, s., wine-merchant
vinazo, ve-nah-tho, s., very strong wine
vínculo, veen-koo-lo, s., tie; link
vindicar, vin-de-kar, v., to vindicate; to avenge
vindicta, vin-dik-tah, s., vengeance
vino, vee-no, s., wine
viña, vee-n'yah, s., vineyard
violado, ve-o-lah-do, a., violet; coloured; violated
violar, ve-o-lar, v., to violate; to ravish; to profane
violento*, ve-o-len-to, a., violent; forced; strained
violín, ve-o-leen, s., violin; fiddle
violón, ve-o-lon, s., bass-viol; double bass
virgen, veer-Hen, s., virgin
viril*, ve-reel, a., virile
virrey, veer-rray'e, s., viceroy
virtud, veer-tood, s., virtue; force; vigour
viruela, ve-roo'ay-lah, s., small-pox
viruta, ve-roo-tah, s., chip. pl., wood-shavings
visaje, ve-sah-Hay, s., grimace; grin
víscera, viss-thay-rah, s., vital organs
visitar, ve-se-tar, v., to visit; to inspect
vislumbrar, viss-loom-brar, v., to have a glimpse
viso, vee-so, s., prospect; outlook   [of
visor, fotografía, ve-sor fo-to-grah-fee-ah, s.,
    view-finder (camera)
víspera, viss-pay-rah, s., eve. pl., vespers
vista, viss-tah, s., sight; view; eye; appearance;
    landscape; purpose
vistazo, viss-tah-tho, s., glance
visto, viss-to, a., obvious; clear. — **que**, — kay,
vistoso*, viss-to-so, a., showy   [whereas

vitalicio, ve-tah-**lee**-the-o, a., during life

¡vítor! vee-tor, interj., long live!

vitualla, ve-too'**ah**-l'yah, s., victuals; food

vituperar, ve-too-pay-**rar,** v., to blame; to curse

viuda, ve'**oo**-dah, s., widow

viudo, ve'**oo**-do, s., widower

vivac, ve-**vahk,** s., bivouac

vivaracho, ve-vah-**rah**-cho, a., lively; frisky

vivaz, ve-**vath,** a., lively; active

víveres, vee-vay-res, s., provisions

viveza, ve-**vay**-thah, s., liveliness

vividero, ve-ve-**day**-ro, a., habitable

vivienda, ve-ve-en-dah, s., dwelling-house

vivir, ve-**veer,** v., to live; to last; to reside

vivo*, vee-vo, a., living; lively; acute; vivid

vizconde, vith-**kon**-day, s., viscount

vocear, vo-thay-**ar,** v., to cry; to vociferate

vocinglería, vo-thin-glay-**ree**-ah, s., clamour; outcry

volandero, vo-lahn-**day**-ro, a., volatile; fortuitous; fleeting

volar, vo-**lar,** v., to fly; to blow up

volatería, vo-lah-tay-**ree**-ah, s., fowling; fowls

volátil, vo-**lah**-til, a., volatile

volatín, vo-lah-**teen,** s., rope-dancer

volcar, vol-**kar,** v., to overturn

voltear, vol-tay-**ar,** v., to whirl; to overset

volteo, vol-**tay**-o, s., whirling; overturning

volumen, vo-**loo**-men, s., volume; size; bulk; tome

voluntad, vo-loon-**tahd,** s., will

volver, vol-**vair,** v., to return; to send back; to turn

vorágine, vo-**rah**-He-nay, s., vortex

voraz*, vo-**rath,** a., voracious

vos, vosotros, vos, vos-o-tros, pron., you

votar, vo-**tar,** v., to vow; to vote

voto, vo-to, s., vow; vote; opinion

voz, voth, s., voice; word; vote; opinion

vuelco, voo'**ell**-ko, s., overturning

vuelo, voo'**ay**-lo, s., flight; projection

vuelta, voo'**ell**-tah, s., turn; return; back side

vuestro, voo'**es**-tro, pron., your; yours

vulgo, vool-go, s., multitude; general public

vulnerar, vool-nay-**rar,** v., to injure the reputation

y, e, conj., and [ing that
ya, yah, adv., now; already. — **que,** — kay, see-
yacente, yah-**then**-tay, a., lying; jacent
yacer, yah-**thair**, v., to lie; to be situated
yedra, **yay**-drah, s., ivy
yegua, yay-goo'ah, s., mare
yelmo, **yell**-mo, s., helmet; helm
yema, yay-mah, s., bud; germ; yolk
yerba, yair-bah, (see **hierba**)
yermo, **yair**-mo, s., desert; wilderness
yerno, yair-no, s., son-in-law
yerro, yair-rro,'s., error; mistake
yerto, yair-to, a., stiff; rigid; motionless
yesca, yess-kah, s., tinder; spunk
yeso, yay-so, s., gypsum; plaster
yo, yo, pron., I
yugo, yoo-go, s., yoke; nuptial tie; oppressive
yunta, yoon-tah, s., yoke (of oxen) [authority
yute, yoo-tay, s., jute

zafio*, **thah**-fe-o, a., coarse; lacking manners
zaga, thah-gah, s., rear part: back of a carriage
zagal, thah-**gahl**, s., swain; shepherd
zaguán, thah-goo'**ahn**, s., porch; vestibule
zaherir, thah-ay-**reer**, v., to censure; to mortify
zahurda, thah'**oor**-dah, s., hovel; pigsty
zalamería, thah-lah-may-**ree**-ah, s., wheedling
zalear, thah-lay-**ar**, v., to shake a thing
zamarra, thah-**mar**-rrah, s., sheep-skin jacket
zambo, **thahm**-bo, a., knock-kneed
zambra, **thahm**-brah, s., noisy mirth; feast
zambucar, thahm-boo-**kar**, v., to hide
zambullida, thahm-boo-l'yee-dah, s., ducking
zambullir, tham-boo-l'**yeer**, v., to plunge
zampar, thahm-**par**, v., to devour eagerly
zampuzar, thah-poo-**thar**, v., to plunge; to dive
zanahoria, thah-nah-o-re-ah, s., carrot
zancada, thahn-**kah**-dah, s., stride
zancajo, thahn-kah-Ho, s., heel
zancarrón, thahn-kar-**rron**, s., fleshless bone
zanco, thahn-ko, s., stilt
zangandongo, thahn-gahn-**don**-go, s., idler

zanganear, thahn-gah-nay-**ar**, v., to live in idleness
zángano, thahn-gah-no, s., drone; sluggard
zanja, thahn-Hah, s., ditch; trench
zanquear, thahn-kay-**ar**, v., to waddle
zaparrastrar, thah-par-rrahs-**trar**, v., to trail
zapata, thah-pah-tah, s., leather hinge
zapatero, thah-pah-tay-ro, s., shoemaker
zapato, thah-pah-to, s., shoe
zaque, thah-kay, s., leather flask; wine bag; [tippler]
zarabanda, thah-rah-bahn-dah, s., saraband
zaranda, thah-rahn-dah, s., screen; sieve
zarandajas, thah-rahn-dah-Hahs, s., trifles
zarandar, thah-rahn-**dar**, v., to winnow; to sift
zarapito, thah-rah-**pee-**to, s., curlew
zaraza, thah-rah-thah, s., chintz
zarceta, thar-**say-**tah, s., moor-hen
zarcillo, thar-**thee-**l'yo, s., ear-ring; tendril
zarpa, thar-pah, s., claw [shabby]
zarrapastroso, thar-rrah-pahs-**tro-**so, a., ragged;
zarria, thar-rre-ah, s., leather thong; dirt on [clothes]
zarzal, thar-**thahl,** s., bramble patch [blackberry]
zarzamora, thar-thah-**mo-**rah, s., blackberry
zarzuela, thar-thoo-**ay**-lah, s., musical comedy;
     vaudeville
zascandil, thahs-kahn-**dil,** s., busybody
zipizape, the-pe-thah-**pay**, s., noisy scuffle
zócalo, tho-kah-lo, s., base; socle
zoclo, tho-klo, s., wooden shoe
zona, tho-nah, s., zone
zonzo*, thon-tho, a., insipid; dull; stupid
zoquete, tho-kay-**tay**, s., block; bit of bread;
zorra, thor-rrah, s., vixen; prostitute [blockhead]
zorro, thor-rro, s., male fox; sly fellow
zorruno, thor-**rroo-**no, a., vulpine; foxlike
zorzal, thor-**thal,** s., thrush
zote, tho-tay, s., ignorant lazy person; dunce
zozobra, tho-**tho-**brah, s., uneasiness; anxiety
zueco, thoo'ay-ko, s., wooden shoe
zumba, thoom-bah, s., carrier's bell; joke; jest
zumbido, thoom-**bee-**do, s., buzzing sound
zumo, thoo-mo, s., sap; juice
zurcir, thoor-**theer**, v., to darn; to patch up

zurdo, thoor-do, a., left handed

zurrapa, thoor-**rrah**-pah, s., lees; dregs   [to flog

zurrar, thoor-**rrar**, v., to curry; to dress; to tan;

zurriago, thoor-rre-**ah**-go, s., leather whip

zurrido, thoor-**rree**-do, s., humming; bustle

zurrón, thoor-**rron**, s., shepherd's bag; husk

DICCIONARIO
INGLÉS-ESPAÑOL
(ENGLISH-SPANISH DICTIONARY)

(Para la explicación de la pronunciación figurada léanse
cuidadosamente las páginas x., xii., y xiii.)

a, ei, art., un; uno; una

aback, *a*-ḥak´, adv., detrás, atrás; **taken —,** sorprendido; desconcertado

abandon, *a*-ban´-dn, v., abandonar; **—ed,** a., abandonado; (morally) vicioso

abase, *a*-beis´, v., humillar

abash, *a*-bash´, v., avergonzar, consternar

abate, *a*-beit´, v., disminuir; (price) rebajar

abbot, Ab´-ot, s., abad m.

abbreviate, *a*-brii´-vi-eit, v., abreviar

abdicate, Ab´-di-keit, v., abdicar

abdomen, Ab´-do-men, s., abdomen m.

abduction, Ab-dŏk´-shon, s., abducción f.; rapto m.

abet, *a*-bet´, v., apoyar; ayudar

abeyance, *a*-bei´-*a*ns, s., expectación f.; suspensión f.; **in —,** en suspenso

abhor, ab-joar´, v., aborrecer

abhorrence, ab-jor´-ens, s., aborrecimiento m.

abide, *a*-baid´, v., permanecer; **— by,** adherirse a

ability, *a*-bil´-i-ti, s., habilidad f., aptitud f.

abject*, Ab´-CHekt, a., abyecto; vil

ablaze, *a*-bleis´, a., en llamas; (emotion) ardiendo

able, ei-´bl, a.,. capaz, hábil; **to be —,** poder

ably, ei´-bli, adv., hábilmente

abnormal, Ab-noar´-mal, a., anormal; (misshapen) disforme

aboard, *a*-bórd´, s., a bordo

abode, *a*-boud´, s., domicilio m., habitación f.

abolish, *a*-bol´-ish, v., abolir; (cancel) anular

abominable, *a*-bom´-in-*a*-bl, a., abominable

abominate, *a*-bom´-in-eit, v., abominar

aboriginal, Ab-o-riCH-in-al, a., aborigen
abortion, a-boar'-shon, s., aborto m.
abound, a-baund', v., abundar
about, a-baut', adv., casi, alrededor. prep., alrededor de; cerca de; por; hacia
above, a-böv', adv., arriba; encima prep., encima de;
abrasion, a-brei'-shon, s., raspadura f. [sobre
abreast, a-brest', adv., de frente
abridge, a-briCH', v., abreviar
abroad, a-broad', adv., (to be —) estar en el extranjero; (to go —) ir al extranjero
abrupt', ab-röpt', a., abrupto, brusco
abscess, Ab'-ses, s., absceso m.
abscond, ab-skond', v., evadirse
absence, ab'-sens, s., ausencia f.; (lack) falta f.
absent, Ab'-sent, a., ausente; — **minded,** -distraído
absentee, Ab-sen-tii', s., ausente m.
absolute', Ab'-so-luut, a., absoluto; categórico
absolve, ab-solv', v., absolver; desligar
absorb, ab-soarb', v., absorber
abstain, ab-stein', v., abstenerse
abstainer, Ab-stein'-a, s., abstinente m.
abstemious, ab-stii'-mi-os, a., abstemio
abstinence, Ab'-sti-nens, s., abstinencia f.
abstract, Ab-strakt', v., abstraer; extractar
abstract, Ab'-strakt, s., abstracto m. a., abstracto
abstruse', Ab-struus', a., abstruso
absurd', ab-särd', a., absurdo
abundant', a-bön-dant, a., abundante
abuse, a-biuus', v., injuriar; abusar de
abuse, a-biuus', s., abuso m.; (insult) injuria f.
abusive, a-biuus'-iv, a., abusivo; injurioso
abut, a-böt', v., colindar
abyss, a-bis', s., abismo m.
academy, a-kad'-i-mi, s., academia f.
accelerate, Ak-sel'-er-eit, v., acelerar
accent, Ak'-sent, s., acento m.; inflexión de voz f.
accentuate, Ak-sent'-tu-eit, v., acentuar
accept, ak-sept', v., aceptar; (opinion) acoger bien
acceptance, ak-sept'-ans, s., aceptación f.
acceptor, ak-sept'-or, s., aceptante m.; (bill) aceptador m.
access, Ak'-ses, s., acceso m., entrada f. [tador m.

accession, ᴀk-se'-shon, s., (throne) advenimiento m.

accessory, ᴀk'-ses-so-ri, s., cómplice m. a., accesorio

accident, ᴀk'-si-dent, s., accidente m.

accidental*, ᴀk-si-den'-tl, a., accidental

acclaim, a-kleim', v., aclamar; aplaudir

acclimatize, a-klai'-met-ais, v., aclimatar

accomodate, a-kom'-o-deit, v., acomodar; (lodge) alojar; (money) prestar dinero

accomodation, a-kom-o-dei'-shon, s., (lodging) alojamiento m.; (agreement) conveniencia f.

accompaniment, a-kŏm'-pa-ni-ment, s., acompañamiento m.

accompanist, a-kŏm'-pa-nist, s., acompañante m.

accompany, a-kŏm'-pa-ni, v., acompañar

accomplice, a-kom'-plis, s., cómplice m.

accomplish, a-kom'-plish, v., efectuar

accomplishment, a-kom'-plish-ment, s., cumplimiento m.; (completion) terminación f. pl., (talents) talentas m. pl., prendas f. pl.

accord, a-ko*ard*', v., conceder; ajustar; conciliar; s., acuerdo m.

according to, a-ko*ard*'-ing tu, prep., según, conforme

accordingly, a-ko*ard*'-ing-li, adv., en conformidad

accordion, a-ko*ard*'-i-on, s., acordeón m.

accost, a-kost', v., acercarse; trabar conversación

account, a-kaunt', s., cuenta f., dar cuenta; (explain) explicar; **on no —**, de ninguna manera

accountable, a-kaunt'-a-bl, a., responsable

accountant, a-kaunt'-ant, s., contador m.; (chartered) contador colegiado m.

accredit, a-kred'-it, v., acreditar

accrue, a-kruu', v., crecer; resultar

accumulate, a-kiuu'-miu-leit, v., (gather) amontonar; (hoard) acumular

accumulator, a-kiuu'-miu-lei-ta, s., acumulador

accuracy, ᴀk'-iu-ra-si, s., exactitud f. [m.

accurate*, ᴀk'-iu-reit, a., exacto

accursed, a-kĕrst', a., maldito, maldecido

accusation, a-kius-ei'-shon, s., acusación f.

accuse, a-kiuus', v., acusar

accustom, *a*-kŭs'-tm, v., acostumbrar, soler

ace, eis, s., (cards) as m.

acetate, ᴀs'-si-teit, s., acetato m.

ache, eik, s., dolor m.; mal m. v., doler

achieve, *a*-chiiv', v., ejecutar; (ambition) lograr

achievement, *a*-chiiv'-ment, s., ejecución f.; (feat) hazaña f.

acid, ᴀs'-id, s. & a., ácido m.

acidity, *a*-sid'-i-ti, s., acidez f.

acknowledge, ak-nol'-ᴇcʜ, v., reconocer; confesar

acknowledgment, ak-nol'-ᴇcʜ-ment, s., reconocimiento m.; gratitud f.; confesión f.; (receipt) acuse de recibo m.

acme, ᴀk'-mi, s., colmo m.

acorn, ei'-koᴀrn, s., bellota f.

acoustics, *a*-kus-tiks, s., acústica f.

acquaint, *a*-kueint', v., familiarizar; informar; (socially) conocer; —**ance**, s., conocimiento m.; (person) conocido m.

acquiesce, ᴀ-kui-es', v., consentir, someterse; —**nce**, s., sumisión f.; consentimiento m.

acquire, *a*-kuair', v., adquirir; —**ment**, s., adquisición f.

acquisition, *a*-kui-si'-shon, s., adquisición f.

acquit, *a*-kuit', v., absolver; libertar

acquittal, *a*-kuit'-l, s., absolución f., descargo m.

acre, ei'-kr, s., acre m.

acrid, ᴀk'-rid, a., acre; mordaz

across, *a*-kros', adv., a través de. prep., a través de

act, ᴀkt, s., (deed) hecho m.; (of a play) acto m.; (law) ley f. v., operar; (in theatre) representar; —**or**, s., actor m.; —**ress**, actriz f.

action, ᴀk'-shon, s., acción f.; (law) proceso m.; (mil.) batalla f.

active*, ᴀk'-tiv, a., activo

actual*, ᴀk'-tiu-al, a., actual, efectivo

actuate, ᴀk'-tiu-eit, v., impulsar; excitar

acumen, *a*-kiuu'-men, s., penetración f.

acute*, *a*-kiuut', a., agudo; (senses) penetrante

acuteness, *a*-kiuut'nes, s., (mind) perspicacia f.; (sharpness) agudeza f.

adage, ᴀd'-eicʜ, s., adagio m.

adamant, Ad'-*a*-mant, a., inexorable

adapt, *a*-dApt', v., adaptar

adaptation, *a*-dAp-tei'-shon, s., adaptación f.

add, Ad, v., añadir; — **up,** sumar

adder, Ad'-*a*, s., (snake) víbora f.

addict, *a*-dikt', v., (oneself to) entregarse a

addicted, *a*-dikt'-id, a., entregado

addition, *a*-di'-shon, s., adición f.; **in —,** además

additional, *a*-di'-shon-l, a., adicional

addle, Ad'-l, a., (egg) huero; (fig.) inepto

address, *a*-dres', v., (letter, etc.) dirigir; (a meeting) hablar; (a crowd) arengar. s., (domicile) señas f. pl.; (speech) discurso m.; (to king, etc.) petición f.

addressee, A-dres'-ii, s., destinatario m.

adduce, *a*-diuus', v., aducir, alegar

adept, Ad'-ept, s., adepto m., a., hábil

adequacy, Ad'-i-kua-si, s., suficiencia f.

adequate*, Ad'-i-kuit, a., adecuado; proporcionado

adhere, Ad-jiir', v., adherir

adherence, Ad-jiir'-ens, s., adhesión f.

adherent, Ad-jiir'-ent, s., (partisan) partidario m. a., adherente

adhesive, *a*d-jii'-siv, s., adhesivo m. a., adhesivo

adjacent, *a*-cHei'-sent, a., contiguo

adjoin, *a*-cHóin', v., estar contiguo; (fields, etc.) colindar; **—ing,** a., contiguo; colindante

adjourn, *a*-cHérn', v., aplazar; suspender

adjournment, *a*-cHérn'-ment, s., suspensión f.

adjudge, *a*-cHócH', v., adjudicar; (prize) conceder

adjudication, A-cHiu-di-kei'-shon, s., adjudicación f.

adjunct, A'-cHóñ-kt, s. & a., accesorio m., adjunto m.

adjust, *a*-cHóst', v., arreglar; (mech.) ajustar

adjustment, *a*-cHóst'-ment, s., arreglo m.; (mech.) ajuste m.

adjutant, A'-cHu-tant, s., ayudante m.

administer, ad-min'-is-t*a*, v., administrar

admirable, Ad'-mi-r*a*-bl, a., admirable

admiral, Ad'-mi-r*a*l, s., almirante m.; **—ty,** s., ministerio de marina m.

admiration, ad-mi-rei'-shon, s., admiración f.

admire, ad-mair', v., admirar

admission, ad-mi'-shon, s., entrada f., acceso m.; (confession) admisión f.

admit, ad-mit', v., (enter) admitir; (acknowledge) reconocer; (confess) confesar

admittance, ad-mit'-ans, s., entrada f., admisión f.

admonish, ad-mon'-ish, v., amonestar, reprender

admonition, ad-mo-ni'-shon, s., amonestación f.

adolescence, ad-o-les'-ens, s., adolescencia f.; pubertad f.

adopt, a-dopt'. v., adoptar

adore, a-dór', v., adorar, idolatrar

adorn, a-doarn', v., adornar

adornment, a-doarn'-ment, s., adorno m.

adrift, a-drift', adv., (naut.) a la deriva, flotando

adroit, a-droit', a., diestro, hábil

adulation, ad-iu-lei'-shon, s., adulación f.

adult, a-dölt', s., adulto m. a., adulto

adulterate, a-döl'-te-reit, v., adulterar

adultery, a-döl'-te-ri, s., adulterio m.

advance, ad-vaans', v., (ahead) adelantar; (push forward) avanzar; (price) encarecer; (lend) anticipar. s., (progress) progreso m.; (money) anticipo m.; (price) alza f.; **in —,** (before) anticipadamente; (payment) por adelantado; **—ment,** s., adelantamiento m., progreso m.

advantage, ad-vaan'-tich, s., ventaja f.

advantageous*, ad-vaan-tei'-chos, a., ventajoso

advent, ad'-vent, s., venida f.; (eccl.) adviento m.

adventitious, ad-ven-tish'-os, a., adventicio

adventure, ad-ven'-tiur, s., aventura f.

adventurer, ad-ven'-tiur-a, s., aventurero m.

adventurous*, ad-ven'-tiur-os, a., aventurero; (bold) valeroso

adversary, ad'-ver-sa-ri, s., adversario m.

adverse*, ad'-vèrs, a., adverso; contrario

advertise, ad'-ver-tais, v., anunciar, avisar, publicar, notificar; **—er,** s., anunciante m.; avisador m.

advertisement, ad-vèr'-tis-ment, s., anuncio m., aviso m.

advertising, ad-ver-tais'-ing, s., publicidad f.

advice, ad-vais', s., (opinion offered) consejo m.; (commerce) aviso m.

advisability, ad-vais'-a-bil'-i-ti, s., prudencia f.; conveniencia f.

advisable, ad-vais'-a-bl, a., aconsejable, prudente

advise, ad-vais', v., aconsejar; avisar, notificar; ill —d, mal aconsejado; well —d, bien aconsejado

adviser, ad-vais'-a, s., consejero m.

advocate, ad-vo-kit', s., abogado m. v., abogar

aerated, ei'-e-rei-tid, — **water,** s., agua gaseosa f.

aerial, e-i'-ri-al, s., antena f. a., aéreo

aerodrome, e'-er-o-droum, s., aeródromo m.

aeroplane, e'-er-o-plein, s., avión m., aeroplano m.

afar (from), a-faar', adv., lejos

affable, Af'-a-bl, a., afable, amable, cortés

affably, Af'-a-bli, adv., afablemente

affair, a-fér', s., negocio m.; (matter) asunto m.

affect, a-fekt', v., (act upon) afectar; (pretend) fingir

affected*, a-fekt'-id, a., (moved) conmovido; (assuming) afectado

affecting, a-fekt'-ing, a., (pathetic) conmovedor

affection, a-fek'-shon, s., afección f.

affectionate*, a-fek'-shon-eit, a., afectuoso, cariñoso [ñoso

affianced, a-fai'-anst, a., desposado

affidavit, ʌ-fi-dei'-vit, s., atestación f.

affiliate, a-fil'-i-eit, v., afiliar

affinity, a-fin'-i-ti, s., afinidad f.

affirm, a-férm', v., afirmar

affirmation, a-fér-mei'-shon, s., afirmación f.

affirmative, a-férm'-at-iv, s., afirmativa f. a.,* afir- [mativo

affix, a-fiks', v., pegar; (not stick) fijar

afflict, a-flikt', v., afligir

affliction, a-flik'-shon, s., aflicción f.; desgracia f.; (by death) duelo m.

affluence, Af'-lu-ens, s., afluencia f.; opulencia f.

affluent, ʌf'-lu-ent, a., afluente m. a., opulento; copioso [pioso

afford, a-fórd', v., tener medios para

affray, a-frei', s., riña f., tumulto m.

affront, a-frönt', v., afrentar, s., afrenta f.

aflame, a-fleim', adv. & a., en llamas

afloat, a-flout', adv., & a., flotante, a flote

aforesaid, a-fór'-sed, a., susodicho
afraid, a-fred', **to be —** (of), v., tener miedo (de)
afresh, a-fresh', adv., de nuevo
aft, aaft, adv., (naut.) a popa, en popa
after, aaft'-a, adv., después; prep., después de; según
aftermath, aft'-er-maaz, s., (fig.) segunda cosecha f.
afternoon, aaft'-er-nuun, si, la tarde f.
afterthought, aaft'-er-zoat, s., reflexión tardía f.
afterwards, aaft'-er-uerds, adv., después
again, a-guein', adv., otra vez, de nuevo
against, a-gueinst', prep., contra
age, eich, s., edad f.; (period) siglo m.; (ancient)
     antigüedad f.; **to be of —,** ser mayor de edad
aged, ei'-CHed, a., viejo, anciano. s., viejo m.
agency, ei'-CHen-si, s., (fig.) mediación f.
agent, ei'-CHent, s., agente m.; comisionista m.
agglomerate, a-glom'-er-eit, v., aglomerar
aggravate, AG'-ra-veit, v., agravar
aggregate, AG'-ri-gueit, s., totalidad f. v., agregar
aggression, a-gre'-shon, s., agresión f.
aggressive*, a-gres'-iv, a., agresivo
aggrieve, a-griiv', v., apenar, afligir, vejar
aghast, a-gaast', a., estupefacto, horrorizado
agile, A'-CHil, a., ágil
agitate, A'-CHi-teit, v., (shake) agitar; (mental) pertur-
     bar; (stir up strife) alborotar
agitation, A-CHi-tei'-shon, s., agitación f.; pertur-
     bación f.
ago, a-gou', adv., hace, ha; **long —,** mucho
     tiempo ha; **how long —?** ¿cuánto tiempo ha?
agog, a-gog', adv. & a., ansiosamente, con curiosidad
agonize, AG'-o-nais, v., agonizar; torturar
agonizing*, AG'-o-nais-ing, a., atroz, angustioso
agony, AG'-o-ni, s., agonía f.; (mental) angustia f.
agree, a-grii', v., concordar; consentir; acceder;
     convenir en; **—able,** a., conveniente; agradable;
     —ment, s., acuerdo m., convenio m.; (contract)
     contrato m.
agricultural, a-gri-cöl'-tiu-ral, a., agrícola
agriculture, AG-ri-cöl-tiur, s., agricultura f.
aground, a-graund', adv., (naut.) encallado
argue, ei'-guiu, s., fiebre intermitente f.

ahead, *a*-jed', adv., delante; adelante

aid, eid, s., ayuda f., socorro m. v., ayudar, socorrer

ail, eil, v., estar enfermo; estar malo; —**ing**, a., enfermizo; —**ment**, s., dolencia f., indisposicion f.

aim, eim, v., (arms) apuntar; (aspire) aspirar a. s., (arms) puntería f.; (ambition) fin m.

aimless, eim'-les, a., sin objeto

air, ér, s., aire m. v., (clothes, etc.) airear; —**con-ditioning**, s., acondicionamiento de aire m.; —**craft**, s., avión m.; —**gun**, s., escopeta de aire comprimido f.; —**ily**, adv., ligeramente; —**port**, s., aeropuerto m.; —**ship**, s., dirigible m.; —**tight**, a., hermético; —**y**, a., aéreo; (manners) airoso

aisle, ail, s., ala f., nave lateral f.; pasillo

ajar, *a*-CHaar', a., entreabierto

akimbo, *a*-kim'-bou, adv., en jarras

akin, *a*-kin', a., emparentado; análogo

alabaster, Al'-*a*-baus-t*a*, s., alabastro m.

alacrity, *a*-lak'-ri-ti, s., viveza f.

alarm, *a*-laarm', v., alarmar. s., alarma f.; — **clock**, despertador m.; —**ing***, a., alarmante, inquie-

alas! *a*-lass', interj., ¡ay! [tante

albeit, Oal-bii'-it, conj., aunque, bien que

album, Al'-bom, s., álbum m.

alcohol, Al'-ko-jol, s., alcohol m.

alderman, Oal'-der-man, s., regidor m.

alert, *a*-lërt', a., alerto, activo; **on the —**, sobre aviso; —**ness**, s., viveza f., vigilancia f.

alias, ei'-li-as, adv., alias, por otro nombre

alibi, Al'-i-bai, s., coartada f.

alien, eil'-yen, s., extranjero m. a., ajeno   [quistar

alienate, ei'-li-en-eit, v., enajenar; (estrange) mal-

alight, *a*-lait', v., bajar; descender; apearse. a., encendido

alike, *a*-laik', adv., igualmente. a., semejante

alimony, Al'-im-o-ni, s., alimento m.

alive, *a*-laiv', a., vivo; activo

all, Oal, a., todo; todos. adv., enteramente, del todo — **along**, todo el tiempo; — **but**, casi; **not at —**, de nada; de ningún modo; — **right**, bien

allay, *a*-lei', v., aliviar, calmar

allege, *a*-leCH', v., alegar, sostener

allegiance, *a*-lii'-CHi-*a*ns, s., lealtad f., fidelidad f.

alleviate, *a*-li'-vi-eit, v., aliviar; calmar

alley, Al'-i, s., callejuela f., callejón m.

alliance, *a*-lai'-*a*ns, s., alianza f.; unión f.

allied, *a*-laid', a., aliado; confederado

allocate, Al'-lou-keit, v., asignar, distribuir

allot, *a*-lot', v., asignar; (distribute) repartir;
—**ment,** s., (issue) reparto m.; (portion) lote m.

allow, *a*-lau', v., permitir, admitir; rebajar

allowance, *a*-lau'-*a*ns, s., (monetary) pensión f.;
(food) ración f.; (rebate) descuento m.

alloy, *a*-loi', s., aleación f.; mezcla v.; alear

allude, *a*-liuud', v., aludir, referirse

allure, *a*-liur', v., atraer, fascinar, seducir

alluring, *a*-liur'-ing, a., atractivo, tentador, se-
allusion, *a*-liuu'-**sh**on, s., alusión f.   [ductivo
(food) ración f.; (rebate) descuento m.

ally, Al'-lai, s., aliado m. v., aliar, unir

almanac, Oal'-ma-nak, s., almanaque m.

Almighty, Oal-mai'-ti, s., El Omnipotente m. a.,
omnipotente

almond, aa'-mond, s., almendra f.

almost, Oal'-moust, adv., casi, cerca de

alms, aams, s., limosna f.; —**-house,** hospicio m.

aloft, *a*-loft', adv., arriba en alto

alone, *a*-loun', a., solo, solitario

along, *a*-long', adv., a lo largo; — **with,** prep., con

alongside, *a*-long'-**s**aid, adv., al lado; (a ship) al
costado

aloof, *a*-luuf', adv., lejos, lejos de; (reserved) apar-

aloud, *a*-laud', adv., alto, en alta voz   [tado

already, Oal-red'-i, adv., ya

also, Oal'-sou, adv., también

altar, Oal'-ta, s., altar m.

alter, Oal'-ta, v., alterar, cambiar, reformar

alteration, Oal-ter-ei'-shon, s., alteración f., cambio m., reforma f.

alternate, Oal-tĕr'-neit, a., alternativo

alternating, Oal-tĕr-nei'-ting, a., alternante

alternative, Oal-tĕr'-na-tiv, s., alternativa f. a.,*
alternativo

although, oal-Dou', conj., aunque, bien que

altitude, Al'-ti-tiuud, s., altitud f., altura f.

altogether, oal-tug-eD'-a, adv., en conjunto; completamente

alum, Al'-am, s., alumbre m.

aluminium, al-iu-min'-i-ŏm, s., aluminio m.

always, oal'-ues, adv., siempre

amass, a-mas', v., acumular

amateur, Am'-a-tiur, s., aficionado m.

amaze, a-meis', v., asombrar, pasmar

amazement, a-meis'-ment, s., asombro m., pasmo

amazing*, a-meis'-ing, a., asombroso, pasmoso [m.

ambassador, Am-bas'-a-dr, s., embajador m.

amber, Am'-br, s., ámbar m.

ambiguous*, am-big'-iu-os, a., ambiguo, equívoco

ambiguousness, Am-bi'-gui-os-nes, s., ambigüedad f.

ambition, Am-bi'-shon, s., ambición f.

ambitious*, vm-bi'-shos, a., ambicioso

ambulance, Am'-biu-lans, s., ambulancia f.

ambush, Am'-bush, s., emboscada f. v., asechar

ameliorate, a-mii'-lyor-eit, v., mejorar

amenable, a-mii'-na-bl, a., sujeto a

amend, a-mend', v., enmendar; reformarse

amendment, a-mend'-ment, s., enmienda f.

amends, a-mends', s., compensación f.; make —v., compensar

amethyst, Am'-i-zist, s., amatista f.

amiable, ei'-mi-a-bl, a., amable, afable

amicable, Am'-i-ka-bl, a., amigable, amistoso

amicably, Am'-i-ka-bli, adv., amigablemente

amid, amidst, a-mid', a-midst', prep., entre; en medio de; —ships, adv., en medio del buque

amiss, a-mis', adv., mal; fuera de lugar. a., malo; irregular

amity, Am'-i-ti, s., amistad f.; concordia f.

ammonia, a-mou'-ni-a, s., amoníaco m.

ammunition, a-miu-ni'-schon, s., munición f.

amnesty, Am'-nes-ti, s., amnistía f.

among, amongst, a-mŏng', a-mŏngst', prep., entre; en medio de; con; al

amorous*, Am'-or-os, a., enamorado

amount, a-maunt', s., importe m.; suma f. v., importar

ample, Am'-pl, a., amplio, abundante

amplifier, Am'-pli-fair, amplificador m.

amplify, Am'-pli-fai, v., ampliar

amputate, Am'-piu-teit, v., amputar

amuck, a-mok', adv., furiosamente

amuse, a-miuus', v., entretener, divertir

amusement, a-miuus'-ment, s., diversión f., entretenimiento m.

amusing*, a-miuus'-ing, a., divertido

an, an, art., un; uno; una (see **a**)

analogous*, a-nal'-og-os, a., análogo

analysis, a-nal'-i-sis, s., análisis f.

analyze, An'-a-lais, v., analizar

anarchy, An'-aar-ki, s., anarquismo m.

anathema, a-naz'-i-ma, s., anatema m.

ancestor, An'-ses-tr, s., antepasado m.

ancestral, an-ses'-tral, a., hereditario

ancestry, An'-ses-tri, s., linaje m.

anchor, Añ'-ker, s., ancla m. (in the plural, f.)

anchorage, Añ'-ker-eich, s., anclaje m.

anchovy, An-chou'-vi, s., anchoa f.

ancient*, ein'-shent, a., antiguo

ancillary, An'-sil-a-ri, a., auxiliar

and, And, conj., y; e

angel, ein'-chel, s., ángel m.

anger, An'-guer, s., ira f., cólera f. v., enfurecer, irritar; enfadar

angle, Añ'-gl, s., ángulo m.; (of a street) esquina f. v., (to fish) pescar con caña

angler, Añ'-gla, s., pescador de caña m.

angling, Añ'-gling, s., pesca con caña

angrily, Añ'-gri-li, adv., coléricamente

angry, Añ'-gri, a., enfadado; enojado

anguish, Añ'-guish, s., ansia f., angustia f.

animal, An'-i-mal, s., animal m. a., animal

animate, An'-i-meit, v., animar. a., animado

animated, An'-i-mei-tid, a., vivo

animation, An-i-mei'-shon, s., animación f.; viveza f.

animosity, An-i-mou'-si-ti, s., animosidad f.

aniseed, An'-i-siid, s., anís m.

ankle, Añ'-kl, s., tobillo m.

annals, An'-als, s., anales m.

annex, An'-neks, s., anexo m.

annihilate, a-nai'-jil-eit, v., aniquilar

annihilation, a-nai-jil-ei'-shon, s., aniquilación f.

anniversary, An-i-vers'-a-ri, s., aniversario m.

annotate, An'-nou-teit, v., anotar, apuntar

announce, a-nauns', v., anunciar, publicar

announcement, a-nauns'-ment, s., anuncio m.

annoy, a-noi', v., molestar, dar la lata m . . .

annoying, a-noi'-ing, a., molesto, fastidioso

annual, An'-iu-al, a.,* anual, s., anuario m.

annuity, a-niuu'-i-ti, s., anualidad f.; renta vitalicia f.

annul, a-nŏl', v., anular, cancelar

annulment, a-nŏl'-ment, s., anulación f.

anode, An'-oud, s., ánodo m.

anoint, a-noint', v., untar, ungir

anomalous*, a-nom'-a-los, a., anómalo

anon, a-non', adv., pronto; en seguida

anonymous*, a-non'-i-mos, a., anónimo

another, a-nŏD'-r, pron. & a., otro; diferente

answer, aan'-sr, s., respuesta f., contestación f.; solución f. v., responder; contestar

answerable, aan'-ser-a-bl, a., responsable

ant, Ant, s., hormiga f.

antagonist, An-tag'-o-nist, s., antagonista m.

antecedent, An-ti-sii'-dent, s. & a., antecedente m.

antechamber, An'-ti-cheim'-br, s., antecámara f.

antedate, An'-ti-deit, v., antedatar

antediluvian, An'-ti-di-luu'-vi-an, a., antediluviano

antelope, An'-ti-loup, s., antílope m.

anterior, an-ti'-ri-or, a., anterior, precedente

anteroom, An'-ti-ruum, s., antesala f.; vestíbulo m.

anthem, An'-zem, s., antífona f.; (national anthem) himno nacional m.

anthracite, An'-zra-sait, s., antracita f.

anthrax, An'-zraks, s., antrax m.

anticipate, An-tis'-i-peit, v., esperar, prever

anticipation, An-tis'-i-pei'-shon, s., anticipación f.; expectación f.

antics, ʌn′-tiks, s. pl., zapateta f., farsa f.

antidote, ʌn′-ti-dout, s., antídoto m.

anti-freeze, ʌn′-ti-friis, s., anticogelante m.

antipathy, ʌn-tip′-a-zi, s., antipatía f.

antiquary, ʌn′-ti-kua-ri, s., anticuario m.

antiquated, ʌn′-ti-kueit-id, a., anticuado

antique, ʌn-tiik′, s., antigüedad f. a., antiguo

antiseptic, ʌn-ti sep′ tik, s. & a., antiséptico m.

antler, ʌnt′-la, s., asta del venado f.; cuerno m.

anvil, ʌn′-v-il, s., yunque m.

anxiety, ʌñk-sai′-i-ti, s., ansiedad f., inquietud f.

anxious*, ʌñk′-shos, a., ansioso, inquieto

any, en′-i, a. & adv., cualquier, cualquiera, cualesquiera; alguno, algunos; alguna, algunas

anybody, en′-i-bo-di, pron., alguien, cualquiera

anyhow, en′-i-jau, adv., de cualquier manera

anything, en′-i-zing, pron., algo, cualquier cosa

anyway, en′-i-ouei, adv., de cualquier modo

anywhere, en′-i-uèr, adv., en cualquier parte; donde quiera

apart, a-paart′, adv., aparte, a un lado, separadamente

apartment, a-paart′-ment, s., (lodgings) cuarto m., habitación f.; (flat) piso m., apartamento m.

apathetic, ʌp-a-zet′-ik, a., apático

apathy, ʌp′-a-zi, s., apatía f.

ape, eip, v., imitar, s., mono m., mona f.

aperient, a-pí′-ri-ent, s., laxante m.

aperture, ʌp′-er-tiur, s., abertura f.

apex, ei′-peks, s., ápice m.   [uno

apiece, a-píis′, adv., por persona, por cabeza, cada

apologize, a-pol′-o-chais, v., excusarse, excusar

apology, a-pol′-o-chi, s., apología f., justificación f.   macéutico m.

apostle, a-pos′-l, s., apóstol m.

apothecary, a-poz′-i-ka-ri, s., boticario m., farmacéutico m.

appal, a-pool′, v., espantar, aterrar

appalling, a-pool′-ing, a., espantoso, aterrador

apparatus, ʌp-a-rei′-tos, s., aparato m., aparejo m.

apparel, a-pʌr′-el, s., vestido m.; traje m.; adorno m.

apparent*, a-pei′-rent, a., aparente, manifiesto, obvio

apparition, ᴀᴘ-*a*-ri'-shon, s., aparición f.

appeal, *a*-piil', s., súplica f.; (legal) apelación f. v., apelar; suplicar

appear, *a*-pir', v., aparecer; (in courts) comparecer

appearance, *a*-pir'-ans, s., apariencia f.; (in courts) comparecencia

appease, *a*-piis', v., calmar; apaciguar

appeasement, *a*-piis'-ment, s., apaciguamiento m.

appellant, *a*-pel'-ant, s., apelante m. a., apelante

append, *a*-pend', v., añadir, agregar; **—age,** s., dependencia f.; accesorio m.

appendix, *a*-pen'-diks, s., apéndice m.

appertain, ᴀᴘ-er-tein', v., pertenecer

appetite, ᴀᴘ'-*i*-tait, s., apetito m.; gana f.

appetizer, ᴀᴘ'-*i*-tais-a, s., aperitivo m.

appetizing, ᴀᴘ'-*i*-tais-ing, a., apetitoso, tentador

applaud, *a*-plo*a*d', v., aplaudir; alabar

applause, *a*-plo*a*s', s., aplauso m.; aprobación f.

apple, ᴀᴘ'-el, s., manzana f.; **—tree,** manzano m.

appliance, *a*-plai'-ans, s., utensilio m.; aparato m.

applicant, ᴀᴘ'-li-kant, s., candidato m.; pretendiente m.; (petitioner) suplicante m.

application, ᴀᴘ-li-kei'-shon, s., aplicación f.; uso m.

apply, *a*-plai', v., aplicar; (for employment, license, etc.) solicitar; **— to,** dirigirse a, recurrir a

appoint, *a*-point', v., nombrar; (time) señalar; **—ment,** s., (engagement) cita f.; (position) empleo m.; (official) nombramiento m.

apportion, *a*-pór'-shon, v., distribuir, repartir; **—ment,** s., repartimiento m.

apposite*, ᴀᴘ'-*o*-sit, a., adaptado; oportuno

apposition, ᴀᴘ-*o*-si'-shon, s., aposición f.

appraise, *a*-pres', v., valuar, tasar, estimar; **—ment,** s., valuación f., tasación f.

appraiser, *a*-pres'-a, s., avaluador m., tasador m.

appreciable, *a*-prii'-shi-a-bl, a., apreciable

appreciate, *a*-prii'-shi-eit, v., apreciar, valuar, tasar; (in value) subir en valor

appreciation, *a*-prii'-shi-ei'-shon, s., valuación f., tasa f., aprecio m.; (in value) alza f.

apprehend, ᴀᴘ'-ri-jend, v., aprehender, arrestar; (understand) comprender; (fear) temer

apprehension, ʌp-ri-jen′-shon, s., temor m.; comprensión f.; arresto m.

apprehensive*, ʌp-ri-jen′-siv, a., aprensivo

apprentice, a-pren′-tis, s., aprendiz m. v., poner en aprendizaje

apprise, a-prais′, v., informar, avisar

approach, a-proach′, s., acceso m.; entrada f. v., acercarse

approbation, ʌp-ro-bei′-shon, s., aprobación f.

approbative, ʌp′-ro-bat-iv, a., aprobativo

appropriate, a-prou′-pri-eit, v., apropiar; destinar. a.,* apropiado; conveniente

appropriateness, a-prou′-pri-eit′-nes, s., aptitud f.

approval, a-pruu′-val, s., aprobación f.

approve, a-pruu′-v, v., aprobar

approvingly, a-pruu′-ving-li, adv., con aprobación

approximate, a-prox′-i-meit, a., aproximado, v., aproximar, acercarse

appurtenance, a-pĕr′-ten-ans, s., pertenencia f.

apricot, ei′-pri-kot, s., albaricoque m.

April, ei′-pril, s., abril m.

apron, ei′-pron, s., delantal m.; (coarse) mandil m.

apse, apsis, ʌps, ʌp′-sis, s., ábside m.

apt*, ʌpt, a., apto; (inclined) propenso

aptitude, aptness, ʌp′-ti-tiuud, apt′-nes, s., aptitud f.; (inclination) tendencia f.

aqueduct, ʌk′-ui-dŏkt, s., acueducto m.

aqueous, ei′-kui-os, a., ácueo

aquiline, ʌk′-uil-in, a., aguileño

arable, ʌr′-a-bl, a., arable

arbitrary, aar′-bi-tra-ri, a., arbitrario

arbitrate, aar′-bi-treit, v., arbitrar

arbitration, aar′-bi-trei′-chon, s., arbitraje m.

arbitrator, aar′-bi-treit-a, s., árbitro m.

arbour, aar′-ba, s., emparrado m., glorieta f.

arc, aark, s., arco m.; —lamp, arco voltáico m.

arcade, aar′-keid, s., arcada f.

arch, aarch, s., arco m., bóveda f. v., arquear. a., principal

archbishop, aarch-bish′-op, s., arzobispo m.

archdeacon, aarch-dii′-kn, s., arcediano m.

archer, aarch′-a, s., arquero m.

architect, aar'-ki-tekt, s., arquitecto m.

archive, aar'-kaiv, s., archivo m.

archway, aarch'-uei, s., arcada f., bóveda f.

arctic, aark'-tik, a., ártico

ardent*, aar'-dent, a., ardiente

ardour, aar'-d_a_, s., ardor m., pasión f.

arduous*, aar'-diu-os, a., arduo

area, é'-ri-_a_, s., área f., superficie f.

arena, a-rii'-na, s., arena f.; (bull ring) redondel m.

argue, aar'-guiuu, v., discutir, disputar

argument, aar'-guiu-ment, s., argumento m.

aright, a-rait', adv., rectamente

arise, a-rais', v., elevarse, levantarse

aristocracy, Ar-is-tok'-ra-ci, s., aristocracia f.

aristocratic, Ar-is-tok-rat'-ik, a., aristocrático

arithmetic, a-riz'-met-ik, s., aritmética f.

ark, aark, s., arca f.

arm, aarm, s., brazo m.; (gun) arma f. v., armar, armarse

armament, aar'-m_a_-ment, s., armamento m., equipo m.

arm-chair, aarm'-chér, s., sillón m.　　　　　[m.

armful, aarm'-ful, s., brazada f.

armlet, aarm'-let, s., brazalete m.

armour, aar'-m_a_, s., armadura f., coraza.f

armourer, aar'-mor-_a_, s., armero m.

armoury, aar'-mor-i, s., armería f., arsenal m.; museo de armas m.

arm-pit, aarm'-pit, s., sobaco m.

arms, aarms, s., armas f.; (crest) cota de armas f.

army, aar'-mi, s., ejército m.

aromatic, Ar-o-mAt'-ik, a., aromático

around, a-raund', adv., alrededor. prep., cerca de

arouse, a-raus', v., despertar, excitar

arraign, a-rein', v., citar, acusar

arrange, a-reinch', v., arreglar, colocar; convenir

arrant*, Ar'-ant, a., insigne, consumado

array, a-rei', v., vestir, adornar. s., pompa f.; aparato m.

arrear, a-rir', s., atraso m. **—s** s.pl., atrasos m. pl.

arrest, a-rest', s., prision f., detención f.; (goods) arresto m. v., prender

arrival, a-rai'-val, s., llegada f., arribo m.

arrive, *a*-raiv', v., llegar
arrogant*, A'-*ro*-gant, a., arrogante
arrow, A'-rou, s., flecha f., saeta f.
arsenal, aar'-sen-al, s., arsenal m.
arson, aar'-son, s., incendio premeditado m.
art, aart, s., arte m.
artery, aar'-ter-i, s., arteria f.
artful*, aart'-ful, a., artificioso, astuto
artichoke, aar'-ti-chouk, s., alcachofa f.
article, aar'-ti-kl, s., (news) artículo m.; (commodity) objeto m.; (clause) estipulación f. v., contratar; poner en aprendizaje
articulate, aar-tik'-iu-leit, v., articular
artificial*, aar-ti-fish'-al, a., artificial
artillery, aar-til'-a-ri, s., artillería f.
artisan, aar-ti-saN', s., obrero m., artesano m.
artist, aar'-ist, s., artista m.
artless*, aart'-les, a., natural, cándido; sin arte
artlessness, aart'-les-nes, s., candidez f.
as, As, conj., como; tan; mientras; según; igualmente; pues que; — **for,** — **to,** en cuanto a; — **soon** —, tan pronto como; — **well,** también; — **yet,** hasta ahora
asbestos, as-bes'-tos, s., amianto m., asbesto m.
ascend, *a*-send', v., ascender, subir
ascendency, *a*-send'-en-si, s., ascendencia f., poder
ascent, *a*-sent', s., subida f., ascensión f.   [m.
ascertain, A-sa-tein', v., averiguar
ascribe, as-kraib', v., atribuir; asignar
ash, Ash, s., ceniza f.; (tree) fresno m.; —**tray,** cenicero m.
ashamed, *a*-sheimd', a., avergonzado
ashore, *a*-shór', adv., en tierra, a., (aground) varado
aside, *a*-said', adv., al lado; a un lado; aparte
ask, aask, v., preguntar; — **for,** pedir
askance, askew, aslant, *a*-skans', *a*-skiuu', *a*-slaant', adv., al sesgo, oblicuamente
asleep, *a*-sliip', a., dormido
asp, asp, s., (snake) áspid m.
asparagus, as-par'-a-gos, s., espárrago m.
aspect, As'-pekt, s., aspecto m.

aspen, Asp'-n, s., álamo temblón m.

asperse, As-pĕrs', v., calumniar

aspersion, As-pĕr'-shon, s., difamación f.

asphyxia, As-fik'-si-a, s., asfixia f.

aspirate, As'-pi-reit, v., aspirar. a., aspirado

aspire, as-pair', v., aspirar

ass, As, s., asno m., borrico m.

assail, a-seil', v., asaltar

assailant, a-sei-lant, s., agresor m.

assassinate, a-sas'-si-neit, v., asesinar

assault, a-soalt', s., asalto m. v., asaltar, acometer

assay, a-sei', s., prueba f.; aquilatamiento m. v., aquilatar

assemble, a-sem'-bl, v., congregar, reunir

assembly, a-sem'-bli, s., asamblea f.; congreso m.

assent, a-sent', v., asentir. s., asentimiento m.

assert, a-sĕrt', v., sostener, asegurar

assertion, a-sĕr'-shon, s., aserción f.

assess, a-ses', v., (taxes) señalar; (damages) fijar; **—ment,** s., amillaramiento m.; valoración f.

assets, A'-sets, s.pl., haber m., capital m.; activo m.

assiduous, a-sid'-iu-os, a., asiduo

assign, a-sain', v., asignar; (law) transferir; **—ee,** s., apoderado m.; **—ment,** s., asignación f., cesión f.

assist, a-sist', v, ayudar; (charity) socorrer; (to be present) asistir; **—ant,** s., ayudante m.; auxiliar m.; asistente m.

assizes, a-sais', s.pl. tribunal de justicia m.

associate, a-sou'-shi-eit, s., (partner) socio m. (companion) asociado m. v., asociar, asociarse

assort, a-soart', v., surtir, clasificar, ordenar; **—ment,** s., surtido variado m.; clasificación f.

assuage, a-sueich', v., mitigar, apaciguar

assume, a-siuum', v., presumir, usurpar

assuming, a-siuum'-ing, a., presuntuoso

assumption, a-sŏmp'-shon, s., suposición f.; postulado m.

assurance, a-shúr'-ans, s., seguridad f.; (insurance) seguro m.

assure, a-shúr', v., afirmar; (insure) asegurar

asterisk, as'-te-risk, s., asterisco m.

astern, a-stẽrn', adv., en popa

asthma, az'-ma, s., asma f.

astir, a-stẽr', a., activo, en movimiento

astonish, as-ton'-ish, v., asombrar, pasmar

astound, as-taund', v., aturdir, aterrar

astray, a-strei', adv., extraviado

astride, a-straid', adv., a horcajadas

astute, as-tiut', a., astuto, sagaz

astuteness, as-tiut'-ness, s., astucia f.

asunder, a-sön'-da, adv., separadamente, en dos

asylum, a-sai'-lom s., (mental) asilo m.; (alms-house) hospicio m.

at, At, prep., a, en, sobre; — **all events,** en todo caso; — **home,** en casa; — **once,** enseguida; — **times,** de vez en cuando

athlete, Az'-liit, s., atleta m. [de

athwart, a-zuoart', adv., al través, prep., a través

atom, At'-om, s., átomo m.; —**ic,** a., atómico; —**ic energy,** s., energía atómica f.

atone, a-toun', v., expiar, reparar

atonement, a-toun'-ment, s., expiación f.

atrocious', a-trou'-shos, a., atroz; espantoso

atrophy, At'-ro-fi, s., atrofia f. v., atrofiar

attach, a-tAch, v., (tie) atar; (stick) pegar; (annex) juntar; (law) secuestrar

attachment, a-tach'-ment, s., adherencia f.; (liking) afecto m.; (law) secuestro m.

attack, a-tAk', s., ataque m., agresión f. v., atacar

attain, a-tein', v., lograr, alcanzar

attainment, a-tein'-ment, s., logro m.; —**s,** (ac-quirements) conocimientos m. pl., alcances m. pl.

attempt, a-tempt', v., intentar, ensayar; (risk) em-prender; (attack) atentar. s., empresa f.; (attack) atentado m.

attend, a-tend', v., asistir a; — **to,** atender; (serve) servir; (nurse) cuidar

attendance, a-tend'-ans, s., servicio m.

attendant, a-tend'-ant, s., sirviente m.; criado m.; compañero m.

attention, a-ten'-shon, s., atención f.

attest, a-test', v., atestiguar, atestar, certificar

attic, At-'ik, s., desván m., guardilla f.

attire, a-tair', s., atavío m. v., vestir, adornar

attitude, A'-ti-tiuud, s., actitud f.; postura f.

attorney, a-tĕr'-ni, s., procurador m.; (commercial) apoderado m.

attract, a-trakt', v., atraer

attraction, a-trak'-shon, s., atracción f.

attractive*, a-trakt'-iv, a., atractivo

attribute, a-trib'-iut, v., atribuir, imputar

attribute, At'-ri-biut, s., atributo m.; símbolo m.

attune, a-tiuun', v., acordar, armonizar

auburn, oa'-ban, a., castaño rojizo

auction, oak'-shon, s., subasta f.; almoneda f.

auctioneer, oak'-shon-ir, s., subastador m.

audacious*, oa-dei'-shos, a., audaz

audacity, oa-das'-i-ti, s., audacia f.

audible, oa'-di-bl, a., perceptible

audience, oa'-di-ens, s., auditorio m.

audit, oa'-dit, v., intervenir, verificar una cuenta

auditor, oa'-dit-or, s., revisor de cuentas m.

augment, oag'-ment, s., aumento m.

augur, oa'-ga, s., presagio m. v., augurar, pronosticar

August, oa'-gost, s., agosto m.

august, oa-göst', a., augusto, majestuoso

aunt, aant, s., tía f.

auspicious*, oas-pi'-shos, a., propicio, favorable

austere*, oas-tir', a., austero

authentic, oa-zen'-tik, a., auténtico

author, oa'-za, s., autor m., escritor m.

authoritative*, oa-zor'-i-ta-tiv, a., autoritivo

authority, oa-zor'-i-ti, s., autoridad f.

authorize, oa'-zor-ais, v., autorizar

automatic, oa-to-mat'-ik, a., automático

autumn, oa'-tom, s., otoño m.

auxiliary, oag-zil'-i-a-ri, a., auxiliar

avail, a-veil', s., provecho m. ventaja f., v., ser útil; — **oneself of,** valerse de

available, a-veil'-a-bl, a., disponible

avalanche, av'-a-laanch, s., avalancha f., alud f.

avarice, av'-a-ris, s., avaricia f.

avaricious*, av-a-ri'-shos, a., avaro

avenge, a-vench', v., vengar

avenue, AV′-e-niuu, s., avenida f., alameda f.

average, AV′-a-richly, s., término medio m. a., medio

averse, a-vèrs′, a., adverso

aversely, a-vĕrs′-li, adv., con repugnancia

aversion, a-vĕr′-shon, s., aversión f.

avert, a-vèrt′, v., prevenir

aviary, ei′-vi-a-ri, s., pajarera f.

aviation, ei-vi-ei′-shon, s., aviación f.

avidity, a-vid′-i-ti, s., avidez f., voracidad f.

avoid, a-void′, v., evitar

avow, a-vau′, v., confesar, declarar

avowal, a-vau′-al, s., confesión f., declaración f.

await, a-ueit′, v., aguardar, esperar

awake, awaken, a-ueik′, a-ueik′-n, v., despertarse; (to call) despertar. a., despierto

awakening, a-ueik′-ning, s., despertar m.

award, a-ouoard′, s., sentencia f. v., conceder

aware, a-uér′, a., enterado, cauto

away, a-uei′, adv., (absent) ausente; **far—,** lejos

awe, oa, s., temor m.; (terror) pavor m. v., atemorizar; **—struck,** a., aterrado

awful*, oa′-ful, a., horroroso, terrible

awhile, a-uail′, adv., poco tiempo; un rato

awkward*, oak′-uerd, a., (clumsy) desmañado; (inconvenient, embarrassing) embarazoso; **—ness,** s., (clumsiness) torpeza f.

awl, oal, s., punzón m.

awning, oan′-ing, s., toldo m.

awry, oa-rai′, adv., de través. a., sesgado; oblicuo

axe, Aks, s., hacha f.

axle, Aks′-l, s., eje m.

azure, A′-sher, s., azul celeste m.

babble, BAB′-l, s., balbuceo m. v., balbucear

babe, baby, beib, bei′-bi, s., bebé m., nene m.

bacchanal, BAK′-a-nal, s., bacanal f. [infante m.

bachelor, BACH′-el-or, s., soltero m.; (degree) bachiller m.

back, BAK, s., espalda f.; (animal) dorso m. v., (support) apoyar; (bet) apostar. adv., (behind) atrás. interj., ¡atrás! **—bone,** s., espina dorsal f.;

— **door**, puerta trasera f.; —**ground**, fondo m.; —**ing**, apoyo m.; endoso m.; — **seat**, asiento de detrás m.; —**slide**, v., reincidir; —**ward**, adv., atrás. a., lento; atrasado; —**wards**, adv., atrás; —**water**, s., remanso m.

backer, bak'-a, s., partidario m.; (sport) apostador m.

bacon, bei'-kn, s., tocino m. [m.

bad*, bad, a., malo; (health) enfermo

badge, badch, s., divisa f., símbolo m.

badger, badch'-a, s., tejón m. v., molestar

badness, bad'-nes, s., maldad f.

baffle, baf'-l, v., frustrar, dejar perplejo

bag, bag, s., saco m.; bolsa f., v., ensacar

baggage, bag'-ich, s., equipaje m.

bagpipe, bag'-paip, s., gaita f.

bail, beil, s., caución f., fianza f. v., caucionar

bailer, beil'-a, s., fiador m.

bailiff, bei'-lif, s., alguacil m.

bait, beit, s., (lure) anzuelo m. v., azuzar; (molest) molestar

baize, beis, s., bayeta f.,

bake, beik, v., cocer; (in oven) cocer en horno

baker, beik'-a, s., panadero m.

bakery, beik'-er-i, s., panadería f.

balance, bal'-ans, s., (poise) balance m.; (accounts) saldo m.; (scale) balanza f. v., (poise) balancear; (accounts) saldar

balcony, bal'-ko-ni, s., balcón m.

bald, boald, a., calvo; —**ness**, s., calvicie f.

bale, beil, s., bala f.

baleful*, beil'-ful, a., triste, funesto

balk, baulk, boak, v., frustrar, fracasar

ball, boal, s., bola f., pelota f.; (dance) baile m.; —**point** (pen), s., bolígrafo m.

ballast, bal'-ast, s., lastre m.

ballet, bal'-ei, s., baile m.; ballet m.

balloon, ba-luun', s., balón m.; (toy) globo m.; globo dirigible m.

ballot, bal'-ot, s., votación f. v., votar

balm, baam, s., bálsamo m. v., embalsamar

balsam, boal'-sam, s., bálsamo m.

bamboo, bam-buu', s., bambú m.

ban, bᴀn, v., proscribir, maldecir. s., bando m.; (excommunication) pregón m.

banana, ba-naa′-na, s., plátano m.

band, bᴀnd, s., (brass) banda f.; (string) orquesta f.; (ligature) venda f.; (company) bandería f. v., vendar

bandage, bᴀn′dich, s., vendaje m.

band-master, bᴀnd′-maas-tr, s., director de orquesta m.

bandy (legged), bᴀn′-di (legd), a., estevado

bane, bein. s., veneno m.

baneful*, bein′-ful, a., venenoso, funesto

bang, bᴀñg, s., ruido m., detonación f. v., (knock) golpear; (door) cerrar la puerta con estrépito

banish, bᴀn′-ish, v., desterrar

banister, bᴀn′-is-ta-s., baranda f., barandilla f.

bank, bᴀñk, s., banco m.; (river) orilla f. v., (money, etc.) poner dinero en un banco; **—book,** s., libreta de banco f.; **—er,** banquero m.; **—holiday,** día feriado m.; **— note,** billete de banco m.; **—rupt,** fallido m. a., insolvente, quebrazo; **—ruptcy,** s., bancarrota f., quiebra f.

banner, bᴀn′-a, s., insignia f., bandera f.

banquet, bᴀñ′-kuet, s., banquete m. v., banquetear

banter, bᴀn′-ta, s., zumba f., burla f. v., burlarse

baptism, bᴀp′-tism, s., bautismo m.

bar, baar, s., bar m.; (metal) barra f.; (courts) tribunal m. v., atrancar; (impede) impedir; **—maid,** s., camarera de bar f.

barb, baarb, s., (implement) púa f.

barbarian, baar-be′-ri-an, s., bárbaro m. a., bárbaro

barbarity, baar-bᴀr′-i-ti, s., barbaridad f.

barbed, baarbd, a., barbado

barber, baar′-ba, s., barbero m.

bard, baard, s., (implement) poeta m.

bare, bér, v., desnudar. a., desnudo; **—faced,** descarado; **—footed,** descalzo; **—headed,** descubierto; **—ness,** s., desnudez f.; pobreza f.

barely, bér′-li, adv., apenas, escasamente

bargain, baar′-guin, s., ocasión f., ganga f. v., regatear; **—ing,** s., regateo m.

barge, baarch, s., bote m.

bark, baark, s., (dog) ladrido m.; (tree) corteza f.
v., ladrar; (tree) descortezar

barley, baar'-li, s., cebada f.

barn, baarn, s., granero m.

barometer, ba-rom'-it-a, s., barómetro m.

barracks, bar'-aks, s., cuartel m.

barrel, bar'-el, s., barril m.; (gun) cañón de escopeta m.

barren, bar'-en, a., estéril, infructuoso

barrenness, bar'-en-nes, s., esterilidad f.

barrier, bar'-i-a, s., barrera f.

barring, baar'-ing, prep., salvo, excepto

barrister, bar'-is-ta, s., abogado m.

barrow, bar'-ou, s., carretón m., carretilla f.

barter, baar'-ta, v., trocar. s., tráfico m., cambio m.

base, beis, v., basar, fundar. s., base f. a., *(vile) vil
(metal, etc.) bajo

baseless, beis'-les, a., infundado

basement, beis'-ment, s., sótano m.

baseness, beis'-nes, s., bajeza f., infamia f.

bashful*, bash'-ful, a., tímido, modesto; **—ness,**
s., timidez f., modestia f.

basin, bei'-sn, s., (ablution) bacía f.; (dish) tazón m.

basis, bei'-sis, s., base f

bask, baask, v., ponerse al sol

basket, baas'-kit, s., cesta f., canasta f.

basketful, baas-kit-ful, s., cesta llena f,

bass, beis, s., (music) bajo, profundo m.

bassoon, ba-suun', s., bajón m.

bastard, bas'-tard, s., bastardo m. a., bastardo

baste, beist, v., pringar

bat, bat, s., (mammal) murciélago m.; (games)
pala f.

batch, bach, s., (bakery) hornada f.; (things) cantidad f.

bath, baaz, s., baño m.; **—chair,** silla de ruedas f.;
—room, sala de baño f.; **shower—,** ducha f.

bathe, beiD, v., bañar, bañarse

bather, beiD'-a, s., bañero m.

batter, bat'-a, v., batido m. v., apalear

battery, bat'-a-ri, s., (car) batería f.

battle, bat'-l, s., batalla f. v., batallar

battleship, BAT´-l-ship, s., buque de guerra m., acorazado m.

bauble, boa´-bl, s., baratija f., chuchería f.

bawd, boad, s., alcahuete m., alcahueta f.

bawdy, boa´-di, a., impúdico, obsceno, indecente

bawl, boal, v., gritar

bay, bei, s., (geographical) bahía f.; (tree, leaf) laurel m. a., (colour) bayo. v., (dog, etc.) aullar

b'e, bi, v., ser; estar

beach, biich, s., playa f.

beacon, bii´-kon, s., fanal m.; (naut.) boya f.

bead, biid, s., (adornment) cuenta f.; (drop) gota f.

beadle, bii´-dl, s., bedel m., macero m.

beagle, bii´-gl, s., (hound) sabueso m.

beak, biik, s., pico m., punta f.

beam, biim, s., (wood) viga f.; (light) rayo m.

beaming, biim´-ing, a., radiante

bean, biin, s., judía f,. haba f., alubia f.

bear, bér, s., oso m.; (Stock-Exchange) bajista m. v., (suffer) soportar; (burden) cargar; (produce) producir; (birth) dar a luz

bearable, bér´-a-bl, a., soportable

beard, biird, s., barba f.

bearded, bird´-id, a., barbudo

beardless, bird´-les, a., imberbe

bearer, bér´-a, s., portador m.; (mech.) soporte m.

beast, biist, s., bestia f.; **wild —,** fiera f.

beastly, biist´-li, a.,* bestial; repugnante

beat, biit, v., (thrash) batir, golpear; (drum) tocar; (pulsate) palpitar; (vanquish) vencer; (time) marcar el compás. s., (stroke) golpe m.; (pulse, etc.) pulsación f.; (police) ronda f.

beating, biit´-ing, s., pulsación f.; (thrashing) paliza f.

beautiful*, biuu´-ti-ful, a., hermoso, bello

beautify, biuu´-ti-fai, v., hermosear

beauty, biuu´-ti, s., hermosura f.; **— spot,** lunar m.

beaver, bii´-va, s., castor m.

becalm, bi-kaam´, v., calmar; (naut.) encalmar

because, bi-koas´, conj., porque; **— of,** a causa de

beckon, bek´-on, v., llamar por señas

become, bi-kŏm´, v., hacerse ; ponerse ; llegar a ser ; convenir a
becoming, bi-kŏm´-ing, a., decoroso ; conveniente
bed, bed, s., cama f., lecho m. ; **—ding,** s., ropa de cama f. ; **—ridden,** a., postrado en cama ; **—room,** s., alcoba f.
bedeck, bi-dek´, v., adornar
bee, bii, s., abeja f. ; **—hive,** s., colmena f.
beech, biich, s., haya f.
beef, biif, s., carne de vaca f.
beer, bir, s., cerveza f.
beet, biit, s., acelga f. **-root,** remolacha f.
beetle, bii´-tl, s., escarabajo m.
befall, bi-fóal´, v., suceder, acontecer
befitting, bi-fit´-ing, a., conveniente, propio
before, bi-fór´, antes ; ya. prep., delante de ; enfrente de ; ante ; **—hand,** adv., de antemano
befriend, bi-frend´, v., amparar, patrocinar
beg, beg, v., (alms) mendigar ; (request) rogar ; (implore) implorar
beget, bi-guet´, v., engendrar
beggar, beg´-a, s., mendigo m.
beggarly, beg´-ar-li, adv., pobremente. a., pobre
begging, be´-guing, s., mendiguez f.
begin, bi-guin´, v., empezar, comenzar
beginner, bi- guin´-a, s., novato m., principiante m.
beginning, bi-guin-ing, s., principio m., origen m., comienzo m.
begone! bi-goon´, interj., ¡fuera! ¡véte!
begrime, bi-graim´, v., enlodar
begrudge, bi-grŏCH´, v., envidiar
beguile, bi-gail´, v., engañar ; seducir
behalf, bi-jaaf´, on **- of,** por ; en nombre de ; en favor de
behave, bi-jeiv´, v., conducirse, comportarse bien
behaviour, bi-jeiv´-ia, s., conducta f., proceder m.
behead, bi-jed´, v., decapitar
behest, bi-jest´, s., mandato m., orden m.
behind, bi-jaind´, s., posterior m. adv., atrás ; por detrás. prep., detrás
behindhand, bi-jaind´-jand, adv., con atraso. a., atrasado

behold, bi-jould', v., mirar, observar. interj., ¡he aquí! ¡mirad!

beholden, bi-joold'-n, a., obligado, deudor

being, bii'-ing, s., existencia f.; (human) ser m., ente m.

belabour, bi-lei'-ba, v., apalear

belated, bi-lei'-tid, a., atrasado; tardío

belch, belch, v., (vulgar) eructar

belfry, bel'-fri, s., campanario m.

belie, bi-lai', v., desmentir, contradecir

belief, bi-liif', s., creencia f.; opinión f.

believable, bi-liiv'-a-bl, a., creíble

believe, bi-liiv', v., creer

believer, bi-liiv'-a, s., creyente m., fiel m.

bell, bel, s., campana f.; (small size) campanilla f.; (sleigh) cascabel m.; (door, etc.) timbre m.

belligerent, bel-li'-che-rent, a., beligerante m.

bellow, bel'-ou, v., vociferar; (bull, etc.) mugir

bellows, bel'-ous, s., fuelle m.

bellringer, bel-ring'-a, s., campanero m.

belly, bel'-i, s., vientre m.; panza f.

belong, bi-lŏng', v., pertenecer, atañer

belongings, bi-lŏng'-ings, s. pl., posesiones f. pl.; bienes m. pl.

beloved, bi-lŏv'-id, a., querido, amado

below, bi-lou', adv., abajo; debajo. prep., bajo

belt, belt, v., ceñir, s., cinturón m.; (silk, etc.) faja f.

bemoan, bi-moun', v., lamentar, deplorar

bench, bench, s., banco m., tribunal de justicia m.

bend, bend, v., encorvar, plegar, curvar. s., curva f.

bending, bend'-ing, s., recodo m. a., encorvado

beneath, bi-niiz', adv. & prep., debajo; (unworthy) indigno de

benediction, ben-e-dik'-shon, s., bendición f.

benefactor, ben-i-fak'-ta, s., bienhechor m.

beneficial*, ben-i-fi'-shal, a., beneficioso, provechoso

beneficiary, ben-i-fi'-sha-ri, s., beneficiario m.

benefit, ben'-i-fit, v., beneficiar, aprovechar. s., beneficio m.; provecho m.

benevolence, bi-nev'-o-lens, s., benevolencia f.

benevolent*, bi-nev'-o-lent, a., benévolo

benighted, bi-nait′-id, a., anochecido

benign*, bi-nain′, a., benigno

bent, bent, a., torcido. s., (fig.) inclinación f.

benumb, bi-nŏm′, v., entorpecer entumecer

benzine, ben′-siin, s., bencina f.

bequeath, bi-kuiiz′, v., legar

bequest, bi-kuest′, s., legado m.

bereave, bi-riiv′, v., despojar; (death) desolar; privar; **—ment,** s., aflicción f.; (death) duelo m.

berry, be′-ri, s., baya f.; (coffee) grano m.

berth, berz, s., (dock) anclaje m.; (on a train or ship, etc.) camarote m.; (employment) emple om. v., amarrar

beseech, bi-siich′, v., suplicar, implorar

beset, bi-set′, v., importunar, perseguir

beside, bi-said′, prep., al lado de

besides, bi-saids′, adv., además. prep., además de

besiege, bi-siich′, v., (mil.) sitiar; (fig.) acosar

besmear, bi-smir′, v., ensuciar

besotted*, bi-sot′-id, a., tonto

bespangle, bi-spaÑ′-gl, v., adornar con lentejuelas

bespatter, bi-spat′-a, v., salpicar

besprinkle, bi-spriñ′-kl, v., rociar, regar

best, best, adv., más bien. a., mejor. s., lo mejor n.

bestial*, bes′-ti-al, a., bestial, brutal

bestir (oneself), bi-stĕr′ (uŏn-self′), v., moverse

bestow, bi-stou′, v., dar, conferir

bestowal, bi-stou′-al, s., donación f., presente m.

bestrew, bi-struu′, v., rociar, esparcir

bet, bet, v., apostar. s., apuesta f.; **—ter** s., apostador m.; **—ting,** s., apuesta f.

betide, bi-taid′, v., suceder, acontecer

betimes, bi-taims′, adv., con tiempo

betoken, bi-tou′-kn, v., anunciar, indicar

betray, bi-trei′, v., (treason) traicionar; (seduce) vender; (secret) revelar; **—al,** s., traición f.

betroth, bi-trouD′, v., desposar; **—al,** s., esponsales m. pl.

better, bet′-a, s., superior f.; (gambler) apostador m. a., mejor. adv., más, mejor. v., mejorar; **—ment,** s., (physically) mejora f.; (materially) mejoramiento m.

between, betwixt, bi-tuiin', bi-tuikst', adv., en medio. prep., entre

bevel, bev'-l, v., sesgar. s., bisel m. a., sesgo

beverage, bev'-er-ich, s., bebida f., brebaje m.

bevy, bev'-i, s., bandada f.

bewail, bi-ueíl', v., llorar; lamentar

beware, bi-uér', v., guardarse de

bewilder, bi-uil'-da, v., descaminar, aturdir

bewilderment, bi-uil'-der-ment, s., aturdimiento m.

bewitch, bi-uich', v., embrujar; fascinar

beyond, bi-iond', adv., lejos. prep., tras; más allá; fuera de

bias, bai'-as, v., influir. s., prejuico m.

Bible, bai'-bl, s., Biblia f.

bibulous, bib'-iu-los, a., poroso

bicker, bik'-a, v., reñir, disputar

bickering, bik'-er-ing, s., disputa f., riña f.

bicycle, bai'-si-kl, s., bicicleta f.

bid, bid, s., postura f. v., licitar, ofrecer; **to — good-bye,** v., despedirse

bidder, bid-a, s., postor m., pujador m.

bidding, bid'-ing, s., postura f., subasta f.

bide, baid, v., soportar

bier, bir, s., féretro m.

big, big, a., grande, vasto

bigot, big'-ot, s., fanático m.

bigoted*, big'-ot-id, a., fanático

bile, bail, s., bilis f.

bilious, bil'-i-os, a., bilioso

bill, bil, s., cuenta f.; (of exchange) letra de cambio f.; (poster) cartel m.; (parliamentary) proyecto de ley m.; (bird) pico m.; **— of fare,** lista de platos f.; **— of lading,** conocimiento de embarque m.

billet, bil'-et, s., (mil.) boleta f. v., alojar

billiards, bil'-iards, s. pl., billar m.

billion, bil'-yon, s., billón m.

bimonthly, bai-mönz'-li, a., bimestral

bin, bin, s., hucha f.; (wine) portabotellas m.; (refuse) cubo de la basura m.

bind, baind, v., atar; (-up) ligar; (books) encuadernar; **— over,** obligar a comparecer

binding, baind'-ing, s., (of books) encuadernación f. a., obligatorio

binocular(s), bai-nok'-iu-la(s), s. binóculo m., s. pl., gemelos m. pl.

biography, bai-og'-ra-fi, s., biografía f.

biology, bai-ol'-o-сні, s., biología f.

biped, bai'-ped, s., bípedo m.

birch, bĕrch, s., (tree) abedul m.; (punitive) férula f.

bird, bĕrd, s., ave m.; pájaro m.

bird's-eye view, bĕrds'-ai-viuu, adv., a vista de pájaro

birth, bĕrz, s., nacimiento m.

birthday, bĕrz'-dei, s., cumpleaños m.

birthplace, bĕrz'-pleis, s., suelo natal m.

birthrate, bĕrz'-reit, s., natalidad f.

biscuit, bis'-kit, s., bizcocho m.

bisect, bai-sekt', v., bisecar

bishop, bish'-op, s., obispo m.

bit, bit, s., pedazo m.; (horse) bocado del freno m.

bitch, bich, s., perra f.

bite, bait, v., morder. s., mordedura f.; (insect) picadura f.

biting*, bai'-ting, a., (fig.) cáustico

bitter*, bit'-a, a., amargo; —**ness,** s., amargura f.

black, blak, a., color negro m. a., **negro;** oscuro. v., ennegrecer; (shoes) embetunar

blackbeetle, blak-bii'-tl, s., cucaracha f.

blackberry, blak'-be-ri, s., zarzamora f.

blackbird, blak'-bĕrd, s., mirlo m.

blackcurrant, blak'-kör-rent, s., grosella negra f.

blacken, blak'-en, v., ennegrecer

blackguard, blá'-guard, s., pillo m., pícaro m.

blacking, blak'-ing, s., betún m.

blacklead, blak'-led, s., grafito m.

blackleg, blak'-leg, s., petardista m.

blackmail, blak'-meil, s., chantage m. v., sacar dinero con amenazas

blacksmith, blak'-smiz, s., herrero m., forjador m.

blackthorn, blak'-zoarn, s., endrino m.

bladder, blád'-a, s., vejiga f.

blade, bleid, s., (cutting part) hoja f.; (grass) brizna f.; (oar) pala de remo f.

blame, bleim, v., reprobar, censurar, s., censura f., culpa f.; **—less***, a., irreprochable

blanch, blaanch, v., blanquear

bland, bland, a., suave, blando

blandishment, blan'-dish-ment, s., caricia f.

blank, blañk, s., blanco m.; (lottery) billete en blanco m. a.; (mental) desconcertado; (vacant) blanco

blanket, blañ'-ket, s., manta f.

blare, blér, v., trompetear

blaspheme, blas-fiim', v., blasfemar

blasphemy, blas'-fi-mi, s., blasfemia f.

blast, blaast, v., (explode) minar; (blight) marchitar. s., (gust) ráfaga f.; (trumpet) llamada f.

blatant, blei'-tant, a., ruidoso

blaze, bleis, v., flamear. s., (flame) llama f.; (conflagration) hoguera f.; **—of light,** luz brillante f.

bleach, bliich, v., blanquear; s., cloruro de cal

bleak*, bliik, a., (cold) frío; (desolate) desierto

bleat, bliit, v., balar, s., balido m.

bleed, bliid, v., sangrar

bleeding, bliid'-ing, s., sangría f.

blemish, blem'-ish, s., imperfección f.; (character) deshonra f. v., infamar

blend, blend, v., mezclar. s., mezcla f.

bless, bles, v., bendecir; **—ed,** a., bendito

blight, blait, v., (disease) tizón m.

blind, blaind, a., (sight) ciego. v., cegar; **—fold,** vendar los ojos; **—man,** s., ciego m.; **—ness,** ceguera f.

blind, blaind, s., (window) persiana f.; (venetian) celosía f.

blink, bliñk, v., pestañear; **—er,** s., (horse) anteojera

bliss, blis, s., felicidad f., gloria f. [f.

blissful*, blis'-ful, a., bienaventurado, dichoso

blister, blis'-ta, s., ampolla f.

blithe*, blaiD, a., alegre, contento

blizzard, blis'-ard, s., ventisca f.

bloat, blout, v., hinchar, hincharse

bloater, blout'-a, s., arenque ahumado m.

block, blok, v., bloquear. s., bloque m.; (traffic) embotellamiento m. v., embotellar, bloquear

blockade, blok'-eid, s., bloqueo m. v., bloquear

blood, blŏd, s., sangre f.
blood-hound, blŏd'-jaund, s., sabueso m.
bloodshed, blŏd'-shed, s., matanza f.
bloodthirsty, blŏd'-zẽrs-ti. a., sanguinario
bloody, blŏd-i, a., sangriento
bloom, bluum, s., flor f. v., florecer
blossom, blos'-om, s., capullo m. v., florecer
blot, blot, v., emborronar, secar. s., borrón m.; (character) mancha f.
blotch, bloch, s., roncha f., mancha f.
blotting-paper, blot'-ing-pei'-pa, s., papel secante
blouse, blaus, s., blusa f.   [m.
blow, blou, v., soplar; (wind) ventear; (nose, trumpet, etc.) sonar. s., (knock) golpe m.
blow-pipe, blou'-paip, s., soplete m.
blubber, blŏb'-a, s., grasa de ballena f. v., gimotear
bludgeon, blŏch'-en, s., porra f.; garrote m. v., garrotear
blue, bluu, a., azul; —**bell**, s., campanilla f.; —**stocking**, s., literata f.
bluff, blŏf, s., fanfarronada f. v., alardear
bluish, bluu'-ish, a., azulado, azulino
blunder, blŏn'-da, v., desatinar. s., disparate m.
blunt, blŏnt, v., embotar, a.,* embotado; (brusque) brusco; —**ness**, s., embotadura f.; (manner) grosería f.
blur, blẽr, v., hacer borrones. s., borrón m.
blush, blŏsh, v., sonrojarse. s., rubor m., sonrojo m.
bluster, blŏs'-ta, v., bravear. s., bravata f.; —**er**, fanfarrón m.; —**ing***, a., ruidoso; (gusty) tempestuoso
boar, bór, s., verraco m.; **wild** —, jabalí m.
board, bórd, s., (wood) tabla f.; (directors, etc.) consejo m.; (food) pensión f. v., (carpentering) entablar; —**er**, s., huésped m.; (school) interno m.; —**ing-house**, casa de huéspedes f., pensión f.; —**ing-school**, internado f.
boast, boust, v., jactarse. s., fanfarronada f., alarde
boaster, boust'-a, s., fanfarrón m., jaque m.   [m.
boat, bout, s., barco m.; vapor m.; (rowing) bote de remos m.; **motor**—, lancha automóvil f.; **steam**—, buque de vapor m.

boat-hook, bout′-juk, s., bichero m.
boating, bout′-ing, s., paseo en bote m.
boatman, bout′-man, s., barquero m.
boatswain, bou′-s'n, s., contramaestre m.
bob, bob, v., bambolearse, oscilar
bobbin, bob′-in, s., bobina f.
bode, boud, v., presagiar
bodice, bod′-is, s., corpiño m.
bodily, bod′-i-li, adv., corporalmente. a., corpóreo
bodkin, bod′-kin, s., punzón m.
body, bod′-i, s., cuerpo m.; (vehicle) carrocería f.
bog, bog, s., pantano m.
bogey, bou′-gui, s., (children's) coco m.; (goblin) duende m.; (truck) carretilla f.
boggy, bo′-gui, s., pantanoso
boil, boil, v., (fluids) hervir; (food in fluids) cocer. s., (tumour) furúnculo m.
boiler, boil′-a, s., olla f.
boisterous*, boist′-er-os, a., tempestuoso, borrascoso
bold*, bould, a., intrépido, audaz [coso, violento
boldness, bould′-nes, s., intrepidez f., audacia f.
bolster, boul′-sta, v., apoyar. s., travesaño m.
bolt, boult, v., cerrar con cerrojo; (horse) desbocarse. s., cerrojo m.; **thunder—,** rayo m.
bomb, bom, s., bomba f.
bombard, bom-baard′, v., bombardear
bombastic, bom-bas′-tik, a., rimbombante ampuloso
bond, bond, s., (obligation; stock) obligación f.; (tie) ligadura f.; (customs) **in —,** en depósito m.
bondage, bon′-dich, s., esclavitud f.; servidumbre f.
bone, boun, s., hueso m.; (fish) espina f.
bonfire, bon′-fair, s., hoguera f.
bonnet, bon′-et, s., gorro m., gorra f.
bonus, bou′-nas, s., bonificación f.
bony, bou′-ni, a., osudo, huesudo
book, buk, v., registrar. s., libro m.; **—binder,** s., encuadernador m.; **—case,** s., librería m.; **—ing-office,** s., taquilla f.; **—keeper,** s., tenedor de libros m.; **—seller,** s., librero m.; **—shop,** s., librería f.; **—stall,** s., puesto de libros m.; **—worm,** s., ratón de biblioteca m.

boom, buum, s., (business) prosperidad f.; (noise) estampido m.; (ship) cadena de puerto f. v., (noise) dar bombo; (prices) estar en auge

boon, buun, s., dádiva f., dicha f.

boor, búr, s., patán m., villano m.

boorish*, búr'-ish, a., rústico

boot, buut, s., bota f.; **——-maker,** zapatero m.

booth, buuÞ, s., barraca f., cabaña f.

booty, buu'-ti, s., botín m., saqueo m.

border, boar'-da, s., (ornamental edge) orilla f.; (frontier) frontera f. v., orillar

bordering, boar'-der-ing, a., contiguo, lindante

bore, bór, v., (pierce) perforar; (drill) taladrar, s., barreno m.; (calibre) calibre m.; (person) majadero m.

born, boarn, a., nacido

borough, bŏr'-o, s., burgo m.

borrow, bor'-ou, v., pedir prestado

bosom, bu'-som, s., seno m.

botanist, bot'-a-nist, s., botánico m.

botany, bot'-a-ni, s., botánica f.

both, bouz, a., ambos conj., tanto como

bother, boÞ'-a, v., fastidiar, incomodarse s., molestia f.

bottle, bot'-el, s., botella f. v., embotellar

bottom, bot'-om, s., fondo m.; (seat) posterior m.

bottomless, bot'-om-les, a., sin fondo

boudoir, buu'-duaar, s., tocador de (habitación) m.

bough, bau, s., rama de árbol f.

bounce, bauns, v., saltar s., salto m. f.

bound, baund, v., limitar; (jump) saltar s., (jump) salto m.; **—— for,** a., destinado

boundary, baun'-da-ri, s., frontera f., límite m.

bounteous*, bountiful*, baun'-ti-os, baun'-ti-ful, a., generoso; liberal

bounty, baun'-ti, s., generosidad f.; (gift) prima f.

bouquet, bu'-kei, s., ramillete f.; (wine) olor m.

bout, baut, s., turno m.

bow, bau, v., saludar; inclinarse; (bend) doblarse, s., inclinación f., reverencia f.; (ship) proa f.

bow, bou, s., (archery) arco m.; (tie) corbata de lazo f.; (violin) arco de violín m.; (knot) nudo m.

bowels, bau'-els, s.pl., intestinos m. pl.

bower, bau'-a, s., glorieta f., cenador m.

bowl, baul, v., bolear. s., tazón m.; (ball) bola f.

bowling-green, baul'-ing-griin, s., boleo m.

box, boks., v., boxear. s., (small) cajita f.; (medium size) caja f.; (large) cajón m.; (theatre) palco m.; (on the ear) bofetada f.

boxing, bok'-sing, s., boxeo m.

boy, boi, s., muchacho m.; niño m.; chico m.

boycott, boi'-kot, s., boicoteo m. v., excluir, boicotear

boyhood, boi'-jud, s., niñez f.

boyish, boi'-ish, a., pueril, juvenil

brace, breis, v., atar; (invigorate) bracear. s., abrazadera f.; (two) par m.; **—s,** pl., tirantes m. pl.

bracelet, breis'-let, s., brazalete m.; pulsera f.

bracing, breis'-ing, a., tónico

bracken, brak'n, s., helecho m.

bracket, brak'-et, s., paréntesis m.; (wall) modillón m. v., poner en paréntesis

brackish, brak'-ish, a., salobre

brag, brag, v., jactarse. s., jactancia f.

braggart, brag'-aart, s., fanfarrón m.

braid, breid, s., trenza f.; galón m. v., trenzar

brain, brein, s., cerebro m.; sesos m. pl.

brainless, brein'-les, a., tonto

braise, breis, v., cocer en marmita

brake, breik, s., freno m. v., frenar

bramble, bram'-bl, s., zarza f.

bran, bran, s., salvado m., afrecho m.

branch, braanch, s., rama f.; (business) sucursal f. v., ramificarse

brand, brand, s., (trade mark) marca f.; (fire) tizón m.; (stigma) estigma f. v., marcar; estigmatizar; (cattle) herrar

brandish, bran'-dish, v., blandir

brandy, bran'-di, s., brandy m.

brass, braas, s., latón m., bronce m.

brat, brat, s., rapaz m., chico m.

bravado, bra-vaa'-dou, s., bravata f.

brave, breiv, a.,* bravo, valiente. v., bravear

bravery, breiv'-er-i, s., valentía f.

brawl, bro*a*l, v., alborotar. s., alboroto m.

brawn, bro*a*n. s., carne de cerdo f.; (muscle) fuerza muscular f.

brawny, bro*a*'-ni, a., musculoso

bray, brei, v., rebuznar

brazen, brei'-*s*en, a., bronceado; (insolent) desvergonzado

brazier, br*e*i'-si-*a*, s., latonero m.; (fire) brasero m.

Brazil-nut, bre-sill'-nŏt, s., nuez del Brasil f.

breach, briich, s., (aperture) brecha f.; (contract) rotura f.; (law) violación f.

bread, bred, s., pan m.

breadth, bredz, s., anchura f.

break, breik, v., romper; (tame) domar; (limb) fracturar; (law) violar; (contract, promise) romper. s., rotura f.; (pause) pausa f.

breakage, breik'-icH, s., fractura f.; rotura f.

breakdown, breik'-d*a*un, s., derrumbamiento m.

breaker, breik'-*a*, s., rompedor m.; (law) infractor m.

breakers, breik'-*a*s, s. pl. (sea) rompientes m. pl.

breakfast, brek'-f*a*st, s., desayuno m. v., desayunarse

breakthrough, breik-zruu, v., salvar un obstáculo

breakwater, breik'-u*oa*-tr, s., rompeolas m.

bream, briim, s., (river) sargo m.; (sea) besugo m.

breast, brest, s., seno m.; (chest) pecho m.

breast-bone, brest'-b*o*un, s., esternón m.

breath, brez, s., respiración f.; (vapour) aliento m.

breathe, briiD, v., respirar

breathless, brez'-les, a., falto de aliento

bred, bred, a., criado; educado

breech, briich, s., (arms) culata f.

breeches, briich'-is, s. pl., pantalones m. pl.

breed, briid, v., criar; multiplicarse. s., raza f.

breeder, briid'-*a*, s., criador m., productor m.

breeding, briid'-ing, s., cría f.; educación f.

breeze, briis, s., brisa f.

breezy, brii'-si, a., fresco

brethren, breD'-ren, s. pl., hermanos m. pl.

brevity, brev'-i-ti, s., brevedad f., concisión f.

brew, bruu, v., hacer cerveza. s., mezcla f.

brewer, bruu'-a, s., cervecero m.

brewery, bruu'-ar-i, s., fábrica de cerveza f.

briar, brier, brai'-a, s., zarza f.

bribe, braib, v., sobornar. s., soborno m.

bribery, brai-ber-i, s., corrupción f.

brick, brik, s., ladrillo m.

bricklayer, brik'-lei-a, s., albañil m.

bridal, brai'-dl, s., boda f. a., nupcial

bride, braid, s., novia f.

bridegroom, braid'-gruum, s., novio m.

bridesmaid, braids'-meid, s., madrina de boda f.

bridge, briCH, s., puente m. v., levantar un puente

bridle, brai'-dl, s., brida f., freno m. v., embridar; — **path**, s., camino de herradura

brief, briif, s., relación f. a., breve. v., instruir

brigade, bri-gueid', s., brigada f.

bright*, brait, a., claro; (lively) brillante

brighten, brait'-n, v., pulir; (weather) aclarar, despejarse

brightness, brait'-nes, s., claridad f.; brillantez f.; (mental) viveza f.

brilliancy, bril'-yan-si, s., brillantez f., fulgor m.

brilliant, bril'-yant, a.,* brillante. s., brillante m.

brim, brim, s., borde m., orilla f.; (glass) labio m., borde m.; (hat) ala f.; — **over**, v., desbordar

brimstone, brim'-stoun, s., azufre m.

brine, brain, s., salmuera f.

bring, bring, v., traer, llevar; — **forward**, (accounts) llevar una suma a otra cuenta; — **in**, (receipts) presentar; — **up**, (educate) educar; (rear) criar

bringer, bring'-a, s., portador m.

brink, brink, s., borde m.; (river) orilla f.

briny, brai'-ni, a., salado

brisk*, brisk, a., (lively) vivo; (agile) activo

brisket, brisk'-et, s., pecho de buey m.

briskness, brisk'-nes, s., vivacidad f., despejo m.

bristle, bris'-l, v., erizarse. s., cerda f.

bristly, bris'-li, a., cerdoso

brittle, brit'-el, a., quebradizo, frágil

brittleness, brit'-el-nes, s., fragilidad f.

broad*, broad, a., ancho; (accent) marcado

broadcast, broad'-kaast, s., emisión f.; difusión f. v., radiar, difundir, emitir. adv., esparcidamente; **—ing,** s., transmisión f.

brocade, bro-keid', s., brocado m.

broccoli, brok'-o-li, s., bróculi m. paseo m.

brogue, broug, s., acento m.; (shoe) zapato de

broil, broil, v., asar, tostar. s., (dispute) riña f.

broker, brou'-ka, s., corredor m.; **stock-—,** agente de bolsa m.

bromide, brou'-maid, s., bromuro m.

bronchitis, bron-kai'-tis, s., bronquitis f.

bronze, brons, s., bronce m. v., broncear

brooch, brouch, s., broche m., prendedero m.

brood, bruud., s., pollada f., nidada f. v., empollar; meditar

brook, bruk, s., arroyo m.

broom, bruum, s., escoba f.; (shrub) retama f.

broth, broaz, s., caldo m.

brothel, broD'-el, s., burdel m.; lupanar m.

brother, brŏD'-a, s., hermano m.; **—in-law,** cuñado m.; **—hood,** s., hermandad f.; **—ly,** a., fraternal

brow, brau, s., frente f.

browbeat, brau'-biit, v., intimidar, amedrentar

brown, braun, a., moreno. v., poner tostado, tostar

brownish, braun'-ish, a., pardo

browse, braus, v., pacer

bruise, bruus, v., magullar, s., magulladura f.

brunette, bru-net', s., morena f., trigueña f.

brunt, brŏnt, s., choque m., embate m.

brush, brŏsh, s., cepillo m.; (paint) pincel m.; (dynamo) cepillo m. v., acepillar

brushwood, brŏsh'-u'ud, s., breñal m., zarzal m.

brusque, brŏsk, a., brusco

brussels sprouts, brŏs'-els sprauts, s. pl., coles [de Bruselas m. pl.

brutal*, bruu'-tl, a., brutal [de Bruselas m. pl.

brutality, bruu-tal'-i-ti, s., brutalidad f.

brute, bruut, s., bruto m., bestia f. a., bruto, bestial

bubble, bŏb'-l, s., burbuja f. v., burbujear

buccaneer, bŏk-a-nir', s., filibustero m.

buck, bŏk, s., lejía f., gamo m.

bucket, bŏk'-et, s., cubo m., balde m.
buckle, bŏk'-l, s., hebilla f. v., hebillar, abrochar; (bend) doblarse
buckram, bŏk'-ram, s., bucarán m., cinturilla f.
buckthorn, bŏk'-zŏrn, s., cambrón m.
bud, bŏd, s., yema f.; (rose) capullo m. v., brotar
budge, bŏcH, v., moverse, menearse
budget, bŏcH'-it, s., presupuesto m.
buff, bŏf, s., (colour) color de ante m.
buffalo, bŏf'-a-lou, s., búfalo m.
buffer, bŏf'-a, s., (railway) tope m.
buffet, bŏf'-it, s., (refreshments) cantina f. v., (hit) abofetear
buffoon, bo-fuun', s., bufón m.
bug, bŏg, s., chinche m.
bugbear, bŏg'-bér, s., espantajo m.
bugle, biuu'-gl, s., (military) corneta f.
build, bild, v., edificar. s., estructura f.
builder, bil'-da, s., constructor m.
building, bil'-ding, s., edificio m.; construcción f.
bulb, bŏlb, s., (plant) bulbo m.; (lamp) ampolla f.
bulge, bŏlcH, v., combarse
bulk, bŏlk, s., volumen m.; **in —,** a granel m.
bulky, bŏl'-ki, a., voluminoso
bull, bul, s., toro m.; (papal) bula f.; (stock exchange) alcista m.; **—dog,** s., perro de presa m.; **—fight,** s., corrida de toros f.
bullet, bul'-et, s., bala f.
bulletin, bul'-i-tin, s., boletín m.
bullion, bul'-yon, s., (gold) oro en barras m.; (silver) plata en barras f.
bullock, bul'-ok, s., buey m., cebón m.
bull's eye, buls'-ai, s., (target) centro de blanco m.
bully, bul'-i, v., maltratar. s., matón m.
bulrush, bul'-rŏsh, s., junco m.
bulwark, bul'-uĕrk, s., baluarte m.
bumble-bee, bŏm'-bl-bii, s., abejarrón m.
bump, bŏmp, г., chocar. s., topetazo m.; (bruise) chichón m.
bumper, bŏm'-pa, s., (shock) tope m.
bumpkin, bŏmp'-kin, s., (yokel) patán m.
bumptious, bŏmp'-shos, a., presumido

bun, bŏn, s., bollo m.

bunch, bŏnch, s., **— of flowers,** manojo de flores m.; **— of violets,** ramillete de violetas m.; **— of grapes,** racimo de uvas m.; **— of keys,** puñado de llaves m.

bundle, bŏn′-dl, s., paquete m. v., empaquetar

bung, bŏng, s., tapón m.

bungalow, bŏñ′-ga-lou, s., chálet m.; casa de un piso f.

bungle, bŏñ′-gl, v., chapucear. s., chapucería f.

bungler, bŏñ′-gla, s., chapucero m.

bunion, bŏn′-yon, s., juanete m.

bunk, bŏnk, s., tarima f.

bunker, bŏñ′-ka, s., (ship's) carbonera f.

bunkum, bŏñ′-kom, s., patraña f.

bunting, bŏn′-ting, s., estameña f.

buoy, boi, v., boyar, s., boya f.

buoyancy, boi′-an-si, s., ligereza f., vivacidad f.

buoyant, boi′-ant, a., flotante; vivo

burden, bẽr′-dn, s., carga f.; (responsibility) fardo m. v., cargar; gravar; (oppress) agobiar

burdensome, bẽr′-den-som, a., (expensive) oneroso; (encumbrance) molesto   [(desk) papelera f.

bureau, biu′-rou, s., (office) oficina f., escritorio m.;

bureaucracy, biu-ro′-kra-si, s., burocracia f.

burgess, bẽr′-ches, s., burgués m.

burglar, bẽr′-gla, s., ladrón m.

burglary, bẽr′-gla-ri, s., hurto m.; robo m.

burial, be′-ri-al, s., entierro m.

burial-ground, be′-ri-al-graund, s., cementerio m.

burlesque, ber-lesk′, s., burlesco m. a., burlesco. v., parodiar

burly, bẽr′-li, a., corpulento, robusto

burn, bẽrn, v., quemar, arder. s., quemadura f.

burner, bẽrn′-a, s., mechero m.

burnish, bẽrn′-ish, v., bruñir

burrow, bŏr′-ou, v., minar; (by animals) horadar. s., conejera f.

bursar, bẽr′-sa, s., tesorero m.

burst, bẽrst, v., reventar; (tears) brotar. s., explosión

bury, ber′-i, v., enterrar   [f.; (crack) reventón m.

bus, bŏs, s., autobus m.

bush, bush, s., arbusto m.; mata f.

bushel, bush'-l, s., medida inglesa de áridos f. (unos 36 litros

bushy, bush'-i, a., matoso

busily, bis'-i-li, adv., activamente

business, bis'-nes, s., negocio m., or negocios pl.

business-like, bis'-nes-laik, a., serio; práctico

bust, bŏst, s., busto m.

bustle, bŏs'-l, v., bullir, menearse. s., bullicio m.

bustling, bŏs'-ling, a., bullicioso, ruidoso

busy, bis'-i a., ocupado

busybody, bis'-i-bŏd-i, s., entrometido m.

but, bŏt, conj., pero, mas; sin embargo. prep., excepto, menos. adv., solamente, no . . . mas que, no . . . sino

butcher, buch'-a, s., carnicero m., matar

butler, bŏt'-la, s., despensero m., mayordomo m.

butt, bŏt, s., extremidad f.; (gun) culata f.; (cask) tonel m. v., topetar

butter, bŏt'-a, s., manteca f., mantequilla f. v., untar con manteca; **—-dish,** mantequera f.

buttercup, bŏt'-er-kŏp, s., botón de oro m.

butterfly, bŏt'-er-flai, s., mariposa f.

buttock, bŏt'-ok, s., nalga f., anca f.

button, bŏt'-n, s., botón m. v., abotonar; (refl.) abotonarse; **—-hole,** s., ojal m.

buttress, bŏt'-res, s., contrafuerte m., estribo m.

buxom, bŏk'-som, a., (woman) rolliza

buy, bai, v., comprar

buyer, bai'-a, s., comprador m.

buzz, bŏs, v., zumbar, s., zumbido m.

buzzard, bŏs'-erd, s., buharro m., modrego m.

by, bai, adv., ahí; allí. prep., por; a; en; de; cerca de; sobre; según

bye-law, bai'-loa, s., reglamento m.

by-pass, bai'-paas, s., paso m., desvío m. v., pasar, desviar

bygone, bai'-goan, a., pasado

bystander, bai'-stAn-dr, s., espectador m.

by the by, bai-Di-bai, adv., de paso

byway, bai'-uei, s., camino desviado m.

byword, bai'-uĕrd, s., proverbio m.

cab, kAB, s., (motor) taxi m.; (horse) coche m.; **—by, —man,** s., cochero m.

cabal, ka-bAl', v., maquinar, intrigar. s., cábala f.

cabbage, kAB'-icH, s., col f.

cabin, kAB'-in, s., camarote m.; (hut) choza f.

cabinet, kAB'-in-et, s., gabinete m.; ministerio m.

cabinet-maker, kAB'-in-et-meik'-a, s., ebanista m.

cable, kei'-bl, s., cable m. v., cablegrafiar

cablegram, kei'-bl-grAm, s., cablegrama m.

cackle, kAk'-l, v., cacarear. s., cacareo m.

cactus, kAk'-tus, s., cacto m.

cad, kAD, s., sinvergüenza m.

caddy, kAD, s., (tea) cajita para té f.

cage, keicH, s., jaula f. v., enjaular

cajole, ka-cHoul', v., lisonjear

cake, keik, s., pastel m.; tarta f.; torta; (soap) pastilla de jabón f. v., coagularse

calamitous*, ka-lAm'-i-tos, a., calamitoso

calamity, ka-lAm'-i-ti, s., calamidad f.

calculate, kAl'-kiu-leit, v., calcular

calendar, kAl'-en-da, s., calendario m.

calender, kAl'-en-da, s., calandria f.

calf, kaaf, s., ternero m.; (leg) pantorrilla f.

calico, kAl'-i-kou, s., estampado m., indiana f., percal m.

call, koal, s., llamada f.; (visit) f. v., llamar; visitar; **—ing,** s., profesión f.

callous*, kAl'-os, a., calloso; (unfeeling) endurecido

callow, kAl'-ou, a., inexperto

calm, kaam, s., calma f.; (weather) bonanza f. a.,* quieto. v., calmar

calmness, kaam'-nes, s., tranquilidad f., sosiego m.

calory, kAl'-o-ri, s., caloría f.

calumny, kAl'-om-ni, s., calumnia f.

cambric, keim'-brik, s., batista f.

camel, kAm'-l, s., camello m.

cameo, kAm'-i-ou, s., camafeo m.

camera, kAm'-er-a, s., cámara f.; cámara fotográfica f.

camisole, kAm'-i-soul, s., camiseta f.

camomile, kAm'-o-mail, s., camomila f.   [encubrir

camouflage, kAm'-o-flaarcH, s., camuflage m. v.

camp, kamp, v., acampar. s., campo m., campamento m.; —**stool,** silla plegadiza f.

campaign, kam-pein', s., campaña f. v., servir en campaña

camphor, kam'-fa, s., alcanfor m.

can, kan, s., lata f. v., (preserve) enlatar

can, kan, v., (to be able) poder; (to know how) saber

canal, ka-nal', s., canal m.

canary, ka-nei'-ri, s., canario m.

cancel, kan'-sl, v., cancelar, anular

cancer, kan'-sa, s., cáncer m.

candid, kan'-did, a., cándido, sincero

candidate, kan'-di-deit, s., candidato m.

candied, kan'-did, a., confitado

candle, kan'-dl, s., vela f., candela f.

candlestick, kan'-del-stik, s., palmatoria f.

candour, kan'-da, s., sinceridad f.

candy, kan'-di, s., confite m. v., confitar

cane, kein, s., caña f.; (walking-stick) bastón m.

canine, kei'-nain, a., canino

canister, kan'-is-ta, s., canastillo m.; (tin) lata f.

canker, kañ'-ka, s., gangrena f.

cannibal, kan'-i-bal, s., caníbal m.

cannon, kan'-on, s., cañón m.; (billiards) carambola f.

canoe, ka-nuu', s, canoa f.

canon, kan'-on, s., (title) canónigoim.; (law) canon m.

canopy, kan'-o-pi, s., baldaquín m.; (of bed) pabellón m.

cant, kant, s., hipocresía f., hablar en caló

cantankerous, kan-tañ'-ker-os, a., pendenciero

canteen, kan-tiin'- s., cantina f.

canter, kan'-ta, s., medio galope m. v., andar e caballo a paso largo

canticle, kan'-ti-kl, s., cántico m.

canting, kant'-ing, s., falso devoto m. a., hipócrita

canvas, kan'-vas, s., (cloth) lona f,; (sail) vela f.; (painting) lienzo m.

canvass, kan'-vas, v., solicitar. s., solicitación f.

cap, kap, s., gorra f.; (metal) cápsula f.

capable, kei'-pa-bl, a., capaz

capacity, ka-pass'-i-ti, s., capacidad f.

cape, keip, s., (geographical) cabo m.; (cloak) capa f.

caper, kéi'-pa, v., hacer cabriolas. s., (pickle) alcaparra f.

capital, káp'-i-tl, s., (city) capital f.; (money) capital m.; (letter) mayúscula f.

capitulate, ka-pit'-iu-leit, v., capitular

capon, kéi'-pn, s., capón m.

capricious*, ka-prish'-os, a., caprichoso

capsize, kap-sáis', v., volcar; (naut.) zozobrar

capstan, káp'-stan, s., cabrestante m.

capsule, káp'-siul, s., cápsula f.

captain, káp'-tin, s., capitán m.

captive, káp'-tiv, s. & a., cautivo m., prisionero m.

captivity, kap-tiv'-i-ti, s., cautiverio m.

capture, káp'-tiur, v., capturar. s., captura f.

car, kaar, s., coche m.; automóvil m.; (horse) carro m.; (tramcar) tranvía m.; (aero) barquilla f.

caramel, kár'-a-mel, s., caramelo m.

carat, kár'-at, s., quilate m.

caravan, kár'-a-van, s., caravana f.

caraway, kár'-a-uei, s., (seed) alcaravea f.

carbide, kaar'-baid, s., carburo m.

carbine, kaar'-bain, s., carabina f.

carbolic, kaar-bol'-ik, s., ácido fénico m. a., afenicado

carbon, kaar'-bon, s., carbón m., carbono m.;
——**paper,** papel carbón m.

carbuncle, kaar'-bŏn-kl, s., (med.) carbunclo m.

carburettor, kaar'biu-ret-a, s., carburador m.

carcase, carcass, kaar'-kas, s., res muerta f.

card, kaard, s., carta f.; (playing) naipe m.; (visiting) tarjeta f.; ——**board,** s., cartón m.

cardigan, kaar'-di-gan, s., chaqueta de punto sin solapas

cardinal, kaar'-di-nal, s., cardenal m. a., cardinal

care, kér, s., cuidado m., atención f.; (anxiety) inquietud, f. cuidar; —— **for,** (persons) querer a; (things) gustar de; **take —— of,** cuidar de; c/o, al cuidado de

career, ka-rir, s., carrera f., profesión f.

careful*, kér'-ful, a., cuidadoso, atento

careless*, kér'-les, a., descuidado; indiferente

carelessness, kér'-les-nes, s., descuido m.
caress, ka-res', v., acariciar. s., caricia f.
caretaker, kér'-tei'-ka, s., guardián m., conserje m.
cargo, kaar'-gou, s., carga f., cargamento m.
caricature, kar'-i-ka-tiur, s., caricatura f. v., ridiculizar
carman, kaar'-man, s., carretero m.
carmine, kaar'-min, s., carmín m.
carnage, kaar'-nich, s., matanza f., carnicería f.
carnal*, kaar'-nl, a., carnal, sensual
carnation, kaar-nei'-shon, s., (flower) clavel m.
carnival, kaar'-ni-vl, s., carnaval m.
carol, kar'-ol, s., (cantata) villancico m.
carousal, ka-rau-sl, s., francachela f., orgía f.
carp, kaarp, s., carpa f. v., criticar
carpenter, kaar'-pen-ta, s., carpintero m.
carpet, kaar'-pet, s., alfombra f.
carping, kaarp'-ing, s., censura f. a., capcioso
carriage, kar'-ich, s., (vehicle) coche m.; (freight) porte m.; (deportment) porte m.
carrier, kar'-i-a, s., (vehicle) coche m.; (carter) carretero m.; (mule) arriero m.
carrion, kar'-i-on, s., carroña f.
carrot, kar'-ot, s., zanahoria f.; **—y,** a., pelirrojo
carry, kar'-i, v., llevar; transportar
cart, kaart, s., carro m.; (long and narrow) carreta f. v., carretear; **—age,** s., acarreo m.; **—er,** s., carretero m.; **—load,** s., carretada f.
cartoon, kaar-tuun', s., caricatura f.
cartridge, kaar'-trich, s., cartucho m.
carve, kaarv, v., (wood) tallar; (meat, etc.) trinchar
carving, kaarv'-ing, s., (wood) talla f.
cascade, kas-keid', s., cascada f.
case, keis, s., caso m.; (box) caja f.; (cigarette, jewel, or spectacle) estuche m.; **in —,** en caso
casement, keis'-ment, s., alféizar m.
cash, kash, s., dinero m.; (paying) dinero contante m. v., cobrar; **—-book,** s., libro de caja m.; **—-box,** s., caja para dinero f.; **—ier,** s., cajero [m.
cashmere, kash'-mir, s., casimir m.
cask, kaask, s., barril m., tonel m.; (for water) cuba f.

casket, kaas'-ket, s., estuche para joyas f.

cassock, kas'-ok, s., sotana f.

cast, kaast, s., (throw) tiro m.; (theatre) reparto m.; (metal) molde m. v., tirar; fundir, modelar

castanet, kas'-ta-net, s., castañuela f.

caste, kaast, s., casta f.

castigate, kas'-ti-gueit, v., castigar

casting, kaas'-ting, s., moldura f.

castle, kaa'-sl, s., castillo m.; (fortress) fortaleza f.; (chess) torre f. v., enrocar

castor, kaas'-tor, s., (furniture bearings) ruedecilla f.; —**oil,** aceite de ricino m.

casual, kash'-iu-al, a., casual

casualties, kash'-iu-al-tes, s. pl., pérdidas f. pl.; (war) bajas f. pl.

casualty, kash'-iu-al-ti, s., accidente m.

cat, kat, s., gato m.

catalogue, kat'-a-log, s., catálogo m.

catarrh, ka-taar', s., catarro m.

catastrophe, ka-tas'-tro-fi, s., catástrofe f.

catch, kach, v., coger; (seize) asir; —**up,** alcanzar. s., presa f.; (door, etc.) cerradera f.

catching, kach'-ing, a., contagioso

catchword, kach'-uërd, s., reclamo m.; slogan m.

category, kat'-i-gori, s., categoría f.

cater, kei'-ta, v., abastecer, proveer

caterer, kei'-ter-a, s., abastecedor m., proveedor m.

caterpillar, kat'-er-pil-a, s., oruga f.

cathedral, ka-zii'-dral, s., catedral f.

catholic, kaz'-o-lik, a., católico

cattle, kat'-l, s., ganado m.

cauldron, koal'-dron, s., caldero m.

caucus, koa'-kos, s., junta secreta f.

cauliflower, ko'-li-flau-er, s., coliflor f.

caulk, koak, v., calafatear

cause, koas, s., causa f.; origen m. v., causar

causeway, koas'-uei, s., calzada f.

caustic, koas'-tik, s., cáustico m. a., cáustico

cauterize, koa'-ter-ais, v., cauterizar

caution, koa'-shon, s., precaución f.; cuidado m.; (warning) aviso m. v., caucionar, prevenir

cautious*, koa'-shos, a., cauto, prudente

cavalier, kav-a-lir', s., caballero m.
cavalry, kav'-al-ri, s., caballería f.
cave, keiv, s., cueva f., caverna f.
cavernous, kav'-ern-os, a., cavernoso
cavil, kav'-il, v., cavilar
cavity, kav'-i-ti, s., hueco m.; (tooth) cavidad f.
caw, koa, v., graznar
cease, sis, v., cesar, parar; —**less***, a., incesante
cedar, sii'-da, s., cedro m.
cede, siid, v., ceder
ceiling, siil'-ing, s., techo m.
celebrate, sel'-i-breit, v., celebrar; solemnizar
celebrated, sel'-i-breit-id, a., célebre
celerity, si-ler'-i-ti, s., celeridad f.
celery, sel'-e-ri, s., apio m.
celestial, si-les'-ti-al, a., celeste
celibacy, sel'-i-ba-si, s., celibato m.
cell, sel, s., calabozo m.; (anatomy) célula f.; (battery) par m.
cellar, sel'-a, s., sótano m.; (wine) bodega f.
celluloid, sel'-iu-loid, s., celuloide f.
cement, si-ment', s., cemento m. v., argamasar
cemetery, sem'-i-ta-ri, s., cementerio m.
cenotaph, sen'-o-taf, s., cenotafio m.
censer, sen'-sa, s., incensario m.
censor, sen'-sr, s., censor m.
censorship, sen'-sr-ship, s., censura f.
census, sen'-sos, s., censo m.
cent, sent, s., ciento m., centavo m.; céntimo m.
centenary, sen'-ti-ner-i, s., centenario m.
central*, sen'-tral, a., central; — **heating,** s., calefacción central f.; —**ize,** v., centralizar
centre, sen'-tr, s., centro m. v., centralizar
centruy, sen'-tiu-ri, s., siglo m.
ceramics, ser-am'-iks, s., cerámica f.
cereals, sii'-rii-als, s. pl., cereales m. pl.
ceremonious*, ser-i-mou'-ni-os, a., ceremonioso
ceremony, ser'-i-mou-ni, s., ceremonia f.
certain*, ser'-tin, a., cierto; —**ty,** s., certeza f.
certificate, ser-tif'-i-keit, s., certificado m.; testimonio m.
certify, ser'-ti-fai, v., certificar

certitude, sĕr'-ti-tiuud, s., certidumbre f.

cessation, se-sei'-shon, s., cesación f.; suspensión f.

cesspool, ses'-puul, s., sumidero m.

chafe, cheif, v., (rub) calentar frotando; (fret) irritar

chafing dish, chei'-fing dish, s., escalfeta f.

chaff, chaaf, s., paja f.; (tease) burla f. v., burlarse

chaffinch, chaf'-inch, s., pinzón m.

chain, chein, v., encadenar, s., cadena f.; — **up,** v., [encadenar

chair, chér, s., silla f.

chairman, chér'-man, s., presidente m.

chalice, chal'-is, s., cáliz m.

chalk, choak, s., yeso m., greda f.; (crayon) tiza f.

chalky, choa'-ki, a., gredoso

challenge, chal'-inch, s., desafío m.; (duel) provocación f. v., desafiar; provocar

chamber, cheim'-ba, s., (apartment) cuarto m.; (gun) cámara f.; —**s,** pl., (lawyers', etc.) estudio de abogado m.

chamberlain, cheim'-ber-lin, s., chambelán m.

chambermaid, cheim'-ber-meid, s., doncella f.

chamois, shAm'-uaa, shAm'-i, s., gamuza f.

champagne, shAm-pein', s., champaña f.

champion, chAm'-pi-on, s., campeón m. v., defender

chance, chaans, s., ventura f., azar m.; (opportunity) oportunidad f. a., casual v., acaecer

chancel, chaan'-sl, s., santuario m.

chancellor, chaan'-se-la, s., canciller m.

chancery, chaan'-se-ri, s., cancillería f.

chandelier, shAn-di-lir', s., candelabro m.

chandler, shaand-la, s., cerero m., velero m.

change, cheinch, s., (money, alteration, exchange) cambio m.; (residence) mudanza f. v., (money, opinion, habits, trains, gear, etc.) cambiar; (clothing) mudar; —**able,** a., variable

changeless, cheinch'-les, a., inmutable

channel, chAn'-l, s., canal f. v., acanalar

chant, chaant, v., cantar. s., canto llano m.

chaos, kei'-os, s., caos m.

chap, chAp, v., agrietar. s., grieta f.

chapel, chAp'-l, s., capilla f.

chaperon, shAp'-roun, s., acompañante m. & f. v.,

chaplain, chAp'-lin, s., capellán m. [escoltar

chaplet, chʌp´-let, s., guirnalda f.; rosario m.

chapter, chʌp´-ta, s., capítulo m.

char, chaar, v., carbonear; (clean) trabajar a jornal;
—**woman,** s., jornalera f.

character, kʌr´-ak-ta, s., carácter m.

charcoal, chaar´-koul, s., carbón de leña m.

charge, chaarch, s., coste m.; ataque m.; acusación
f. v., acusar; atacar; (price) cobrar; (battery)
cargar; **to be in** —, estar encargado

chariot, chʌr´-i-ot, s., carroza f.

charitable, chʌr´-it-a-bl, a., caritativo

charity, chʌr´-i-ti, s., caridad f.

charm, chaarm, v., encantar. s encanto m.;
—**ing***, a., ancantador; (bewitching) hechicero

charnel-house, chaar´-nel-jaus, s., osario m.

chart, chaart, s., carta de navegar f.

charter, chaar´-ta, v., (ship) fletar. s., (grant) carta
de privilegio f.

chary, ché´-ri, a., cauteloso

chase, cheis, v., cazar; perseguir. s., caza f.

chasm, kʌsm, s., abismo m.

chaste, cheist, a., casto, virtuoso

chastise, chas-tais´, v., castigar

chastisement, chʌs´-tis-ment, s., castigo m.

chastity, chʌs´-ti-ti, s., castidad f.

chat, chʌt, s., charla f. v., charlar

chattel, chʌt´-l, s., bienes muebles m. pl.

chatter, chʌt´-a, v., charlar; (teeth) castañetear;
—**box,** s., charlador m.; —**ing,** charla f.

chauffeur, shof´-a, s., chófer m.

cheap*, chiip, a., barato; —**en,** v., abaratar;
—**er,** a., más barato; —**ness,** s., baratura f.

cheat, chiit, v., trampear. s., trampa f.

cheating, chiit´-ing, s., timo m.

check, chek, s., (restraint) rechazo m.; (verifica-
tion) revisión f.; (chess) jaque m.; (pattern) cua-
drados m. pl. v., refrenar; revisar; (stop) parar;
—**mate,** s., jaque mate m. v., dar jaque mate

cheek, chiik, s., mejilla f.; (fam.) descaro m.

cheer, chir, s., alegría f.; (applause) vivas m. pl.
v., dar vivas; (brighten) alegrar; —**ful***, a.,
alegre, animado; —**less,** triste, desanimado

cheese, chiis, s., queso m.

chemical*, kem′-i-kl, a., químico (producto)

chemise, shi-miis′, s., camisa de señora f.

chemist, kem′-ist, s., químico m.; (shop) farma-céutico m.; —**ry,** química f.

cheque, chek, s., cheque m.

cheque-book, chek′-buk, s., libro de cheques m.

chequered, chek′-erd, a., variado

cherish, cher′-ish, v., querer

cherry, cher-i, s., cereza f.; —**tree,** cerezo m.

cherub, cher′-ob, s., querubín m.

chess, ches, s., ajedrez m.

chest, chest, s., (human) pecho m.; (trunk) cofre m.; (box) cajón m.; — **of drawers,** cómoda f.

chestnut, ches′-nŏt, s., castaña f. a., castaño; —**tree,** s., castaño m.; **horse**—, castaña de Indias f.

chew, chuu, v., masticar; (tobacco, etc.) mascar —**ing gum,** s., chicle m.

chicken, chik′-n, s., gallina f., pollo m.

chicken-pox, chik′-n-poks, s., viruelas locas f. pl.

chide, chaid, v., regañar, reprender

chief, chiif, s., jefe m. a.,* principal

chilblain, chil′-blein, s., sabañón m.

child, chaild, s., niño m.; —**ish*,** a., infantil

chill, chil, s., escalofrío m. v., enfriar; (liquids) helar

chilly, chil′-i, a., frío

chime, chaim, v., repiquetear. s., tañido de cam-panas m. juego de campanas m.

chimney, chim′-ni, s., chimenea f.

chimney-sweep, chim′-ni-suiip, s., deshollinador [m.

chin, chin, s., barbilla f.

china, chai′-na s., porcelana f.; loza f.

chink, chiñk, s., hendidura f. v., sonar

chintz, chints, s., zaraza f.

chip, chip, v., desmenuzar. s., trozo m., astilla f.

chiropodist, ki-rop′-o-dist, s., pedicuro m.

chirp, chĕrp, v., chirriar, gorjear

chisel, chis′-l, s., cincel m. v., cincelar

chivalrous, shiv′-al-ros, a., caballeresco

chive, chaiv, s., cebolleta f.

chloride, klŏ′-raid, s., cloruro m.

chlorine, klō′-rin, s., cloro m.
chloroform, klou′-rou-form, s., cloroformo m.
chocolate, chok′-o-leit, s., chocolate m.
choice, chois, s., elección f. a., escogido, selecto
choir, kuair, s., coro m.
choke, chouk, v., (suffocate) sofocar; (strangle) ahogar; (block up) obstruir
choler, kol′-a, s., cólera f.
cholera, kol′-er-a, s., cólera-morbo m.
choose, chuus, v., escoger, elegir
chop, chop, s., chuleta f., costilla f. v., cortar; — **off,** tajar
chopper, chop′-a, s., cortante m., cuchilla f.
choral, kó′-ral, a., coral
chord, koard, s., cuerda f.; acorde m.
chorister, kor′-is-ta, s., corista f.
chorus, kó′-ros, s., coro m.
Christ, kraist, s., Cristo m.
christen, kris′-n, v., bautizar
christening, kris′-ning, s., bautismo m.
Christianity, kris-ti-an′-i-ti, s., cristianismo m.
Christmas, kris′-mas, s., Navidad f.; —**box,** aguinaldo m.; — **-tree,** árbol de Navidad m.
chronic, kron′-ik, a., crónico
chronicle, kron′-ik-l, s., crónica f. v., contar
chrysanthemum, kri-san′-ze-mom, s., crisantemo m.
chubby, chöb′-i, a., mofletudo, rechoncho   [m.
chuckle, chŏk′-l, v., reir entre dientes. s., risa ahogada f.
chum, chöm, s., camarada m.
chunk, chöñk, s., trozo m.; pedazo m.
church, chêrch, s., iglesia f.
churchyard, chêrch-yaard, s., cementerio m.
churl, chêrl, s., rústico m.
churlish*, chêr′-lish, a., rudo
churn, chern, s., mantequera f. v., batir la leche
cider, sai′-da, s., sidra f.
cigar, si-gaar′, s., cigarro m.
cigarette, sig-a-ret′, s., cigarrillo m.
cinder, sin′-da, s., escoria f.
cine-film, sin′-i film, s., película de cine
cinema, sin′-i-ma, s., cinema m.

cinnamon, sin´-na-mon, s., canela f.

cipher, sai´-fa, s., cifra f. v., cifrar

circle, ser´-kl, s., círculo m. v., circundar

circlet, ser´-klet, s., (headband) corona f.

circuit, ser´-kit, s., circuito m.

circuitous*, ser-kiu´-it-os, a., tortuoso

circular, ser´-kiu-lar, s., circular f. a.,* circular

circulate, ser´-kiu-leit, v., circular; poner en circulación

circulating, ser´-kiu-leit-ing, a., circulante; — **library,** s., gabinete de lectura m.

circumcise, ser-kom-sais´, v., circuncisar

circumference, ser-kom´-fer-ens, s., circunferencia f.

circumflex, ser´-kom-fleks, s., circunflejo m.

circumscribe, ser´-kom-skraib, v., circunscribir

circumspect, ser´-kom-spect, a., circunspecto, prudente

circumstance, ser´-kom-stans, s., circunstancia f.; —**s,** pl., (financial) medios m. pl.

circumstantial*, ser-kom-stan´-shal, a., circunstancial;—**evidence,** s., indicios vehementes

circumvent, ser-kom-vent´, v., engañar   [m.pl.

circus, ser´-kos, s., circo m.

cistern, sis´-tern, s., cisterna f.

citadel, sit´-a-del, s., ciudadela f.

cite, sait, v., citar

citizen, sit´-i-sn, s., ciudadano m.

citizenship, sit´-i-sn-ship, s., ciudadanía f.

citron, sit´-ron, s., (fruit) cidra f.; (tree) cidro m.

city, sit´-i, s., ciudad f.

civet, siv´-et, s., civeta f.

civil*, siv´-il, a., civil; (courteous) cortés

civilian, siv-il´-yan, s., paisano m., burgués m.

civilisation, siv-il-ai-sei´-shon, s., civilización f.

claim, kleim, s., demanda f.; (inheritance) título m.; (mine, etc.) pertenencia f. v., reclamar

claimant, kleim´-ant, s., reclamante m.; (throne) pretendiente m.

clamber, klam´-ba, v., trepar, gatear

clamorous*, klam´-or-os, a., ruidoso, tumultuoso

clamour, klam´-er, s., clamor m. v., gritar, vociferar

clamp, klʌmp, s., grapa f. v., empalmar

clan, klʌn, s., tribu f.; clan m.

clandestine, klʌn-des'tin, a., clandestino

clang, klʌñg, s., rechinamiento m. v., rechinar

clank, klʌñk, (see **clang**)

clap, klʌp, s., aplauso m.; (thunder) trueno m. v., aplaudir

clapping, klʌp'-ing, s., aplauso m.

clap-trap, klʌp'-trap, s., engañabobos m. pl.

claret, klʌr'-et, s., clarete m.

clarify, klʌr'-i-fai, v., clarificar

clarinet, klʌr'-i-net, s., clarinete m.

clarion, klʌr'-yon, s., clarín m.

clash, klʌsh, s., (noise) choque m.; (differing) conflicto m. v., chocar; oponerse

clasp, klaasp, s., corchete m.; (embrace) abrazo m. v., abrozar; abrazar

class, klaas, s., clase f.; (quality) calidad f. v., clasificar

classify, klʌs'-i-fai, v., clasificar

clatter, klʌt'-a, v., resonar. s., ruido m.

clause, kloas, s., cláusula f., estipulación f.

claw, kloa, s., garra f., uña f. v., arañar

clay, klei, s., arcilla f., barro m.

clayey, klei'-i, a., arcilloso

clean, kliin, v., limpiar. a.,* limpio

cleaning, kliin'-ing, s., limpieza f.

cleanliness, cleanness, klen'-li-nes, kliin'-nes, s., limpieza f., aseo m.

cleanse, kienz, v., limpiar; purificar

clear*, klir, a., claro; (profit) neto v., desembarazar; (sky) aclarar; (customs) despacho m.; —**ness,** claridad f.

cleave, kliiv, v., hender

cleft, kleft, s., hendedura f., grieta f.

clematis, kiem'-a-tis, s., clemátide f.

clemency, klem'-en-si, s., clemencia f.

clench, klench, v., remachar; (teeth, etc.) cerrar

clergy, klėr'-CHi, s., clero m.; —**man,** clérigo m., eclesiástico m.

clerical, kier'-ik-l, a., clerical; —**error,** s., error de escritura m.

clerk, klaark, s., dependiente m., escribiente m.

clever*, klev'-*a*, a., inteligente; hábil; (manually) diestro

cleverness, klev'*er*-nes, s., habilidad f.; (manual) destreza f.

click, klik, v., hacer tictac. s., golpe seco m.

client, klai'-ent, s., cliente m.

clientele, klai'-ent-íl, s., clientela f.

cliff, klif, s., acantilado m.

climate, klai'-met, s., clima m.

climax, klai'-maks, s., colmo m.

climb, klaim, v., trepar, escalar; **—er,** s., trepador m.; (plant) enredadera f.

clinch, klinch, (see **clench**)

cling, kling, v., pegarse; (fig.) adherirse

clinical, klin'-i-kal, a., clínico

clink, klińk, v., hacer resonar; (metallic) retiñir;

clinker, klińk'-*a*, s., escoria f.   [retintín m.

clip, klip, s., grapa f. v., engrapar—; (cut) cortar

cloak, klouk, s., capa f.; manto m. v., encapotar; (conceal) encubrir; **—room,** s., (theatre, restaurant) guardarropa f., (railway) consigna f.

clock, klok, s., reloj m.; **alarm —,** despertador m.; **—maker,** relojero m.; **—work,** mecanismo de reloj m.

clod, klod, s., terrón m.

clog, klog, s., traba f.; (shoe) chanclo m. v., (mech.) trabar; (obstruct) obstruir

cloister, klois'-ta, s., claustro m.

close, klous, s., fin m., conclusion f. v., cerrar; (terminate) terminar. a., (weather) pesado. adv., (near) cerca. prep., cerca de

closet, klos'-et, s., gabinete m.; **water —,** (private) excusado m.; (public) retrete m.

closure, klou'-shur, s., clausura f., fin m.

clot, klot, s., cuajarón m. v., cuajarse

cloth, kloz, s., tela f., paño m.; **table —,** mantel m.

clothe, klouD, v., vestir

clothes, klouDs, s. pl., vestidos m. pl.; **bed—,** ropa de cama f.; **—brush,** cepillo m.

clothier, klouD'-ya, s., pañero m.

clothing, klouD'-ing, s., vestidos m. pl., ropa f.

cloud, klaud, s., nube f. v., anublarse; **—burst,** s., chaparrón m.; **—less,** a., sin nubes; **—y,** nublado

clout, klaut, s., trapo m.; (nail) clavo m.; (slap) bofetada f. v., remendar; abofetear

clove, klouv, s., clavo m.

cloven, klouv'-n, **-footed,** a., patihendido

clover, klou'-va, s., trébol m.

clown, klaun, s., payaso m.

club, klob, s., círculo m.; (stick) porra f.; (cards) bastos m. pl.; **— foot,** pateta m.

cluck, klok, v., cloquear, s., cloqueo m.

clue, kluu, s., guía f.; pista f.; indicio m.

clump, klomp, s., tarugo m.

clumsiness, klom'-si-nes, s., torpeza f.

clumsy, klom'-si, a., torpe, desmañado

cluster, klos'-ta, s., grupo m.; (fruit) racimo m. v., agruparse; arracimarse

clutch, kloch, s., garra f., presa f.; (motor) embrague m. v., agarrar

coach, kouch, s., coche m.; (state) carroza f.; (tutor) preceptor m. v., (teaching) enseñar; **—man,** s., cochero m.

coagulate, kou-a'-giuu-leit, v., coagular; (refl.) coagularse

coal, koul, s., carbón de piedra m.; **-cellar,** carbonera f.; **—mine,** mina de carbón f.

coalition, kou-a-li'-shon, s., coalición f.

coarse', kours, a., tosco; (manner) grosero

coarseness, kours'-nes, s., grosería f.

coast, koust, s., costa f., litoral m. v., costear; **—guard,** s., guarda costas m.

coat, kout, s., levita f., chaqueta f., abrigo m.; (animal) pelaje m.; (paint) capa de pintura f. v., vestir; **—ing,** s., revestimiento m.; **—of arms,** escudo de armas m.; **over—,** abrigo m.

coax, kouks, v., engatusar

cob, kob, s., (horse) jaca f.

cobbler, kob'-la, s., remendón m.

cobweb, kob'-ueb, s., telaraña f.

cocaine, kou-kein', s., cocaína f.

cochineal, koch-i-niil', s., cochinilla f.

cock, kok, s., (bird) gallo m.; (gun) gatillo m.; (turn-valve) llave f.; **—ade,** escarapela f.; **—erel,** pollo m.

cockle, kok'-l, s., coquina f.; (plant) cáscara f.

cockney, kok'-ni, s., indígena de Londres m.

cockroach, kok'-rouch, s., cucaracha f.

cocoa, kou'-kou, s., cacao m.; **—nut,** coco m.

cocoon, ko-kuun', s., capullo del gusano de seda m.

cod, kod, s., abadejo m., bacalao m.; **—liver oil,** aceite de higado de bacalao m.

coddle, kod'-l, v., mimar, acariciar

code, koud, s., código m.

codicil, kod'-i-sil, s., codicilo m.

coerce, kou-ĕrs', v., forzar

coffee, kof'-i, s., café m.; **—house,** café m.

coffee-pot, kof'-i-pot, s., cafetera f.

coffer, kof'-*a*, s., cofre m.; **—s,** pl., tesoro m.

coffin, kof'-in, s., ataúd m., féretro m.

cog, kog, s., diente de rueda m. v., dentar una rueda; **—wheel,** s., rueda dentada f.

cogency, kou'-chen-si, s., fuerza logica f.; fuerza moral f.

cogitate, koch'-i-teit, v., pensar; meditar

cogitation, koch-i-tei'-shon, s., meditación f.

cognac, ko-ñak', s., coñac m.

cognate, kog'-neit, a., consanguíneo; análogo

cognizance, kog'-ni-sans, s., conocimiento f.

cognizant, kog'-ni-sant, a., informado, enterado

coherence, kou-ji'-rens, s., coherencia f.

coherent*, kou-ji'-rent, a., coherente

cohesion, kou-jii'-shon, s., cohesión f.

cohesive*, kou-jii'-siv, a., cohesivo

coil, koil, s., rollo m.; bobina f. v., enrollar

coin, koin, s., moneda f. v., acuñar

coincide, kou-in-said', v., coincidir

coke, kouk, s., coque m.

cold, kould, s., frío m.; (head) resfriado m. a.,* frío

colic, kol'-ik, s., cólico m.

collaborate, ko-lab'-o-reit, v., colaborar

collapse, ko-laps', v., hundirse. s., hundimiento m.

collar, kol'-r, s., cuello m.; (dog) collar m.; **—bone,** clavícula f.

collate, ko-leit', v., comparar

collateral*, ko-lăt'-er-al, a., colateral; accesorio

collation, ko-lei'-shon, s., cotejo m.

colleague, kol'-iig, s., colega m.

collect, ko-lekt', v., (stamps, art) coleccionar; (money) cobrar; **—ed,** a., reunido; **—ion,** s., colección f.; (money) cobro m.; **—ive,** a., colectivo; **—or,** s., (tax, etc.) cobrador m.; (stamps, art, etc.) coleccionador m.

college, kol'-ich, s., colegio m.

collide, ko-laid', v., chocar

collier, kol'-ya, s., minero m., carbonero m.

colliery, kol'-yer-i, s., mina de carbón f.

collision, ko-li'-shon, s., choque m.

collop, kol'-op, s., tajada f., rebanada f.

colloquial, ko-lou'-küi-al, a., familiar

collusion, ko-luu'-shon, s., colusión f.

colon, kou'-lon, s., dos puntos m.pl.

colonel, kër'-nel, s., coronel m.

colonist, kol'-on-ist, s., colono m.

colonnade, ko-lon-eid', s., columnata f.

colony, kol'-o-ni, s., colonia f.

colossal, ko-los'-l, a., colosal

colour, köl'-a, s., color m. v., colorar; **—bar,** s., discriminación racial; **—ing,** s., colorido m.; color m.

colt, koult, s., potro m.

column, kol'-om, s., columna f.

coma, kou'-ma, s., coma f., letargo m.

comb, koum, s., (hair) peine m.; (bird) cresta f.; (honey) panal m. v., peinar

combat, kom'-bat, s., combate m. v., combatir; **—ant,** s., combatiente m.; **—ive,** a., belicoso

combination(s), kom-bi-nei'-shon(s), s., combinación f.; combinaciones f. pl.

combine, köm-bain', v., asociación f. v., combinar

combustion, kom-böst'-yon, s., combustión f.

come, köm, v., venir; **—back,** volver; **—down,** bajar; **— in,** entrar; **— off,** (unfasten, disjoin, loose) separarse; **— out,** salir; **— up,** subir

comedian, ko-mii'-di-an, s., comediante m., cómico m.

comedy, kom'-i-di, s., comedia f.
comeliness, kŏm'-li-nes, s., (grace) gracia f.; (beauty) belleza f.
comet, kom'-et, s., cometa m.
comfit, kŏm'-fit, s., confite m.
comfort, kŏm'-fort, s., (physical) comodidad f.; (solace) consuelo m.; (relief) alivio m. v., consolar; aliviar; **—able,** a., cómodo, agradable
comic, kom'-ic, a., cómico
comma, kom'-a, s., coma f.
command, ko-maand', v., mandar; dominar. s., orden f.; (knowledge) dominio m.; (mil.) mando m. **—er,** comandante m.
commandment(s), ko-maand'-ment(s), s., mandamiento(s) de la ley de Dios m.(pl).
commence, ko-mens', v., comenzar, principiar; **—ment,** s., comienzo m., principio m.
commend, ko-mend', v., recomendar; (praise) alabar
commendation, ko-men-dei'-shon, s., elogio m.
comment, ko-ment', v., comentar, s., comentario m.
commerce, kom'-ẽrs, s., comercio m.
commercial, kom-mer'-shal, a., comercial
commiserate, ko-mis'-er-eit, v., compadecer
commission, ko-mish'-on, s., comisionar, s., comisión f.; (pay) patente f.; **—aire,** factor m.
commit, ko-mit', v., (bind) comprometerse; (fault) cometer; (sentence) encarcelar
committal, ko-mit'-l, s., encarcelamiento m.
committee, ko-mit'-i, s., comité m.
commodious*, ko-moud'-i-os, a., cómodo
commodity, ko-mod'-i-ti, s., géneros m. pl., productos m. pl.
commodore, kom'-o-dór, s., jefe de escuadra m.
common, kom'-on, a.,* común; ordinario; vulgar. s., (public land) ejido m.
commoner, kom'-on-a, s., plebeyo m.
commonplace, kom'-n-pleis, a., común, trivial
commonwealth, kom'-on-uelz, s., el estado m.; la nación f.
commotion, ko-mou'-shon, s., conmoción f.
commune, ko-miuun', v., conferir; conversar

communicate, ko-miuu′-ni-keit, v., comunicar; (eccl.) comulgar

communication, ko-miuu-ni-kei′-shon, s., comunicación f.

Communion, ko-miuu′-ni-on, s., (eccl.) comunión f.

community, ko-miuu′-ni-ti, s., comunidad f.

commute, ko-miuut′, v., conmutar; —**er,** s., viajero de cercanía

compact, kom-pʌkt′, s., pacto m. a.,* compacto

companion, kom-pʌn′-yon, s., compañero m.; —**ship,** compañerismo m.

company, kŏm′-pa-ni, s., compañía f.

comparative*, kom-pʌr′-a-tiv, a., comparativo

compare, kom-pér′, v., comparar; compararse

comparison, kom-pʌr′-is-n, s., comparación f.

compartment, kom-paart′-ment, s., compartimiento m.

compass, kŏm′-pas, s., (magnetic) brújula · f.; (range) alcance m.; (a pair of)—**es,** pl., compás m.

compassionate*, kom-pʌsh′-on-eit, a., compasivo

compel, kom-pel′, v., forzar, constreñir

compensate, kom′-pen-seit, v., compensar; indemnizar

compensation, kom-pen-sei′-shon, s., compensación f.

compete, kom-piit′, v., concurrir, competir

competence, kom′-pi-tens, s., competencia f.

competition, kom-pi-ti′-shon, s., (commercial) concurrencia f.; (games) concurso m.

competitor, kom-pet′-i-ta, s., competidor m., rival m.

compile, kom-pail′, v., compilar

complacent*, kom-plei′-sent, a., complaciente

complain, kom-plein′, v., quejarse

complaint, kom-pleint′, s., queja f.; (malady) mal m.

complement, kom′-plii-ment, s., complemento m.

complete, kom-pliit′, v., completar; terminar a.,* completo; —**ly,** adv., completamente; —**ness,** s., integridad

completion, kom-plii′-shon, s., acabamiento m.

complex, kom′-plex, s., complejo m. a., complejo

complexion, kom-plek'-shon, s., (face) cutis m.
compliance, kom-plai'-ans, s., consentimiento m.
compliant*, kom-plai'-ant, a., complaciente
complicate, kom'-pli-keit, v., complicar
compliment, kom'-pli-ment, s., cumplimiento m.
v., cumplementar; —s, s.pl., saludos m. pl.
comply, kom-plai', v., conformarse
component, kom-pou'-nent, s. & a., componente m.
comport, kom-port', v., comportarse
compose, kom-pous', v., componer; calmar
composer, kom-pou'-sa, s., compositor m.
composite, kom'-po-sit, a., compuesto
composition, kom-pou-si'-shon, s., (essay, music) composición f.
compositor, kom-pos'-i-tr, s., compositor m.
composure, kom-pou'-sher, s., calma f.; compostura f.
compound, kom-paund', v., componer, a., compuesto; —fracture, fractura múltiple f. —interest, interés compuesto m.
comprehend, kom-pri-jend', v., comprender
comprehension, kom-pri-jen'-shon, s., comprensión f.
compress, kom-pres', v., comprimir, s., compresa f.
comprise, kom-prais', v., contener
compromise, kom'-pro-mais, s, compromiso m. v., comprometer
compulsion, kom-pöl'-shon, s., compulsión f.
compulsory, kom-pöl'-so-ri, a., obligatorio
compunction, kom-pönk'-shon, s., contrición f.
compute, kom-piuut', v., computar; calcular; —er, s., aparato computador m.
comrade, kom'-reid, s., camarada m.
concave, kon'-keiv, a., cóncavo
conceal, kon-siil', v., esconder, ocultar; —ment, s., escondite m., secreto m.
concede, kon-siid', v., conceder
conceit, kon-siit', s., vanidad f., presunción f.
conceited*, kon-sii'-tid, a., presumido, vano
conceive, kon-siiv', v., concebir; imaginar
concentrate, kon'-sen-treit, v., concentrar
conception, kon-sep'-shon, s., concepción f.

concern, kon'-sĕrn, s., (affair) negocio m.; (firm) empresa f.; (disquiet) preocupación f. v., concernir; **to be —ed,** (anxious) estar inquieto; (involved, interested) estar mezclado

concert, kon'-sĕrt, s., concierto m.

concession, kon-sesh'-on, s., concesión f.

conciliate, kon-sil'-i-eit, v., conciliar

concise*, kon-saiss', a., conciso

conclude, kon-kluud', v., concluir

conclusion, kon-kluu'-shon, s., conclusión f.

conclusive*, kon-kluu'-siv, a., concluyente

concoct, kon-kokt', v., confeccionar; inventar

concord, kon'-koard, s., concordia f. v., concordar

concordant, kon-koar'-dant, a., conforme

concourse, kŏn'-kórs, s., concurso m., afluencia f.

concrete, kon'-kriit, s., hormigón m. a., concreto

concur, kon-kĕr', v., concurrir, estar de acuerdo

concurrence, kon-kŏr'-ens, s., cooperación f.

concussion, kon-kŏsh'-on, s., concusión f.

condemn, kon-dem', v., condenar

condense, kon-dens, v., condensar

condescend, kon-dí'-send', v., condescender

condescension, kon-di-sen'-shon, s., condescendencia f.

condiment, kon'-di-ment, s., condimento m.

condition, kon-di'-shon, s., condición f.

conditional*, kon-di'-shon-al, a., condicional

condole, kon-doul', v., condolerse, dar el pésame

condolence, kon-dou'-lens, s., pésame m.

condone, kon-doun', v., condonar

conduce, kon-diuus', v., conducir

conducive, kon-diuu'-siv, a., conducente

conduct, kon-dŏkt, s., conducta f.; proceder m. v., conducir, dirigir

conductor, kon-dŏkt'-a, s., (guide) guía m.; (bus) cobrador m.; (music) director de orquesta m.

conduit, kŏn'-dit, s., conducto m.; (pipe) caño m.

cone, koun, s., cono m.; (fir) piña f.

coney, (see **cony**)

confabulate, kon-fAb'-iu-leit, v., confabular

confectioner, kon-fek'-sho-na, s., confitero m.; (shop) confitería f.; **—y,** (sweetmeats) dulces m.pl.

confederate, kon-fed′-er-eit, s., confederado m., cómplice m. [ración f.
confederation, kon-fed′-er-ei-shon, s., confede-
confer, kon-fër′, v., conferenciar; (bestow) conferir
confess, kon-fes′, v., confesar, reconocer
confession, kon-fesh′-on, s., confesión f.
confide, kon-′faid, v., confiar
confidence, kon′-fi-dens, s., confianza f., confidencia f.
confident*, kon′-fi-dent, a., seguro; (trustful) confiado
confidential*, kon-fi-den′-shal, a., confidencial
confine, kon-fain′, v., limitar; (lock up) aprisionar.
s., confín m., límite m.; **—ment,** prison f.;
(lying-in) parto m.
confirm, kon-fërm′, v., confirmar [f.
confirmation, kon-fër-mei′-shon, s., confirmación
confiscate, kon′-fis-keit, v., confiscar
conflagration, kon-fla-grei′-shon, s., incendio m.
conflict, kon′-flikt, s., conflicto m.; (combat) lucha f.
v., contender; **—ing,** a., contradictorio
confluent, kon′-flu-ent, a., confluente
conform, kon-foarm′, v., conformar; **—to,** conformarse; **—able,** a., conforme
confound, kon-faund′, v., (confuse) consternar;
(mistake) confundir; **—ed,** a., maldito
confront, kon-frönt′, v., confrontar
confuse, kon-fiuus′, v., confundir
confusion, kon-fiuu′-shon, s., confusión f.
confutation, kon-fiu-tei′-shon, s., refutación f.
congeal, kon-chii′l, v., congelar
congenial, kon-chii′-ni-al, a., congenial, simpático
congenital, kon-chen′-i-tl, a., congénito
congest, kon-chest′, v., aglomerar; congestionar;
—ion, s., acumulación f.; (med.) congestión f.
congratulate, kon-grat′-iu-leit, v., felicitar
congratulation, kon-grat′-iu-lei′-shon, s., con-
gratulación f., enhorabuena f.
congregate, koñ-gri-gueit, v., congregar, juntarse
congregation, koñ-gri-guei′-shon, s., asamblea f.;
(eccl.) congregación f.
congress, koñ-gres, s., congreso m.

congruous*, koñ'-gru-*os*, a., congruo

conjecture, kon-сник-'tiur, v., conjeturar. s., conjetura f.

conjointly, kon-сноint'-li, adv., conjuntamente

conjugal, kon'-сніuu-gal, a., conyugal

conjunct, kon-сноnkt', a., conjunto, unido

conjuncture, kon-сноnk'-tiur, s., coyuntura f., sazón f.

conjure, kŏn'-снer, v., hacer juegos de mano, escamotear

conjurer, kŏn'-снer-*a*, s., prestidigitador m.

connect, ko-nect', v., juntar, unir; (mech.) acoplar; —**ion**, s., conexión f.; relación f.; clientela f.

connive (at), ko-naiv'(At), v., hacer la vista gorda

connoisseur, kon-is-ĕr', s., conocedor m.

conquer, koñ'-ker, v., conquistar; vencer; —**or**, s., conquistador m.; vencedor m.

conquest, koñ'-kuest, s., conquista f.

conscience, kon'-shens, s., conciencia f.

conscientious*, kon-shi'-en-shos, a., concienzudo

conscious*, kon'-shos, a., consciente

consciousness, kon'-shos-nes, s., conocimiento m.

conscript, kon'-skript, s., recluta m. a., conscripto. v., reclutar

consecrate, kon'-si-kreit, v., consagrar

consecutive*, kon-sek'-iu-tiv, a., consecutivo

consent, kon-sent', v., consentir. s., consentimiento m.

consequence, kon'-si-kuens, s., consecuencia f.

consequential*, kon-si-küen'-shal, a., importante

consequently, kon'-si-küent'-li, adv., por consiguiente, consiguientemente

conservative*, kon-sĕr'-va-tiv, s., conservador m. a., conservador

conservatory, kon-sĕr'-va-to-ri, a., (plants) invernadero m.; (music) conservatorio m.

conserve, kon-sĕrv', v., conservar

consider, kon-sid'-*a*, v., (opinion) considerar; (ponder) reflexionar; —**ate**, a., considerado, atento; —**ation**, s., consideración f.; in —**ation, of**, en consideración de; —**ing**, prep., visto que, en atención a., considerando

considerable, kon-sid'-er-a-bl, a., considerable

consign, kon-sain', v., consignar, enviar; —**ee**, s., consignatario m.; —**ment**, consignación f.; envío m.; expedición f.; —**or**, consignador m.

consist, kon-sist', v., consistir

consistency, kon-sis'-ten-si, s., consistencia f.

consistent*, kon-sis'-tent, a., consistente; compatible

consolation, kon-so-lei'-shon, s., consolación f.

console, kon-soul', v., consolar

consoler, kon-soul'-a, s., consolador m.

consolidate, kon-sol'-i-deit, v., consolidar

consols, kon'-sols, s. pl., títulos de la deuda consolidada m. pl.

consonant, kon'-so-nant, s., consonante f.

consort, kon-soart, s., cónyuge m. v., asociarse

conspicuous*, kon-spik'-iu-os, a., (noticeable) visible; (distinguished) notable

conspiracy, kon-spir'-a-si, s., conspiración f.

conspirator, kon-spir'-ei-ta, s., conspirador m.

conspire, kon-spair', v., conspirar

constable, kon'-sta-bl, s., agente de policía m.

constabulary, kon-stab'-iu-la-ri, s., policía f.

constancy, kon'-stan-ci, s., constancia f.

constant*, kon'-stant, a., constante   [m.

constipation, kon-sti-pei'-shon, s., estreñimiento

constituency, kon-stit'-iu-en-si, s., distrito electoral m.

constituent, kon-stit'-iu-ent, s., elector m.

constitute, kon'-sti-tiuut, v., constituir

constitution, kon-sti-tiuu'-shon, s., constitución f.

constrain, kon-strein', v., constreñir

constraint, kon-streint', s., constreñimiento m.

constriction, kon-strik'-shon, s., constricción f.

construct, kons-tr̄okt', v., construir, edificar

construction, kons-tr̄ok'-shon, s., construcción f.; interpretación f.

construe, kon-struu', v., interpretar; construir

consul, kon'-sel, s., cónsul m.

consulate, kon'-siul-eit, s., consulado m.

consult, kon-sŏlt', v., consultar

consultation, kon-sel-tei'-shon, s., consulta f.

consume, kon-si**uu**m', v., consumir

consumer, kon-si**uu**'-ma, s., consumidor m.

consummate, kon'-som-e**it**, v., consumar

consummation, kon'-som-e**i**'-shon, s., consumación f.

consumption, kon-sŏm'-shon, s., (use) consumo m.; (med.) tisis f.

consumptive, kon-sŏm'-tiv, a., tísico

contact, kon'-tAkt, s., contacto m.; —**lenses**, s. pl., lentes corneales de contacto

contagious, kon-tei'-CHos, a., contagioso

contain, kon-tein', v., contener

contaminate, kon-tAm'-i-neit, v., contaminar

contemplate, kon'-tem-pleit, v., contemplar

contemporary, kon-tem'-po-ra-ri, s., contemporáneo m.

contempt, kon-temt', s., desprecio m.

contemptible, kon-tem'-ti-bl, a., despreciable

contend, kon-tend', v., contender; (maintain) sostener

content, kon-tent', v., contentar. a., contento

contention, kon-ten'-shon, s., contención f., disputa f.

contentious, kon-ten'-shos, a., contencioso

contents, kon-tents', s. pl., contenido m.

contest, kon'-test, s., contienda f.; disputa f. v., competir; disputar

contiguous, kon-ti-guiu'-os, a., contiguo

continent, kon'-ti-nent, s., continente m.

contingency, kon-tin'-CHen-si, s., eventualidad f.; contingencia f.

contingent, kon-tin'-CHent, a., contingente; casual

continual, kon-tin'-iu-al, a., continuo, incesante

continuation, kon-tin'-iu-ei'-shon, s., continua-

continue, kon-tin'-iuu, v., continuar   [ción f.

continuous, kon-tin'-iu-os, a., continuo

contortion, kon-toar'-shon, s., contorsión f.

contraband, kon'-tra-bAnd, s., contrabando m.

contract, kon-trakt', s., contrato m. v., contraer; (marriage) contraer; —**for**, —**ion**, s., contracción f., abreviación f.; —**or**, contratante m.; (builder) maestro de obras m.

contradict, kon-tra-dikt', v., contradecir
contradiction, kon-tra-dik'-shon, s., contradic-
  ción f. [ción f.
contrary, kon'-tra-ri, s., contrario m.
contrary, kon'-tra-ri, a., opuesto
contrast, kon'-trast, s., contraste m. v., contrastar
contravene, kon-tra-viin', v., contravenir, infringir
contravention, kon-tra-ven'-shon, s., contraven-
contribute, kon-trib'-iut, v., contribuir [ción f.
contribution, kon-trib-iuu'-shon, s., contribución
  f.; (gift) dádiva f.; (literary) artículo m.
contrite, kon'-trait, a., contrito
contrivance, kon-trai'-vans, s., invención f.; artificio m.; disposición f.
contrive, kon-traiv', v., imaginar; ingeniar
control, kon- troul', v., dirigir; (feelings) refrenar,
  s., dominio m.; (authority) dirección f.
controller, kon-troul'-a, s., director m.; inspector m.
controls, kon-trouls', s., (mech.) mandos m. pl.
controversial, kon-tro-vêr'-shal, a., contencioso
controversy, kon'-tro-ver-si, s., controversia f.
controvert, kon'-tro-vert, v., controvertir
contumely, kon'-tiu-me-li, s., contumelia f.; desdén m.
conundrum, ko-nŏn'-drom, s., acertijo m., adi-
  vinanza f.
convalescence, kon-va-les'-ans, s., convalecencia f.
convalescent, kon-va-les'-ent, a., convaleciente
convene, kon-viin', v., convocar
convenience, kon-vii'-ni-ens, s., conveniencia f.;
  (lavatory) excusado m.
convenient, kon-vii'-ni-ent, a., conveniente
convent, kon'-vent, s., convento m.
convention, kon-ven'-shon, s., convención f.;
  (assembly) asamblea f.
converge, kon-vêrcH', v., converger
conversant, kon'-ver-sant, a., versado en; experto
conversation, kon-ver-sei'-shon, s., conversación f.
converse, kon-vêrs', v., conversar
conversion, kon-ver'-shon, s., conversión f.
convert, kon-vêrt', v., convertir; (alter) cambiar;
  (religion) convertirse
convert, kon'-vêrt, s., convertido m.

convex, kon′-veks, a., convexo

convey, kon-vei′, v., transportar; (impart) transmitir, participar; **—ance,** s., transporte m.; vehículo m.; (law) cesión f.

conveyancer, kon-vei′-ans-a, s., escribano m.

convict, kon′-vikt, s., convicto m., presidario m. v., condenar; **—ion,** s., convicción f.; (crime) condenación f.

convince, kon-vins′, v., convencer

convivial, kon-viv′-i-al, a., sociable, festivo

conviviality, kon-viv-i-al′-i-ti, s., jovialidad f.

convocation, kon-vou-kei′-shon, s., convocatoria f., asamblea f.

convoy, kon-voi′, s., convoy m. v., convoyar

convulse, kon-vols′, v., convulsionarse; (geological) sacudir

convulsion, kon-vŏl′-shon, s., convulsión f.; (geological) sacudida f.

convulsive*, kon-vŏl′-siv, a., convulsivo

coo, kuu, v., arrullar

cook, kuk, s., cocinero m. v., hacer la comida; (in oil) guisar; (in water) cocer

cookery, kuk′-er-i, s., arte de cocina m.

cool, kuul, v., enfriar. a.,* fresco; **—ness,** s., frescura f.; indiferencia f.; sangre fría f.

coop, kuup, v., enjaular. s., jaula f.

cooper, kuu′-pa, s., tonelero m.

co-operate, kou-op′-er-eit, v., cooperar

co-operator, kou-op′-er-ei-ta, s., cooperador m.

cope, koup, v., contender

copious*, kou′-pi-os, a., copioso, abundante

copper*, kop′-a, s., cobre m., cobrizo

coppice, copse, kop′-is, kops, s., soto m., maleza f.

copy, kop′-i, v., copiar. s., copia f.; ejemplar m.

copy-book, kop′-i-buk, s., cuaderno de escribir m.

copyright, kop′-i-rait, s., derechos de autor m.

coquetry, kou′-ket-ri, s., coquetería f.

coracle, kor′-a-kl, s., barquilla de cuero f.

coral, kor′-al, s., coral m.

cord, koard, s., cuerda f. v., encordelar

cordial*, koar′-di-al, a., cordial

corduroy, koar-diu-roi′, s., pana f.

core, k**ó**r, s., centro m.

co-respondent, kou-ri-spon'-dent, s., cómplice m.

cork, k**oa**rk, s., corcho m.; (stopper) tapón m. v. tapar con corchos

corkscrew, k**oa**rk'-scruu, s., tirabuzón m., sacacorchos m.

cormorant, k**oa**r'-mo-rant, s., corvejón m.

corn, k**oa**rn, s., trigo m., grano m.; (foot) callo m.

corner, k**oa**r'-na, s., esquina f.; (of a room) rincón m.

cornflower, k**oa**rn'-fl**au**-a, s., coronilla f.

cornice, k**oa**r'-nis, s., cornisa f.

coronation, ko-ro-nei'-shon, s., coronación f.

coroner, kor'-o-na, s., médico forense m.

coronet, kor'-o-net, s., corona de un título m.

corporal, k**oa**r'-po-ral, s., cabo m. a., corporal

corporate, k**oa**r'-po-rit, a., incorporado

corporation, k**oa**r'-po-rei'-shon, s., corporación f.

corps, k**ó**r, s., cuerpo militar m.

corpse, k**oa**rps, s., cadáver m.

corpulency, k**oa**r'-piu-len-si, s., corpulencia f., gordura f.

corpulent, k**oa**r'-piu-lent, a., corpulento, gordo

corpuscle, k**oa**r'-pos-l, s., corpúsculo m.

correct, 'ko-rekt, a.,* correcto. v., corregir; (admonish) reprender; **—ness,** s., exactitud f.; (manners) corrección f.

corrective, ko-rek'-tiv, a., correctivo

correspond, kor-i-spond', v., corresponder; **—ence,** s., correspondencia f.; **—ent,** correspoudiente m.

corridor, kor'-i-d**oa**r, s., corredor m.; pasillo m.

corroborate, ko-rob'-o-reit, v., corroborar

corroboration, ko-rob'-o-rei'-shon, s., corroboración f.

corrode, ko-r**ou**d, v., corroer   [yente

corrosive, ko-r**ou**'-siv, s., corrosivo m. a., corro-

corrugated, kor'-u-guei-tid, a., (iron) ondulado; (cardboard) acanalado

corrupt, ko-r**ö**pt', v., corromper, a.,* corrupto

corruption, ko-r**ö**p'-shon, s., corrupción f.

corsair, k**oa**r'-s**é**r, s., corsario m.

corset, k**oa**r'-set, s., corsé m.

cortege, ko*ar*-te**sh**′, s., comitiva f., séquito m.

corvette, ko*ar*-vet′, s., corbeta f.

cost, kost, s., precio m.; —**s**, pl. (law) costas f. pl. v., costar; —**ly**, a., caro, costoso

costermonger, kos′-ter-mŏn̄-ga, s., vendedor ambulante

costume, kos′-tiuum, s., traje m.; vestido m.

cosy, kou′-zi, a., cómodo

cot, kot, s., (hut) cabaña f.; (child's) cuna f.

cottage, kot′-ich, s., choza f., casita de campo f.

cotton, kot′-n, s., algodón m.; (thread) hilo m.

cotton-wool, kot′-n-uul, s., algodón en rama m.

couch, kauch′, s., cama f., lecho m.

cough, ko*af*, s., tos f. v., toser

council, kaun′-sil, s., concejo m.; (state) consejo m.

councillor, kaun′-sil-a, s., concejal m.

counsel, kaun′-sl, s., (lawyer) abogado consejero m. v., aconsejar

counsellor, kaun′-sel-a, s., consultor m.; (law) consejero m.

count, kaunt, v., contar; —**-less**, a., innumerable

countenance, kaun′-te-nans, s., rostro m. v., (tolerate) apoyar, favorecer

counter, kaun′-ta, s., mostradorm.; (games) ficha f.; —**act**, v., impedir, frustrar; —**felt**, s., falsificación f. v., falsificar. a., falso; —**foil**, s., talón m.; —**mand**, v., contramandar; —**pane**, s., cubrecama f.; —**part**, contraparte f.; —**sign**, santo y seña m.

country, kŏn′-tri, s., (rural) campo m.; (state) país m.; —**man**, compatriota m.; (rural) campesino

county, kaun′-ti, s., condado m. [m.

couple, kŏp′-l, s., par m.; (people) pareja f. v., unir

courage, kŏr′-ich, s., valor m.

courageous*, ko-rei′-chos, a., valiente

course, kó*r*s, s., (direction) curso m.; (tuition) serie f.; (race) carrera f.; (ship's) rumbo m.; (meal) plato m.; **of** —, desde luego

court, kó*r*t, s., (royal) corte f.; (law) tribunal m. v., cortejar; —**ier**, s., cortesano m.; —**-martial**, consejo de guerra m.; —**ship**, corte f., noviazgo m.; —**yard**, patio m.

courteous*, kĕr′-ti-os, a., cortés, afable

courtesy, kĕr′-ti-si, s., cortesía f.

cousin, kŏs′-n, s., primo m., prima f.

cove, kouv, s., ensenada f.

covenant, kŏv′-i-nant, s., convención f. v., estipular

cover, kŏv′-a, s., cubierta f.; (lid) tapa f.; (shelter) abrigo m. v., cubrir

covet, kŏv′-et, v., codiciar

cow, kau, s., vaca f. v., intimidar; **—hide,** s., cuero vacuno m.; **—slip,** s., primavera f.

coward, kau′-uerd, s., cobarde m.; **—ice,** cobardía f.

cower, kau′-a, v., agacharse

cowl, kaul, s., (hood) capucha f.; (chimney) caballete m.

coxcomb, koks′-koum, s., mequetrefe m.

coxswain, kok′-sn, s., (steersman) timonel m.

coy*, koi, a., tímido, modesto, reservado

crab, krAb, s., cangrejo m.; **—-apple,** manzana silvestre f.; **—-bed*,** a., aspero; (writing) ilegible

crack, krAk, s., hendedura f., grieta f.; (glass) raja f.; (noise) crujido m.; (of a whip) chasquido m. v., (noise) crujir; (fissure) hender, agrietar; (whip) chasquear; (nuts) cascar

cracker, krAk′-er, s., (firework) carretilla f.; (nut) cascanueces m.; (Xmas) triquitraque m.

crackle, krAk′-l, v., crujir; (fire) crepitar

cradle, krei′-dl, s., (crib) cuna f.

craft, kraaft, s., (trade) oficio m.; (ship) embarcación f.; (cunning) astucia f.

craftsman, kraafts′-man, s., artífice m.

crafty, kraaf′-ti, a., astuto

crag, krAg, s., risco escarpado m.

cram, krAm, v., apretar; (coach) preparar para examen

cramp, krAmp, s., calambre m. v., apretar

cranberry, krAn′-be-ri, s., arándano m.

crane, krein, s., (bird) grulla f.; (hoist) grúa f. v., extender

crank, krAnk, s., manivela f.; (fig) maniático m.

cranny, krAn′-i, s., grieta f.

crape, kreip, s., crespón m.

crash, krAsh, v., (collide) chocar; (break) romper;

(crash down) desplomarse. s., choque m.; (noise) estrépito m.; (financial) quiebra f.

crater, kreit'-*a*, s., cráter m.

crave, kreiv, v., suplicar; (desire) ansiar

craving, krei'-ving, s., deseo vehemente m.

crawfish, crayfish, kroa'-fish, krei'-fish, s., (river) cangrejo de río m.; (sea) cangrejo de mar m.

crawl, kroal, v., arrastrarse; — **up,** trepar

crayon, krei'-on, s., lápiz de color m.

craze, kreis, s., demencia f.; (mania) manía f.

crazy, krei'-si, a., demente; (structure) desvencijado

creak, kriik, v., crujir

cream, kriim, s., nata f.; (whipped) crema f.

creamy, krii'-mi, a., qué contiene nata

crease, kriis, s., (press) pliegue m.; (crush) arruga f. v., plegar; arrugar

create, kri-eit', v., crear; causar; producir

creature, krii'-ti*ur*, s., criatura f.

credentials, kri-den'-sh*a*ls. s. pl., credenciales f. pl.; (diplomatic) cartas credenciales f. pl.

credible, kred'-i-bl, a., creíble

credit, kred'-it, s., crédito m. v., acreditar; — **able,** a., estimable; honorífico; — **or,** s., acreedor m.

credulous, kred'-iu-los, a., crédulo

creed, kriid, s., creencia f.

creep, kriip, v., deslizarse; (reptile) arrastrarse

creeper, krii'-p*a*, s., enredadera f.

cremate, kri-meit', v., incinerar

cremation, kri-mei'-shon, s., cremación f.

creole, krii'-oul, s., criollo m.

crescent, kres'-ent, s., creciente m.

cress, kres, s., (watercress) berro m.

crest, krest, s., (bird's) cresta f.; (heraldry) cimera f.; (hill) cima f.; — **fallen,** a., abatido

crevice, krev'-is, s., hendedura f.; griet*a* f.

crew, kruu, s., tripulación f.

crick, krik, s., tortícolis m.

cricket, krik'-et, s., grillo m.; (game) criquet m.

crime, kraim, s., crimen m.

criminal, krim'-i-n*a*l, s., criminal m.; delincuente m. a., criminal

crimson, krim'-son, s., carmesí m. a., carmesí

cringe, krincн, v., rebajarse, humillarse
crinkle, kriñ'-kl, v., rizar. s., sinuosidad f.
cripple, krip'-l, s., lisiado m. v., lisiar
crisis, krai'-sis, s., crisis f.
crisp, krisp, a., tostado crespo
criterion, krai-ti´-ri-on, s., criterio m.
critical*, krit'-i-kal, a., crítico; difícil
criticism, krit'-i-sism, s., crítica f.
criticize, krit'-i-sais, v., criticar
croak, krouk, v., (crow) graznar; (frog) croar. s., (crow) graznido m.; (frog) canto m.
crochet, krou'-she, s., (needle) aguja de gancho f. v., hacer crochet
crockery, krok'-er-i, s., vajilla f.
crocodile, krok'-o-dail, s., cocodrilo m.
crocus, krou'-kos, s., azafrán m.
crook, kruuk, s., gancho m.; (rogue) petardista m.; **—ed*,** a., corvo; deshonesto
crop, krop, s., cosecha f. v., cosechar
cross, kros, a., cruz f. a., (veexd) mal humorado. v., cruzar; **—examine,** repreguntar; **—ing,** s., (railway, road) cruce m.; (sea) travesía f.; **—out,** v., rayer; **—over,** atravesar; **—road,** s., encrucijada f.
crotchet, krót'-shit, s., (music) corchea f.
crouch, krauch, v., agacharse
crow, krou, s., cuervo m. v., cacarear
crowbar, krou'baar, s., palanca f.; barra f.
crowd, kraud, s., (people) Muchedumbre f.; (things) montón m. v., amontonar; (people) apiñarse
crown, kraun, s., corona f.; (cranium) coronilla f. v., coronar
crucible, kruu'-si-bel, s., crisol m.
crucifix, kruu'-si-fiks, s., crucifijo m.
crucify, kruu'-si-fai, v., crucificar
crude*, kruud, a., (raw) crudo; (rough) tosco
cruel*, kruu'-el, a., cruel; **—ty,** s., crueldad f.
cruet, kruu'-et, s., vinagrera f.
cruise, kruus, s., viaje por mar m. v., navegar en corso
cruiser, kruu'-sa, s., crucero m.
crumb, krŏm, s., miga f.

crumble, krŏm'-bl, v., desmoronarse
crumple, krŏm'-pl., v., estrujar; arrugar
crunch, krŏnch, v., mascar
crush, krŏsh, s., apiñamiento m. v., aplastar
crust, krŏst, s., (bread) corteza f.; (pastry) pasta f.; (earth) capa f.; **—y,** a., tostado
crutch, krŏch, s., muleta f., horquilla f.
cry, krai, s., grito m. v., (call) gritar; (weep) llorar
cryptic, krip'-tik, a., escondido, secreto
crystal, kris'-tl, s., cristal m.   [(lion) leoncillo m.
cub, kŏb, s., (dog) cachorro m.; (bear) osezno m.;
cube, kiuub, s., cubo m.
cuckoo, ku'-kuu, s., cuclillo m.
cucumber, kiuu'-kŏm-ba, s., pepino m.
cud, kŏd, s., rumia f.
cuddle, kŏd'-l, v., abrazar, abrazarse
cudgel, kŏch'-l, s., palo m. v., apalear
cue, kiuu, s., (acting) apunte m.; (billiard) taco m.
cuff, cŏf, s., puño m.; (slap) bofetada f.
culinary, kiuu'-li-na-ri, a., culinario
culminate, kŏl'-mi-neit, v., culminar
culpability, kŏl-pa-bil'-i-ti, s., culpabilidad f.
culpable, kŏl-pa-bl, a., culpable
culprit, kŏl-prit, s., reo m., culpable m.
cultivate, kŏl'-ti-veit, v., cultivar
culture, kŏl'-tiur, s., cultura f.
cumbersome, kŏm'-ber-som, a., embarazoso; pesado
cunning, kŏn'-ing, s., astucia f. a.,* astuto
cup, kŏp s., taza f.; (trophy) copa f.
cupboard, kŏb'-erd, s., armario m.
cupola, kiuu'-po-la, s., cúpula f., domo m.
cur, kẽr, s., perro de mala raza m.; hombre vil m.
curate, kiu'-reit, s., vicario m.
curb, kẽrb, v., refrenar s., freno m.; **—stone,** piedra que forma el reborde de la acera f.
curd, kẽrd, s., cuajada f., requesón m.
curdle, kẽr'-dl, v., cuajar
cure, kiur, s., (treatment) cura f.; (remedy) remedio m. v., curar; (meat, fish, etc.) salar
curiosity, kiu-ri-os'-i-ti, s., curiosidad f.
curious*, kiu-ri-os, a., curioso; (peculiar) raro
curl, kẽrl, s., rizo m. v., rizarse

urlew, kĕr'-liuu, s., chorlito m.
urrant, kŏr'-ant, s., grosella f.; (dried) pasa de Corinto f.
urrency, kŏr'-en-si, s., moneda f.
urrent, kŏr'-ent, s., corriente f. a.,* corriente
urry, kŏr'-i, s., condimento de India m.
urse, kĕrs, s., maldición f. v., maldecir
ursory, kĕr'-so-ri, a., de carrera, somero
urt*, kĕrt, a., brusco; (restrict) restringir
urtail, ker-teil', v., acortar; (restrict) restringir
urtailment, ker-teil'-ment, s., cercenamiento m.
urtain, kĕr'-tin, s., cortina f.; (theatre) telón m.
urtsy, kĕrt'-si, s., (obeisance) reverencia f.
urve, kĕrv, s., curva f. v., encorvar
ushion, kush'-on, s., cojín m., almohada f.
ustard, kŏs'-terd, s., natillas f. pl. [m.
ustody, kŏs'-to-di, s., encierro m.; (care) cuidado
ustom, kŏs'-tom, s., costumbre f.; (trade) parroquia f.; **—house,** aduana f.; **—s-duty,** derechos de aduana m. pl.
ustomary, kŏs'-tom-a-ri, a., usual
ustomer, kŏs'-tom-a, s., parroquiano m.
ut, kŏt, s., corte m.; (joint, etc.) tajada f. v., cortar; separar; (cards) alzar; (snub) desairar; **—off,** amputar; (decapitar; (phone) cortar
uticle, kiuu'-ti-kl, s., cutícula f.
utlass, kŏt'-las, s., cuchilla f. machete m.
utler, kŏt'-la, s., cuchillero m.
utlery, kŏt'-la-ri, s., cuchillería f.
utlet, kŏt'-let, s., chuleta f.; costilla f.
utter, kŏt'-a, s., (tailor) cortador m.; (ship) cúter m.
uttle-fish, kŏt'-l-fish, s., calamar m.
yclamen, sik'-la-men, s., artanita f.
ycle, sai'-kl, s., ciclo m.; bicicleta f.
ylinder, sil'-in-da, s., cilindro m.
ynical, sin'-i-kal, a., cínico
ypress, sai'-pres, s., ciprés m.

ïab, dᴀb, s., (fish) barbada f. v., tocar
ïaffodil, daf'-o-dil, s., narciso atrompetado m.
ïagger, dᴀg'-a, s., daga f., puñal m.
ïahlia, dᴀl'-i-a, s., dalia f.

daily, dei'-li, adv., diariamente, a., cotidiano

dainty, dein'-ti, s., golosina f. a., delicado; elegant

dairy, dei'-ri, s., lechería f.

daisy, dei'-si, s., margarita f., maya f.

dale, deil, s., valle m.

dam, dAm, s., pantano m. v., estancar

damage, dAm'-ich, s., daño m.; (average) avería f v., dañar; averiar

damask, dAm'-ask, s., damasco m.

damn, dAm, v., maldecir. interj., ¡maldito!

damnation, dAm-nei'-shon, s., condenación f.

damp, dAmp, s., humedad f. a., húmedo. v., hu medecer

damson, dAm'-sn, s., ciruela damascena f.

dance, daans, s., baile m., danza f. v., bailar

dancer, daans'-a, s., bailador m.; bailarín m.

dandelion, dAn'-di-lai-on, s., amargón m.

dandruff, dAn'-drof, s., caspa f.

danger, dein'-cHa, s., peligro m.

dangerous*, dein'-cHer-os, a., peligroso

dangle, dAn'-gl, v., colgar

dapper, dAp'-a, a., apuesto

dare, dér, v., atreverse; (challenge) desafiar

daring, dé'-ring, s., audacia f. a.,* audaz, osado

dark, daark, a., oscuro; **—ness,** s., obscuridad f.

darling, daar'-ling, s., querido m. a., querido

darn, daarn, v., zurcir, s., zurcido m.

dart, daart, s., dardo m. v., lanzar

dash, dAsh, s., (short line) raya f. v., (throw) ar rojar; (rush) lanzarse

dashing*, dAsh'-ing, a., fogoso

dastard, dAs'-tard, s., cobarde m. a.,* cobarde

data, dei'-ta, s. pl., datos m. pl., antecedentes m. pl

date, deit, s., fecha f.; (fruit) dátil m. v., fechar

daughter, doa'-ta, s., hija f.; **—in-law,** nuera f.

dauntless*, doant'-les, a., intrépido

dawdle, doa'-dl, v., callejear; (lag) tardar

dawn, doan, s., alba m. v., amanecer

day, dei, s., día m.; **—break,** (see dawn)

daylight, dei'-lait, s., luz del día f.

dazzle, dAs'-l, v., deslumbrar; (fig.) ofuscar

deacon, dii'-kn, s., diácono m.

dead, ded, a., muerto

deaden, ded'-n, v., amortiguar

deadlock, ded'-lok, s., paro m., desacuerdo m.

deadly, ded'-li, adv., mortalmente, a., mortal

deaf, def, a., sordo

deafen, def'-n, v., ensordecer

deafness, def'-nes, s., sordera f.

deal, diil, s., (business) trato m.; (quantity) cantidad f.; (wood) madera de pino f. v., (trade) negociar; (treat, attend to) tratar; (cards) distribuir; **a great —,** mucho

dealer, diil'-a, s., negociante m.; (small) tratante m.; (cards) mano f.

dean, diin, s., deán m.

dear, dir, a.,* querido; (expensive) caro, costoso

dearth, dĕrz, s., escasez f.

death, dez, s., muerte f.

debar, di-báar', v., excluir; (deprive) privar

debase, di-beis', v., envilecer; degradar

debate, di-beit', v., debatir, s., debate m.

debater, di-bei'-ta, s., orador m.; polemista m.

debauch, di-boach', v., corromper; pervertir

debauchery, di-boa'-cher-i, s., libertinaje m.

debenture, di-ben'-tiur, s., obligación f.

debility, di-bil'-i-ti, s., debilidad f.

debit, deb'-it, s., debe m. v., debitar

debt, det, s., deuda f.

debtor, det'-a, s., deudor m.

decadence, dek'-a-dens, s., decadencia f.

decamp, di-kamp', v., escaparse

decant, di-kant', v., trasegar

decanter, di-kan'-ta, s., garrafa f.

decarbonize, di-kaar'-bon-ais, v., descarbonizar

decay, di-kei', s., (decline) decadencia f.; (rot) podredumbre f. v., decaer; (rot) pudrirse; (tooth) v., cariarse. a., cariado

decease, di-siis', v., morir. s., fallecimiento m.

deceased, di-siist', s. & a., muerto m., difunto m.

deceit, di-siit', s., engaño m.

deceitful, di-siit'-ful, a., engañoso; falso

deceive, di'-siiv', v., engañar; (illusion) alucinar

December, di-sem'-ba, s., diciembre m.

decency, dii'-sen-si, s., decencia f.

decent', dii'-sent, a., decente

deception, di-sep'-shon, s., decepción f.; (trick) engaño m.

deceptive, di-sep'-tiv, a., engañoso

decide, di-said', v., decidir; resolver

decided, di-sai'-did, a., resuelto; firme

decimal, des'-i-mal, a., decimal

decipher, di-sai'-fa, v., descifrar

decision, di-si'-shon, s., decisión f.

decisive*, di-sai'-siv, a., decisivo

deck, dek, v., adornar s., cubierta f., puente m.

declaim, di-kleim', v., declamar

declaration, dek-la-rei'-shon, s., declaración f.

declare, di-klér', v., declarar

declension, di-klen'-shon, s., decadencia f.; (grammar) declinación f.

decline, di-klain', s., disminución f.; (values) baja f.; (ground) declive m.; (decadence) decadencia f. v., decaer; (reject) rehusar; (grammar) declinar

declutch, dii-klöch', v., desembragar

decompose, di-kom-pous', v., descomponer

decorate, dek'-o-reit, v., decorar, adornar

decoration, dek-o-rei'-shon, s., decoración f.

decorous*, dek'-o-ros, a., decoroso, decente

decoy, di-koi', s., (thing) seducción f.; (person) entruchón m.; (bird) señuelo m. v., entruchar

decrease, di-kriis', v., disminuir, decrecer

decrease, dii'-kriis, s., disminución f.

decree, di-krii', v., decretar, s., decreto m.

decry, di-krai', v., denigrar, desacreditar

dedicate, ded'-i-keit, v., dedicar; consagrar

deduct, di-dökt', v., rebajar, deducir

deduction, di-dök'-shon, s., deducción f., rebaja f.

deed, diid, s., acto m.; hecho m.; (valour) hazaña f.; (document) escritura f.

deem, diim, v., juzgar

deep, diip, s., piélago m. a.,* profundo, hondo

deepen, dii'-pn, v., profundizar

deer, dir, s., venado m.

deface, di-feis', v., desfigurar

defamation, def-a-mei'-shon, s., difamación f.

defame, di-feim', v., difamar

default, di-foalt', s., (business) suspensión de pagos f. v., dejar de pagar; (law) estar en rebeldía

defaulter, di-foalt'-a, delincuente m.; (payment) que no paga

defeat, di-fiit', s., derrota f. v., derrotar; frustrar

defect, di-fekt', s., defecto m., imperfección f.

defective*, di-fek'-tiv, a., defectuoso

defence, di-fens', s., defensa f.; protección f.

defenceless, di-fens'-les, a., indefenso

defend, di-fend', v., defender; proteger

defendant, di-fen'-dant, s., demandado m.

defender, di-fen'-da, s., defensor m.

defensible, di-fen'-si-bl, a., defendible

defensive*, di-fen'-siv, a., defensivo

defer, di-fër', v., diferir

deference, def'-er-ens, s., consideración f.

defiance, di-fai'-ans, s., reto m.; (challenge) desafío m.

deficiency, di-fish'-en-si, s., falta f.; (money) déficit m.

deficient, di-fish'-ent, a., deficiente

deficit, def'-i-sit, s., déficit m.

defile, di-fail', v., (soil) ensuciar; (moral) manchar

define, di-fain', v., definir, determinar

definite*, def'-i-nit, a., definido, preciso

definition, def-i-ni'-shon, s., definición f.

deflect, di-flekt', v., desviar; apartar; desviarse

deflection, di-flek'-shon, s., desviación f.

deform, di-foarm', v., deformar; desfigurar

defraud, di-froad', v., defraudar; estafar; frustrar

defray, di-frei', v., costear, pagar

deft*, deft, a., diestro, mañoso, hábil

defunct, di-fönkt', a., difunto

defy, di-fai', v., desafiar, retar

degenerate, di-chen'-er-et, v., degenerar. s., degenerado m.

degradation, deg-ra-dei'-shon, s., degradación f.; envilecimiento m.

degrade, di-greid', v., degradar; envilecer

degree, di-grii', s., grado m.

deign, dein, v., dignarse, condescender

deject, di-CHEKT', v., abatir, desalentar
dejection, di-CHEK'-shon, s., abatimiento m.
delay, di-le', s., dilación f.; (late) retraso m. v., retardar; (linger) tardar
delectable, di-lek'-ta-bl, a., deleitable
delegate, del'-i-guet, s., delegado m. v., delegar
delete, di-liit', v., borrar
deleterious, di-li-tii'-ri-os, a., deletéreo, pernicioso
deletion, di-lii'-shon, s., tachadura f.
deliberate, di-lib'-er-eit, v., deliberar. a., circunspecto, prudente; premeditado
delicacy, del'-i-ka-si, s., delicadeza f.; (food) golosina f.
delicate*, del'-i-keit, a., delicado
delicious*, di-lish'-os, a., delicioso
delight, de-lait', v., deleitar. s., deleite m., delicia f.
delightful*, de-lait'-ful, a., delicioso
delineate, di-lin'-i-eit, v., delinear
delinquent, di-lin'-kuent, s. & a., delincuente m. &
delirious, di-lir'-i-os, a., delirante   [f.
delirium, di-lir'-i-om, s., delirio m.
deliver, di-liv'-a, v., (letters, goods) entregar; (rib) librar; (set free) libertar; (speech) pronunciar; —y, s., entrega f.; (letters) distribución f.
delude, di-liuud', v., engañar; (mental) alucinar
delusion, di-liuu'-shon, s., ilusión f.; engaño m.
delve, delv, v., cavar
demand, di-maand', s., demanda f. v., demandar, exigir
demean (oneself), di-miin', v., comportarse
demeanour, di-mii'-ner, s., conducta f., porte m.
demented, di-men'-tid, a., loco, demente
demise, di-mais', s., muerte f.
democratic, dem-ou-krat'-ik, a., democrático
demolish, di-mol'-ish, v., demoler
demon, dii'-mon, s., demonio m.
demonstrate, dem'-on-streit, v., demostrar
demoralize, di-mor'-a-lais, v., desmoralizar
demur, di-mer', v., oponerse, objeción f.
demure*, di-miuur', a., reservado, modesto
den, den, s., antro m.; (wild beast) cuchitril m.
denial, di-nai'-al, s., negativa f., denegación f.

denizen, den'-i-sn, s., vecino m., habitante m. & f.

denomination, di-nom-i-nei'-shon, s., denominación f.; (religion) secta f.

denote, di-nout', v., denotar

denounce, de-nauns', v., denunciar, delatar

dense*, dens, a., espeso, denso

density, dens'-i-ti, s., densidad f.

dent, dent, s., abolladura f. v., abollar

dentist, den'-tist, s., dentista m.

dentistry, den'-tist-ri, s., cirugía dental f.

denude, di-niuud', v., desnudar, despojar

deny, di-nai', v., negar; (refuse) rehusar

deodorizer, di-ou'-der-ai-sa, s., desodorante m.

depart, di-paart', v., partir; (decease) morir

department, di-paart'-ment, s., departamento m.

departure, di-paar'-tiur, s., partida f.; salida f.;
——**platform,** andén m.

depend (upon), di-pend', v., (contingent) depender de; (trust) confiar en

dependant, di-pen'-dant, s., dependiente m. & f.

depict, di-pikt', v., pintar, representar

deplete, di-pliit', v., agotar, disipar

depletion, di-plii'-shon, s., agotamiento m.

deplore, di-plór', v., deplorar

deport, di-pórt', v., deportar

deportment, di-pórt'-ment, s., porte m.; conducta f.

depose, di-pous', v., deponer

deposit, di-pos'-it, s., (bank, sediment, on account, etc.) depósito m. v., depositar

depositor, di-pos'-i-ta, s., depositante m. & f.

depository, di-pos'-i-to-ri, s., (store) almacén m.

depot, di'-pou, s., almacén m.; (station) estación f.

deprave, di-preiv', v., depravar, viciar

deprecate, dep'-ri-keit, v., deprecar

depreciate, di-prii'-shi-eit, v., depreciar; rebajar

depredation, dep-ri-dei'-shon, s., pillaje m.

depress, di-pres', v., deprimir; desanimar

depression, di-presh'-on, s., (trade) depresión f.; (spirits) abatimiento m.; (glen) hondonada f.

deprivation, dep-ri-vei'-shon, s., privación f., pérdida f.

deprive, di-praiv', v., privar, despojar

depth, depz, s., profundidad f., hondo m.

deputation, di-piu-tei'-shon, s., diputación f.

deputy, dep'-iu-ti, s., substituto m.; delegado m.

derailment, di-reil'-ment, s., descarrilamiento m.

derange, di-reinch', v., desarreglar; —ment, s., desarreglo m.; trastorno mental m.

derelict, der'-i-likt, a., abandonado. s., derelicto m.

deride, di-raid', v., mofar, escarnecer

derision, di-rii'-shon, s., mofa f., escarnio m.

derisive*, di-rai'-siv, a., irrisorio, burlesco

derive, di-raiv', v., derivar; (knowledge) deducir

derogatory, di-rog'-a-to-ri, a., despectivo

descend, di-send', v., bajar; (lineage) descender

descendant, di-send'-ant, s., descendiente m.

descent, di-sent', s., bajada f.; (lineage) descendencia f.

describe, di-skraib', v., describir

description, di-skrip'-shon, s., descripción f.

desecrate, des'-i-kreit, v., profanar

desert, des'-ert, s., (wilderness) desierto m.

desert, di-sert', v., abandonar; (mil.) desertar

deserter, di-sert'-a, s., desertor m.

desertion, di-ser'-shon, s., abandono m.; (mil.) deserción f.

deserve, di-serv', v., merecer

deservedly, di-ser'-ved-li, adv., merecidamente

desiccate, di-sik'-eit, v., desecar, secar

design, di-sain', s., (sketch) diseño m.; (intention) designio m.; (pattern) patrón m. v., (plan) proyectar; (sketch) diseñar

designing, di-sai'-ning, a., intrigante, artero

desireable, di-sai'-ra-bl, a., deseable

desire, di-sair', v., deseo m v., desear

desirous, di-sai'-ros, a., deseoso

desist, di-sist', v., desistir, cesar

desk, desk, s., pupitre m.; escritorio m.

desolate, des'-o-leit, a., desolado. v., desolar

despair, di-sper', v., desesperar. s., desesperación f.

despatch, dis-pach', s., (message) despacho m. v., despachar

desperate*, des'-per-eit, a., desesperado

despicable, des'-pi-ka-bl, a., despreciable
despise, di-spais', v., despreciar
despite, di-spait', prep., a pesar de
despoil, di-spoil', v., despojar
despond, di-spond', v., desalentarse
despondency, di-spon'-den-si, s., desaliento m.
despot, des'-pot, s., déspota m., tirano m.
dessert, di-sért', s., postres m. pl.
destination, des-ti-nei'-shon, s., destinación f.
destine, des'-tin, v., destinar
destiny, des-tin'-i, s., destino m., hado m.
destitute, des'-ti-tiuut, a., destituído
destitution, des-ti-tiuu'-shon, s., destitución f.;
   privación f.
destroy, di-stroi', v., destruir
destruction, dis-trök'-shon, s., destrucción f.
destructive*, dis-trök'-tiv, a., destructivo
desultory, des'-ol-to-ri, a., variable, inconstante
detach, di-tach', v., separar; (mil.) destacar
detachable, di-tach'-a-bl, a., movible
detail, di-teil', v., detallar
detail, dii'-teil, s., detalle m., pormenor m.
detain, di-tein', v., detener
detect, di-tekt', v., descubrir; sorprender
detective, di-tek'-tiv, s., detective m.
detention, di-ten'-shon, s., detención f.
deter, di-tĕr', v., disuadir, acobardar
detergent, di-tĕr'-chent, s., detergente m.
deteriorate, di-tii'-ri-o-reit, v. deteriorar, desmejorar
determine, di-tĕr'-min, v., determinar, resolverse
detest, di-test', v., detestar
dethrone, di-zroun', v., destronar
detonation, di-to-nei'-shon, s., detonación f.
detour, di-túr', s., vuelta f., rodeo m.
detract, di-trakt', v., detraer; (value) disminuir
detrimental, det-ri-men'-tal, a., perjudicial
deuce, diuus, s., (cards, dice, two) dos m.; (equality) a patas f. pl.
devastate, dev'-as-teit, v., devastar
develop, di-vel'-op, v., desenvolver, desarrollar
development, di-vel'-op-ment, s., desarrollo m.

deviate, diï'-vi-eit, v., desviarse

device, di-vais', s., medio m.; invención f.

devil, dev'-l, s., diablo m., demonio m.

devilry, dev'-il-ri, s., diablura f.

devise, di-vais', v., inventar, tramar; (law) disponer

devoid, di-void', a., falto, desprovisto

devote, di-vout', v., dedicar

devour, di-vaur', v., devorar

devout*, di-vaut', a., devoto, piadoso

dew, diuu, s., rocío m.

dexterous*, deks'-ter-os, a., diestro; hábil

diabetes, dai-a-bii'-tis, s., diabetes f.

diabolical*, dai-a-bol'-i-kal, a., diabólico

diagnose, dai-ag-nous', v., diagnosticar

diagonal, dai-ag'-o-nal, s., diagonal m. a.,* diagonal

diagram, dai'-a-gram, s., diagrama m.

dial, dai'-al, s., (clock) esfera f.; (sun) reloj de sol m.

dialect, dai'-a-lekt, s., dialecto m.

dialogue, dai'-a-log, s., diálogo m.

diameter, dai-am'-i-ta, s., diámetro m.   [m. pl.

diamond, dai'-a-mond, s., diamante m.; (cards) oros

diarrhœa, dai-a-rii'-a, s., diarrea f.

diary, dai'-a-ri, s., diario m.; (business) agenda f.

dice, dais, s. pl., dados m. pl.

dictate, dik-teit', v., dictar

dictionary, dik'-shon-a-ri, s., diccionario m.

die, dai, v., morir, fallecer. s., (stamp) cuño m.;
(mould) matriz f.

diet, dai'-et, s., dieta f., alimento m., régimen m.;
to put on a —, v., poner a dieta; **to be on a
—,** estar a dieta

differ, dif'-a, v., diferir, diferenciarse; (disagree) disentir

difference, dif'-er-ens, s., diferencia f., disputa f.

different*, dif'-er-ent, a., diferente

difficult, dif-ik-elt, a., difícil; **—y,** s., dificultad f.

diffident*, dif'-id-ent, a., desconfiado; (fig) corto

diffuse, dif-iuus', v., difundir s., difuso

dig, dig, v., cavar, excavar

digest, di-cнest', v., digerir. s., recopilación f.

digestion, di-cнes'-tion, s., digestión f.

dignified, dig'-ni-faid, a., grave, digno

dignitary, dig'-ni-ta-ri, s., dignatario m.

dignity, dig'-ni-ti, s., dignidad f.

digression, di-gresh'-on, s., digresión f.

dike, daik, s., dique m., presa f.

dilapidated, di-lap'-i-deit-id, a., dilapidado

dilapidation, di-lap'-i-dei-shon, s., dilapidación f.

dilate, di-leit', v., dilatar; dilatarse

dilatory, dil'-a-to-ri, a., dilatorio, lento

dilemma, di-lem'-a, s., dilema m.

diligence, dil'-i-chens, s., diligencia f.

diligent*, dil'-i-chent, a., diligente

dilute, di-liuut', v., diluir, aguar

dim, dim, v., obscurecer. a.,* obscuro; (sight) turbio

dimension, di-men'-shon, s., dimensión f., medida f.

diminish, di-min'-ish, v., disminuir

dimness, dim'-nes, s., obscuridad f.

dimple, dim'-pel, s., hoyuelo m.   [m.

din, din, v., ensordecer. s., estruendo m., estrépito

dine, dain, v., comer

dingy, din'-chi, a., deslustrado, deslucido

dining-car, dain'-ing-kaar, s., coche restauran m.

dining-room, dain'-ing-ruum, s., comedor m.

dinner, din'-a, s., comida f.; (=supper) cena f.

dip, dip, s., inmersión f. v., sumergir; (moisten) mojar; (slope) bajar

diphtheria, dif-zii'-ri-a, s., difteria f.

diplomacy, di-plou'-ma-si, s., diplomacia f.

dire, dair, a., terrible, horrendo

direct, di-rekt', v., dirigir. a., directo

direction, di-rek'-shon, s., dirección f.; (instruction) orden f.

directly, di-rekt'-li, adv., directamente, en seguida. conj., luego que

director, di-rek'-ta, s., director m., administrador m.

directory, di-rek'-to-ri, s., directorio m.; (small) guía f.

dirt, dërt, s., basura f., lodo m., suciedad f.

dirty, dër'-ti, v., ensuciar. a., sucio

disability, dis-a-bil'-i-ti, s., inhabilidad f.; incapacidad f.

disable, dis-ei'-bl, v., mutilar; inutilizar

disadvantage, dis-ad-vaan'-tich, s., desventaja f.

disagree, dis-*a*-grii', v., disentir; discrepar; incomodar

disagreeable, dis-*a*-grii'*a*-bl, a., desagradable

disallow, dis-*a*-lau', v., desaprobar; rechazar

disappear, dis-*a*-pir', v., desaparecer

disappearance, dis-*a*-pi'rans, s., desaparición f.

disappoint, dis-*a*-point', v., chasquear, desengañar, desilusionar; frustrar; (promise) dar chasco; —**ment,** s., desengaño m., chasco m., desilusión f.

disapprove, dis-*a*-pruuv', v., desaprobar

disarm, dis-aarm', v., desarmar

disaster, dis-aas'-ta, s., desastre m.

disastrous*, dis'-aas-tros, a., desastroso

disavow, dis-*a*-vau', v., repudiar; desconocer

disc, disk, s., disco m.

discard, dis-kaard', v., descartar; (cast off) desechar

discern, di-sĕrn', v., discernir

discharge, dis-chaarch', s., (dismissal) despedida f.; (gun) descarga f.; (merchandise) descargo m.; (med.) derrame m. v., despedir; descargar; (fulfil) cumplir; (acquit) absolver; (release) poner en libertad

disciple, dis-ai'-pl, s., discípulo m.

discipline, dis'-i-plin, s., disciplina f.

disclaim, dis-kleim', v., renunciar; (deny) desconocer

disclose, dis-klous', v., revelar; descubrir

disclosure, dis-klou'-shur, s., revelación f.

discolour, dis-kal'-*a*, v., descolorar; desteñir

discomfit, dis-kŏm'-fit, v., desconcertar; —**ure,** s., desconcierto m.

discomfort, dis-kŏm'-fort, s., incomodidad f.

disconnect, dis-ko-nekt', v., desunir; desconectar

discontent, dis-kon-tent', s., descontento m.; —**ed,** a., descontento

discontinue, dis-kon-tin'-iuu, v., interrumpir; (deter) aplazar

discord, dis-koard', s., discordia f.

discount, dis-kaunt', v., descontar, s., descuento m.

discourage, dis-kŏr'-ich, v., desalentar

discourse, dis-kŏrs', v., discurrir; conversar, s., discurso m.; conversación f.

discourteous*, dis-k0ar´-ti-os, a., descortés
discover, dis-kŏv´-a, v., descubrir
discovery, dis-kŏv´er-i, , descubrimiento m.
discreet*, dis-kriit´, a., discreto
discrepancy, dis-krep´-ans-i, s., discrepancia f.
discriminate, dis-krim´-i-neit, v., discernir
discuss, dis-kŏs´, v., discutir
disdain, dis-dein´, v., desdeñar, s., desdén m.
disdainful*, dis-dein´-ful, a., desdeñoso
disease, di-siis´, enfermedad f., dolencia f.
disengaged, dis-en-geich´, a., libre; vacante
disentangle, dis-en-taŋg´-gl, v., desenredar
disfigure, dis-fig´-a, v., desfigurar
disgrace, dis-greis´, s., deshonra f. v., deshonrar
disguise, dis-gais´, s., disfraz m. v., disfrazar; (feelings) ocultar
disgust, dis-gŏst´, v., disgustar. s., repugnancia f.
dish, dish, s., fuente f.; (meal) plato m.; — **cloth,** rodilla f.; — **up,** v., servir
dishearten, dis-jaar´-tn, v., desalentar
dishevelled, di-shev´-eld, a., desgreñado
dishonest, dis-on´-ist, a., deshonrado
dishonour, di-son´-a, v., deshonrar. s., deshonra f.
disillusionize, dis-i-liuu´-shon-ais, v., desilusiona
disinclination, dis-in-klin-ei´-shon, s., aversión f.
disinfect, dis-in-fekt´, v., desinfectar
disinherit, dis-in-jer´-it, v., desheredar
disjoin, dis-choin´, v., descoyuntar, separar; —**ted,** a., dislocado; separado; desarticulado
dislike, dis-laik´, v., tener aversión a, s., aversión f.
dislocate, dis´-lo-keit, v., dislocar; (joint) descoyuntar
disloyal, dis-loi´-al, a., desleal; infiel
dismal*, dis´-mal, a., triste; (gloomy) lúgubre
dismay, dis-mei´, v., aterrorizar, s., consternación f.
dismiss, dis-mis´, v., despedir; (mentally) descartar
dismount, dis-maunt´, v., desmontar
disobedient*, dis-o-bii´-di-ent, a., desobediente
disobey, dis-ou-bei´, v., desobedecer
disorder, dis-oar´-da, s., desorden m. v., desordenar
disown, dis-oun´, v., repudiar; desconocer
disparage, dis-par´-ich, v., rebajar

dispatch, (see despatch)

dispel, dis-pel', v., dispersar; disipar

dispensary, dis-pen'-sa-ri, s., dispensario m.

dispensation, dis-pen-sei'-shon, s., distribución f.

disperse, dis-pörs', v., dispersar [(eccl.) dispensa f.

display, dis-plei', v., exhibir. s., exhibición f.

displease, dis-pliis', v., desagradar

displeasure, dis-plesh'-er, s., desagrado m.

disposal, dis-pou'-sal, s., disposición f.; venta f.

dispose, dis-pous', v., disponer; vender

disprove, dis-pruuv', refutar

disputable, dis-piuu'-ta-bl, a., disputable; controvertible

dispute, dis-piuut', v., disputar. s., disputa f.

disqualify, dis-kuou'-li-fai, v., descalificar

disquiet, dis-kuai'-et, v., inquietar [(quietud) inquietud f.

disregard, dis-ri-gaard', v., desatender. s., desatención f.

disrepute, dis-ri-piuut', s., descrédito m.

disrespect, dis-ri-spekt', s., desatención f.; **—ful***, a., desatento

dissatisfy, di-sAT'-is-fai, v., descontentar

dissect, dis-sekt', v., disecar

dissent, di-sent', v., disentir. s., disensión f.

dissimilar, di-sim'-i-lar, a., diferente, disímil

dissipate, dis'-si-peit, v., disipar, esparcir

dissociate, di-sou-shi-eit, v., desunir, disociar

dissolute, dis'-o-liuut, a., disoluto, libertino

dissolve, dis-solv', v., disolver

dissuade, di-sueid', v., disuadir

distance, dis'-tans, s., distancia f.

distant*, dis'-tant, a., distante; esquivo; frío

distasteful*, dis-teist'-ful, a., desagradable

distemper, dis-tem'-pa, s., (paint) destemple m.; (veterinary) moquillo m.; (peevish) mal humor m.

distend, dis-tend', v., distender, dilatar

distil, dis-til', v., destilar

distinct*, dis-tiñkt, a., distinto; diferente

distinction, dis-tiñk'-shon, s., distinción f.; diferencia f.

distinguish, dis-tiñ'-güish, v., distinguir

distort, dis-toart', v., falsear; torcer

distract, dis-trakt', v., distraer; perturbar; **—ion,** s., distracción f.; perturbación f.

distress, dis-tres', s., pena f.; angustia ·f. v., angustiar; **to be in —,** (naut.) estar en apuros; **—ing,** a., penoso

distribute, dis-trib'-**iuut,** v., distribuir; clasificar

distributor, dis-trib'-**iuut**-*a*, s., (mech.) mecanismo distribuidor m.; (comm.) comerciante distribuidor m.; concesionario m.

district, dis'-trikt, s., distrito m.; región f.

distrust, dis-tröst', v., desconfiar, s., desconfianza f.

disturb, dis-tĕrb', v., perturbar; **—ance,** s., interrupción f.; disturbio m.; (mob) tumulto m.

disuse, dis-iuus's, s., desuso m.

ditch, dich, s., zanja f.; foso m.

ditto, dit'-oh, adv., idem [m.

dive, daiv, v., zambullirse; sumergirse; **—r,** s., buzo

diverge, di-vĕrch', v., divergir

diverse, dai-vĕrs', a., varios; diversos

diversion, di-vĕr'-shon, s., desviación f.; distracción f.

divert, dai-vĕrt', v., desviar; (attention) distraer

divest, di-vest', v., desnudar; (deprive) despojar

divide, di-vaid', v., dividir; separar; (distribute) repartir

divine, di-vain', v., adivinar. a.,* divino

division, di'-vi-shon, s., división f.; partición f.

divorce, di-vórs', v., divorciar. s., divorcio m.

divulge, di-vŏlch', v., revelar

dizzy, diz'-i, a., vertiginoso; (faint) desvanecido

do, duu, v., hacer; servir; bastar; cocer; hallarse

docile, dos'-il, a., dócil, sumiso

dock, dok, s., dársena f.; (court) barra f.; **dry—,** astillero m.; **—yard,** astillero m.

doctor, dok -ta, s., médico m. v., curar

doctrine, dok'-trin, s., doctrina f.; dogma m.

document, dok'-iu-ment, s., documento m.; **—ary,** s., (film) película documental f.

dodge, doch, v., evadir; esquivar. s., evasiva f.

dog, dog, s., perro m.; **—ged,** a., tenaz; terco

dole, doul, v., distribuir. s., distribución f.; dádiva f.

doleful*, doul'-ful, a., doloroso; lastimoso

doll, dol, s., muñeca f.

domain, do-mein', s., propriedad f.; dominio f.

dome, doum, s., cúpula f., domo m.

domestic, do-mes'-tik, s., criado m.; doméstico m.; a., doméstico; — **ated,** a., domesticado

domicile, dom'-i-sail, s., domicilio m. v., domiciliar

dominate, dom'-i-neit, v., dominar

domineer, dom-i-nir', v., dominar; tiranizar

donation, do-nei'-shon, s., donación f.

donkey, dong'-ki, s., asno m., burro m.

donor, do'-na, s., donador m.; donante m.

doom, duum, s., sentencia f.; destino m.; ruina f. v., predestinar; — **sday,** s., día del juicio universal m.

door, dór, s., puerta f.; — **keeper,** portero m.; — **knocker,** picaporte m.; — **mat,** felpudo m.; — **step,** escalera de entrada f.

dormant, dor'-mant, a., desuso, inactivo

dormitory, dor'-mi-to-ri, s., dormitorio m.

dormouse, dor'-maus, s., lirón m.

dose, dous, s., dosis f. v., dosificar

dot, dot, s., punto m. v., puntear

double, dób'-l, s., doble m.; duplicado m. v., doblar

doubt, daut, v., dudar. s., duda f.; — **ful*,** a., dudoso; — **less,** adv., sin duda

douche, dush, s., ducha f.

dough, dou, pasta f., masa f.

dove, dóv, s., paloma f.; — **cot,** palomar m.

down, daun, adv. & prep., abajo. s., plumón m.; — **cast,** a., abatido; — **fall,** s., caída f., ruina f.; — **pour,** aguacero m.; chaparrón m.; — **wards,** adv., hacia abajo

dowry, dau'-ri, s., dote f.

doze, dous, v., dormitar. s., sueño ligero m.

dozen, dós'-n, s., docena f.

drab, drab, a., pardusco

draft, draaft, s., (money) giro m.; (sketch) boceto m.; (writing) borrador m. v., redactar

drag, drag, v., arrastrar, tirar. s., draga f.

dragon, drag'-on, s., dragón m.; — **fly,** libélula f.

drain, drein, v., desaguar. s., desaguadero m.; (trench) zanja f.; — **age,** desagüe m.

drake, dreik, s., pato m.

dram, drAm, s., dracma f.

dramatic, drAm-a'-tick, a., dramático

draper, drei'-pa, s., pañero m.

drastic, drAs'-tik, a., drástico

draught, draaft, s., (air) corriente de aire f. ; (med.) poción f. ; (liquor) trago m. ; (sketch) diseño m. ; (ship) calado m. ; **—board**, tablero de damas m. ; **—s**, pl., juego de damas m.

draughtsman, draafts'-man, s., delineante m.

draw, droa, v., (pull) tirar ; (attract) atraer ; (sketch) dibujar ; (bill) girar ; (money) cobrar

drawback, droa'-bak, s., desventaja f.

drawer, droa'-a, s., (furniture) cajón m. ; (bill) girador m. ; **—s**, pl., calzoncillos m. pl.

drawing, droa'-ing, s., tiro m. ; (sketch) dibujo m.

drawl, droal, v., arrastrar las palabras

dray, drei, s., carromato m.

dread, dred, s., miedo m. v., temer

dreadful, dred'-ful, a., terrible

dream, driim, s., sueño m. v., soñar

dreary, dri'-ri, a., triste ; sombrío ; fatigante

dredge, drech, v., dragar ; **—r**, s., draga f.

dregs, dregs, s. pl., heces f. pl. ; sedimento m.

drench, drench, v., empapar, mojar

dress, dres, s., vestido m., traje m. v., vestir, vestirse ; (wounds) curar ; (hair) peinar

dressing, dres'-ing, s., (med.) vendajes m. pl. ; (culinary) condimento m. ; **—-case**, neceser m. ; **—-gown**, bata f. ; **—-room**, tocador m.

dressmaker, dres'-meik-a, s., modista f.

dribble, drib'-l, v., gotear

drift, drift, s., deriva f. ; (snow, etc.) torbellino m. ; (tendency) tendencia f., giro m. v., derivar ; impeler

drill, dril, s., (mil.) ejercicio m. ; (tool) taladro m. v., enseñar el ejercicio ; taladrar

drink, dring-k, s., bebida f. v., beber

drip, drip, v., gotear, chorrear. s., gotera f.

dripping, drip'-ing, s., (fat) pringue m.

drive, draiv, v., conducir, guiar. s., (approach) calzada para coches f. ; (outing) paseo en coche m.

driver, drai'-v*a*, s., cochero m.; chófer m.; (owner) conductor m.; (engine) maquinista m.

drizzle, dris'-l, v., lloviznar. s., llovizna f.

droll, droul, a., jocoso

drone, droun, s., zángano m. v., zumbar

droop, druup, v., inclinarse; (plants) marchitarse

drop, drop, s., caída f.; (liquid) gota f. v., caer; (let fall) dejar caer

dropsy, drop'-si, s., hidropesía f.

drought, draut, s., sequía f., sequedad f.

drove, drouv, s., manada f., rebaño m.

drown, draun, v., ahogar, ahogarse

drowsy, drau'-si, a., soñoliento, adormecido

drudge, dröch, v., afanarse

drudgery, dröch'-*a*-ri, s., faena f.

drug, drög, v., jaropar, s., droga f.

druggist, drö'-guist, s., boticario m., droguero m.

drum, drom, s., tambor m.; (ear) tímpano m.; (container) bidón m.; **—mer,** tambor m.

drunk, dröng'-k, a., borracho; **—ard,** s., borrachón m.; **—enness,** embriaguez f.

dry, drai, v., secar, a., *seco; **—ness,** s., sequedad f.

dubious*, diuu'-bi-os, a., dudoso

duchess, döch'-es, s., duquesa f.

duck, dök, s., pato m. v., (immerse) zambullir; (stoop) esquivar

due, diuu, s., (owing) debido n.; (toll, rights, etc.) derechos m. pl.; (deserts) merecido m. a., (owing) debido; (bill) vencido

duel, diuu'-el, s., duelo m.

duet, diu-et', s., dúo m.

duke, diuuk, s., duque m.

dull, döl, a., (mind) lerdo; (markets) desanimado; (weather) cubierto; (blunt) sin filo

duly, diuu'-li, adv., oportunamente, a su tiempo

dumb, döm, a., mudo

dumbfound, döm-faund', v., confundir

dummy, döm'-i, s., (lay figure) maniquí m.; (sham) imitado m.; (cards) mudo m.

dump, dömp, s., depósito m., estiba f. v., verter

dung, döng, s., boñiga f.; (manure) estiércol m.

dungeon, dön'-chen, s., calabozo m.

dupe, diuup, s., incauto m. v., embaucar

duplicate, diuu'-pli-keit, s., duplicado m., doble m. v., duplicar

durable, diu'-ra-bl, a., durable; duradero

duration, diu-rei'-shon, s., duración f.

during, diu'-ring, prep., durante

dusk, dösk, s., obscuridad f.; (evening) crepúsculo m.; **—y,** a., obscuro; (colour) moreno

dust, döst, s., polvo m. v., despolvorear

dust-bin, döst'-bin, s., (refuse) basurero m.

duster, döst'-a, s., plumero m.; (cloth) trapo m.

dutiful*, diuu'-ti-ful, a., obediente; respetuoso

duty, diuu'-ti, s., deber m.; (customs) derechos m. pl.; (service) servicio m.

dwarf, duoarf, s. & a., enano m. v., achicar

dwell, duel, v., habitar, residir; **—er,** s., habitante m.; residente m.; **—ing,** domicilio m.

dwindle, duin'-dl, v., mermar; disminuirse

dye, dai, s., tinte m., tintura f. v., teñir

dynamite, dai'-na-mait, s., dinamita f.

dynamo, dai'-na-mou, s., dínamo m.

dysentery, dis'-n-tri, s., disentería f.

each, iich, pron., cada uno, todos a., cada todo; **— other,** pron., el uno al otro, mutuamente

eager, ii'-ga, a.,* deseoso; **—ness,** s., ansia f.

eagle, ii'-gl, s., águila m.

ear, ir, s., oreja f.; (music) oído m.; (corn) espiga f.; **—mark,** v., marcar; **—phone,** s., auricular m. **—ring,** s., pendiente m.; **—wig,** s., tijereta f.

earl, ĕrl, s., conde m.

early, ĕr'-li, adv., temprano a., matinal; primitivo

earn, ĕrn, v., ganar; **—ings,** s. pl., salario m.

earnest*, ĕr'-nest, a., serio; sincero

earth, ĕrz, s., tierra f., suelo m. v., (electrical) ligar con la tierra; **—enware,** s., loza de barro f.; **—ly,** a., terrestre; **—quake,** s., terremoto m.

ease, iis, s., (comfort) comodidad f.; (relief) alivio m.; (facility) facilidad f. v., aliviar; **not at —,** mal a gusto

easel, ii'-sl, s., caballete de pintor m.

easily, ii'-si-li, adv., fácilmente

east, iist, s. este m., oriente m.; **—erly,** a., del este; **—ern,** oriental

Easter, iis'-ta, s., Pascua de Resurrección f.

easy, ii'-si, a., fácil; cómodo, **—chair,** s., sillón m.

eat, iit, v., comer; (worm; acid) roer

eatable, ii'-ta-bl, a., comestible; **—s,** s. pl., comestibles m. pl.   [escondido; curioso

eavesdropper, iivs'-drop-a, s., el que escucha

ebb, eb, v., menguar s., reflujo m.

ebony, eb'-o-ni, s., ébano m.

eccentric, ek-sen'-trik, a., excéntrico

echo, ek'-ou, s., eco m.

eclipse, i-klips', s., eclipse m. v., eclipsar

economize, i-kon'-o-mais, v., economizar

economy, i-kon'-o-mi, s., economía f.

ecstasy, ek'-sta-si, s., extasis m.

edge, eCH, v., (border) ribetear. s., (knife) filo m.; (brink) borde m.

edible, ed'-i-bl, a., comestible

edify, ed'-i-fai, v., edificar

edit, ed'-it, v., redactar, editar; **—ion,** s., edición f.; **—or,** editor m.; (press) director m.; **—orial,** a., artículo de fondo m.

educate, ed'-iu-keit, v., educar; (rear) criar

education, ed-iu-kei'-shon, s., educación f.

eel, iil, s., anguila f.

efface, ef-eis', v., borrar

effect, ef-ekt', v., efectuar. s., efecto m.

effective*, ef-ek'-tiv, a., eficaz; operativo

effeminate, ef-em-i-neit, a., afeminado

effervescing, ef-er-ves'-ing a., efervescente

effete, i'-fiit, a., estéril; agotado

efficacious*, ef-i-kei'-shos, a., eficaz

efficient, ef-i'-shent, a., competente; eficaz

effort, ef'-ert, s., esfuerzo m.

effusive*, ef-iuu'-siv, a., expansivo

egg, eg, s., huevo m.; **—cup,** huevera f.

egotism, eg'-ou-tism, s., egotismo m.

eiderdown, ai'-der-daun, s., edredón m.; colcha f.

eight, eit, s. & a., ocho m.; **—h,** octavo m.; **—een,** s. & a., diez y ocho m.; **—eenth,** décimoctavo m.; **—y,** s. & a., ochenta m.

either, ai'-Da, pron., uno u otro; cualquiera de los dos. adv., tampoco
eject, i-chekt', v., arrojar; expeler; despedir
elaborate, i-lab'-o-reit, v., elaborar. a.,* elaborado
elapse, i-laps', v., pasar, transcurrir
elastic, i-las'-tik, s. & a., elástico m.
elate, i-leit', v., exaltar; elevar. a., exaltado
elbow, el'-bou, s., codo m. v., codear
elder, el'-da, s., mayor m. & f.; (tree) saúco m.
elderly, el'-der-li, a., anciano [a., mayor
eldest, el'-dest, a., el mayor; primogénito
elect, i-lekt', v., elegir. s. & a., electo m.
election, i-lek'-shon, s., elección f.
electric(al*), i-lek'-trik(al), a., eléctrico
electrician, i-lek-trish'-an, s., electricista m.
electricity, i-lek-tri'-si-ti, s., electricidad f.
electrify, i-lek'-tri-fai, v., electrizar
electronic*, i-lek-tron'-ik, a., electrónico
electro-plate, i-lek'-troh-pleit, s., artículo galvanizado m. v., galvanizar
elegance, el'-i-gans, s., elegancia f.
elegant*, el'-i-gant, a., elegante
element, el'-i-ment, s., elemento m.
elementary, el-i-men'-ta-ri, a., elemental, rudimentario
elephant, el'-i-fant, s., elefante m.
elevate, el'-i-veit, v., elevar, alzar; exaltar
elevated, el'-i-vei-tid, a., elevado; exaltado
eleven, il-ev'-n, s. & a., once m.; —th, undécimo m.
elicit, il-is'-it, v., deducir; (draw out) sonsacar
eligible, el'-i-chi-bl, a., elegible; apropiado
eliminate, i-lim'-i-neit, v., eliminar
elite, ei-liit', s, lo selecto m., la flor f.
elk, elk, s., alce m
elm, elm, s., olmo m.
elongate, ii-long'-eit, v., alargar
elope, i-loup', v., fugarse; —ment, s., fuga f.
eloquent, el'-o-kuent, a., elocuente
else, els, a., otro. adv., o bien; **where,** en otra parte
elucidate, i-liuu'-si-deit, v., aclarar
elude, i-liuud', v., eludir; escapar
elusive*, i-liuu'-siv, a., evasivo, esquivo

emaciate, i-mei'-shi-eit, v., extenuar, adelgazar
emanate, em'-a-neit, v., emanar
emancipate, i-mʌn'-si-peit, v., emancipar
embalm, em-baam', v., embalsamar
embankment, em-bang-k'-ment, s., terraplén m.;
(water) malecón m.
embargo, em-baar'-gou, s., embargo m. v., embargar
embark, em-baark', v., embarcar, embarcarse
embarrass, em-bar'-ass, v., turbar; (commercial)
apurar; **—ment,** s., turbación f.
embassy, em'-bas-j, s., embajada f.
embellish, em-bel'-ish, v., embellecer; adornar
ember, em'-ber, s., ascua f.; **—s,** pl., rescoldo m.
embezzle, em-bez'-l, v., desfalcar
embitter, em-bit'-a, v., amargar; agriar
embody, em-bod'-i, v., incorporar
embolden, em-boul'-dn, v., animar; envalentonar
embrace, em-breis', v., abrazar, abrazo m.
embrocation, em-brou-kei'-shon, s., ungüento m.
embroider, em-broi'-da, v., bordar; **—y,** s., bor-
dado m.
embroil, em-broil', v., embrollar; confundir
emerald, em'-e-rald, s., esmeralda f.
emerge, i-mĕrch', v., emerger; surgir; **—ney,** s.,
emergencia f.; necesidad urgente f.
emetic, i-met'-ik, s., emético m.
emigrant, em'-i-grant, s., emigrante m. K f.
emigrate, em'-i-greit, v., emigrar
eminence, em'-in-ens, s., altura f.; eminencia f.
eminent*, em'-in-ent, a., eminente
emissary, em'-is-a-ri, s., emisario m.
emit, i-mit', v., emitir, arrojar; exhalar
emotion, i-mou'-shon, s., emoción f.; sensación f.
emperor, em'-per-a, s., emperador m.
emphasis, em'-fa-sis, s., énfasis f.
emphasize, em'-fa-sais, v., acentuar, recalcar
emphatical*, em-fat'-i-kl, a., enfático
empire, em'-pair, s., imperio m., dominio m.
employ, em-ploi', v., emplear; **—er,** s., (principal)
jefe m.; (master) patrón m.; **—ment,** s., empleo m.
emporium, em-pou'-ri-om, s., emporio m.
empower, em-pau'-a, v., autorizar, comisionar

empress, em'-pres, s., emperatriz f.

empty, em'-ti, v., vaciar; evacuar. a., vacío

emulate, em'-iu-leit, v., emular; imitar

emulation, em-iu-lei'-shon, s., emulación f.

enable, en-ei'-bl, v., habilitar, facilitar, permitir

enact, en-akt', v., decretar; estatuir; efectuar

enamel, en-am'-l, s., esmalte m. v., esmaltar

enamoured, en-am'-erd, a., enamorado

enchant, en-chaant', v., hechizar; (delight) encantar; —ment, s., (fascination) encanto m.

encircle, en-ser'-kl, v., circundar, cercar; (roundup) rodear

enclose, en-klous', v., cercar; incluir

enclosure, en-klou'-shur, s., cercado m.; (in envelope, parcel, etc.) contenido m.

encore, ang-koar', v., pedir la repetición. interj., ¡bis! ¡que se repita!

encounter, en-kann'-ta, s., encuentro m.; combate m. v., encontrar; batirse

encourage, en-kor'-ich, v., alentar; (spur) fomentar; —ment, s., estímulo m.; fomento m.

encroach, en-krouch', v., abusar; usurpar; —ment, s., abuso m.; usurpación f.

encumber, en-kom'-ba, v., estorbar; (law) gravar

encumbrance, en-kom'-brans, s., embarazo m.; (burden) estorbo m.; (legal) gravámen m.

encyclopaedia, en-sai'-klo-pii'-di-a, s., enciclopedia f.

end, end, s., fin m.; conclusión f.; final f.; extremo m. v., acabar, terminar; cesar

endanger, en-dein'-cha, v., arriesgar, poner en peligro

endear, en-dir', v., hacerse querer; encarecer

endearment, en-dir'-ment, s., encarecimiento m.

endeavour, en-dev'-a, v., esforzarse. s., esfuerzo m.

endive, en'-div s., escarola f.

endless, end'-les, a., sin fin; perpetuo

endorse, en-doars', v., endosar; (ratify) sancionar; —ment, s., endoso m.; sanción f.

endow, en-dau', v., dotar; fundar

endurance, en-diúr'-ans, s., resistencia f.; paciencia f.

endure, en-diúr', v., soportar; tolerar
enema, en'-i-ma, s., jeringa f., lavativa f.
enemy, en'-i-mi, s., enemigo m.
energetic, en-er-CHET'-ik, a., enérgico
energy, en'-er-CHI, s., energía f.
enervate, en'-er-veit, v., enervar; debilitar
enfeeble, en-fíi'-bl, v., debilitar
enforce, en-fórs', v., hacer observar; forzar
engage, en-gueich', v., (employ) emplear; (reserve) retener; (enemy) atacar; (bind) comprometerse
engaged, en-gueichd', a., (affianced) prometido, comprometido; (occupied) ocupado; (reserved) retenido
engagement, en-gueich'-ment, s., obligación f.; (mil.) combate m.; (betrothal) esponsales m. pl.; (appointment) cita f.
engaging, en-guei'-ching, a., simpático, atractivo
engender, en-chen'-da, v., engendrar
engine, en'-chin, s., máquina f.; locomotora f.
engineer, en-chi-nír', s., ingeniero m.
engineering, en-chi-nír'-ing, s., ingeniería f.
engrave, en-greiv', v., grabar; —r, s., grabador m.
engross, en-grous', v., absorber; absorber
engulf, en-gölf', v., engolfar
enhance, en-jaans', v., realzar, mejorar
enjoin, en-choin', v., ordenar; prescribir
enjoy, en-choi', v., gozar; — oneself, divertirse
enjoyment, en-choi'-ment, s., goce m., placer m.
enlarge, en-laarch', v., agrandar; dilatar
enlargement, en-laarch'-ment, s., ampliación f.
enlighten, en-lai'-tn, v., iluminar, instruir
enlist, en-list', v., alistar; alistarse
enliven, en-lai'-vn, v., animar; alegrar
enmity, en-mi-ti, s., enemistad f.; hostilidad f.
enormous*, i-nóar'-mos, a., enorme
enough, i-nöf', adv., bastante. interj., ! basta ¡
enquire, enquiry, (see **inquire**)
enrage, en-reich', v., exasperar, enfurecer
enrapture, en-rap'-tiur', v., extasiar, arrobar
enrich, en-rich', v., enriquecer; (adorn) embellecer
enrol(l), en-roul', v., alistar; alistarse; registrar

ensign, en′-sain, s., (flag) bandera f.; (naval flag) pabellón m.; (rank) alférez m.

enslave, en-sleiv′, v., esclavizar

ensnare, en-snér′, v., tender un lazo; (fig) entrampar

ensue, en-siuu′, v., seguir, sobrevenir

entail, en-teil′, ocasionar; (law) vincular

entangle, en-tang′-l, enmarañar; implicar

enter, en′-ta, v., entrar; — **up,** asentar

enterprise, en′-ter-prais, s., empresa f.; (originality, boldness) acometimiento m.

entertain, en-ter-tein′, v., entretener; hospedar; —**ment,** s., entretenimiento m. hospitalidad f.; acogida f.

enthusiasm, en-ziuu′-si-Asm, s., entusiasmo m.

entice, en-tais′, v., tentar, atraer

entire*, en-tair′, a., entero, íntegro; completo

entitle, en-tai′-tl, v., dar derecho, intitular

entomb, en-tuum′, v., enterrar, sepultar

entrance, en′-trans, s., entrada f.

entrance, en-traans′, v., extasiar

entreat, en-triit′, v., suplicar; implorar; exortar

entrench, en-trench′, v., atrincherar

entrust, en-tröst′, v., entregar; confiar

entry, en′-tri, s., entrada f.; (record) asiento m.

entwine, en-tuain′, v., entrelazar

enumerate, i-niuu′-mer-eit, v., enumerar

envelop, en-vel′-op, v., envolver, cubrir

envelope, en′-vel-op, s., sobre m., cubierta f.

envious*, en′-vi-os, a., envidioso

environs, en-vai′-rons, s. pl., alrededores m. pl.

envoy, en′-voi, s., enviado m.

envy, en′-vi, v., envidiar. s., envidia f.

epicure, ep′-i-kiúr, s., epicúreo m., gastrónomo m.

epidemic, ep-i-dem′-ik, s., epidemia f.

episode, ep′-i-soud, s., episodio m.

epistle, ep-is′-l, s., epístola f.; (letter) carta f.

epoch, ii′-pok, ep′-ok, s., época f., era f.

equal, ii′-kual, v., igualar. a., *igual. s., igual m.

equality, i-kual′-i-ti, s., igualdad f.

equalize, ii′-kua-lais, v., igualar

equator, i-kuei′-ta, s., ecuador m.

equerry, ek′-ue-ri, s., caballerizo m.
equilibrium, i-kui-lib′-ri-om, s., equilibrio m.
equip, i-kuip′, v., equipar
equitable, ek′-ui-ta-bl, a., equitativo; imparcial
equity, ek′-ui-ti, s., equidad f.
equivalent, i-kui′-va-lent, s. & a., equivalente m.
era, i′-ra, s., era f., época f.
eradicate, i-rAd′-i-keit, v., desarraigar; extirpar
erase, i-reis′, v., (delete) borrar
eraser, i-rei′-sa, s., (metal, etc.) raspador m.;
  (rubber) goma para borrar f.
erect, i-rekt′, v., erigir. a., erguido, derecho
ermine, ěr′-min, s., armiño m.
err, ěr, v., errar; desviarse
errand, er′-and, s., recado m.; —**boy,** mensajero m.
erratic, e-rat′-ik, a., errático
erroneous*, e-rou′-ni-os, a., erróneo
error, er′-or, s., error m., yerro m.
eruption, i-rap′-shon, s., erupción f.
escape, es-keip′, s., escapada f. escape m.; fuga f.,
  huída f. v., escapar, evitar
escort, es-koart′, v., escoltar. s., escolta f.
especially, es-pesh′-al-i, adv., especialmente
espy, es-pai′, v., divisar; observar
essay, es′-ei, s., ensayo m.
essential*, es-en′-shal, a., esencial
establish, es-tAb′-lish, v., establecer; —**ment,** s.,
  establecimiento m.
estate, es-teit′, s., propiedades f. pl., bienes m. pl.;
  (possessions) herencia f.; (status) rango m.
esteem, es-tiim′, v., estimar. s., estima f.
estimate, es′-ti-meit, s., (costs) estimación f. v.,
  estimar, computar
estrange, es-treinch′, v., apartar, desviar
etching, ech′-ing, s., aguafuerte m.
eternal*, i-těr′-nal, a., eterno
eternity, i-těr′-ni-ti, s., eternidad f.
ether, ii′-zer, s., éter m.
euphony, iuu′-fo-ni, s., eufonía f.
evacuate, i-vAk′-iu-eit, v., evacuar
evade, i-veid′, v., evadir, eludir
evaporate, i-vAp′-or-eit, v., (refl.) evaporarse

evasion, i-vei′-sh*o*n, s., evasión f.; evasiva f.

evasive*, i-vei′-siv, a., evasivo

eve, iiv, s., víspera f.; (evening) tarde f.

even, ii′-vn, adv., aun. a.,* igual; (smooth) liso

evening, iiv′-ning, s., tarde f., noche f.; — **dress,** traje de etiqueta m.; (ladies') vestido de noche m.

evensong, ii′-vn-song, s., vísperas f. pl

event, i-vent′, s., acontecimiento m., caso m.; —**ful,** a., memorable; —**ually,** adv., al fin

ever, ev′-*a*, adv., siempre; (at any time) jamás; —**lasting*,** a., perdurable, eterno

every, ev′-ri, a., cada, todo, todos, toda, todas, —**body,** s., todo el mundo m.; —**thing,** todo m.; —**where,** adv., en todas partes

evict, i-vikt′, v., desposeer; —**ion,** s., desahucio m.

evidence, ev′-i-dens, s., evidencia f., prueba f.; testimonio m.; **give —,** v., dar testimonio

evident*, ev′-i-dent, a., evidente

evil, ii′-vl, s., mal m., maldad f.; desgracia f. a., malo

evince, i-vins′, v., probar, manifestar

evoke, i-vouk′, v., evocar, llamar

evolve, i-volv′, v., desenvolver; evolucionar

ewe, iuu, s., oveja f.

exact, eg-s*a*kt′, a.,* exacto. v., exigir; —**ing,** a., exigente; —**itude,** s., exactitud f.

exaggerate, eg-s*a*ch′-*e*r-eit, v., exagerar

exaggeration, eg-s*a*ch′-*e*r-ei′-sh*o*n, s., exageración f.

exalt, eg-so*a*lt′, v., exaltar

examination, eg-s*a*m′-i-nei′-sh*o*n, s., examen m.; inspección f.; (legal) interrogatorio m.

examine, eg-s*a*m′-in, v., examinar; (excise) registrar

example, eg-s*a*am′-pl, s., ejemplo m.

exasperate, eg-s*a*s′-per-eit, v., exasperar

excavate, eks′-k*a*-veit, v., excavar

exceed, ek-siid′, v., exceder; —**ingly,** adv., excesivamente, muy

excel, ek-sel′, v., sobresalir; superar

excellent*, ek′-sel-ent, a., excelente

except, ek-sept′, v., exceptuar. prep., excepto, fuera de; —**ion,** s., excepción f.; **take —ion,** v., objetar a; —**ional,** a., excepcional

excerpt, ek'-serpt, s., extracto m. v., extractar
excess, ek-sess', s., exceso m.; —**ive***, a., excesivo
exchange, eks-cheinch', s., cambio m.; (telephone) central f.; (money) cambio m. v., cambiar
exchequer, eks-chek'-a, s., tesorería f., erario m.
excise, ek-sais', s., alcabala f.
excitable, ek-sai'-ta-bl, a., excitable
excite, ek-sait', v., excitar; —**ment,** s., excitación f.; conmoción f.; agitación f.
exciting, ek-sai'-ting, a., excitante; (thrilling) conmovedor
exclaim, eks-kleim', v., exclamar
exclamation, eks-kla-mei'-shon, s., exclamación f.
exclude, eks-kluud', v., excluir
exclusive*, eks-kluu'-siv, a., exclusivo
excruciating, eks-kruu'-shi-ei-ting, a., penosísimo
excursion, eks-kër'-shon, s., excursión f.
excuse, eks-kiuus', s., excusa f.
excuse, eks-kiuus', v., excusar; (pardon) dispensar
execrate, eks'-si-kreit', v., execrar
execute, ek'-si-kiuut, v., ejecutar
executioner, ek-si-kiuu'-shon-a, s., verdugo m.
executor, ek-sek'-iu-ta, s., testamentario m.
exempt, eg-sempt', v., eximir, a., exento
exemption, eg-semp'-shon, s., exención f.
exercise, eks'-er-sais, s., ejercicio m. v., ejercitarse; (mil.) hacer el ejercicio; (profession) ejercer
excert, eg-sërt', v., esforzarse, empeñarse
exertion, eg-sër'-shon, s., esfuerzo m., conato m.
exhale, eks-jeil', v., exhalar, emitir
exhaust, eg-soast', s., escape m. v., agotar; rendirse
exhaustive*, eg-soast'-iv, a., completo
exhibit, eg-sib'-it, v., exhibir, s., objeto m.
exhibition, eks-i-bish'-on, s., exposición f.
exhilarate, eg-sil'-a-reit, v., regocijar, alegrar
exhilarating, eg-sil'-a-rei-ting, a., vigorizante
exhort, eg-soart', v., exhortar
exile, ek-sail', v., desterrar, s., destierro m.; (person) desterrado m.
exist, eg-sist', v., existir
existence, eg-sis-tens, s., existencia f.
exit, ek'-sit, s., salida f.; (departure) partida f.

exodus, ek'-so-dus, s., éxodo m.; emigración f.
exonerate, eg-son'-er-eit, v., exonerar, aliviar
exorbitant*, ek-soar'-bi-tant, a., exorbitante
expand, eks-pand', v., dilatar; —**ing,** a., elástico
expansion, eks-pan'-shon, s., expansión f.
expect, eks-pekt', v., esperar
expectation, eks-pek-tei'-shon, s., expectación f.
expedient, eks-pii'-di-ent, s., expediente m. a.,* conveniente; pronto
expedite, eks'-pi-dait, v., expedir; acelerar
expel, eks-pel', v., expeler; expulsar
expend, eks'-pend, v., gastar; —**iture,** s., gasto m.; desembolso m.
expense, eks-pens', s., gasto m., coste m.
expensive*, eks-pen'-siv, a., caro, costoso
experience, eks-pi'-ri-ens, s., experiencia f., ensayo m. v., experimentar, probar
experiment, eks-per'-i-ment, v., experimentar, s., experimento m.
expert, eks-pĕrt', s., experto m.; perito m. a., experto, perito
expire, eks-pair', v., espirar
explain, eks-plein', v., explicar
explanation, eks-pla-nei'-shon, s., explicación f.
explicit*, eks-plis'-it, a., explícito, categórico
explode, eks-ploud', v., estallar, explotar
exploit*, eks-ploit', s., hazaña f. v., explotar [m.
explore, eks-plór', v., explorar; —**r,** s., explorador
export, eks-pórt', v., exportar; —**er,** s., exportador m.; —**s,** exportaciones f. pl
expose, eks-pous', v., exponer; (fraud) desenmascarar; (plot) revelar; (danger) arriesgar
expostulate, eks-pos'-tiu-leit, v., reconvenir
exposure, eks-pou'-shur, s., exposición f., revelación f.
expound, eks-paund', v., exponer; explicar
express, eks-pres', s., expreso m. a., expreso, v., expresar
expression, eks-presh'-on, s., expresión f.
expulsion, eks-pŏl'-shon, s., expulsión f.
exquisite*, eks'-kui-sit, a., exquisito
extempore, eks-tem'-po-ri, a., improvisado

extend, eks-tend', v., extender, extenderse
extensive*, eks-ten'-siv, a., extenso vasto
extent, eks-tent', s., extensión f., grado m.
extenuate, eks-ten'-iu-eit, v., atenuar; extenuar
exterior, eks-ti'-ri-a, s., exterior m. a., exterior
exterminate, eks-tër'-min-eit, v., exterminar
external*, eks-tër'-nal, a., externo; exterior
extinct, eks-ting'-kt, a., extinto; (fire) apagado
extinguish, eks-ting'-uish, v., extinguir, apagar
extort, eks-to*art*, v., arrancar; **—ion,** s., extorsión f.
extra, eks-trA, a., adicional. s., suplemento m.; **—ordinary,** a., extraordinario
extract, eks-trAct', v., extraer. s., extracto m.
extravagant*, eks-trav'-*a*-gant, a., extravagante; pródigo
extreme, eks-triim', s., extremo m. a., extremado
extremely, eks-triim'-li, adv., sumamente
extricate, eks'-tri-keit, v., desembrollar
eye, ai, s., ojo m.; **—ball,** globo ocular m.; **—brow,** ceja f.; **—glass,** monóculo m.; **—glasses,** lentes m. pl.; gafas f. pl.; **—lash,** pestaña f.; **—let,** ojete m.; **—lid,** párpado m.; **—sight,** vista f.; **—witness,** testigo ocular m.

fable, féi'-bel, s., fábula f.
fabric, fAb'-rik, s., tejido m.; textura f.; (edifice) fábrica f.; **—ation,** fabricación f.; ficción f.
fabulous*, fAb'-iu-los, a., fabuloso, ficticio
facade, fa-seid', s., fachada f.
face, feis, s., cara f., rostro m.; (clock) cuadrante m. v., afrontar. **—cream,** s., crema facial f.; **—massage,** masaje facial m.
facetious*, fa-sii'-shos, a., chistoso, jocoso
facilitate, fa-sil'-i-teit, v., facilitar
facsimile, fAk-si'-mi-li, s., facsímile m.
fact, fakt, s., hecho m.; realidad f.
factory, fAk'-to-ri, s., fábrica f.
faculty, fak'-ul-ti, s., facultad f.; aptitud f.
fade, feid, v., marchitarse; (colour) descolorarse
faggot, fAg'-ot, s., haz de leña m.

fail, feil, v., (neglect) faltar a; (omit to) dejar de; (miscarry) fracasar; (examination) suspender; (insolvency) quebrar; **without —,** sin falta

failing, feil'-ing, s., falta f.

failure, feil'-iur, s., falta f.; (plans) fracaso m.; (insolvency) quiebra f.

faint, feint, v., desmayarse. s., desmayo m. a.,* lánguido; indistinto

fair, fér, a., justo; (hair) rubio; (pleasing) bello; (weather) sereno. s., feria f.; **—ness,** equidad f.; belleza f.

fairy, fé-ri, s., hada f.

faith, feiz, s., fe f.; confianza f.; fidelidad f.; **—ful,** a., fiel; **—less,** infiel

fake, feik, s., falsificación f.; impostura f. v., falsificar

falcon, foal'-kn, s., halcón m.

fall, foal, s., decadencia f.; (tumble) caída f.; (prices) baja f.; (water) cascada f. v., caer; bajar

fallacy, fal'-a-si, s., falacia f., sofisma f.

false,* foals, a., falso; (artificial) postizo

falsehood, foals'-jud, s., falsedad f.

falsification, foal-si-fi-kei'-shon, s., falsificación f.

falsify, foal'-si-fai, v., falsificar

falter, foal'-ta, v., vacilar; (speech) titubear

fame, feim, s., fama f.; **—d,** a., famoso; renombrado

familiar*, fa-mil'-ya, a., familiar

family, fam'-i-li, s., familia f.

famine, fam'-in, s., carestía f. hambre f.

famish, fam'-ish, v., morir de hambre

famous*, fei'-mos, a., famoso

fan, fan, s., abanico m.; ventilador m. (admirer) aficionado m. v., abanicar

fanatic, fa-nat'-ik, s., fanático m. a., fanático m.

fanaticism, fa-nat'-i-sism s., fanatismo m.

fancy, fan'-si, s., imaginación f.; (liking) gusto m.; (preference) inclinación f. v., imaginar; desear; **—dress,** s., disfraz m.

fang, fang, s., colmillo m.

fantastic, fan-tas'-tik, a., fantástico

fantasy, fan'-ta-si, s., fantasía f.

far, faar, adv., lejos. a., lejano, distante

farce, faars, s., farsa f.

fare, fér, s., tarifa f.; (food) comida f.

farewell, fér'-uel, interj., ¡ adiós ! s., despedida f.

farm, faarm, s., granja f., cortijo m. v., cultivar

farmer, faar'-ma, s., granjero m., agricultor m.

farrier, far'-i-a, s., herrador m.

farther, faar'-Da, adv., más lejos; además. a., más lejano; otro; ulterior

fascinate, fas'-in-eit, v., fascinar

fascinating, fas'-in-eit-ing, a., fascinador

fashion, fash'-on, s., moda f. v., formar; —**able**, a., de moda; **to be in** —, estar de moda

fast, faast, a., rápido; firme; (colour) fijo a., ayuno m. v., ayunar

fasten, faas'-n, v., atar; (close) cerrar; (dress) abrochar

fastidious*, fas-tid'-i-os, a., difícil, quisquilloso, descontentadizo

fat, fat, s., grasa f. a., grueso, gordo; —**ness**, s., gordura f.; —**ten**, v., engordar; —**ty**, a., gordo

fatal*, fei'-tl, a., fatal; mortal

fate, feit, s., destino m., suerte f.; —**d**, a., predestinado

father, faa'-Da, s., padre m.; —**-in-law,** suegro m.; —**ly,** a., paternal

fathom, faD'-om, s., braza f. v., sondear

fatigue, ta-tig', v., fatigar. s., fatiga f.

fault, foalt, s., culpa f.; (defect) falta f.; —**less,** a., intachable; —**y,** defectuoso

favour, fei'-va, s., favor m.; (commercial) atenta f. v., favorecer; —**able,** a., favorable; —**ite,** s., favorito m. a., favorito

fawn, foan, s., cervato m. v., halagar

fear, fir v., temer, recelar. s., miedo m., temor m.; —**ful,** a.,* terrible; (timorous) medroso; —**less*,** impertérrito

feasible, fii'-si-bl, a., factible, practicable

feast, fiist, v., festejar, regalar. s., fiesta f.; banquete m.

feat, fiit, s., hazaña f.; (skill) proeza f. [f. pl.

feather, feD'-a, s., pluma f., v., emplumar

feature, fii'-tiur, s., rasgo m.; —**s,** s. pl., facciones f. pl.

February, feb'-ru-a-ri, s., febrero m.

federation, fed-*er*-**ei**'-shon, s., confederación f.

fee, fii, s., honorarios m. pl., gajes m. pl.

feeble, fii'-bl, a., débil; enclenque

feed, fiid, v., alimentar; comer; (cattle) pastar

feel, fiil'-la, v., (touch) palpar, tocar; (affect) sentir; —**ing,** s., tacto m.; sentimiento m. a., tierno

feeler, fiil'-*la*, s., antena f., tentáculo m., prueba f.

feign, fein, v., fingir, pretender

feint, feint, s., disimulación f.; (fencing) ataque fingido m.

fell, fel, v., (trees) desmontar, cortar; (animals) derribar

fellow, fel'-**ou,** s., (member) socio m.; —**ship,** compañía f.; sociedad f.

felony, fel'-*o*-ni, s., felonía f., traición f.

felt, felt, s., fieltro m.

female, fii'-**meil,** s., hembra f.; mujer f.

feminine, fem'-i-nin, s., femenino f.

fen, fen, s., pantano m.

fence, fens, s., valla f.; (wooden) palizada f. v., (enlose) cercar; (swordsmanship) esgrimir

fencing, fen'-sing, s., esgrima f. [f.

fender, fen'-*da*, s., guarda-fuegos m.; (ship) defensa

ferment, fer-**ment**', v., fermentar. s., fermento m.

fern, fern, s., helecho m.

ferocious*, fi-**rou**'-shos, a., feroz

ferret, fer'-et, s., hurón m. v., huronear

ferrule, fer'-ul, s., herrete m.

ferry, fer'-i, s., transbordador m.

fertile, fer'-**tail,** a., fértil

fertilize, fer-ta-**lais**', v., fertilizar

fervent*, fer'-vent, a., ferviente, ardiente

fester, fes'-*ta*, v., ulcerarse

festival, fes'-ti-vl, s., fiesta f. a., festivo

festive, fes'-tiv, a., festivo, alegre

festoon, fes-tuun', s., festón m. v., festonear

fetch, fech, v., ir a buscar; traer; producir

fetter, fet'-*a*, v., encadenar; —**s,** s. pl., grillos m. pl.

feud, fiuud, s., feudo m.; —**al,** a., feudal

fever, fii'-**va,** s., fiebre f.; —**ish,** a., febril

few, fiuu, a., pocos; unos; **a —,** algunos '

fibre, fai'-*ba*, s., fibra f.

fickle, fik'-l, a., inconstante, variable

fiction, fik'-shon, s., ficción f.; literatura novelesca f.

fictitious*, fik-ti'-shos, a., ficticio; falso

fiddle, fid'-l, s., violín m. v., tocar el violín

fidelity, fi-del'-i-ti, s., fidelidad f.; lealtad f.

fidget, fich'-et, v., agitarse; molestar

fidgety, fich'-et-i, a., agitado; inquieto

field, fiild, s., campo m.

fiend, fiind, s., demonio m.; arpía f.; —ish, a
diabólico

fierce*, firs, a., fiero; cruel; impetuoso; feroz

fiery, faif'-er-i, a., ardiente; fogoso

fife, faif, s., pífano m.

fifteen, fif-tiin', s. & a., quince m.; —th, décimo-
quinto m.; quinzavo m.

fifth, fifz, s. & a., quinto m.; (fraction) quinta parte f.

fiftieth, fif'-ti-iz, s. & a., quincuagésimo m.;
cincuentavo m.

fifty, fif'-ti, s. & a., cincuenta m.

fig, fig, s., higo m.; — **tree,** higuera f.

fight, fait, v., pelear; combatir. s., combate m.;
lucha f.; pelea f.; —er, s., (person) luchador m.;
(plane) avión de caza m.

figure, fi'-guer, s., cuerpo m.; figura f. número m.;
(number) cifra f. v., figurar; —head, s., mascarón
[de proa m.

filbert, fil'-bert, s., avellana f.

filch, filch, v., ratear, sisar, hurtar

file, fail, s., (tool) lima f.; (office) carpeta m. v.,
limar; archivar; (mil.) marchar en fila

fill, fil, v., llenar; satisfacer; (position) ocupar

filly, fil'-i, s., potranca f.

film, film, s., (snapshots, etc.) película f.; (cinema)
film m.; (eye) membrana f.

filter, fil'-ta, v., filtrar. s., filtro m.

filth, filz, s., basura f.; —y, a., sucio; obsceno

fin, fin, s., aleta f.

final*, fai'-nal, a., final; último; decisivo

finance, fi'-nans, s., hacienda pública f.; ciencia
financiera f. v., (loans) negociar; (undertaking)
respaldar

financial*, fi-nan'-shal, a., monetario, bancario

finch, finch, s., pinzón m.

find, faind, v., encontrar; descubrir; (law) fallar

fine, fain, s., (penalty) multa f. v., multar. a.,* fino; delicado; bello; sutil; excelente

finger, fing′-ga, s., dedo m. v., tocar

finical, fin′-i-kl, a., afectado, remilgado

finish, fin′-ish, v., acabar; terminar. s., fin m.

finite, fai′-nait, a., finito; limitado

fir, fẽr, s., pino m., abeto m.; —**cone,** piña f.

fire, fair, s., fuego m.; (conflagration) incendio m. v., encender; (gun etc.) tirar; —**alarm,** s., alarma de incendio f.; —**brigade,** servicio de bomberos m.; —**engine,** bomba de incendios f.; —**escape,** aparato de salvamento m.; —**fly,** luciérnaga f.; —**man,** bombero m.; —**place,** hogar f.; chimenea f.; —**proof,** a., incombustible; —**works,** s. pl., fuegos artificiales m. pl

firm, fẽrm, s., firma f. a.,* sólido; (resolute) firme

first, fẽrst, adv., primeramente, a., primero

firth, fẽrz, s., estuario m., brazo de mar m

fish, fish, v., pescar. s., (live) pez m.; (food) pescado m.; —**bone,** espina f.; —**erman,** pescador m.; —**hook,** anzuelo m.; —**monger,** pescadero m.

fishing, fish′-ing, s., pesca f.; —**rod,** caña de pescar f.

fissure, fish′-ur, s., grieta f.; hendedura f.

fist, fist, s., puño m. [a.,* apto, propicio

fit, fit, v., ajustar; (clothes) entallar. s., convulsión f.

fittings, fit′-ings, s. pl., guarniciones f. pl.

five, faiv, s. & a., cinco m.

fix, fiks, v., fijar. s., apuro m., aprieto m.

fixture, fiks′-tiur, s., mueble fijo m.; instalación f.

flabby, flab′-i, a., fofo, blando

flag, flag, s., bandera f., pabellón m.; —**ship,** buque almirante m.; —**staff,** asta de la bandera

flagon, flag′-on, s., frasco m., botella f. [m.

flagrant,* flei′-grant, a., flagrante, enorme

flake, fleik, s., laminilla f.; (snow, etc.) copo m.

flaky, fleik′-i, a., (pastry) hojaldrado

flame, fleim, s., llama f. v., llamear

flaming, flei′-ming, a., llameante; ardiente

flange, flanch, s., reborde m.; pestaña f.; acoplo m.

flank, flang-k, s., flanco m.; (animal) ijada f. v., flanquear

flannel, flĂn'-l, s., franela f.

flap, flap, s., (table) hoja f.; (pocket) cartera f.; (trap) trampa f.; (wings) aleta f. v., aletear

flare, flér, s., llamarada f. v., brillar

flash, flash, s., (light) resplandor m.; (lightning) relámpago m.; (gun, etc.) fogonazo m.; **—bulb,** s., bombilla de flas f.; **—light,** al magnesio m.

flask, flaask, s., frasco m., redoma f.; (vacuum) termos m.

flat, flat, s., (music) bemol m.; (dwelling) piso m.; (land) llano m. a., llano; insípido; (market) flojo

flatten, flat'-n, v., allanar

flatter, flat'-ĕr, v., lisonjear, adular; **—ing,** a., halagüeño; **—y,** s., lisonja f.

flavour, flei'-va, v., sazonar. s., sabor m.; aroma m.

flaw, floa, s., defecto m.; (crack) grieta f.

flax, flaks, s., lino m.

flea, flii, s., pulga f.

fledged, flechd, a., cubierto de plumas

flee, flii, v., huir

fleece, fliis, s., vellón m. v., esquilar; (fig.) despojar

fleet, fliit, s., flota f. a., veloz

flesh, flesh, s., carne f.

flexible, fleks'-i-bl, a., flexible

flicker, flik'-a, v., vacilar, temblar. s., vacilante m.; tembleteo m.

flight, flait, s., huída f.; (birds) vuelo m.; (stairs) tramo m.

flimsy, flim'-si, a., (material, paper) ligero; delgado; (structure) débil

flinch, flinch, v., acobardarse; vacilar

fling, fling v., lanzar, arrojar

flint, flint, s., pedernal m.

flippant*, flip'-ant, a., ligero; petulante

flirt, flĕrt, s., coqueta f. v., coquetear

float, flout, s., (raft) balsa f.; (angler's) corcho m. v., flotar; (a company, etc.) lanzar

flock, flok, s., (sheep) rebaño m., manada f.; (birds) bandada f. v., ir en tropel, congregarse

flog, flog, v., azotar

flood, flŏd, v., inundar. s., Diluvio m.; inundación f.

floor, flōr, s., suelo m.; (storey) piso m.

florid*, flŏr-id, a., florido, vivo

florist, flor'-ist, s., florista f.

flounce, flauns, s., (dress) volante m.

flour, flaur, s., harina f.

flourish, flŏr'-ish, s., adorno m.; (signature) rúbrica f. v., (brandish) blandir; (prosper) prosperar

flout, flaut, v., mofar, burlarse

flow, flou, v., fluir, correr. s., flujo m.; efusión f.

flower, flau'-a, s., flor f. v., florecer

fluctuate, flŏk'-tiu-eit, v., fluctuar; vacilar

flue, fluu, s., cañón de chimenea m.

fluency, fluu'-en-si, s., fluidez f., soltura f.

fluent*, fluu'-ent, a., fluente, fácil

fluffy, flŏf'-i, a., con plumón, con vello

fluid, fluu'-id, s., flúido m. a., flúido

fluke, fluuk, s., (chance) chiripa f.

flurry, flŏr'-i, s., aturdimiento m. v., aturdir

flush, flŏsh, v., (redden) sonrojar; (rinse) fluir, chorrear. s., rubor m.; a., al ras de

fluster, flŏs'-ta, v., aturdir. s., agitación f.

flute, fluut, s., flauta f. v., (groove) estriar

flutter, flŏt'-a, s., aleteo m.; palpitación f.; emoción f. v., aletear

fly, flai, s., mosca f. v., volar; (flag) enarbolar

fly-leaf, flai'-liif, s., guarda f.

fly-wheel, flai'-juiil, s., volante m.

foal, foal, s., potro m. v., parir

foam, foum, s., espuma f. v., espumar

fob, fob, s., faltriquera del reloj f.

f.o.b. = free on board, franco a bordo

focal, fou'-kl, a., focal, céntrico; — **point,** s., punto céntrico; punto focal

focus, fou'-kos, s., foco m. v., enfocar

fodder, fod'-a, s., forraje m.

foe, fou, s., enemigo m.

fog, fog, s., niebla f., bruma f.; —**gy,** a., brumoso; —**horn,** s., sirena f.

foil, foil, s., (fencing) florete m.; (metal) hoja f. v., frustrar

foist, foist, v., imponer

fold, fould, s., (cloth, etc.) pliegue m.; (sheep) redil m. v., plegar; (arms) cruzar

foliage, fou'-li-ich, s., follaje m.

folk, fouk, s., gente f.

follow, fol'-ou, v., seguir; suceder; —**er,** s., seguidor m.; discípulo m.; admirador m.

folly, fol'-i, s., locura f., tontería f.

foment, fo-ment', v., fomentar

fond, fond, a., (affection) afectuoso; **to be — of,** v., (affection) ser aficionado a, querer; (taste, recreation) gustar

fondle, fon'-dl, v., mimar, acariciar

fondness, fond'-nes, s., afecto m.; (inclination) afición f.

font, font, s., pila bautismal f.

food, fuud, s., alimento m.; comida f.; (fodder) pasto [m.

fool, fuul, s., tonto m. v., embromar; —**ery,** s., tontería f.; —**hardy,** a., temerario; —**ish**', tonto; —**proof,** a., a prueba de imprudencia

foot, fut, s., pie m.; —**ball,** balón m.; (game) fútbol m.; —**board,** (bus, train) plataforma f.; —**ing,** posición f.; —**man,** lacayo m.; —**path,** senda f.; (pavement) acera f.; —**step,** paso m.; (print) huella f.; —**stool,** escabel m.

fop, fop, s., pisaverde m., gomoso m.

for, for, prep., por; a causa de; para; en nombre de. conj., porque; para que; como; pues

forage, for'-ich, s., forraje m. v., forrajear

forbear, for-bér', v., soportar; abstenerse

forbearance, for-bér'-ans, s., indulgencia f.

forbid, for'-bid, v., prohibir; —**ding,** a., aborrecible

force, fórs, s., fuerza f.; vigor m. v., forzar

forceful, fórs'-ful, a., fuerte, poderoso

forcible, fórs'-i-bl, a., fuerte; concluyente

ford, fórd, v., vadear. s., vado m.

fore, fór, s., proa f. a., delantero. adv., delante

forearm, fór'-aarm, s., antebrazo m.

forebode, fór'boud', v., presagiar, pronosticar

foreboding, fór-'boud'-ing, s., presagio m.

forecast, fór'-kaast, s., pronóstico m.

foreclose, fór-klous', v., excluir

foredoom, fór-duum', v., predestinar

forefather, fór'-faa-Da, s., antecesor m.
forefinger, fór'-fiñ-ga, s., dedo índice m.
forego, fór-gou', v., renunciar a.; abandonar
foregoing, fór-gou'-ing, a., precedente
foregone, fór-goun', a., anticipado
foreground, fór'-graund, s., primer plano m.
forehead, fór'-jed, fór'-ed, s., frente f.
foreign, fór'-in, a., extranjero; —**er,** s., extranjero
foreman, fór'-mn, s., capataz m.   [m.
foremost, fór'-moust, a., primero; principal
forenamed, fór'-neimd, a., susodicho
forenoon, fór'-nuun, s., mañana f.
forerunner, fór-rön'-a, s., precursor m.
foresee, fór-sii', v., prever
foresight, fór'-sait, s., previsión f.
forest, fór'-est, s., bosque m., selva f.
forestall, fór-stoal', v., anticipar; prevenir
foretaste, fór'-teist, s., goce anticipado m.
foretell, fór-tel', v., predecir
forethought, fór'-zoat, s., previsión f.; premeditación f.
forewarn, fór-uoarn', v., prevenir
forfeit, fór'-fit, s., multa f.; perder
forge, fórch, v., forjar; falsificar. s., fragua f., forja f.
forgery, fórch'-er-i, s., falsificación f.
forget, for-guet', v., olvidar; —**ful,** a., olvidadizo;
—**fulness,** s., olvido m.
forgive, for-guiv', v., perdonar; —**ness,** s., perdón
m.
fork, fóark, s., tenedor m.; (tool) horca f.; (road)
bifurcación f. v., ahorquillarse
forlorn, for-loarn', a., abandonado; desesperado
form, fóarm, s., forma f.; (figure) figura f.; (a form
to fill up) formulario m.; (seat) banco m.; (class)
clase f. v., formar
formal*, foar'-mal, a., formal; ceremonioso; —**ity,**
s., formalidad f.; etiqueta f.
formation, foar-mei'-shon, s., formación f.
former, foar'-ma, a., anterior; —**ly,** adv., antes,
antiguamente
formula, foar'-miu-la, s., fórmula f.; receta f.
forsake, for-seik', v., dejar, abandonar

fort, fórt, s., fuerte m.; **—ress,** fortaleza f.
forth, fórz, adv., adelante; fuera; **—coming,** a.,
futuro; que viene; **—with,** adv., sin dilación
fortieth, foar'-ti-iz, s., & a., cuadragésimo m.;
cuarentavo m.
fortification, foar-ti-fi-kei'-shon, s., fortificación f.
fortify, foar'-ti-fai, v., fortificar; (health) fortalecer
fortitude, foar'-ti-tiuud, s., firmeza f.; valor m.
fortnight, foart'-nait, s., quincena f., dos semanas
f. pl.
fortunate*, foar'-tiu-net, a., afortunado, dichoso
fortune, foar'-tiun, s., fortuna f.; (fate) suerte f.
forty, foar'-ti, s. & a., cuarenta m.
forward, foar'-uard, v., enviar, expedir. adv., adelante. a., adelantado; (pert) descarado; **—ing-
agent,** s., agente expedidor m.; **—ness,** descaro
m.
fossil, fos'-il, s., fósil m.   [m.
foster, fost'-a, v., criar; (encourage) fomentar;
—parents, s. pl., padres adoptivos m. pl.
foul, faul, v., ensuciar, a.,* sucio; impuro; obsceno
found, faund, v., fundar; (metal) fundir
foundation, faund-ei'-shon, s., fundación f.; (building, etc.) cimiento m.; (fig.) fundamento m.
founder, faun'-da, v., hundirse s., fundador m.
foundling, faund'-ling, s., niño expósito m.
foundry, faun'-dri, s., fundición f.
fountain, faun'-tin, s., fuente f.
fountain-pen, faun'-tin-pen, s., pluma estilográfica f.
four, foar, s. & a., cuatro m.; **—fold,** a., cuádruplo;
—teen, s. & a., catorce m.; **—th,** cuarto m.
fowl, faul, s., ave f.; (chicken) pollo m.
fox, foks, s., zorro m.; **—glove,** dedalera f.;
—terrier, perro zorrero m.
fraction, frak'-shon, s., fracción f.; fragmento m.
fracture, frak'-tiur, s., fractura f. v., fracturar
fragile, frach'-il, a., frágil; (health) delicado
fragment, frag'-ment, s., fragmento m.
fragrance, frei'-grans, s., fragancia f.; perfume m.
fragrant*, frei'-grant, a., fragante, perfumado
frail, freil, a., frágil; (health) débil, endeble
frame, freim, s., marco m. v., formar; (picture, etc.)

poner en marco; —**work**, s., armazón m.

franchise, fran'-chais, s., sufragio m.

frank, frang-k, a., franco; —**ness,** s., franqueza f.

frantic, fran'-tik, a., frenético, furioso

fraternal*, fra-ter'-nal, a., fraternal

fraud, froad, s., fraude m.

fraudulent*, froa'-diu-lent, a., fraudulento

fray, frei, v., deshilachar. s., riña f., refriega f.

freak, friik, s., rareza f.; fenómeno m.

freckle, frek'-l, s., peca f.

free, frii, v., libertar, librar. a.,* libre; gratuito; —**dom,** s., libertad f.; —**hold,** dominio absoluto m.; —**mason,** francmasón m.

freeze, friis, v., helar; congelarse

freezing, frii'-sing, s., congelación f. a., glacial

freight, freit, s., carga f.; (cost) flete m. v., fletar

frenzy, fren'-si, s., frenesí m.

frequency, frii'-kuen-si, s., frecuencia f.

frequent*, frii'-kuent, a., frecuente. v., frecuentar

fresh, fresh, a., fresco; puro

freshness, fresh'-nes, s., frescura f.; pureza f.

fret, fret, v., angustiarse; inquietarse; —**ful,** a., irritable, enojadizo; —**saw,** s., sierra de calados f.; —**work,** calados m.

friar, frai'-a, s., fraile m.

friary, frai'-er-i, s., convento de frailes m.

friction, frik'-shon, s., fricción f., frotación f.

Friday, frai'-di, s., viernes m.; **Good —,** viernes santo m.

friend, frend, s., amigo m.; —**liness,** amistad f.; —**ly,** a., amigable; —**ship,** s., amistad f.

fright, frait, s., susto m., terror m.

frighten, frai'-tn, v., espantar, aterrorizar

frightful*, frait'-ful, a., espantoso, horrible

frigid*, fricH'-id, a., frígido; indiferente

frill, fril, s., escarola f., faralá f. v., escarolar

fringe, frincH, s., franja f. v., franjear

frisk, frisk, v., brincar, cabriolar

frisky, frisk'-i, a., juguetón, vivaracho

fritter, frit'-a, s., fritura f. v., desperdiciar; —**away,** malgastar

frivolous*, friv'-ol-os, a., frívolo

frizzle, friz'-l, v., rizar; (fig.) achicharrar

fro, frou, adv., atrás; **to and —,** de un lado á ot o

frock, frok, s., vestido m.

frog, frog, s., rana f.

frolic, frol'-ik, v., juguetear. s., travesura f.

from, from, prep., de; desde; de parte de; según

front, front, s., frente f.; (mil.) frente m a., delantero

frontier, fron'-tir, s., frontera f. a., fronterizo

frost, froast, s., helada f v., escarchar; **—-bitten,** a., helado; **—y,** helado

froth, froaz, s., espuma f v., espumar

frown, fraun, s., ceño m v., fruncir el ceño

frugal*, fruu'-gl, a., frugal, económico

fruit, fruut, s., fruta f.; fruto m.; **—erer,** frutero m.; **—ful,** a., fructífero; **—-knife,** s., cuchillo de postres m.; **—less*,** a., infructuoso; estéril; **—tart,** s., tarta de frutas f.

fruition, fru-ish'-on, s., fruición f., goce m.

frustrate, fros-treit', v., frustrar

fry, frai, v., freir; **—ing pan,** s., sartén f.

fuchsia, fiuu'-shi-a, s., fucsia f.

fuel, fiu'-el, s., combustible m.

fugitive, fiuu'-chi-tiv, s., fugitivo m. a., fugitivo

fugue, fiuug, s., fuga f.

fulcrum, föl'-krom, s., alzaprima f.

fulfil, ful-fil', v., cumplir; realizar; **—ment,** s., realización f., cumplimiento m.

full, ful, a., lleno; completo; saciado

fullness, ful'-nes, s., plenitud f.; abundancia f.

fulsome, ful'-som, a., repugnante; grosero; bajo

fume, fiuum, s., humo m. v., humear

fun, fön, s., broma f.; (joke) chiste m.; **—ny,** a., cómico; chistoso

function, föng-k'-shon, s., función f. v., funcionar

fund, fönd, s., fondo m. v., fundar

fundamental*, fönd-a-men'-tl, a., fundamental

funeral*, fiuu'-ner-al, s., entierro m.

funnel, fön'-l, s., embudo m.; (smoke) chimenea f.

fur, fër, s., piel f.; incrustación f. v., incrustarse

furbish, fër'-bish, v., acicalar, pulir

furious*, fiuu'-ri-os, a., furioso

furlong, fër'-long, s., estadio m.

furlough, fĕr'-lou, s., licencia f.
furnace, fĕr'-nis, s., horno m.; (small) hornillo m.
furnish, fĕr'-nish, v., amueblar; equipar
furniture, fĕr'-ni-tiur, s., muebles m. pl.
furrier, fĕr'-i-a, s., peletero m.
furrow, fĕr'-ou, v., surcar, s., surco m.
further, fĕr'-Da, a., adicional. adv., más allá. v.,
     apoyar; —**ance,** s., adelantamiento m.; promo-
     ción f.
furtive, fĕr'-tiv, a., furtivo
fury, fiu'-ri, s., furor m., furia f.
fuse, fiuus, s., (slow match) mecha f.; (time) espoleta
     graduada f.; (electric) corta-circuitos m.; fusible
     m. v., fundirse
fuss, fŏs, s., barullo m. v., causar revuelo
fustiness, fŏs'-ti-nes, s., enmohecimiento m.
fusty, fŏs'-ti, a., mohoso
futile, fiuu'-tail, a., fútil; frívolo
future fiuu-tiur, s., porvenir m. a., futuro

gable, guei'-bl, s., gablete m.
gadfly, gAd'-flai, s., tábano m.
gag, gag, s., mordaza f. v., amordazar
gaff, gAf, s., arponcillo m.
gaiety, gue'-i-ti, s., alegría f.
gaily, gue'-i-li, adv., alegremente
gain, guein, s., ganancia f. v., (win, earn) ganar;
     (attain) alcanzar; (watch) adelantar
gait, gueit, s., marcha f.; (horse) andadura f.
gaiter, guei'-ta, s., polaina f.
galaxy, gAl'-ak-si, s., (astronomical) galaxia f.;
     — **of,** grupo notable de
gale, gueil, s., ventarrón m.
gall, gôal, s., (bile) bilis f., hiel f.; v., amargar,
     irritar; —**stones,** s., cálculos biliarios m. pl.
gallant*, gAl'-ant, a., valeroso
gallantry, gAl'-ant-ri, s., valor m.; galantería f.
gallery, gAl'-ar-i, s., galería f.
gallop, gAl'-op, s., galope m. v., galopar
gallows, gAl'-ous, s., horca f., patíbulo m.
galoshes, ga-losh'-os, s.pl., chanclos m.pl.
galvanism, gAl'-van-ism, s., galvanismo m.

gamble, GAM′-bl, s., jugado m. v., jugar

gambler, GAM′-bla, s., jugador m., tahur m.

gambol, GAM′-bl, s., cabriola f. v., brincar

game, gueim, s., juego m.; (animals) caza f.

game-keeper ,gueim-kiip′-a, s., guardabosque m.

gaming-house, guei′-ming-jaus, s., garito m.

gammon, GAM′-on, s., jamón m.

gander, GAN′-da, s., ganso m., ánsar m.

gang, gang-g, s., cuadrilla f.; (robbers, etc.) banda f.;
—**way**, (passage) pasillo m.; (ship's) pasamano m.

gaol, CHeil, s., cárcel f.

gap, GAP, s., brecha f., boquete m., laguna f.

gape, gueip, v., abrir la boca; (open) abrirse

garage, gaa-riCH′, s., garage m.

garb, gaarb, s., vestido m.

garbage, gaarb′-iCH, s., basura f., desperdicios m. pl.

garden, gaar′-dn, s., jardín m.; (kitchen) huerto m.;
—**er**, jardinero m.; —**ing**, jardinería f.

gargle, gaar′-gl, v., hacer gárgaras

garland, gaar′-land, s., guirnalda f. v., enguirnaldar

garlic, gaar′-lik, s., ajo m.

garment, gaar′-ment, s., prenda de vestir f.

garnish, gaar′-nish, v., aderezar. s., aderezo m.

garret, GAR′-et, s., desván m., buhardilla f.

garrison, GAR′-i-s′n, s., guarnición f.

garrulity, ga-ruu′-li-ty, s., locuacidad f.

garrulous, GAR′-u-los, a., locuaz

garter, gaar′-ta, s., liga f.; (order) jarretera f.

gas, gas, s., gas m.; —**burner**, mechero m.;
—**eous**, a., gaseoso; —**works**, s.pl., fábrica de
gas f.

gash, gash, s., cuchillada f. v., acuchillar

gasket, gas′-kit, s., obturador m.; junta elástica f.

gasp, gaasp, s., boqueada f. v., boquear

gastric, gas′-trik, a., gástrico

gate, gueit, s., puerta f.; entrada f.; (field, etc.)
barrera f.

gather, gaD′-a, v., reunir; (pluck) recoger; (infer)
inferir; —**ing**, s., reunión f.; (med.) absceso m.

gaudy, goa′-di, a., llamativo

gauge, gueiCH, s., (tool) calibrador m.; (rail) entrevía
f.; (size) calibre m. v., mediar; estimar

gaunt, goant, a., enjuto, descarnado, desvaído
gauntlet, goant'-let, s., manopla f.
gauze, goas, s., gasa f.; (wire) tela metálica f.
gawky, goa'-ki, a., desgarbado
gay, guei, a., alegre, festivo
gaze, gueis, v., mirar, contemplar
gazelle, ga-sel', s., gacela f.
gazette, ga-set', s., gaceta f. v., nombrar oficialmente
gear, guir, s., engranaje m.; —**box,** caja de engranajes f.
gelatine, CHel'-a-tin, s., gelatina f.
gem, CHem, s., joya f., gema f.
gender, CHen'-da, s., género m.
general, CHen'-er-al, s., general m. a., general
generalize, CHen'-er-a-lais, v., generalizar
generally, CHen'-er-a-li, adv., generalmente
generate, CHen'-er-eit, v., engendrar; producir
generation, CHen-er-ei'-shon, s., generación f.
generator, CHen'-er-eit-a, s., (elec.) generador m.; alternador m.
generosity, CHen-er-os'-i-ti, s., generosidad f.
generous*, CHen'-er-os, a., generoso, liberal
genial*, CHii'-ni-al, a., genial, cordial
genius, CHii'-ni-os, s., genio m.
genteel, CHen-tiil', a., gentil, elegante; distinguido
Gentile, CHen'-tail, s., & a. gentil m., pagano m.
gentility, CHen-til'-i-ti, s., nobleza f., gentileza f.
gentle, CHen'-tl, a., suave, dulce; —**man,** s., caballero m.; —**ness,** suavidad f.
gently, CHen'-tli, adv., suavemente
genuine, CHen'-iu-in, a., genuino; auténtico; puro; sincero; —**ness,** s., autenticidad f.; pureza f.
genus, CHiin'-os, s., género m.
geography, CHi'-og'-ra-fi, s., geografía f.
geology, CHi-ol'-o-CHi, s., geología f.
geometry, CHi-om'-a-tri, s., geometría f.
geranium, CHi-rei'-ni-om, s., geranio m.
germ, CHerm, s., germen m.; (disease) microbio m.
germinate, CHĕr'-mi-neit, v., germinar
gesticulate, CHes-tik'-iu-leit, v., gesticular
gesticulation, CHes-tik'-iu-lei-shon, s., gesticulación f.

gesture, CHes'-tiur, s gesto m.

get, guet, v., obtener; (earn) ganar; (attain) llegar; (fetch) traer; — **away**, escaparse; — **back**, volver; (recover) recobrar; —**down**, bajar; —**in**, entrar; —**on**, avanzar; —**out**, salir; —**up**, levantarse

geyser, guii'-sa, s., calentador de agua m.; géiser m.

ghastly, gaast'-li, a., lívido; (horrible) espantoso

gherkin, guér'-kin, s., pepinillo m.

ghost, goust, s., fantasma m., espíritu m.

giant, CHai'-ant, s., gigante m. a., gigantesco

gibberish, guib'-er-ish, s., jerigonza f.

gibbet, CHib'-et, s., horca f., patíbulo m.

gibe, CHaib, s., mofa f., burla f. v., mofarse

giblets, CHib'-lets, s. pl., menudillos de ave m. pl.

giddiness, guid'-i-nes, s., vértigo m.

giddy, guid'-i, a., vertiginoso

gift, guift, s., regalo m.; donación f.

gifted, guif'-tid, a., talentoso

gigantic, CHai-gan'-tik, a., gigantesco

giggle, guig'-l, v., reírse por nada

gild, guild, v., dorar; —**ing**, s., doradura f.

gills, guils, s. pl., branquias f. pl.

gilt, guilt, a., dorado

gimlet, guim'-let, s., barrena f.

gin, CHin, s., (spirit) ginebra f.; (snare) trampa f.

ginger, CHin'-CHer, s., jengibre m.; —**bread**, pan de jengibre m.

gipsy, CHip'-si, s., gitano m., gitana f. a., gitanesco

giraffe, CHi-raf', s., jirafa f.

gird, guérd, v., ceñir; (encompass) cercar

girder, guér'-da, s., travesaño m., viga f.

girdle, guér'-dl, s., cinturón m. v., ceñir

girl, guérl, s., muchacha f.; —**hood**, doncellez f.

girth, guérz, s., cincha f.; (measure) periferia f.

give, guiiv, v., dar, entregar; — **in**, asentir; — **up**, renunciar

giver, guiv'-a, s., dador m., donante m.

gizzard, guiz'-erd, s., molleja de ave f.

glacier, gla'-si-a, s., ventisquero m.

glad*, glad, a., contento, alegre

gladden, glad'-n, v., alegrar

glade, gleid, s., claro m.

gladness, glăd'-nes, s., alegría f., regocijo m.

glamour, glăm-or, s., encanto m.; hechizo m.

glance, glans, s., ojeada f. v., mirar de prisa; **— off,** desviarse

gland, glănd, s., glándula f.

glare, glér, s., (sun) resol m.; (light) deslumbramiento m.; (stare) mirada rencorosa f. v., deslumbrar; (stare) mirar con enojo

glaring*, glér'-ing, a., deslumbrante; (striking) manifiesto

glass, glaas, s., vidrio m., cristal m.; (vessel) vaso m.; (wine) copa f.; (mirror) espejo m.; **—es,** s. pl., lentes f. pl., espejuelos m. pl.; **— -ware,** s., cristalería f.; **—y,** a., vidrioso

glaze, gleis, v., vidriar, lustrar

glazier, glei'-sher, s., vidriero m.

gleam, gliim, s., (shimmer) fulgor m.; (ray) rayo m.; v., rielar; brillar

gleaning, glii'-ning, s., rebusca f.

glee, glii, s., alegría f.

glen, glen, s., cañada f., valle m.

glib,* glib, a., liso, voluble

glide, glaid, s., resbalón m.; deslizamiento m. v., resbalar; (air) planear; **—r,** s., (aircraft) planeador m.

glimmer, glim'-a, s., vislumbre m. v., alborear

glimpse, glimps, s., vislumbre m.

glint, glint, s., destello m. v., destellar

glisten, glis'-n, v., relucir

glitter, glit'-a, v., brillar, centellear, s., centelleo m.

gloat, glout, v., deleitarse

globe, gloub, s., globo m.

globular, gloub'-iu-la, a., esférico

gloom, gluu⌐m, s., obscuridad f.; (dismal) tristeza f.

gloomy, gluu'-mi, a., obscuro; sombrío; triste

glorify, glou'-ri-fai, v., glorificar; exaltar

glorious*, gló'-ri-os, a., glorioso; magnífico

glory, gló'-ri, s., gloria f. v., (in) gloriarse (de)

gloss, glos, s., lustre m. v., lustrar; **—y,** a., lustroso

glove, glóv, s., guante m.; **—r,** s., guantero m.

glow, glou, s., brillo m.; (sky) fulgor m. v., brillar

glue, gluu, s., cola f.

glum, glöm, a., displicente, malhumorado

glut, glöt, s., exceso m. v., (market) inundar

glutton, glöt'-n, s., glotón m.

gnarled, naarld, a., nudoso

gnash, nash, v., crujir los dientes; **—ing**, s., rechinamiento m.

gnat, nat, s., mosquito m., cinife m.

gnaw, noa, v., roer

go, gou, v., ir; (mech.) andar; **—away**, irse, partir, marcharse; **—back**, volver; **—down**, bajar; **—off**, partir; (gun) dispararse; **—out**, salir; **—up**, subir; **—without**, pasarse de

goad, goud, s., aguijón m. v., aguijonear

goal, goul, s., objeto m.; (posts) meta f.; (score) tanto m.; gol m.

goat, gout, s., cabra f.; cabrón m.

gobble, gob'-l, v., tragar; **—r**, s., tragón m.

goblet, gob'-let, s., copa f.

goblin, gob'-lin, s., trasgo m.

God, god, s., Dios m.; **-fearing**, a., temeroso de Dios

god, god, s., ídolo m.; **—child**, ahijado m.; **—dess**, diosa f.; **—father**, padrino m.; **—less**, a., impío, ateo; **—liness**, s., piedad f.; **—ly**, a., piadoso; **—mother**, s., madrina f.

goggle-eyed, gog'-l-aid, a., de ojos saltones

goggles, gog'-ls, s. pl., anteojeras f. pl.

going, gou'-ing, s., paso m.; (horse) andadura f.

goitre, goi'-ta, s., papera f.

gold, gould, s., oro m. a., de oro; **—en**, en oro; **—finch**, s., cardelina f.; **—fish**, pez de colores m.; **—leaf**, pan de oro m.; **—smith**, orfebre [m.

golf, golf, s., golf m.

gone, gon, p.p., ido; pasado; (dead) muerto

gong, gong, s., batintín m.

good, gud, s., bien m.; ventaja f. a., bueno; válido. adv., bien; **—bye**, interj., ¡adiós!; **—ly**, a., considerable; **—morning**, interj., ¡ buenos días!; **—natured**, a., bonachón; **—ness**, s., bondad f.; **—will**, buena voluntad f.; (business) clientela f.

Good Friday, gud-frai'-di, s., Viernes Santo m.

goods, guds, s., mercancía f.; — **train,** tren de mercancías m.

goose, guus, s., ganso m., gansa f., oca f., ánsar m.

gooseberry, guus'-be-ri, s., grosella f.

gore, gór, s., sangre cuajada f.; (gusset) contrete m. v., acornear

gorge, goarch, s., garganta f. v., hartarse

gorgeous*, goar'-chos, a., suntuoso, esplendoroso

gorilla, go-ril'-la, s., gorila m.

gorse, goars, s., argomón m.

gosling, gos'-ling, s., gansarón m.

gospel, gos'-pl, s., evangelio m.

gossamer, gos'-a-ma, s., telaraña f.

gossip, gos'-ip, s., chismoso m. v., chismear

gouge, gauch, s., gubia f. v., escoplear; sacar

gout, gaut, s., gota f.; —**y,** a., gotoso

govern, gov'-ern, v., gobernar; —**ess,** s., institutriz f.; —**ment,** gobierno m.; —**or,** gobernador m.; (mech.) regulador m.

gown, gaun, s., vestido de mujer m.; (official) toga f.

grab, grab, v., asir, agarrar. s., (mech.) gancho m.

grace, greis, s., gracia f.; favor m.; —**ful*,** a., gracioso; —**fulness,** s., gracia f.; gentileza f.; —**less,** a., réprobo

gracious*, grei'-shos, a., gracioso; benévolo

gradation, gra-dei'-shon, s., gradación f.

grade, greid, s., grado m.; rango m. v., graduar

gradient, gre'-di-ent, s., rampa f., pendiente f.

gradual*, grad'-iu-al, a., gradual

graduate, grad'-iu-eit, s., graduado m. v., graduarse

graft, graaft, s., corrupción f., (trees) injertar

grain, grein, s., grano m.; (wood, etc.) veta f.; (leather) flor f. v., (paint) vetear

grammar, gram'-a, s., gramática f.

gramophone, gram'-o-foun, s., gramófono m.

granary, gran'-a-ri, s., granero m.

grand*, grand, a., grandioso, magnífico; —**child,** s., nieto m., nieta f.; —**daughter,** nieta f.; —**father,** abuelo m.; —**mother,** abuela f.; —**son,** nieto m.

grange, greinch, s., granja f.; (estate) quinta f.

grant, graant, v., conceder; (law) otorgar. s., concesión f.; (gift) don m.

grape, greip, s., uva f.; **—fruit,** toronja f.; **—shot,** metralla f.

graphic*, graf'-ik, a., gráfico

grapple, grap'-l, s., arpeo m. v., agarrar; **— with,** (confront boldly) luchar

grasp, graasp, v., empuñar; (mentally) comprender. s., asimiento m.

grasping, graas'-ping, a., avaro

grass, graas, s., hierba f., yerba f.; **—hopper,** saltamontes m.; **—y,** a., herboso, herbáceo

grate, greit, s., (fire) parrilla f. v., raspar; irritar

grateful*, greit'-ful, a., agradecido

gratefulness, greit'-ful-nes, s., gratitud f.

gratification, grat'-i-fi-kei'-shon, s., satisfacción f.; recompensa f.

gratify, grat'-i-fai, v., gratificar; **—ing,** a., agradable

grating, grei'-ting, s., reja f. a., (sound) chirriant

gratitude, grat'-i-tiuud, s., gratitud f.

gratuitous*, gra-tiuu'-i-tos, a., gratuito

gratuity, gra-tiuu'-i-ti, s., recompensa f.; (tip) propina f.

grave, greiv, s., sepultura f., tumba f. a.,* grave; **—digger,** s., sepulturero m.; **—stone,** lápida sepulcral f.; **—yard,** cementerio m.

gravel, grav'-l, s., gravilla f.; (med.) litiasis f.

graven, grei'-vn, a., grabado

gravitate, grav'-i-teit, v., gravitar

gravity, grav'-i-ti, s., gravedad f.

gravy, grei'-vi, s., jugo m., salsa f.

graze, greis, v., rozar; (feed) pacer

grease, griis, s., grasa f. v., engrasar; lubricar

greasy, grii'-si, a., grasiento

great*, greit, a., gran; ilustre

greatness, greit'-nes, s., grandeza f.

greed, griid, s., voracidad f.; (avarice) codicia f.; **—ily,** adv., vorazmente; **—iness,** s., voracidad f.; avaricia f.; **—y,** a., voraz; glotón; avaro

green, griin, s., verde m. a., verde; **—gage,** s., ciruela verdal f.; **—grocer,** verdulero m.;

—house, invernadero m.; **—ish,** a., verdoso
greet, griit, v., saludar
greeting, griit'-ing, s., saludo m., salutación f.
grenade, gre-neid', s., granada f., bomba f.
grey, grei, a., gris, pardo
greyhound, grei'-jaund, s., galgo m., galga f.
gridiron, grid'-ai-ern, s., parrilla f.
grief, griif, s., pena f., dolor m., aflicción f.
grievance, grii'-vans, s., agravio m., perjuicio m.
grieve, griiv, v., afligir, afligirse; agraviar
grievous, grii'-vos, a., penoso, doloroso; cruel
grill, grill, s., parrilla f. v., asar en parrilla
grim*, grim, a., ceñudo, horrendo; formidable
grimace, gri-meis', s., mueca f., visaje m.
grime, graim, s., tizne m., mugre f.
grin, grin, s., sonrisa burlona f. v., sonreír burlonamente
grind, graind, v., moler; (sharpen) afilar
grinder, grain'-da, s., (for knives, etc.) afilador m.; (coffee, etc.) molino m.
grip, grip, s., (action) presa f., agarro m.; (hand) apretón m.; (handle) mango m.; puño m. v., agarrar, empuñar
gripe, graip, v., (bowels) dar cólico
grisly, gris'-li, a., espantoso, horroroso
grist, grist, s., molienda f.
grit, grit, s., cascajo m.; (particle) arena f.
gritty, grit'-i, a., arenoso
groan, groun, s., gemido m. v., gemir
groats, grouts, s.pl., sémola f.
grocer, grou'-sa, s., tendero de ultramarinos m.
grocery, grou'-sa-ri, s., tienda de ultramarinos f.
grog, grog, s., grog m., ponche m.
groggy, gro'-gui, a., vacilante
groin, groin, s., ingle f.; (arch) arista f.
groom, gruum, s., mozo de cuadra m.
groove, gruuv, s., ranura f. v., acanalar
grope, group, v., andar a tientas
gross, grous, s., (12 dozen) gruesa f.; (weight) bruto m. a.,* (coarse) grosero; (flagrant) enorme
ground, graund, v., (vessel) encallar. s., tierra f., suelo m.; motivo m.; **—floor,** piso bajo m.;

—less*, a., infundado ; **—s**, s.pl. (park, etc.) jardines m.pl. ; **—work**, s., plan m., base f.

group, gruup, s., grupo m. v., agrupar

grouse, graus, s., gallina silvestre f.

grove, grouv, s., arboleda f., alameda f.

grovel, grov'-l, v., arrastrarse

grow, grou, v., crecer ; cultivar ; **—er**, s., cultivador m., productor n **n up**, adulto m.

growl, graul, s., gruñido m. v., gruñir

growth, gruuz, s., crecimiento m., tumor m.

grub, gröb, s., gorgojo m., larva f.

grudge, gröch, s., ojeriza f. v., envidiar

gruel, gruu'-el, s., avenate m.

gruesome, gruu'-som, a., horrendo

gruff, gröf, a., áspero, seco

grumble, gröm'-bl, v., refunfuñar

grunt, grönt, s., gruñido m. v., gruñir

guarantee, ga-ran-tii', v., garantizar, garantía f.

guard, gaard, s., guardia f. ; (railway) conductor m. v., guardar

guarded, gaar'-did, a., circunspecto

guardian, gaar'-di-an, s., guardián m. ; (trustee) tutor m.

gudgeon, göch'-n, s., gobio m.

guess, gues, v., adivinar, conjeturar. s., conjetura f. ; **—work**, conjetura f.

guest, guest, s., (visitor ; lodger) huésped m. ; (for meals only) convidado m. ; (hotel) cliente m.

guidance, gai'-dans, s., dirección f. ; gobierno m.

guide, gaid, v., guiar. s., guía m.

guide-book, gaid'-buk, s., guía de viajes f.

guild, guild, s., gremio m. ; corporación f.

guile, gail, s., engaño m. ; **—less**, a., cándido

guilt, guilt, s., culpabilidad f. ; (moral) pecado m.

guilty, guil'-ti, a., culpable

guinea, guin'-i s., guinea f. ; **—-fowl**, pintada f. ; **—-pig**, conejillo de Indias m.

guise, gais, s., manera f., apariencia f.

guitar, gui-taar', s., guitarra f.

gulf, gölf, s., golfo m. ; abismo m.

gull, göl, s., gaviota f. v., engañar

gullet, göl'-et, s., gaznate m.

gulp, gŏlp, s., trago m. v., tragar
gum, gŏm, s., goma f.; (teeth) encía f. v., engomar
gun, gŏn, s., fusil m.; (sports) escopeta f.; (artillery) cañón m.; **—ner,** artillero m.; **—powder,** pólvora f.; **—smith,** armero m.
gurgle, guĕr′-gl, v., gorgotear. s., gorgoteo m.
gush, gŏsh, v., borbotar. s., borbotón m.
gust, gŏst, s., ráfaga f., racha f.; **—y,** a., rafagoso, ventoso, borrascoso
gut, gŏt, s., tripa f. v., destripar
gutter, gŏt′-a, s., (roof) gotera f.; (street) arroyo m.
guy, gai, s., mamarracho m.
gymnasium, CHim-nei′-si-om, s., gimnasio m.
gymnastics, CHim-nas′-tiks, s.pl., gimnástica f.

N.B.—La H debe pronunciarse siempre, excepto en las voces marcadas §

haberdasher, jab′-er-dash-a, s., mercero m.
habit, jab′-it, s., hábito m., costumbre f.
habitable, jab′-it-a-bl, a., habitable
habitual′, ja-bit′-iu-al, a., habitual, acostumbrado
hack, jak, s., caballo de alquiler m. v., tajar
hackneyed, jak′-nid, a., (subject) trillado
haemorrhage, ji′-mor-ich, s., hemorragia f.
hag, jag. s., bruja f.
haggard′, jag′-ard, a., (appearance) ojeroso
haggle, jag′-l, v., regatear
hail, jeil, s., granizo m. v., granizar; (call) llamar
hair, jér, s., pelo m., cabello m.; (horse) crin m.; **—brush,** cepillo para el pelo m.; **—dresser,** peluquero m.; **—drier,** s., secador para el pelo m.; **—pin,** horquilla f.; **—y,** a., peludo
hake, jeik, s., merluza f.
hale, jeil, a., sano, robusto
half, jaaf, s., mitad f. a., medio. adv., a medias
halibut, jal′-i-bŏt, s., mero m., hipogloso m.
hall, joal, s., vestíbulo m.; **—mark,** marca del contraste f.; **—porter,** conserje m.
hallow, jal′-ou, v., santificar
hallucination, ja-liu′-si-nei′-shon, s., alucinación f.
halo, jei′-lou, s., halo m., aureola f.

halt, jo*a*lt, s., parada f. v., pararse, interj., ¡alto!

halter, jo*a*l'-ta, s., cabestro m.

halve, jaav, v., partir en dos mitades

ham, jam, s., jamón m.

hamlet, jam'-let, s., aldea f., villorrio m.

hammer, jam'-*a*, s., martillo m. v., martillar

hammock, jam'-ok, s., hamaca f.

hamper, jam'-pa, s., canasto m. v., estorbar

hand, jand, s., (human, clock, cards) mano f.
v., dar; **—bag**, s., bolsa f.; **—bill**, s., cartel m.;
—book, manual m.; **—cuffs**, s. pl., esposas
f. pl.; **—ful**, s., puñado m.; **—kerchief**,
pañuelo m.; **—made**, a., hecho á mano f.;
—rail, s., barandal m.; **second—**, de
segundamano; **—y**, a., mañoso

handle, jan'-dl, s., mango m.; (bag) asa f.; (door)
botón m. v., manejar

handsome*, jan'-som, a., bello; elegante; generoso

hang, jang, v., (execute) ahorcar; **—er**, s., colgadero m.; **—man**, verdugo m.; **—up**, v., colgar

hangar, jang'-ga, s., hangar m.

hank, jang-k, s., madeja f.

hanker, jang'-ka, v., ansiar, apetecer

hapless, jap'-les, a., desventurado

happen, jap'-n, v., acontecer, ocurrir

happily, jap'-i-li, avd., felizmente

happiness, jap'-i-nes, s., felicidad f., dicha f.

happy, jap'-i, a., feliz, dichoso

harangue, ja-rang', s., arenga f. v., arengar

harass, jar'-as, v., acosar

harbinger, jaar'-bin-cha, s., precursor m.

harbour, jaar'-br, s., puerto m.

hard, jaard, a., duro

harden, jaar'-dn, v. endurecer; (refl.) endurecerse

hardly, jaard'-li, avd., apenas; severamente

hardness, jaard'-nes, s., dureza f.; dificultad f.

hardship, jaard'-ship, s., pena f.; privación f.

hardware, jaard'-uér, s., quincallería f.

hardy, jaar'-di, a., robusto; atrevido

hare, jér, s., liebre f.

hark, jaark, v., escuchar. interj. ¡oye!

harlequin, jaar'-li-küin, s., arlequín m.

harlot, jaar'-lot, s., prostituta f.

harm, jaarm, s., daño m. v., dañar; **—ful*,** a., dañoso; **—less*,** inofensivo

harmonious*, jaar-mou'-ni-os, a., armonioso

harmonize, jaar'-mon-ais, v., armonizar

harness, jaar'-nes, s., (horses, armour) arnés m. v., enjaezar; (forces) acoplar

harp, jaarp, s., arpa f.

harpoon, jaar-puun', s., arpón m.

harrow, jar'-ou, s., grada f. v., gradar (feelings) perturbar

harsh*, jaarsh, a., (sound) discordante; (severe) áspero; (colour) duro

hart, jaart, s., ciervo m.

harvest, jaar'-vest, s., cosecha f. v., cosechar

hash, jash, s., picadillo m., salpicón m. v., picar

hassock, jas'-ok, s., cojín m.

haste, jeist, s., prisa f.; **—n,** v., apresurarse

hastily, jeis'-ti-li, adv., precipitadamente

hat, jat, s., sombrero m.; **—-box,** sombrerera f.; **—-pin,** alfiler de sombrero m.; **—-stand,** percha f.; **—ter,** sombrerero m.

hatch, jach, s., (naut.) escotilla f. v., empollar; (plot) tramar

hatchet, jach'-et, s., hacha f.

hate, jeit, v., odiar s., odio m.

hateful*, jeit'-ful, a., odioso, detestable

haughty, joa'-ti, a., altivo, soberbio

haul, joal, s., arrastre m.; (catch) redada f. v., tirar de, arrastrar; **—age,** s., tracción f.

haunch, joanch, s., anca f.

haunt, joant, s., (animal) guarida f. v., rondar

have, jav, v., haber; tener; poseer; (to cause) hacer

haven, jei'-vn, s., puerto m., abra f.; (refuge) asilo m.

haversack, jav'-er-sak, s., mochila f.

havoc, jav'-ok, s., estrago m., ruina f.

hawk, joank, s., halcón m. v., revender

hawker, joa'-ka, s., buhonero m.

hawthorn, joa'-zoarn, s., espino m.

hay, jei, s., heno m.; **—-fever,** fiebre del heno f.; **—-loft,** henil m.; **—-making,** siega del heno f.; **—-stack,** almiar m., niara f.

hazard, jʌsˈ-erd, s., azar m., acaso m.; (risk) riesgo m. v., aventurar; **—ous'**, a., arriesgado
haze, jeis, s., bruma f., neblina f.
hazel, jeiˈ-sl, s., avellano f.; **—nut,** avellana f.
hazy, jeiˈ-si, a., brumoso
he, jii, pron. pers., él
head, jed, s., cabeza f.; (chief) jefe m. a., (main) principal
headache, jedˈ-eik, s., dolor de cabeza m.
heading, jedˈ-ing, s., encabezamiento m., título m.
headland, jedˈ-land, s., cabo m.
headlights, jedˈ-laits, s. faros m. pl.
headline, jedˈ-lain, s., título m.
headlong, jedˈ-long, adv., de cabeza. a., temerario
headmaster, jedˈ-maas-ta, s., principal m.
headquarters, jedˈ-kuoar-tas, s., cuartel general
headstrong, jedˈ-strong, a., testarudo, terco   [m.
head-waiter, jed-ueiˈ-ta, s., camarero principal m.
headway, jedˈ-uei, s., progreso m.
heady, jedˈ-i, a., temerario; (wine) capitón
heal, jiil, v., sanar; curar
healing, jiiˈ-ling, s., curación f. a., curativo
health, jelz, s., salud f.
healthy, jelˈ-zi, a., sano
heap, jiip, s., montón m. v., amontonar
hear, jir, v., oír; **—er,** s., oyente m.; **—ing,** oído m.; (judicial) audiencia f.
hearsay, jirˈ-sei, s., rumor m.
hearse, jêrs, s., carro fúnebre m.; féretro m.
heart, jaart, s., corazón m.; (cards) copas m. pl.; **—broken,** a., transido de dolor; **—burn,** s., acedía f.; **—ily,** adv., cordialmente; **—iness,** s., cordialidad f.; **—less,** a., sin corazón; **—y,** cordial
hearth, jaarz, s., hogar m.
heat, jiit, s., calor m. v., calentar
heater, jiitˈ-a, s., calentador m., calorífero m.
heath, jiiz, s., (land) brezal m.
heathen, jiiˈ-Den, s. & a., pagano m.; (fig) ateo m.
heather, jeDˈ-a, s., brezo m.
heating, jiiˈ-ting, s., calefacción f.
heave, jiiv, v., alzar; (naut.) izar

heaven, jev'-n, s., cielo m.; firmamento m.
heavenly, jev'-n-li, a., celestial
heaviness, jev'-i-nes, s., pesadez f.
heavy, jev'-i, a., pesado
hedge, jeCH, s., seto m.; —**hog,** erizo m.
heed, jiid, v., atender. s., atención f.
heedful*, jiid'-ful, a., atento, vigilante
heedless*, jiid'-les, a., descuidado, distraído
heel, jiil, s., talón m.; (shoe) tacón m.
heifer, jef'-a, s., ternera f.
height, jait, s., altura f.; (person) estatura f.
heighten, jai'-ten, v., elevar, realzar
heinous*, jei'-ños, a., atroz, odioso
§**heir,** ér, s., heredero m.
§**heiress,** ér'-es, s., heredera f.
§**heirloom,** ér'-lum, s., herencia f.
helicopter, jel'-i-kop-ta, s., helicóptero m.
hell, jel, s., infierno m.; —**ish,** a., infernal
helm, jelm, s., timón m.; —**sman,** timonero m.
helmet, jel'-met, s., yelmo m., casco m.
help, jelp, s., ayuda f.; (in distress) socorro m.
interj., ¡socorro ! v., ayudar; socorrer; —**er,**
s., asistente m.; —**ful,** a., útil; servicial; —**less,**
desamparado; impotente; —**mate,** s., compañero m.   [(surround) rodear
hem, jem, s., dobladillo m. v., dobladillar; — **in,**
hemisphere, jem'-i-sfiir, s., hemisferio m.
hemp, jemp, s., cáñamo m.
hen, jen, s., gallina f.; —**pecked,** a., marido que se
deja mandar; —**roost,** gallinero m.
hence, jens, adv., de aquí; por lo tanto
henceforth, jens-fórz, adv., en adelante
her, jér, pers. pron. la; le; ella; a ella. poss. adj.
su, sus (de ella)
herald, jer'-ald, s., heraldo m. v., anunciar
herb, jérb, s., yerba f.; —**alist,** s., herbolario m.
herd, jérd, s., manada f., hato m. v., reunir el ganado; ir en hatos; —**sman,** s., vaquero m.
here, jir, adv., aquí; acá; por aquí
hereabout, jir-a-baut', adv., por aquí cerca
hereafter, jir-aaft'-a, adv., en lo futuro
hereby, jir-bai', adv., por éstas; por la presente

hereditary, ji-red'i-ta-ri, a., hereditario

herein, jir-in', adv., aquí dentro; incluso

hereof, jir-ov', adv., de esto; de aquí

hereon, jir-on', adv., sobre esto

heresy, jer'i-si, s., herejía f.

heretic, jer'i-tik, s., hereje m.

hereto, jir-tuu', adv., a esto, a este fin

heretofore, jir-tuu-fór', adv., hasta agur

hereupon, jir-öp-on', adv., sobre esto

herewith, jir-uiD', adv., con esto; adjunto

hermetic, jer'-met-ik, a., hermético

hermit, jêr'-mit, s., ermitaño m.

hermitage, jêr'-mi-tiCH, s., ermita f.

hernia, jêr'-ni-a, s., hernia f.

hero, ji'-rou, s., héroe m.; (stage, etc.) protagonista m.

heroic, ji'-rou-ik, a., heroico, épico

heroine, ji'-ro-in, s., heroína f.; (stage, etc.) protagonista f.

heroism, ji'-ro-ism, s., heroísmo m.

herring, jer'-ing, s., arenque m.

hers, jêrs, pron., f., suyo, suya, de ella; el suyo, la suya, los suyos, las suyas (de ella)

herself, jêr-self', pron., ella misma

hesitate, jes'-i-teit, v., vacilar, dudar, titubear

hesitation, jes-i-tei'-shon, s., duda f.; indecisión f.

hew, jiuu, v., tajar; (stone) picar

hiatus, jai-ei'-tos, s., hiato m.

hiccough, hiccup, jik'-op, s., hipo m.

hide, jaid, s., cuero m., piel f. v., esconder

hideous*, jid'-i-os, a., horrible, espantoso

hiding, jai'-ding, s., (flogging) paliza f. a., (in hiding) escondido; **—place,** s., escondite m.

high*, jai, a., alto; (status) eminente; (elevated) elevado; (food) pasado; (cost) caro; **—est,** a., el más alto; supremo; **—ness,** s., altura f.; (title) Alteza f.

highbrow, jai'-brau, s., snob intelectual m. a., docto, erudito

highlander, jai'-land-a, s., montañés m.

highlight, jai'-lait, s., punto sobresaliente m.; realce m. v., poner de relieve

highway, jai'-uei, s., carretera f., camino real m.

hilarity, ji-lar'-i-ti, s., hilaridad f.

hill, jil, s., colina f.; (road) cuesta f.; **—y,** a., montañoso

hilt, jilt, s., puño de espada m.

him, jim, pers. pron., le; él; a él

himself, jim-self', pron., él, él mismo

hind, jaind, s., cierva f. a., trasero

hinder, jin'-da, v., impedir, estorbar

hindermost, jin'-der-moust, a., postrero, último

hindrance, jin'-drans, s., impedimento m.

hinge, jinch, s., bisagra f.; (door) gozne m.

hint, jint, s., indirecta f., sugestión f., insinuación f. v., sugerir; insinuar

hip, jip, s., cadera f.

hire, jair, s., alquiler m. v., alquilar; **— purchase,** s., venta a plazos

his, jis, pron., m., suyo suya, de él; el suyo, la suya, los suyos, las suyas (de él). poss. adj., su, sus (de él)

hiss, jis, v., (steam) silbar; (derision) chiflar. s. silbido m.; (derision) rechifla f.

historical*, jis-to'-rikal, a., histórico

history, jis'-to-ri, s., historia f.

hit, jit, v., pegar; (target, etc.) acertar. s., golpe m.

hitch, jich, s., (pull) tirón m.; (obstacle) tropiezo m. v., enganchar; (naut.) amarrar

hither, jiD'-a, adv., aquí; acá; por aquí; por acá

hitherto, jiD'-er-tu, adv., hasta ahora

hive, jaiv, s., colmena f.

hoar, jór, **—y,** a., canoso; **—frost,** s., escarcha f.

hoard, jórd, v., (money, jewels) atesorar; (food, etc.) acaparar. s., tesoro m.

hoarse*, jórs, a., ronco, enronquecido

hoax, jouks, s., chasco m. v., chasquear

hobble, job'-l, s., cojera f. v., (walk) cojear

hobby, job'-i, s., pasatiempo m.

hock, jok, s., vino del Rin m.; (animal) jarrete m.

hoe, jou, s., azada f. v., cavar

hog, jog, s., puerco m., cerdo m.

hoist, joist, v., alzar; (flag) izar

hold, jould, v., tener, agarrar; (capacity) contener,

s., presa f.; (ship) cala f.; — **back**, v., retener;
— **good,** ser válido; — **on,** agarrarse; — **over,**
aplazar

holder, joul'-da, s., tenedor m., poseedor m.;
(handle) mango m.; (receptacle) asa f.; (bracket)
brazo m.; **share—,** accionista m. & f.

holding, joul'-ding, s., tenencia f.; (share) acción f.

hole, joul, s., agujero m.

holiday, jol'-i-dei, s., fiesta f.

holidays, jol'-i-deis, s. pl., vacaciones f. pl.

holiness, jol'-i-nes, s., santidad f.

hollow, jol'-ou, s., hueco m. a., hueco v., ahuecar

holly, jol'-i, s., acebo m.

holy, jou'-li, a., santo; sagrado; — **water,** s., agua
bendita f.; — **week,** Semana Santa f.

homage, jom'-ich, s., homenaje m.

home, joum, s., casa f.; (circle) hogar m.; (home-
land) patria f.; **at —,** en casa; **—less,** sin
hogar; **—ly,** a., casero

homesick, joum'-sik, a., nostálgico

homeward, joum'-uerd, adv., hacia casa;
—bound, de regreso

homœopathic, jou'-mi-o-paz'-ik, a., homeopático

hone, joun, s., piedra de afilar f. v., (blades) asentar

§**honest,** on'-est, a., honrado; honesto; sincero

§**honesty,** on'-est-i, s., honradez f., honestidad f.

honey, jon'-i, s., miel f.; **—moon,** luna de miel f.;
—suckle, madreselva f.

§**honorary,** on'-er-a-ri, a., honorario

§**honour,** on'-a, s., honor m.

§**honourable,** on'-er-a-bl, a., honorable

hood, jud, s., capucha f.; (vehicle) capota f.

hoodwink, jud'-uingk, v., enganar

hoof, juf, s., pezuña f.; (horse) casco m.

hook, juk, s., gancho m., garfio m.; (fish) anzuelo m.
v., enganchar; **—and eye,** s., corchete m.;
(hook) macho m.; (eye) hembra f.; **by — or by
crook,** adv., a tuertas o a derechas

hoop, jup, s., cerco m., arco m.; aro m.

hoot, juut, s., (owl) grito m.; (derision) grita f.;
(motor) bocinazo m. v., gritar; (derision) dar
grita; (motor) bocinar

hop, jop, s., brinco m.; (plant) lúpulo m. v., brincar

hope, joup, s., esperanza f. v., esperar, **—ful***, a., prometedor; **—less***, desesperado; irremediable

horizon, jo-rai´-son, s., horizonte m.

horizontal*, jo-ri-son´-tal, a., horizontal

horn, joarn, s., cuerno m., asta f.; (motor) bocina f.; (hunt) cuerno de caza m.

hornet, joar´-net, s., moscardón m.

horrible, jor´-i-bl, a., horrible

horrid*, jor´-id, a., hórrido

horrify, jor´-i-fai, v., horrorizar

horror, jor´-or, s., horror m., terror m.

horse, joars, s., caballo m.; **—back (on)**, adv., a caballo; **—hair**, s., crin f.; **—man**, jinete m.; **—power**, caballos de fuerza m. pl.; **—radish**, jaramago m.; **—shoe**, herradura f.

hose, jous, s., manga de riego f.; (stocking) media f.; **half—**, calcetines m. pl.

hosier, jou´-sha, s., mediero m., calcetero m.

hosiery, jou´-sher-i, s., calcetería f.

hospitable, jos´-pi-ta-bl, a., hospitalario

hospital, jos´-pi-tal, s., hospital m.

host, joust, s., (inn) anfitrión m.; (friend) huésped m.; (army) hueste f.; (sacrament) hostia f.

hostage, jos´-tich, s., (mil.) rehén m.

hostelry, jos´-tel-ri, s., posada f., hostelería f.

hostess, jous´-tes, s., huéspeda f., anfitriona f.; (inn) posadera f.

hostile, jos´-tail, a., hostil, enemigo

hot*, jot, a., caliente, cálido; (condiment) picante

hotel, jo-tel´, s., hotel m.; (inn) posada f.

hothouse, jot´-jaus, s., invernadero f.

hound, jaund, s., perro de caza m. v., cazar; perseguir

§**hour,** auer, s., hora f.; **—ly**, adv., a cada hora

house, jaus, v., albergar. s., casa f.; **—agent**, agente de casas m.; **—hold**, familia f.; **—holder**, amo de casa m.; **—keeper**, ama de llaves f.; **—maid**, criada f.

hovel, jov´-l, s., cabaña f., choza f.

hover, jov´-a, v., revolotear; (fig.) dudar

how, jau, adv., cómo; cuán, cuánto; por qué;

—ever, como quiera que sea. conj., sin embargo; **— far,** a qué distancia; **— much, many,** cuánto, cuánta, cuántos, cuántas

howl, jaul, v., aullar. s., aullido m.

hub, jŏb, s., cubo de la rueda m.

huddle, jŏd´-l, v., arrebujar   [m.

hue, jiuu, s., color m.; tinte m.; **—and cry,** alarma

hug, jŏg, v., abrazar. s., abrazo m.

huge, jiuch, a., vasto, enorme inmenso

hulk, jŏlk, s., casco m.

hull, jŏl, s., casco m.

hum, jŏm, v., (insect, engine) zumbar; (voice) tararear. s., zumbido m.

human, jiuu´-man, a., humano; **—ity,** s., humanidad f.

humane*, jiuu-mein´, a., humano, humanitario

humble, jŏm´-bl, a., humilde. v., humillar

humidity, jiuu-mid´-i-ti, s., humedad f.

humiliate, jiuu-mil´-i-eit, v., humillar

humiliation, jiuu-mi-li-ei´-shon, s., humillación f.

humorist, jŏn´-mer-ist, s., humorista m.

humorous*, jiuu´-mer-os, a., jocoso, cómico

humour, jiuu´-ma, s., humor m. v., complacer

hump, jŏmp, s., joroba f.; **—** back, jorobado m.

hunch, jŏnsh, s., giba f.; **—back,** joroba f.

hundred, jŏn´-dred, s. & a., ciento m.; cien m.; **—fold,** a., céntuplo; **—th,** centésimo; **—weight,** s., quintal m.

hunger, jŏn´-ga, s., hambre m. v., sufrir hambre

hungry, jŏn´-gri, a., hambriento

hunt, jŏnt, s., caza f. v., cazar; **—er,** s., cazador m.

hurdle, jŏr´-dl, s., zarzo m., valla f.

hurl, jĕrl, v., arrojar; precipitar

hurricane, jŏr´-i-kan, s., huracán m.

hurry, jŏr´-i, v., apresurarse. s., prisa f.

hurt, jŏrt, v., herir, dañar. s., mal m.

hurtful*, jĕrt´-ful, a., nocivo; perjudicial

husband, jŏs´-band, s., marido m. v., economizar, ahorrar

hush, jŏsh, interj.; ¡ chitón ! v., **— up,** ocultar

husk, jŏsk, s., cáscara f., vaina f.; **—y,** a., ronco

hussy, jŏs´-i, s., pícara f.

hustle, jŏs'-l, v., darse prisa; (jostle) empujar

hut, jŏt, s., choza f., cabaña f.

hutch, jŏch, s., (rabbit) conejera f.

hyacinth, jai'-*a*-sinz, s., jacinto m.

hydrant, jai'-drant, s., boca de riego f.

hydraulic, jai'-drou-lik, a., hidráulico

hydro, jai'-drou, **—gen,** s., hidrógeno m.; **—pathic,** a., hidropático; **—phobia,** s., rabia f.; **—plane,** hidroplano m.

hygienic, jai-CHi-en'-ik, a., higiénico

hymn, jim, s., himno m.

hyphen, jai'-fen, s., guión m.

hypocrisy, jip-o'-kri-si, s., hipocresía f.; disimulo m.

hypocrite, jip'-o-krit, s., hipócrita m. & f.

hysterical, jis-ter'-i-kal, a., histérico

I, ai, pron., yo

ice, ais, s., hielo m.; **—bound,** a., aprisionado por el hielo; **—cream,** s., helado m.

icicle, ais'-i-kl, s., carámbano m., cerrión m.

icy, ais'-i, a., helado

idea, ai-dii'-*a*, s., idea f.

ideal, ai-dii'-*al*, s., ideal m. a., ideal

idealise, ai-dii'-*al*-is, v., idealizar

identical*, ai-den'-ti-kl, a., idéntico

identify, ai-den'-ti-fai, v., identificar

identity, ai-den'-ti, s., identidad f.

idiom, id'-i-om, s., (phrase) modismo m.

idiot, id'-i-ot, s., idiota m. & f.

idiotic, id-i-ot'-ik, a., tonto; absurdo

idle, ai'-dl, a., ocioso. v., holgazanear; **—ness,** s., ociosidad f.; **—r,** holgazán m.

idol, ai'-dol, s., ídolo m.

idolize, ai'-dol-ais, v., idolatrar

idyll, id'-dil, s., idilio m.

idyllic, id-dil'-ik, a., idílico, pastoril

if, if, conj., si; **even —,** aunque

ignite, ig-nait', v., encender

ignition, ig-ni'-shon, s., ignición f.

ignoble, ig-nou'-bl, a., innoble, vil

ignominious*, ig-no-min'-i-os, a., ignominioso

ignominy, ig'-no-min-i, s., ignominia f.

ignoramus, ig-nor-ei'-mos, a., ignorante

ignorance, ig'-nor-ans, s., ignorancia f.

ignore, ig-nór', v., no hacer caso, pasar por alto

ill, il, a., enfermo, malo; (nausea) mareado; **—ness,** s., enfermedad f.

illegal*, i-líi'-gal, a., ilegal

illegible, i-lecH'-i-bl, a., ilegible

illegitimate*, i-lecH-it'-i-met, a., ilegítimo

illiberal*, i-líb'-er-al, a., avaro, mezquino

illiterate, i-lít'-er-eit, s. & a., analfabeto m.; ignorantem.

illogical*, i-locH'-i-kl, a., ilógico

illuminate, i-liuu'-mi-neit, v., iluminar; **—d,** adj., iluminado

illumination, i-liuu-mi-nei'-shon, s., iluminación

illusion, i-liuu'-shon, s,, ilusión f. [f.

illusive*, i-liuu'-siv, a., ilusivo

illusory, i-liuu'-so-ri, a., ilusorio

illustrate, i-lus'-treit, v., ilustrar

illustration, i-lus-trei'-shon, s., ilustración f.

illustrious*, i-lus'-tri-os, a., ilustre

image, im'-icH, s., imagen f. [f.

imagination, i-macH'-in-ei'-shon, s., imaginación

imagine, i-macH'-in, v., imaginar; figurarse

imbecile, im'-bi-sail, a., imbécil

imbibe, im-baib', v., beber; (absorb) embeber

imbue, im-biuu', v., imbuir; infundir

imitate, im'-i-teit, v., imitar, remedar

immaculate*, i-mʌk'-iu-let, a., inmaculado

immaterial*, i-ma-tíi'-ri-al, a., inmaterial; indiferente

immature*, i-ma-tiúr', a., inmaturo; prematuro

immeasurable, i-mesh'-iu-ra-bl, a., inmensurable

immediately, i-mii'-di-et-li, adv., inmediatamente, en seguida

immense*, i-mens', a., inmenso

immensity, i-mens'-i-ti, s., inmensidad f.

immerse, i-mérs', v., sumergir

immigrant, i'-mi-grant, s., inmigrante m.

immigrate, i'-mi-greit, v., inmigrar

imminent*, i'-mi-nent, a., inminente

immobilize, i-mo'-bi-lais, v., inmovilizar, paralizar

immoderate*, i-mod'-er-et, a., inmoderado
immodest*, i-mod'-ist, a., inmodesto; impúdico
immoral*, i-mor'-al, a., inmoral
immortal, i-mor'-tal, a., inmortal; **—ize**, v., inmortalizar
immovable, i-muu'-va-bl, a., inmóvil; inamovible; inmueble
immune, i-miuun', a., inmune; exento
imp, imp, s., diablillo m.
impact, im'-pakt, s., choque m.; impacto m.
impair, im-pér', v., deteriorar; perjudicar
impale, im-peil', v., empalar
impanel, im-pan'-l, v., nombrar los jurados
imparity, im-par'-i-ti, s., disparidad f.
impart, im-paart', v., comunicar; dar
impartial*, im-paar'-shal, a., imparcial
impassable, im-pass'-a-bl, a., impracticable
impassion, im-pash'-on, v., apasionar; conmover
impassive*, im-pas'-iv, a., impasible
impatience, im-pei'-shens, s., impaciencia f.
impatient*, im-pei'-shent, a., impaciente
impeach, im-piich', v., acusar
impeachment, im-piich'-ment, s., acusación f.
impecunious, im-pi-kiuu'-ni-os, a., sin dinero, pobre
impede, im-piid', v., impedir
impediment, im-ped'-i-ment, s., impedimento m.
impel, im-pel', v., impeler; incitar
impending, im-pen'-ding, a., inminente
imperative, im-per'-a-tiv, s. & a., imperativo m.
imperfect*, im-per'-fekt, a., imperfecto
imperfection, im-per-fek'-shon, s., imperfección f.
imperial*, im-pi'-ri-al, a., imperial
imperil, im-per'-il, v., poner en peligro
imperious, im-pi'-ri-os, a., imperioso; perentorio
imperishable, im-per'-i-sha-bl, a., imperecedero; indestructible
impermeable, im-per'-mi-a-bl, a., impermeab`e
impersonal*, im-per'-son-al, a., impersonal
impersonate, im-per'-son-eit, v., personificar; (stage) representar
impertinence, im-per'-ti-nens, s., impertinencia f.

impertinent*, im-pĕr'-ti-nent, a., impertinente
(not appertaining) fuera de propósito
impervious*, im-pĕr'-vi-os, a., impenetrable
impetuosity, im-pet'-iu-os'-i-ti, s., impetuosidad f
impetuous*, im-pet'-iu-os, a., impetuoso
impetus, im'-pi-tos, s., ímpetu m.; (fig.) impulsión f
impiety, im-pai'-et-i, s., impiedad f.
impious*, im'-pi-os, a., impío
implement, im'-pli-ment, s., instrumento m.
herramienta f.
implicate, im'-pli-keit, v., implicar
implicit*, im-plis'-it, a., implícito, absoluto
implore, im-plór', v., implorar
imply, im-plai', v., implicar; denotar; insinuar
impolite*, im-po-lait', a., descortés
import, im-pórt', v., importar. s., importación f.
— **duty**, derechos de entrada m. pl.; —**er**, im-
portador m.
importance, im-pór'-tans, s., importancia f.
important*, im-pór'-tant, a., importante
importunate, im-pór'-tiu-neit, a., importuno
impose, im-pous', v., imponer; — **upon**, abusar
imposing, im-pou'-sing, a., imponente
imposition, im-po-si'-shon, s., imposición f.; impostura f.; (tax) impuesto m.
impossibility, im-pos-i-bil'-i-ti, s., imposibilidad f.
impossible, im-pos'-i-bl, a., imposible
impostor, im-pos'-tr, s., impostor m.
impotence, im-po'-tens, s., impotencia f.
impound, im-paund', v., encerrar; (judicial) depositar
impoverish, im-pov'-er-ish, v., empobrecer
imprecation, im-pri-kei'-shon, s., imprecación f.
impregnable, im-preg'-na-bl, a., inexpugnable
impregnate, im-preg'-neit, v., impregnar; (fertilize) empreñar
impress, im'-pres, v., imprimir, estampar; (feelings) impresionar; —**ion**, s., impresión f.;
(stamp) marca f.; —**ive**, a., solemne; grandioso
imprint, im-print', s., marca f.; impresión f.; v.,
marcar; (mind) fijar   [encarcelación f
imprison, im-pris'-n, v., encarcelar; —**ment**, s.

mprobable, im-prob′-a-bl, a., improbable

mproper*, im-prop′-a, a., impropio, indecente

mpropriety, im-pro-prai′-i-ti, s., impropiedad f.

mprove, im-pruuv′, v., mejorar; mejorarse;
—**ment,** s., mejora f.; progreso m.

mprovident,* im-prov′-i-dent, a., impróvido

mprudent*, im-pruu′-dent, a., imprudente

mpudence, im′-piu-dens, s., descaro m

mpudent*, im′-piu-dent, a., descarado

mpulse, im′-pöls, s., impulso m.

mpure*, im-piúr′, a., impuro; (morally) manchado

mpurity, im-piú′-ri-ti, s., impureza f.

mpute, im-piuut′, v., imputar

n, in, adv., dentro, adentro. prep., en; por; sobre;
a; con; de; mientras

nability, in-a-bil′-i-ti, s., inhabilidad f.

naccessible, in-ak-sess′-i-bl, a., inaccesible

naccuracy, in-ak′-iu-ra-si, s., inexactitud f.

naccurate*, in-ak′-iu-ret, a., inexacto

nadequate, in-ad′-i-kuet, a., inadecuado

nadvertent*, i-nad-vêr′-tent, a., inadvertido

nane, i-nein′, a., inepto, fútil

nanimate i-nan′-i-met, a., inanimado

napt, i-nap′-t, a., inepto

nasmuch as, in-as-möch′-as, conj., visto que

naudible, in-oa′-di-bl, a., inaudible

naugurate, in-oa′-guiu-reit, v., inaugurar

nborn, inbred, in′-boarn, in′-bred, a., innato

ncalculable, in-kal′-kiu-lei-bl, a., incalculable

ncapable, in-kei′-pa-bl, a., incapaz

ncapacitate, in-ka-pas′-i-teit, v., incapacitar

ncapacity, in-ka-pas′-i-ti, s., incapacidad f.

ncarnation, in-kar-nei′-shon, s., encarnación f.

ncautious*, in-koa′-shos, a., incauto

ncense, in-sens′, s., incienso m. v., (incite) provocar; (anger) encolerizar

ncentive, in-sen′-tiv, s., incentivo m.; estímulo m.

ncessant*, in-ses′-ant, a., incesante

nch, inch, s., pulgada f.

ncident, in′-si-dent, s., incidente m.

ncidental*, in-si-den′-tl, a., incidental

ncipient, in-sip′-i-ent, a., incipiente

incision, in-sish'-on, s., incisión f.

incite, in-sait', v., incitar

incivility, in-si-vil'-i-ti, s., descortesía f.

inclination, in-kli-nei'-shon, s., inclinación f.; (disposition) tendencia f.

incline, in-klain', v., inclinar; inclinarse

incline, in'-klain, s., (slope) declive m.

include, in-kluud', v., incluir, encerrar

including, in-kluud'-ing, adv. & a., inclusive; incluyendo

inclusive, in-kluu'-siv, a., inclusivo

incoherent, in-ko-ji'-rent, a., incoherente

income, in'-kom, s., ingresos m. pl.; renta f. —**tax,** impuesto sobre la renta m.

incoming, in'-kom-ing, a., entrante

incommode, in-kom-oud', v., incomodar

incommodious*, in-kom-ou'-di-os, a., incómodo

incomparable, in-kom'-pa-ra-bl, a., incomparable

incompatible, in-kom-pat'-i-bl, a., incompatible

incompetent, in-kom'-pi-tent, a., incompetente

incomplete*, in-kom-pliit', a., incompleto

incomprehensible, in-kom'-pri-jen'-si-bl, a., incomprensible

inconceivable, in-kon-sii'-va-bl, a., inconcebible

inconclusive*, in-kon-kluu'-siv, a., inconcluyente

incongruous*, in-kon'-gru-os, a., incongruo

inconsiderable, in-kon-si'-de-ra-bl, a., insignificante

inconsiderate, in-kon-si'-der-eit, a., poco considerado

inconsistent*, in-kon-sis'-tent, a., incompatible, contradictario

inconsolable, in-kon-soul'-a-bl, a., inconsolable

inconstant, in-kon'-stant, a., inconstante

inconvenience, in-kon-vii'-ni-ens, v., perturbar molestar. s., inconveniencia f.; moles f.

inconvenient, in-kon-vii'-ni-ent, a., inconveniente

incorporate, in-kor'-po-reit, v., incorporar

incorrect*, in-ko-rekt', a., incorrecto, inexacto

incorrigible, in-kor'-i-chi-bl, a., incorregible

increase, in-kriis', v., aumentar; crecer

increase, in'-kriis, s., aumento m.

incredible, in-kred'-i-bl, a., increíble
incredulous, in-kred'-iu-los, a., incrédulo
incriminate, in-krim'-i-neit, v., incriminar
incumbent, in-kŏm'-bent, a., obligatorio; (eccl.) beneficiado
incur, in-kŏr', v., incurrir
incurable, in-kiú'-ra-bl, a., incurable
incursion, in-kŏr'-shon, s., incursión f., algarada f.
indebted, in-det'-id, a., empeñado; reconocido; adeudado
indecent*, in-dii'-sent, a., indecente
indecision, in-di-si'-shon, s., indecisión f.
indecisive*, in-di-sai'-siv, a., indeciso, irresoluto
indecorous, in-di-kó'-ros, a., indecoroso, indecente
indeed, in-diid', adv., verdaderamente, de veras
indefatigable, in-di-fat'-i-ga-bl, a., infatigable
indefensible, in-di-fen'-si-bl, a., indefendible
indefinite, in-def'-i-nit, a., indefinido
indelible, in-del'-i-bl, a., indeleble
indelicacy, in-del'-i-ka-si, s., indecoro m.
indemnify, in-dem'-ni-fai, v., indemnizar
indemnity, in-dem'-ni-ti, s., indemnización f.
indent, in-dent', v., (to dent) dentar; —ation, s., indentación f. [f.
independence, in-di-pen'-dens, s., independencia
independent*, in-di-pen'-dent, a., independiente
indescribable, in-di-skrai'-ba-bl, a., indescriptible
indestructible, in-di-strŏk'-ti-bl, a., indestructible
index, in'-dex, s., índice m. ; — **finger,** dedo índice
India-rubber, in-di-a-rab'-a, s., (eraser) goma f.
indicate, in'-di-keit, v., indicar
indication, in-di-kei'-shon, s., indicación f.
indicator, in-di-kei-ta, s., indicador m.
indict, in-dait', v., procesar, encausar
indifference, in-dif'-er-ens, s., indiferencia f.
indifferent*, in-dif'-er-ent, a., indiferente ; mediano
indigestible, in-di-CHes'-ti-bl, a., indigesto
indigestion, in-di-CHest'-ion, s., indigestión f.
indignant*, in-dig'-nant, a., indignado
indignity, in-dig'-ni-ti, s., indignidad f.
indirect*, in-di-rekt', a., indirecto

indiscreet*, in-dis-kriit', a., indiscreto
indiscriminate, in-dis-krim'-i-net, a., promiscuo; **—ly**, adv., indistintamente
indispensable, in-dis-pen'-sa-bl, a., indispensable
indisposed, in-dis-pouzd', a., indispuesto
indisputable, in-dis'-piuu-ta-bl, a., indisputable
indistinct*, in-dis-tiñ-kt', a., indistinto
indistinguishable, in-dis-ting'-gui-sha-bl, a., indistinguible
indite, in-dait', v., redactar
individual, in-di-vid'-iu-al, a.,* individual. s., individuo m.
indolent, in'-do-lent, a., indolente
indoors, in-dórs', adv., en casa
induce, in-diuus', v., inducir, mover; **—ment**, s., móvil m., aliciente m.
indulge (in), in-dólch', v., entregarse a
indulgent*, in-dôl'-chent, a., indulgente
industrial, in-dôs'-tri-al, a., industrial
industrious*, in-dôs'-tri-os, a., industrioso
industry, in'-dos-tri, s., industria f.
inebriated, in-ii'-bri-ei-tid, a., borracho
ineffective*, in-ef-ek'-tiv, a., ineficaz
ineffectual*, in-ef-ek'-tiu-al, a., ineficaz
inefficient*, in-ef-ish'-ent, a., ineficaz
inept*, i-nept', a., inepto; absurdo
inequality, in-i-kuol'-i-ti, s., desigualdad f.
inert*, in-ërt', a., inerte
inestimable, in-es'-ti-ma-bl, a., inestimable
inevitable, in-ev'-i-ta-bl, a., inevitable
inexact, in-eg-sakt', a., inexacto; incorrecto
inexhaustible, in-eg-sous'-ti-bl, a., inagotable
inexpedient*, in-eks-pii'-di-ent, a., inoportuno
inexpensive*, in-eks-pen'-siv, a., barato
inexperience, in-eks-pii'-ri-ens, s., inexperiencia f.
inexperienced, in-eks-pii'-ri-enst, a., inexperto
inexplicable, in-eks'-pli-ka-bl, a., inexplicable
inexpressible, in-eks-press'-i-bl, a., indecible
infallible, in-fal'-i-bl, a., infalible
infamous*, in'-fa-mos, a., infame
infamy, in'-fa-mi, s., infamia f.
infancy, in'-fan-si, s., infancia f.; (law) minoridad f.

infant, in'-fant, s., infante m.; niño m.; (law) menor

infantry, in-fan'-tri, s., infantería f.   [m.

infatuation, in-fAt'-iu-ei'-shon, s., infatuación f.

infect, in-fekt', v., infectar; contagiar

infectious, in-fek'-shos, a., infeccioso; contagioso

infer, in-fër', v., inferir; **—ence**, s., inferencia f.

inferior, in-fi'-ri-or, s. & a., inferior m.

infernal, in-fër'-nal, a., infernal

infest, in-fest', v., infestar; (molest) plagar

infidel, in-fi-del, s. & a., infiel m.

infinite*, in'-fi-nit, a., infinito

infirm, in-fërm', a., doliente, enfermizo, inválido

infirmary, in-fër'-ma-ri, s., enfermería f.

inflame, in-fleim', v., inflamar

inflammable, in-flam'-a-bl, a., inflamable

inflammation, in-fla-mei'-shon, s., inflamación f.

inflate, in-fleit', v., inflar, hinchar

inflexible, in-fleks'-i-bl, a., inflexible

inflict, in-flikt', v., infligir, imponer

influence, in'-flu-ens, s., influencia f. v., influir

influential, in-flu-en'-shal, a., influyente

influenza, in-flu-en'-sa, s., gripe f.

inform, in-foarm', v., informar, enterar, comunicar; **—al**, a., informal; sin ceremonia; **—ality**, s., informalidad; **—ant**, s., informante m.; denunciador m.; **—ation**, s., información f.

infrequent*, in-frii'-ku-ent, a., infrecuente

infringe, in-frinch', v., infringir, contravenir; **—ment**, s., infracción f.; contravención f.

infuriate, in-fiuu'-ri-eit, v., enfurecer

infuse, in-fiuus', v., infundir; (tea) poner en infusión

ingenious, in-CHii'-ni-os, a., ingenioso

ingenuity, in-CHin-iuu'-i-ti, s., ingeniosidad f.

ingot, in'-got, s., lingote m.; barra f.

ingratiate, in-grei'-shi-eit, v., insinuarse

ingratitude, in-grAt'-i-tiuud, s., ingratitud f.

ingredient, in-grii'-di-ent, s., ingrediente m.

inhabit, in-jab'-it, v., habitar; **—able**, a., habitable; **—ant**, s., habitante m.

inhale, in-jeil', v., inhalar; (smoke) tragar

inherent*, in-ji'-rent, a., inherente   [f.

inherit, in-jer'-it, v., heredar; **—ance**, s., herencia

inhibition, in-jib-i'-schon, s., inhibición f., prohibición f.

inhospitable, in-jos'-pit-a-bl, a., inhospitable

inhuman, in-jiuu'-man, a., inhumano

iniquitous, in-ik'-ui-tos, a., inicuo

initial, in-ish'-al, s., letra inicial f. a., inicial

initiate, i-nish'-i-eit, v., iniciar

inject, in-CHekt', v., inyectar; —**ion,** s., inyección f.

injudicious, in-CHiu-dish'-os, a., poco juicioso

injunction, in-CHongk'-shon, s., mandato m.; (law)
entredicho m.

injure, in'-CHiúr, v., agraviar; (spoil) dañar;
(bodily) lastimar

injurious*, in-CHiú'-ri-os, a., perjudicial; dañoso

injury, in'-CHer-i, s., daño m.; (bodily) lesión f.

injustice, in-CHös'-tis, s., injusticia f.

ink, ingk, s., tinta f.; —**stand,** tintero m.

inlaid, in-leid', a., incrustado

inland, in'-land, s. & a., interior m.

inlet, in'-let, s., entrada f., abra f.; estuario m.

inmate, in'-meit, s., interno m.; acogido m.

inmost, in'-moust, a., recóndito; íntimo

inn, in, s., posada f., fonda f.; —**keeper,** hospedero m.

inner, in'-a, a., interior

innocent*, in'-o-sent, a., inocente

innocuous, in-o'-kiu-os, a., innocuo

innovation, in-o-vei'-shon, s., innovación f.

innumerable, in-niu'-mer-a-bl, a., innumerable

inoculate, in-o'-kiu-leit, v., inocular

inoffensive*, in-o-fen'-siv, a., inofensivo

inopportune, in-o'-por-tiuun, a., inoportuno

inquest, in'-kuest, s., pesquisa judicial f.

inquire, in-kuair', v., informarse; (ask) preguntar;
(law) inquirir

inquiry, in-kuai'-ri, s., investigación f.; (law) pesquisa f.; —**office,** oficina de información f.

inquisition, in-kui-si'-shon, s., inquisición f.

inquisitive*, in-kuis'-it-iv, a., curioso, inquisitivo

insane*, in-sein', a., loco, demente

insanity, in-san'-i-ti, s., locura f., demencia f.

insatiable, in-sei'-shi-a-bl, a., insaciable

inscription, in-skrip'-shon, s., inscripción f.

insect, in'-sekt, s., insecto m.

insecure, in-si-kiúr', a., inseguro

insensible, in-sen'-si-bl, a., insensible; (unconscious) sin sentido

inseparable, in-sep'-a-ra-bl, a., inseparable

insert, in-sert', v., insertar; —**ion,** s., inserción f.; (advertisement) anuncio m.

inside, in'-said, adv., en, dentro. s., entrañas f. pl.; interior m. a., interior

insidious*, in-sid'-i-os, a., insidioso

insight, in'-sait, s., penetración f.; perspicacia f.

insignificant, in-sig-nif'-i-kant, a., insignificante

insincere, in-sin-sir', a., insincero, hipócrita

insinuate, in-sin'-iu-eit, v., insinuar

insipid, in-sip'-id, a., insípido, soso

insist, in-sist', v., insistir

insolence, in'-so-lens, s., insolencia f.

insolent*, in'-sou-lent, a., insolente

insolvency, in-sol'-ven-si, s., insolvencia f.

inspect, in-spekt', v., inspeccionar; —**ion,** s., inspección f.; —**or,** inspector m.

inspiration, in-spi-rei'-shon, s., inspiración f.

inspire, in-spair', v., inspirar; —**d,** a., inspirado

install, in-stoal', v., instalar; montar; —**ation,** s., instalación f.; (mech.) montaje m.

instalment, in-stoal'-ment, s., plazo m.; (books, serials) entrega f.

instance, in'-stans, s., caso m.; ejemplo m.

instant, in'-stant, s., instante m.; —**aneous*,** a., instantáneo; —**ly,** adv., al instante

instead, in-sted', adv., en cambio; — **of,** en vez de

instep, in'-step, s., empeine m.

instigate, in'-sti-gueit, v., instigar

instil, in-stil', v., instilar; infundir

instinct, in'-sting-kt, s., instinto m.

institute, in'-sti-tiut, s., instituto m., v., instituir

instruct, in-strōkt', v., instruir; —**or,** s., instructor m.; maestro m.; tutor m.; —**ion,** s., instrucción f.

instrument, in'-stru-ment, s., instrumento m.

insubordinate, in-sub-or'-di-neit, a., insubordin-

insufferable, in-suf'-fer-a-bl, a., insufrible   [ado

insufficient*, in-*suf*-ish'-ent, a., insuficiente
insulation, in-siu-lei'-shon, s., aislamiento m.
insult, in-sólt', v., insultar. s., insulto m.
insurance, in-shúr'-ans, s., seguro m.
insure, in-shúr', asegurar
insurrection, in-ser-rek'-shon, s., insurrección f.
integrate, in'-ti-greit, v., integrar, completar
intelligence, in-tel'-i-chens, s., inteligencia f., talento m.; (information) informe m.
intelligent*, in-tel'-i-chent, a., inteligente
intemperate, in-tem'-per-et, a., inmoderado
intend, in-tend', v., intentar; destinar
intense*, in-tens', a., intenso; vehemente
intent, in-tent', s., designio m.; **—ion**, intención f.; **—ional***, a., intencional
inter, in-ter', v., enterrar; **—ment**, s., entierro m.
intercept, in-ter-sept', v., interceptar
interchange, in'-ter-cheinch, cambiar. s., intercambio m.
intercourse, in'-ter-kórs, comercio m.; relaciones f. pl.
interdict, in-ter-dikt', v., interdecir; prohibir
interest, in'-ter-rest, v., interesar. s., interés m.; (money) rédito m.; **—ing**, a., interesante
interfere, in-ter-fír', v., mezclarse, meterse
interference, in-ter-fír'-ens, s., ingerencia f.
interior, in-tii'-ri-or, s. & a., interior m.
interlace, in-ter-leis', v., entrelazar
interloper, in'-ter-lou-pa, s., intruso m.
interlude, in'-ter-luud, intermedio m.
intermediate, in-ter-mii'-di-et, a., intermedio
intermingle, in-ter-ming'-gl, v., mezclarse
intermission, in-ter-mish'-on, s., interrupción f.
intermittent*, in-ter-mit'-ent, a., intermitente
intermix, in-ter-miks', v., entremezclar
intern, in-tern', v., internar
internal*, in-ter'-nl, a., interno
international, in-ter-nash-o-nal, a., internacional
interpret, in-ter'-pret, v., interpretar; **—er**, s., intérprete m.; traductor m.
interrogate, in-ter'-o-gueit, v., interrogar
interrupt, in-ter-rópt, v., interrumpir

interval, in-ter-vl, s., intervalo m.
intervene, in-ter-viin, v., intervenir
intervention, in-ter-ven-shon, s., intervención f.
interview, in-ter-viuu, untrevista f. v., avistarse con
intestate, in-tes'-tet, a., intestado
intestine, in-tes'-tin, s., intestino m.
intimacy, in'-ti-ma-si, s., intimidad f.
intimate in'-ti-meit, v., intimar; insinuar
intimate*, in'-ti-met, a., íntimo
intimation, in-ti-mei'-shon, s., intimación f.
intimidate, in-tim'-i-deit, v., intimidar
into, in'-tu, prep., en, dentro
intolerable, in-tol'-er-a-bl, a., intolerable
intoxicate, in-tok'-si-keit, v., embriagar
intrepid*, in-trep'-id, a., intrépido
intricate*, in'-tri-ket, a., intrincado
intrigue, in-triig', s., intriga f. v., intrigar
intriguing, in-trii'-guing, a., intrigante
intrinsic, in-trin'-sik, a., intrínseco
introduce, in-tro-diuus', v., introducir; presentar
introductory, in-tro-dŏk'-to-ri, a., preliminar
intrude, in-truud', v., ingerir; forzar; —r, s., intruso m.
intuition, in-tiu-ish'-on, s., intuición f.
inundation, in-on-dei'-shon, s., inundación f.
inure, in-iur', v., habituar, acostumbrar
invade, in-veid', v., invadir; —r, s., invasor m.
invalid, in'-va-liid, s., inválido m.; —chair, silla de inválido f.
invalid, in-val'-id, a., inválido; nulo
invaluable, in-val'-iu-a-bl, a., inapreciable
invariable, in-véi'-ri-a-bl, a., invariable
invasion, in-vei'-shon, s., invasión f.
invent, in-vent', v., inventar; —ion, s., invención f.; —or, inventor m.
inventory, in'-ven-to-ri, s., inventario m.
inverse, in-vŏrs', a., inverso
invert, in-vŏrt', v., invertir
invest, in-vest', v., investir; (capital) invertir
investigate, in-ves'-ti-gueit, v., investigar
investment, in-vest'-ment, s., inversión de fondos f.

inveterate*, in-vet´-er-et, a., inveterado
invidious*, in-vid´-i-os, a., envidioso, odioso
invigorate, in-vig´-or-eit, v., vigorizar
invincible, in-vin´-si-bl, a., invencible
invisible, in-vis´-i-bl, a., invisible
invitation, in-vi-tei´-shon, s., invitación f.
invite, in-vait´, v., invitar, convidar
invoice, in´-vois, s., factura f.
invoke, in-vouk´, v., invocar
involuntary, in-vol´-ön-ta-ri, a., involuntario
involve, in-volv´, v., envolver, implicar, complicar
inward, in´-uerd, a., interior; interno. adv., hacia
dentro
iodine, ai´-o-din, s., yodo m.
I.O.U., ai ou yuu, s., vale m., pagaré m.
ire, air, s., ira f.
iris, ai´-ris, s., flor de lis f.; (eye) iris m.
irksome*, ĕrk-´-som, a., tedioso, fastidioso
iron, ai´-ern, v., planchar. s., hierro m.; (flat) plancha f.; (steam) plancha de vapor; **—monger**,
ferretero m.; **—ware**, ferretería f.
ironical*, ai-ron´-i-kl, a., irónico
irony, ai´-ron-i, s., ironía f.
irreconcilable, i-rek´-on-sai´-la-bl, a., irreconcili-
able
irregular*, i-re´-guiu-lar, a., irregular
irrelevant*, i-rel´-i-vant, a., inaplicable ajeno
irreproachable, i-re-prou´-cha-bl, a., irreprochable
irresistible, i-re-sis-ti-bl, a., irresistible
irrespective (of), i-re-spek´-tiv, a., sin consideración de; independiente de
irresponsible, i-ri-spon´-si-bl, a., irresponsable
irretrievable, i-ri-trii´-va-bl, a., irrecuperable
irreverent*, i-rev´-er-ent, a., irreverente
irrigate, i´-rri-gueit, v., irrigar
irritable, ir´-ri-ta-bl, a., irritable, irascible
irritate, i´-ri-teit, v., irritar
island, ai´-land, s., isla f.; **—er**, isleño m.
isle, ail, s., isla f.
islet, ai´-let, s., islote m.
isolate, ai´-sol-eit, v., aislar
isolation, ai-so-lei´-shon, s., aislamiento m.

issue, i'-shiuu, s., edición f.; progenie f.; (currency) emisión f. v., emitir; producir

isthmus, is'-mos, s., istmo m.

it, it, pron., él; ella; ello; lo; la; le

italic, i-tal'-ik, s., (type) letra cursiva f.

itch, ich, v., picar. s., comezón f.

item, ai'-tem, s., item f.; artículo m.; (news) noticia f.

itinerant, i-tin'-er-ant, s., viandante m. a., ambulante

its, its, pron., su; suyo; sus

itself, it-self', pron., el mismo; la misma; lo mismo; sí mismo

ivory, ai'-ver-i, s., marfil m.

ivy, ai'-vi, s., hiedra f.

jabber, CHAb'-a, v., charlar. s., jerigonza f.

jack, CHAk, s., (mech.) cric m.

jackal, CHAk'-oal, s., chacal m.

jackass, CHAk'-as, s., garañón m.; (fig.) borrico m.

jacket, CHAk'-et, s., chaqueta f.

jade, CHeid, s., (stone) lemanita f.; **—d,** a., cansado

jag, CHag, s., mella f. v., mellar, dentar

jail, CHeil, s., cárcel f.; **—er,** carcelero m.

jam, CHam, s., (conserve) confitura f. v., (lock) apretar

jangle, CHang'-gl, v., rechinar; (quarrel) altercar

January, CHAn'-iu-a-ri, s., enero m.

jar, CHaar, s., tarro m.; **—ring,** a., chirriante

jaundice, CHoan'-dis, s., ictericia f.

jaunt, CHoant, s., excursión f.; **—y,** a., ligero; alegre

jaw, CHoa, s., mandíbula f.; (animal) quijada f.

jay, CHei, s., grajo m.

jealous, CHel'-os, a., celoso; **—y,** s., celos m. pl.

jeer, CHir, v., mofarse, s., mofa f.

jelly, CHel'-i, s., jalea f.; **—fish,** medusa f.

jeopardize, CHep-er-dais', v., arriesgar

jeopardy, CHep'-er-di, s., riesgo m.; peligro m.

jerk, CHĕrk, v., sacudir, s., sacudida f.

jersey, CHĕr'-si, s., jersey m.

jest, CHest, s., chanza f. v., chancearse

jester, CHes'-ta, s., chancero m.; (court) bufón m.

jet, CHet, s., (ornament) azabache m.; (nozzle) caño de salida m.; (liquid) chorro m.; (engine) motor de chorro; propulsor de chorro; (plane) avión de retropropulsión a chorro v., brotar

jettison, CHet'-ti-son, v., arrojar

jetty, CHet'-i, s., muelle m.

jew, CHiuu, s., judío m.

jewel, CHiuu'-el, s., joya f.; **—lery**, joyas f. pl.

jeweller, CHiuu'-el-a, s., joyero m.

jig, CHig, s., jiga f.

jilt, CHilt, v., dar calabazas

jingle, CHing'-gl, v., retiñir, s., retintín m.

job, CHob, s., empleo m.; (task) tarea f.

jobber, CHob'-ba, s., (stock) corredor de bolsa m.

jocular*, CHok-iu-lar, a., jocoso, alegre

join, CHoin, v., juntar; unirse; (fit) encolar; (a club, etc.) asociarse

joiner, CHoin'-a, s., ensamblador m.; carpintero m.

joint, CHoint, s., juntura f.; (anatomy) articulación f.; (meat) trozo de carne m. a., unido; colectivo. s., (Jt. Stock Co.) compañía anónima f.

jointly, CHoint'-li, adv., juntamente; colectivamente

joke, CHouk, s., chiste m. v., chancear

jolly, CHol'-i, a., alegre, jovial

jolt, CHoult, s., sacudida f.; traqueteo m.

jostle, CHos'-l, v., empujar, dar empellones

journal, CHĕr'-nal, s., periódico m.; diario m.; **—ism**, periodismo m.; **—ist**, periodista m.

journey, CHĕr'-ni, s., viaje m. v., viajar

jovial*, CHou'-vi-al, a., alegre, jovial

joy, CHoi, s., gozo m.; **—ful**, a., gozoso; **—less**, sin alegría; triste; **—ous**, festivo

jubilant, CHuu'-bi-lant, a., alborozado

jubilee, CHuu'-bi-li, s., jubileo m.

judge, CHŏCH, s., juez m. v., juzgar

judgment, CHŏCH'-ment, s., discernimiento m.; sentencia f.

judicial*, CHu-dish'-al, a., judicial

judicious*, CHu-dish'-os, a., juicioso

jug, CHŏg, s., jarro m.; cántaro m.

juggle, CHŏg'-l, v., hacer juegos de mano

juggler, CHŏg'-la, s., prestidigitador m.

juice, CHuus, s., jugo m., zumo m.

juicy, CHuu'-si, a., jugoso

July, CHu-lai', s., julio m.

jumble, CHŏm'-bl, s., mezcla f. v., mezclar

jump, CHŏmp, v., saltar. s., salto m.

jumper, CHŏmp'-*a*, s., saltador m.

junction, CHŏngk'-shon, s., unión f.; (rail) empalme m.

juncture, CHŏngk'-tiur, s., juntura f.; ocasión f.

June, CHuun, s., junio m.

jungle, CHŏng-gl, s., jungla f., matorral m.

junior, CHuu'-ni-or, s., más joven m. & f.; (son) hijo m.

juniper, CHuu'-ni-p*a*, s., junípero m.

junk, CHŏngk, s., (rubbish) basura f.; desecho m.

jurisdiction, CHú-ris-dik'-shon, s., jurisdicción f.

juror, CHú'-ror, s., jurado m.

jury, CHú'-ri, s., jurado m.

just, CHŏst, adv., justamente; apenas. a.,* justo; exacto; **—ice,** s., justicia f.; (judge) juez m.; **—ification,** justificación f.; **—ify,** v., justificar

jut, CHŏt, sobresalir

jute, CHuut, s., yute m.

juvenile, CHuu'-vi-nail, juvenil

kale, keil, s., bretón m.

kangaroo, KAN-ga-ruu', s., canguro m.

keel, kiil, s., quilla f.

keen,* kiin, a., agudo, afilado; ansioso

keenness, kiin'-nes, s., agudeza f.; penetración f.

keep, kiip, v., guardar; tener; mantener; continuar; quedarse con. s., mantenimiento m.; **— back,** v., retener; **— off,** impedir; tener a distancia; **— to,** adherirse a; **—er,** s., guardián m.; **—sake,** recuerdo m.

keg, keg, s., barrilito m.

kennel, ken'-l, s., perrera f.

kerb, kĕrb, s., bordillo m.

kernel, kĕr'-nl, s., almendra f.; (pip) pepita f.

kettle, ket'-l, s., hervidor m.; **—-drum,** timbal m.

key, kii, s., llave f.; (piano) tecla f.; **—-board,** teclado m.; **—-hole,** ojo de la cerradura m.

kick, kik, s., patada f.; coz f. v., dar puntapiés; (animal) cocear

kid, kid, s., cabrito m.; **—gloves,** guantes de cabritilla m. pl.; **—nap,** v., secuestrar personas

kidney, kid'-ni, s., riñón m.

kill, kil, v., matar

kiln, kiln, s., horno m.

kin, kin, s., parentesco m.; **—sfolk,** parientes m. pl.; **—sman,** pariente m.; **—swoman,** parienta f.

kind, kaind, a.,* bueno, benévolo. s., especie f.

kindle, kin'-dl, v., encender

kindness, kaind'-nes, s., bondad f.

kindred, kind-red, s., parentesco m. a., emparentado

king, king, s., rey m.; **—dom,** reino m.

kipper, kip'-a, s., arenque ahumado m.

kiss, kis, s., beso m. v., besar

kit, kit, s., equipo m.

kitchen, kit'-shin, s., cocina f.

kite, kait, s., cometa f.

kitten, kit'-n, s., gatito m., gatita f.

klaxon, klAks'-on, s., claxon m.; bocina de automóvil f.

knack, nAk, s., destreza f.; arte m.; maña f.

knapsack, nAp'-sak, s., mochila f.

knave, neiv, s., bribón m.; (cards) sota f.

knead, niid, v., amasar

knee, nii, s., rodilla f.; **—cap,** rótula f.

kneel, niil, v., arrodillarse

knell, nel, s., toque de difuntos m.

knickers, nik'-ers, s. pl., pantalones m. pl.

knife, naif, s., cuchillo m.; **pocket—,** naraja f.

knight, nait, s., caballero m.; (chess) caballo m.

knit, nit, v., hacer calceta

knitting, nit'-ing, s., trabajo de punto m.

knob, nob, s., pomo m.; (of a stick, etc.) puño m.

knock, nok, s., golpe m. v., (call) llamar; (strike) golpear; **—against,** tropezar contra; **—down,** derribar; **—er,** s., (door) aldaba f.

knoll, noul, v., doblar las campanas s., montecillo m.

knot, not, s., nudo m.; (naut.) milla náutica f. v. anudar; **—ty,** a., nudoso; (fig.) intrincado

know, nou, v., conocer; saber

knowledge, nou'-ⁱᴄʜ, s., conocimiento m.; saber m.

knuckle, nok'-l, s., nudillo m.

label, lei'-bl, s., etiqueta f., rótulo m. v., rotular

laboratory, lᴀʙ-o'-ra-to-ri, s., laboratorio m.

laborious*, la-bó'-ri-os, a., laborioso; penoso

labour, lei'-ba, v., trabajar. s., trabajo m.

labourer, lei'-ba-ra, s., trabajador m., obrero m.

laburnum, la-bĕr'-nom, s., laburno m.

lace, leis, s., encaje m.; (shoe, etc.) cordón m. v., lazar

lacerate, lᴀs'-er-eit, v., lacerar

lack, lak, v., faltar de, carecer de. s., falta f., carencia f.

lacquer, lᴀᴋ'-a, s., laca f. v., charolar

lad, lᴀd, s., mozo m.; muchacho m.

ladder, lᴀd'-a, s., escalera f.

lading, lei'-ding, s., carga f.; **bill of —,** conocimiento de embarque m.

ladle, leid'-l, s., cucharón m., cacillo m. v., servir

lady, lei'-di, s., señora f.; **—bird,** mariquita f.; **—'s-maid,** doncella f.

lag, lᴀg, v., remolonear; **— behind,** rezagarse

lagoon, la-guun', s., laguna f.

lair, lér, s., guarida f.

lake, leik, s., lago m.

lamb, lᴀm, s., cordero m.

lame, leim, a.,* cojo. v., lisiar; **—ness,** s., cojera f.

lament, la-ment', v., lamentar. s., lamento m.

lamp, lᴀmp, s., lámpara f.; (street lamp) farol m.; (electric bulb) bombilla eléctrica f.

lance, laans, s., lanza f. v., lancear; (surgery) abrir; **—r,** s., lancero m.

land, lᴀnd, v., desembarcar. s., tierra f.; (home) país m.; **—-agent,** corredor de fincas m.; **—ing,** desembarco m.; (quay) desembarcadero m.; **—lady,** patrona f.; **—lord,** propietario m.; **—mark,** mojón m.; **—scape,** paisaje m.; **—slide,** derrumbamiento m.

lane, lein, s., (country) callejuela f.   [lenguaje m.

language, lᴀng'-güich, s., lengua f., idioma m.;

languid*, lan*g*'-güid, a., lánguido
languish, lan*g*'-güish, v., languidecer, descaecer
lank, langk, a., flaco; **—y,** alto y delgado
lantern, lan'-tern, s., linterna f.
lap, lap, s., regazo m. v., lamer
lapel, la-pel', s., solapa f.
lapse, laps, v., pasar. s., curso m.; error m.
larceny, laar'-si-ni, s., hurto m.
lard, laard, s., manteca de cerdo f.
larder, laar'-da, s., despensa f.
large*, laar*ch*, a., grande; fuerte; considerable
lark, laark, s., alondra f.
lash, lash, s., (whip) látigo m.; (stroke) latigazo m.
v., (whip) azotar; (bind) amarrar
lass, las, s., mozuela f., muchacha f.
lassitude, las-i-tiuud, s., cansancio m.
last, laast, v., durar. s., (shoe) horma f. a.,* último; **—ing***, durable; permanente
latch, lach, s., picaporte m. v., cerrar
latch-key, latch'-kii, s., llavín m.
late, leit, adv., tarde. a., tardío; reciente; difunto
lately, leit'-li, adv., recientemente, poco ha
latent, lei'-tent, a., latente; oculto
lathe, leiD, s., torno m.
lather, laD'-a, s., jabonadura f. v., enjabonar
latitude, lat'-i-tiuud, s., latitud f.
latter, lat'-ta, a., último. adv., recientemente
lattice, lat'-is, s., celosía f.
laudable, loa'-da-bl, a., loable
laugh, laaf, v., reír. s., risa f.; **—able,** a., risible;
—ing-stock, s., hazmerreír m.; **—ter,** risa f.,
hilaridad f.
launch, loanch, s., (boat) lancha f. v., botar al
agua; (enter upon) lanzar
laundry, loan'-dri, s., lavadero m.
laurel, loa'-rl, s., (tree) laurel m.; honor m.
lavatory, lav'-a-to-ri, s., lavatorio m.; excusado m.
lavender, lav'-en-da, s., espliego m.
lavish, lav'-ish, a.,* pródigo. v., prodigar
law, loa, s., ley f.; **—ful***, a., legal; legítimo;
lícito; **—less,** ilegal; **—suit,** s., pleito m.,
proceso m.; **—yer,** abogado m., jurista m.

lawn, lo*an*, s., césped m.

lax*, laks, a., laxo, flojo [m.

laxative, lak'-*sa*-tiv, s. & a., laxativo m., purgante

lay, lei, v., poner; (place) colocar. a., lego; **—man,** s., lego m.

layer, lei'-*a*, s., (strata) capa f., estrato m.

layout, lei'-*ant*, s., trazado m.; disposición f.

laziness, lei'-si-nes, s., pereza f.

lazy, lei'-si, a., perezoso, holgazán

lead, led, s., plomo m.; (sounding) sondalesa f. v., emplomar

lead, liid, v., conducir; guiar. s., (cards) salida f.; **—er,** conductor m., jefe m.; **—ership,** dirección f.; **—ing,** a., principal; primero; **—ing article,** s., artículo de fondo m.

leaf, liif, s., hoja f.; **—y,** a., frondoso

leaflet, liif'-let, s., folleto m.

league, liig, s., liga f.; (measure) legua f.

leak, liik, v., gotear, hacer agua. s., gotera f.

lean, liin, a., delgado. s., (meat) magro m.; **—against,** v., apoyarse; **—out,** asomarse

leap, liip, v., saltar s., salto m.

leap-year, liip'-yir, s., año bisiesto m.

learn, lẽrn, v., aprender; (news) saber

learned, lẽrn'-id, a., docto, erudito

learner. lẽrn'-*a*, s., estudiante m.; aprendiz m.

learning, lẽrn'-ing, s., estudio m., (knowledge) saber m.

lease, liis, v., arrendar. s., arriendo m.

leasehold, liis'-jould, s., arriendo m.

leash, liish, s., traílla f. v., atraillar

least, liist, adv., menos. a., mínimo; **at—,** al menos

leather, leD'-*a*, s., cuero m.; **patent —,** charol m.

leave, liiv, s., permiso m.; (farewell) despedida f. v., partir; dejar, abandonar; **—behind,** dejar atrás; **—off,** cesar; **—out,** omitir; **—to,** dejar a

lecture, lek'-*tiur*, v., dar una conferencia; sermonear. s., conferencia f., admonición f.

lecturer, lek'-tiur-*a*, s., conferenciante m.; profesor

ledge, lecH, s., (shelf) repisa f.; (mountain) borde m.

ledger, lecH'-*a*, s., libro mayor m.

leech, liich, s., sanguijuela f.

leek, liik, s., puerro m.

leer, lir, v., mirar de soslayo

left, left, a., izquierdo; **—-handed,** zurdo

leg, leg, s., pierna f.; (furniture) pie m.; (animal) pata f.; **—ging,** polaina f.

legacy, leg'-*a*-si, s., legado m.; herencia f.

legal*, lii'-gal, a., legal; **—ize,** v., legalizar

legation, li-gei'-shon, s., legación f.

legend, lecH'-end, s., leyenda f.

legible, lecH'-i-bl, a., legible

legion, lii'-cHon, s., legión f.

legislate, lecH'-is-leit, v., legislar

legislation, lecH-is-lei'-shon, s., legislación f.

legitimacy, lecH-it'-i-ma-si, s., legitimidad f.

legitimate*, lecH-it'-i-met, a., legítimo

leisure, lesh'-er, s., ocio m.; comodidad f.

leisurely, lesh'-er-li, adv., despacio

lemon, lem'-on, s., limón m.; **—ade,** limonada f.

lend, lend, v., prestar

length, leng'-gz, s., longitud f.; (time) duración f.

lengthen, leng-gzn, v., alargar, prolongar

lengthways, leng'-gzues, adv., a lo largo

lengthy, leng'-gzi, a., largo, difuso

leniency, lii'-ni-ens-i, s., indulgencia f.

lenient*, lii'-ni-ent, a., indulgente

lens, lens, s., lente f.

Lent, lent, s., cuaresma f.

lentil, len'-til, s., lenteja f.

leopard, lep'-ard, s., leopardo m.

leper, lep'-a, s., leproso m.

leprosy, lep'-ro-si, s., lepra f.

less, les, adv., menos, a., menor

lessee, les-ii, s., arrendatario m.

lessen, les'-n, v., disminuir; (pain) aliviar

lesson, les'-n, s., lección f.

let, let, v., dejar; permitir; (lease) arrendar

letter, let'-a, s., carta f.; (alphabet) letra f.; **—-box,** buzón m.; **— of credit,** carta de crédito f.

lettuce, let'-is, s., lechuga f.

level, lev'-l, s., nivel m. v., nivelar. a., llano, igual; **— crossing,** s., paso a nivel m.

lever, lii′-*va*, s., palanca f.; (watch) escape m.
levity, lev′-i-ti, s., levedad f., ligereza f.
levy, lev′-i, v., (taxes) recaudar. s., impuesto m.
lewd, liuud, a., lascivo; —**ness,** s., lascivia f.
liabilities, lai-*a*-bil′-i-tes, s. pl., el pasivo m.
liability, lai-*a*-bil′-i-ti, s., obligación f., responsabilidad f.
liable, lai′-*a*-bl, a., expuesto; responsable
liar, lai′-*a*, s., mentiroso m., embustero m.
libel, lai′-bl, s., libelo m. v., difamar
libellous, lai′-bel-os, a., difamatorio
liberal, lib′-er-*a*l, s. & a.,* liberal m.
liberate, lib′-er-eit, v., libertar
liberty, lib′-er-ti, s., libertad f.
librarian, lai-bré-ri-*a*n, s., bibliotecario m.
library, lai′-bre-ri, s., biblioteca f., librería f.
license, lai′-sens, s., licencia f. v., licenciar
licentious*, lai-sen′-shos, a., licencioso, libertino
lichen, lai′-ken, s., liquen m.
lick, lik, v., lamer
lid, lid, s., tapa f.; (eye) párpado m.
lie, lai, s., (untruth) mentira f. v., mentir; (in a place) estar; (situate) estar situado; —**about,** (disorder) estar esparcido; —**down,** (repose) acostarse
lieutenant, lef-ten′-ant, s., teniente m.
life, laif, s., vida f.; (vivacity) viveza f.; —**belt,** salvavidas m.; —**boat,** lancha salvavidas f.; —**guard,** (mil.) guardia de corps m.; —**insurance,** seguro de vida m.; —**less,** a., inanimado; muerto; —**like,** natural; —**long,** de toda la vida; —**size,** de tamaño natural; —**time,** s., curso de la vida m.
lift, lift, s., ascensor m. v., levantar
light, lait, s., luz f.; claridad f. a.,* ligero; claro. v., encender; (illuminate) alumbrar; —**en,** aligerar; —**er,** s., encendedor m.; (boat) gabarra f.; —**house,** faro m.; —**ing,** alumbrado m.; —**ness,** s., ligereza f.
lightning, lait′-ning, s., relámpago m.; —**conductor,** pararrayos m.
like, laik, v., gustar. a., (similar) semejante,

parecido; (equal) igual

likelihood, laik'-li-jud, s., probabilidad f.

likely, laik'-li, adv., probablemente. a., probable

likeness, laik'-nes, s., semejanza f.; parecido m.

likewise, laik'-uais, adv., también; asimismo

liking, lai'-king, s., gusto m.; inclinación f.

lilac, lai'-lak, s., lila f.

lily, lil'-i, s., lirio m.; — **of the valley,** lirio del
campo m.

limb, lim, s., (body) miembro m.

lime, laim, s., cal f.; (bird-lime) liga f.; (fruit)
lima f.; (tree) tilo m.

lime-juice, laim'-chuus, s., zumo de lima m.

limekiln, laim'-kiln, s., calera f.

lime-light, laim'-lait, s., luz de calcio f.

limit, lim'-it, s., límite m.; término m. v., limitar;
determinar; **Ltd. Co.,** sociedad anónima f.

limp, limp, v., cojear. a., flojo

limpet, lim'-pet, s., lapa f.

line, lain, s., línea f.; (business) ramo m.; (goods) renglón m.; (rope) cuerda f.; (fishing) sedal m.,
cuerda f.; (railway) riel m. v., (garment) forrar

lineage, lain'-i-ech, s., linaje m., genealogía f.

linen, lin'-en, s., hilo m.; (laundry) ropa blanca f.

liner, lain'-a, s., paquebote m., vapor de línea m.

linger, ling'-guer, v., tardar; languidecer

linguist, ling'-uist, s., lingüista m. & f.

lining, lain'-ing, s., (of clothes) forro m.

link, lingk, v., eslabonar; unir. s., eslabón m.;
(cuff links) gemelos m. pl.

linnet, lin'-net, s., jilguero m.

linseed, lin'-siid, s., linaza f.

lint, lint, s., hilaza f., hilas f. pl.

lion, lai'-on, s., león m.; — **ess,** leona f.

lip, lip, s., labio m.; — **stick,** barra de labios f.

liquefy, lik'-ui-fai, v., derretir, liquidar

liqueur, li-ker', s., licor f.

liquid, lik'-uid, s., líquido m. a., líquido

liquidate, lik'-ui-deit, v., liquidar; (debts) saldar

liquidation, lik'-ui-dei'-shon, s., liquidación f.

liquor, lik'-er, s., (alcoholic) licor m.; (cookery)
jugo m.

lisp, lisp, v., cecear. s., ceceo m.

list, list, s., lista f.; (naut.) bandeo m. v., catalogar, alistar, registrar, (naut.) escorar

listen, lis'-n, v., escuchar; **—er,** s., escuchador m.

literal*, lit'-er-al, a., literal

literary, lit'-er-a-ri, a., literario

literature, lit'-er-a-tiur, s., literatura f. [fiar

lithograph, liz'-o-graf, s., litografía f. v., litogra-

litigate, lit'-i-gueit, v., litigar

litter, lit'-a, s., (stretcher) camilla f.; (untidi-ness) desorden m.; (bedding) cama de paja f.; (young) lechigada f. v., esparcir

little, lit'-l, a., (quantity, time) poco; (size) pe-queño. adv., poco

live, liv, v., vivir; habitar [fiar

live*, laiv, a., vivo; **—ly,** animado

liver, liv'-a, s., hígado m.

livery, liv'-er-i, s., librea f.

livid, liv'-id, a., lívido

living, liv'-ing, s., vida f.; (eccl.) beneficio m. a., vivo

lizard, liz'-erd, s., lagarto m.

load, loud, v., cargar. s., carga f.

loaf, louf, s., (bread) pan m.; **—-sugar,** azúcar de pilón m.

loafer, lou'-fa, s., (idler) haragán m.

loam, loum, s., marga f.; **—y,** a., margoso

loan, loun, s., (personal) préstamo m.; (public) em-préstito m. v., prestar

loathe, louD, v., aborrecer, detestar

loathing, louD'-ing, s., repugnancia f.

loathsome, louD'-som, a., odioso, repugnante

lobby, lob'-i, s., vestíbulo m.

lobe, loub, s., lóbulo m.

lobster, lob'-sta, s., langosta f.

local*, lou'-kl, a., local; **—ity,** s., localidad f.

locate, lou'-keit, v., situar; (find) encontrar

location, lou-kei'-shon, s., sitio m.; emplaza-miento m.

lock, lok, s., cerradura f.; (hair) rizo m.; (canal) es-clusa f. v., cerrar; **—et,** s., medallón m.; **— in** (or **up**), v., encerrar; **—jaw,** s., teta-no m.; **— out,** v., dejar fuera; **—smith,** s., cerrajero m.

locomotive, lou'-ko-mou-tiv, s., locomotora f.

locust, lou'-kust, s., langosta f.

lodge, loch, s., (masonic) logia f. v., hospedarse

lodger, loch'-a, s., huésped m.

lodging, loch'-ing, s., alojamiento m.

loft, loft, s., desván m.; —**y,** a., elevado; sublime

log, log, s., tronco m.; —**book,** diario de navegación m.

logic, loch'-ik, s., lógica f.; —**al*,** a., lógico

loin, loin, s., lomo m.

loiter, loi'-ta, v., haraganear; —**er,** s., haragán m.

loll, lol, v., recostarse; (tongue) sacar la lengua

lone(ly), loun(ly), a., & adv., solo, solitario

loneliness, loun'-li-ness, s., soledad f.

long, long, a., largo; (time) mucho; — **for,** v., suspirar por; —**ing,** s., ansia f., anhelo m.; — **to,** v., ansiar

longitude, lon'-chi-tiuud, s., longitud f.

look, luk, s., mirada f. v., mirar; (seem) aparecer; — **after,** (take care of) cuidar de; — **at,** mirar; — **for,** buscar; —**er on,** s., espectador m.; —**ing-glass,** espejo m.; — **out,** vigía f. v., asomarse, interj., ¡cuidado! **good —ing,** a., bien parecido

loom, lum, s., telar m. v., aparecer a lo lejos

loop, luup, s., lazo m.; —**hole,** tronera f.; — **the loop,** v., describir círculos

loose, luus, a., flojo; (morals) disoluto; —**n,** v., aflojar; (to free) soltar; —**ning,** s., aflojamiento

loot, luut, s., pillaje m. v., saquear [m.

lop, lop, v., (prune) podar; — **off,** tajar; —**sided*,** a., asimétrico, desequilibrado

loquacious,* lo-kuei'-shos, a., locuaz, hablador

Lord, loard, s., (Deity) el Señor m., Dios m.

lord, loard, s., lord m.; señor m.

lorry, lor'-i, s., camión m.

lose, luus, v., perder; (clock) atrasar

loser, luu'-sa, s., perdedor m.

loss, los, s., pérdida f.; (damage) daño m.

Lost Property Office, lost prop'-er-ti of'-is, s., oficina de objetos perdidos f.

lot, lot, s., (auction) lote m.; (fate) suerte f.; (many) cantidad f.

lotion, lou'-shon, s., loción f.

lotion, lou'-shon, s., loción f.

lottery, lot'-er-i, s., lotería f. [m.

loud*, laud, a., alto; **—-speaker,** s., (radio) altavoz

lounge, launch, v., haraganear. s., (room) salón m.

louse, laus, s., piojo m.

lout, laut, s., patán m.; rústico m.

love, lov, v., amar; querer; (like) gustar, s., amor m.;
   —liness, hermosura f.; **—-ly,** a., hermoso;
   (charming) encantador; **—-r,** s., (illicit) amante m.

low, lou, v., mugir. a.,* bajo; vil; **—-er,** v., bajar;
   humillar; (flag) arriar; (price) rebajar; **—-land,**
   s., tierra baja f.

loyal*, loi'-al, a., leal, fiel; **—-ty,** s., lealtad f.

lozenge, los'-ench, s., pastilla f.; (geometry) rombo

   lubricate, liuu'-bri-keit, v., lubricar [m.

lubrication, liuu-bri-kei'-shon, s., lubricación f.

lucid*, liuu'-sid, a., lúcido, claro

luck, lok, s., suerte f., fortuna f.

lucky, lok'-i, a., afortunado, dichoso, venturoso;
   (charm) para buena suerte

lucrative*, liuu-kra-tiv, a., lucrativo, provechoso

ludicrous, liuu'-di-kros, a., risible, ridículo

luggage, log'-ech s., equipaje m.; **—- office,**
   oficina de equipajes f.; **— rack,** s., portaequipajes m.

lukewarm, liuuk'-uo*arm*, a., tibio

lull, lol, v., adormecer; (baby) arrullar. s., calma f.

lullaby, lol'-a-bai, s., canción de cuna f.

lumbago, lom-bei'-gou, s., lumbago m.

lumber, lom'-ba, s., trastos m.; pl.; (timber) madera
   de construcción f.

luminous*, liuu'-mi-nos, a., luminoso

lump, lomp, s., pedazo m.; **—-y,** a., aterronado, gru-
   moso

lunacy, luu'-na-si, s., locura f.

lunar, luu'-nar, a., lunar

lunatic, luu'-na-tik, s., lunático m., loco m.; **—-
   asylum,** manicomio m.

lunch(eon), lonch'(-n), s., almuerzo m. v., almorzar

lung, long-g, s., pulmón m.

lurch, lĕrCH, s., sacidida f.; (ship) bandazo m.;
     to leave in the —, v., dejar en el atolladero
lure, liu*r*, v. atraer; inducir. s. señuelo m.
lurid, liu'-rid a. (colour) cárdeno
lurk, lĕrk, v., espiar, acechar; (hide) esconderse
luscious, lŏ'-shos, a., suculento
lust, lŏst, s., lujuria f.; (greed) codicia f. v., codiciar;
     —ful, a., lujurioso, sensual
lustre, lŏs'-tr, s., brillo m.; (pendant) lustro m.
lute, liuut, s., laúd m.
luxurious*, lŏk-siu'-ri-os, a., lujoso; exuberante
luxury, lŏk'-sher-i, s., lujo m.; suntuosidad f.
lymph, limf, s., linfa f.
lynch, linch, v., linchar

macaroni, mak-*a*-rou'-ni, s., macarrones m. pl.
macaroon, mak-*a*-ruun', s., almendrado m.
mace, meis, s., maza f.
machine, ma-shiin', s., máquina f.
machine-gun, ma-shiin'-gŏn, s., ametralladora f.
machinery, ma-shiin'-er-i, s., maquinaria f.
machinist, ma-shiin'-ist, s., maquinista m.
mackerel, mak'-er-el, s., escombro m.
mackintosh, mak'-in-tosh, s., impermeable m.
mad, mAd, a., loco; (dogs) rabioso; **—man,** s.,
     loco m.; **—ness,** s., locura f.
madam, mAd'-m, s., señora f.; (unmarried) señorita f.
magazine, mA-ga-siin', s., (periodical) revista f.;
     (powder) polvorín m.; (gun) cámara f.
maggot, mAg'-ot, s., evesa f.
magic, mACH'-ik, s., magia f. a., mágico
magistrate, mACH'-is-treit, s., magistrado m.   [f.
magnanimity, mAg-nan-im'-i-ti, s., magnanimidad
magnanimous*, mAg-nan'-i-mos, a., magnánimo
magnesia, mAg-nii'-sha. s., magnesia f.
magnesium, mAg-nii'-shi-om, s., magnesio m.
magnet, mAg'-net, s., imán m.; **—ic,** a., magnético;
     —ism, s., magnetismo m.; **—ize,** v., magnetizar
magneto, mAg-nii'-tou, s., magneto m.
magnificent*, mAg-nif'-i-sent, a., magnífico
magnify, mAg'-ni-fai, v., aumentar; ampliar;
     —ing-glass, s., lupa f.

magnitude, mag'-ni-tiuud, s., magnitud f.

magpie, mag'-pai, s., picaza f.

mahogany, ma-jog'-a-ni, s., caoba f.

maid, meid, s., (young girl) doncella f.; (servant) sirvienta f.; **—en,** doncella f.; vírgen f.; **old —,** solterona f.

mail, meil, s., (post) correo m.; (armour) cota de malla f.; (mail-bag) valija f.; (mail-boat) vapor correo m. v., enviar por correo

maim, meim, v., mutilar

main, mein, a., principal, mayor. s., (pipe) cañería maestra f.; **—land,** continente m.

maintain, mein-tein', v., mantener, er, sostener

maintenance, mein'-te-nans, s., mantenimiento m.

maize, meis, s., maíz m.

majestic, ma-ches'-ti, a., majestuoso　　　　[f.

majesty, mach'-es-ti, s., (His or Her) Su Majestad

major, meich'-or, s., mayor m.; (mil.) comandante m. a., mayor

majority, mach-o'-ri-ti, s., mayoría f.

make, meik, v., hacer; causar; (manufacture) fabricar. s., hechura f.; (commercial) marca f.; **—believe,** pretexto m. v., pretender; **—r,** s., fabricante m.; constructor m.; **—shift,** expediente m.; **— up,** (face) maquillaje m. v., maquillarse

malady, mal'-a-di, s., enfermedad f.

malaria, mal-ei'-ri-a, s., paludismo m.

male, meil, s., varón m.; (animal) macho m.

malevolent*, mal-ev'-o-lent, a., malévolo

malice, mal'-is, s., malicia f.

malicious*, ma-lish'-os, a., malicioso

malign, ma-lain', v., difamar. a.,* maligno

malignant*, ma-lig'-nant, a., maligno; nocivo

malinger, ma-ling'-a, v., fingirse enfermo

mallet, mal'-et, s., mazo m., mallo m.

mallow, mal'-ou, s., malva f.

malnutrition, mal'-niuu-trish-an, s., desnutrición f.

malt, moalt, s., malta f.　　　　[f.

maltreat, mal-triit', v., maltratar

mammal, mam'-mal, s., mamífero m.

man, man, v., (a ship) tripular. s., hombre m.;

—**hood,** virilidad f.; —**kind,** género humano m.; —**ly,** a., viril; —**servant,** s., criado m.

manacle, MAN'-*a*-kl, s., manilla f. v., maniatar

manage, MAN'-ICH, v., (business) administrar, dirigir; (accomplish) lograr, suceder; (control) manejar, gobernar; —**ment,** s., administración f., dirección f.

manager, MAN'-ICH-*a*, s., gerente m., director m.

mandate, MAN'-deit, s., mandato m., orden f.

mandoline, MAN'-dou-lin, s., mandolina f.

mane, mein, s., (of a horse, lion) crin m.

manger, mein'-CHa, s., pesebre m.

mangle, MANG'-gl, s., calandria f. v., pasar por la calandria

mania, mei'-ni-*a*, s., manía f.

maniac, mei'-ni-ak, s., maniático m.

manicure, MAN'-i-kiur, s., manicura f. v., curar las uñas

manifest, MAN'-i-fest, s. & a.,* manifiesto m. v., manifestar

manifold, MAN'-i-fould, a., múltiple, diverso

manipulate, MAN-ip'-iuu-leit, v., manipular

manner, MAN'-*a*, s., manera f., forma f.; modo m.; costumbre f.; género m.; —**s,** pl., modales m. pl.

manœuvre, m*a*-nuu'-ver, s., maniobra f. v., maniobrar

manor, MAN'-*or*, s., casa solariega f.

mansion, MAN'-shon, s., mansión f. [m.

manslaughter, MAN'-sloa-ta, homicidio m.

mantel-piece, MAN'-tl-piis, s., manto de chimenea

mantle, MAN'-tl, s., manto m.; (gas) manguito incandescente m.

manual, MAN'-iu-al, s., manual m. a.,* manual

manufacture, MAN-iu-fak'-tiur, s., manufactura f.; fabricación f. fabricar; —**r,** s., fabricante m.

manure, m*a*-niúr, s., abono m., estiércol m. v., abonar, engrasar

manuscript, MAN'-iu-skript, s., manuscrito m.

many, men'-i, a., muchos

map, MAP, s., mapa m.; (town) plan m.

maple, mei'-pl, s., arce m.

mar, maar, v., estropear; dañar; desfigurar

marble, maar′-bl, s., mármol m.; —**s,** (game) bolas
march, maarch, v., marchar. s., marcha f.   [f. pl.
March, maarch, s., marzo m.
mare, meir, s., yegua f.
margarine, maar′-ga-rin, s., margarina f.
margin, maar′-chin, s., margen m. & f. v., marginar;
  —**al note,** s., nota marginal f.
marigold, mar′-i-gould, s., maravilla f.
marine, ma-riin′, s., soldado de marina m. a., marino
mariner, maar′-in-a, s., marino m., marinero m.
maritime, ma′-ri-tim, a., marítimo
mark, maark, v., marcar. s., marca f.; **book-—,**
  señal f.; **trade-—,** marca de fábrica f.; —**ing-
  ink,** tinta de marcar f.
market, maar′-ket, s., mercado m.
marmalade, maar′-ma-leid, s., mermelada de
marmot, maar′-mot, s., marmota f. [naranjas f.
maroon, ma-ruun′, a., marrón m., abandonar, aislar
marquee, maar-kii′, s., marquesina f.
marriage, maar′-ich, s., matrimonio m.; boda f.
married, mar′-id, a., (life) conyugal; — **couple,**
  s., matrimonio m.
marrow, mar′-ou, s., médula f.; tuétano m.;
  (vegetable) calabaza f.
marry, mar′-i, v., casarse; (ceremony) casar
marsh, maarsh, s., pantano m.
marshal, maar′-shal, s., mariscal m.
mart, maart, s., mercado m.
marten, maar′-ten, s., marta f.
martial,* maar′-shal, a., marcial, militar; **court-
  —,** s., consejo de guerra m.; —**law,** ley marcial f.
martyr, maar′-ta, v., martirizar. s., mártir m. & f.;
  —**dom,** martirio m.
marvel, maar′-vl, s., maravilla f. v., maravillarse;
  —**lous,** a., maravilloso
masculine, mas′-kiu-lin, a., masculino
mash, mash, v., machacar. s., (vegetable) masa f.
mask, mask, s., máscara f. v., enmascarar
mason, mei′-s′n, s., albañil f.; (stone worker) can-
  tero m.; (freemason) francmasón m.
masonic, mei-son′-ik, a., masónico
masonry, mei′-son-ri, s., albañilería f.

masquerade, MAS-ker-eid', v., disfrazarse
mass, MAS, s., masa f.; (eccl.) misa f. v., amontonar
massacre, MAS'-a-ker, s., matanza f., carnicería f.
massage, ma-saaCH', s., masaje m. v., dar masaje
massive*, MAS'-iv, a., macizo
mast, maast, s., mástil m., palo m.
master, maas'-ta, v., domar; vencer. s., amo m.;
    (teacher) maestro m., profesor m.; **—ful,** a.,
    dominante; **—ly,** magistral. adv., magistral-
    mente; **—piece,** s., obra maestra f.
masticate, MAS'-ti-keit, v., masticar
mastiff, MAS'-tif, s., mastín m.
mat, MAT, s., estera f.
match, MACH, s., (safety) fósforo m.; (wax) cerilla f.;
    (game) partido m.; (boxing) pugilato m. v., igualar
matchless, MACH'-les, a., incomparable
mate, meit, v., aparear. s., compañero m.
material, ma-tii'-ri-al, s., material m.; (cloth)
    paño m., tela f.; **—ist,** s., materialista
materialize, ma-tii'-ri-a-lais, v., materializar
maternal*, ma-têr'-nal, a., materno
mathematics, maz-i-MAT'-iks, s., matemáticas f. pl.
matrimony, MAT'-ri-mo-ni, s., matrimonio m.
matrix, mei'-trix, s., matriz f.; (mould) molde m.
matron, mei'-tron, s., matrona f.
matter, MAT'-a, s., materia f., substancia f.; (pus)
    pus m.; (affair) asunto m.; (business) negocio m.
    v., importar
matting, MAT'-ing, s., estera f.
mattress, MAT'-res, s., colchón m.
mature, ma-tiúr', v., madurar; (bill) vencer. a.,
    maduro
maturity, ma-tiúr'-i-ti, s., madurez f.; vencimiento
maul, moal, v., aporrear; (claw) magullar   [m.
mauve, mouv, s., color de malva m.
maxim, MAK'-sim, s., máxima f.
maximum, MAK'-si-mom, s., máximum m.
may, mei, v., poder; **—be,** adv., acaso, quizás
May, mei, s., mayo m.; **—flower,** s., maya f.
mayor, mei'-or, s., alcalde m.; **—ess,** corregidora f.
maze, meis, s., laberinto m.; confusión f.
me, mii, pron., me; mí; (to me) a mí

meadow, med'-ou, s., prado m.; pradera f.

meagre, mii'-ga, a., magro; (scanty) insuficiente

meal, miil, s., harina f.; (repast) comida f.

mean, miin, a.,* avaro; (action) bajo. v., querer decir; —**ing,** s., significación f.; (sense) sentido m.; —**ingless,** a., insensato

means, miins, s. pl., medios m. pl.; recursos m. pl.

meanwhile, miin'-uail, adv., entretanto

measles, mii'-sls, s. pl., sarampión m.

measure, mesh'-a, s., medida f.; (tape) metro m. v., medir; —**d,** a., medido; —**ment,** s., medida f.

meat, miit, s., carne f., vianda f.

mechanic, mi-kan'-ik, s., mecánico m.; —**al,** a., mecánico; —**s,** s. pl., mecánica f.

mechanism, mek'-an-ism, s., mecanismo m.

mechanization, mek-an-ais-ei'-shon, s., mecanización f.

medal, med'-l, s., medalla f.

meddle, med'-l, v., meterse, entremeterse

meddlesome, med'-l-som, a., entremetido, intruso

mediaeval, med-i-i'-vl, a., medioeval

mediate, mii'-di-eit, v., mediar, intervenir

medical, med'-i-kl, a., médico

medicine, med'-sin, s., medicina f.

mediocre, mii'-di-ou'-kr, a., mediocre; vulgar

meditate, med'-i-teit, v., meditar; reflexionar

medium, mii'-di-om, s., medio m.; vía f. a., mediano

meek*, miik, a., manso, humilde

meet*, miit, v., encontrar; (obligations) honrar; —**ing,** s., encuentro m., reunión f.; (Board) junta

melancholy, mel'-an-kol-i, s., melancolía f.   [f.

mellow, mel'-ou, a., maduro; (tone) meloso

melodious*, mi-lou'-di-os, a., melodioso

melody, mel'-o-di, s., melodía f.

melon, mel'-on, s., melón m.

melt, melt, v., derretir, fundir; —**ing,** s., fusión f.

member, mem'-ba, s., miembro m.; (club) socio m.; (parliament) diputado m.; —**ship,** calidad de socio f.

membrane, mem'-brein, s., membrana f.   [m.

memento, mi-men'-tou, s., recuerdo m.; memento

memoir, mem'-uaar, s., memoria f., relación f.

memorandum, mem-or-*an'*-dom, s., memorandum m.; **—-book,** libro de memorias m.

memorial, mi-*mou'*-ri-al, s., monumento conmemorativo m.

memory, mem'-*o*-ri, s., memoria f.

menace, men'-*as*, v., amenazar. s., amenaza f.

menagerie, mi-NACH'-er-i, s., colección de fieras f.

mend, mend, v., reparar; corregirse

mendacious*, men-dei'-shos, a., mendaz; mentiroso [so

menial, mii'-ni-al, s., criado m. a., servil

mental*, men'-tl, a., mental

mention, men'-shon, v., mencionar. s., mención f.

menu, men'-iuu, s., menú m., lista de platos f.

mercantile, mer'-kan-tail, a., mercantil; comercial

merchandise, mer'-chan-dais, s., mercadería f., mercancía f.

merchant, mer'-chant, s., comerciante m., mercader m. a., comercial; (fleet) mercante

merciful*, mer'-si-ful, a., misericordioso, clemente

mercury, mer'-kiu-ri, s., mercurio m.

mercy, mer'-si, s., misericordia f.; gracia f.

mere, mir, a., puro, mero s., lago m.

merge, merch, v., fundir; absorber; **—er,** s., unión f.; consolidación f.

meridian, mi-ri'-di-an, s., meridiano m. a., de mediodía

merit, mer'-it, s., mérito m. v., merecer

meritorious*, mer-i-tó'-ri-os, a., meritorio

mermaid, mer'-meid, s., sirena f.

merriment, mer'-i-ment, s., alegría f.; júbilo m.

merry*, mer'-i, a., alegre; **—-go-round,** s., caballitos m. pl.; tiovivo m.

mesh, mesh, s., malla f.

mesmerize, mes'-mer-ais, v., hipnotizar

mess, mes, s., (mil.) rancho de los oficiales m.; (dirt) porquería f.; lío m. v., manchar

message, mes'-ich, s., mensaje m., recado m.

messenger, mes'-en-cha, s., mensajero m.

metal, met'-l, s., metal m.; **—lic,** a., metálico

meteor, mii'-ti-or, s., meteoro m.

meter, mii'-ta, s., (gas. etc.) contador m.

method, mez'-od, s., método m.

methylated spirit, mez'-i-lei-tid spi'-rit, s., alcohol metílico m.

metre, mii'-ta, s., (measure, rhythm) metro m.

metropolis, mi-trop'-o-lis, s., metrópoli f.

mica, mai'-ka, s., mica f.

Michaelmas, mik'-el-mas, s., la San Miguel f.

microphone, mai'-kro-foun, s., micrófono m.

microscope, mai'-kros-koup, s., microscopio m.

middle, mid'-l, s., medio m.; centro m.; **—age,** edad media f.; **—class,** (people) clase media f.; **—man,** intermediario m.

middling, mid'-ling, a., mediano

midge, mich, s., mosquito m.

midget, mich'-et, s., enano m.

midnight, mid'-nait, s., media noche f.

midshipman, mid'-ship-man, s., guardia marina m.

midst, midst, prep., entre, en medio de

midwife, mid'-uaif, s., partera f.

mein, miin, s., semblante m.; facha f.

might, mait, s., fuerza f., poder m.

mighty, mait'-i, a., poderoso; fuerte

mignonette, min-yon-et', s., reseda f.

migrate, mai-greit', v., emigrar

mild*, maild, a., suave; benigno, templado

mildew, mil'-diuu, s., moho m.; (plants) tizón m.

mile, mail, s., milla f.; **—stone,** piedra miliaria f.

military, mil'-i-ta-ri, a., militar

milk, milk, s., leche f. v., ordeñar; **—y,** a., lácteo

milky-way, mil'-ki-uei, s., vía láctea f.

mill, mil, v., moler. s., molino m.; **—er,** molinero m.

milliner, mil'-i-na, s., modista f.

millinery, mil'-i-ner-i, s., modas f. pl. [m.

million, mil'-yon, s., millón m.; **—aire,** millonario

mimic, mim'-ik, v., remedar. s., mimo m. a., mímico

mince, mins, v., (meat, etc.) picar; (words) medir

mind, maind, s., mente f.; opinión f.; intención f.; v., atender a; (nurse) cuidar; **—ful,** a., atento

mine, main, poss. pron., mío, mía; míos, mías

mine, main, s., mina f. v., minar; **—r,** s., minero m.

mineral, min'-er-al, s. & a., mineral m.

mingle, ming'-gl, v., mezclar; **— with,** mezclarse con

minimize, min'-i-m**ais,** v., reducir, disminuir

minister, min'-is-t**a,** s., clérigo m.; (government) ministro m. v., administrar; servir; proveer

ministry, min'-is-tri, s., ministerio m., gabinete m.

mink, mink, s., visón m.

minor, mai'-n**a,** s., menor de edad m. a., menor

minority, mi-nor'-i-ti, s., minoría f.

minster, min'-st**a,** s., catedral f.; monasterio m.

minstrel, min'-strel, s., trovador m.

mint, mint, s., casa de la moneda f.; (plant) menta f. v., acuñar

minuet, min-iu-et', s., minueto m., minué m.

minus, mai'-n**os,** a. & adv., menos. prep., sin

minute, min'-it, s., minuto m.; (records) minuta f.

minute, mai-ni**uut',** a., menudo; minucioso

miracle, mi'-r**a**-kl, s., milagro m.

miraculous, mi-rak'-iu-los, a., milagroso

mirage, mi-raa**sh',** s., espejismo m.

mire, mair, s., fango m., lodo m., cieno m.

mirror, mir'-**or,** s., espejo m. v., reflejar

mirth, mĕrz, s., alegría f., regocijo m.

mis, mis, ——**adventure,** s., desventura f.; ——**apprehension,** equivocación f.; error m.; ——**appropriate,** v., malversar; ——**behave,** portarse mal; ——**believer,** s., incrédulo m.; ——**carriage,** aborto m.; ——**carry,** v., abortar; ——**conduct,** s., mala conducta f.; ——**construction,** mala interpretación f.; error m.; ——**count,** v., contar mal; ——**deed,** s., fechoría f.; (law) delito m.; ——**demeanour,** mala conducta f.; (law) delito m.; ——**direct,** v., dirigir erradamente; ——**fit,** s., lo que no ajusta bien; ——**fortune,** desdicha f.; calamidad f.; ——**giving,** recelo m.; ——**govern,** v., gobernar mal; ——**guide,** descaminar; ——**hap,** s., accidente m.; contratiempo m.; ——**inform,** v., informar mal; ——**judge,** juzgar mal; ——**lay,** extraviar, perder; ——**lead,** descarriar; (fraud) engañar; ——**manage,** administrar mal; ——**place,** extraviar; colocar mal; ——**print,** s., errata f.; ——**pronounce,** v., pronunciar mal; ——**represent,** desfigurar; pervertir; ——**statement,** s., relación inexacta f.; ——**take,** v., equivocarse.

s., equivocación f.; **—taken**, a., erróneo; **—trust**, v., desconfiar. s., desconfianza f.; **—understand**, v., entender mal; **—understanding**, s., equivocación f., mala inteligencia f.; **—use**, v., abusar de

miscellaneous*, mis-*el*'-*ei*'-ni-os, a., misceláneo

mischief, mis'-chif, s., daño m., perjuicio m.

mischievous*, mis'-chi-vos, a., malicioso; perjudicial [m.

miscreant, mis'-krii-*ant*, s., malandrín m.; bellaco

miser, mai'-*sa*, s., avaro m.; **—ly**, a., avaricioso

miserable, mis'-*er*-a-bl, a., miserable; (sad) angustiado

misery, miis'-ri, s., miseria f.; dolor m.

Miss, mis, s., señorita f.

miss, mis, v., perder; (someone's absence) echar de menos; **—ing**, a., extraviado, perdido

missile, mis'-il, s., proyectil m.

mission, mish'-on, s., misión f.

missionary, mish'-on-*a*-ri, a., (eccl.) misionero m.

mist, mist, s., bruma f.; neblina f.

Mister (Mr.), mis'-*ta*, s., señor m.

mistletoe, mis'-s'l-tou, s., muérdago m.

mistress, mis'-tres, s., (house) ama f.; dueña f.; (school) maestra f.; (kept) querida f.; (Mrs.) señora f.

misty, mis'-ti, a., brumoso

mitigate, mit'-i-gu*eit*, v., mitigar, suavizar

mitre, mai'-*ta*, s., mitra f.; (joint) inglete m.

mix, miks, v., mezclar; (salad) aderezar; **—ed**, a., mezclado; **—er**, s., mezclador m.; **—ture**, s., mezcla f.

moan, moun, v., gemir. s., gemido m.

moat, mout, s., foso m.

mob, mob, s., chusma f.; turba f. v., asaltar en tropel; (enthusiasm) cercar por la multitud

mobile, mou'-bil, a., móvil, movible

mobilize, mo'-bi-l*ais*, v., movilizar

mock, mok, v., burlarse. a., falso; imitado; **— at**, v., burlarse de; **—ery**, s., mofa f., burla f.; **—ingly**, adv., burlonamente

mode, moud, s., manera f.; (fashion) moda f

model, mod'-l, s., modelo m. v., modelar
moderate, mod'-er-eit, v., moderar
moderate*, mod'-er-et, a., moderado; mediocre
moderation, mod-er-ei'-shon, s., moderación f.
modern, mod'-ern, a., moderno
modest*, mod'-ist, a., modesto
modify, mod'-i-fai, v., modificar [tano m.
Mohammedan, mou-jam'-me-dan, s., mahome-
moist, moist, a., húmedo; **—en,** v., humedecer
moisture, mois'-tiur, s., humedad f.
mole, moul, s., topo m.; (mark) lunar m.; **—-hill,**
topinera f.
molecule, mol'-e-kiuul, s., molécula f.
molest, mo-lest', v., molestar
mollify, mol'-i-fai, v., ablandar
molten, moul'-tn, a., fundido
moment, mou'-ment, s., momento m.
momentous,* mou-men'-tos, a., importante; grave
momentum, mou-men'-tom, s., ímpetu m., impulsión f.
monarch, mon'-ark, s., monarca m.
monarchy, mon'-ar-ki, s., monarquía f.
monastery, mon'-as-tri, a., monasterio m.
Monday, mön'-di, s., lunes m.
monetary, mön'-e-ta-ri, a., monetario
money, mön'-i, s., dinero m.; moneda f.; **—-order,**
libranza postal f.
monger, mõng'-ga, s., traficante m.
mongrel, mõng'-grel, a., mestizo
monk, mõngk, s., monje m., fraile m.
monkey, mõng'-ki, s., mono m.
monocle, mon'-o-kl, s., monóculo m.
monogram, mon'-ou-gram, s., monograma m.
monopolize, mo-nop'-o-lais, v., monopolizar
monopoly, mo-nop'-o-li, s., monopolio m.
monotonous*, mon-ot'-o-nos, a., monótono
monster, mon'-sta, s., monstruo m.
monstrous*, mon'-stros, a., monstruoso
month, mönz, s., mes m.; **—-ly,** a., mensual
monument, mon'-iu-ment, s., monumento m.
mood, muud, s., (temper) humor m.; (grammar)
modo m.; **—-y,** a., caprichoso

moon, muun, s., luna f.; **—light,** luz de la luna f.

moor, muur, s., páramo m. v., amarrar

Moor, muur, s., moro m.; **—ish,** a., morisco

moot, muut, a., discutible

mop, mop, s., estropajo m. v., limpiar

mope, moup, v., abatirse; atontarse

moral, moar**'-al,** a., (lesson) moraleja f. a.,* moral; **—ity,** s., moralidad f.; **—s,** s. pl., costumbres f.

morass, mo-ras', s., ciénaga f.; marisma f.   [pl.

moratorium, mou-ra-tou'-ri-om, s., moratoria f.

morbid*, moar**'-bid,** a., mórbido; enfermizo

more, mór, adv., más; **—over,** además

morning, moar**'-ning,** s., mañana f.; **early —,** madrugada f.; **good —,** buenos días

morocco, mo-rok'-ou, s., (leather) tafilete m.

morose, mo-rous', a., enfermizo

morphia, moar**'-fi-a,** s. morfina f.

morrow, mor'-ou, s., mañana m.

morsel, moar**'-sl,** s., bocado m.

mortal, moar**'-tl,** s. & a.,* mortal m.

mortality, mor-tal'-i-ti, s., mortalidad f.

mortar, moar**'-tr,** s., mortero m.

mortgage, moar**'-guich,** s., hipoteca f.; **—e,** acreedor hipotecario m.; **—r,** deudor hipotecario m.

mortification, moar**'-ti-fi-kei'-shon,** s., mortificación f.

mortuary, moar**'-tiu-a-ri,** s., depósito de cadáveres

mosaic, mou-sei'-ik, s. & a., mosaico m.   [m.

mosque, mosk, s., mezquita f.

mosquito, mos-kii'-tou, s., mosquito m.

moss, mos, s., musgo m.

most, moust, adv., sumamente; muy; más. s., la mayor parte f. a., lo más; **—ly,** adv., principalmente

moth, moz, s., polilla f.

mother, mŏD'-er, s., madre f.; **—hood,** maternidad f.; **—in-law,** suegra f.; **—of-pearl,** nácar m., madreperla f.; **—ly,** adv., maternal

motion, mou'-shon, s., movimiento m.

motionless, mou'-shon-les, a., inmóvil

motive, mou'-tiv, s., motivo m., móvil m. a., motriz

motor, mou'-ta, s., motor m.; **—-bus,** autobus m.; **—-car,** coche m.; automóvil m.; **—-cycle,** motocicleta f.; **—ing,** automovilismo m.; **—ist,** automovilista m. & f.

mottled, mot'-ld, a., moteado; abigarrado

motto, mot'-ou, s., divisa f.; mote m.

mould, mould, v., moldear. s., molde m.; matriz f.; (mildew) moho m.; (earth) mantillo m.; **—er,** moldeador m.; **—ing,** moldura f.; **—y,** a., mohoso

moult, moult, v., mudar el pelo; (birds) desplumar

mound, maund, s., montículo m.; (mil.) terraplén m. v., aterraplenar

mount, maunt, v., monte m.; (horse) caballería f.; (picture) marco m.; (jewels) engaste m. v., subir; (jewels) engastar, engarzar; **—ed,** a., (horseback) montado, de a caballo

mountain, maun'-tin, s., montaña f.; monte m.; **—eer,** montañés m.; **—ous,** a., montañoso; **— range,** s., sierra f.

mourn, moarn, v., lamentar, llorar; **—er,** s., miembro del duelo m.; plañidero m.; **—ful,** a., lúgubre, triste, fúnebre; **—ing,** s., lamento m.; (apparel) luto m.

mouse, maus, s., ratón m.; **—-trap,** ratonera f.

moustache, mus-taash', s., bigote m.

mouth, mauz, s., boca f.; (animal) hocico m.; (river) desembocadura f.; **—ful,** bocado m.; **—-piece,** boquilla f.; (fig.) intérprete m.

movable, muu'-va-bl, a., móvil; mueble

move, muuv, v., mover; (removal) mudarse; (propose) proponer. s., movimiento m.; (fig.) golpe m.

mow, mou, v., segar; **—er,** s., segadora f.

much, môch, adv., mucho; muy; **how—?** ¿cuánto?

mud, môd, s., barro m.; **—dy,** a., barroso; fangoso; **—guard,** s., guardabarro m.

muddle, môd'-l, s., desorden m.; confusión f.

muff, môf, s., manguito m.

muffle, môf'-l, v., embozar; (sound) amortiguar

muffler, môf'-la, s., bufanda f.

mug, môg, s., cubilete m.; (pot) pichel m.

mulatto, miu-lat'-ou, s., mulato m.; mulata f.

mulberry, mŏl'-be-ri, s., mora f; **—-tree,** morera f.

mule, miuul, s., mulo m., mula f.

mullet, mŏl'-et, s., múgil m.; **red —,** salmonete m.

multifarious*, mŏl-ti-fé'-ri-os, a., variado, diverso

multiplication, mŏl'-ti-pli-kei'-shon, s., multiplicación f.

multiply, mŏl'-ti-plai, v., multiplicar; multiplicarse

multi-purpose, mŏl'-ti pér'-pos, a., de aplicaciones varias

multitude, mŏl'-ti-tiuud, s., multitud f.

mummy, mŏm'-i, s., momia f.

mumps, mŏmps, s. pl., parótidas f. pl.

munch, mŏnch, v., mascar

municipal, miu-nis'-i-pal, a., municipal

munificent*, miu-nif'-i-sent, a., munífico; generoso

munition, miu-nish'-on, s., municiones f. pl.

murder, mêr'-da, v., asesinar. s., asesinato m.;
—er, asesino m.; **—ess,** ascsina f.; **—ous,** a.,
asesino

murky, mêr'-ki, a., obscuro, sombrío, lóbrego

murmur, mêr'-mr, v., murmurar, s., murmullo m.

muscle, mŏs'-l, s., músculo m.

muse, miuus, v., meditar. s., musa f.

museum, miu-zii'-om, s., museo m.

mushroom, mŏsh'-rum, s., seta f.

music, miuu'-sik, s., música f.; **—al,** a., musical

musician, miu-sish'-on, s., músico m.

musk, mŏsk, s., almizcle m.

musket, mŏs'-ket, s., mosquete m.; fusil m.

muslin, mŏs'-lin, s., muselina f.

mussel, mŏs'-l, s., mejillón f.

must, mŏst, v., deber, haber de, tener que, s., (wine)
mosto m.; **—y,** a., mohoso

mustard, mŏs'-tard, s., mostaza f.

muster, mŏs'-ta, v., congregar; (mil.) pasar lista

mute, miuut, s., mudo m. a.,* mudo

mutilate, miuu'-ti-leit, v., mutilar [m.

mutineer, miuu-ti-nír, s., amotinador m., rebelde

mutinous, miuu'-ti-nos, a., amotinado

mutiny, miuu'-ti-ni, s., motín m. v., amotinarse

mutter, mŏt'-a, v., murmurar

mutton, mŏt'-on, s., carne de carnero f.

mutual, miuu'-tiu-al, a., mutuo, mutual
muzzle, mŏz'-l, s., (for dogs, etc.) bozal m.; (snout) hocico m.; (gun) boca f.
my, mai, poss., mi, mis; **—self,** pron., yo mismo
myrrh, mer, s., mirra f.
myrtle, mĕr'-tl, s., mirto m.
mysterious*, mis-ti'-ri-os, a., misterioso
mystery, mis'-ter-i, s., misterio m.
mystify, mis'-ti-fai, v., confundir
myth, miz, s., mito m.; **—ology,** mitología f.

nag, nag, v., regañar. s., (horse) jaca f.
nail, neil, s., clavo m.; (human) uña f. v., clavar, enclavar; **—brush,** s., cepillo para las uñas m.; **—file,** lima para las uñas f.
naive*, ne'-iv, a., ingenuo
naked, nei'-kid, a., nudo, desnudo
name, neim, v., nombrar, llamar. s., nombre m.; **—less,** a., anónimo; **—ly,** adv., a saber, es decir; **—sake,** s., tocayo m.; **Christian —,** nombre de bautismo m.; **sur—,** apellido m.
nap, nap, s., siesta f.; (cloth) lanilla f.
nape, neip, s., nuca f.
naphtha, nap'-za, s., nafta f.
napkin, nap'-kin, s., servilleta f.
narcissus, nar-sis'-os, s., narciso m.
narcotic, nar-kot'-ik, s. & a., narcótico m.
narrate, nar-eit', v., narrar, relatar
narrative, nar'-a-tiv, s., narrativa f. relación f.
narrow*, nar'-ou, a., estrecho; **—minded,** mezquino; **—ness,** s., estrechura f.; estrechez f.
nasal*, nei'-sal, a., nasal
nasturtium, nas-tĕr'-shom, s., capuchina f.
nasty, naas'-ti, a., indecente; desagradable
nation, nei'-shon, s., nación f.
national, nash'-o-nal, a., nacional
nationality, nash-o-nal'-i-ti, s, nacionalidad f.
native, nei'-tiv, s., natural m. & f.; indígena m. & f. a., natal
natural*, nat'-iu-ral, a., natural; **—ization,** s., naturalización f.
nature, nei'-tiur, s., naturaleza f.; índole f.

naught, noat, nada. s., cero m.

naughty, noa'-ti, a., travieso, revoltoso

nausea, noa'-sia, s., náusea f.; asco m.

nautical*, noa'-ti-kl, a., náutico

naval, nei'-val, a., naval; — **engagement,** s., batalla naval f.; — **officer,** oficial de marina m.

navel, nei'-vel, s., ombligo m.

navigate, nav'-i-gueit, v., navegar

navigation, na-vi-guei'-shon, s., navegación f.

navigator, na-vi-guei'-ta, s., navegante m.

navvy, nav'-i, s., bracero m., peón m.

navy, nei'-vi, s., marina de guerra f.; armada f.

near, nir, a., cercano. prep., cerca de. adv., cerca, v., acercarse; —**ly,** adv., casí, cerca de; —**ness,** s., proximidad f.; —**side,** s., lado cercano (in Spain); lado izquierdo (en Inglaterra) —**sighted,** a., miope

neat, niit, a., (spruce) pulcro; (dainty) pulido, delicado; (tidy) aseado; (not diluted) puro; —**ness,** s., pulcritud f.; delicadeza f.; aseo m.

necessarily, nes'-es-a-ri-li, adv., necesariamente

necessary, nes'-es-a-ri, a., necesario

necessitate, ne-ses'-i-teit, v., requerir

necessity, ne-ses'-i-ti, s., necesidad f.; miseria f.

neck, nek, s., cuello m.; (bottle, etc.) gollete m.; —**lace,** collar m.; —**tie,** corbata f.

need, niid, v., necesitar. s., necesidad f.; —**ful*,** a., necesario; —**less,** innecesario, inútil

needle, nii'-dl, s., aguja f.; —**woman,** modista f.; costurera f.

needy, nii'-di, a., indigente, necesitado

negation, ni-guei'-shon, s., negación f.

negative, neg'-a-tiv, s., negativa f.; (photo) negativo m. a.,* negativo

neglect, nig-lekt', v., descuidar. s., descuido m.; —**ful*,** a., negligente, descuidado

negligence, neg'-lich-ens, s., negligencia f.

negligent, neg'-lich-ent, a., negligente, descuidado

negotiate, ni-gou'-shi-eit, v., negociar

negotiation, ni-gou-shi-ei'-shon, s., negociación f.

negress, nii'-gres, s., negra f.

negro, nii'-grou, s., negro m.

neigh, nei, v., relinchar. s., relincho m.

neighbour, nei'-ba, s., vecino m.; **—hood,** vecindad f.; vecindario m.; **—ly,** adv., sociablemente. a., sociable

neither, nai'-Da, pron. & a., ni uno ni otro; . . .**nor,** conj., ni . . .ni. adv., tampoco

nephew, nev'-iu, s., sobrino m.

nerve, nërv, s., nervio m.; (pluck, etc.) valor m., sangre fría f.

nervous*, nër'-vos, a., nervioso; tímido

nest, nest, s., nido m. v., anidar

nestle, nes'-l, v., acogerse; (birds) anidar

net, net, s., red f. a., neto; **—work,** s., red f.; cadena f.

nett, net, a., neto [f. (radio, TV)

nettle, net'-l, s., ortiga f.

neuralgia, niu-ral'-CHI-a, s., neuralgia f.

neuritis, niuu'-rai-tis, s., neuritis f.

neorotic*, niuu-rot'-ik, a., neurótico

neuter, niuu'-ta, s. & a., neutro m.

neutral*, niuu'-tral, a., neutral

never, nev'-a, adv., nunca, jamás; **— more,** nunca más; **—theless,** sin embargo

new*, niuu, a., nuevo; reciente; fresco; tierno; **— year,** s., red f., año nuevo m.

news, niuus, s., noticias f pl.; **—agent,** vendedor de periódicos m.; **—paper,** periódico m., diario m.

next, nekst, a., próximo; siguiente; (beside) contiguo, de al lado. adv., después

nib, nib, s., (pen) plumilla f., pico m.

nibble, nib'-l, v., mordiscar; (rodents) roer

nice*, nais, a., amable, simpático, agradable; (good) bueno, exquisito; (pretty) lindo, bonito

nick, nik, s., muesca f.

nickel, nik'-l, s., níquel m.

nickname, nik'-neim, s., apodo m. v., apodar

nicotine, ni'-ko-tiin, s., nicotina f.

niece, niis, s., sobrina f.

night, nait, s., noche f.; **—club,** s., cabaret m.; café cantante m.; **—dress,** s., camisón m.; **—fall,** anochecer m.; **—ingale,** ruiseñor m.; **—ly,** adv., cada noche; **—mare,** s., pesadilla f.

nimble, nim'-bl, a., ágil, ligero; veloz
nine, nain, s. & a., nueve m.; **—teen,** diez y
nueve m.; **—teenth,** décimonono m.; **—tieth,**
nonagésimo m.; **—ty,** noventa m.
ninth, nainz, s. & a., nono, noveno m.
nip, nip, v., pellizcar; **— off,** desmochar
nipple, nip'-l, s., pezón m.
nitrate, nai'-treit, s., nitrato m.
nitrogen, nai'-trou-cHen, s., nitrógeno m.
no, nou, adv., no
nobility, no-bil'-i-ti, s., nobleza f.; aristocracia f.
noble, nou'-bl, s. & a., noble m.
nobody, nou'-bod-i, nadie, ninguno
nod, nod, v., cabecear. s., cabeceo m.; saludo m.
noise, nois, s., ruido m.; **—less*,** silencioso
noisily, noi'-si-li, adv., ruidosamente
noisy, noi'-si, a., ruidoso
nominal*, nom'-i-nal, a., nominal
nominate, nom'-i-neit, v., nombrar; elegir
nominee, nom-i-nii', s., nómino m.; candidato m.
none, nõn, pron. & a., ninguno, nadie
nonplussed, non'-plõst, a., confundido
nonsense, non'-sens, s., disparate m., tontería f.
non-skid, non'-skid, a., antirresbaladizo
non-stop, non'-stop, a., continuo; (train, etc.)
directo
nook, nuk, s., ángulo m.; (fig.) rincón m.
noon, nuun, s., mediodía m.
noose, nuus, s., lazo corredizo m.
nor, noar, conj., ni
normal*, noar'-mal, a., normal
north, noarz, s., norte m.   [nal
northerly, noar'-Der-li, a., del norte, septentrio-
nose, nous, s., nariz f.; (of a ship) proa f.
nostril, nos'-tr'l, s., ventana de la nariz f.
not, not, adv., no
notable, nou'-ta-bl, a., notable
notch, noch, v., hacer muescas. s., muesca f.
note, nout, v., notar. s., nota f.; (currency) billete m.; **—book,** libreta f.; **—paper,** papel
para cartas m.; **—d,** a., afamado, célebre
noteworthy, nout'-uèr-Di, a., notable

nothing, nŏ'-zing, adv., nada; **for —,** de balde

notice, nou'-tis, v., notar. s., aviso m.; (newspaper) noticia f.; (to quit) notificación f.

noticeable, nou'-tis-*a*-bl, a., notable, reparable

notify, nou'-ti-fai, v., notificar

notion, nou'-shon, s., noción f.; idea f.

notoriety, nou-to-rai'-i-ti, s., notoriedad f.

notorious*, no-tou'-ri-os, a., notorio

notwithstanding, not-uiD-stan'-ding, prep. & conj., a pesar de, no obstante

nought, nout, nada. s., cero m.

noun, naun, s., nombre m., substantivo m.

nourish, nŏr'-ish, v., nutrir, alimentar; **—ing,** a., nutritivo; **—ment,** s., alimento m.

novel, nov'-l, s., novela f. a., nuevo

novelist, nov'-el-ist, s., novelista m. & f.

novelty, nov'-el-ti, s., novedad f.

November, no-vem'-ba, s., noviembre m.

novice, nov'-is, s., novicio m.

now, nau, adv., ahora; **— and then,** de vez en cuando

nowadays, nau'-*a*-deis, adv., hoy día

nowhere, nou'-juér, adv., en ninguna parte

noxious*, nok'-shos, a., nocivo, pernicioso

nozzle, nos'-l, s., (of hose) boquerel de manguera m.

nuclear, niuu'-klir, a., nuclear

nucleus, niuu'-kli-os, s., núcleo m.

nude, niud, a., desnudo

nudge, nŏCH, s., codazo m. v., dar codazos

nugget, nŏ'-guit, s., pepita f.

nuisance, niuu'-sens, s., (annoyance) fastidio m., molestia f.; (bother) calamidad f.

null, nŏl, a., nulo. v., anular

numb, nŏm, a., entumecido; (frm cold) aterido. v., entumecer; **—ness,** s., entumecimiento m.

number, nŏm'-ba, s., número m. v., numerar

numberless, nŏm'-ber-les, a., innumerable

numerous*, niuu'-mer-os, a., numeroso

nun, nŏn, s., monja f., religiosa f.

nunnery, nŏn'-er-i, s., convento de monjas m.

nurse, nčrs, s., enfermera f.; (male) enfermero m.; (maid) niñera f. v., cuidar; (suckle) criar

nursery, nĕrs'-er-i, s., cuarto de los niños m.; (plants) plantel m., semillero m.

nursery-ryhme, nĕrs'-er-i-raim, s., cuento de niños m.

nut, nŏt, s., nuez f.; (hazel) avellana f.; (pea) cacahué m.; (bolt) tuerca f.; **—cracker,** cascanueces m.; **—meg,** nuez moscada f.; **—shell,** cascara de nuez m.

nutriment, niuu'-tri-ment, s., alimento m.

nutritious*, niuu-trish'-os, a., nutritivo

oak, ouk, s., roble m.

oakum, ou'-kom, s., estopa f.

oar, our, s., remo m.

oarsman, ours'-man, s., remero m.

oasis, ou-ei'-sis, s., oasis m.

oat, out, s., avena f.; **—meal,** harina de avena f.

oath, ouz, s., juramento m.; maldición f.

obdurate*, ob'-diu-ret, a., obstinado; terco

obedience, o-bii'-di-ens, s., obediencia f.

obedient*, o-bii'-di-ent, a., obediente

obese, o-biis', a., obeso

obesity, o-bes'-i-ti, s., obesidad f.

obey, o-bei', v., obedecer

obfuscate, ob-fŏs'-keit, v., ofuscar

obituary, ob-it'-iuu-a-ri, s., obituario m. a., mortuorio

object, ob-chekt', v., (resent) objetar; (oppose) oponerse

object, ob'-chekt, s., objecto m.; (aim) propósito m.; (grammar) complemento m.; **—ion,** objeción f.; **—ionable,** a., objetable; **—ive,** s. & a., objetivo m.

obligation, ob-li-guei'-shon, s., obligación f.

obligatory, ob'-li-guei-to-ri, a., obligatorio

oblige, ob-laich', v., obligar; complacer

obliging*, ob-laich'-ing, a., servicial

obliterate, ob-lit'-er-eit, v., borrar

oblivion, ob-liv'-i-on, s., olvido m.

oblivious*, ob-liv'-i-os, a., olvidadizo

oblong, ob'-long, a., oblongo

obnoxious*, ob-nok'-shos, a., ofensivo

obscene*, ob-siin', a., obsceno
obscure, ob-skiúr', v., obscurecer. a.,* obscuro
observant, ob-sër'-vant, a., atento
observation, ob-sër-vei'-shon, s., observación f.
observatory, ob-sër'-va-to-ri, s., observatorio m.
observe, ob-sërv', v., observar
obsess, ob-ses', v., obsesionar; —**ion**, s., obsesión f.
obsolete, ob'-so-liit, a., anticuado; desusado
obstacle, ob'-sta-kl, s., obstáculo m.
obstinacy, ob'-sti-na-si, s., obstinación f.
obstinate*, ob'-sti-net, a., obstinado, terco
obstruct, ob-strökt', v., obstruir; impedir
obstruction, ob-strök'-shon, s., obstrucción f.
obtain, ob-tein', v., obtener, conseguir, alcanzar
obtrude, ob-truud', v., imponer; entrometerse
obtrusive, ob-truu'-siv, a., intruso; importuno
obviate, ob'-vi-eit, v., evitar; impedir
obvious*, ob'-vi-os, a., obvio, evidente, claro
occasion, o-kei'-shon, v., ocasionar. s., ocasión f.;
    causa f.; —**al**, a., ocasional; —**ally**, adv., alguna
    vez
occult, ok-költ', a., oculto, secreto
occupation, ok-kiu-pei'-shon, s., ocupación f.;
    empleo m.
occupier, o'-kiu-uai-a, s., ocupador m.; (tenant)
    inquilino m.
occupy, o'-kiu-pai, v., ocupar; (mil.) apoderarse
    de; (oneself) ocuparse
occur, ok-ker', v., ocurrir; —**rence**, s., ocurrencia f.
ocean, ou'-shan, s., océano m.; mar m. & f.
ochre, ou'-ker, s., ocre m.
o'clock, o-klok', s., . . .hora f.
octagon, ok'-ta-guon, s., octágono m.
octagonal, ok-ta'-guon-al, a., octagonal
octave, ok'-teiv, s., octava f.
October, ok-tou'-ba, s., octubre m.
octopus, ok'-tou-pus, s., pulpo m., pólipo m.
oculist, ok'-iu-list, s., oculista m.
odd, od, a., (number) impar; (single) suelto;
    (strange) extraño; —**ly**, adv., extrañamente;
    —**s**, s. pl., (betting) ventaja f.; —**s and ends**,
    restos m. pl., despojos m. pl.

odious*, ou'-di-os, a., odioso; detestable

odour, ou'-da, s., olor m.; (sweet) fragancia f.

of, ov, prep., de

off, of, adv., lejos; a distancia; a lo largo; **—hand**, adv., improvisado, de repente; **—side**, s., lado exterior (in Spain), lado derecho (en Inglaterra); a., (games) fuera de juego, offside

offal, of'-l, s., desperdicios m. pl.; bazofia f.

offence, o-fens', s., ofensa f.; (law) delito m.

offend, o-fend', v., ofender; (law) delinquir [f.

offensive, o-fen'-siv, a.,* ofensivo m.; (mil.) ofensiva

offer, of'-a, v., ofrecer. s., oferta f.

offering, of'-er-ing, s., tributo m.; sacrificio m.

office, of'-is, s., oficio m.; (business) oficina f.

officer, of'-is-a, s., funcionario m.; (mil.) oficial m.

official, o-fish'-l, s., funcionario m. a.,* oficial

officious*, o-fish'-os, a., oficioso; solícito

offspring, of'-spring, s., vástago m., prole f.

oft, often, oft, of'-n, adv., a menudo

ogle, ou'-gl, v., mirar al soslayo

oil, oil, s., aceite m. v., lubricar; **—cloth**, s., hule m.; **—y**, a., aceitoso, oleoso

ointment, oint'-ment, s., ungüento m.

old, ould, a., viejo, anciano; antiguo

old-fashioned, ould-fash'-nd, a., anticuado

olive, ol'-iv, s., aceituna f.; **— oil**, aceite de oliva m.

omelet, om'-e-let, s., tortilla f.

omen, ou'-men, s., agüero m., presagio m.

ominous, ou'-mi-nos, a., ominoso; presagioso

ommission, o-mish'-on, s., omisión f.; (neglect) descuido m.

omit, o-mit', v., omitir; (neglect) descuidar

omnibus, om'-ni-bos, s., ómnibus m.

omnipotent, om-nip'-o-tent, a., omnipotente

on, on, prep., (upon) en sobre, encima de; (date) el, adv., (onward) adelante; **— foot**, a pie

once, uöns, adv., una vez; (formerly) antes, en otro tiempo; **all at —**, de repente; **at —**, inmediatamente; **— more**, otra vez

one, uön, s., un, uno, una f.; (impersonal) uno m., una f. a., un, uno, una; **—self**, pron., se, sí mismo; **—way**, (street), calle con dirección única

onerous*, on'-*er*-os, a., oneroso

onion, ŏn'-i-on, s., cebolla f.

only, ōun'-li, a., sólo, único; adv., sólo, solamente

onslaught, on'-slŏat, s., asalto m.

onward, on'-uerd, adv., hacia, adelante

onyx, on'-lks, s., ónice m.

ooze, uus, v., manar, fluir. s., fango m.

opal, ou'-pal, s., ópalo m.

opaque, o-peik', a., opaco

open, ou'-pn, v., abrir. a.,* abierto; —**er**, s., (tool) abridor m.; —**ing**, abertura f.; oportunidad f.

opera, op'-e-ra, s., ópera f.; —**glass**, gemelos de teatro m. pl.; —**hat**, clac m.; —**house**, teatro de la ópera m.

operate, op'-er-eit, v., funcionar; (med.) operar

operation, op'-er-ei'-shon, s., operación f.

operator, op'-e-rei-ta, s., operario m., (med.) operador m.

opinion, o-pin'-yon, s., opinión f.

opium, ou'-pi-om, s., opio m.

opossum, ou-pos'-som, s., zarigüeya f.

opponent, o-pou'-nent, s., adversario m.; rival m.

opportune*, o'-por-tiuun, a., oportuno

opportunity, o-por-tiuun'-i-ti, s., oportunidad f.

oppose, o-pous', v., oponer; combatir

opposite, op'-o-sit, a., opuesto; (facing) enfrente, s., opuesto m.

opposition, op-pou-si'-shon, s., oposición f.

oppress, o-pres', v., oprimir

oppression, o-presh'-on, s., opresión f.; pesadez f.

oppressive*, o-pres'-siv, a., opresivo; tiránico

optical, op'-tik-al, a., óptico, relativo a la vista

optician, op-tish'-an, s., óptico m.

option, op'-shon, s., opción f.; —**al***, a., facultativo

opulence, op'-iu-lens, s., opulencia f.

opulent, op'-iu-lent, a., opulento

or, or, conj., o, u; sea, sea que; —**else**, o sino

oral*, ó'-ral, verbal

orange, or'-inch, s., naranja f.

orator, or'-a-ta, s., orador m.

oratory, or'-a-to-ri, s., oratoria f., elocuencia f.

orb, oarb, s., (sphere) globo m., orbe m., esfera f.

orbit, oαrb'-it, s., órbita. v., volar en círculo

orchard, oαr'-cherd, s., huerta f.; (poetical) verjel

orchestra, oαr'-kes-trα, s., orquesta f. [m.

orchid, oαr'-kid, s., orquídea f.

ordain, oαr-dein', v., ordenar

ordeal, oαr'-diil, s., dura prueba f.

order, oαr'-dα, s., orden f.; (goods) pedido m.; (command) orden m.; (decoration) condecoración f. v., ordenar; (goods) hacer un pedido

orderly, oαr'-der-li, a.,* ordenado; (quiet) tranquilo. s., ordenanza f.

ordinary, oαr'-di-nα-ri, a., ordinario

ordnance, oαrd'-nαns, s., artillería f.

ore, ór, s., mineral m.

organ, oαr'-gαn, s., órgano m.

organic, oαr-guan'-ik, a., orgánico

organization, oαr-guan-ai-sei'-shon, s., organización f.

organize, oαr'-gαn-ais, v., organizar

orgy, oαr'-chi, s., orgía f.

orient, ó'-ri-ent, s., oriente m.

oriental, ou-ri-en'-tαl, s. & a., oriental m. & f.

origin, or'-i-chin, s., origen m.; **—al*,** a., original

originate, o-rich'-in-eit, v., originar; originarse

ornament, oαr'-nα-ment, s., adorno m. v., adornar

ornamental, oαr-nα-men'-tαl, a., decorativo

orphan, oαr'-fαn, s., huérfano m.; **—age,** asilo de huérfanos m.

orthodox, or'-zo-doks, a., ortodoxo

orthography, oαr-zog'-rα-fi, s., ortografía f.

oscillate, os'-il-eit, v., oscilar

ostentatious*, os-ten-tei'-shos, a., ostentoso

ostrich, os'-trich, s., avestruz m.

other, ðD'-α, a., otro; **another time,** adv., otra vez; **the other one,** pron., el otro; **—wise,** adv., de otro modo

otter, ot'-α, s., nutria f.

ought, oat, v., deber; convenir

ounce, αuns, s., onza f. (28 gr. 35)

our, aúr, poss. adj., nuestro

ours, aúrs, poss. pron., el nuestro

ourselves, aúr-selvs', pron., nosotros mismos

out, aut, adv., fuera. a., (extinguish) apagado; (issue) publicado; **—bid,** v., pujar más alto; **—break,** s., insurrección f.; epidemia f.; **—burst,** explosión f.; **—cast,** proscrito m.; **—come,** s., resultado m.; fruto m.; **—cry,** clamor m.; alboroto m.; **—do,** v., exceder; **—fit,** s., equipo m.; **—fitter,** proveedor m.; (ship) armador m.; **—grow,** v., crecer más que; crecer demasiado para; durar más; **—last,** v., durar más; **—law,** s., bandido m.; v., poner fuera de la ley; **—lay,** s., desembolso m., gasto m.; **—let,** salida f., desagüe m.; **—line,** v., bosquejar. s., contorno m.; **—live,** v., sobrevivir; **—look,** s., aspecto m.; perspectiva f.; **—lying,** a., distante; exterior; **—number,** v., exceder en número; **—post,** s., avanzada f.; **—put,** producción f.; **—rage,** ultraje m.; **—rageous*,** ultrajante; exagerado; **—right,** adv., completamente; **—run,** v., correr más que otro; pasar; **—side,** adv., afuera. s. & a., exterior; **—sider,** s., extraño m.; (racing) forastero m.; **—size,** tamaño extra m.; **—skirts,** inmediaciones f. pl.; **—spoken*,** a., abierto, franco; **—standing,** a., prominente; (debts) pendiente; **—ward,** adv., fuera. a., exterior; **—ward bound,** (shipping) en viaje de ida; **—wit,** v., engañar

oval, ou'-vl, s., óvalo m. a., oval

ovation, ou-vei'-shon, s., ovación f.

oven, ŏ'-vn, s., horno m.

over, ou'-va, adv., sobre, por encima. prep., sobre; encima de; **—alls,** s.pl., zahones m.pl.; **—bearing,** a., arrogante; **—board,** adv., al mar, al agua; **—cast,** a., nublado; **—charge,** s., (price) extorsión f. v., sobrecargar; **—coat,** s., sobretodo m.; **—come,** v., triunfar de; **—do,** v., excederse en; **—dose,** s., dosis excesiva f.; **—draw,** v., exceder el crédito; **—due,** a., vencido y no pagado; **—flow,** v., desbordar; **—grow,** crecer con exceso; **—hang,** sobresalir; suspender; **—haul,** examinar; **—hear,** oir por casualidad; **—joy,** arrebatar de alegría; **—land,** a. & adv., por tierra; **—lap,** v., traslapar; **—load,** sobrecargar; **—look,** dominar; (forget) descuidar; (pardon) pasar por alto; **—power,** vencer; subyugar; **—rate,** encarecer; **—rule,** (set aside) denegar; **—run,** invadir; infestar; **—seas,** a., ultramar; **—see,** v., superintender; **—seer,** s., superintendente m.; **—sight,** inadvertencia f.; **—sleep,** v., dormir demasiado; **—step,** exceder; **—take,** alcanzar; **—throw,** (vanquish) vencer; **—time,** s., (work) horas de trabajo extraordinarias f. pl.; **—ture,** propuesta f.; (mus.) obertura f.; **—turn,** v., volcar; (deliberate) derribar; **—weight,** s., exceso de peso m.; **—whelm,** v., abrumar; **—work,** sobrecargar de trabajo

owe, ou, v., deber

owing, ou'-ing, a., debido; **— to,** debido a

owl, aul, s., buho m., mochuelo m.

own, oun, v., poseer; confesar. a., propio

owner, ou'-na, s., dueño m., propietario m.

ox, ox, s., buey m.

oxygen, ok'-si-chen, s., oxígeno m.

oyster, ois'-ta, s., ostra f.; **—bed,** ostrero m.

pace, peis, s., paso m. v. (measure) medir; pasear

pacify, pas'-i-fai, v., pacificar

pack, pak, v., empaquetar. s., (bundle) paquete m.; (bale) fardo m.; (cards) baraja f.; (gang) cuadrilla f.; (hounds) hato m.; **—age,** bulto m.

packet, pak'-et, s., paquete m.

packing, pak'-ing, s., embalaje m.; (mech.) empaque m.

pact, pakt, s., pacto m.

pad, pad, v., (to stuff) rellenar, emborrar. s., (stamp pad) almohadilla para entintar f.; (writing) bloc de papel m.

paddling, pad'-dling, s., (stuffing) relleno m.

paddle, pad'-dl, v., remar con canalete; (feet) chapotear. s., canalete m.; **—steamer,** vapor de ruedas m.; **—wheel,** rueda de paleta f.

paddock, pad'-ok, s., (meadow) dehesa f.

padlock, pad'-lok, s., candado m. v., cerrar con candado

pagan, peiʹ-*gan*, s., pagano m. a., pagano

page, peiCH, s., (book) página f.; (court) paje m.;
   —boy, (at hotels, etc.) botones m., mozo m.

pageant, paCHʹ-*ent*, s., procesion f.

pail, peil, s., cubo m.

pain, pein, s., dolor m. v., doler; **—ful***, a.,
   doloroso; **—less,** sin dolor.

paint, peint, v., pintar. s., pintura f.; (art) color
   m.; (face) colorete m.; **—brush,** brocha f.;
   (art) pincel m.; **—er,** pintor m.; **—ing,** cuadro
   m.; pintura f.

pair, pér, s., par m.; pareja f.

palace, palʹ-*is*, s., palacio m.

palatable, palʹ-*a-ta*-bl, a., sabroso

palate, palʹ-*et*, s., paladar m.

pale, peil, a., pálido. v., palidecer; **—ness,** s., palidez f.

palette, palʹ-*et*, s., paleta f.

paling, peiʹ-ling, s., (fence) palizada f.

palm, paam, s., (hand) palmera f.; (hand) palma f.; **—ist,**
   quiromántico m.; **—istry,** quiromancia f.;
   — Sunday, domingo de Ramos m.

palpitation, pal-pi-teiʹ-shon, s., palpitación f.

paltry, po*al*ʹ-tri, a., mezquino; vil, miserable

pamper, pamʹ-*pa*, v., (indulge) mimar

pamphlet, pamʹ-flet, s., folleto m.

pan, pan, s., (frying) sartén f.; **—cake,** buñuelo m.

pander, panʹ-*da*, v., alcahuetear

pane, pein, s., vidrio m., cristal m.

panel, panʹ-l, s., (persons) lista f.

pang, pang, s., ansia f.; dolor m.

panic, panʹ-ik, s., pánico m.

pansy, panʹ-si, s., pensamiento m.

pant, pant, v., jadear

panther, panʹ-*zer*, s., pantera f.

pantry, panʹ-tri, s., despensa f.

pants, pants, s. pl., calzoncillos m. pl.

pap, pap, s., (food) papilla f.

papal, peiʹ-pʹl, a., papal

paper, peiʹ-*pa*, s., papel m.; **news—,** periódico m.,
   diario m.; **wall—,** papel de empapelar m.

par, paar, s., par m.

parable, ᴘᴀʀ'-*a*-bl, s., parábola f.

parachute, ᴘᴀʀ'-*a*-shut, s., paracaídas m.

parade, p*a*-reid', s., parada f. v., ostentar

paradise, ᴘᴀʀ'-*a*-dais, s., paraíso m.

paraffin, ᴘᴀʀ'-*a*-fin, s., parafina f.

paragraph, ᴘᴀʀ'-*a*-graaf, s., párrafo m.; parágrafo

parallel, ᴘᴀʀ'-*a*-lel, a., paralelo   [m.

paralysis, ᴘᴀʀ-*a*'-lai-sis, s., parálisis f.

paralyze, ᴘᴀʀ'-*a*-lais, v., paralizar

parasite, ᴘᴀʀ'-*a*-sait, s., parásito m.

parcel, paar'-sl, s., paquete m.

parched, paart'-sht, a., reseco, mustio

parchment, paart'-shment, s., pergamino m.

pardon, paar'-dn, v., perdonar, s., perdón m.; (official) indulto m.

parents, peɪ'-rents, s. pl., padres m. pl.

parish, ᴘᴀʀ'-ish, s., parroquia f.

park, paark, s., parque f.; —ing, (motors) estacionamiento m.; —ing place, plaza de estacionamiento f.

parley, paar'-li, v., parlamentar

parliament, paar'-li-ment, s., parlamento m.

parlour, paar'-la, s., recibidor m.

parochial, p*a*-rou'-ki-*a*l, a., parroquial

parrot, ᴘᴀʀ'-ot, s., papagayo m.

parry, ᴘᴀʀ'-i, v., parar. s., quite m.

parse, paars, v., (grammar) analizar

parsimonious*, paar'-si-mou'-ni-*o*s, a., tacaño

parsley, paars-li, s., perejil m.

parsnip, paar'-snip, s., chirivía f.

parson, paar'-sn, s., clérigo m.; (parish) párroco m.

parsonage, paar'-son-ɪᴄʜ, s., rectoría f., vicaría f.

part, paart, v., partir; (separate) separar; (hair) hacer la raya, s., parte f.; (actor's) papel m.; —time, s., horas de jornada incompleta

partake, paar-teik', — in, v., tomar parte en; —of, participar

partial*, paar'-shal, a., parcial; —ity, s., parcialidad f.; prejuicio m.; predilección f.

participate, paar-tis'-i-peit, v., participar

participle, paar'-ti-si-pl, s., participio m.

particle, paar'-ti-kl, s., partícula f.

particular*, par-tik′-iu-lr, a., particular; (fastidious) exigente, quisquilloso; (exact) exacto; **—s**, s. pl., detalles m. pl.

parting, paar′-ting, s., separación f.; (hair) raya f.

partition, paar-tish′-on, s., (wall) partición f.

partner, paart′-na, s., (business) socio m.; (cards) compañero m.; (dance) pareja f.

partnership, paart′-ner-ship, s., sociedad f.

partridge, paar′-trich, s., perdiz f.

party, paar′-ti, s., partido m.; (social) reunión f., tertulia f.

pass, paas, v., pasar; (examination) aprobar s.; (mountain) puerto m.; **—book,** libreta de banco f.; **—port,** pasaporte m.

passage, pas′-ich, s., pasaje m.; (in a house) pasillo m.; (sea) travesía f.

passenger, pas′-in-cha, s., pasajero m.

passer-by, pas′-r-bai, s., transeúnte m.

passion, pash′-on, s., pasión f.; (anger) cólera f.

passionate*, pash′-on-et, a., apasionado

past, paast, s., pasado m. a., pasado

paste, peist, v., engrudar. s., engrudo m.; (cakes, gems, etc.) pasta f.

pastime, paas′-taim, s., pasatiempo m.

pastries, peis′-treis, s. pl., pastas f. pl.

pastry, peis′-tri, s., pastelería f.; **—cook′s,** pastelería f.

pasture, paas′-tiur, s., pasto m.

pat, pat, v., dar una palmadita

patch, pach, s., remiendo m. v., remendar

patent, pei′-tent, a., patente, visible, manifiesto. s., patente f.; diploma f.; **— leather,** charol m.; hule m.

paternal*, pa-ter′-nal, a., paternal, paterno

path, paaz, s., senda f., camino m.

pathetic, pa-ze′-tik, a., patético, conmovedor

patience, pei′-shens, s., paciencia f.

patient, pei′-shent, a.,* paciente. s., enfermo m.

patriot, pei′-tri-ot, s., patriota m.

patriotic, pei-tri-ot′-ik, a., patriótico

patrol, pa-troul′, s., patrulla f. v., patrullar

patronize, pat′-ron-ais, v., patrocinar; proteger

pattern, pʌt'-ern, s., modelo m.; (sample) muestra f.; (paper) patrón m.

paunch, poanch, s., panza f.

pauper, poa͟,-pr, s., pobre m.

pause, poas, s., pausa f. v., pausar

pave, peiv, v., pavimentar

pavement, peiv'-ment, s., pavimento m.

pavilion, pa-vil'-yon, s., pabellón m.

paw, poa, s., garra f. v., (as a horse) piafar

pawn, poan, v., empeñar. s., prenda f.; (chess) peón m.; **—broker's shop,** casa de empeños f.

pay, pei, v., pagar. s., paga f.; **—able,** a., pagadero; **—er,** s., pagador m.; **—load,** s., carga rentable f.; carga explosiva f.; **—ment,** pago m.

pea, pii, s., guisante m.; **—nut,** cacahuete m.

peace, piis, s., paz f.; **—ful,** a., pacífico, tranquilo

peach, piich, s., melocotón m.; **—-tree,** melocotonero m.

peacock, pii'-kok, s., pavo real m.

peak, piik, s., pico m., cima f.

peal, piil, v., repicar. s., (bells) repique m.; (thunder) tronido m.

pear, pér, s., pera f.; **—-tree,** peral m.

pearl, pêrl, s., perla f.

peasant, pes'-ant, s., campesino m.

peat, piit, s., turba f.

pebble, peb'-l, s., guija f.

peck, pek, v., picotear

peculiar', pi-kiuu'-li-a, a., peculiar; **—ity,** s., peculiaridad f.

pecuniary, pi-kiuu'-ni-a-ri, a., pecuniario

pedal, ped'-al, s., pedal m.

pedantic, pi-dan'-tik, a., pedantesco

pedestal, ped'-es-tal, s., pedestal m.

pedestrian, pi-des'-tri-an, s., peatón m., caminante m.

pedigree, ped'-i-grii, s., genealogía f.

pedlar, ped'-la, s., buhonero m.

peel, piil, v., pelar. s., corteza f.

peep, piip, v., atisbar. s., ojeada f.

peer, pir, v., escudriñar. s., par m.; **—age,** dignidad de par f.

peerless, pir-les, a., sin par

peevish*, pii'-vish, a., quisquilloso

peg, peg, s., clavija f.; (for hats, etc.) colgador m. v., enclavijar

pellet, pel'-et, s., pella f.; (shot) perdigón m.

pell-mell, pel'-mel, adv., a trochemoche

pelt, pelt, v., apedrear. s., (skin) piel f.

pen, pen, v., escribir; encerrar. s., pluma f.; (cattle, etc.) corral m.; **—holder,** portapluma m.; **—knife,** navaja f. [m.

penal, pii'-nl, a., penal; **—servitude,** s., presidio

penalty, pen'-al-ti, s., castigo m.; (fine) multa f.

penance, pen'-ans, s., penitencia f.

pencil, pen'-sl, s., lápiz m.

pendant, pen'-dant, s., medallón m.

pending, pen'-ding, a., pendiente. prep., durante

pendulum, pen'-diu-lom, s., péndulo m.

penetrate, pen'-i-treit, v., penetrar

penguin, pen'-guin, s., pingüino m.

peninsula, pen-in'-siu-la, s., península f.

penitent*, pen'-i-tent, a., penitente

penniless, pen'-i-les, a., sin dinero, sin blanca; pobre

penny, pen'-i, s., penique m.

pension, pen'-shon, s., pensión f.; (mil.) retiro m. v., pensionar; **—er,** s., pensionado m.; (services) inválido m.

pensive*, pen'-siv, a., pensativo

people, pii'-pl, s., gente f.; nación f. v., poblar

pepper, pep'-a, s., pimienta f.; **—mint,** menta f.

per, per, prep., por; **—cent,** por ciento; **—centage,** s., porcentaje m.

perambulator, per-Am'-biu-lei-ta, s., cochecillo de niño m.

perceive, per-siiv', v., percibir, comprender, entender

perception, per-sep'-shon, s., percepción f.

perch, perch, s., percha f.; (fish) perca f.

perchance, per-chaans', adv., acaso; tal vez, quizá

percolate, per'-ko-leit, v., colar, filtrar

peremptory, per-emp'-to-ri, a., perentorio

perfect, per'-fikt, a.,* perfecto, acabado. v., perfeccionar; **—ion,** s., perfección f.

perfidious*, p*er*-fĭd′-i-os, a., pérfido
perforate, per′-fo-reit, v., perforar, horadar
perform, per-foarm′, v., hacer, ejecutar; (stage) representar; **—ance**, s., ejecución f.; (stage) representación f.
perfume, pĕr′-fiuum, s., perfume m. v., perfumar
perhaps, per-japs′, adv., quizá, acaso
peril, per′il, s., peligro m.; **—ous***, a., peligroso
period, pi′-ri-od, s., periodo m.; **—ical**, revista f.
periscope, pi′-ris-koup, s., periscopio m.
perish, per′-ish, v., perecer; (spoil) pasarse
perishable, per′-i-sha-bl, a., perecedero
perjury, pĕr′-CHiu-ri, s., perjurio m.
permanent*, pĕr′-ma-nent, a., permanente
permeate, pĕr′-mi-eit, v., penetrar; (liquid) calar
permission, per-mish′-on, s., permiso m.
permit, per-mit′, v., permitir
permit, per′-mit, s., permiso m.
pernicious, per-nish′os, a., pernicioso
perpendicular, per-pen-dik′-iu-l*a*, s. & a.,* perpendicular f.
perpetrate, pĕr′-pi-treit, v., perpetrar, cometer
perpetual*, per-pet′-iu-al, a., perpetuo
perplex, per-pleks′, v., confundir, aturrullar
persecute, pĕr′-si-kiuut, v., perseguir
persecution, pĕr-si-kiu′-shon, s., persecución f.
perseverance, per-si-vii′-rans, s., perseverancia f.
persevere, per-si-vir′, v., perseverar
persist, per-sist′, v., persistir
person, pĕr′-son, s., persona f.; **—al**, a., personal; **—ality**, s., personalidad f.
personify, per-son′-i-fai, v., personificar
perspective, per-spek′-tiv, s., perspectiva f.
perspicacity, pĕr-spi-kas′-i-ti, s., perspicacia f.
perspiration, pĕr-spi-rei′-shon, s., sudor m., transpiración f.
perspire, pĕr-spair′, v., sudar, transpirar
persuade, per-sueid′, v., persuadir
persuasion, per-suei′-shon, s., persuasión f.
pert*, pĕrt, a., petulante, atrevido
pertain, per-tein′, v., pertenecer
pertinacity, per-ti-nas′-i-ti, s., pertinacia f.

pertinent*, pĕr'-ti-nent, a., pertinente
perturb, per-tĕrb', v., perturbar; agitar
perusal, pe-ruu'-sal, s., examen m.
peruse, pe-ruus', v., recorrer, examinar
perverse*, per-vĕrs', a., perverso; depravado
pervert, per-vĕrt'r; falsear
pest, pest, s., peste f., pestilencia f.
pester, pes'-ta, v., molestar; importunar
pet, pet, s., favorito m.; (child) niño mimado m. v.,
mimar; acariciar
petal, pet'-l, s., pétalo m.
petition, pi-tish'-on, s., petición f.; memorial m.
v., pedir; dirigir un memorial
petitioner, pi-tish'-on-a, s., solicitante m.
petrify, pet'-ri-fai, v., petrificar
petrol, pet'-rol, s., gasolina f.; — guage, s.,
indicador de nivel de gasolina
petroleum, pi-trou'-li-om, s., petróleo m.
petticoat, pet'-i-kout, s., enaguas f. pl.; combinación f.
petty, pet-i, a., pequeño; mezquino; despreciable
petulance, pet'-iu-lans, s., petulancia f.
pew, piuu, s., banco de iglesia m.
pewter, piuu'-ta, s., peltre m.
phantom, fan'-tom, s., fantasma m., espectro m.
phase, feis, s., fase f.
pheasant, fes'-ant, s., faisán m.
phenomenon, fi-nom'-i-non, s., fenómeno m.
philosopher, fi-los'-o-fa, s., filósofo m.
phlegm, flem, s., flema f.
phosphate, fos'-feit, s., fosfato m.
phosphorus, fos'-fo-ros, s., fósforo m.
photograph, fou'-to-graf, s., fotografía f.
photographer, fou-tog'-raf-a, s., fotógrafo m.
phrase, freis, s., frase f.
physic, fis'-ik, s., medicina f.; —al*, a., físico m.
physician, fi-sish'-an, s., médico m.; físico m.
piano, pi-a'-nou, s., piano m.; grand —, piano
de cola m.
pick, pik, v., picar; (choose) escoger; (gather) recoger; (teeth) mondar. s., pico m.; —pocket,
ratero m. — up, v., coger

pickle, pik´-l, v., encurtir; **—s,** s. pl., encurtidos m.

picnic, pik´-nik, s., merienda en el campo f. [pl.

picture, pik´-tiur, s., pintura f., cuadro m.; ilustración f.; (portrait) retrato m.

pie, pai, s., pastel m., empanada f.

piece, piis, s., pedazo m.; fragmento m.; (length) pieza f.; (music, etc.) pieza f.; **—meal,** adv., en pedazos; **—work,** obra a destajo f.

pier, pir, s., muelle m., embarcadero m.

pierce, pirs, v., taladrar; (ears) horadar

piercing, pir´-sing, a., penetrante, agudo

piety, pai´-i-ti, s., piedad f., devoción f.

pig, pig, s., cerdo m., puerco m.; **—iron,** hierro en lingotes, m.; **—sty,** pocilga f.

pigeon, pich´-in, s., paloma f., pichón m.

pigeon-hole, pich´-in-joul, s., casilla f.

pike, paik, s., pica f.; (fish) lucio m.

pilchard, pil´-cherd, s., sardina f.

pile, pail, s., estaca f.; (heap) montón m.; (carpet, etc.) pelo m. v., amontonar

piles, pails, s. pl., hemorroides f. pl.

pilfer, pil´-fд, v., ratear, hurtar

pilgrim, pil´-grim, s., peregrino f.

pilgrimage, pil´-gri-mich, s., peregrinación f.

pill, pil, s., píldora f.

pillage, pil´-ich, v., pillar. s., pillaje m.

pillar, pil´-a, s., pilar m.; columna f.; **—box,** buzón m.

pillory, pil´-o-ri, s., picota f.

pillow, pil´-ou, s., almohada f.

pilot, pai´-lot, s., piloto m. v., pilotear

pimpernel, pim´-per-nel, s., pamplina f.

pimple, pim´-pl, s., grano m., botón m.

pin, pin, s., alfiler m.; (safety) imperdible m. v., prender con alfileres

pinafore, pin´-a-fór, s., delantal m.

pincers, pin´-sers, s. pl., pinzas f. pl., tenazas f. pl.

pinch, pinch, s., pellizco m. v., pellizcar; (press) apretar

pine, pain, v., languidecer. s., (tree) pino m.

pine-apple, pain´-ap-el, s., piña f.

pinion, pin´-yon, s., piñón m. v., maniatar

pink, pingk, s., color de rosa m.; (flower) clavel m. a., rosado

pinnacle, pin'-*a*-kl, s., pináculo m.

pint, paint, s., pinta f. (0·57 litre)

pioneer, pai-o-nir', s., colono m.; explorador m.; (mil.) gastador m.

pious*, pai'-os, a., pío, devoto

pip, pip, s., pepita f.

pipe, paip, s., tubo m.; (water, gas, etc.) cañería f.; (tobacco) pipa f.; — **dream**, s., sueño m.; ilusión m.

piquant*, pii'-kant, a., picante

pirate, pai'-ret, s., pirata m.

pistol, pis'-tl, s., pistola f.

piston, pis'-ton, s., émbolo m., pistón m.   [m.

pit, pit, s., hoyo m.; (theatre) platea f.; (mine) pozo

pitch, pich, s., pez f.; tono m. v., (naut.) cabecear

pitcher, pich'-*a*, s., cántaro m.

pitchfork, pich'-fo*a*rk, s., horca f.

piteous*, pi'-ti-os, a., lastimoso

pitfall, pit'-fo*a*l, s., trampa f.

pith, piz, s., (spinal) médula f.; (plant) meollo m.

pitiful*, pit'-i-f*u*l, a., lastimoso

pitiless*, pit'-i-les, a., despiadado, cruel

pity, pit'-i, s., piedad f., compasión f.

pivot, piv'-ot, s., pivote m., eje m.

placard, pl*A*k'-aard, s., cartel m.; anuncio m.

place, pleis, s., lugar m.; (locality) localidad f. v., poner, colocar

placid*, pl*A*s'-id, a., plácido, apacible

plagiarism, plei'-chi-*a*-rism, s., plagio m.

plague, pleig, s., plaga f., peste f. v., molestar

plaice, pleis, s., platija f.

plain*, plein, a., (looks, etc.) ordinario; (simple) sencillo; (clear) claro. s,. llano m.; llanura f.; (in S. America) pampa f.

plaint, pleint, s., queja f.; lamento m.; (legal) alegato de quejas m.; —**iff**, demandante m.; —**ive***, a., (complaining) quejoso; (sorrow) dolorido

plait, pl*A*t, s., trenza f. v., trenzar; (fold) plegar

plan, plan, s., plan m., proyecto m.; (drawing) plano m. v., proyectar

plane, plein, v., cepillar, s., plano m.; (tool) cepillo m.; **—-tree,** plátano m.

planet, plan'-et, s., planeta m.

plank, plangk, s., tabla f.

plant, plaant, v., plantar. s., planta f.; (mech.) maquinaria f.; **—ation,** plantío m.; (coffee) cafetal m.; (sugar) ingenio m.; (tobacco) tabacal m.

plaster, plaas'-ta, v., enyesar. s., yeso m.; emplasto m.; **sticking —,** esparadrapo m.; **— of Paris,** yeso mate m.

plastic, plas'-tik, s., materia plástica. a., plástico

plate, pleit, v., (chromium) cromar; (nickel) niquelar; (gold) dorar; (silver) platear. s., plato m.; (family) vajilla de plata f.; (photo) placa f.; **—-glass,** vidrio cilindrado m.; luna f.

platform, plat'-foarm, s., plataforma f.; (station) andén m.

platinum, plat'-i-nom, s., platino m.

play, plei, v., (game) jugar; (music) tocar. s., juego m.; (theatre) representación f.; **—er,** jugador m.; músico m.; actor m.; actriz f.; **—ful,** a., juguetón, s., **—ground,** s., campo de juego m. **—ing-cards,** naipes m. pl.

plea, plii, s., proceso m.; defensa f.; pretexto m.

plead, pliid, v., alegar; (law) pleitear

pleasant*, ples'-ant, a., agradable, placentero

please, pliis, v., agradar; satisfacer. interj., sírvase; haga el favor; **to be —d,** v., complacerse, estar contento

pleasing, pliis'-ing, a., agradable, amable

pleasure, plesh'-er, s., placer m., gusto m.

pledge, plech, s., (pawn) prenda f.; (oath) promesa f. v., (pawn) empeñar; (oath) comprometerse a

plenty, plen'-ti, s., abundancia f.

pleurisy, pliuu'-ri-si, s., pleuresía f.

pliable, plai'-a-bl, a., flexible; dócil

pliers, plai'-as, s. pl., alicates m. pl.

plight, plait, s., apuro m., aprieto m.

plod, plod, v., afanarse; **— along,** (walk) andar penosamente; **—der,** s., tardón m.

plot, plot, v., conspirar. s., intriga f.; (land) terreno m., (story, etc.) acción f.; **—ter,** conspirador m.

plough, pl**au**, v., arar. s., arado m.; **—man,** arador m.

plover, plŏv'-**a**, s., frailecillo m.

pluck, plŏk, v., arrancar; desplumar. s., valor m.

plug, plŏg, v., taponar. s., tapón m.; obturador m.; (elec.) enchufe m.; **sparking —,** bujía (para tapón) f.

plum, plŏm, s., ciruela f.

plumage, plu-**meich**, s., plumaje m.

plumb, plŏm, v., sondar. adv., a plomo. s., plomo m,

plumber, plŏm'-**a**, s., plomero m.

plump, plŏmp, a., rollizo ; (animal) gordo

plunder, plŏn'-**da**, v., saquear. s., pillaje m.

plunderer, plŏn'-der-**a**, s., saqueador m.

plunge, plŏnch, v., sumergirse, zambullirse; (dagger) hundir. s., zambullida f.

plural, pluu'-r**al**, s., plural m a., plural

plus, plŏs, adv., más

plush, plŏsh, s., felpa f.; peluche m.

ply, pl**ai**, v., (trade) ejercer. s., (three-ply-wood) madera de tres chapas f.; (three-ply-wool) lana de tres hilos f.; **— between,** v., hacer el servicio entre...

pneumatic, niu-mat'-ik, a., neumático

pneumonia, niu-mou'-ni-**a**, s., pulmonía f.

poach, p**o**ach, v., cazar en vedado ; (eggs) escalfar; **—er,** s., cazador furtivo m.

pocket, pok'-it, v., embolsar. s., bolsillo m.

pod, pod, s., cápsula f. ; (peas, etc.) vaina f.

poem, p**o**u'-em, s., poema m.

poet, p**o**u'-et, s., poeta m.

poetry, p**o**u'-et-ri, s., poesía f.; versos m. pl.

point, point, v., indicar, apuntar; (sharpen) aguzar. s., punto m.; (tip) punta f.; **—er,** apuntador m.; (dog) pachón m.

poise, pois, v., equilibrar. s., (deportment) equilibro m.; (grace) donaire f.

poison, poi'-sn, s., veneno m.; v., envenenar

poisonous, pois'-nos, a., venenoso

poke, p**o**uk, s., empujón m. v., empujar; (fire) atizar; **—r,** s., atizador m.; (cards) póker m.

pole, p**o**ul, s., pértiga f.; (geographical) polo m.

police, po-lis', s., policía f.; —**man**, policía m., guardia m.; —**-station**, comisaría f., puesto de guardia m.

policy, pol'-i-si, s., política f.; (insurance) póliza f.

polish, pol'-ish, s., (gloss) brillo m.; (for shoes) betún m.; (furniture, etc.) barniz m. v., pulir; (shoes) limpiar

polite*, po-lait', a., cortés; —**ness**, s., cortesía f.

political, po-lit'-i-kal, a., político

politician, pol-i-tish'-an, s., estadista m.

politics, pol'-i-tiks, s., política f.

poll, poul, s., elección f. v., votar

pollute, po-liuut', v., manchar, contaminar, corromper

pomade, pou-meid', s., pomada f.

pomegranate, pŏm'-grA-net, s., granada f.

pomp, pomp, s., pompa f.; —**ous***, a., pomposo

pond, pond, s., estanque m.

ponder, pon'-da, v., ponderar; —**ous***, a., ponderoso

pontiff, pon'-tif, s., Pontífice m.

pony, pou'-ni, s., haca f., jaco m., poney m.

poodle, puu'-dl, s., perro de lanas m.

pool, puul, s., (water) balsa f. v., (funds) mancomunar intereses

poop, puup, s., popa f.

poor*, púr, a., pobre. s., los pobres m. pl.

pop, pop, s., (of a cork) taponazo m. v., saltar

Pope, poup, s., Papa m.

poplar, pop'-la, s., álamo m.

poppy, pop'-i, s., amapola f.

populace, pop'-iu-las, s., pueblo m.

popular*, pop'-iu-lr, a., popular

populate, pop'-iu-leit, v., poblar

population, po-piu-lei'-shon, s., población f.

populous, pop'-iu-los, a., populoso

porcelain, pórs'-lin, s., porcelana f.

porch, pórch, s., pórtico m., porche m.

porcupine, por'-kiu-pain, s., puerco espín m.

pore, pór, s., poro m.; —**over**, v., estudiar

pork, pórk, s., carne de puerco f.

porous, pó'-ros, a., poroso

porpoise, pôar'-pos, s., puerco marino m.

porridge, por'-ich, s., gachas de avena f. pl.

port, pôrt, s., (wine) oporto m.; (harbour) puerto m.; (naut.) babor m.; ——**hole,** babor m., porta f.

portable, pôr'-ta-bl, a., portátil

portend, poar-tend', v., pronosticar

portentous*, por-ten'-tos, a., portentoso

porter, pôr'-ta, s., (door) portero m.; (luggage) mozo de cordel m.; ——**age,** porte m.

portfolio, pôrt-fou'-li-ou, s., cartera f.; (government) ministerio m.

portion, pôr'-shon, s., porción f.; (share) parte f.

portly, pôrt'-li, a., corpulento; majestuoso

portmanteau, pôrt-man'-tou, s., maleta f.

portrait, pôr'-tret, s., retrato m.

portray, pôr'-trei', v., retratar; (describe) describir

pose, pous, s., postura f. v., colocar; —— **as,** pasar por

position, po-sish'-on, s., posición f.; (job) colocación f.

positive*, pos'-i-tiv, a., positivo; (certain) cierto

possess, po-ses', v., poseer; ——**ion,** s., posesión f.

possessor, po-ses'-er, s., poseedor m.

possibility, pos-i-bil'-i-ti, s., posibilidad f.

possible, pos'-i-bl, a., posible

possibly, pos'-i-bli, adv., posiblemente

post, poust, a., correo m.; (wood, etc.) poste m.; (job) empleo m. v., echar al correo; ——**age,** s., franqueo m.; ——**card,** tarjeta postal f.; ——**date,** v., posfechar; ——**er,** s., cartel m.; —— **free,** a., franco de porte; ——**man,** s., cartero m.; ——**master,** administrador de correos m.; —— **mortem,** autopsia f.; ——**office,** correos m. pl.; ——**pone,** v., diferir, posponer; ——**script,** s., posdata f.

posterior, post-i'-ri-a, a., posterior

posterity, po-stěr'-i-ti, s., posteridad f.

posture, pos'-tiur, s., postura f.

pot, pot, s., pote m.; (flower) tiesto m.; (cooking) olla f.

potash, pot'-ash, s., potasa f.

potato, pou-tei'-tou, s., patata f.

potent*, pou'-tent, a., potente; eficaz; ——**ial,** s.,

potencial m.; a., potencial, eficaz
potion, pou'-shon, s., poción f.
pottery, pot'-er-i, s., alfarería f.
pouch, pauch, s., bolsillo m.; (tobacco) tabaquera f.
poulterer, poul'-ter-a, s., pollero m., gallinero m.
poultice, poul'-tis, s., cataplasma f.
poultry, poul'-tri, s., aves de corral f. pl.
pounce, pauns, v., (on, upon) echarse sobre
pound, paund, s., libra esterlina f.; (weight) libra f.;
(animals) corral m. v., (pulverise) machacar
pour, pór, v., verter; (rain) llover a cántaros
pour out, pór aut, echar; (serve) servir
pout, paut, v., enfurruñarse
poverty, pov'-er-ti, s., pobreza f.
powder, pau'-da, s., polvo m.; (gun) pólvora f.;
(face) polvos m. pl. v., pulverizar; (face) darse
polvos
power, pau'-a, s., poder m.; (mech.) fuerza f.;
(state) potencia f.; **—ful***, a., poderoso;
—less*, impotente
pox, poks, **small—,** s., viruelas f. pl.; **chicken—**, viruelas locas f. pl.
practicability, prak-ti-ka-bil'-i-ti, s., posibilidad
practical*, prak'-ti-kl, a., práctico [f.
practice, prak'-tis, s., práctica f.; (custom) costumbre f.; (professional) clientela f.; (exercise)
ejercicio m.
practise, prak'-tis, v., ejercitarse; (profession) ejercer
practitioner, prak-tish'-on-a, s., médico m.
praise, preis, v., alabar. s., alabanza f., elogio m.
praiseworthy, preis'-uér-Di, a., digno de alabanza
prance, praans, v., cabriolar; (fig.) pavonearse
prank, prangk, s., travesura f., jugarreta f.
prattle, prat'-l, v., charlar. s., charla f.
prawn, proan, s., langostino m.
pray, prei, v., orar, rezar
prayer, preir, s., oración f.; **—book,** devocionario
m.; **Lord's Prayer,** Padre Nuestro m.
preach, priich, v., predicar; **—er,** s., predicador m.
preamble, prii'-am-bel, s., preámbulo m.
precarious*, pri-ké'-ri-os, a., precario

precaution, pri-ko*a*'-shon, s., precaución f.
precede, pri-siid', v., preceder
precedence, prii-sii'-dens, s., precedencia f.
precedent, pres'-ii-dent, s., (example) precedente m.
precept, pri'-sept, s., precepto m.
preceptor, pri-sep'-ta, s., preceptor m.
precinct, prii'-singkt, s., recinto m.
precious*, presh'-os, a., precioso
precipice, pres'-i-pis, s., precipicio m.
precise*, pri-sais', a., exacto; **—ness,** s., exactitud
precision, pri-sish'-on, s., precisión f.   [f.
preclude, pri-kiuud', v., excluir; impedir
precocious*, pri-kou'-shos, a., precoz
predatory, pred'*a*-to-ri, a., de rapiña, rapaz
predecessor, prii-dii-ses'*a*, s., predecesor m.
predicament, pri-dik'*a*-ment, s., predicamento m.
predicate, pred'-i-ket, s., (grammar) atributo m.
predict, pri-dikt', v., predecir
prediction, pri-dik'-shon, s., predicción f.
predominant*, pri-dom'-i-nant, a., predominante
pre-eminent*, prii-em'-i-nent, a., preeminente
preface, pref'-is, s., prefacio m.
prefect, prii'-fekt, s., prefecto m.
prefer, pri-fër', v., preferir
preferable, pref'*er*-a-bl, a., preferible
preference, pref'*er*-ens, s., preferencia f.
prefix, prii-fiks', v., anteponer. s., prefijo m.
pregnancy, preg'-nan-si, s., preñez f.
pregnant, preg'-nant, a., embarazada, encinta;
   (animals) preñada
prejudice, pre'-cHiu-dis, v., perjudicar; predisponer. s., perjuicio m.; **without —,** sin perjuicio
prejudicial*, precH-u-dish'-al, a., perjudicial
prelate, prel'-et, s., prelado m.
preliminary, prii-lim'-i-na-ri, s. & a., preliminar f.
prelude, pre'-liuud, v., preludiar. s., preludio m.
premature, prem'*a*-tiúr, a., prematuro
premeditate, pri-med'-i-teit, v., premeditar
premier, prii'-mi-*a*, s., primer ministro m. a., primero
premises, prem'-i-sis, s. pl., posesiones f. pl.;

edificio m.

premium, prii'-mi-om, s., premio m., prima f.

preparation, prep-a-rei'-shon, s., preparación f.

prepare pri-pér', v., preparar

prepay, pri-pei', v., pagar adelantado

prepossessing, pri-po-ses'-ing, a., simpático, atractivo

preposterous*, pri-pos'-ter-os, a., absurdo

prerogative, prii-rog'-g-tiv, s., prerrogativa f.

prescribe, pri-skraib', v., prescribir

prescription, priis-krip'-shon, s., prescripción f.

presence, pres'-ens, s., presencia f.; — **of mind,** presencia de ánimo f.

present, pri-sent', v., presentar; (gift) regalar

present, pres'-ent, s., regalo m. a., presente; —**ation,** s., presentación f.; —**ly,** adv., luego, en seguida

presentiment, pri-sen'-ti-ment, s., presentimiento m.

preservation, pres-er-vei'-shon, s., (state, condition) preservación f.

preserve, pri-sërv', v., preservar, conservar; guardar; (fruit) confitar; —**s,** s. pl. confitura f.

preside, pri-said', v., presidir

president, pres'-i-dent, s., presidente m.

press, pres, s., prensa f. v., apretar; (fruit) exprimir; (clothes) prensar; —**ing,** a., urgente

pressman, pres'-mʌn, s., periodista m.

pressure, presh'-er, s., presión f.; urgencia f.

presume, pri-siuum, v., presumir; (dare) atreverse

presumption, pri-sömp'-shon, s., presunción f.

pretence, pri-tens', s., pretencia f.; pretexto m.

pretend, pri-tend', v., pretender

pretentious*, pri-ten'-shos, a., presuntuoso

pretext, pri-text', s., pretexto m.

pretty, pri'-ti, a., lindo, bonito

prevail, pri-veil', v., prevalecer; —**upon,** persuadir

prevalent*, prev'-a-lent, a., prevaleciente

prevaricate, pri-var'-i-keit, v., prevaricar

prevent, pri-vent', v., impedir; —**ion,** s., prevención f.; —**ive,** a., preventivo

previous*, prii'-vi-os, a., previo, anterior

prevision, pri-vi'-shon, s., previsión f.

prey, prei, s., presa f.; víctima f. v., robar

price, prais, s., precio m.; **—less,** a., inapreciable

prick, prik, v., picar. s., picadura f.; **—le,** espina f.; **—ly,** a., espinoso

pride, praid, s., orgullo m. v., enorgullecerse

priest, priist, s., sacerdote m.

priggish, prig'-ish, a., afectado, petulante

prim, prim, a., etiquetero; (dress) peripuesto

primary, prai'-ma-ri, a., primario; fundamental

primate, prai'-met, s., primado m.

prime, praim, s., (of life) flor f. a., (quality) selecto. v., preparar; **— minister,** s., presidente del consejo m.

primer, praim'-a, s., libro de prima instrucción m.

primitive, prim'-i-tiv, a., primitivo

primrose, prim'-rous, s., primavera f.

prince, prins, s., príncipe m.

princely, prins'-li, a., grande, noble, regio

princess, prin'-ses, s., princesa f.

principal, prin'-si-pal, s., director m., jefe m.; (funds) principal m. a.,* principal

principle, prin'-si-pl, s., principio m.

print, print, v., imprimir. s., impresión f.; (photo) positiva f.; **—er,** impresor m.; **—ing,** impresión f.; **—ing-works,** imprenta f.

prior, prai'-or, s., prior m. a., anterior. adv., antes de; **—ity,** s., prioridad f.; **—y,** priorato m.

prism, prism, s., prisma m.; **—atic,** a., prismático

prison, pri-sn, s., prisión f.; cárcel f.

prisoner, prii'-son-a, s., prisionero m., preso m.

privacy, prai'-va-si, s., retraimiento m.

private*, prai-vet, a., privado; personal; secreto

privation, prai-vei'-shon, s., privación f.

privilege, priv'-i-lich, s., privilegio m. v., privilegiar

prize, prais, s., premio m. v., apreciar

probable, prob'-a-bl, a., probable

probate, prou-beit, s., adveración de un testamento f.

probation, prou-bei'-shon, s., probación f.; prueba f.; **—er,** meritorio m.; (eccl.) novicio m.

probe, proub, v., sondar. s., sonda f.

probity, prob'-i-ti, s., probidad f.

problem, prob'-lem, s., problema m.

procedure, pro-sii'-diúr, s., proceder m.; (law) procedimiento m.

proceed, pro-siid', v., proceder, continuar; **—ings,** s. pl., procedimiento m.; (law) proceso m.

proceeds, pro'-siids, s. pl., producto m.

process, prou'-ses, s., proceso m.; curso m.

procession, pro-sesh'-on, s., procesión f.

proclaim, pro-kleim', v., proclamar; publicar [f.

proclamation, prok-la-mei'-shon, s., proclamación

proclivity, pro-kliv'-i-ti, s., propensión f. [f.

procastination, pro-kras-ti-nei'-shon, s., dilación

proctor, prok'-ta, s., (university) censor m.

procurable, pro-kiú'-ra-bl, a., asequible

procure, pro-kiúr', v., conseguir; procurar; (pimp) alcahuetear

prod, prod, v., aguijonear. s., aguijón m.

prodigal, prod'-i-gal, a., pródigo

prodigious*, pro-dich'-os, a., prodigioso

prodigy, prod'-ich-i, s., prodigio m.

produce, pro'-diuus', s., producto m.; producción f.

produce, pro-diuus', v., producir. s., producto m.; **—r,** productor m.; (stage) director m.

product, prod'-ökt, s., producto m.; **—ion,** producción f.; (stage) representación f.

profane, pro-fein', v., profanar. a.,* profano

profess, pro-fes', v., profesar; declarar; **—ion,** s., profession f., carrera f.; **—ional,** a., profesional

professor, pro-fess'-a, s., profesor m.

proficiency, pro-fish'-en-si, s., adelanto m.

proficient*, pro-fish'-ent, a., adelantado; versado

profile, prou'-fail, s., perfil m.

profit, prof'-it, s., ganancia f., utilidad f. v., ganar; **—able,** a., provechoso; **—eer,** s., acaparador m.

profligate, prof'-li-guet, a., licencioso, disoluto

profound*, pro-faund', a., profundo

profuse*, pro-fiuus', a., profuso

prognosticate, prog-nos'-ti-keit, v., pronosticar

programme, prou'-gram, s., programa m.

programmer, prou'-gram-a, s., programador m.

progress, pro-gres', v., progresar, adelantar
progress, prou'-gres, s., progreso m., curso m.
prohibit, prou-jib'-it, v., prohibir
prohibition, prou-jib-i'-shon, s., prohibición f.
project, pro-cнekt', v., proyectar, sobresalir.
  s., proyecto m.; **—ile,** proyectil m.; **—ion,**
  proyección f.; **—or,** proyector m.
proletarian, prou-li-té'-ri-an, s. & a., proletario m.
prologue, prou'-log, s., prólogo m.
prolong, prou-long', v., prolongar
promenade, prom-i-naad', s., paseo m. v., pasearse
prominent*, prom'-i-nent, a., prominente
promiscuous*, pro-mis'-kiu-os, a., promiscuo
promise, pro'-mis, s., promesa f. v., prometer
promissory note, prom'-is-o-ri nout, s., pagaré m.
promote, pro-mout', v., promover; fomentar
promoter, pro-mou'-ta, s., promotor m.; **Company —,** fundador m.
promotion, pro-mou'-shon, s., promoción f.
prompt, prompt, a., pronto. v., sugerir; (stage)
  apuntar; **—er,** s., apuntador m.; **—ly,** adv.,
  en punto
promulgate, pro'-mul-gueit, v., promulgar
prone, proun, a., propenso, inclinado
prong, prong, s., púa f., punta f.
pronoun, prou'-naun, s., pronombre m.
pronounce, pro-nauns', v., pronunciar; (sentence) dar
pronunciation, pro-nön-si-ei'-shon, s., pronunciación f.
proof, pruuf, s., prueba f. a., a prueba de
prop, prop, s., apoyo m., puntal m. v., sostener
propaganda, prop-a-guan'-da, s., propaganda f.
propagate, prop'-a-gueit, v., propagar
propel, pro-pel', v., impeler; **—lent,** s., propulsor
  a., propulsante; **—ler,** s., hélice m. & f.
proper*, prop'-a, a., propio; apto; decoroso
property, prop'-er-ti, s., propiedad f., bienes m. pl.
prophecy, prof'-i-si, profecía f.
prophesy, prof'-i-sai, v., profetizar
prophet, prof'-et, s., profeta m., profetisa f.
propitious*, pro-pish'-os, a., propicio

proportion, pro-pór'-shon, s., proporción f.

proposal, pro-pou'-sal, s., propuesta f.; (marriage) declaración f.

propose, pro-pous', v., proponer; declararse

proposition, pro-pos-ish'-on, s., proposición f.

proprietor, pro-prai'-e-ta, s., propietario m.; dueño m.

propriety, pro-prai'-e-ti, s., propiedad f.; decoro m.

propulsion, pro-pól'-shon, s., propulsión f.; impulso [m.

proscribe, pro-skraib', v., proscribir

prose, prous, s., prosa f.

prosecute, pros'-i-kiut, v., (law) procesar

prosecution, pros-i-kiu'-shon, s., prosecución f.

prosecutor, pros'-i-kiu-ta, s., acusador m.

prospect, pros'-pekt, s., perspectiva f. v., explorar

prospective*, pros-pek'-tiv, a., en perspectiva

prospectus, pros-pek'-tos, s., prospecto m.

prosper, pros'-pa, v., prosperar; **—ity,** s., prosperidad f.; **—ous*,** a., próspero

prostitute, pros'-ti-tiuut, s., prostituta f.

prostrate, pros-treit', v., prosternarse. a., postrado

prostration, pros-trei'-shon, s., postración f.

protect, pro-tekt', v., proteger

protection, pro-tek'-shon, s., protección f.

protest, pro-test', v., protestar. s., protesto m.

protract, pro-trakt', v., prolongar, diferir

protrude, pro-truud', v., sobresalir

proud*, praud, a., orgulloso

prove, pruuv, v., probar

proverb, prov'-erb, s., proverbio m.

provide, pro-vaid', v., proveer; estipular

providence, prov'-i-dens, s., providencia f.

provident*, prov'-i-dent, a., providente

provider, pro-vai'-da, s., proveedor m.

province, prov'-ins, s., provincia f.; (sphere) incumbencia f.

provision, pro-vish'-on, provisión f.; estipulación f.; **—al,** a.,* provisorio

provisions, pro-vish'-ons, s. pl., comestibles m. pl.

provocation, prov-o-kei'-shon, s., provocación f.

provoke, pro-vouk', v., provocar

provost, prov'-ost, s., preboste m.

prowl, praul, v., rondar

proximity, prok-sim'-i-ti, s., proximidad f.

proxy, prok'-si, s., apoderado m.; **by —,** por poder

prude, pruud, s., mojigata f.; **—nce,** prudencia f.; **—nt,** a., prudente; **—ry,** s., mojigatería f.

prudish*, pruu'-dish, a., remilgado

prune, pruun, s., ciruela pasa f. v., (trees) podar

pry, prai, v., escudriñar; acechar

psalm, saam, s., salmo m.

pseudonym, siuu'-do-nim, s., seudónimo m.

psychiatry, sai-kai-a-tri, s., psiquiatría f.

psychology, sai-kol'-o-chi, s., psicología f.

public, pŏb'-lik, s., el público m. a.,* público; **—an,** s., tabernero m.; **—house,** taberna f.

publication, pŏb-li-kei'-shon, s., publicación f.; (notification) promulgación f.

publish, pŏb'-lish, v., publicar; (books) editar

publisher, pŏb'-lish-a, s., editor m.

pucker, pŏk'-a, v., fruncir s., pliegue m.

pudding, pud'-ing, s., pudín m.; **black —,** morcilla

puddle, pŏd'-l, s., charco m. [f.

puerile, piu'-er-ail, a., pueril

puff, pŏf, v., soplar. s., (breath) soplo m.; (of wind) ráfaga f.; **powder —,** polvora f. varse f.

puffy, pŏf'-i, a., hinchado, inflado

pug, pŏg, s., (dog) perro faldero m.; **—nacious,** a., pugnaz; **—nosed,** nacho

pull, pul, s., tirón m.; (tension) tirantez f. v., tirar; **— down,** derrumbar; (lower) bajar; **— out,** sacar, extraer; **— up,** levantar, alzar

pullet, pul'-et, s., pollito m., pollita f.

pulley, pul'-i, s., polea f., garrucha f.

pulp, pŏlp, s., f.; **wood—,** pulpa de madera f.

pulpit, pul'-pit, s., púlpito m.

pulse, pŏls, s., pulso m.

pumice-stone, pŏm'-is-ston, s., piedra pómez f.

pump, pŏmp, v., dar a la bomba. s., bomba f.

pumpkin, pŏmp'-kin, s., calabaza f.

pun, pŏn, s., juego de palabras m.

punch, pŏnch, v., dar metidos; perforar; s., metido m.; perforador m.; (drink) ponche m.; (Punch and Judy show) títeres m. pl.

punctilious*, pŏng-ktil'-i-os, a., puntilloso

punctual*, pŏng'-ktiu-al, a., puntual

punctuate, pŏng'-ktiu-eit, v., puntuar

punctuation, pŏng-ktiu-ei'-shon, s., puntuación f.

puncture, pŏng'-ktiur, s., punción f.; (tyre) pinchazo m. v., punzar; (tyre) pinchar

pungency, pŏn'-CHen-si, s., picante m., acerbidad f.

pungent, pŏn'-CHent, a., picante, acre

punish, pŏn'-ish, v., castigar; —**able**, a., punible

punishment, pŏn'-ish-ment, s., castigo m.

punitive, piuu'-ni-tiv, a., penal, punitivo

punt, pŏnt, s., lancha de fondo plano f.

puny, piuu'-ni, a., encanijado; débil

pupil, piuu'-pil, s., alumno m.; (eye) pupila f.

puppet, pŏp'-et, s., muñeco m.; títere m.

puppy, pŏp'-i, s., cachorro m.

purchase, pẽr'-chis, v., comprar. s., compra f.; — **tax**, s., impuesto sobre la compra

purchaser, pẽr'-chis-a, s., comprador m.

pure*, piúr, a., puro; (chaste) casto

purgative, pẽr'-ga-tiv, s., purgante m.

purgatory, pẽr'-ga-to-ri, s., purgatorio m.

purge, pẽrCH, v., purgar; purificar; (med.) purgar

purify, piú'-ri-fai, v., purificar

purity, piú'-ri-ti, s., pureza f.

purloin, pẽr-loin', v., hurtar, robar

purple, pẽr'-pl, s., púrpura f. a., purpúreo

purport, pẽr'-port, s., sentido m. v., significar

purpose, pẽr'-pos, s., intención f., objeto m. v., proponerse

purposely, pẽr'-pos-li, adv., de propósito

purr, pẽr, v., rononear [m.

purse, pẽrs, s., bolsa f., porta-monedas m.; monedero

purser, pẽr'-sa, s., sobrecargo m.

pursue, pẽr-siuu', v., perseguir [f. pl.

pursuit, pẽr-siuut', s., persecución f.; —**s**, tareas

purveyor, pẽr-vei-a, s., proveedor m.

pus, pŏs, s., pus m., materia f.

push, push, v., empujón m. v., empujar

pushing, push'-ing, a., (enterprising) emprendedor

puss, pus, s., micho m.

put, put, v., poner, colocar; — **off**, posponer;

s—18

— **on**, ponerse

putrefy, piuu'-tri-fai, v., pudrirse, corromperse

putrid, piuu'-trid, a., podrido, pútrido

putty, pŏt'-i, s., masilla f.

puzzle, pŏs'-l, v., confundir. s., problema m.; (pastime) rompecabezas m.; **cross word —,** palabras cruzadas f.

pyjamas, pi-chaa'-mas, s. pl., pijamas m. pl.

pyramid, pir'-a-mid, s., pirámide f.

python, pai'-zŏn, s., boa f., pitón m.

quack, kuak, v., graznar. s., curandero m.; charlatán m.; **—ing,** graznido m.

quadrant, kuod'-rant, s., cuadrante f.

quadrille, kua-dril', s., contradanza f.

quadruped, kuod'-ru-ped, s., cuadrúpedo m.

quadruple, kuod'-ru-pl, a., cuadruplo m.

quagmire, kuag'-mair, s., tremadal m.

quail, kueil, s., codorniz f.   [dad f.

quaint*, kueint, a., curioso; **—ness,** s., singulari-

quake, kueik, v., temblar. s., temblor m.; **earth— ,** terremoto m.

quaker, kuei'-ka, s., cuáquero m.

qualification, kuol'-i-fi-kei'-shon, s., calificación f.; resquisito m.

qualify, kuol'-i-fai, v., calificar; habilitarse; (degree) obtener un grado   [pl.

qualities, kuol'-i-tes, s. pl. (things) propiedades f.

quality, kuol'-i-ti, s., calidad f.; (nobility) distinción f.

quandary, koun'-da-ri, s., perplejidad f.

quantity, koun'-ti-ti, s., cantidad f.

quarantine, kour'-an-tiin, s., cuarentena f.

quarrel, kour'-el, s., riña f., pendencia f. v., reñir

quarrelsome, kour'-el-som, a., pendenciero

quarry, kuor'-i, s., cantera f.; (prey) presa f.

quart, kuoart, s., cuarto de galón m.

quarter, kuoar'-ta, v., hacer cuartos. s., cuarto m.; (period) trimestre m.; **—day,** fin de trimestre m.; **—ly,** a., trimestral; **—master,** comisario ordenador m.; (naut.) cabo de brigadas

quartet, kuoar'-tet, s., cuarteto m.   [m.

quartz, kuo*arts,* s., cuarzo m.

quash, kuosh, v., exprimir; (a verdict) anular

quaver, kueí'-v*a,* v., gorjear. s., (mus.) corchea f.

quay, kii, s., muelle m.

queen, kuiin, s., reina f.

queer*, ukir, a., raro, extraño

quell, kuel, v., reprimir; (allay) aquietar

quench, kuench, v., apagar; (thirst) calmar

querulous*, kuer'-u-los, a., querelloso, quejoso

query, (see **question**)

quest, kuest, s., busca f.; investigación f.; informe m.

question, kues'-tyon, v., interrogar; (doubt) dudar. s., pregunta f.; **—able,** a., cuestionable; **—mark,** s., punto de interrogación m.

queue, kiuu, s., cola f., fila f.

quibble, kui'-bl, v., hacer uso de argucias, s., subterfugio m.

quick*, kuik, a., rápido; (wit, etc.) vivo, **—en,** v., animar; (hasten) apresurar; **—lime,** s., cal viva f.; **—ness,** rapidez f.; **—sands,** arena movediza f.; **—silver,** s., azogue m.

quiet, kuai'-et, s., quietud f. a.,* quieto, tranquilo

quill, kuil, s., (pen) pluma de ave f.

quilt, kuilt, s., colcha f.

quince, kuins, s., membrillo m.

quinine, kuiin'-in, s., quinina f.

quire, kua*ir,* s., mano de papel f.

quit, kuit, v., salir de; **—s,** adv., en paz

quite, kuait, adv., enteramente; totalmente

quiver, kuiv'-*a,* v., temblar. s., (sheath) aljaba f.

quoit, koit, s., tejo m.

quota, kuou'-ta, s., cuota f.

quotation, kuou-tei'-shon, s., citación f.; (price) cotización f.

quote, kuout, v., citar; (price) cotizar

rabbi, rab'-ai, s., rabí m.; rabino m.

rabbit, rab'-it, s., conejo m.

rabble, rab'-l, s., populacho m., gentuza f.

rabid*, rab'-id, a., rabioso; (temper) furioso

rabies, rei'-bi-iis, s., rabia f.; hidrofobia f.

race, reis, v., correr. s., (breed) raza f.; (contest)

carrera f.; —**-course,** campo de carreras m.;
—**-horse,** caballo de carrera m.

races, rei'-ses, s., (horse) carreras de caballos f. pl.;
(motor) carreras de automóviles f. pl.

racial, rei'-shal, a., racial, étnico

rack, rak, ε., (torture) rueda f.; (clothes) tendedor
m.; (luggage) percha f.

racket, racquet, rak'-et, s., (sports) raqueta f.

racy, rei'-si, a., picante

radiant, rei'-di-ant, a., radiante, brillante

radiate, rei'-di-eit, v., radiar, irradiar

radiation, rei-di-ei'-shon, s., radiación f., irradia-
ción f.

radiator, rei'-di-ei-ta, s., radiador f.

radio, rei'-di-o, s., radio f.; —**active,** a., radio-
activo; —**activity,** s., radioactividad f.

radish, rad'-ish, s., rábano m.; **horse —,** rábano
picante m.

radium, rei'-di-om, s., radium m.   [picante m.

radius, rei'-di-os, s., radio m.

raffle, raf'-l, s., rifa f. v., rifar

raft, raaft, s., balsa f., almadía f.

rafter, raaf'-ta, s., cabrio m., viga f., traviesa f.

rag, rag, s., trapo m.; —**ged,** a., harapiento

rage, reich, s., rabia f.; furor m. v., enfurecerse

raid, reid, v., invadir. s., incursión f.

rail, reil, v., injuriar. s., (railway) riel m.; (stair)
baranda f.; —**lery,** chocarrería f.

railway, reil'-uei, s., ferrocarril m.

raiment, rei'-ment, s., ropa f.

rain, rein, v., llover. s., lluvia f.; —**bow,** arco
iris m.; —**coat,** impermeable m.; —**fall,**
aguacero m.; (measure) caída de agua f.;
—**water,** agua de lluvia f.; —**y,** a., lluvioso

raise, reis, v., (pick up) recoger; (heighten) elevar;
(pull up) levantar; (crops) cultivar

raisin, rei'-sin, s., pasa f.

rake, reik, s., rastrillo m.; libertino m. v., rastrillar;
(fire) atizar

rally, ral'-i, v., reunir; reanimar   [v., apisonar

ram, ram, s., morueco m.; (battering) ariete m.

ramble, ram'-bl, s., paseo m.; correteo m. v.,
pasearse

rampant, RAM'-pant, a., rampante; (fig.) exuberante

rampart, RAM'-paart, s., terraplén m.; muralla f.

rancid, RAN'-sid, a., rancio

rancour, RAN'-ka, s., rencor m.

random, RAN'-dom, **at —,** adv., al azar

range, REINCH, s., (kitchen) cocina f.; (extent) extensión f.; (mountain) cordillera f.; (practice) campo de tiro m.; (projectile) alcance m. v., arreglar, ordenar; **—-finder,** s., (photog.) telémetro m.; **—r,** s., guardabosque m.

rank, RANGK, a., (taste, smell) rancio. s., grado m.; (row) fila f.; **— and file,** la tropa f.

ransack, RAN'-sak, v., saquear; escudriñar

ransom, RAN'-som, s., rescate m. v., rescatar

rap, RAP, s., golpe seco m. v., (hit) golpear; (knock) llamar, tocar

rape, reip, s., rapto m.; violación f. v., violar

rapid*, RAP'-id, a., rápido; (stream) raudo; **—ity,** s., rapidez f.; **—s,** rabión m.

rapture, RAP'-tiur, s., rapto m.; éxtasis m.

rapier, rei'-pi-a, s., espadín m.

rare*, rér, a., raro; (precious) valioso; (thin) ralo

rarefy, rei'-ri-fai, v., enrarecer, enralar

rarity, ré'-ri-ti, s., rareza f.

rascal, raas'-kl, s., pícaro m.; bribón m.

rash, RASH, a., (skin) sarpullido m. a., temerario; **—er,** s., magra f., lonja f.; **—ness,** temeridad f.

rasp, raasp, s., raspador m. v., raspar

raspberry, raas'-ber-i, s., frambuesa f.

rat, RAT, s., rata f.; **—-trap,** ratonera f.

rate, reit, s., (proportion) razón f.; (exchange) tipo m.; (tax) contribución f.; (price) precio m.; (speed) razón f. v., (value) tasar

rather, raaD'-a, adv., algo; (prefer) más bien, mejor

ratify, RAT'-i-fai, v., ratificar

ratio, rei'-shi-ou, s., proporción f.

ration, rei'-shon, s., ración f.

rational*, RASH'-on-al, a., racional; razonable

rattle, RAT'-l, v., matraquear. s., matraqueo m.; (instrument) matraca f.; (toy) sonajero m.

rattlesnake, RAT'-l-sneik, s., culebra de cascabel f.

ravage, RAV'-ich, s., asolamiento m. v., asolar

rave, reiv, v., enfurecerse; — **about,** entusiasmarse locamente

raven, rei'-n, s., cuervo m.

ravenous*, rav'-en-os, a., voraz

ravine, ra-viin', s., barranca f., garganta f.

raving, rei'-ving, a., delirante; — **mad,** loco rematado

ravish, rav'-ish, v., arrebatar; violar; (charm) encantar; —**ing,** a., encantador

raw, roa, a., crudo; (wound) en carne viva

ray, rei, s., rayo m.

raze, reis, v., arrasar

razor, rei'-sa, s., navaja de afeitar f.; (safety —) maquinilla de afeitar f.; (electric —) maquina de afeitar; —**-blade,** hoja de afeitar f.; —**-strop,** pasador m.

reach, riich, v., (extend to) alcanzar; (arrive) llegar

react, rii-akt', v., reaccionar; —**ion,** s., reacción f.; —**or,** s., reactor

read, riid, v., leer; estudiar; —**er,** s., lector m.; corrector m.; —**ing,** s., lectura f., interpretación f.

readily, red'-i-li, adv., prontamente; de buena gana

readiness, red'-i-nes, s., prontitud f.; buena voluntad f.

ready, red'-i, a., listo, pronto; —**made,** ya hecho

real*, rii'-al, a., real, verdadero

realize, rii'-a-lais, v., darse cuenta; (cash) realizar

realm, relm, s., reino m.

ream, riim, s., resma f.

reap, riip, v., segar; recoger; —**er,** s., segador m.; —**ing machine,** segadora mecánica f.

reappear, rii-a-pir', v., reaparecer

rear, riir, v., criar; (prance) encabritarse. s., (mil.) retaguardia f.; (background) fondo m.

rear-admiral, riir-ad'-mi-ral, s., contralmirante m.

reason, rii'-sn, v., razonar. s., razón f.

reasonable, rii'-sn-a-bl, a., razonable

reassure, rii-a-shúr', v., tranquilizar

rebate, rii-beit', v., rebajar. s., rebaja f.

rebel, reb'-l, s., rebelde m.

rebel, ri-bel', v., rebelarse; —**lion,** s., rebelión f.

rebound, ri-baund', v., rebotar. s., rebote m.

rebuff, ri-bŭf′, v., desairar. s., repulsa f.

rebuke, ri-biuuk′, v., reprender. s., reprensión f.

recall, ri-koal′, v., revocar; recordar

recant, ri-kant′, v., retractarse

recapitulate, ri-ka-pit′iu-leit, v., recapitular

recede, ri-siid′, v., retroceder; cejar

receipt, ri-siit′, s., recibo m. v., dar recibo

receipts, ri-siits′, s. pl., (business) ingresos m. pl.

receive, ri-siiv′, v., recibir; **—r,** s., receptor m.; (bankruptcy) síndico m.

recent*, rii′-sent, a., reciente

receptacle, ri-sep′-ta-kl, s., receptáculo m.

reception, ri-sep′-shon, s., recepción f.

recess, ri-ses′, s., nicho m.; vacaciones f. pl.

recipe, res′-i-pi, s., récipe m., receta f.

reciprocate, ri-sip′-ro-keit, v., reciprocar

recital, ri-sai′-tl, s., relato m.; recital m.

recite, ri-sait′, v., recitar; relatar; declamar

reckless*, rek′-les, a., temerario

reckon, rek′-n, v., contar, calcular, computar

reclaim, ri-kleim′, v., reclamar; (land) rellenar

recline, ri-klain′, v., reclinarse, recostarse

recluse, ri-kluus′, s. & a., recluso m.

recognition, rek-og-nish′-on, s., reconocimiento m.

recognize, rek-og-nais′, v., reconocer

recoil, ri-koil′, v., recular; retroceder. s., retroceso m.

recollect, rek-o-lekt′, v., recordar, acordarse

recollection, rek-o-lek′-shon, s., recuerdo m.

recommence, rii-ko-mens′, v., empezar de nuevo

recommend, rek-o-mend′, v., recomendar; **—ation,** s., recomendación f.

recompense, rek′-om-pens, v., recompensar. s., recompensa f.

reconcile, rek′-on-sail, v., reconciliar

reconsider, rii-kon-sid′-a, v., considerar de nuevo

record, ri-koard′, v., registrar; (tape, disc) grabar

record, rek′-oard, s., registro m.; (gramophone) disco m.

recourse, ri-kórs′, s., recurso m.; remedio m.

recover, ri-kŏv′-a, v., (retrieve) recuperar; (health) restablecerse; **—y,** s., recuperación f.; restablecimiento m.

re-cover, ri-kŏv′-*a,* v., volver a cubrir
recreation, rek-rii-ei′-shon, s., recreo m., diversión f.; **—ground,** campo de recreo m.
recruit, ri-kruut′, s., recluta m. v., reclutar
rectangular, rek-tang′-iuu-lar, *a.,* rectangular
rectify, rek′-ti-fai, v., rectificar; refinar
rector, rek′-ta, rector m.; **—y,** rectoría f.
recumbent, ri-kŏm′-bent, *a.,* recostado, reclinado
recuperate, ri-kiuu′-per-eit, v., restablecerse
recur, ri-kĕr′, v., repetirse, volver
red, red, *a.,* rojo; **—breast,** s., petirrojo m.; **—den,** v., enrojecer; (blush) ruborizarse **—dish,** *a.,* rojizo; **—hot,** candente; **—ness,** s., rojez f.; **—skin,** piel roja f.
redeem, ri-diim′, v., (promise) cumplir; (bonds, etc.) amortizar; (pledge) desempeñar; (soul) redimir
redemption, ri-demp′-shon, s., redención f.; (commercial) amortización f.
redouble, ri-dŏb′-l, v., redoblar
redress, ri-dres′, s., reparación f. reparar
reduce, ri-diuus′, v., reducir; (disgrace) degradar
reduction, ri-dŏk′-shon, s., reducción f.; rebaja f.
reed, riid, s., caña f.
reef, riif, s., arrecife m.; (sail) rizo m. v., arrizar
reek, riik, s., vapor m., humo m. v., humear
reel, riil, s., (cotton, film, fishing) carrete m.; (yarn) devanadera f. v., (sway) tambalear
refer, ri-fĕr′, v., referir, consultar
referee, ref-er-ii′, s., árbitro m.
reference, ref′-er-ens, s., referencia f.; (testimonial) recomendación f.
refine, ri-fain′, v., refinar; **—d*,** *a.,* refinado; culto; **—ment,** s., cultura f.
reflect, ri-flekt′, v., reflejar; meditar; **—ion,** s., reflejo m.; (thought) reflexión f.; (blame) reproche m.; **—or,** s., reflector m.
reflex, rii′-fleks, s., reflejo m.
reform, ri-foarm′, v., reformar; reformarse; **—ation,** s., reformación f.; (church) Reforma f.
refrain, ri-frein′, v., abstenerse
refresh, ri-fresh′, v., refrescar

refreshment, ri-fresh'-ment, s., refrescos m. pl.
refrigerator, ri-frich'-a-rei-ta, s., refrigerador m.; (ice box) nevera f.
refuel, rii-fiu-el, v., reaprovisionar
refuge, ref'-iuuch, s., refugio m.; asilo m.
refugee, ref'-iuu-chi, s., refugiado m.
refund, ri-fönd', v., reembolsar, restituir
refusal, ri-fiuu'-sl, s., negativa f.
refuse, ri-fiuus'. v., rehusar, negar
refuse, ref'-iuus, s., basura f.
refute, ri-fiuut', v., refutar
regain, ri-guein', v., recuperar
regal*, rii'-gl, a., real, regio
regale, ri-gueil', v., agasajar, regalar
regard, ri-gaard', v., observar; considerar. s., consideración f.; —less, a., indiferente
regards, ri-gaards', s. pl.; (greetings) expresiones [f. pl.]
regenerate, ri-chen'-er-eit, v., regenerar
regent, ri'-chent, s., regente m. & f.
regiment, rech'-i-ment, s., regimiento m.
region, rii'-chon, s., región f.; territorio m.; provincia f.
register, rech'-is-ta, s., registro m. v., registrar; (letters) certificar
registrar, rech'-is-traar, s., registrador m.
registration, rech-is-trei'-shon, s., registro m.; inscripción f.
registry, rech'-is-tri, s., oficina de registros f.
regret, ri-gret', v., sentir; arrepentirse. s., sentimiento m.; remordimiento m.
regrettable, ri-gret'-a-bl, a., lamentable
regular*, re'-guiu-la, a., regular
regulate, reg'-iu-leit, v., regularizar, regular
regulation, re'-guiu-lei'-shon, s., regulación f.; regla f.; (official) reglamento m.
rehearsal, ri-jěr'-sl, s., ensayo m.
rehearse, ri-jěrs', v., ensayar, repetir
reign, rein, s., reinar. s., reino m.
reimburse, rii-im-běrs', v., reembolsar
rein, rein, s., rienda f.
reindeer, rein'-dir, s., reno m.
reinforce, rii-in-fórs', v., reforzar

reinstate, rii-in-steit', v., reintegrar

reject, ri-cHekt', v., rechazar; (spurn) desechar

rejoice, ri-chois', v., regocijarse, alegrarse

rejoicings, ri-chois'-ings, s. pl., (public) fiestas f. pl.

rejuvenate, ri-cHuu'-ven-eit, v., rejuvenecer

relapse, ri-laps', s., recaída f. v., recaer

relate, ri-leit', v., relatar; —**d,** a., relacionado

relation, ri-lei'-shon, s., relación f.; pariente m.

relative, rel'-a-tiv, s., pariente m. a.,* relativo

relax, ri-laks', v., relajar; —**ing,** a., enervante

relay, ri-lei', v., (radio) transmitir. s., trasmisión f.

release, ri-liis', v., soltar, libertar. s., alivio f.

relent, ri-lent', v., aplacarse; —**less***, a., implacable

relevant, rel'-i-vant, a., aplicable, apropiado

reliable, ri-lai'-a-bl, a., seguro; veraz

reliance, ri-lai'-ans, s., confianza f.

relic, rel'-ik, s., reliquia f.; resto m.

relief, ri-liif', s., (anxiety, pain) alivio m.; (help) socorro m.; (raised) relieve m.

relieve, ri-liiv', v., aliviar; socorrer

religion, ri-licH'-on, s., religión f.

religious*, ri-licH'-os, a., religioso

relinquish, ri-ling'-kuish, v., abandonar; ceder

relish, rel'-ish, v., saborear. s., sabor m.

reluctance, ri-lók'-tans, s., repugnancia f.

reluctant*, ri-lók'-tant, a., recalcitrante

rely, ri-lai', v.. confiar

remain, ri-mein', v., quedar; permanecer; —**der,** s., residuo m.; —**s,** restos m. pl.

remand, ri-maand', v., (law) devolver a la cárcel

remark, ri-maark', s., observación f. v., observar

remarkable, ri-maark'-a-bl, a., notable

remedy, rem'-i-di, s., remedio m. v., remediar

remember, ri-mem'-ba, v., acordarse de, recordar

remembrance, ri-mem'-brans, s., recuerdo m.

remind, ri-maind', v., recordar

remit, ri-mit', v., remitir; —**tance,** s., remisa f.

remnant, rem'-nant, s., resto m.; —**s,** retazos m. pl.; retal m.

remonstrate, ri-mon'-streit, v., reconvenir, objetar

remorse, ri-moars', s., remordimiento m.

remote*, ri-mout', a., remoto, distante

removal, ri·muu'·val, s. mudanza f.

remove, ri·muuv', v., mudar.

remunerate, ri·miuu'·ner·eit, v., remunerar

remunerative*, ri·miuu'·ner·ei·tiv, a., lucrativo

rend, rend, v., rasgar; — **er,** (aid, service) prestar; (account) presentar; —**ing,** s., traducción f.

renegade, ren'·i·gueid, s., renegado m.

renew, ri·niuu', v., renovar

renewal, ri·niuu'·al, s., renovación f.

renounce, ri·nauns', v., renunciar

renovate, ren'·o·veit, v., renovar

renown, ri·naun', s., renombre m.; fama f.

rent, rent, s., renta f.; (tear) rasgón m. v., alquilar

renunciation, ri·nön·si·ei'·shon, s., renunciación f.

repair, ri·pér', s., reparación f. v., reparar

reparation, rep·a·rei'·shon, s., reparación f.

repartee, rep·ar·tii', s., réplica f.

repeal, ri·piil', v., revocar. s., revocación f.

repeat, ri·piit', v., repetir

repel, ri·pel', v., repeler; —**lent,** a., repulsivo

repent, ri·pent', v., arrepentirse

repetition, rep·i·tish'·on, s., repetición f.

replace, ri·pleis', v., reponer; reemplazar

replenish, ri·plen'·ish, v., volver a llenar, rellenar

reply, ri·plai', s., respuesta f. v., responder

report, ri·pórt', s., informe m.; (school) notas f. pl.; (noise) estampido m. v., informar; denunciar

reporter, ri·pór'·ta, s., (journalist) reporter m.

repose, ri·pous', v., reposar

repository, ri·pos'·i·to·ri, s., depósito m.

represent, rep·ri·sent', v., representar; —**ation,** s., representación f.; —**ative,** representante m.

reprieve, ri·priiv', v., indultar. s., indulto m.

reprimand, rep·ri·maand', v., reprender. s., reprimenda f.

reprint, ri·print', v., reimprimir. s., reimpresión f.

reprisal, ri·prai'·al, s., represalia f.

reproach, ri·prouch', v., reprochar. s., reproche m.

reprobate, rep'·ro·bet, s., réprobo m.

reproduce, rii·pro·diuus', v., reproducir [f.

reproduction, rii·pro·dök'·shon, s., reproducción

reproof, ri·pruuf', s., reprobación f.

reprove, ri-pruuv', v., reprobar, reprender
reptile, rep'-tail, s., reptil m.
republic, ri-pŏb'-lik, s., república f.
repudiate, ri-piuu'-di-eit, v., repudiar
repugnant*, ri-pŏg'-nænt, a., repugnante
repulse, ri-pŏls', v., repulsar, repeler
repulsive*, ri-pŏl'-siv, a., repulsivo
reputation, rep-iu-tei'-shon, s., reputación f.
repute, ri-piuut', s., fama f.
request, ri-kuest', s., ruego m.; petición f. v., rogar
require, ri-kuair', v., necesitar; requerir; **—ment,**
    s., necesidad f.; requerimiento m.
requisite, rek'-ui-sit, s., requisito m. a.. necesario
rescind, ri-sind', v., rescindir, anular
rescue, res'-kiuu, v., salvar. s., salvación f.
research, ri-sĕrch', s., investigación f.
resemble, ri-sem'-bl, v., parecerse
resent, ri-sent', v., resentirse; **—ful*,** a., resen-
    tido; **—ment,** s., resentimiento m.
reservation, ri-sŏr-vei'-shon, s., reservación f.
reserve, ri-sŏrv', v., reserva f. v., reservar
reservoir, res'-ŏr-voar, s., depósito m.
reside, ri-said', v., residir
residence, res'-i-dens, s., residencia f.
resident, res'-i-dent, a., residente. s., habitante m.
resign, ri-sain', v., abandonar; (a post) dimitir;
    (oneself) resignarse
resin, res'-in, s., resina f.; (violin) colofonia f.
resist, ri-sist', v., resistir; **—ance,** s., resistencia f.
resolute*, res'-o-liuut, a., resoluto, determinado
resolution, res-o-liuu'-shon, s., resolución f.
resolve, ri-solv', v., resolver, decidir
resort, ri-soart', v., recurrir
resound, ri-sound', v., resonar, retumbar   [m. pl.
resource, ri-sŏrs', s., recurso m.; **—s,** recursos
respect, ri-spekt', v., respetar. s., respeto m.;
    —ability, respetabilidad f.; **—able,** a., respe-
    table; **—ful*,** respetuoso; **—ive*,** respectivo
respire, ri-spair', v., respirar
respite, res'-pit, s., tregua f.
respond, ri-spond', v., responder
respondent, ri-spon'-dent, s., demandado m.

response, ri-spons', s., respuesta f.

responsible, ri-spon'-si-bl, a., responsable

rest, rest, s., descanso m.; (sleep) reposo m.; (re-mainder) resto m. v., descansar; **—ful,** a., tranquilo; **—ive,** impaciente; **—less,** inquieto

restaurant, res'-tou-rant, s., restaurante m.; **—car,** coche restaurant m.

restore, ri-stór', v., restituir; (health) restaurar

restrain, ri-strein', v., refrenar; (law) prohibir; **—t,** s., refrenamiento m.; sujeción f.

restrict, ri-strikt', v., restringir; coartar

restriction, ri-strik'-shon, s., restricción f.

result, ri-sölt', v., resultar; s., resultado m.

resume, ri-siuum', v., resumir, continuar

resumption, ri-sömp'-shon, s., reasunción f.

resurrection, res-er-rek'-shon, s., resurrección f.

retail, ri-teil', v., vender al por menor. s., venta al por menor f.; **—er,** revendedor m.

retain, ri-tein', v., retener; (keep) guardar

retaliate, ri-tal'-i-eit, v., desquitarse

retard, ri-taard', v., retardar, demorar

reticent*, ret'-i-sent, a., reservado

retinue, ret'-i-niuu, s., comitiva f., séquito m.

retire, ri-tair', v., retirarse; retirar; **—ment,** s., retiro m.; retraimiento m.

retort, ri-toart', v., replicar. s., réplica f.

retract, ri-trakt', v., retractar; retractarse

retreat, ri-triit', v., retirarse. s., retreta f.

retrospect, ret'-ros-pekt', s., mirada retrospectiva f.

return, ri-törn', v., volver; (give back) devolver, s., vuelta f.; **—s,** ganancia f.; **—ticket,** billete de ida y vuelta m.

reveal, ri-viil', v., revelar

revel, rev'-l, v., parrandear. s., orgía f.

revenge, ri-vench', v., vengarse. s., venganza f.

revenue, rev'-i-niuu, s., renta f.; ingreso m.

revere, ri-vir', v., reverenciar

reverend, rev'-er-end, a., reverendo

reverse, ri-vörs', v., invertir; (engine) hacer marcha atrás. s., reverso m.; (defeat) revés m. a., contrario

revert, ri-vört', v., volver; retroceder

review, ri-viuu', v., (consider) revisar; (inspect)

revistar; (books, etc.) criticar. s., revista f., (books) crítica f.

revile, ri-vail', v., injuriar; ultrajar; denigrar

revise, ri-vais', v., revisar

revision, ri-vish'-on, s., revisión f.

revive, ri-vaiv', v., avivar; reanimarse; resucitar

revoke, ri-vouk', v., revocar, s., (cards) renuncio m.

revolt, ri-volt', v., rebelarse. s., revuelta f.

revolve, ri-volv', v., revolver; girar

revolver, ri-vol'-va, s., revólver m.

reward, ri-uoard', v., remunerar. s., premio m.

rheumatism, ruu'-ma-tism, s., reumatismo m.

rhinoceros, rai-nos'-e-ros, s., rinoceronte m.

rhubarb, ruu'-baarb, s., ruibarbo m.

rhyme, raim, v., rimar. s., rima f.

rib, rib, s., costilla f.

ribbon, rib'-on, s., cinta f.; (medal) condecoración f.

rice, rais, s., arroz m.

rich*, rich, a., rico; —es, s. pl., riqueza f.

rick, rik, s., niara f.

rickets, rik'-ets, s., raquitismo m.

rickety, rik'-et-i, a., (shaky) desvencijado

rid, rid, v., desembarazar; librar

riddle, rid'-l, s., enigma m. v., acribillar

ride, raid, v., ir a caballo; ir en auto: ir en bicicleta

ridge, rich, s., (mountain) cumbre f.

ridicule, rid'-i-kiuul, v., ridiculizar. s., ridículo m.

ridiculous*, ri-dik'-iu-los, a., ridículo; risible

rifle, rai'-fl, v., robar; pillar. s., fusil m.

rift, rift, s., (crack) grieta f.; (cleft) hendedura f.

rig, rig, v., (naut.) aparejar. s., (ship) aparejo m.

right, rait, s., derecho m. v., enderezar. a.,* derecho; justo

rigid*, rich'-id, a., rígido; tieso

rigorous*, rig'-or-os, a., rigoroso; duro

rigour, rig'-a, s., rigor m.

rim, rim, s., borde m.; (wheel) llanta f.

rind, raind, s., corteza f.; (bacon) pellejo m.

ring, ring, v., tocar. s., anillo m., (circus) redondel

ringleader, ring'-lii-da, s., cabecilla m.   [m.

rinse, rins, v., enjuagar

riot, rai'-ot, s., tumulto m. v., amotinarse

rip, rip, v., hender; (cloth) rasgar
ripe, raip, a., maduro; **—n,** v., madurar
ripple, rip'-l, s., onda f.
rise, rais, v., subir; (stand up, revolt, etc.) levantarse; (river) crecer; (sun) salir. s., subida f.
risk, risk, s., riesgo m.; peligro m. v., arriesgar
rite, rait, s., rito m.; **—s,** (funeral) exequias f. pl.
rival, rai'-vl, a., rival. s., rival m.; competidor m.
river, riv'-a, s., río m.
rivet, riv'-et, s., remache m. v., remachar
road, roud, s., camino m.
roam, roum, v., vagar
roar, rór, v., rugir. s., rugido m.
roast, roust, v., asar. s., asado m.
rob, rob, v., robar, hurtar; **—ber,** s., ladrón m.
robbery, rob'-er-i, s., robo m., hurto m.
robe, roub, s., traje m.; (eccl.) vestimenta f.
robin, rob'-in, s., petirrojo m.
robust*, ro-böst', a., robusto; vigoroso
rock, rok, v., (roll) bambolear; (cradle) mecer. s., roca f.; **—y,** a., peñascoso
rocket, rok'-et, s., cohete m.
rod, rod, s., vara f.; (fishing) caña de pescar f.
roe, rou, s., (deer) corzo m.; (fish) hueva f.
rogue, roug, s., bribón m.; **—ry,** bribonada f.
roll, roul, v., rodar; (-up) enrollar. s., rollo m.; (bread) bollo m.; **—-call,** acto de pasar lista m.; **—er,** rodillo m.; **—er-skate,** patín de ruedas m.
romance, rou-mans', s., romance m.; novela f.
romp, romp, v., retozar
roof, ruuf, s., tejado m.; (mouth) paladar m.
rook, ruk, s., corneja f.
room, ruum, s., cuarto m.; (space) espacio m.
roost, ruust, v., descansar en una percha
root, ruut, s., raíz f. v., arraigarse
rope, roup, s., cuerda f.; (naut.) cordaje m.
rosary, rou'-sa-ri, s., jardín de rosales m.
rose, rous, s., rosa f.; **—-bush,** rosal m.
rosemary, rous'-ma-ri, s., romero m.
rosy, rou'-si, a., rosado, sonrosado
rot, rot, v., pudrirse. s., putrefacción f.
rotate, rou'-teit, v., girar

rotten, rot'-n, a., podrido, putrefacto

rouge, ruush, s., colorete m.

rough*, rŏf, a., (coarse) áspero; (manners) grosero; (crude) tosco; (sea, wind) borrascoso; (bumpy) escabroso; **—ness,** s., aspereza f.; groseria f.; tosquedad f.

round, raund, a.,* redondo; circular. v., redondear. s., círculo m.; **—about,** a., indirecto. s., tiovivo m.; **—ness,** redondez f.

rouse, raus, v., provocar; (awaken) despertar

rout, raut, v., (mil.) derrotar. s., derrota f.

route, ruut, s., ruta f.; itinerario m

routine, ru-tiin', s., rutina f.

rove, rouv, v., errar, vagar

row, rou, v., remar. s., hilera f., fila f.

row, rau, s., riña f.

royal*, roi'-αl, a., real; **—ty,** s., realeza f.; (payment) derechos de autor m. pl.

rub, rŏb, v., frotar; **—** frotamiento m.; **—off,** limpiar; **—out,** borrar; **—ber,** s., caucho m.; (eraser) goma de borrar f.

rubbish, rŏb'-ish, s., escombro m., basura f.; (nonsense) disparate m.

ruby, ruu'-bi, s., rubí m.; (colour) carmín m.

rudder, rŏd'-α, s., timón m.

rude, ruud, a., descortés; (manner) brusco

rudiment, ru'-di-ment, s., rudimento m.

rue, ruu, v., lamentar; **—ful,** a., lamentable

ruffian, rŏf'-i-αn, s., rufián m.

ruffle, rŏf'-l, v., desordenar; incomodar

rug, rŏg, s., manta f.; (mat) tapete m.

rugged*, rŏ'-guid, a., (scenery) escarpado

ruin, ruu'-in, v., arruinar. s., ruina f.

rule, ruul, v., gobernar; (lines) reglar. s., (regulation) regla f.; reglamento m.

ruler, ruu'-lα, s., (drawing) regla f.

rum, rŏm, s., rón m.

rumble, rŏm'-bl, s., ruido sordo m.

rummage, rŏm'-ech, v., revolver

rumour, ruu'-mα, s., rumor m.

run, rŏn, v., correr; (colours) extenderse; **—away,** huir. s., (horse) caballo desbocado m.

rupture, rŏp′-tiur, s., hernia f.; ruptura
rural*, ru′-rl, a., campestre
rush, rŏsh, s., carrera precipitada f.; (water) torrente m.; (people) agolpamiento m.; (reed) junco m. v., precipitarse, agolparse; — **hour,** s., hora punta, hora de afluencia f.
rust, rŏst, v., oxidarse. s., orín m.; —**y,** a., oxidado
rustic, rŏs′-tik, a. & s., rústico m.
rustle, rŏs′-l, v., susurrar; (silk) crujir. s., susurro m.; crujido m.
rut, rŏt, s., rodada f.; surco m.
rye, rai, s., centeno m.

sable, sei′-bl, s., marta f., cebellina f.
sack, sak, s., saco m. v., (mil.) saquear
sacrament, sak′-ra-ment, s., sacramento m.
sacred*, sei′-krid. a., sagrado; consagrado
sacrifice, sak′-ri-fais, v., sacrificar. s., sacrificio m.
sacrilege, sak′-ri-liCH, s., sacrilegio m.
sad*, sad, a., triste; —**ness,** s., tristeza f.
saddle, sad′-l, s., silla de montar f. v., ensillar
saddler, sad′-la, s., sillero m.
safe, seif, a., seguro. s., caja fuerte f.; (ice) frigorífico m.; —**guard,** salvaguardia f. v., proteger; —**ty,** s., seguridad f.
sag, sag, v., combarse
sagacious*, sa-guei′-shos, a., sagaz
sage, seiCH, s., sabio m.; (herb) salvia f. a., sabio
sail, seil, v., navegar; (leave) zarpar s., vela f.
sailor, seil′-a, s., marinero m.
saint, seint, s., santo m., santa f. a., santo
sake, seik, s., causa f.; consideración f.; amor m.
salad, sal′-ad, s., ensalada f.
salary, sal′-a-ri, s., salario m.; sueldo m.
sale, seil, s., venta f.; liquidación f.; —**able,** a., vendible; —**sman,** s., vendedor m.
salient, sei′-li-ent, a., saliente, saledizo
saliva, sa-lai′-va, s., saliva f.
sallow, sal′-ou, a., cetrino
salmon, sam′-on, s., salmón m.
saloon, sa-luun′, s., salón m.; **dining**—, comedor m.

salt, s<small>O</small>alt, s., sal m. & f. a., salado; **—-cellar,** salero m.

salute, s<small>a</small>-luut', v., saludar. s., saludo m.

salvage, s<small>A</small>l'-vich, s., salvamento m. v., salvar

salvation, s<small>A</small>l-vei'-shon, s., salvación f.; **— army,** Ejército de Salvación m.

salver, s<small>A</small>l'-v<small>a</small>, s., bandeja f.

same, seim, a. & pron., mismo

sample, saam'-pl, v., probar. s., muestra f.

sanctimonious*, s<small>A</small>ng<small>k</small>-ti-m<small>o</small>u'-ni-os, a., devoto

sanction, s<small>A</small>ng<small>k</small>'-shon, s., sanción f. v., sancionar

sanctity, s<small>A</small>ng<small>k</small>'-ti-ti, s., santidad f.

sanctuary, s<small>A</small>ng<small>k</small>'-tiu-<small>a</small>-ri, s., santuario m.

sand, s<small>A</small>nd, s., arena f.; **—y,** a., arenoso, de arena

sandal, s<small>A</small>n'-dl, s., sandalia f.

sandwich, s<small>A</small>nd'-uich, s., bocadillo m.

sane*, sein, a., cuerdo

sanguine*, s<small>A</small>ng'-guin, a., sanguíneo; vehemente

sanitary, s<small>A</small>n'-i-ta-ri, a., sanitario; **— towel,** s., paño higiénico m.

sanity, s<small>A</small>n'-i-ti, s., cordura f.

sap, s<small>A</small>p, v., zapar. s., savia f.; **—per,** zapador m.

sapphire, s<small>A</small>f'-air, s., zafiro m.

sarcasm, saar'-kasm, s., sarcasmo m.

sarcastic, s<small>A</small>r-k<small>A</small>s'-tik, a., sarcástico

sardine, s<small>A</small>r-diin', s., sardina f.

sash, s<small>A</small>sh, s., (belt) faja f.

satchel, s<small>A</small>tsh'-l, s., mochila f.; (school) bolsa f.

satellite, s<small>A</small>t'-e-lait, s., satélite m.

satiate, sei'-shi-eit, v., saciar, hartar

satin, s<small>A</small>t'-in, s., raso m. a., de raso

satire, s<small>A</small>t'-air, s., sátira f.

satisfaction, s<small>A</small>t-is-f<small>A</small>k'-shon, s., satisfacción f.

satisfactory, s<small>A</small>t-is-f<small>A</small>k'-to-ri, a., satisfactorio

satisfy, s<small>A</small>t'-is-fai, v., satisfacer

saturate, s<small>A</small>t'-iu-reit, v., saturar

Saturday, s<small>A</small>t'-er-di, s., sábado m.

satyr, s<small>A</small>t'-er, s., sátiro m.

sauce, s<small>O</small>as, s., salsa f.; **—pan,** cacerola f.

saucer, s<small>O</small>a'-sa, s., platillo m.

saucy, s<small>O</small>a'-si, a., (fam.) descarado

saunter, s<small>O</small>an'-ta, v., vagar

sausage, so'-sich, s., salchicha f.

savage*, sav'-ich, a., salvaje; feroz. s., salvaje m.

save, seiv, v., salvar; (economize) ahorrar; (keep) guardar

saving, sei'-ving, a., económico; frugal. s., ahorro m.; economía f.

saviour, sei'-vi-a, s., salvador m.; (Jesus) el Redentor m.

savour, sei'-va, s., sabor m.

savoury, sei'-va-ri, s., entremés m. a., sabroso

saw, soa, s., sierra f. v., serrar

say, sei, v., decir

saying, sei'-ing, s., dicho m., proverbio m.

scabbard, skab'-erd, s., (sword) vaina de espada f.

scaffold, skaf'-old, s., (building) andamio m.; (execution) patíbulo m.; **—ing,** andamiada f.

scald, skoald, v., escaldar

scale, skeil, v., escamar; (climb) escalar. s., (fish) escama f.; (measure) escala f.; (music) gama f.

scales, skeils, s. pl., balanza f.

scallop, skal'-op, s., (fish) venera f.

scalp, skalp, s., cuero cabelludo m.

scamp, skamp, s., bribón m., pícaro m.

scamper, skam'-pa, v., escaparse

scan, skan, v., escudriñar

scandal, skan'-dl, s., escándalo m.

scandalous*, skan'-dal-os, a., escandaloso

scanty, skan'-ti, a., escaso

scapegoat, skeip'-gout, s., víctima propiciatoria f.

scar, skaar, s., cicatriz f. v., marcar con una cicatriz

scarce*, skérs, a., escaso

scarcity, skér'-si-ti, s., escasez f., carestía f.

scare, skér, s., susto m. v., asustar; **—away,** espantar; **—crow,** s., espantajo m.

scarf, skaarf, s., banda f.

scarlet, skaar'-let, a., de color escarlata. s., escarlata f.; **—fever,** escarlatina f.

scathing*, skei'-Ding, a., dañoso

scatter, skat'-a, v., esparcir; (wealth) disipar; **— brained,** a., atolondrado

scavenger, skav'-en-cha, s., basurero m.

scene, siin, s., escena f.

scenery, sii'-ner-i, s., paisaje m.; vista f.; (theatre) decoraciones f. pl.

scent, sent, s., perfume m.; (flowers) fragancia f.; (track) pista f. v., perfumar

sceptical*, skep'-ti-kal, a., escéptico

sceptre, sep'-ta, s., cetro m.

schedule, shed'-iuul, s., cédula f.; anexo m.

scheme, skiim, s., proyecto m., plan m. v., proyectar

schism, sism, s., cisma f.

schist, shist, s., esquisto m.

scholar, skol'-a, s., escolar m.; (pupil) alumno m.

scholarship, skol'-er-ship, s., (prize) beca f.

school, skuul, s., escuela f.; **—master,** maestro de escuela m.; **—mistress,** maestra de escuela f.

schooner, skuun'-a, s., goleta f.

sciatica, sai-At'-i-ka, s., ciática f.

science, sai'-ens, s., ciencia f.

scientific, sai'-en-ti-fik, a., científico

scion, sai'-on, s., vástago m., descendiente m.

scissors, sis'-ers, s. pl., tijeras f. pl.

scoff, skof v., burlarse

scold, skould, v., regañar; reñir

scoop, skuup, s., pala de mano f. v., ahuecar

scope, skoup, s., esfera f.; (aim) objeto m.

scorch, skoarch, v., chamuscar; (sun) abrasar

score, skór, s., (number) veintena f.; (games) puntos m. pl. v., ganar; (cut) hacer muescas; (record) marcar

scorn, skoarn, s., desdén m. v., desdeñar

scornful, skoarn'-ful, a., desdeñoso

scoundrel, skaun'-drel, s., pícaro m.

scour, skaur, v., fregar; estregar, rascar

scourge, skërch, v., azotar. s., azote m.

scout, skaut, s., escucha m.; (boy) explorador m. v., explorar

scowl, skaul, v., mirar con ceño s., ceño m.

scraggy, skra'-gui, a., (thin) flaco

scramble, skram'-bl, s., (struggle) arrebatiña f. v., (climb) trepar; **— for,** arrebatarse

scrap, skrap, s., fragmento m.; (cloth) retal m.

scrape, skreip, v., raspar. s., raspadura f.

scraper, screi'-pa, s., raspador m.

scratch, skrach, s., arañazo m., rasguño m.; (sport) línea de partida f. v., arañar; (rub oneself) rascar; (glass) rayar; (sports) abandonar

scream, skriim, v., chillar. s., chillido m.

screen, skriin, s., (fire, cinema, light) pantalla f.; (wind) biombo m.; (partition) tabique m. v. proteger

screw, skruu, s., tornillo m. v., atornillar; **—driver,** s., destornillador m.

scribble, skrib'-l, v., borrajear, garabatear s. garabatos m. pl.

scrip, skrip, s., cédula f.; certificado provisional m.

Scripture, skrip'-tiur, s., Sagrada Escritura f.

scrofula, skrof'-iuu-la, s., escrófula f.

scroll, skroul, s., rollo de papel m.; lista f.

scrub, skröb, s., fregar; frotar. s., (bush) matorral m.

scruple, skruu'-pl, v., tener escrúpulos s., escrúpulo [m.

scrupulous*, skruu'-piu-los, a., escrupuloso

scrutinize, skruu'-ti-nais, v., escudriñar

scuffle, sköf'-l, v., pelear. s., pelea f.; riña f.

scull, sköl, v., bogar con espadilla. s., remo de es-[padilla m.

scullery, sköl'-er-i, s., fregadero m.

sculptor, skölp'-ta, s., escultor m.

sculpture, skölp'-tiur, s., escultura f. v., esculpir

scum, sköm, s., espuma f.; espumar

scurf, skörf, s., caspa f.

scurrilous*, skör'-i-los, a., grosero; injurioso

scurvy, skör'-vi, s., escorbuto m a., vil, ruín

scuttle, sköt'-l, s., (coal) cubo para carbón m. v. echar a pique

scythe, saiD, s., guadaña f.

sea, sii, s., mar m. & f.; **—man,** marino m.; **—sick,** a., mareado; **—side,** s., costa f.; playa f.; **—weed,** s., alga marina f.; **—worthy,** a., capaz de navegar

seal, siil, v., sellar. s., sello m.; (animal) foca f.; **—ing-wax,** lacre m.; **—skin,** piel de foca f.

seam, siim, v., coser. s., costura f.; (mine) vena f.; filón m.; **—stress,** costurera f.

sear, sir, v., (dry up) agostar; (burn)⁹ quemar; (brand) herrar a fuego. a., (withered) marchito

search, sĕrch, v., buscar; examinar. s., busca f.; (Customs) examen m.; —**light**, reflector m.

season, sii´-sn, v., sazonar; (timber) secar. s., estación f.; (fashionable) temporada f.; —**able**, del tiempo; —**ticket**, s., abono m.

seasoning, sii´-son-ing, s., condimento m.

seat, siit, s., asiento m.; (bench) banco m.; (country estate) quinta f. v., sentar

secluded, si-kluu´-did, a., retirado

seclusion, si-kluu´-shon, s., reclusión f., retiro m.

second, sek´-ond, v., (support) secundar. s., (time; number) segundo m.; (duel, etc.) padrino m a., segundo; —**-hand**, de ocasión

secrecy, sii´-kri-si, s., secreto m., reserva f.

secret, sii´-krit, s., secreto m. a.,* secreto

secretary, sek´-ri-ta-ri, s., secretario m.

secrete, si-kriit´, v., esconder; (separate) secretar

secretion, si-krii´-shon, s., secreción f.

sect, sekt, s., secta f.

section, sek´-shon, s., sección f.; (cross) corte transversal m.

secular, sek´-iuu-la, a., secular; seglar

secure, si-kiúr´, v., asegurar, a.,* seguro

securities, si-kiúr´-i-tis, s. pl., valores m. pl.

security, si-kiú´-ri-ti, s., seguridad f.; garantía f.

sedate, si-deit´, a., sosegado; formal

sedative, sed´-a-tiv, a., calmante m.; sedativo m.

sedentary, sed´-en-ta-ri, a., sedentario

sediment, sed´-i-ment, s., sedimento m., hez f.

sedition, si-dish´-on, s., sedición f.

seditious, si-dish´-os, a., sedicioso

seduce, si-diuus´, v., seducir

see, sii, v., ver; — **through**, ver a través; (fig.) penetrar; — **to**, cuidar

seed, siid, s., semilla f., simiente f.

seek, siik, v., buscar; (strive) ambicionar

seem, siim, v., parecer; —**ly**, a.,* decente

seethe, siiD, v., hervir; bullir; (unrest) fermentar

seize, siis, v., asir, tomar; (law) embargar

seizure, sii´-sher, s., asimiento m.; (law) embargo m.; (stroke) ataque m.

seldom, sel´-dm, adv., raramente

select, si-lekt′, v., escoger. a., selecto, escogido
selection, si-lek′-shon, s., selección f.
self, self, a., mismo; **one—,** pron., sí mismo; **—ish,** a., egoísta; **—ishness,** s., egoísmo m.; **—starter,** (motor) arranque automático m.
sell, sel, v., vender; **—er,** s., vendedor m.
semblance, sem′-blans, s., semejanza f.
semi, sem′-i, semi, medio; **—circle,** s., semi-círculo m.; **—colon,** punto y coma m.
semolina, sem-o-li′-na, s., sémola f.
senate, sen′-et, s., senado m.
send, send, v., enviar o despachar; **— away,** (dis-miss) despedir; **— back,** devolver; **—er,** s., remitente m.; **— for,** v., enviar por; **— in advance,** enviar por adelantado
senile, sii′-nail, a., senil, caduco
senior, sii′-ni-a, a., mayor. s., mayor m.; **—-partner,** socio principal m.
sensation, sen-sei′-shon, s., sensación f.
sense, sens, s., sentido m.; **—less,** a., sin sentido
sensible, sen′-si-bl, a., sensato
sensitive, sen′-si-tiv, a., sensitivo
sensual*, sen′-shu-al, a., sensual
sentence, sen′-tens, s., frase f.; (law) sentencia f. v., condenar
sentiment, sen′-ti-ment, s., sentimiento m.; opi-nión f.
sentry, sen′-tri, s., centinela m.; **—-box,** garita f.
separable, sep′-a-ra-bl, a., separable
separate, sep′-a-reit, v., separar; dividir
separation, sep-a-rei′-shon, s., separación f.; (law) separación judicial f.
September, sep-tem′-ba, s., septiembre m.
septic, sep′-tik, a., séptico
sequel, sii′-kuel, s., secuela f.; consecuencia f.
sequence, sii′-kuens, s., serie f.; orden de sucesión
serenade, ser-i-neid′, s., serenata f. [m.
serene*, si-riin′, a., sereno; tranquilo
serge, sẽrCH, s., sarga f., estameña f.
sergeant, saar′-chent, s., sargento m.
serial, sii′-ri-al, a, consecutivo, s. folletín m.; serial m.
series, si′-riis, s., serie f.

serious*, si′-ri-os, a., serio
sermon, sĕr′-mon, s., sermón m.
serpent, sĕr′-pent, s., serpiente f.
serum, sir′-um, s., suero m.
servant, sĕr′-vant, s., criado m.; (maid) criada f.
serve, sĕrv, v., servir; (law) ejecutar
service, sĕr′-vis, s., servicio m.; (divine) oficio m.
serviceable, sĕr′-vis-a-bl, a., servible
servile, sĕr′-vail, a., servil
servitude, sĕr′-vi-tiuud, s., servidumbre f.; (penal) trabajo forzado m.
session, sesh′-on, s., sesión f.
set, v., (type, music) componer; (clock) regular; (trap) tender; (task) imponer; (example) dar; (tools) asentar; (fracture) entablillar; (solidify) cuajar; (jewels) engastar; s., colección f.; serie f.; (buttons, etc.) juego m.; (china) servicio m.; — **dog at**, v., excitar; — **on fire**, pegar fuego a.
settee, set′-ii, s., sofá m.
settle, set′-l, v., (accounts) ajustar, liquidar; (finish) poner fin a; (decide) resolver; (assign) asignar; (in a place) establecerse; —**ment**, s., colonia f.; (dowery) dote f.; (agreement) convenio m.; (accounts) liquidación f.; —**r**, colono m.
seven, sev′-n, s. & a., siete m.; —**teen**, diecisiete m.; —**th**, séptimo m.; —**ty**, setenta m.
sever, sev′-a, v., separar; (cut) cortar
several, sev′-er-al, a., diversos, varios
severe*, si-vir′, a., severo; riguroso; violento
severity, si-ver′-i-ti, s., severidad f.
sew, sou, v., coser; —**ing**, s., costura f.; —**ing-cotton**, hilo de coser m.; —**ing-machine**, máquina de coser f.
sewage, siuu′-eich, s., aguas de albañal f. pl.
sewer, siuu′-a, s., albañal m., cloaca f.
sex, seks, s., sexo m.; —**ual**, a., sexual
shabbiness, shab′-i-nes, s., desaseo m.
shabby, shab′-i, a., raído; (unkempt) desaseado
shackle, shak′-l, s., (feet) grillete m.; (hands) esposas f. pl. v., encadenar
shade, sheid, s., sombra f.; (of colours) matiz m.; (lamp) pantalla f.; (eyes) visera f. v., sombrear
shadow, shad′-ou, s., sombra f. v., (follow) seguir

shady, shei'-di, a., umbroso; (fig.) sospechoso

shaft, shaaft, s., (arrow) asta f.; (mech.) eje m.; (mine) pozo de mina m.; **—s,** pl., (vehicle) limonera f.

shaggy, shag'-gui, a., lanudo, hirsuto

shake, sheik, v., agitar; (quake) sacudir; (tremble) temblar; (hands) estrechar. s., sacudida f.; (hands) apretón de manos m.

shaky, shei-ki, a., trémulo, vacilante; inseguro

shallow, shal'-ou, a., somero, superficial

sham, sham, s., ficción f.; fingimiento m. v., fingir a., fingido

shame, sheim, s., vergüenza f.; (modesty) pudor m. v., avergonzar; **—ful,** a., vergonzoso; **—less,** a., desvergonzado

shampoo, sham'-puu, s., champú m.

shamrock, sham-rok, s., trébol m.

shape, sheip, s., forma f. v., dar forma; modelar

share, shér, s., participación f.; (stock) acción f. v., repartir; participar; **—holder,** s., accionista m.

shark, shaark, s., tiburón m.

sharp, shaarp, a., afilado; (point) puntiagudo; (mind) agudo; (taste) picante; **—en,** v., afilar; **—ness,** s., agudeza f.

sharper, shaar'-pa, s., estafador m.; (cards) tramposo m.

shatter, shat'-a, v., estrellar, quebrantar

shave, sheiv, v., afeitar, afeitarse

shaving, shei'-ving, **—brush,** s., brocha de afeitar f.; **—s,** (wood) raspaduras f. pl.

shawl, shoal, s., chal m.; toquilla f.

she, shii, pers. pron., ella

sheaf, shiif, s., haz m.; (corn) gavilla f.; (papers) legajo m.

shear, shir, v., esquilar; **—s,** s. pl., tijeras f. pl.

sheath, shiiz, s., (scabbard) vaina f.

shed, shed, s., cobertizo m. v., (tears, blood) derramar; (hair, feathers) pelechar; (leaves) perder

sheen, shiin, s., brillo m., lustre m

sheep, shiip, s., carnero m., oveja f.

sheer, shir, a., puro; (steep) escarpado

sheet, shiit, s., (bed) sábana f.; (paper) hoja f. cuartilla f.; (metal) plancha f.; — **lightning,** fucilazo m.

shelf, shelf, s., anaquel m.; estante m., (a set) estantería f.

shell, shel, s., (hard) cascara f.; (soft) pellejo m.; (fish) concha f.; (artillery) bomba f. v., descascarar; bombardear; —**fish,** s., marisco m.

shelter, shel'-ta, s., abrigo m., albergue m. v. resguardarse, refugiarse

shepherd, shep'-erd, s., pastor m.

sheriff, sher'-if, s., alguacil mayor m.

sherry, sher'-i, s., vino de Jerez m.

shield, shiild, s., escudo m. v., escudar

shift, shift, s., (working) tanda f. v., mudar, remover

shilling, shil'-ing, s., chelín m.

shin, shin, s., canilla f., tibia f.

shine, shain, s., lustre m. v., brillar, lucir

shingle, shing'-gl, s., ripia f. v., (hair) rapar

ship, ship, s., buque m., barco m. v., embarcar; —**ment,** embarque m., cargamento m.; —**owner,** naviero m., armador m.; —**ping,** (traffic) navegación f.; —**wreck,** naufragio m.; —**yard,** astillero m.; arsenal m.

shire, shair, s., condado m.

shirk, shĕrk, v., esquivar, evadir; —**er,** s., tumbón m.

shirt, shĕrt, s., camisa de hombre f.

shiver, shiv'-a, v., tiritar, temblar. s., estremecimiento m.; (fever) escalofrío m.

shoal, shoal, s., multitud f.; (fish) cardume m.; (shallows) bajío m.

shock, shok, s., (jolt) choque m.; (electric, etc.) sacudida f.; (fright) susto m.; (med.) postración f. v., (disgust) ofender; —**absorber,** s., amortiguador m.; —**ing,** a., espantoso; ofensivo

shoddy, shod'-i, s., paño burdo m. a., burdo

shoe, shuu, s., zapato m.; (horse) herradura f. v., (horse) herrar; —**black,** s., limpiabotas m.; —**horn,** calzador m.; —**lace,** cordón, m.; —**maker,** zapatero m.; —**polish,** bétun m. lustre m.

shoot, sh*u*ut, v., disparar; (kill) matar; (execute) fusilar; (grow) brotar. s., caza f.; (growth) retoño m.; **—ing,** tiro m.; **—ing-star,** estrella fugaz f.

shop, shop, s., tienda f.; (stores) almacenes m. pl. v., ir de compras; **—keeper,** s., tendero m.

shopping, shop'-ing. s., compras f. pl.

shore, sh*ó*r, s., costa f.; (land) tierra f.; (support) puntal m. v., apuntalar

shorn, shorn, a., mocho; (deprived) despojado

short, sho*art*, a., corto; (persons) pequeño; (need) escaso; **—age,** a., déficit m.; **—circuit,** s., cortocircuito m.; **—en,** v., acortar; abreviar; **—hand,** s., taquigrafía f.; **—ly,** adv., dentro de poco; pronto; **—ness,** s., cortedad f.; brevedad f.; deficiencia f.; **—sighted,** a., miope

shot, shot, s., tiro m.; (marksman) tirador m.; (pellet) perdigones m. pl.

shoulder, shoul'-d*a*, s., hombro m. v., cargar al hombro; **—blade,** s., omoplato m.

shout, sh*au*t, s., grito m. v., gritar

shove, shov, s., empujón m. v., empujar

shovel, shov'-l, s., pala f. v., traspalar

show, shou, s., espectáculo m.; exposición f. v., mostrar; (teach) enseñar; **—room,** s., sala de exposición f.; **—y,** a., (gaudy) vistoso

shower, shau'-*a*, s., chaparrón m.; **—bath,** ducha m.; **—y,** a., lluvioso

shred, shred, s., triza f.; (tatter) harapo m. v., picar

shrew, shruu, s., arpía f.; **—d*,** a., astuto

shriek, shr*ii*k, v., chillar. s., chillido m.

shrill, shril, a., agudo, penetrante

shrimp, shrimp, s., camarón m.

shrine, shr*ai*n, s., relicario m., santuario m.

shrink, shri*n*gk, v., encogerse

shrivel, shriv'-l, v., arrugarse

shroud, shr*au*d, s., mortaja f. v., amortajar

Shrove Tuesday, shr*ou*v-tiuus'-di, s., martes de carnaval m.

shrub, shrob, s., arbusto m.

shrug, shrog, v., encoger los hombros

shudder, shŏd'-*a*, v., estremecerse. s., estremecimiento m.

shuffle, shŏf'-l, v., (gait) arrastrar los pies; (cards)
barajar

shun, shŏn, v., rehuir, esquivar

shunt, shŏnt, v., (trucks, etc.) desviar

shut, shŏt, v., cerrar; **—ter,** s., persiana f.; (camera)
obturador m.

shuttle, shŏt'-l, s., (sewing) lanzadera f.

shy, shai, a.,* tímido, reservado. v., asustarse

shyness, shai'-nes, s., timidez f., reserva f.

sick, sik, a., enfermo; mareado; **—en,** v., enfermar; **—ly,** adv., enfermizo; **—ness,** s., enfermedad f.; náusea f.

sickle, sik'-l, s., hoz f.

side, said, s., lado m.; (hill) falda f.; (river) orilla f.
v., tomar parte; **—board,** s., aparador m.

sideways, said'-ueis, adv., de lado

siding, sai'-ding, s., desviadero m.

siege, siiCH, s., sitio m.; asedio m.

sieve, siiv, s., tamiz m., criba f.

sift, sift, v., tamizar, cribar; investigar

sigh, sai, s., suspiro m. v., suspirar

sight, sait, v., avistar. s., (eye) vista f.; (spectacle) espectáculo m.; (gun) mira f.; **at —,** a
la vista; **by —,** de vista

sign, sain, v., firmar. s., señal f.; (board) muestra
de establecimiento f.; **—post,** poste de guía m.

signal, sig'-nal, s., señal f. v., señalar

signature, sig'-na-tiur, s., firma f.

significant*, sig-nif'-i-kant, a., significante

signification, sig-ni-fi-kei'-shon, s., significación f.

signify, sig'-ni-fai, v., significar; manifestar

silence, sai'-lens, s., silencio m.; (quiet) sosiego m.
interj., ! silencio ! v., hacer callar

silencer, sai'-len-sa, s., (engine) silencioso m.

silent*, sai'-lent, a., silencioso, callado; taciturno

silhouette, sil'-luu-et, s., silueta f.

silicon, sil'-i-kon, s., silicio m.

silk, silk, s., seda f.; (thread) hilo de seda m.;
—en, a., de seda; **—worm,** s., gusano de
seda m.; **—y,** a., sedoso

sill, sill, s., (door) umbral m.; (window) antepecho [m.

silly, sil'-i, a., tonto, bobo

silver, sil'-va, s., plata f. a., de plata. v., platear

silversmith, sil'-ver-smiz, s., platero m.

similar*, sim'-i-la, a., semejante; **—ity,** s., semejanza f.

simile, sim'-i-li, s., comparación f.

simmer, sim'-a, v., hervir a fuego lento

simple, sim'-pl, a., simple; **—ton,** s., simplón m.

simplicity, sim-plis'-i-ti, s., sencillez f.

simplify, sim'-pli-fai, v., simplificar

simultaneous*, si-mol-tei'-ni-os, a., simultáneo

sin, sin, v., pecar. s., pecado m.; **—ful,** a., pecaminoso; **—less,** sin pecado; **—ner,** s., pecador m.

since, sins, prep., desde. adv., desde entonces, conj., desde que, después que; ya que, pues que, puesto que

sincere*, sin-sir', a., sincero [m.

sinew, sin'-iuu, s., tendón m.; músculo m.; nervio

sing, sing, v., cantar; **—er,** s., cantor m.; cantante m. or f.

singe, sinch, v., chamuscar

single, sing'-gl, a., solo; (unmarried) soltero

single-handed, sing'-gl-jan-did, a., solo

singly, sing'-gli, adv., uno a uno

singular*, sing'-guiu-lr, a., singular; peculiar

sinister, sin'-is-ta, a., siniestro

sink, singk, s., vertedero m.; (drain) albañal m. v., hundir; (scuttle) echar a pique; (shaft) fijar

sip, sip, v., sorber; libar. s., sorbo m.

siphon, sai'-fn, s., sifón m.

siren, sai'-ren, s., sirena f.

sirloin, sër'-loin, s., lomo m., solomillo m.

sister, sis'-ta, s., hermana f.; **—in-law,** cuñada f.

sit, sit, v., sentarse; (incubate) empollar; **—down,** sentarse; **—ting,** a., sentado. s., sesión f.; **—ting-room,** sala f.

site, sait, s., sitio m.; (building) solar m.

situated, sit'-iu-ei-tid, a., situado

situation, sit-iu-ei'-shon, s., situación f.; (post) colocación f.

six, six, s. & a., seis m.; **—teen,** dieciséis m.;

—**teenth,** décimosexto m.; —**th,** sexto m.;
—**tieth,** sexagésimo m.; —**ty,** sesenta m.
size, sais, s., tamaño m.; talla f.; (measure) medida
f.; (glue) cola f. v., encolar.
skate, skeit, v., patinar. s., patín m.; (fish) raya f.
skein, skein, s., madeja f.
skeleton, skel'-e-ton, s., esqueleto m.
sketch, skech, v., bosquejar. s., bosquejo m.
skewer, skiuu'-a, s., espetón m., boceto m.
skid, skid, v., patinar
skiff, skif, s., esquife m.
skilful*, skil'-ful, a., diestro, hábil   [f.
skill, skil, s., habilidad f., destreza f.; (natural) maña
skim, skim, v., rasar; espumar; (cream) desnatar
skin, skin, s., piel f., cutis m.; (hide) cuero m.;
(peel) pellejo m. v., desollar; (fruit) pelar
skip, skip, v., omitir; saltar
skipper, skip'-a, s., patrón de buque m.
skirmish, skër'-mish, s., escaramuza f.
skirt, skërt, s., falda f.; (border) borde m. v., fal-
dear; bordear
skittles, skit'-ls, s. pl., juego de bolos f.
skull, sköl, s., cráneo m.
skunk, sköñk, s., mofeta f.
sky, skai, s., cielo m.; —**light,** claraboya f.
sky-scraper, skai-skrei'-pa, s., rascacielos m.
slab, slab, s., losa f.; (large) lastra f.
slack, slak, s., escoria f. a., flojo; —**en,** v., aflojar
slander, slaan'-da, v., calumniar. s., calumnia f.
slanderer, slaan'-da-rer, s., calumniador m.
slang, slang, s., argot m.
slant, slaant, v., sesgarse, oblicuar. s., sesgo m.,
oblicuidad f.; —**ing,** a., sesgado, oblicuo
slap, slap, v., dar una manotada. s., manotada f.
slash, slash, s., (cut) corte m. v., cortar
slate, sleit, v., empizarrar. s., pizarra f.
slaughter, sloa'-ta, v., matar; (massacre) degollar.
s., matanza f.; —**er,** matador m.
slave, sleiv, v., trabajar como un esclavo. s., esclavo m.; —**ry,** esclavitud f.
slay, slei, v., matar
sledge, slecH, s., trineo m.; —**hammer,** macho m.

sleek*, sliik, a., liso; (manners) suave
sleep, sliip, v., dormir. s., sueño m.; **—ing-car,** coche cama m.; **—less,** a., insomne; desvelado; **—lessness,** s., insomnio m.; **—y,** a., soñoliento
sleet, sliit, s., aguanieve f.
sleeve, sliiv, s., manga f.
sleigh, slei, s., trineo m.
sleight, slait, s., maña f.; **— of hand,** juego de manos m.
slender*, slen'-da, a., delgado; (means) escaso
slice, slais, s., tajada f.; (bread) rebanada v., cortar en lonjas
slide, slaid, s., resbalón m.: (microscopic, photo-graphic, etc.) placa f. v., resbalar
slight, slait, s., desaire m. a., ligero. v., desairar
slim, slim, a., delgado. v., adelgazar
slime, slaim, s., limo m.; (mud) fango m.
slimy, slai'-mi, a., viscoso, fangoso
sling, sling, s., (med.) cabestrillo m. v., (throw) lanzar
slink, slingk, v., escabullirse
slip, slip, v., resbalar, s., caída f.; **—pery,** a., res-baladizo
slipper, slip'-a, s., zapatilla f.
slit, slit, v., rajar. s., raja f.
sloe, slou, s., endrina f.
slop, slop, s., agua sucia f.; **—-pail,** cubo para agua sucia m.
slope, sloup, v., sesgarse. s., declive m.
slot, slot, s., muesca f., ranura f.; **— machines,** s., máquina de servicios automáticos f.
sloth, slouz, s., pereza f.; (animal) perezoso m.
slouch, slauch, v., andar cabizbajo
slough, slau, s., (fig.) abismo m.
slovenly, slöv'-n-li, a., desaliñado
slow*, slou, a., lento, despacio. v., (clock, etc.) atrasar
slug, slög, s., babosa f.; (missile) posta f.
sluggish, slö'-guish, a., perezoso, indolente
sluice, sluus, s., (gate) compuerta f.
slum, slöm, s., barrio bajo m.
slumber, slöm'-ba, v., dormitar. s., sueño ligero m.

slump, slŏmp, s., baja repentina en los valores f.

slur, slẽr, s., mancha f. v., manchar

slush, slŏsh, s., lodo m., fango m.

slut, slŏt, s., perra f.

sly*, slaı, a., socarrón

smack, smᴀk, s., (hand) cachete f.; (lips) rechupete m.; (kiss) beso sonado m.; (boat) queche m. v., (beat) pegar; (lips) rechuparse

small, smoᴀl, a., pequeño; **—ness,** s., pequeñez f.

small-pox, smoᴀl'-poks, s., viruelas f. pl.

smart, smaart, a., vivo; (clever) listo; (spruce) elegante. v., escocer

smash, smᴀsh, s., colisión f.; (commercial) fracaso m. v., romper; destrozar

smattering, smᴀt'-er-ing, s., conocimiento superficial m.

smear, smir, v., untar. s., mancha f.

smell, smel, v., oler. s., olor m.; **—ing-salts,** sales aromáticas f. pl.

smelt, smelt, v., fundir. s., eperlano m.

smile, smaıl, v., sonreírse. s., sonrisa f.

smite, smaıt, v., herir; afligir

smith, smiz, s., forjador m.; **—y,** s., forja f.

smoke, smouk, s., humo m. v., fumar; **—less,** a., sin humo; **—r,** s., fumador m.

smoky, smouk'-i, a., ahumado

smooth, smuuᴅ, a.,* suave; liso. v., alisar

smother, smŏᴅ'-a, v., sofocar

smoulder, smoul'-da, v., arder en rescoldo

smudge, smŏᴄн, s., tiznón m. v., tiznar

smug, smŏg, a., pimpante, presumido

smuggle, smŏg'-l, v., hacer contrabando

smuggler, smŏg'-gla, s., contrabandista m.

smut, smŏt, s., tiznón m.

snack, snᴀk, s., piscolabis m.; taco m., bocadillo m.

snail, sneıl, s., caracol m.

snake, sneık, s., serpiente f.; culebra f.

snap, snᴀp, s., chasquido m.; (bite) dentellada f. v., chasquear; (break) romperse; (fingers) castañetear; (animal) dentellear

snapshot, snᴀp'-shot, s., instantánea f.

snare, sner, s., lazo m., trampa f. v., poner trampas

snarl, snaarl, v., gruñir

snatch, snAch, — **from,** v., arrebatar; — **at,** echar mano

sneak, sniik, s., soplón m. v., (steal) ratear; — **away,** escabullirse

sneer, snír, v., mofarse. s., mofa f.

sneeze, sniis, v., estornudar. s., estornudo m.

sniff, snif, v., husmear; (smell) olfatear

snip, snip, s., tijeretada f. v., tijeretear

snipe, snaip, s., agachadiza f.; —**r,** tirador m.

snore, snór, v., roncar

snort, snoart, v., resoplar. s., resoplido m.

snout, snaut, s., hocico m.; (pig) jeta f.

snow, snou, v., nevar. s., nieve f.; —**bound,** a., sitiado por la nieve; —**drop,** campanilla blanca f.; —**storm,** nevada f.

snub, snöb, s., desaire m. v., desairar

snub-nose, snöb'-nous, s., nariz chata f.

snuff, snöf, s., rapé m., tabaco en polvo m.

snug, snög, a., cómodo; abrigado

so, sou, adv., así; así pues; por tanto; tan

soak, souk, v., remojar, empapar

soap, soup, s., jabón m.

soar, sór, v., remontarse, cernerse

sob, sob, s., sollozo m. v., sollozar

sober*, sou'-ba, a., sobrio; moderado

sociable, sou'-sha-bl, a., sociable

social*, sou'-shal, a., social; —**ism,** s., socialismo m.; —**ist,** socialista m.

society, so-sai'-i-ti, s., sociedad f.

sock, sok, s., calcetín m.

socket, sok'-it, s., encaje m.; (eyes) cuenca f.; (teeth) alvéolo m.

sod, sod, s., témpano m.

soda, sou'-da, s., sosa f.; —**water,** agua de soda f.

soft*, soft, a., blando, muelle; —**en,** v., ablandar

softness, soft'-nes, s., blandura f.

soil, soil, s., tierra f. v., manchar; ensuciar

sojourn, sŏch'-ern, s., estancia f. v., morar

solace, sol'-as, s., consuelo m. v., consolar

solder, sol'-da, v., soldar. s., soldadura f.

soldier, soul'-chа, s., soldado m.

sole, soul, s., suela f.; (fish) lenguado m. v., echar suelas. a.,* único, solo

solemn*, sol'-em, a., solemne

solicit, so-lis'-it, v., solicitar

solicitor, so-lis'-i-ta, s., abogado m.

solicitude, so-lis'-i-tiuud, s., solicitud f.

solid*, sol'-id, a., sólido; macizo; firme; **—arity,** s., solidaridad f.; **—ify,** v., solidificar

solitary, sol'-i-ta-ri, a., solitario

solitude, sol'-i-tiuud, s., soledad f.

soluble, sol'-iu-bl, a., soluble

solution, so-liuu'-shon, s., solución f.

solve, solv, v., resolver

solvency, sol'-ven-si, s., solvencia f.

solvent, sol'-vent, a., solvente; s., solvente m.

sombre*, som'-ber, a., sombrío

some, sŏm, a. & pron., alguno, un, algún, cierto, un poco de; algo de, unos pocos; **—body,** s., alguien m.; **—how,** adv., de algún modo; **—one,** s., alguno m.; **—thing,** algo m.; **—times,** adv., a veces, algunas veces; **—what,** algo, un poco; **—where,** en alguna parte

somersault, sŏm'-er-sŏult, s., salto mortal m.

somnambulist, som-nam'-biu-list, s., somámbulo

son, sŏn, s., hijo m.; **—in-law,** yerno m. [m.

sonata, so-naa'-ta, s., sonata f.

song, song, s., canción f., canto m.

soon, suun, adv., pronto; **as — as,** tan pronto como; **how —?** ¿ cuándo ?

soot, sut, s., hollín m.

soothe, suuD, v., calmar; (pacify) apaciguar

sorcerer, sór'-ser-a, s., hechicero m.; brujo m.

sorcery, sór'-ser-i, s., hechicería f.; brujería f.

sordid*, sóar'-did, a., sórdido; bajo; vil

sore, sóar, s., llaga f.; (animal's) matadura f. a.,* dolorido, doloroso; (throat, etc.) mal de . . .

sorrel, sor'-el, s., acedera f. a., alazán

sorrow, sor'-ou, s., dolor m., pesar m. v., afligirse

sorrowful*, sor'-ou-ful, a., afligido, triste

sorry, sor'-i, a., pesaroso; **I am —,** lo siento

sort, sóart, s., especie f.; clase f. v., clasificar

soul, soul, s., alma f.

sound, saund, v., sonar; (naut.) sondear. a., (health) robusto; (character) recto; (sleep) profundo. s., sonido m.; (bells) tañido m.; (channel) estuario m.; **—ing,** s., (naut.) sondeo m.; **— track,** s., cinta fotofónica f.; pista sonora f.

soup, suup, s., sopa f.; **—tureen,** sopera f.

sour*, saur, a., agrio; (fig.) desabrido, rancio

source, sórs, s., fuente f.; origen m.

south, sauz, s., sur m., sud m.

southerly, soz'-er-li, a., del sur; meridional

souvenir, su-vi-niir', s., recuerdo m.

sovereign, sov'-er-in, s., soberano m. a., supremo; (remedy) eficaz

sow, sau, s., cerda f., puerca f.

sow, sou, v., sembrar; **—er,** s., sembrador m.

space, speis, s., espacio m.; período m.; **—craft,** s., nave espacial f.

spacious*, spei'-shos, a., espacioso

spade, speid, s., azada f.; (cards) espadas f. pl.

span, span, s., palmo m.; (architecture) tramo m. v., extenderse sobre

spangle, spang'-gl, s., lentejuela f.

spaniel, span'-yel, s., perro de aguas m.

spanner, span'-a, s., llave de tuercas f.

spar, spaar, v., boxear. s., (naut.) mástil m.

spare, spér, v., perdonar; (grant) hacer el favor de

sparing*, spé'-ring, a., frugal, económico

spark, spaark, v., chispear. s., chispa f.

sparkle, spaar'-kl, v., centellear; (wine) espumar

sparrow, spar'-ou, s., gorrión m.

spasm, spasm, s., espasmo m.; **—odic,** a., espasmódico

spatter, spat'-a, v., salpicar

spawn, spoan, s., huevas f. pl. v., desovar

speak, spiik, v., hablar; **—er,** s., orador m.

spear, spir, s., lanza f. v., alancear

special*, spesh'-al, a., especial

speciality, spesh-i-al'-i-ti, s., especialidad f.

specie, spii'-shii, s., moneda f.

species, spii'-shii-es, s., especie f.; género m.

specification, spes-i-fi-kei'-shon, s., especificación

specify, spes'-i-fai, v., especificar; detallar   [f.

specimen, spes'-i-men, s., ejemplar m.; muestra f.
specious*, spil'-shos, a., especioso, plausible
speck, spek, s., mota f.
spectacle, spek'-ta-kl, s., espectáculo m.
spectacles, spek'-ta-kls, s., (optical) gafas f. pl.
spectator, spek-tei'-ta, s., espectador m.
spectre, spek'-tr, s., espectro m., fantasma m.
speculate, spek'-iu-leit, v., especular; reflexionar
speech, spiich, s., habla m.; (discourse) discurso m.; **—less,** a., (fig.) mudo
speed, spiid, s., rapidez f., velocidad f.; **—ometer,** s., velocímetro m.; **—y,** a., veloz
spell, spel, s., hechizo m. v., deletrear
spend, spend, v., gastar; **—thrift,** s., pródigo m.
sphere, sfir, s., esfera f.
spice, spais, s., especia f. v., condimentar
spicy, spai'-si, a., aromático; (fig.) picante
spider, spai'-da, s., araña f.
spike, spaik, s., alcayata f.; clavo m. v., clavar con alcayatas
spill, spil, v., derramar
spin, spin, v., hilar; (turn) girar; **—drier,** s., máquina secadora f.; **—ning,** s., hilado m.
spinach, spin'-ich, s., espinaca f.
spinal, spai'-nl, a., espinal, vertebral
spindle, spin'-dl, s., huso m.; (axle) eje m.
spine, spain, s., espina dorsal f.
spinster, spin'-sta, s., soltera f.
spiral, spai'-rl, a., espiral. s., espira f.
spire, spair, s., chapitel m.; aguja f.
spirit, spir'-it, s., espíritu m.; alcohol m.; (animation) brío m.; **—ed,** a., brioso; (bold) valiente; **—ual,** espiritual; **—ualist,** s., espiritista m.
spit, spit, v., escupir. s., salvia f.; (roasting) asador m.; **—toon,** s., escupidera f.
spite, spait, v., despechar; vejar. s., despecho m.; **—ful*,** a., despechado, rencoroso; **in — of,** a pesar de
splash, splash, v., salpicar; (play) chapotear
splendid*, splen'-did, a., espléndido, magnífico
splendour, splen'-dr, s., esplendor m.
splint, splint, s., (surgical) tablilla f.

splinter, splin'-ta, s., astilla f. v., hacer astillas
split, split, v., hender. s., hendedura f.
spoil, spoil, v., echar a perder; (child, etc.) mimar
spoke, spouk, s., rayo de rueda m.
spokesman, spouks'-man, s., portavoz m.
sponge, sponch, s., esponja f. v., esponjar
sponsor, spon'-sr, s., fiador m.; (baptism) padrino m.
spontaneous*, spon-tei'-ni-os, a., espontáneo
spool, spuul, s., canilla f., carrete m., bobina f. v., devanar
spoon, spuun, s., cuchara f.; **—ful,** cucharada f.
sport, sport, s., deporte m.; **—ive,** a., deportivo
sportsman, sports'-man, s., deportista m.
spot, spot, v., manchar. s., mancha f.; (place) sitio m.; lugar m.; **—less,** a., sin mancha
spouse, spaus, s., esposo m., esposa f.
spout, spaut, s., (outlet) canalón m.; (jug or pot) pico m. caño m. v., brotar, borbotar
sprain, sprein, v., torcer, discolarse. s., torcedura f.
sprat, sprat, s., arenque m.
sprawl, sproal, v., despatarrar
spray, sprei, s., (branch) ramita f.; (water) rociada f. v., rociar; (med.) pulverizar
sprayer, sprei'-a, s., pulverizador m.
spread, spred, v., extender; (on bread, etc.) untar; (news) divulgar; **— out,** desplegar
sprig, sprig, s., ramito m.; (off-shoot) vástago m.
sprightly, sprait'-li, a., alegre; vivo, despierto
spring, spring, s., primavera f.; (leap) salto m.; (water) manantial m.; (metal) resorte m., muelle m. v., saltar
sprinkle, spring'-kl, v., espolvorear; (water) rociar
sprout, spraut, v., brotar. s., brote m.
spruce, spruus, s., abeto m. a., elegante
spur, spör, s., espuela f. v., espolear
spurious*, spiu'-ri-os, a., falso
spurn, spörn, v., desdeñar, despreciar
spy, spai, s., espía m. v., espiar
squabble, skuob'-l, s., riña f. v., reñir; disputar
squad, skuod, s., (mil.) pelotón m.; **—ron,** (mil.) escuadrón m.; (naval) escuadrilla f.
squalid*, skuol'-id, a., escuálido

squall, skuoal, s., (wind) chubasco m. v., (scream) chillar

squalor, skuoal'-r, s., escualidez f.; suciedad f.

squander, skuon'da, v., derrochar, malgastar

square, skuér, s., cuadrado m.; (public) plaza f. a.,* cuadrado

squash, skuosh, v., aplastar; (fig.) apretar. s., presión m.

squat, skuot, v., ponerse en cuclillas, agacharse. a., rechoncho

squeak, skuíik, v., chillar; (bearings, etc.) chirriar

squeeze, skuiis, v., estrujar; (cuddle) apretar

squint, skuint, v., bizquear. s., bizco m.

squirrel, skuir'-l, s., ardilla f.

squirt, skuért, v., jeringar. s., jeringa f.

stab, stAb, v., apuñalar. s., puñalada f.

stability, sta-bil'-i-ti, s., estabilidad f.

stable, stei'-bl, s., caballeriza f.; establo m. a., estable, fijo

stack, stAck, s., (wood) pila f.; (hay) niara f.; (chimney) chimenea f. v., amontonar

staff, staaf, s., cayado m.; (employees) personal m.; (mil.) estado mayor m.; **flag—**, s., asta f.

stag, stAg, s., ciervo m.

stage, steich, s., escenario m., escena f.; (hall) tablado m.; (period) fase f, v., poner en escena

stagger, stAg'-a, v., tambalearse; (fig.) asombrar

stagnate, stAg'-neit, v., estancarse

staid*, steid, a., grave; sosegado

stain, stein, v., teñir; (soil) manchar. s., tinte m.; mancha f.; **—less,** a., (steel) inoxidable

stair, ster, s., peldaño m.; escalón m.; **—s,** escalera f.

stake, steik, s., estaca f.; (wager) apuesta f. v., estacar; (wager) apostar

stale, steil, a., (bread, etc.) viejo; (beer) pasada

stalk, stoalk, s., tallo m. v., cazar al acecho

stall, stoal, s., (market) puesto m.; (theatre) buta-

stalwart, stoal'-uert, a., fornido, membrudo [ca f.

stamina, stAm'-i-na, s., vigor m.

stammer, stAm'-a, v., tartamudear

stamp, stAmp, s., (rubber, etc.) seal) estampador m.; (postage) sello de correo m. v., estampar;

(postage) timbrar ; (foot) patear

stampede, stam-piid', s., estampida f.

stand, stand, v., estar de pie ; (place) colocar ; (endure) soportar. s., tribuna f. ; pedestal m. (market) puesto m. ; (resistance) resistencia f. ; **— still,** parada f.

standard, stan'-dard, s., estandarte m. a., de ley ; clásico ; **—ize,** v., uniformar, unificar, tipificar

standing, stan'-ding, a., permanente. s., posición f. ; **— room,** sitio para estar de pie m.

staple, stei'-pl, s., armella f. a., corriente

star, staar, s., estrella f. ; **—ry,** a., estrellado

starboard, staar'-bórd, s. (naut.) estribor m.

starch, staarch, s., almidón m. v., almidonar

stare, stér, v., fijar la vista. s., mirada fija f.

starling, staar'-ling, s., estornino m.

start, staart, s., comienzo m. principio m. ; (shock) sobresalto m. v., (commence) comenzar, principiar ; (mech.) poner en marcha ; (leave) salir

startle, staar'-tl, v., asustar

starvation, staar-vei'-shon, s., hambre m., inanición f.

starve, staarv, v., morir de hambre

state, steit, v., declarar. s., estado m. ; (condition) condición f. ; (pompa) pompa f. ; **—ly,** a., majestuoso ; **—ment,** s., declaración f. ; (account) estado de cuentas m.

statesman, steits'-man, s., estadista m.

station, stei'-shon, s., estación f. ; (position) posición f. v., apostar

stationary, stei'-shon-a-ri, a., estacionario

stationer, stei'-shon-a, s., papelero m.

stationery, stei'-shon-a-ri, s., papelería f.

statistics, sta-tis'-tiks, s., estadística f.

statue, stat'-iu, s., estatua f.

statute, stat'-iuut, s., estatuto m., ley f.

staunch, stoanch, a.,* constante. v., estancar

stave, steiv, s., duela f. ; **— in,** v., desfondar

stay, stei, s., estancia f. v., permanecer, quedarse

stays, steis, s., corsé m.

stead, sted, s., lugar m., sitio m. ; **in— of,** adv., en lugar de

steadfast, sted'-fast, a., constante; determinado

steady, sted'-i, a., firme; (reliable) formal, estable; (markets) firme

steak, steik, s., (beef) biftec m.

steal, stiil, v., robar, hurtar

stealth, stelz, s., recato m., cautela f.; **by —,** a hurtadillas

steam, stiim, s., vapor m.

steamer, stii'-ma, s., buque de vapor m.

steel, stiil, s., acero m.

steep, stiip, v., empapar. a., empinado

steeple, stii'-pl, s., campanario m.

steer, stiir, v., gobernar; (motor) conducir. s., novillo m.; **—age,** proa f., entrepuente m.

stem, stem, s., tallo m.; (glass) pie m. v., contrarrestar

stench, stench, s., hedor m.

stenographer, sten-og'-raf-a, s., taquígrafa f., estenógrafa f.

step, step, v., dar un paso. s., paso m.; (stair) peldaño m.; **—father,** padrastro m.; **—mother,** madrastra f.

stereophonic*, ster-rio-fon'-ik, a., estereofónico

sterile, ster'-ail, a., estéril

sterilize, ster'-i-lais, v., esterilizar

sterling, stêr'-ling, s., esterlina f.; genuino, puro

stern, stêrn, s., (naut.) popa f. a.,* austero, severo

stevedore, stii'-vi-dor, s., estibador m.

stew, stiuu, s., estofado m. v., estofar

steward, stiuu'-erd, s., camarero m.; (estate) mayordomo m.; **—ess,** camarera f.

stick, stik, v., (affix) pegar. s., palo m.; (walking) bastón m.; **—y,** a, pegajoso

stiff, stif, a., tieso; yerto; **—en,** v., atiesar

stifle, stai'-fl, v., sofocar, ahogar

stigmatize, stig'-ma-tais, v., estigmatizar

stile, stail, s., portillo m.; **turn—,** torniquete m.

still, stil, s., (distil) alambique m. v., (to calm) calmar. a., quieto. adv., aún, todavía. conj., (yet) sin embargo

stimulate, stim'-iu-leit, v., estimular

sting, sting, v., picar; (nettle) ortigar. s., aguijón m.

stingy, stin'-CHi, a., avaro, mezquino

stink, stink, v., heder, apestar. s., hedor m.

stint, stint, v., limitar, restringir; escatimar

stipend, stai'-pend, s., (eccl.) estipendio m.

stipulate, stip'-iu-leit, v., estipular

stipulation, stip-iu-lei'-shon, s., estipulación f.

stir, stër, v., revolver; moverse. s., alboroto m.

stirrup, stër'-op, s., estribo m.

stitch, stich, v., dar puntadas. s., puntada f.; (pain) punzada f.

stock, stok, v., vender; poner en surtido s., (tree) tronco m.; (gun) caja f.; (flower) alelí m.; (goods) existencias f. pl.; (live) ganado m.; **—-book,** libro de inventarios m.; **—-broker,** corredor de bolsa m.; **—-exchange,** bolsa f.; **—s,** (securities) acciones f. pl.; valores m. pl.; (pillory) cepo m.; **—-size,** tamaño normal m.; **—-taking,** inventario m.

stocking, stok'-ing, s., media f.; calceta f.

stoke, stouk, v., alimentar; **—r,** s., fogonero m.

stolid,* stol'-id, a., estólido, impasible

stomach, stöm'-ak, s., estómago m.; **—-ache,** dolor de estómago m.

stone, stoun, v., apedrear. s., piedra f.; (pebble) guijo m.

stool, stuul, s., banqueta f.; (med.) bacín m.

stoop, stuup, v., agacharse; (fig.) humillarse

stop, stop, s., parada f.; (interruption) pausa f.; (punctuation) punto m. v., parar, pararse; (payment) suspender; (teeth) empastar; (cease) cesar; **— up,** cegar

stopper, stop'-a, s., tapón m., obturador m.

storage, stor'-reich, s., almacenaje m.

store, stór, s., (shop) tienda f.; (departmental) almacén m. v., almacenar

stork, stoark, s., cigüeña f.

storm, stoarm, v., asaltar. s., tempestad f.

stormy, stoar'-mi, a., tempestuoso

story, stó'-ri, s., cuento m. historia f.; (floor) piso m.

stout,* staut, a., corpulento; (strong) fuerte

stove, stouv, s., estufa f.; (range) fogón m.

stow, stou, v., hacinar; (naut.) estivar

stowaway, stou'-*a*-uei, s., polizón m.

straggle, strag'-l, v., desparramarse; (stray) extraviarse

straight*, streit, a., derecho, directo; **—en**, v., enderezar; **—forward,*** a., recto; sincero

strain, strein, s., esfuerzo m.; (music) acorde m.; (pull) tirantez f. v., esforzarse; (strecht) estirar; (tendon) torcer; (liquid) colar

strainer, strei'-na, s., colador m.

straits, streits, s. pl., (channel) estrecho m.

strand, strand, v., (naut.) encallar. s., playa f.; (hair) trenza f.

strange*, streinch, a., extraño; (peculiar) raro

stranger, strein'-cha, s., forastero m.; extraño m.

strangle, strang'-gl, v., estrangular

strap, strap, v., atar con correas. s., correa f.

straw, stroa, s., paja f.

strawberry, stroa'-ber-i, s., fresa f.

stray, strei, v., extraviarse, descarriarse. a., extraviado

streak, striik, s., raya f. v., rayar

streaky, striik'-i, a., rayado

stream, striim, v., correr. s., corriente f.; (small) arroyo m.

street, striit, s., calle f.

strength, strengz, s., fuerza f.; **—en**, v., fortificar, reforzar; (health) fortalecer

strenuous*, stren'-iu-os, a., estrenuo; enérgico

stress, stres, s., (pressure) fuerza f.; (urge) urgencia f. v., acentuar

stretch, strech, v., estirar. s., extensión f.; distancia f.

stretcher, strech'-a, s., camilla f.; tendedor m.

strew, struu, v., esparcir, desparramar

strict*, strikt, a., estricto; riguroso

stride, straid, v., andar a trancos. s., tranco m.

strife, straif, s., contienda f., riña f.; disputa f.

strike, straik, v., (work) declararse en huelga; (smite) pegar, golpear; (lightning) herir; (match) encender. s., huelga f., paro m.; **— off, — out**, v., (delete) borrar

striker, straik'-a, s., (work) huelguista m.

string, string, s., cordel m.; (thin) bramante f.; (violin) cuerda f. v., (beads) ensartar

stringency, strin'-cHen-si, s., rigor m.; aprieto m.

strip, strip, s., tira f. v., desnudar

stripe, straip, s., raya f.; (mil.) galón m. v., rayar

strive, straiv, v., esforzarse

stroke, strouk, s., toque m.; (med.) ataque m.; (piston) carrera f.; (pen) trazo m. v., acariciar

stroll, stroul, v., pasearse s., paseo m.

strong*, strong, a., fuerte; sólido; (light) brillante

strop, strop, s., asentador m. v., asentar

structure, strŏk'-tiur, s., construcción f.

struggle, strog'-l, v., luchar s., lucha f.

strut, strŏt, v., pavonearse. s., (brace) riostra f.

stubborn*, stŏb'-ern, a., testarudo, obstinado

stud, stŏd, s., tachón s.; (collar) botón m.; (breeding) yeguada f. v., tachonar

student, stiuu'-dent, s., estudiante m.

studio, stiuu'-di-ou, s., estudio m.

studious*, stiuu'-di-os, a., estudioso

study, stŏd'-i, s., estudio m.; (room) escritorio m. v., estudiar

stuff, stŏf, v., rellenar; (preserve) empajar. s., (cloth) tela f.; (suiting) paño m.

stuffing, stŏf'-ing, s., relleno m.

stumble, stŏm'-bl, v., dar un traspié, tropezar

stump, stŏmp, s., tocón m.; (arm, leg) muñón m.; (tooth) raigón m.; (cricket) palo m.

stun, stŏn, v., aturdir; **—ning,** a., (fig.) pasmoso

stunt, stŏnt, s., maniobra sensacional f.

stunted, stŏnt'-id, a., achaparrado

stupefy, stiuu'-pi-fai, v., causar estupor

stupendous*, stiu-pen'-dos, a., estupendo

stupid*, stiuu'-pid, a., tonto, estúpido

stupidity, stiuu-pi'-di-ti, s., estupidez f.

stupor, stiuu'-pr, s., estupor m.

sturdy, stěr'-di, a., fuerte, vigoroso

sturgeon, stěr'-cHon, s., esturión m.

stutter, stŏt'-a, v., tartamudear

sty, stai, s., pocilga f.; (med.) orzuelo m.

style, stail, s., estilo m.; moda f.

stylish, stai'-lish, a., elegante, a la moda

subdue, sŏb-diuu′, v., sojuzgar; (tame) amansar

subject, sŏb-CHekt′, v., sujetar; obligar

subject, sŏb′-CHekt, s., sujeto m.; (national) súbdito m.

subjection, sŏb-chek′-shon, s., sujeción f.

subjunctive, sŏb-CHŏngk′-tiv, s., subjuntivo m.

sublime, sŏb-laim′, a., sublime

submarine, sŏb-ma-riin′, s. & a., submarino m.

submerge, sŏb-mērch′, v., sumergir

submission, sŏb-mish′-on, s., sumisión f.

submit, sŏb′-mit′, v., someter, someterse

subordinate*, sŏb-or′-di-neit, v., subordinado

subscribe, sŏb-skraib′, v., subscribir; (papers) abonarse; —**r,** s., subscriptor m., abonado m.

subscription, sŏb-skrip′-shon, s., subscripción f.; abono m.

subsequent*, sŏb-si-kuent′, a., subsecuente

subservient, sŏb-sĕr′-vi-ent, a., subordinado

subside, sŏb-said′, v., hundirse; (water) bajar

subsidy, sŏb′-si-di, s., (grant) subvención f.

subsist, sŏb-sist′, v., subsistir

substance, sŏb′-stance, s., sustancia f.; esencia f.

substantial*, sŏb-stan′-shal, a., substancial

substantiate, sŏb-stan′-shi-eit, v., verificar

substitute, sŏb-sti-tiuut, s., substituto m.; (proxy) suplente m. v., substituir

subterranean, sŏb-ter-rei′-nii-an, a., subterráneo

subtle, sŏt′-l, a., sutil

subtract, sŏb-trakt′, v., substraer

suburb, sŏb′-ĕrb, s., suburbio m.

subversive, sŏb-ver′-siv, a., subversivo

subway, sŏb′-uei, s., pasaje subterráneo m.; túnel m.

succeed, sŏk-siid′, v., suceder; (achieve) lograr; — **to,** (inherit) heredar

success, sŏk-ses′, s., éxito m.; acierto m.; —**ful*,** a., eficaz; próspero; —**ion,** s., sucesión f.

successor, sŏk-ses′-a, s., sucesor m.

succour, sŏk′-er, s., socorro m. v., socorrer

succumb, sŏk-ŏm′, v., sucumbir

such, sŏch, a., tal; igual; — **a,** tal; igual

suck, sŏk, v., chupar; —**le,** amamantar

suction, sŏk'-shon, s., succión f.

sudden*, sŏd'-n, a., repentino, súbito

sue, siuu, v., demandar en justicia

suet, siuu'-et, s., sebo en rama m.

suffer, sŏf'-a, v., sufrir; soportar; **—ing**, s., sufrimiento m. a., paciente **on —ance**, con tolerancia

suffice, sŏ-fais', v., bastar, ser suficiente [cia

sufficient*, sŏ-fish'-ent, a., suficiente

suffocate, sŏf'-o-keit, v., sofocar [f. pl.

sugar, shu'-ga, s., azúcar m.; **—-tongs**, tenacillas

suggest, sŏ-chest', v., sugerir; (advise) aconsejar; **—ion**, s., sugestión f., idea f.; **—ive**, a., sugestivo

suicide, siuu'-i-said, s., suicidio m.

suit, siuut, v., convenir; (dress, climate) sentar bien. s., traje m.; (law) pleito m.; **—able**, a., apropiado; **—or**, s., (wooer) pretendiente m.

suite, suiit, s., (retinue) séquito m.; apartamento m.; (furniture) juego m.

sulk, sŏlk, v., amurriarse; **—y**, a., murriático

sullen*, sŏl'-n, a., sombrío, hosco

sulphur, sŏl'-fr, s., azufre m.

sultry, sŏl'-tri, a., bochornoso

sum, sŏm, s., suma f.; **— up**, v., resumir

summary, sŏm'-a-ri, s., resumen m. a., (law) sumario

summer, sŏm'-a, s., verano m.

summit, sŏm'-it, s., cima f., cumbre f.

summon, sŏm'-n, v., citar; (call) llamar

summons, sŏm'-ns, s., (legal) citación f.

sumptuous*, sŏmp'-tiu-os, a., suntuoso

sun, sŏn, s., sol m.; **—beam**, rayo de sol m.; **—-dial**, reloj de sol m.; **—ny**, a., soleado; **—rise**, s., salida del sol f.; amanecer m.; **—set**, puesta del sol f.; **—shine**, luz del sol f.; **—stroke**, insolación f.

Sunday, són-di, s., domingo m.

sundries, sŏn'-dris, s., géneros varios m. pl.

sundry, sŏn'-dri, a., vario, diverso

sunken, sŏng'-kn, a., hundido

sup, sŏp, v., cenar; **—per**, s., cena f.

super, siuu'-per, s., (theatrical) comparsa m. & f.; **—annuation**, s., pensión f.; **—cilious**, a., arrogante; **—ficial**, superficial; **—fine**, superfino; **—intend,** v., vigilar; **—intendent,** superintendente m.; **—natural,** lo sobrenatural n.; **—sede,** v., reemplazar; **—vise,** inspeccionar; **—vision,** s., vigilancia f.

superb*, siu-pĕrb', a., soberbio

superfluous*, sŏp'-ĕr-flu-os, a., supérfluo

superior*, siuu-pi'-ri-a, a., superior [m.

superlative*, siuu-pĕr'-la-tiv, s. & a*., superlativo

superstitious*, siuu-pĕr-stish'-os, a., supersticioso

supplant*, so-plaant', v., suplantar

supple, sŏp'-l, a., flexible

supplement, sŏp'-li-ment, s., suplemento m.

supplicant, sŏp'-li-kant, s. & a., suplicante m. & f.

supplier, sŏp'-lai-a, s., proveedor m.; suministrador

supply, so-plai', v., proveer. s., provisión f. [m.

support, so-pórt', s., (prop.) puntal m.; (moral) sostén m.; (maintenance) manutención f. v., apuntalar; sostener; mantener

suppose, so-pous', v., suponer

supposition, so-pous-i'-shon, s., suposición f.

suppress, so-pres', v., suprimir; (conceal) ocultar

supremacy, siu-prem'-a-si, s., supremacía f.

supreme, siu-priim', a., supremo

surcharge, sĕr-chaardch', (postal) recargo m. v., recargar

sure*, shúr, a., seguro cierto

surety, shúr'-ti, s., (bail) fianza f.; (person) fiador m.

surf, sĕrf, s., oleado m.

surface, sĕr'-fis, s., superficie f.

surge, sĕrch, v., embravecerse. s., oleaje m.

surgeon, sĕr'-chon, s., cirujano m.

surgery, sĕr'-cher-i, s., cirugía f.

surgical, sĕr'-chi-kal, a., quirúrgico

surly, sĕr'-li, a., rudo; (dog) arisco

surmise, ser-mais', v., conjeturar. s., conjetura f.

surmount, ser-maunt', v., (overcome) vencer

surname, sĕr'-neim, s., apellido m.

surpass, ser-pass', v., superar, aventajar

surplus, sĕr'-plos, s., sobrante m., excedente m.

surprise, ɛer-prais', v., sorprender. s., sorpresa f.

surrender, ɛe-ren'-da, s., (mil.) rendición f. v., rendirse; (cede) ceder

surround, se-raund', v., rodear; (mil.) cercar

surroundings, se-raund'-ings, s., alrededores m. pl.

survey, sèr'-vei, s., (land, etc.) medición f. v., medir; (look at) inspeccionar; **—or,** s., topógrafo m.

survival, ser-vai'-vl, s., supervivencia f.

survive, ser-vaiv', v., sobrevivir

survivor, ser-vai'-vr, s., sobreviviente m.

susceptible, so-sep'-ti-bl, a., susceptible

suspect, sos-pekt', v., sospechar. s., sospechosa f.

suspend, sos-pend', v., suspender; (defer) aplazar

suspenders, sos-pen'-ders, s. pl., ligas f. pl.

suspense, sos'-pens, s., incertidumbre f.

suspension, sos-pen'-shon, s., suspensión f.; **—bridge,** puente colgante m.

suspicion, sos-pish'-on, s., sospecha f.

suspicious*, sos-pish'-os, a., sospechoso

sustain, sos-tein', v., sostener; mantener; sufrir

sustenance, sos'-ten-ans, s., sustento m.

swagger, suag'-a, v., fanfarronear

swallow, suol'-ou, s., trago m. v.; sorbo m.; (bird) golondrina f. v., tragar

swamp, suomp, s., pantano m. v., (boat) echar a pique

swan, suon, s., cisne m.

swarm, suoarm, s., nube f.; (bees) enjambre m.; (people) multitud f. v., enjambrar; hormiguear

sway, suei, v., oscilar; dominar; influir; (reel) tambalear. s., (power) poder m.; (influence) influjo m.

swear, suér', v., jurar; (curse) blasfemar

sweat, suet, s., sudor m. v., sudar

sweep, suiip, v., barrer; (chimney) deshollinar, s., (chimney) deshollinador m.; **—er,** barrendero m.; (carpet) escoba mecánica f.

sweet, suiit, a., dulce. s., (confection) golosina f.; (dinner, etc.) dulces m. pl.; **—bread,** lechecillas de ternera f. pl.; **—en,** v., endulzar; **—heart,** s., novio m., novia f.; **—ness,** dulzura f.; (smell) fragancia f.; **—pea,** guisante de olor m.

swell, suel, s., (sea) oleaje m. v., hinchar

swelling, suel'-ing, s., hinchazón f.

swerve, suérv, desviarse, apartarse

swift, suift, a., veloz, rápido

swim, suim, v., nadar. s., natación f.
swimmer, suim'-ma, s., nadador m.
swindle, suin'-dl, v., estafar. s., estafa f.
swindler, suin'-dla, s., estafador m.
swine, suain, s., cerdo m., puerco m.
swing, suing, s., oscilación f.; (child's) columpio m.
v., oscilar, balancear; columpiarse; (whirl) remolinar
switch, suich, s., (riding) latiguillo m.; (electric) con-
mutador m. v., (train) desviar; — **off,** (electric) cortar; — **on,** poner
swivel, sui'-vel, s., eslabón giratorio m.
swoon, swuun, v., desmayarse. s., desmayo m.
swoop, swuup, v., precipitarse; (bird) arrebatar
sword, sórd, s., espada f.
sworn, suórn, a., juramentado
syllable, sil'-a-bl, s., sílaba f.
syllabus, sil'-a-bos, s., sílabo m.; horario m.
symbol, sim'-bol, s., símbolo m.
symmetry, sim'-et-ri, s., simetría f.
sympathetic, sim-pa-zet'-ik, a., simpático
sympathize, sim-pa-zais', v., simpatizar
sympathy, sim'-pa-zi, s., simpatía f.
symptom, simp'-tom, s., síntoma m.
syndicate, sin'-di-keit, s., sindicato m.
synonymous, si-non'-i-mos, a., sinónimo
synchronize, sin'-kro-nais, v., sincronizar
syphilis, sif'-i-lis, s., sífilis f.
syphon, sai'-fon, s., sifón m.
syringe, sir'-inch, s., jeringa f. v., jeringar
syrup, sir'-op, s., jarabe m.; **fruit —,** jarabe de
system, sis'-tem, s., sistema m.   [frutas m.

tabernacle, tab'-er-nak'l, s., tabernáculo m.
table, tei'-bl, s., mesa f.; (list) cuadro m.; **—cloth,**
mantel m.; **—land,** meseta f.
table-spoon, tei'-bl-spuun, s., cuchara f.
tablet, tab'-let, s., tableta f.; placa f.; pastilla f.
tack, tak, s., tachuela f. v., clavar; (sew) hilvanar;
(naut.) virar
tackle, tak'-l, s., (fishing) avíos de pescar m. pl.;
(naut.) aparejo m. v., (attack) atajar

tact, takt, s., tacto m.; **—ful***, a., diplomático; **—less,** falto de tacto; **—ics,** s., táctica f.

tadpole, taḏ'-poul, s., renacuajo m.

tail, teil, s., rabo m.; (comet) cola f.; (dress) faldón m.

tailor, tei'-lr, v., sastre m.

taint, teint, v., manchar; infeccionar, s., mancha f.

take, teik, v., tomar, coger; (medicine) tomar; (accept) aceptar; (along) llevar; **— away,** llevar; **— care of,** cuidar de; **— off,** quitarse; (aero) elevarse

takings, tei'-kings, s. pl., ingresos m. pl.

tale, teil, s., narración f.; (fairy) cuento m.

talent, tɑl'-ent, s., talento m.

talk, toɑk, v., hablar, conversar. s., conversación f.

talkative, toɑk'-a-tiv, a., locuaz, charlatán

tall, toɑl, a., alto

tallow, tɑl'-ou, s., sebo m.

tally, tɑl'-i, v., (agree) concordar

talon, tɑl'-on, s., garra f.

tame, teim, a.,* domesticado; manso, v., domesticar; (animals) domar; **—ness,** s., mansedumbre f.; **—r,** domador m.

tamper, tɑm'-pa, **— with,** v., entremeterse en

tan, tɑn, v., curtir; (sun) tostar. s., casca f.; **—ner,** curtidor m.; **—nery,** tenería f.

tangerine, tɑn'-CHe-rin, s., mandarina f.

tangible, tɑn'-CHi-bl, a., tangible, palpable

tangle, tɑng'-gl, s., enredo m., embrollo m. v., enredar

tank, tɑngk, s., aljibe m.; (mil.) tanque m.

tankard, tɑng'-kerd, s., pichel m.

tantalize, tɑn'-ta-lais, v., atormentar

tantamount, tɑn'-ta-maunt, a., equivalente

tap, tɑp, s., golpecito m.; (on shoulder, etc.) palmada f.; (cock) grifo m.; (barrel) espita f. v., llamar; (tree) sangrar; (barrel) horadar

tape, teip, s., cinta f.; (adhesive) cinta adhesiva; (magnetic) cinta magnética, v., (record) registrar cinta magnética; **—measure,** s., cinta métrica; **—worm,** solitaria f.; **red —,** (fig.) formalismo

taper, tei'-pa, v., hacer punta. s., cirio m.   [m.

tapestry, tɑp'-es-tri, s., tapicería f.; (piece) tapiz m.

tappet, tᴀp-*et*, s., tope de empuje m.

tar, taar, s., brea f. alquitrán m. v., embrear

tardiness, taar'-di-nes, s., lentitud f.

tardy, taar'-di, a., tardo; (late) tardío

tare, tèr, s., (plant) cizaña f.; (weight) tara f.

target, taar'-guet, s., blanco m.

tariff, tᴀr'-if, s., tarifa f.

tarnish, taar'-nish, v., deslustrar; empañar

tarpaulin, taar'-po*a*'-lin, s., lienzo empegado m.

tart, taart, s., tarta f. a.,* ácido

task, taask, s., tarea f. faena f.

tassel, tas'-el, s., borla f.

taste, teist, v., gustar. s., gusto m.; sabor m.;
—**ful,** a., de buen gusto; —**less,** insípido, soso

tasty, teis'-ti, a., sabroso

tatter, tᴀt'-a, s., andrajo m., harapo m.

tattered, tᴀt'-erd, a., andrajoso

tattoo, ta-tuu', s., (mil.) retreta f. v., (the skin) ta-
tuar

taunt, to*a*nt, v., vituperar. s., vituperio m.

tavern, tᴀv'-ern, s., taberna f.

tawdry, to*a*'-dri, a., charro, chillón

tax, taks, v., poner impuestos. s., impuesto m.
contribución f.; —**payer,** contribuyente m.

taxi, tᴀks-i, s., taxi m.

tea, tii, s., té m.; —**pot,** tetera f.

teach, tiich, v., enseñar; —**er,** s., maestro m.;
profesor m.

teaching, tiich'-ing, s., enseñanza f.

team, tiim, s., (sport) equipo m.; (horses) tronco m.; (oxen) yunta f.

tear, tér, v., (rend) rasgar. s., rasgón m.

tear, tir, s., lágrima f.

tease, tiis, v., molestar; (joke) embromar

teat, tiit, s., teta f.; (dummy) chupete m.

technical*, tek'-ni-kl, a., técnico

technique, tek-niik', s., técnica f.

technology, tek-nol'-o-cHi, s., tecnología f.

tedious*, tii'-di-os, a., aburrido, pesado

tedium, tii'-di-öm, s., tedio m., fastidio m.

teem, tiim, v., abundar

teething, til'-Ding, s., dentición f.

teetotaller, tii'-tou-t'l*a*, s., abstemio m.

telegram, tel'-i-gram, s., telegrama f.

telegraph, tel'-i-graf, v., telegrafiar. s., telégrafo m.

telephone, tel'-i-foun, v., telefonear. s., teléfono m.

telephoto, tel'-i-fou-to, s., telefoto m.

telescope, tel'-i-skoup, s., telescopio m.

telescope, tel'-i-skoup, s., telescopio m.

television, tel'-i-vish-on, s., televisión f.

tell, tel, v., decir; (relate) contar

temper, tem'-p*a*, s., humor m.; (steel) temple m. v., templar

temperance, tem'-per-ans, s., moderación f.; sobriedad f. a., sobrio

temperate, tem'-per-et, a., moderado; (habits) morigerado

temperature, tem'-per-a-tiur, s., temperatura f. (fever) calentura f.

tempest, tem'-pest, s., tempestad f., tormenta f.

temple, tem'-pl, s., templo m.; (head) sien f.

temporary, tem'-po-ra-ri, a., temporario

tempt, tempt, v., tentar; **—ation,** s., tentación f.

ten, ten, s. & a., diez m.; **—th,** décimo m.

tenable, ten'-a-bl, a., defensible

tenacious*, ti-nei'-shos, a., tenaz

tenacity, ti-nas'-i-ti, s., tenacidad f.

tenancy, ten'-an-si, s., tenencia f.; inquilinato m.

tenant, ten'-ant, s., inquilino m.

tend, tend, v., guardar; (nurse) cuidar

tendency, ten'-den-si, s., tendencia f.

tender, ten'-d*a*, v., ofrecer. s., oferta f.; (public) sumisión f. a.,* tierno; (sensitive) sensitivo; **—hearted,** compasivo; **—ness,** s., (affection) ternura f.

tenement, ten'-i-ment, s., habitación f., vivienda f.

tennis, ten'-is, s., tenis m.

tenor, ten'-or, s., tenor m.; (purport) substancia f.

tense, tens, a.,* tenso, tirante. s., (grammar) tiempo m.

tension, ten'-shon, s., tensión f., tirantez f. [m.

tent, tent, s., tienda de campaña f.

tentative*, ten'-ta-tiv, a., tentativo

tenure, ten'-iur, s., tenencia f.

tepid, tep'-id, a., tibio

term, těrm, s., término m.; (time) período m.
terminate, těr'-mi-neit, v., terminar
terminus, těr'-mi-nos, s., estación terminal f.
terms, těrms, s. pl., condiciones f. pl.; (instalments) plazos m. pl.
terrace, ter'-is, s., terraplén m.
terrible, ter'-i-bl, a., terrible
terrific, ter-if'-ik, a., terrífico, formidable
terrify, ter'-i-fai, v., aterrar
territory, ter'-i-to-ri, s., territorio m.
terror, ter'-or, s., terror m., espanto m.
terrorize, ter'-or-ais, v., aterrorizar
terse*, těrs, a., conciso, breve
test, test, v., probar, ensayar. s., prueba f., ensayo m.; examen m.; **—ify,** v., testificar; **—imonial,** s., recomendación f.; (presentation) testimonial m.; **—imony,** testimonio m.
testicle, tes'-ti-kl, s., testículo m.
tether, teD'-a, s., traba f. v., estacar
text, text, s., texto m.; **—book,** libro de texto m.
textile, tex'-tail, a., textil
texture, tex'-tiur, s., tejido m.; textura f.
than, Dan, conj., que; de
thank, zangk, v., agradecer; **— you!** interj., ¡ gracias ! **—ful,** a., agradecido; **—less,** desagradecido; **—s,** s. pl., gracias f. pl.; **—s to,** gracias a
thanksgiving, zangks'-guiv-ing, s., acción de gracias f.
that, Dat, a., ese m., esa f.; aquel m., aquella f. pron., ése m., ésa f., eso n.; aquel m., aquella f., aquello n. relative pron., que. conj., que, para que; **— is,** es decir; **— one,** aquel, aquella
thatch, zach, s., barda f. v., bardar
thaw, zoa, s., deshielo m. v., deshelar
the, De, art., el; la; lo; los; las
theatre, zii'-a-ta, s., teatro m.
theft, zeft, s., robo m.; (petty) hurto m.
their, Dér, poss. adj., su; suyo; suya; de ellos; de ellas
theirs, Dérs, pron., el suyo; la suya; los suyos; las suyas

them, Dem, pron., los; las; les; ellos; ellas

theme, ziim, s., tema m.

themselves, Dem-selvs', pron., ellos mismos; ellas mismas; sí mismos

then, Den, adv., entonces; luego. conj., pues

thence, Dens, adv., desde allí

thenceforth, Dens-fórz', adv., desde entonces

theology, zi-ol'-*o*-CHi, s., teología f.

theoretical*, zi-o-ret'-i-kal, a., teórico

theory, zii'-*o*-ri, s., teoría f.

there, Dér, adv., allí; allá; ahí; —**about,** por allí; —**after,** después; —**by,** de este modo; —**fore,** por consiguiente; —**from,** de allí; de allá; —**in,** en eso; en esto; —**upon,** en consecuencia; —**with,** con eso

thermal, zěr'-ml, a., termal

thermometer, zěr-mom'-i-ter, s., termómetro m.

thermostat, zěr-mou-stat, s., termostato m.

these, Diis, pron. & a., estos; estas

thesis, zi'-sis, s., tesis f.; disertación f.

they, Dei, pers, pron., ellos m., ellas f.

thick*, zik, a., grueso; denso; (liquids) espeso; —**en,** v., espesar; —**et,** s., matorral m.; —**ness,** grosor m.; espesura f.; densidad f.

thief, ziif, s., ladrón m.

thieve, ziiv, v., (theft) hurtar; (robbery) robar

thigh, zai, s., muslo m.

thimble, zim'-bl, s., dedal m.

thin, zin, a., delgado; (sparse) ralo, escaso, v., adelgazar; (plants, etc.) enralecer; —**ness,** s., delgadez f.

thine, Dain, pron. & a., tuyo; tuya

thing, zing, s., cosa f.; (business) asunto m.

think, zingk, v., pensar; (believe) creer; — **of,** pensar en; (opinion) pensar de; — **over,** pensarlo

third, zěrd, s., tercio m. a., tercero

thirdly, zěrd'-li, adv., en tercer lugar

thirst, zěrst, s., sed f.; **to be —y,** tener sed

thirteen, zěr'-tiin, s. & a., trece m.

thirteenth, zěr'-tiinz, s. & a., décimotercero m.

thirtieth, zěr'-ti-iiz, s. & a., trigésimo m.

thirty, zěr'-ti, s. & a., treinta m.

this, Dis, pron., éste, ésta, esto. a., este, esta

thistle, zis'-l, s., cardo m.

thither, DiD'-*α*, adv., allí, allá

thong, zong, s., correa f.

thorn, zoαrn, s., espina f.; **—y,** a., espinoso

thorough*, zŏr'-*o*, a., entero; perfecto; real; **—bred,** de pura raza; **—fare,** s., vía pública f.; (main street) calle principal f.; **no —fare,** prohibido el paso

those, Dous, pron. & a., esos m.; esas f.; aquellos m.; aquellas f.

though, Dou, conj., aunque; sin embargo

thought, zoαt, s., pensamiento m.; **—ful*,** a., pensativo; considerado; atento; **—less*,** atolondrado; inconsiderado

thousand, zau'-sαnd, s. & a., mil m.

thousandth, zau'-sαnds, s. & a., milésimo m.

thrall, zrŏαl, s., esclavo m.; esclavitud f.

thrash, zrash, v., trillar; (flog) azotar; **—ing,** s., trilla f.; (flogging) zurra f.; **—ing-machine,** s., trilladora mecánica f.

thread, zred, s., hilo m. v., enhilar; **—bare,** a., raído

threat, zret, s., amenaza f.; **—en,** v., amenazar

threatening, zret'-ning, a., amenazador

three, zrii, s. & a., tres m.; **—fold,** a., triple

threshold, zresh'-jould, s., umbral m.

thrice, zrais, adv., tres veces

thrift, zrift, s., economía f.; **—less,** a., pródigo

thrifty, zrift'-i, a., económico

thrill, zril, v., causar una emoción. s., conmoción f.

thrive, zraiv, v., prosperar; (plants; physically) medrar [medrar]

throat, zrout, s., garganta f.

throb, zrob, v., vibrar; (heart) latir

throes, zrous, s., dolores m. pl.; (fig.) congojas f. pl.

throne, zroun, s., trono m.

throng, zrong, s., tropel m., multitud f. v., apiñarse

throttle, zrot'-l, s., (mech.) gollete m. v., (kill) ahogar

through, zruu, prep., por, a través de, a causa de; **—out,** por entre, todo. adv., (everywhere) en todas partes; **—train,** s., tren directo m.

throw, zrou, v., echar, lanzar. s., toro m.; echada f.

thrush, zrŏsh, s., tordo m.

thrust, zrŏst, v., empujar; (sword) embestir, s., empuje m.; (sword) estocada f.

thud, zŏd, s., baque m.

thumb, zŏm, s., pulgar m.

thump, zŏmp, s., porrazo m. v., aporrear

thunder, zŏn´-da, v., tronar. s., trueno m.; **— bolt,** rayo m.; **—-storm,** tronada f.

Thursday, zĕrs´-di, s., jueves m.

thus, Dŏs, adv., así; de ese modo

thwart, zuoart, v., frustrar

thyme, taim, s., tomillo m.

tick, tik, v., (clock) hacer tic-tac; (check) contramarcar. s., (cattle) garrapata f.; (cover) terliz m.; **—ing,** tic-tac m.

ticket, tik´-et, s., billete m.; (label) etiqueta f.; **season—,** abono m.

tickle, tik´-l, v., hacer cosquillas

ticklish, tik´-lish, a., cosquilloso

tidal, tai´-dl, a., de marea

tide, taid, s., marea f.; **high —,** plenamar f.; **low —,** bajamar f.; marea meguante f.

tidings, tai´-dings, s. pl., noticias f. pl., nuevas f. pl.

tidy, tai´-di, a., ordenado; (neat) pulcro. v., poner en orden

tie, tai, s., (bow) lazo m.; (neck) corbata f. v., atar, liar; unir; (surgery) ligar

tier, tir, s., fila f.; (theatre) fila de palcos f.

tiff, tif, s., pique m., disgusto m.

tiger, tai´-ga, s., tigre m.

tight', tait, a., cerrado; (garments) estrecho, apretado; **air—,** herrmético; **en,** v., estrechar; (a screw) apretar; **water—,** a., estanco

tights, taits, s. pl., calzas ajustadas f. pl

tile, tail, s., (roof) teja f.; (glazed) azulejo m.; (floor) baldosa f. v., tejar

till, til, v., (land) labrar. conj., hasta que. prep., hasta

tiller, til´-a, s., (naut.) caña del timón f.

tilt, tilt, v., inclinar, ladear

timber, tim-ba, s., madera de construcción f.

time, taim, v., medir el tiempo. s., tiempo m.; (occasion) vez f.; (hour) hora f.; (music; in marching) compás m.; **—keeper,** marcador de tiempo m.; **—ly,** a. & adv., oportuno

time-table, raim-tei'-bl, s., horario m.

timid*, tim-id, a., tímido

tin, tin, v., estañar. s., (metal) estaño m., lata f.; **—box,** caja de lata f.; **—foil,** hoja de estaño f.; **—ned,** (food) en lata; **—plate,** hoja de lata f.

tincture, tingk'-tiur, s., tintura f.

tinder, tin'-da, s., mecha f.

tinge, tinch, v., colorar. s., tinte m.; (fig.) dejo m.

tingle, ting'-l, v., sentir hormigueo

tinkle, tingk'-l, v., retiñir. s., retintín m.

tinsel, tin'-sl, s., oropel m., brocadillo m.

tint, tint, s., tinte m. v., teñir

tiny, tai'-ni, a., minúsculo, pequeño, chico

tip, tip, v., (cart. etc.) volcar; (give) dar propina. s., propina f.; (point) punta f.; **on —toe,** adv., de puntillas

tire, tair, s., (rim) llanta f. v., cansar, fatigar; **—d,** a., cansado; **— of,** v., cansarse de

tiresome, tair'-som, a., fastidioso

tissue, tish'-iu, s., tejido m.; (veiling) gasa f.

tissue-paper, tish'-iu-pei'-pa, s., papel de seda f.

tithe, taiD, s., diezmo m.

title, tai'-tl, s., título m.; **— deed,** título de propiedad m.; **— page,** portada f.

titter, tit'-a, v., reír entre dientes

to, tu, prep., a, en, de, por, hasta, con

toad, toud, s., sapo m.

toast, toust, s., (bread) tostada f. v., tostar [m.

toast, toust, v., (propose health) brindar s., brindis

tobacco, to-bak'-ou, s., tabaco m.; **—nist,** estanquero m.; **—pouch,** bolsa para tabaco f.

toboggan, to-bog'-an, s., tobogán m.

to-day, tu-dei, adv., hoy

toe, tou, s., dedo del pie m.

toffee, tof'-i, s., caramelo m.

together, to-gueD'-a, adv., juntos, juntamente

toil, toil, v., afanarse s., faena f., trabajo penoso m.

toiler, toi´-l*a*, s., trabajador m.

toilet, toi´-let, s., tocado m.; (W.C.) retrete m.

token, tou´-kn, s., señal f.; (gift) recuerdo m.

tolerable, tol´-er-a-bl, a., tolerable, pasadero

tolerance, tol´-er-ans, s., tolerancia f.

tolerant*, tol´-er-ant, a., tolerante

tolerate, tol´-er-eit, v., tolerar

toll, toul, s., (due) portazgo m.; (bell) tañido m. v., doblar

tomato, to-maa´-tou, s., tomate m.

tomb, tuum, s., tumba f.; **—stone,** lápida sepulcral f.

tomboy, tom´-boi, s., moza retozona f.

tomcat, tom´-kat, s., gato m.

tomfoolery, tom-fuul´-er-i, s., mentecatada f.

to-morrow, tu-mor´-ou, adv., mañana

tomtit, tom´-tit, s., paro m.

ton, tŏn, s., tonelada f.; **—nage,** tonelaje m.

tone, toun, s., tono m.

tongs, tongs, s. pl., tenazas f. pl.

tongue, tŏng, s., lengua f.; **—tied,** a., con frenillo

tonic, ton´-ik, s. & a., tónico m.

to-night, tu-nait´, adv., esta noche

tonsil, ton´-sil, s., tonsila f.; **—itis,** tonsilitis f.

too, tuu, adv., demasiado; (also) también; **—much,** demasiado

tool, tuul, s., herramienta f.

tooth, tuuz, s., diente m.; **—ache,** dolor de muelas m.; **—brush,** cepillo de dientes m.; **—paste,** pasta dentífrica f.; **—pick,** mondadientes m.; **—powder,** polvos dentífricos m. pl.

top, top, s., (upper part) parte de arriba f.; (mountain) cumbre f.; (of tree) copa f.; (school) primero m.; (spinning) peonza f.; **—boots,** botas de montar f. pl.; **—gear,** marcha directa f.; **—hat,** chistera f.; **on —,** encima

topic, top´-ik, s., tópico m., tema m.

topple (over), top´-l, v., volcarse

topsy-turvy, top´-si-tër´-vi, adv., trastornado

torch, toarch, s., antorcha f., hacha f.

torment, to*ar*´-ment, s., tormento m. v., atormentar

tornado, to*ar*-nei´-dou, s., tornado m.

torpedo, to*ar*-pii'-dou, s., torpedo m.; —**-boat,** torpedero m.

torpid, to*ar*'-pid, a., entorpecido, aletargado

torpor, to*ar*'-pr, s., torpor m.; estupor m.

torque, to*ar*k, s., (mech.) momento de torsión m.; (necklace) collar m.

torrent, to*ar*'-ent, s., torrente m.

torrid, to*ar*'-id, a., tórrido

tortoise, to*ar*'-tos, s., tortuga f.; —**-shell,** concha f.

torture, to*ar*'-tiur, v., torturar s., tortura f.

toss, tos, s., sacudida f. v., lanzar; (coin) echar a cara o cruz; (bull, etc.) revolcar; —**about,** revolverse

total, tou'-tl, s., total m. a.,* total, completo v., sumar, totalizar; —**isator,** s., totalizador m.

totter, tot'-*a*, v., bambolear; —**ing,** a., ruinoso

touch, tŏch, s., contacto m., tocar. v. m. v., tocar; (emotion) conmover; —**ing,** a., commovedor

touchy, tŏch'-i, a., susceptible

tough*, tŏf, a., duro; correoso

tour, túr, s., excursión f. v., viajar por —**ist,** s., turista m. & f.; —**nament,** torneo m.

tout, taut, s., gancho m. v., enganchar

tow, tou, v., (haul) remolcar. s., (flax) estopa f.; —**ing,** remolque m.; —**ing-path,** camino de sirga m.; —**rope,** sirga f.

towards, tou'-*erds*, prep., con, para con; (direction) hacia

towel, tau-*el*, s., toalla f., paño de manos m.

tower, tau-*a*, s., torre f.

town, taun, s., ciudad f.; —**-hall,** ayuntamiento m.

toy, toi, s., juguete m. v., juguetear

trace, treis, s., (track) huella f., rastro m.; (harness) jaez n. v., seguir la pista; (draw) trazar

tracing, treis'-ing, s., trazo m.; —**-paper,** papel de calcar m.

track, trak, s., rastro m.; (race) pista f.; (railway) via f. v., seguir la pista

tract, trakt, s., trecho m.; (religious) opúsculo m.

traction, trak'-shon, s., arrastre m.; —**-engine,** locomotora de arrastre m.

trade, treid, v., comerciar. s., comercio m.; (craft)

oficio m.; **—mark,** marca de fábrica f.; **—sman,** tendero m.; **—s-union,** sindicato m.

trading, tre´-ding, s., comercio m. a., mercantil

tradition, tra-dish´-on, s., tradición f.

traditional*, tra-dish´-on-al, a., tradicional

traffic, traf´-ik, s., circulación f.; (trade) intercambio m.; **— lights,** s., luces de tráfico f. pl.

tragedian, tra-chii´-di-an, s., trágico m.

tragedy, trach´-i-di, s., tragedia f.

tragic, trach´-ik, a., trágico

trail, treil, v., seguir el rastro; (drag) arrastrar s., rastro m., pista f.; **—er,** (van) remolque m.

train, trein, s., tren m.; (dress) cola f.; (retinue) séquito m. v., instruir; educar; disciplinar; (animals) amaestrar; (sport) entrenar; **—ing,** s., instrucción f.; (sport) entrenaje m.

traitor, trei´-ta, s., traidor m.

tram, tram, s., tranvía m.

tramp, tramp, s., vagabundo m. v., ir a pie

trample, tram´-pl, v., hollar, pisotear

trance, traans, s., síncope m.; éxtasis m.

tranquil*, trang´-kuil, a., tranquilo

transact, tran-sakt´, v., tramitar

transaction, tran-sakt´-shon, s., negociación f.

transcribe, tran-skraib´, v., transcribir

transfer, trans-fër´, v., transferir. s., traspaso m.

transform, trans-foarm´, v., transformar

tranship, tran-ship´, v., transbordar

transit, tran´-sit, s., tránsito m.

translate, trans-leit´, v., traducir

translation, trans-lei´-shon, s., traducción f.

translator, trans-lei´-ta, s., traductor m.

transmit, trans-mit´, v., negociar

transparent*, ৰans-pé´-rent, a., transparente

transpire, trans-pair´, v., transpirar   [m.

transport, trans-pórt´, v., transportar, s., transporte

transpose, trans-pous´, v., transponer

trap, trap, v., atrapar. s., trampa f.

trap-door, trap´-dór, s., escotillón m.

trash, trash, s., (fig.) desperdicios m. pl.; hojarasca f.; **—y,** a., hojarascoso

travel, trav´-l, v., viajar; **—ler,** s., viajero m.

traverse, trav'-*ers*, v., atravesar. a., transversal

trawler, trou'-*la*, s., (ship) buque para la pesca a la rastra m.

tray, trei, s., bandeja f.

treacherous*, trech'-*er-os*, a., traidor

treachery, trech'-*er-i*, s., traición f.

treacle, trii'-kl, s., meladura f.

tread, tred, v., pisar. s.,¶ paso m.; (stair) escalón m.

treason, trii'-sn, s., traición f.

treasure, tresh'-*er*, s., tesoro m. v., atesorar

treasurer, tresh'-*er-a*, s., tesorero m.

treasury, tresh'-*er-i*, s., tesorería f.

treat, triit, s., (entertainment) festín m.; (outing) excursión campestre f. v., (negotiate) tratar

treatise, trii'-tis, s., tratado m., memoria f.

treatment, triit'-ment, s., trato m.; tratamiento m.

treaty, trii'-ti, s., tratado m., pacto m.

treble, treb'-l, a., triple v., triplicar. s., (mus.) tiple f.

tree, trii, s., árbol m.; **family —,** árbol genealógico

trellis, trel'-is, s., enrejado m. [m.

tremble, trem'-bl, v., temblar

tremendous*, tri-men'-dos, a., tremendo

tremulous*, trem'-iu-los, a., trémulo

trench, trench, s., zanja f.; (mil.) trinchera f.

trend, trend, s., curso m. v., inclinarse

trespass, tres'-pas, v., traspasar; infringir

trespasser, tres'-pas-*a*, s., transgresor m.

trestle, tres'-l, s., caballete m.

trial, trai'-*al*, s., prueba f.; (law) juicio m.

triangle, trai'-Ang-gl, s., triángulo m.

triangle, trai'-Ang-gl, s., triángulo m.

triangular, trai-Ang'-giuu-*la*, a., triangular

tribe, traib, s., tribu f.

tribunal, trai-biuu'-*nal*, s., tribunal m.

tributary, trib'-iu-ta-ri, s. & a., tributario m.

tribute, trib'-iuut, s., tributo m.

trick, trik, s., (fraud) engaño m., timo m.; (dexterity) juego de manos m.; (cards) baza f.; (joke) broma f. v., engañar, timar; **—ery,** s., engaño m.; **—ster,** s., trapacero m.

trickle, trik'-l, v., (drip) gotear; (flow) escurrir
trifle, trai'-fl, s., bagatela f.; **— with,** v., jugarse de
trifling, trai'-fling, a., insignificante
trigger, trig'-a, s., gatillo m.
trill, tril, v., trinar. s., trino m.
trim, trim, v., (hat; dress) guarnecer; (hair, etc.) recortar; (ship; sails) orientar. a., aseado
trimming, trim'-ing, s., (garments) guarnición f.
trinity, trin'-i-ti, s., trinidad f.
trinket, tring'-ket, s., chuchería f.; (jewel) joya f.
trio, tri'-ou, s., trío m.; (music) terceto m.
trip, trip, s., excursión f., viaje corto m. v., (stumble) tropezar; **—per,** s., excursionista f.; **— up,** v., echar una zancadilla
tripe, traip, s., tripas f. pl.
triple, trip'-l, a., triple
triplets, trip'-lets, s. pl., trillizos m. pl.
tripod, trai'-pod, s., trípode m.
triumph, trai'-omf, s., triunfo m. v., triunfar
trivial*, triv'-i-al, a., trivial, insignificante
trolley, trol'-i, s., carreta baja f.
trombone, trom'-boun, s., trombón m. [m.
troop, truup, s., tropa f.; **—ship,** buque transporte
trooper, truu'-pa, s., soldado de caballería m.
trophy, trou'-fi, s., trofeo m.
tropical, trop'-i-kal, a., tropical
tropics, tro'-piks, s. pl., trópicos m. pl.
trot, trot, v., trotar. s., trote m.
trouble, trob'-l, v., molestar; (perturb) perturbar. s., (cares) afanes m. pl., inquietudes f. pl.; (inconvenience) molestia f.; (disturbance) disturbio m.; alboroto m.; (difficulty) dificultad f.; **—some,** a., (difficult) difícil
trough, tröf, s., artesa f.; (cattle, etc.) pilón m.
trounce, trauns, v., zurrar
trousers, trau'-sers, s. pl., pantalones m. pl.
trout, traut, s., trucha f.
trowel, trau'-el, s., (mason's) llana f.; (garden) desplantador m.
truant, truu'-ant, **play —,** v., hacer novillos
truce, truus, s., tregua f.

truck, trŏk s., carreta f.; (railway) furgón de andén

truculent*, trŏk'-iu-lent, a., truculento; cruel [m.

trudge, trŏCH, v., arrastrarse; — **along,** andar penosamente

true, truu, a., verdadero; (faithful) fiel

truffle, trŏf'-l, s., trufa f.

truism, truu'-ism, s., verdad evidente f.; axioma m.

trump, trŏmp, v., jugar triunfo. s., triunfo m.

trumpery, trŏm'-per-i, s., oropel m. a., de relumbrón

trumpet, trŏm'-pet, s., trompeta f.

truncheon, trón'-shon, s., porra f., garrote m.

trunk, trŏngk s., (tree) tronco m.; (elephant) trompa f.; (travelling) baúl m.; (body) tronco m.; **—call,** conferencia f.

truss, trŏs, s., baz m.; (surgical) braguero m. v., ligar; (poultry) espetar

trust, trŏst, s., confianza f.; (combine) trust m., v., confiar en, fiarse de; (rely) contar con

trustee, trŏs'-tii, s., (public) fideicomisario m.; (bankruptcy) síndico m.

trustworthy, trŏst'-uĕr-Di, a., fidedigno, fiable

truth, truuz, s., verdad f.; **—ful*,** a., veraz

try, trai, v., procurar, tratar de; (taste) probar; (law) procesar, juzgar; **—ing,** a., penoso; **— on,** v., probarse

tub, tŏb, s., tina f., cuba f.; (bath) bañera f.

tube, tiuub, s., tubo m., caño m.; **inner —,** s., cámara de aire f.

tuck, tŏk, s., pliegue m. v., plegar; **— in,** (rug, etc.) arropar; **— up,** arremangar

Tuesday, tiuus'-di, s., martes m.

tuft, tŏft, s., copete m.; (feathers) penacho m.

tug, tŏg, v., tirar de; (boats) remolcar. s., tirón m.

tug-boat, tŏg'-boat, s., remolcador m.

tuition, tiu-ish'-on, s., instrucción f., enseñanza f.

tulip, tiuu'-lip, s., tulipán m.

tumble, tóm'-bl, v., (fall) desplomarse

tumbler, tóm'-bla, s., vaso sin pie m.

tumour, tiuu'-mor, s., tumor m.

tumult, tiuu'-molt, s., tumulto m.; (riot) motín m.

tune, tiuun, v., afinar. s., aire m., tonada f.

tuneful, tiuun'-ful, a., melodioso

tunic, tiuu'-nik, s., túnica f.; (mil.) guerrera f.
tuning-fork, tiuu'-ning-fo**a**rk, s., diapasón m.
tunnel, tŏn'-l, s., túnel m. v., horadar
tunny, tŏn'-i, s., atún m.
turbine, tĕr'-bain, s., turbina f.
turbot, tĕr'-bot, s., rodaballo m.
turbulent*, tĕr'-biu-lent, a., turbulento   [f.
tureen, tiu-riin', s., (soup) sopera f.; (sauce) salsera
turf, tĕrf, s., césped m.; (peat) turba f.
turkey, tĕr'-ki, s., pavo m.
turmoil, tĕr'-moil, s., alboroto m., disturbio m.
turn, tĕrn, s., vuelta f.; (duty) servicio m.; (order
of succession) turno m. v., volver; volverse;
— **about,** girar; — **aside,** desviar; — **back,**
retroceder; — **ing,** s., (corner) vuelta f.; —**ing-
point,** punto decisivo m.; — **into,** v., convertir; — **off,** cerrar; — **on,** abrir; — **out,**
(expel) echar; (light) apagar; — **over,** volver;
volverse, s., (trade) cifra total f.; —**to,** v., acudir
turner, tĕr'-na, s., (artisan) tornero m.
turnip, tĕr'-nip, s., nabo m.
turnstile, tĕrn'-stail, s., torniquete m.
turpentine, tĕr'-pen-tain, s., trementina f.   [f.
turret, tĕr'-et, s., torrecilla f.; (naval) torre blindada
turtle, tĕr'-tl, s., tortuga f.; —**-dove,** tórtola f.;
turn—, v., dar la vuelta
tusk, tŏsk, s., colmillo m.
tussle, tŏs'-l, v., luchar. s., agarrada f.
tutor, tiuu'-ta, s., tutor m.; v., enseñar
twang, tua**n**g, s., tono nasal m.; (sound) estri-
dor m.; (string) punteado m.; (taste) dejo m.
tweezers, tuii'-**sas**, s. pl., pinzas f. pl.; (hair) tenacillas f. pl.
twelfth, tuelfz, s. & a., duodécimo m.
twelve, tuelv, s. & a., doce m.
twentieth, tuen'-ti·iz, s. & a., vigésimo m.
twenty, tuen'-ti, s. & a., veinte m.
twice, tuais, adv., dos veces
twig, tuig, s., ramita f.
twilight, tuai'-lait, s., crepúsculo m.
twill, tuil, s., tela cruzada f.
twin, tuin, s. & a., gemelo m.; mellizo m.

twine, tuain, v., enroscarse. s., guita f.; pita f.
twinge, tuincн, s., punzada f. v., punzar
twinkle, tuing'-kl, v., centellear; (eyes) parpadear
twirl, tuěrl, v., voltear, girar. s., vuelta f.
twist, tuist, v., torcer. s., (turn) vuelta f.
twitch, tuich, s., crispamiento m. v., crisparse
twitter, tuit'-a, v., gorjear. s., gorjeo m.
two, tuu, s. & a., dos m.; —**fold,** a., doble
type, taip, s., tipo m. v., escribir a máquina
typewriter, taip'-rai-ta, s., máquina de escribir f.
typhoid, tai'-fo-id, s., fiebre tifoidea f.
typical*, tip'-i-kal, a., típico
typist, tai'-pist, s., dactilógrafa f.
typography, taip-o'-gra-fi, s., tipografía f.
tyrannical*, ti-raN'-i-kl, a., tiránico
tyrannize, tir'-an-ais, v., tiranizar
tyrant, tai'-rant, s., tirano m.
tyre, tair, s., llanta f.; (pneumatic) neumático m.

ubiquitous, iuu-bik'-ui-tos, a., ubicuo
udder, ŏd'-a, s., ubre f.
ugliness, ŏg'-li-nes, s., fealdad f.
ugly, ŏg'-li, a., feo
ulcer, ŏl'-sa, s., úlcera f.
ulcerate, ŏl'-ser-eit, v., ulcerar
ulterior, ŏl-ti'-ri-or, a., ulterior
ultimate*, ŏl'-ti-met, a., último; fundamental
ultimatum, ŏl-ti-mei'-tŏm, s., ultimátum m.
ultimo, ŏl'-ti-mou, adv., del mes próximo pasado
ultra, ŏl'-tra, ultra, extremo
umbrella, ŏm-brel'-a, s., paraguas m.; —**stand,** paragüero m.
umpire, ŏm-pair, s., árbitro m.
unabashed, ŏn-a-basht', a., descocado
unabated, ŏn-a-bei'-tid, a., completo, cabal
unable, ŏn-ei'-bl, a., incapaz. **to be —,** v., no poder
unacceptable, ŏn-ʌk-sep'-ta-bl, a., inaceptable
unaccountable, ŏn-a-kaun'-ta-bl, a., inexplicable
unacquainted, ŏn-a-kuen'-tid, a., desconocido. **to be — with,** v., desconocer
unaffected*, ŏn-a-fek'-tid, a., inafectado; (un-

moved) impasible
unaided, ŏn-ei'-did, a., sin ayuda
unalterable, ŏn-o̜al'-ter-a-bl, a., inalterable
unaltered, ŏn-o̜al'-terd, a., inalterado
unanimity, iuu-na-ni'-mi-ti, s., unanimidad f.
unanimous*, iuu-nan'-i-mos, a., unánime
unanswerable, ŏn-aan'-ser-a-bl, a., incontestable
unapproachable, ŏn-a-prouch'-a-bl, a., inaccesible
unarmed, ŏn-aarmd', a., desarmado
unashamed*, ŏn-a-sheimd', a., desvergonzado
unassailable, ŏn-a-sei'-la-bl, a., inatacable
unattainable, ŏn-a-tei'-na-bl, a., inasequible
unattended, ŏn-a-ten'-did, a., solo
unattractive, ŏn-a-trakt'-iv, a., inatractivo
unavoidable, ŏn-a-voi'-da-bl, a., inevitable
unaware, ón-a-uér', a., ignorante
unawares, ŏn-a-uérs, adv., desprevenido
unbearable, ŏn-bér'-a-bl, a., intolerable
unbecoming*, ŏn-bi-kŏm'-ing, a., impropio
unbeliever, ŏn-bi-liiv'-a, s., incrédulo m.
unbend, ŏn-bend', v., enderezar
unbending, ŏn-ben'-ding, a., inflexible
unbiassed, ŏn-bai'-ast, a., imparcial
unbleached, ŏn-bliicht', a., crudo
unblemished, ŏn-blem'-isht, a., sin tacha, puro
unbounded, ŏn-baun'-did, a., ilimitado
unbreakable, ŏn-breik'-a-bl, a., irrompible
unburden, ŏn-bér'-dn, v., descargar
unbutton, ŏn-bŏt'-ön, v., desabotonar, desabrochar
uncalled for, ŏn-k̜oald'-fór, a., immerecido; (remark) gratuito
uncanny, ŏn-kan'-i, a., misterioso
uncared for, ŏn-kérd'-for, a., abandonado
unceasing*, ŏn-siis'-ing, a., incesante
uncertain*, ŏn-sér'-tin, a., incierto
unchangeable, ŏn-chein'-cha-bl, a., invariable
uncivil, ŏn-siv'-il, a., incivil, descortés
unclaimed, ŏn-kleimd', a., no reclamado
uncle, oug'-kl, s., tío m.
unclean*, ŏn-kliin', a., sucio; impuro
uncomfortable, ŏn-kom'-for-ta-bl, a., incómodo

uncommon*, ŏn-kom´-on, a., raro ; extraordinario
unconcern*, ŏn-kón-sĕrn´, s., indiferencia f.
unconditional*, ŏn-kon-dish´-o-nl, a., incondicional
uncongenial*, ŏn-kon-CHii´-ni-al, a., antipático
unconscious*, ŏn-kon´-shos, a., sin sentido ; ignorante
uncontrollable, ŏn-kon-trou´-la-bl, a., indomable
unconventional*, ŏn-kon-ven´-shon-l, a., informal
uncork, ŏn-koark´, v., descorchar
uncouth*, ŏn-kuuz´, a., (manners) grosero
uncover, ŏn-kŏv´-a, v., descubrir
uncultivated, ŏn-kŏl´-ti-vei-tid, a., inculto
undated, ŏn-dei´-tid, a., sin fecha
undaunted*, ŏn-doan´-tid, a., impávido
undecided, ŏn-di-sai´-did, a., indeciso
undefiled, ŏn-di-faild´, a., impoluto, puro
undelivered, ŏn-di-liv´-erd, a., sin entregar
undeniable, ŏn-di-nai´-a-bl, a., innegable
under, ŏn´-da, adv., debajo, prep., bajo, debajo de ;
— **age**, a., menor de edad
undercarriage, ŏn´-da-kar-ich, s., bastidor m.
underclothing, ŏn´-da-klouD-ing, s., ropa interior f.
underdone, ŏn´-da-dŏn, a., poco cocido
underfed, ŏn´-da-fed, mal alimentado
undergo, ŏn´-da-gou, v., sufrir
underground, ŏn´-da-graund, a., subterráneo. s.,
(railway) metro m.
undergrowth, ŏn´-da-grouz, s., maleza f.
underhand, ŏn´-da-jand, a., clandestino
underline, ŏn´-da-lain, v., subrayar
undermine, ŏn´-da-main, v., minar
underneath, ŏn´-da-niiz´, adv., debajo. prep., bajo
under-proof, ŏn´-da-pruuf, a., de baja graduación
underrate, ŏn-da-reit´, v., menospreciar
undersell, ŏn-da-sel´, v., vender más barato
undersigned, ŏn´-da-saind, a., infrascrito
undersized, ŏn-da-saisd´, achaparrado ; (children
raquítico
understand, ŏn-da-stand´, v., entender ; —**ing**, s.
entendimiento m. ; inteligencia f.
understate, ŏn-da-steit´, v., quedarse corto
understudy, ŏn´-da-stŏd-i, s., sobresaliente f.

undertake, ŏn'-da-**te**ik, v., emprender; encargarse de

undertaker, ŏn'-da-**te**ik-a, s., director de pompas fúnebres m.

undertaking, ŏn'-da-**te**ik-ing, empresa f.

undertone, ŏn'-da-**to**un, tono bajo m.; voz baja f.

underwear, ŏn'-da-u**è**r, ropa interior f.

underwriter, ŏn'-da-**ra**i-ta, asegurador m.

undeserved,* ŏn-di-**sê**rvd', a., inmerecido; injusto

undesirable, ŏn-di-**sa**i'-ra-bl, a., indeseable

undignified, ŏn-dig'-ni-faid, a., sin dignidad

undiminished, ŏn-di-**mi**'-nisht, a., íntegro

undisclosed, ŏn-dis-**klo**usd', a., no revelado

undismayed, ŏn-dis-**me**id', a., impávido

undisturbed, ŏn-dis-**tê**rbd', a., sereno, tranquilo

undo, ŏn-**du**u', v., deshacer; (untie) desatar

undoubted, ŏn-**da**u'-tid, a., fuera de duda

undress, ŏn-**dr**es', v., desnudar, desnudarse

undue, ŏn-**di**uu', a., indebido; excesivo

unearned, ŏn-**ê**rnd', a., desmerecido; (money) no ganado

unearthly, ŏn-**ê**rz'-li, a., sobrenatural

uneasy, ŏn-**ii**'-si, a., inquieto, ansioso

uneducated, ŏn-ed'-**iu**u-kei-tid, a., indocto; ignorante; inculto

unemployed, ŏn-em-**plo**id', a., sin empleo

unemployment, ŏn-em-**plo**i'-ment, s., falta de trabajo f.

unequalled, ŏn-**ii**'-kuald, a., sin igual, sin par

unerring*, ŏn-**ê**r'-ing, a., infalible

uneven*, ŏn-**ii**'-vn, a., desigual; (road) escabroso

unexpected*, ŏn-eks-**pe**k'-tid, a., inesperado

unfailing*, ŏn-**fe**i'-ling, a., infalible, seguro

unfair*, ŏn-**fé**r', a., injusto

unfaithful*, ŏn-**fe**iz'-ful, a., infiel; desleal

unfaltering*, ŏn-**fo**al'-ter-ing, a., firme

unfasten, ŏn-**fa**s'-n, v., desatar; (dress) desabrochar

unfathomable, ŏn-**fa**D'-om-a-bl, a., insondable

unfavourable, ŏn-**fe**i'-vor-a-bl, a., desfavorable

unfeeling*, ŏn-**fi**i'-ling, a., insensible; cruel

unfit, ŏn-**fi**t', a., incapacitado; incompetente

unflagging*, ŏn-**fla**'-guing, a., infatigable

unflinching*, ŏn-**fli**nch'-ing, a., firme, resuelto

unfold, ŏn-fō**u**ld', v., desplegar; revelar
unforseen, ŏn-fō**a**r-sin', a., imprevisto
unfortunate*, ŏn-fō**a**r'-tiu-net, a., desgraciado
unfounded*, ŏn-fa**o**un'-did, a., infundado
unfriendly, ŏn-frend'-li, a., poco amistoso; hostil
unfulfilled, ŏn-f**u**l-fild', a., incumplido
unfurl, ŏn-f**ė**rl', v., desplegar; (naut.) desaferrar
unfurnished, ŏn-f**ė**r'-nisht, a., desamueblado
ungainly, ŏn-gu**ė**in'-li, a., desgarbado, sin gracia, desmañado
ungrateful*, ŏn-gr**ė**it'-ful, a., ingrato
unguarded*, ŏn-gaa**r**'-did, a., (uncontrolled) desprevenido
unhappily, ŏn-j**A**p'-i-li, adv., desdichadamente
unhappiness, ŏn-j**A**p'-i-nes, s., infelicidad f.j desgracia f.; desdicha f.
unhappy, ŏn-j**A**p'-i, a., desdichado infeliz
unharness, ŏn-jaar'-nes, v., desenjaezar
unhealthy, ŏn-jelz'-i, a., enfermizo; insalúbre
unheard, ŏn-j**ė**rd', a., inaudito;—of, sin ejemplo
unheeded, ŏn-jii'-did, a., desatendido
unhinge, ŏn-jin**CH**', v., desgoznar
unhinged, ŏn-jin**CH**d', a., (mind) turbado
unhurt, ŏn-j**ė**rt', a., ileso, indemne
unification, iuu-ni-fi-k**ė**i'-shon, s., unificación f.
uniform, iuu'-ni-fo**a**rm, s. & a., uniforme m.
uniformity, iuu-ni-fo**a**rm'-i-ti, s., uniformidad f.
unilateral* uu-ni-l**A**t'-te-ral, a., unilateral [ble
unimaginable, ŏn-im-**A**ch'-i-na-bl, a., inimagina-
unimaginative, ŏn-im-**A**ch'-i-na-tiv, a., sin imaginación
unimpaired, ŏn-im p**ė**rd', a., intacto, inalterado
unimpeachable, ŏn-im-piich'-**a**-bl, a., irreprensible
unimportant, ŏn-im-por'-tant, a., sin importancia
uninhabitable, ŏn-in-jab'-i'ta-bl, a., inhabitable
unintelligible, ŏn-in-tel'-ich-i-bl, a., ininteligible
unintentional, ŏn-in-ten'-shon-al, a., sin intención
uninviting, ŏn-in-v**ai**'-ting, a., poco atrayente
union, yuu'-ni-on, s., unión f.
unique, yu-n**ii**k', a., único
unit, yuu'-nit, s., unidad f.

unite, yu-nait', v., unir; juntar
unity, yuu'-ni-ti, s., unidad f.; concordia f.
universal*, yuu-ni-věr'-sl, a., universal
universe, yuu'-ni-věrs, s., universo m.
university, yuu-ni-věr'-si-ti, s., universidad f.
unjust*, ŏn-chŏst', a., injusto
unkind, ŏn-kaind', a., poco amable, desatento
unknown, ŏn-noun', a., desconocido; ignorado
unlawful*, ŏn-loa'-ful, a., ilegal, ilícito [excepto
unless, ŏn-les', conj., a menos que; como no sea]
unlike, ŏn-laik', a., desemejante
unlikely, ŏn-laik'-li, a., improbable
unlimited, ŏn-lim'-i-tid, a., ilimitado
unload, ŏn-loud', v., descargar
unlock, ŏn-lok', v., abrir; (fig.) revelar
unlooked for, ŏn-lukt' fór, a., inesperado
unlucky, ŏn-lŏk-i, a., desdichado, desgraciado;
(portend) de mal agüero
unmannerly, ŏn-man'-er-li, a., descortés, grosero
unmarried, ŏn-mar'-id, a., célibe, soltero
unmerciful*, ŏn-mŏr'-si-ful, a., inclemente, cruel
unmistakable*, ŏn-mis-tei'-ka-bl, a., inequívoco
unmoved, ŏn-muuvd', a., impasible, frío
unnatural*, ŏn-nat'-iu-rl, a., desnaturalizado; inhumano
unnecessary, ŏn-nes'-esa-ri, a., innecesario, su-
perfluo
unnerve, ŏn-něrv', v., amedrentar; enervar
unnoticed, ŏn-nou'-tist, a., inadvertido
unobtainable, ŏn-ob-tei'-na-bl, a., inasequible
unoccupied, ŏn-ok'-iu-paid, a., vacante; des-
unofficial, ŏn-o-fish'-l, a., no oficial [ocupado
unopposed, ŏn-o-posd', a., sin oposición
unorthodox, ŏn-or'-zo-doks, a., no ortodoxo
unpack, ŏn-pak', v., desembalar
unpardonable, ŏn-paar'-dŏn-a-bl, a., imperdona-
unpleasant*, ŏn-ples'-ant, a., desagradable [ble
unpopular, ŏn-pop'-iu-la, a., impopular
unprecedented, ŏn-pres'-i-den-tid, a., sin precedente
unprepared, ŏn-prii-peird', a., sin preparación;
desprevenido

unproductive*, ŏn-pro-dŏk'-tiv, a., improductivo
unprofitable, ŏn-prof'-i-ta-bl, a., no provechoso, improductivo
unpromising, ŏn-prom'-is-ing. a., que no promete
unprotected, ŏn-pro-tek'-tid, a., desamparado
unprovided, ŏn-pro-vai'-did, a., desprovisto; destituido
unpunctual, ŏn-pŏngk'-tiu-al, a., no puntual
unquestionable, ŏn-kues'-tion-a-bl, a., indisputable
unravel, ŏn-ʀav'-l, v., desenredar; (solve) resolver
unread, ŏn-red', a., sin leer; (person) inculto
unreadable, ŏn-ʀii'-da-bl. a., ilegible; malo
unreasonable, ŏn-ʀii'-son-a-bl, a., irracional
unrelated, ŏn-ri-lei'-tid, a., sin conexión
unrelenting, ŏn-ri-len'-ting, a., inexorable
unreliable, ŏn-ri-lai'-a-bl, a., inseguro
unremitting, ŏn-ri-mit'-ing, a., perseverante
unreserved, ŏn-ri-sĕrvd', a., sin reserva
unrest, ŏn-rest', s., inquietud f., desasosiego m.
unrestrained, ŏn-ri-streind', a., desenfrenado
unrestricted, ŏn-ri-strik'-tid, a., sin restricción
unripe, ŏn-raip, a., verde
unroll, ŏn-roul', v., desarrollar
unruly, ŏn-ruu'-li, a., ingobernable, turbulento
unsafe, ŏn-seif', a., poco seguro, inseguro
unsaleable, ŏn-seil-a-bl, a., invendible
unsatisfactory, ŏn-sat-is-fak'-to-ri, a., poco satisfactorio
unscrew, ŏn-skruu', v., destornillar
unscrupulous, ŏn-skruu'-piu-los, a., sin escrúpulo
unseasonable, ŏn-sii-sn-a-bl, a., intempestivo
unseemly, ŏn-siim'-li, a., indecente
unseen, ŏn-siin', a., invisible
unselfish*, ŏn-sel'-fish, a., desinteresado
unsettled, ŏn-set'-ld, a., inestable; pendiente
unshaken, ŏn-shei'-kn, a., inmovable, firme
unshrinkable, ŏn-shringk'-a-bl, a., que no se encoge
unshrinking, ŏn-shringk'-ing, a., intrépido
unsightly, ŏn-sait'-li, a., feo; disforme; deforme
unskilful*, ŏn-skil'-ful, a., inhábil; inexperto

unskilled, ŏn-skild', a., inexperto

unsociable, ŏn-sou'-sha-bl, a., insociable

unsold, ŏn-sould', a., no vendido

unsolicited, ŏn-so-lis'-i-tid, a., no solicitado

unsolved, ŏn-solvd', a., no resuelto

unsound, ŏn-saund', a., defectuoso; enfermo; erróneo; (credit) poco sólido; (mind) demente

unsparing*, ŏn-spé'-ring, a., pródigo; inhumano

unsteady, ŏn-sted'-i, a., inseguro

unstinted, ŏn-stin'-tid, a., liberal

unsuccessful, ŏn-sŏk-ses'-ful, a., infructuoso; (person) sin éxito

unsuitable, ŏn-siuu'-ta-bl, a., impropio; incapaz

unsuited, ŏn-siuu'-tid, a., no apropiado

unsupported, ŏn-so-por'-tid, a., sin apoyo

unsurpassed, ŏn-sor-paast', a., insuperable

unsuspecting, ŏn-sos-pek'-ting, a., confiado

unsympathetic*, ŏn-sim-pa-zet'-ik, a., indiferente, sin conmiseración

untamed, ŏn-teimd', a., indómito

untarnished, ŏn-taar'-nisht, a., limpio

untenable, ŏn-ten'-a-bl, a., insostenible

untenanted, ŏn-ten-an-tid, a., desalquilado

unthankful*, ŏn-zangk'-ful, a., desagradecido

unthinking, ŏn-zingk'-ing, a., descuidado

untidy, ŏn-tai'-di, a., desarreglado

untie, ŏn-tai', v., desatar

until, ŏn-til', prep., hasta.. conj., hasta que

untimely, ŏn-taim'-li, adv., prematuramente

untiring, ŏn-tai'-ring, a., incansable

untold, ŏn-tould', a., no narrado ; (vast) incalculable

untouched, ŏn-tŏcht', a., intacto

untranslatable, ŏn-trans-lei'-ta-bl, a., intraducible

untried, ŏn-traid', a., no ensayado

untrodden, ŏn-trŏd'-n, a., no pisado

untrue, ŏn-truu', a., falso; infiel

untrustworthy, ŏn-trŏst'-uerD-i, a., indigno de confianza

untruth, ŏn-truuz', s., falsedad f.; mentira f.

untwist, ŏn-tuist', v., destorcer, desenroscar

unusual*, ŏn-iuu'-shu-al, a., inusitado, extraño

unvaried, ŏn-vē´-rid, a., invariable

unveil, ŏn-veil´, v., descubrir, levantar el velo

unwarrantable, ŏn-uor´-*an*-ta-bl, a., injustificable, inexcusable

unwavering, ŏn-uei´-ver-ing, a., firme, determinado

unwelcome, ŏn-uel´-kom, a., mal acogido, importuno

unwell, ŏn-uel´, a., indispuesto, malo

unwholesome, ŏn-joul´-sŏm, a., malsano, dañino

unwieldy, ŏn-uiil´-di, a., pesado

unwilling, ŏn-uil´-ing, a., desinclinado, mal dispuesto

unwind, ŏn-uaind´, v., desdevanar [to

unwise, ŏn-uais´, a., imprudente, indiscreto

unwittingly, ŏn-uit´-ing-li, adv., inconscientemente

unworthy, ŏn-uörD´-i, a., indigno, desmerecedor

unwrap, ŏn-rap´, v., desenvolver; descubrir

unwritten, ŏn-rit´-n, a., oral; tradicional

unyielding, ŏn-yiil´-ding, a., inflexible, rígido

up, ŏp, adv., arriba, hacia arriba. prep., (=up on) sobre. p.p., (risen) levantado; —**and down,** adv., arriba y abajo; — **here,** (position) aquí arriba; — **there,** allá arriba; — **to,** prep., (until) hasta

upbraid, ŏp-breid´, v., echar en cara

upheaval, ŏp-jii´-vl, s., (geological) cataclismo m.

uphill, ŏp-jiil´, adv., cuesta arriba; (fig.) penoso

uphold, ŏp-jould´, v., sostener; mantener

upholsterer, ŏp-joul´-ster-*a*, s., tapicero m.

upholstery, ŏp-joul´-ster-i, s., tapicería f.

upkeep, ŏp-kiip´, s., mantenimiento m.; (expenses) gastos m. pl.

upland, ŏp-land´, s., tierras altas f. pl.

uplift, ŏp-lift´, v., levantar, elevar

upon, ŏp-on´, prep., sobre

upper, ŏp´-a, superior, de encima; —**hand,** s., ventaja f.; —**most,** a., predominante

upper-part, ŏp´-a-paart, s., parte superior f.

upright, ŏp´-rait, a., derecho; (honest) honrado, s., montante m.

uprising, ŏp-rai´-sing, s., levantamiento m.

uproar, ŏp-rór´, s., tumulto m., alboroto m.

uproot, ŏp-ruut´, v., desarraigar

upset, ŏp-set′, v., volcar, trastornar. a., (perturbed) perturbado

upside, ŏp′-said, **—down,** adv., al revés; (fig.) en confusión

upstairs, ŏp′-stėrs, adv., arriba; **go —,** v., subir

upstart, ŏp′-staart, s., advenedizo m.

upwards, ŏp′-uerds, adv., hacia arriba

uranium, yú-rein-i-om, s., uranio m.

urban, ėr′-bn, a., urbano

urchin, ėr′-chin, s., granuja m., pilluelo m.

urge, ėrCH, s., impulso m., v., impeler; incitar

urgency, ėr′-CHen-si, s., urgencia f.

urgent*, ėr′-CHent, a., urgente

urine, yú′-rain, s., orina f.

urn, ėrn, s., urna f.

us, ŏs, pron., nos; nosotros

use, iuus, usar, emplear. s., uso m., utilidad f.; **— up,** v., consumir; utilizar

useful*, iuus′-ful, a., útil

useless*, iuus′-les, a., inútil

usher, ŏsh′-a, s., ujier m., conserje m.; (cinema, theatre) acomodador m.; **—in,** v., anunciar

usual*, yuu′-shu-al, a., usual, habitual; ordinario

usurer, yuu-shúr′-a, s., usurero m., logrero m.

usurp, yu-sėrp′, v., usurpar

usury, yuu′-shú-ri, s., usura f.

utensil, yu-ten′-sil, s., utensilio m.

utility, yuu-til′-i-ti, s., utilidad f.

utilize, yuu-til′-ais, v., utilizar

utmost, ŏt′-moust, a., mayor, sumo. adv., lo más

utter, ŏt′-a, v., pronunciar; emitir. a., total, entero

utterance, ŏt′-er-ans, s., expresión f.; pronunciación f.; habla f.

uttermost, *see* **utmost**

vacancy, vei′-kan-si, s., vacancia f.; (lack) vacío m.

vacant, vei′-kant, a., vacante; (empty) vacío; (free) desocupado; (mind) vago

vacate, va-keit′, v., dejar vacante; (mil.) evacuar

vacation, va-kei′-shon, s., (holidays) vacación f.

vaccinate, vak′-si-neit, v., vacunar

vaccination, vak′-si-nei-shon, s., vacunación f.

vacillate, vas'-i-leit, v., vacilar

vacuum, vak'-iuu-om, s., vacío m.; **—cleaner,** aspirador de polvo m.; **—flask,** termos m.

vagabond, vag'-a-bónd, s., vagabundo m.

vague*, veig, a., vago

vain*, vein, a., vanidoso; **in —,** adv., en vano

vale, veil, s., valle m.

valet, val'-et, s., criado m., lacayo m.

valiant*, val'-i-ant, a., valiente

valid*, val'-id, a., válido

valley, val'-i, s., valle m.

valorous*, val'-o-ros, a., valeroso

valour, val'-r, s., valor m.

valuable, val'-iu-a-bl, a., valioso   [pl.

valuables, val'-iu-a-bls, s. pl., objetos de valor m.

valuation, val'-iu-ei'-shon, s., valuación f.; valía f.

value, val'-iu, v., valorar; estimar. s., valor m.

valuer, val'-iu-a, s., tasador m., valuador m.

valve, valv, s., válvul a f.; (radio) lámpara f.

vamp, vamp, s., pala de zapato f. v., (mus.) improvisar

vampire, vam-pair, s., vampiro m.

van, van, s., camión m.; (train) furgón m.; (mil.) vanguardia f.

vandalism, van-dal-ism, s., vandalismo m.

vane, vein, s., veeta f.; (windmill) aspa f.

vanilla, va-nil'-a, s., vainilla f.

vanish, van'-ish, v., desvanecerse; desaparecer

vanity, van'-i-ti, s., vanidad f.

vanquish, vang'-kuish, v., vencer

vaporize, vei'-por-ais, v., evaporizar

vapour, vei'-pr, s., vapor m.

variable, vei'-ri-a-bl, a., variable

variation, vei-ri-ei'-shon, s., variación f.

varicose vein, vei'-ri-kous vein, s., variz f.

varied, vè'-rid, a., variado; ameno

variegated, vè'-ri-guei-tid, a., abigarrado

variety, va-rai'-i-ti, s., variedad f.; **—-theatre,** teatro de variedades m.

various*, vé'-ri-os, a., vario; diverso; diferente

varnish, vaar'-nish, v., barnizar. s., barniz m.

vary, vè'-ri, v., variar; cambiar

vase, vaas, s., jarrón m.
vaseline, vas'-e-lin, s., vaselina f.
vast*, vaast, a., vasto, inmenso
vat, vat, s., cuba f., tina f.; (tannery) noque m.
Vatican, vat'-i-kan, s., Vaticano m.
vault, voalt, s., bóveda f.; (church, etc.) cripta f.; (burial) tumba f. v., (jump) voltear
veal, viil, s., ternera f.
veer, vir, v., virar; (wind) cambiar
vegetable, vech'-i-ta-bl, a., vegetal
vegetables, vech'-i-ta-b'ls, s. pl., legumbres f. pl.
vegetarian, vech-i-tei'-ri-an, s., vegetariano m.
vegetation, vech-i-tei'-shon, s., vegetación f.
vehement, vii'-ji-ment, a., vehemente
vehicle, vii'-ji-kl, s., vehículo m.
veil, veil, s., velo m. v., velar, esconder
vein, vein, s., vena f.
vellum, vel'-m, s., vitela f.; pergamino m.
velocity, vi-los'-i-ti, s., velocidad f.
velvet, vel'-vet, s., terciopelo m.
velveteen, vel-ve-tiin', s., terciopelo de algodón m.
vendor, ven'-dr, s., vendedor m.
veneer, vi-nir', s., chapa f. v., chapear, enchapar
venerable, ven'-er-a-bl, a., venerable
veneration, ven-er-ei'-shon, s., veneración f.
venereal, vi'-ni-ri-al, a., venéreo
vengeance, ven'-chans, s., venganza f.
venial*, vii'-ni-al, a., venial
venison, ven'-sn, s., carne de venado f.
venom, ven'-m, s., veneno m.
venomous*, ven'-om-os, a., venenoso, ponzoñoso
vent, vent, s., salida f.; (cask) venteo m.; **give — to**, v., desahogar
ventilate, ven'-ti-leit, v., ventilar
ventilator, ven'-ti-lei-ta, s., ventilador m.
ventriloquist, ven-tril'-o-kuist, s., ventrílocuo .m.
venture, ven'-tiúr, v., aventurar; (dare) osar. s., ventura f. riesgo m.; **—some**, a., arriesgado; (individual) emprendedor
veracity, vi-ras'-i-ti, s., veracidad f.
verandah, vi-ran'-da, s., pórtico m., galería f.
verb, vêrb, s., verbo m.

verbal*, ver′-bl, a., verbal, oral
verbatim, ver-bei′-tim, adv., palabra por palabra
verbose, ver-bous′, a., verboso
verdant,' ver′-dant, a., verde, verdoso
verdict, ver′-dikt, s., opinión f.; (legal) fallo m.,
   veredicto m
verdigris, ver′-di-gris, s., verdete m.
verge, vercH, v., aproximarse a., s., borde m.
verger, ver′-CHa, s., sacristán m.
verify, ver′-i-fai, v., verificar
vermilion, ver-mil′-yŏn, s., bermellón m.
vermin, ver′-min, s., sabandija f.; (fig.) piojos m. pl.
vernacular, ver-naK′-iu-lar. s., idioma vernáculo m.
versatile, ver′-sa-tail, a., versátil
verse, vers, s., verso m.; poesía f.
versed, verst, a., versado
version, ver′-shon, s., versión f.; traducción f.
versus, ver′-sos, prep., contra
vertical*, ver′-ti-kal, a., vertical
vertigo, ver′-ti-gou, s., vértigo m.
very, ver′-i, adv., muy; mucho; sumamente, a.,
   mismo; verdadero; idéntico
vessel, ves′-l, s., vasija f.; (naut.) buque m.
vest, vest, v., vestir. s., camiseta f.
vested, ves-tid, a., (rights) poseído; (interest) creado
vestige, ves′-ticH, s., vestigio m.; (sign) señal f.
vestment, vest′-ment, s., vestidura f.; (eccl.) vestimenta f.
vestry, ves′-tri, s., sacristía f.
veteran, vet′-i-ran, s. & a., veterano m.
veterinary, vet′-e-ri-na-ri, a., veterinario; **—sur-**
   geon, s., veterinario m.
veto, vii′-tou, s., veto m. v., poner el veto
vex, veks, v., vejar
vexation, veks-ei′-shon, s., vejación f.
vexatious, veks-ei′-shos, a., vejatorio, molesto
via, vai′-a, prep., por vía de
viaduct, vai′-a-dŏkt, s., viaducto m.
vibrate, vai′-breit, v., vibrar
vibration, vai-brei′-shon, s., vibración f.
vicar, vik′-a, s., vicario m.
vicarage, vik′-er-icH. s., vicaría f.

vice, vais, s., vicio m.; (mech.) tornillo de carpintero m. (prefix) vice-

viceroy, vis'-roi, s., virrey m.

vicinity, vi-sin'-i-ti, s., vecindad f.

vicious*, vish'-os, a., vicioso

viciousness, vish'-os-ness, s., depravación f.; vicio m.

victim, vik'-tim, s., víctima f.

victimize, vik'-tim-ais; v., hacer víctima

victor, vik'-to, s., vencedor m.

victorious*, vik-tó'-ri-os, a., victorioso

victory, vik'-to-ri, s., victoria f.

victual, vit'-l, v., avituallar, abastecer

victuals*, vit'-ls, s. pl., vitualla f., víveres m. pl.

vie, vai, v., rivalizar, competir

view, viuu, s., vista f.; opinión f.;— **finder,** s., (photog.) visor m.

vigil, vich'-il, s., vigilia f.

vigilance, vich'-i-lans, s., vigilancia f.

vigilant*, vich'-i-lant, a., vigilante

vigorous*, vig'-or-os, a., vigoroso, fuerte

vigour, vig'-r, s., vigor m., fuerza f.

vile*, vail, a., vil, bajo

vilify, vil'-i-fai, v., envilecer, difamar

village, vil'-ich, s., aldea f.

villager, vil'-ich-a, s., aldeano m.

villain, vil'-in, s., villano m.

villainous*, vil'-a-nos, a., vil, infame

villainy, vil'-a-ni, s., villanía f.

vindicate, vin'-di-keit, v., vindicar, vengar

vindication, vin-di-kei'-shon, s., vindicación f.; venganza f.

vindictive*, vin-dik'-tiv, a., vengativo;—**ness,** s., caracter vengativo m.

vine, vain, s., vid f., parra f.

vinegar, vin'-i-ga, s., vinagre m.

vineyard, vin'-yaard, s., viña f., viñedo m.

vintage, vin'it-ch, s., vendimia f.

violate, vai'-o-leit, v., violar: (law) infringir

violence, vai'-o-lens, s., violencia f.

violent*, vai'-o-lent, a., violento

violet, vai'-o-let, s., violeta f. **a.,** violado

violin, vai′-o-lin, s., violín m.
violinist, vai-ou′-li-nist, s. violinista m.
viper, vai′-pa, s., víbora f.
virgin, věr′-chin, s., virgen f.
virginia, vir-chii′-ni-a, a., de virginia
virile, vir′-ail, vir′-il, a., viril, varonil
virtual*, věr′-tiu-al, a., virtual
virtue, věr′-tiuu, s., virtud f.
virtuous*, věr′-tiu-os, a., virtuoso
virulent*, vir′-u-lent, a., virulento; venenoso
visa, vii′-sa, s., visado m. v., visar
visibility, vis-i-bil′-i-ti, s., visibilidad f.
visible, vis′-i-bl, a., visible
vision, vish′-on, s., visión f.
visit, vis′-it, v., visitar. s., visita f.; —**ing-card,** tarjeta de visita f.
visitor, vis′-i-ta, s., visita f.
visual*, vish′-iu-al, a., visual
vital*, vai′-tl, a., esencial; vital
vitality, vai-ta′-li-ti, s., vitalidad f.
vitals, vai′-tals, s. pl., órganos vitales m. pl.
vitriol, vit′-ri-ol, s., vitriolo m.
vivacious*, vi-vei′-shos, a., vivaz, animado
vivacity, vi-vas′-i-ti, s., vivacidad f.
vivid*, viv′-id, a., vívido; (colour) brillante
vivify, viv′-i-fai, v., vivificar
vixen, vik′-sen, s., zorra f., raposa f.
viz. =**namely,** neim′-li, adv., a saber, es decir
vocabulary, vou-kab′-iu-la-ri, s., vocabulario m.
vocal, vou′-kal, a., vocal; — **chords,** s.pl., cuerdas vocales f.pl.
vocalist, vou′-kal-ist, s., cantor m.; cantante m.
vocation, vou-kei′-shon, s., vocación f.; profesión f.
vociferous, vo-sif′-er-os, a., vociferador, vocinglero
vogue, voug, s., moda f.
voice, vois, s., voz f.
void, void, a., vacío; (null) nulo. s., vacío m.
volatile, vol′-a-tail, a., volátil
volcano, vol-kei′-nou, s., volcán m.
volley, vol′-i, s., descarga f.; (salute) salva f.
volt, volt, s., voltio m.; —**age,** s., voltaje m.
voluble, vol′-iu-bl, a., voluble

volume, vol'-ium, s., volumen m.; (book) tomo m.
voluminous', vol-iuu'-mi-nos, a., voluminoso
voluntary, vol'-on-ta-ri, a., voluntario
volunteer, vol-on-tir', s., voluntario m. v., ofrecerse
voluptuous', vo-löp'-tiu-os, a., voluptuoso
vomit, vom'-it, v., vomitar
voracious, vo-rei'-shos, a., voraz, devorador
vortex, voar'-teks, s., vórtice m. remolino m.
vote, vout, v., votar; s., voto m.
voter, vout'-a, s., votante m. & f.
vouch, vauch, v., garantizar; **— for,** responder de
voucher, vauch'-a, s., (document) resguardo m.
vow, vau, s., voto m. v., hacer votos
vowel, vau'-l, s., vocal f.
voyage, voi'-ich, s., viaje por mar m.
vulcanite, völ'-kan-ait, s., vulcanita f.
vulgar', völ'-gar, a., vulgar; grosero
vulnerable, völ-ner-a-bl, a., vulnerable
vulture, völ'-tiur, s., buitre m.

wabble, uob'-l, v., bambolearse; (fig.) vacilar
wad, uod, s., (cartridge) taco m.; (cotton wool, etc.)
    borra f., guata f.; **—ding,** s., guata; (padding)
    entretela
waddle, uod'-l, v., andar como un pato
wade, ueid, v., vadear
wafer, uei'-fa, s., (thin biscuit) barquillo m.; (eccl.)
    hostia f.
wag, uag, v., menear. s., chancero m.
wager, uei'-cha, s., apuesta f. v., apostar
wages, uei'-chis, s., salario m.; (daily) jornal m.
waggle, uag'-l, v., menearse
waggon, uag'-n, s., carretón m.; (train) vagón m.
waif, ueif, s., niño abandonado m.
wail, ueil, v., lamentarse. s., lamentación f.
wainscot, ueins'-kot, s., entablamento m.; friso m.
waist, ueist, s., cintura f., talle m.
waistcoat, ues'-kot, s., chaleco m.
wait, ueit, v., esperar, aguardar; (at table) servir;
    —er, s., mozo m., camarero m.; **— for,** v.,
    esperar a; **—ing,** s., espera f.; (service) servicio
    m.; **—ing-room,** sala de espera f.; (professional)

antesala f.; —**ress**, camarera f., moza f.; —**upon**, v., servir; atender a

waive, ueiv, v., renunciar, abandonar

wake, ueik, v., (to awake) despertar; (to be called) llamar. s., (ship's) estela f.

walk, uoak, v., andar; (stroll) pasearse. s., paseo m.; —**er**, caminante m.; peatón m.; (stroller) paseante m.

wall, uoal, s., muro m.; (inside) pared f.; —**-flower**, alelí doble m.; —**-paper**, papel de empapelar m.

wallet, uol'-it, s., (note case) cartera f.

wallow, uol'-ou, v., revolcarse

walnut, uoal'-nöt, s., nuez f.; (wood) nogal m.

walrus, uoal'-ros, s., morsa f.

waltz, uoalts, s., vals m. v., valsar

wan, uoan, a., pálido

wander, uoan'-da, v., vagar; (mentally) delirar

wane, uein, v., menguar

want, uoant, s., (lack) falta f.; (shortage) carencia f.; (distress) indigencia f. v., querer, desear

wanton', uon'-ton, a., (wicked) perverso; (lustful) lascivo; (waste) extravagante

war, uoar, v., guerrear. s. guerra f.; —**fare**, hostilidades f. pl.; —**like**, a., a., belicoso

warble, uoar'-bl, v., trinar, gorjear

ward, uoard, s., (minor) menor en tutela m.; (hospital) sala de hospital f.; —**en**, (guard) guardián m.; (college) preceptor m.; —**er**, carcelero m.; —**off**, v., desviar; evitar; —**robe**, guardarropa m.; —**room**, (naval) cuadro de oficiales m.

ware, uër, s., mercadería f.

warehouse, uër'-jaus, s., depósito m.; almacén m. v., almacenar

warily, uë'-ri-li, adv., cautelosamente

wariness, uë'-ri-nes, s., cautela f., precaución f.

warm', uoarm, a., caliente. v., calentar, calentarse

warmth, uoarmz, s., calor m.

warn, uoarn, v., advertir; notificar, avisar

warning, uoarn'-ing, s., advertencia f.

warp, uoarp, v., (wood) combar, torcer

warrant, uor'-ant, s., (authority) autoridad f.;

(for arrest) orden de arresto f.; (voucher) autorización f.; **—y,** garantía f.

warrior, uor'-i-a, s., guerrero m.

wart, uoart, s., verruga f.

wary, ué'-ri, a., cauto, prudente

wash, uoash, v., lavar, lavarse; **—basin,** s., jofaina f.; **—ing** f.; ropa f.; **—ing machine,** s., máquina lavadora

washer, uoash'-a, s., (mech.) arandela f.

wasp, uoasp, s., avispa f.

waste, ueist, s., derroche m.; (refuse) desperdicios m. pl.; (land) tierra baldía f. v., derrochar; (extravagance) desperdiciar; **— away,** irse consumiendo

wasteful, ueist'-ful, a., pródigo; ruinoso

watch, uoch, v., vigilar, observar; s., reloj m.; (naut.) guardia f.; **—maker,** relojero m.; **—man,** (night) sereno m.; **— over,** v., custodiar; **—word,** s., consigna f.

water, uoa'-tr, v., regar; (cattle, etc.) abrevar. s., agua f.; **hot —bottle,** bolsa para agua caliente f.; **—closet,** (W.C.) excusado m.; **—colour,** acuarela f.; **—cress,** berros m. pl.; **—fall,** cascada f.; **—jug,** jarro m., **—lily,** nenufar m.; **—line,** línea de flotación f.; **—logged,** a., anegado en agua; **—proof,** s. & a., impermeable m.; **—tank,** s., cisterna f.; **—tight,** a., estanco; **—y,** aguanoso

watering, uoa'-ter-ing, s., riego m., irrigación f.; **—can,** regadera f.; **—place,** balneario m.

wave, ueiv, s., ola f., onda f. v., (flags) agitar; (to somebody) hacer señas; (sway) balancearse; (hair) ondear

waver, uei'-va, v., vacilar

wavering, uei'-ver-ing, a., vacilante

wax, uaks, v., encerar. s., cera f.; **—works,** exposición de figuras de cera f.

way, uei, s., camino m.; (manner) manera f. **— in,** entrada f.; **—lay,** v., acechar; **— out,** s., salida f.; **—side,** cuneta f.; borde de camino m.; **— through,** pasaje m.; **—ward,** a., voluntarioso

we, uii, pron., pers., nosotros m., nosotras f.

weak*, uiik, a., débil, flojo; **—en,** v., debilitar; flaquear; **—ening,** a., debilitación; **—ling,** s., encanijado m. & f.; **—ly,** a., enfermizo; **—ness,** s., debilidad f.; flojedad f.

weal, uiil, s., prosperidad f.; (wale) verdugón m.

wealth, uelz, s., riqueza f.

wealthy, uel'-zi, a., rico, opulento

wean, uiin, v., destetar; (fig.) enajenar

weapon, uep'-n, s., arma f.

wear, uèr, s., (by use) desgaste m. v., (carry) llevar; (last) durar; **—out,** gastar; (clothes) ponerse; (fatigue) rendir

weariness, ui'-ri-nes, s., cansancio m.

weary, ui'-ri, v., cansado

weasel, uii'-sl, s., comadreja f.

weather, ueD'a, s., tiempo m. v., aguantar, **—bound,** a., detenido por el mal tiempo; **—cock,** s., veleta f.; **—report,** boletín meteorológico m.

weave, uiiv., tejer; **—r,** s., tejedor m.

web, ueb, s., (spider) tela de araña f.

web-footed, ueb-fut'-id, a., palmípedo

webbing, ueb'-ing, s., cincha f.

wed, ued, v., casarse; (perform ceremony) casar

wedding, ued'-ing, s., boda f.; **—-ring,** anillo nupcial m.

wedge, uecH, s., cuña f. acuñar; **— in,** meter por fuerza

wedlock, ued'-lok, s., matrimonio m.

Wednesday, uens'-di, s., miércoles m.

weed, uiid, v., escardar; s., mala yerba f. cizaña f.

week, uiik, s., semana f.; **—day,** día laborable f.; **—end,** fin de semana m.; **—ly,** a., semanal

weep, uiip, v., llorar, lamentar; **—ing,** s., llanto; dolor; lágrimas; **—ing-willow,** s., sauce llorón m.

weevil, uii'-v'l, s., gorgojo m.

weigh, uei, v., pesar; (mentally) ponderar; **—ing-machine,** s., báscula f.

weight, ueit, s., peso m.

weighty, uei'-ti, a., pesado; (serious) grave

weir, uir, s., presa f., esclusa f.

weird, uírd, a., misterioso; (odd) raro

welcome, uei'-kom, s., bienvenida f. a., bien-venido. v., dar la bienvenida, recibir bien

weld, ueld, v., soldar a martillo

welfare, uel'-fér, s., bienestar m., prosperidad f.

well, uel, s., (water) pozo m. adv., bien. a., bueno;
— **being,** s., bienestar m.; — **bred,** a., bien educado; — **done,** (meat, etc.) bien cocido

wench, uench, s., moza f., muchacha f.

wend, uend, v., encaminarse

west, uest, s., oeste m.; — **erly,** a., del oeste

wet, uet, s., humedad f a., húmedo, mojado. v., mojar, humedecer; — **nurse,** s., nodriza f.

whack, juack, v., golpear, s., golpe m.

whale, juél, s., ballena f.; — **bone,** barba de ballena f.; — **r,** ballenero s.

wharf, juoarf, s., muelle m.; malecón m.; embar-cadero m.

what, juot, relative pron., lo que. interrogative pron., qué. interrogative a., que, cuál

whatever, juot-ev'-a, pron., & a., cuanto, cual-quiera cosa que, todo lo que, sea lo que fuere

wheat, juiit, s., trigo m.

wheedle, juii'-dl, v., halagar; (obtain) sonsacar

wheel, juiil, s., rueda f. v., hacer rodar; **spin-ning—,** s., torno para hilar m.; — **barrow,** carretilla f.; — **wright,** carrero m.

wheezy, juii'-si, a., asmático

when, juen, adv., cuándo. conj., cuando, luego que;
— **ce,** adv., de donde; — **ever,** conj., siempre que, cuando quiera que, todas las veces que

where, juér, adv., donde; — **about(s),** donde;
— **as,** conj., mientras que; — **at,** adv., a lo cual;
— **by,** por lo cual; — **fore,** por eso; — **in,** en donde, en que; — **on,** sobre lo cual

wherever, juér-ev'-a, adv., donde quiera

whet, juet, v., afilar; amolar; (appetite) abrir

whether, jueD'-a, conj., si; sea que

which, juich, interrogative pron., cuál, qué. rela-tive pron., que; el cual, la cual, lo cual; el que, la que, lo que

whichever, juich-ev′-*a*, pron., cualquiera, quienquiera

while, juail, v., pasar. conj., mientras

whim, juim., s., capricho m.; **—sical,** a., caprichoso

whimper, juim′-p*a*, s., lloriqueo m. v., lloriquear

whine, juain, v., gemir, lloriquear

whip, juip, s., látigo m. v., azotar, fustigar

whirl, juĕrl, v., girar; **—pool,** s., remolino de agua m.; **—wind,** torbellino m.

whisk, juisk, s., (brush) escobilla f.; (cookery) batidor m. v., (sweep) barrer; (cookery) batir

whiskers, juis′-k*ers*, s. pl., patillas f. pl.; (cat) bigotes m. pl.

whisky, juis′-ki, s., whisky m.

whisper, juis′-p*a*, v., cuchichear. s., cuchicheo m.

whist, juist, s., (cards) whist m.

whistle, juis′-l, s., pito m.; (sound) silbido m. v., silbar

white, juait, a., blanco. s., blanco m.; **—ness,** blancura f.; **—of egg,** clara de huevo f.

whitewash, juait′-uo*a*sh, s., blanqueo m.

whither, juiD′-*a*, adv., adonde, a que parte

whiting, juai′-*u*ing, s., (fish) merlán m., fice m.

Whitsuntide, juit′-sŏn-taid, s., pascua de Pentecostés f.

whiz, juis, v., zumbar, silbar

who, juu, interrogative pron., quién. relative pron., quien que; el cual, la cual; el que, la que

whoever, juu-ev′-*a*, pron., quienquiera que

whole, joul, s., total m., el todo m. a., total, todo, entero; **—sale,** al por mayor; **—some,** sano, saludable

wholly, joul′-i, adv., enteramente

whom, juum, interrogative pron., a quién. relative pron., a quien, al cual, al que; que

whoop, juup, s., alarido m. v., huchear

whooping-cough, juu′-ping-ko*a*f, s., tos ferina f.

whore, jór, s., prostituta f.

whose, juus, interrogative pron., de quién. relative pron., a., cuyo, cuya

whosoever, juu-so-ev′-*a*, pron., quienquiera que

why, uai, adv., por qué; ¿ por qué ?

wick, uik, s., mecha f.

wicked*, uik'-id, a., malvado, inicuo, perverso

wickedness, uik'-id-nes, s., maldad f., iniquidad f.; perversidad f.

wicker, uik'-*a*, s., mimbre m.

wide, uaid, a., ancho; vasto; **—-awake,** (fig.) despabilado; **—ly,** adv., extensivamente; **—n,** v., ensanchar; **—-spread,** a., esparcido

widow, uid'-ou, s., viuda f.

widower, uid'-ou-*a*, s., viudo m.

width, uidz, s., ancho m., anchura f.

wield, uiild, v., manejar; (power) gobernar

wife, uaif, s., mujer f., esposa f.

wig, uig, s., peluca f.

wild*, uaild, a., salvaje; feroz; (fig.) loco

wilderness, uil'-der-nes, s., desierto m., soledad f.

wile, uail, s., ardid m., engaño m.

wilful*, uil'-*ful*, a., voluntarioso; (act) premeditado

will, uil, s., voluntad f.; testamento m. v., querer; (bequeath) legar

willing*, uil'-ing, a., dispuesto, gustoso

willingness, uil'-ing-nes, s., buena voluntad f.

will-o'-the-wisp, uil-o-Di-uisp', s., fuego fatuo m.

willow, uil'-ou, s., sauce m.

wily, uai'-li, a., astuto, mañoso

win, uin, v., ganar; **—ner,** s., ganador m.; vencedor m.; **—ning,** a., (manners) encantador; **—ning-post,** s., meta f.; **—nings,** ganancias f. pl.

wince, uins, v., retroceder, respingar

winch, uinch, s., manubrio m., cigüeña f.

wind, uaind, v., ovillar; (road, river, etc.) serpear; **—ing,** a., serpentino; **— up,** v., ovillar; (clock) dar cuerda; (business) liquidar

wind, uind, s., viento m.; flatulencia f.; **—fall,** fortuna f.; **—mill,** molino de viento m.; **—pipe,** tráquea f.; **—screen,** s., parabrisas m. pl.; **—screen wipers,** s., limpiaparabrisas m. pl.; **—ward,** adv., a barlovento; **—y,** a., ventoso

windlass, uind'-lass, s., cabrestante m.

window, uin'-dou, s., ventana f.; (shop) escaparate m.

wine, uain, s., vino m.; **—glass,** copa para vino f.

wing, uing, s., ala f.; (theatre) bastidor m.; (mil.) flanco m.

wink, uingk, v., guiñar. s., guiño m.

winkle, uin'-kl, s., (shellfish) bígaro m.

winsome, uin'-som, a., mono, simpático

winter, uin'-ta, s., invierno m. v., invernar

wipe, uaip, v., limpiar; (to dry) secar

wire, uair, s., alambre m.

wireless, uair'-les, s., radio m.; radiotelegrafía f.; (apparatus) radio m., (message) radiotelegrama m. v., radiotelegrafiar

wiring, uair'-ing, s., instalación eléctrica f.; alumbrado m.

wisdom, uis'-dm, s., sabiduría f.; prudencia f.

wise*, uais, a., sabio; prudente

wish, uish, s., deseo m., anhelo m. v., desear, anhelar

wishful, uish'-ful, a., deseoso, anheloso

wistaria, uis-té-ri-a, s., glicina f.

wistful*, uist'-ful, a., pensativo

wit, uit, s., ingenio m.; **to —,** a saber, es decir

witch, uich, s., bruja f.

witchcraft, uich'-kraaft, s., brujería f.

with, uiD, prep., con, de, a; **—draw,** v., retirarse; (money) retirar; (apologise) retractarse; **—hold,** detener; (sanction) rehusar; **—in,** prep., dentro. adv., (outside) fuera; **—stand,** v., resistir a

wither, uiD'-a, v., marchitarse

witness, uit'-nes, s., testigo m. v., atestiguar

wits, uits, s., sentido m.; **to live by one's —,** vivir de gorra

witticism, uit'-sism, s., rasgo de ingenio m.

witty, uit'-i, a., ingenioso

wizard, uis'-erd, s., brujo m., nigromante m.

wobble, uou'-bl, v., bambolearse; vacilar

woe, nou, s., pena f., infortunio m.; **— to him,** interj., ¡ ay de él ! **—ful,** a., triste, afligido

wolf, uulf, s., lobo m.; **she-—,** loba f.

woman, uu'-man, s., mujer f.; **—ly,** a., mujeril

womanhood, uu'-man-jud, s., estado de mujer m.

womb, uum, s., matriz f.
wonder, uŏn'-da, s., maravilla f. v., extrañarse, maravillarse de ; (doubt) preguntarse
wonderful*, uŏn'-der-ful, a., maravilloso, estupendo
woo, uu, v., cortejar ; —**er,** s., cortejador m.
wood, uud, s., madera f. ; (forest) bosque m. ; —**bine,** madreselva f. ; —**cock,** chochaperdiz f. ; —**pecker,** pájaro carpintero m.
wooden, uud'-n, a., de madera
woody, uud'-i, a., (trees) arbolado
wool, uul, s., lana f.
woollen, uul'-en, a., de lana
woolly, uul'-i, a., lanudo
word, uĕrd, s., palabra f. ; (news) nuevas f. pl. v., expresar ; (written) redactar ; — **of honour,** s., palabra de honor f.
wording, uĕrd'-ing, s., redacción f. ; estilo m.
work, uĕrk, v., trabajar ; (mine) explotar ; (mech.) funcionar. s., trabajo m. ; ocupación f. ; (achievement) obra f. ; —**er,** obrero m. ; —**house,** hospicio m. ; —**ing,** (mech.) funcionamiento m. ; (mine) explotación f. ; —**ing, expenses,** gastos de explotación m. pl. ; —**man,** obrero m. ; —**man-ship,** mano de obra f. ; —**shop,** taller m.
works, uĕrks, s. pl., fábrica f. ; (mech.) mecanismo
world, uĕrld, s., mundo m., universo m.   [m.
worldly, uĕrld'-li, a., mundano, mundanal
worm, uĕrm, s., gusano m. ; (intestinal) lombriz f. ; (screw) rosca f. ; —**eaten,** a., carcomido
worry, uĕr'-i, s., cuidado m. ; (anxiety) ansiedad f. v., atormentarse ; (bother) molestar
worse, uĕrs, adv., peor. a., peor, pésimo
worship, uĕr'-ship, v., adorar. s., adoración f. ; (divine) culto m.
worst, uĕrst, adv., pésimamente. s., lo peor n.
worsted, uĕr'-stid, s., (yarn) estambre m.
worth, uĕrz, s., valor m. ; mérito m. a., que vale ; —**ily,** adv., dignamente ; —**less,** a., sin valor ; — **while,** valer la pena ; —**y,** a., digno
would-be, uud'-bii, a., pretendiente, supuesto
wound, uund, s., herida f. v., herir

wrangle, rAng'-gl, v., contender. s., riña f., contienda f.

wrap, rAp, s., manto m. v., envolver; — **up,** (oneself) arroparse

wrapper, rAp'-a, s., envoltura f.; (postal) faja f.

wrath, roaz, s., ira f., furor m.

wreath, riiz, s., corona f.

wreathe, riiD, v., entrelazar

wreck, rek, s., buque naufragado m.; (fig.) ruina f. v., naufragar; (fig.) arruinar; —**age,** s., pecios

wrecked, rekt, a., naufragado; arruinado [m. pl.

wren, ren, s., reyezuelo m.

wrench, rench, s., tirón m.; (sprain) torcedura f.; (tool) llave inglesa f. v., torcer; (pull) arrancar

wrestle, res'-l, v., luchar; —**r,** s., luchador m.

wretch, rech, s., miserable m. & f.; —**ed,** a., triste; (person) miserable; —**edness,** s., miseria f.

wriggle, rig'-l, v., retorcerse

wring, ring, v., torcer, retorcer

wrinkle, ring'-kl, s., arruga f. v., arrugar; (brow) fruncir

wrist, rist, s., muñeca f.

writ, rit, s., escrito m., auto m.

write, rait, v., escribir

writer, rai'-ta, s., escritor m., autor m.

writhe, raiD, v., retorcerse

writing, rai'-ting, s., escritura f.; **hand**—, letra f.; **in** —, adv., por escrito; —**paper,** papel de cartas m.; —**table,** escritorio m.

written, rit'-n, a., escrito

wrong, rong, s., agravio m., injusticia f. v., agraviar. a., falso; errado; malo; inoportuno; injusto; ilegal; —**side,** s., mal lado m.; (material) revés m.; **to be** —, v., no tener razón

wroth, roaz, a., enojado, irritado

wrought iron, toat ai'-ern, s., hierro forjado m.

wry, rai, a., torcido; —**face,** s., mueca f.; — **neck,** torticolis m.; (bird) torcecuello m.

Xmas (=**Christmas**), kris'-mas, s., Navidad f.

X-ray, eks'-rei, s., rayo X m.; (X-ray photograph) fotografía por los rayos X f.

xylophone, sai'-lo-foun, s., xilófono m.

yacht, yŏt, s., yate m.; **—ing,** navegación en yate f.
yard, yaard, s., patio m.; (farm) corral m.; (measure) yarda f.; **ship—,** astillero m.; **timber—,** depósito de madera m.
yarn, yaarn, s., hilo m.
yawn, yoan, v., bostezar. s., bostezo m.
yawning, yoan'-ing, a., (chasm, etc.) abierto
year, yir, s., año m.
yearling, yir'-ling, s., añojo m.
yearly, yir'-li, a.,* anual
yearn, yĕrn, v., anhelar, ansiar; **—ing,** s., anhelo m., ansia f.; **—ingly,** adv., anhelantemente
yeast, yiist, s., levadura f., fermento m.
yellow, yel'-ou, a., amarillo
yelp, yelp, v., latir, gañir, gañido m.
yes, yes, adv., sí
yesterday, yes'-ter-di, adv., ayer
yet, yet, adv., aún, todavía. conj., sin embargo
yew, yuu, s., tejo m.
yield, yiild, v., ceder; producir. s., producto m.
yoke, youk, v., uncir; sujetar. s., yugo m.; opresión f.
yokel, youk'-l, s., patán m.
yolk, youk, s., yema de huevo f.
yonder, yon'-da, adv., allí, allá. a., aquel, aquella
you, yuu, pron., vosotros; usted, ustedes; (fam.) tú
young, yŏng, a., joven
younger, yŏng'-a, a., más joven; menor
youngster, yŏng'-sta, s., jovencito m.
your, yúr, a., vuestro, vuestra, vuestros, vuestras; su, sus; de usted, de ustedes; (fam.) tu, tus
yours, yúrs, pron., el vuestro, la vuestra, los vuestros, las vuestras; el suyo, la suya, los suyos, las suyas; el de usted, la de usted, los de usted, las de usted, el de ustedes, la de ustedes, los de ustedes, las de ustedes; (fam.) el tuyo, la tuya, los tuyos, las tuyas
youth, yuuz, s., juventud f.; (lad) joven m.; **—ful*,** a., juvenil; **—fulness,** s., mocedad f.
Yule-tide, yuul'-taid, s., pascua de Navidad m.

zeal, siil, s., celo m. ardor m.

zealous*, sel'-os, a., celoso, entusiasta

zebra, sii'-bra, s., cebra f.

zenith, sen'-iz, s., cénit m.

zephyr, sef'-r, s., céfiro m.

zero, si'-rou, s., cero m.

zest, sest, s., gusto m.; deleite m.

zinc, sink, s., cinc m. v., recubrir de cinc

zone, soun, s., zona f.

zoological, sou-o-loch-i-kl, a., zoológico

zoology, sou-ol'-o-chi, s., zoología f.

hugo

POCKET DICTIONARIES

*All with Imitated Pronunciation
also issued in*
French-English/English-French
German-English/English-German
Italian-English/English-Italian
Russian-English/English-Russian
Dutch-English/English-Dutch

Without Pronunciation
English

★

POCKET PHRASE BOOKS

for

France, Germany, Spain, Greece,
Italy, Holland, Scandinavia and
Portugal

*Essential words and phrases, with
lots more useful information.*